Network+ Exam Prep 2 Objectives Quick Reference

Continues on Following Page

Network+ Exam Prep 2

Drew Bird
Mike Harwood

Network+ Exam Prep 2

International Standard Book Number: 0-7897-3255-6

Library of Congress Catalog Card Number: 2004118402

Printed in the United States of America

First Printing: July 2005

08 07 06 05   4 3 2 1

Trademarks

All terms mentioned in this book that are known to be trademarks or service marks have been appropriately capitalized. Que Publishing cannot attest to the accuracy of this information. Use of a term in this book should not be regarded as affecting the validity of any trademark or service mark.

Warning and Disclaimer

Every effort has been made to make this book as complete and as accurate as possible, but no warranty or fitness is implied. The information provided is on an "as is" basis. The author(s) and the publisher shall have neither liability nor responsibility to any person or entity with respect to any loss or damages arising from the information contained in this book or from the use of the CD or programs accompanying it.

Bulk Sales

Que Publishing offers excellent discounts on this book when ordered in quantity for bulk purchases or special sales. For more information, please contact

U.S. Corporate and Government Sales

1-800-382-3419

corpsales@pearsontechgroup.com

For sales outside the U.S., please contact

International Sales

international@pearsoned.com

PUBLISHER
Paul Boger

EXECUTIVE EDITOR
Jeff Riley

ACQUISITIONS EDITOR
Jeff Riley

DEVELOPMENT EDITOR
Steve Rowe

MANAGING EDITOR
Charlotte Clapp

PROJECT EDITOR
Mandie Frank

COPY EDITOR
Geneil Breeze

INDEXER
Ginny Bess

PROOFREADER
Linda Seifert

TECHNICAL EDITOR
David L. Prowse

PUBLISHING COORDINATOR
Pamalee Nelson

MULTIMEDIA DEVELOPER
Dan Scherf

PAGE LAYOUT
Juli Cook

CERTIFICATION

Que Certification • 800 East 96th Street • Indianapolis, Indiana 46240

A Note from Series Editor Ed Tittel

Congratulations on your purchase of the finest exam preparation book in the marketplace!

As Series Editor of the highly regarded Training Guide series, I can assure you that you won't be disappointed. You've taken your first step toward passing the exam, and we value this opportunity to help you on your way!

As a "Favorite Study Guide Author" finalist in a 2002 poll of CertCities readers, I know the importance of delivering good books. You'll be impressed with Que Certification's stringent review process, which ensures the books are high-quality, relevant, and technically accurate.

We've also added a preview edition of MeasureUp's powerful, full-featured test engine, which is trusted by certification students throughout the world.

As a 20-year-plus veteran of the computing industry and the original creator and editor of the Exam Cram series, I've brought my IT experience to bear on these books. During my tenure at Novell from 1989 to 1994, I worked with and around its excellent education and certification department. At Novell, I witnessed the growth and development of the first really big, successful IT certification program—one that was to shape the industry forever afterward. This experience helped push my writing and teaching activities heavily in the certification direction. Since then, I've worked on more than 70 certification related books, and I write about certification topics for numerous Web sites and for *Certification* magazine.

In 1997 when Exam Cram was introduced, it quickly became the best-selling computer book series since "*...For Dummies,*" and the best-selling certification book series ever. By maintaining an intense focus on the subject matter, tracking errata and updates quickly, and following the certification market closely, Exam Cram was able to establish the dominant position in cert prep books.

You will not be disappointed in your decision to purchase this book. If you are, please contact me at etittel@jump.net. All suggestions, ideas, input, or constructive criticism are welcome!

Ed Tittel

Contents at a Glance

Table of Contents

Part II: Final Review

About the Authors

Drew Bird (MCSE, MCNE, Network+, Linux+, Server+) has been in the IT industry since 1988. Over the years he has designed, implemented, and administered networks of all shapes and sizes. In addition to technical training and consulting assignments, Drew has authored a number of technical articles and is a frequent contributor to technology websites. Away from work, Drew enjoys most outdoor activities but is especially keen on mountain biking, kayaking, and skiing.

Mike Harwood (MCSE, A+, Network+, Server+, Linux+) has held a number of roles in the computer field, including PC repair, network management, consulting, and technical writing. Mike is also the coauthor of numerous computer books, including *Network+ Prep* from Que Publishing, courseware developer and a regular technology presenter for CBC Radio. When not working, Mike stays as far away from keyboards as possible.

About the Technical Reviewer

David L. Prowse is owner of TSR Data, a Technology Solutions company focusing on security and data communications. He is also the creator of TechnicalBlog.Com, an IT support site.

David has more than a dozen IT certifications, including the CompTIA Network+, which he beta tested twice since its inception. He has also taught the Net+ course to the FAA, CompUSA, Sungard, and many other companies. His vision is of a world where he can sleep more than a few hours a day.

Acknowledgments

We would like to thank our family and friends for putting up with the long hours required to complete this project. Thanks must also go to Nathan Cable for his contributions on the Macintosh material, and to David Prowse for his diligent technical editing.

We would like to say a huge thanks to those at Que Publishing who had the daunting task of producing this book on a seemingly impossible timeline. How they managed to do it we will never know. Finally, thanks to Jeff Riley at Que for his ongoing support.

Tell Us What You Think!

As the reader of this book, you are our most important critic and commentator. We value your opinion and want to know what we're doing right, what we could do better, what areas you'd like to see us publish in, and any other words of wisdom you're willing to pass our way.

As a Publisher or Associate Publisher or Executive Editor for Sams or Que, I welcome your comments. You can fax, email, or write me directly to let me know what you did or didn't like about this book—as well as what we can do to make our books stronger.

Please note that I cannot help you with technical problems related to the topic of this book, and that due to the high volume of mail I receive, I might not be able to reply to every message.

When you write, please be sure to include this book's title and author as well as your name and phone or fax number. I will carefully review your comments and share them with the author and editors who worked on the book.

Fax: 317-581-4770

Email: feedback@quepublishing.com

Mail: Jeff Riley
         Que Publishing
         800 East 96th Street
         Indianapolis, IN 46240 USA

Introduction

The CompTIA Network+ exam has become the leading introductory-level network certification available today. Network+ is recognized by both employers and industry giants such as Microsoft and Novell as providing candidates with a solid foundation of networking concepts, terminology, and skills. The Network+ exam covers a broad range of networking concepts, to prepare candidates for the technologies they are likely to be working with in today's network environments.

This book is your one-stop shop. Everything you need to know to pass the exam is in here. You do not have to take a class in addition to buying this book to pass the exam. However, depending on your personal study habits or learning style, you might benefit from buying this book *and* taking a class.

Exam Preps are meticulously crafted to give you the best possible learning experience for the particular characteristics of the technology covered and the actual certification exam. The instructional design implemented in the *Exam Preps* reflects the task- and experience-based nature of CompTIA certification exams. The *Exam Preps* provide the factual knowledge base you need for the exams but then take it to the next level, with exercises and exam questions that require you to engage in the analytic thinking needed to pass the Network+ exam.

CompTIA recommends that the typical candidate for this exam have a minimum of nine months experience in network support and administration. In addition, CompTIA recommends that candidates have preexisting hardware knowledge such as CompTIA A+ certification.

How This Book Helps You

This book takes you on a self-guided tour of all the areas covered by the Network+ exam and teaches you the specific skills you need to achieve your certification. The book also contains helpful hints, tips, real-world examples, and exercises, as well as references to additional study materials. Specifically, this book is set up to help you in the following ways:

▶ **Organization**—This book is organized by individual exam objectives. Every objective you need to know for the Network+ exam is covered in this book. We present the objectives in an order as close as possible to that listed by CompTIA. However, we do not hesitate to reorganize them where needed to make the material as easy as possible for you to learn. We also make the information accessible in the following ways:

  ▶ The full list of exam units and objectives is included in this introduction.

  ▶ Each chapter begins with a list of the objectives to be covered.

▶ Each chapter also begins with an outline that provides an overview of the material and the page numbers where particular topics can be found.

▶ The objectives are repeated where the material most directly relevant to it is covered.

▶ **Instructional features**—This book provides multiple ways to learn and reinforce the exam material. Following are some of the helpful methods:

  ▶ Study and Exam Tips—Read this section early on to help you develop study strategies. This section also provides valuable exam-day tips and information on exam and question formats, such as adaptive tests and case study-based questions.

  ▶ Objective explanations—As mentioned previously, each chapter begins with a list of the objectives covered in the chapter. In addition, immediately following each objective is an explanation of the objective, in a context that defines it meaningfully.

  ▶ Study strategies—The beginning of each chapter also includes strategies for studying and retention of the material in the chapter, particularly as it is addressed on the exam, but also in ways that will benefit you on the job.

  ▶ Exam Alerts—These provide specific exam-related advice. Such tips might address what material is covered (or not covered) on the exam, how it is covered, mnemonic devices, or particular quirks of that exam.

  ▶ Review breaks and summaries—Crucial information is summarized at various points in the book in lists or tables. Each chapter ends with a summary as well.

  ▶ Key terms—A list of key terms appears at the end of each chapter.

  ▶ Notes—Notes contain various kinds of useful or practical information such as tips on technology or administrative practices, historical background on terms and technologies, or side commentary on industry issues.

  ▶ Warnings—When using sophisticated information technology, there is always the potential for mistakes or even catastrophes to occur because of improper application of the technology. Warnings alert you to such potential problems.

  ▶ In the Field sidebars—These relatively extensive discussions cover material that might not be directly relevant to the exam but that is useful as reference material or in everyday practice. In the Field sidebars also provide useful background or contextual information necessary for understanding the larger topic under consideration.

  ▶ Exercises—Found at the end of the chapters in the "Apply Your Knowledge" section and in the "Challenge Exercises" found throughout chapters, exercises are performance-based opportunities for you to learn and assess your knowledge.

▶ **Extensive practice test options**—The book provides numerous opportunities for you to assess your knowledge and practice for the exam. The practice options include the following:

  ▶ Exam questions—These questions appear in the "Apply Your Knowledge" section. You can use them to help determine what you know and what you need to review or study further. Answers and explanations for these questions are provided in a separate section, titled "Answers to Exam Questions."

  ▶ Practice exam—A practice exam is included in the "Final Review" section of the book. The "Final Review" section and the practice exam are discussed later in this Introduction.

  ▶ MeasureUp—A CD from MeasureUp is included, and it offers even more practice questions for your study.

▶ **Final Review**—This part of the book provides two valuable tools for preparing for the exam:

  ▶ Fast Facts—This condensed version of the information contained in the book is useful for last-minute review.

  ▶ Practice Exam—A practice test is included. Questions on this practice exam are written in styles similar to those used on the actual exam. Use the practice exam to assess your readiness for the real thing. Use the extensive answer explanations to improve your retention and understanding of the material.

The book includes several other features, such as a "Suggested Readings and Resources" section at the end of each chapter that directs you to additional information that can aid you in your exam preparation and your real-life work. Valuable appendixes are provided as well, including a glossary and a description of what is on the CD-ROM (Appendix A).

For more information about the exam or the certification process, refer to the CompTIA website, at www.comptia.org/certification.

Network Hardware and Software Requirements

As a self-paced study guide, *Network+ Exam Prep 2* is meant to help you understand concepts that must be refined through hands-on experience. To make the most of your studying, you need to have as much background on and experience with both common operating systems and network environments as possible. The best way to do this is to combine studying with work on actual networks. These networks need not be complex; the concepts involved in configuring a network with only a few computers follow the same principles as those involved in configuring a network that has hundreds of connected systems. This section describes the recommended requirements you need to form a solid practice environment.

To fully practice some of the exam objectives, you need to create a network with two (or more) computers networked together. To do this, you need an operating system. CompTIA maintains that the exam is vendor neutral, and for the most part it appears to be. However, if there were a slight tilt in the exam questions, it would be toward Microsoft Windows. Therefore, you would do well to set up a small network using a Microsoft server platform such as Windows 2000/2003 server. In addition, you need clients with operating systems such as Windows 2000/XP, Linux, and Mac. When you really get into it, you might want to install a Linux server as well because you are most certainly going to be working with them in the real world. The following is a detailed list of the hardware and software requirements needed to set up your network:

- ▶ A network operating system such as Windows Server or Linux
- ▶ Client operating system software such as Windows XP, Mac OS X, or Linux
- ▶ Modern PC offering up-to-date functionality including wireless support
- ▶ A minimum 1.5GB of free disk space
- ▶ A CD-ROM or DVD drive
- ▶ A network interface card (NIC) for each computer system
- ▶ Network cabling such as Category 5 unshielded twisted-pair
- ▶ A two-port (or more) miniport hub to create a test network
- ▶ Wireless devices

It's easy to obtain access to the necessary computer hardware and software in a corporate business environment. It can be difficult, however, to allocate enough time within the busy workday to complete a self-study program. Most of your study time will occur after normal working hours, away from the everyday interruptions and pressures of your regular job.

Advice on Taking the Exam

More extensive tips are found in the "Study and Exam Prep Tips" section, but keep this advice in mind as you study:

- ▶ Read all the material—CompTIA has been known to include material that is not expressly specified in the objectives. This book includes additional information that is not reflected in the objectives, in an effort to give you the best possible preparation for the examination—and for your real-world experiences to come.

▶ Complete the exercises in each chapter—They will help you gain experience in using the specified methodology or approach. CompTIA exams may require task- and experienced-based knowledge and require you to have an understanding of how certain network procedures are accomplished.

▶ Use the exam questions to assess your knowledge—Don't just read the chapter content; use the exam questions to find out what you know and what you don't know. If you are struggling, study some more, review, and then assess your knowledge again.

▶ Review the objectives—Develop your own questions and examples for each objective listed. If you can develop and answer several questions for each objective, you should not find it difficult to pass the exam.

NOTE

Exam-Taking Advice   Although this book is designed to prepare you to take and pass the Network+ certification exam, there are no guarantees. Read this book, work through the questions and exercises, and when you feel confident, take the practice exam and additional exams provided in the MeasureUp test software. Your results should tell you whether you are ready for the real thing.

When taking the actual certification exam, make sure that you answer all the questions before your time limit expires. Do not spend too much time on any one question. If you are unsure about the answer to a question, answer it as best as you can; then mark it for review after you have finished the rest of the questions. Note that this advice does not apply if you are taking an adaptive exam. In that case, take your time on each question because there is no opportunity to go back to a question.

Remember that the primary objective is not to pass the exam but to understand the material. When you understand the material, passing the exam should be simple. Knowledge is a pyramid; to build upward, you need a solid foundation. This book and the Network+ certification are designed to ensure that you have that solid foundation.

Good luck!

Study and Exam Preparation Tips

These study and exam preparation tips provide some general guidelines to help you prepare for the Network+ exam. The information here is organized into three sections. The first section addresses pre-exam preparation activities and covers general study tips. Following this are some tips and hints for the actual test-taking situation. Before tackling those areas, however, you should think a little bit about how you learn.

Learning As a Process

To best understand the nature of preparation for the exams, it is important to understand learning as a process. You are probably aware of how you best learn new material. You might find that outlining works best for you, or you might be a visual learner who needs to "see" things. Whatever your learning style, test preparation takes place over time. Obviously, you cannot start studying for the Network+ exam the night before you take it. It is important to understand that learning is a developmental process, and as part of that process, you need to focus on what you know and what you have yet to learn.

Learning takes place when we match new information to old. You have some previous experience with computers, and now you are preparing for the Network+ exam. Using this book, software, and supplementary materials will not just add incrementally to what you know; as you study, you will actually change the organization of your knowledge as you integrate this new information into your existing knowledge base. This will lead you to a more comprehensive understanding of the tasks and concepts outlined in the CompTIA objectives and of computing in general. Again, this happens as a repetitive process rather than as a singular event. If you keep this model of learning in mind as you prepare for the exam, you will make the best decisions concerning what to study and how much more studying you need to do.

Study Tips

There are many ways to approach studying, just as there are many different types of material to study. The following tips, however, should work well for the type of material covered on the Network+ exam.

Study Strategies

Although individuals vary in the ways they learn, some basic principles apply to everyone. Adopt some study strategies that take advantage of these principles. One of these principles is that learning can be broken into various depths. Recognition (of terms, for example) exemplifies a surface level of learning in which you rely on a prompt of some sort to elicit recall. Comprehension or understanding (of the concepts behind the terms, for example) represents a deeper level of learning. The ability to analyze a concept and apply your understanding of it in a new way represents an even deeper level of learning.

Your learning strategy should enable you to know the material at a level or two deeper than mere recognition. This will help you do well on the exam. You will know the material so thoroughly that you can easily handle the recognition-level types of questions used in multiple-choice testing. You will also be able to apply your knowledge to solve new problems.

Macro and Micro Study Strategies

One strategy that can lead to this deeper learning includes preparing an outline that covers all the objectives for the exam. You should delve a bit further into the material and include a level or two of detail beyond the stated objectives for the exam. Then you should expand the outline by coming up with a statement of definition or a summary for each point in the outline.

An outline provides two approaches to studying. First, you can study the outline by focusing on the organization of the material. You can work your way through the points and subpoints of your outline, with the goal of learning how they relate to one another. Make sure, for example, that you understand how each of the main objective areas is similar to and different from the others.

Next, you can work through the outline, focusing on learning the details. Memorize and understand terms and their definitions, facts, rules and strategies, advantages and disadvantages, and so on. In this pass through the outline, you should attempt to learn detail rather than the big picture (the organizational information that you worked on in the first pass through the outline).

Research has shown that attempting to assimilate both overall and detail types of information at the same time can interfere with the overall learning process. To best perform on the exam, separate your studying into these two approaches.

Active Study Strategies

Develop and actually exercise an active study strategy. Write down and define objectives, terms, facts, and definitions. In human information-processing terms, writing forces you to engage in more active encoding of the information. Just reading over the information exemplifies more passive processing.

Next, determine whether you can apply the information you have learned by attempting to create examples and scenarios on your own: Think about how or where you could apply the concepts you are learning. Again, write down this information to process the facts and concepts more actively.

Common Sense Strategies

Finally, follow common sense practices when studying. Study when you are alert, reduce or eliminate distractions, take breaks when you become fatigued, and so on.

Pretesting Yourself

Pretesting enables you to assess how well you are learning. One of the most important aspects of learning is metalearning. *Metalearning* has to do with realizing when you know something well or when you need to study some more. In other words, metalearning is the ability to recognize how well or how poorly you have learned the material you are studying.

For most people, metalearning can be difficult to assess objectively. Practice tests are useful in that they objectively reveal what you have learned and what you have not learned. You should practice test information to guide review and further study. Developmental learning takes place as you cycle through studying, assessing how well you have learned, reviewing, and assessing again until you think you are ready to take the exam.

You might have noticed the practice exam included in this book. You can use it as part of the learning process. The MeasureUp software on the CD-ROM also provides a variety of ways to test yourself before you take the actual exam. By using the practice exam, you can take an entire timed, practice test similar in nature to the actual Network+ exam. You can use the MeasureUp Adaptive Exam option to take the same test in an adaptive testing environment. This mode monitors your progress as you are taking the test, to offer you more difficult questions as you succeed. By using the Study Mode option, you can set your own time limit, focus only on a particular domain (for example, configuration), and also receive instant feedback on your answers.

Set a goal for your pretesting. A reasonable goal would be to score consistently in the 90% range.

See Appendix A, "What's on the CD-ROM" for a more detailed explanation of the test engine.

Exam Prep Tips

The Network+ certification exam is a standardized, computerized, fixed-form exam that reflects the knowledge domains established by CompTIA.

The original fixed-form, computerized exam is based on a fixed set of exam questions. The individual questions are presented in random order during a test session. If you take the same exam more than once, you will see the same number of questions, but you won't necessarily see the exact same questions. This is because two or three final forms are typically assembled for such exams. These are usually labeled Forms A, B, and C.

As suggested previously, the final forms of a fixed-form exam are identical in terms of content coverage, number of questions, and allotted time, but the questions differ. You might notice, however, that some of the same questions appear on, or are shared among, different final forms. When questions are shared among multiple final forms of an exam, the percentage of sharing is generally small. Many final forms share no questions, but some older exams might have a 10% to 15% duplication of exam questions on the final exam forms.

Fixed-form exams also have a fixed time limit in which you must complete the exam. The MeasureUp test engine on the CD-ROM that accompanies this book provides fixed-form exams.

Finally, the score you achieve on a fixed-form exam is based on the number of questions you answer correctly. The exam's passing score is the same for all final forms of a given fixed-form exam.

Table 1 shows the format for the exam.

TABLE 1   Time, Number of Questions, and Passing Score for the Network+ Exam

Exam	Time Limit in Minutes	Number of Questions	Passing %
Network+ exam	90	72	72%

Remember that you should not dwell on any one question for too long. Your 90 minutes of exam time can be consumed very quickly.

Given all these different pieces of information, the task now is to assemble a set of tips that will help you successfully tackle the Network+ certification exam.

More Exam Prep Tips

Generic exam-preparation advice is always useful. Tips include the following:

▶ Become familiar with networking terms and concepts. Hands-on experience is one of the keys to success. Review the exercises throughout this book.

- ▶ Review the current exam preparation guide on the CompTIA website.

- ▶ Memorize foundational technical detail, but remember that you need to be able to think your way through questions as well.

- ▶ Take any of the available practice tests. We recommend the ones included in this book and the ones you can create by using the MeasureUp software on the CD-ROM.

- ▶ Look at the CompTIA website for samples and demonstration items.

Tips for During the Exam Session

The following generic exam-taking advice that you have heard for years applies when taking the Network+ exam:

- ▶ Take a deep breath and try to relax when you first sit down for the exam session. It is important to control the stress you might (naturally) feel when taking exams.

- ▶ You will be provided scratch paper. Take a moment to write down on this paper any factual information and technical detail that you committed to short-term memory.

- ▶ Carefully read all information and instruction screens. These displays have been put together to give you information relevant to the exam you are taking.

- ▶ Read the exam questions carefully. Reread each question to identify all relevant details.

- ▶ Tackle the questions in the order in which they are presented. Skipping around will not build your confidence; the clock is always counting down.

- ▶ Do not rush, but also do not linger on difficult questions. The questions vary in degree of difficulty. Don't let yourself be flustered by a particularly difficult or verbose question.

- ▶ Note the time allotted and the number of questions appearing on the exam you are taking. Make a rough calculation of how many minutes you can spend on each question, and use this to pace yourself through the exam.

- ▶ Take advantage of the fact that you can return to and review skipped or previously answered questions. Record the questions you cannot answer confidently, noting the relative difficulty of each question, on the scratch paper provided. After you have made it to the end of the exam, return to the troublesome questions.

- ▶ If session time remains after you have completed all questions (and if you aren't too fatigued!), review your answers. Pay particular attention to questions that seem to have a lot of detail or that involve graphics.

▶ As for changing your answers, the general rule of thumb is don't! If you read a question carefully and completely and you thought you knew the right answer, you probably did. Do not second-guess yourself. If as you check your answers, one clearly stands out as being incorrectly marked, of course you should change it. If you are at all unsure, however, go with your first impression.

If you have done your studying, know the material, and follow the preceding suggestions, you should do well. Good luck!

PART I

Exam Preparation

CHAPTER ONE

Introduction to Networking

Objectives

This chapter covers the following CompTIA-specified objectives for the "Media and Topologies" section of the Network+ exam:

1.1 Recognize the following logical or physical network topologies given a diagram, schematic, or description:

▶ **Star**

▶ **Bus**

▶ **Mesh**

▶ **Ring**

▶ **Wireless**

▶ One of the fundamental network concepts that must be understood by all network administrators is topologies. A handful of topologies are currently defined and in use, and you will be expected to know the characteristics of each one.

1.2 Specify the main features of 802.2 (Logical Link Control), 802.3 (Ethernet), 802.5 (Token Ring), 802.11(wireless), and FDDI (Fiber Distributed Data Interface) networking technologies, including

▶ **Speed**

▶ **Access method (CSMA/CA [Carrier Sense Multiple Access/Collision Avoidance] and CSMA/CD [Carrier Sense Multiple Access/Collision Detection])**

▶ **Topology**

▶ **Media**

▶ Standards enable network components from different manufacturers to work together on the same network. It is important that network administrators understand the characteristics of commonly implemented standards.

1.7 Specify the general characteristics (for example, carrier speed, frequency, transmission type, and topology) of the following wireless technologies:

▶ **802.11 (Frequency hopping spread spectrum)**

▶ **802.11x (Direct sequence spread spectrum)**

▶ **Infrared**

▶ **Bluetooth**

▶ Wireless networking has become commonplace, and as a network administrator it is important that you understand the most commonly used wireless technologies.

1.8 Identify factors that affect the range and speed of wireless service (for example, interference, antenna type, and environmental factors).

▶ Working with wireless technologies requires an understanding of those factors that interfere with wireless transmissions.

Outline

Study Strategies

▶ Review the characteristics of the various network topologies including their strengths and weaknesses.

▶ Identify the features and functions of the IEEE 802 standards.

▶ Review the characteristics of 802.11 standards, including the information provided in Table 1.12.

▶ Identify the components involved in wireless communications.

▶ Review the factors that cause wireless interference.

▶ Review the Notes, Tips, and Exam Alerts in this chapter. Be sure that you understand the information in the Exam Alerts. If you don't understand the topic referenced in an Exam Alert, refer to the information in the chapter text and then read the Exam Alert again.

Introduction

By itself, the computer sitting on your desk is a powerful personal and business tool. Link that system with 1, 2, or even 1,000 other computers, and the possibilities and potential of your system become almost endless. That is the nature of networking.

Companies of all sizes depend on a collection of interconnected computers to conduct business. These computer networks make possible most of the applications and services used in corporate and home environments. Email, printing, real-time communication, file sharing, and videoconferencing would all be unavailable (or pointless) without networks.

The CompTIA Network+ exam is designed to prepare people to work with and around computer networks. The CompTIA objectives introduce basic networking concepts and design, laying the foundation for a solid, comprehensive understanding of networking fundamentals. This book closely follows the CompTIA objectives, clearly explaining each objective and highlighting the important concepts that are most likely to appear on the exam.

This chapter examines some of the fundamental principles that affect modern networking. These include a discussion about peer-to-peer and client/server computing, a discussion of the differences between local area networks (LANs), wide area networks (WANs), and metropolitan area networks (MANs). This chapter also looks at network topologies and how they can affect the basic layout and makeup of a network. Finally, this chapter explores basic wireless concepts including the wireless communication process and the wireless standards used today.

What Is a Network?

By definition, a *network* is a group of connected computers. The group can be as small and simple as two computers and a printer set up in a house or as large and complex as a multisite network that supports thousands of computers and hundreds of printers and other devices. Regardless of the size and complexity of a network, its fundamental function is to allow you to communicate and share data and resources.

Although the basic purpose of a network has not changed since the first network was created, the way in which we build and use networks has evolved in an amazing way. What was once a luxury that only the largest companies and governments could afford has become a vital business tool that hundreds of millions of people rely on every day.

NOTE

The Internet It might seem as though a small network in your house is very different from a network such as the Internet, but you would be surprised how much the two have in common. For example, the PCs on a home network most likely communicate in the same way as systems on the Internet. Also, the Internet has clients and servers just like a small network might have. The Internet uses certain devices, such as network routers, that are not as common in a home network, but the basic building blocks of both networks are the same. In fact, the term *Internet* is derived from the term *internetwork*, which is used to describe a group of connected networks.

The operation of a network should be transparent to the people who use it. Users should, for example, be able to print to a printer connected to the network just as easily as if it were attached to their own PCs. They should also be able to access files this easily. The degree of transparency of a network depends on how good the network's structure is and, to a certain extent, how well the network is managed. (But no matter how well a network is managed, problems will occasionally crop up.)

The Functions of a Network

If the purpose of a network is to share resources among computer systems, what types of information and services are shared on a network—and why? All networks, regardless of their design or size, perform one or all of a number of network functions. The following are some common reasons for implementing a network:

- **Communication**—Increased communication is one of the primary purposes of a network. Networks allow a variety of communications, including videoconferencing, real-time chats, and email. Many organizations have grown so dependent on network communications that without it, they cannot function.

- **Sharing hardware**—Printing is the best example of hardware sharing. Without a network, each computer that requires printing capabilities would need a printer connected directly to it—and that would be impractical and costly. Although printers are almost certainly the most popular devices shared on networks, other devices are often shared as well, including scanners, CD-ROM drives, tape drives, and other removable media.

- **Data sharing**—Linking users on the same system makes it easy for them to share files with others on the network. However, because people can access the data across the network, access to both the data and the network must be carefully controlled. Fortunately, network operating systems provide mechanisms that allow you to secure data so that access can be controlled.

- **Application sharing**—Networking makes it possible for numerous users to share a single application. This makes it unnecessary to install the same application on several computer systems; instead, the application can be run from a central location. Such a strategy is often used on medium to large networks, where it is difficult and time-consuming to install and maintain applications on numerous individual systems. Application sharing is also important for centralized systems such as databases; users rely on networks to access and use such systems.

- **Data backup and retrieval**—A network makes it possible to store data in a central location. When the data is in a central location, it is easier to back up and retrieve. The importance of this benefit cannot be overstated. No matter how much money is invested in a computer network, the data that travels on it has the most value.

Because of these network functions, the majority of businesses and increasing numbers of home users have networks. Given such advantages, the real decision often is not whether to set up a network but what type of network to create. This chapter explores some of the options.

Peer-to-Peer Versus Client/Server Networks

Wired networks use two basic models: peer-to-peer and client/server. The model used by an organization depends on the role of the network and what the users require from it. You will probably encounter both network models; therefore, you need to understand how these models work as well as their strengths and weaknesses.

The Peer-to-Peer Networking Model

Peer-to-peer networking, sometimes referred to as a workgroup, is a low-cost, easily implemented network solution generally used in small network environments that need to share a few files and maybe some hardware, such as printers. As its name suggests, on a peer-to-peer network all systems are equal, or *peers*. Each system can share hardware or files and access the same things on other systems.

> **NOTE**
>
> **Peer-to-Peer Home Networks**   Peer-to-peer networks are often seen in residential settings, where home computers are linked together to share an Internet connection, printers, or files. All popular workstation PC operating systems offer peer-to-peer network functionality.

A peer-to-peer network offers no centralized data storage or centralized control over the sharing of files or resources. In a sense, everyone on a peer-to-peer network is a network administrator and can share resources as they see fit. They have the option to grant all users on the network complete access to their computers, including printers and files, or they can choose not to share anything. Figure 1.1 shows an example of a peer-to-peer network.

The peer-to-peer model works well on networks that have 10 or fewer computers, but as a network grows, it becomes more complicated. Peer-to-peer networking is often referred to as *decentralized networking* because the network files, data, and administration are not handled from a central location. This arrangement can lead to huge problems, especially in large networks. For example, locating specific files can become difficult because the files might be on multiple computers. Data backup cannot be performed from a central location; each computer must be backed up individually. Decentralized networking can also be difficult in terms of network security because security is controlled by individual computer users instead of being administered from a central location. This decentralized security model requires that each user have a user ID and password defined on each and every system that he will access. With no way of synchronizing passwords between the systems, this can quickly become a problem. Many users have problems remembering just one or two passwords—let alone a dozen.

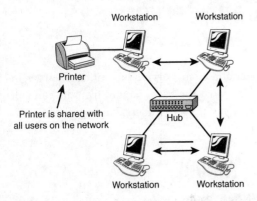

Resources of each system are made available to other systems on the network

FIGURE 1.1 An example of a peer-to-peer network.

Given the complexity and drawbacks of using peer-to-peer networking, you might wonder why anyone would use it. Many small companies begin with a peer-to-peer network because it's the easiest and least expensive type to install. After the networks grow too big, they switch to the client/server model, which is discussed in the next section.

> **NOTE**
>
> **Peer-to-Peer Network Size** A peer-to-peer network can link an unlimited number of PCs; no standards define a maximum. The only limits are the practicality of managing multiple systems in a peer-to-peer model and the restrictions of the operating system being used on the workstations.

Advantages of Peer-to-Peer Networks

The following are some of the advantages of using the peer-to-peer networking model:

▶ **Cost**—Because peer-to-peer networking does not require a dedicated server, such networks are very cost-effective. This makes them an attractive option in environments where money is tight.

▶ **Ease of installation**—The built-in support for peer-to-peer networking in modern operating systems makes installing and configuring a peer-to-peer network a straightforward process.

Disadvantages of Peer-to-Peer Networks

The following are some of the disadvantages of using the peer-to-peer networking model:

▶ **Security**—In a decentralized model, a networkwide security policy cannot be enforced from a server; rather, security needs to be applied to each computer and resource individually.

▶ **Data backup**—Because files and data are located on individual computers, each system must have its data backed up individually.

▶ **Resource access**—In a decentralized approach, it can be difficult to locate resources on the network. Printers and files may be distributed among numerous computer systems.

▶ **Limited numbers of computers**—Peer-to-peer networking is effective only on small networks (fewer than 10 computers).

As you can see, the disadvantages of peer-to-peer networking outweigh the advantages. Therefore, client/server networks are far more popular in corporate or business environments than peer-to-peer networks.

The Client/Server Networking Model

Client/server networking—or *server-based networking*, as it is commonly called—is the network model you are most likely to see in the corporate world. The server-based network model is completely scalable, allowing additional computers or other networked devices to be added with little difficulty. Perhaps the greatest benefit of this model is that it allows for centralized management of all network services, security, and streamlined backup procedures. Figure 1.2 shows an example of a client/server network.

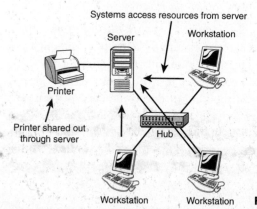

FIGURE 1.2 An example of a client/server network.

As you may have gathered, two different types of computers are required for the server-based model: the client and the server. Figure 1.3 shows the relationship between client and server computers. These two computer systems are often very different from each other, and each plays a unique role on a network.

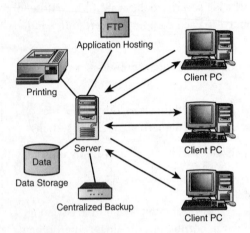

FIGURE 1.3   The relationship between client and server computers.

Servers

Servers are the workhorses of the network. They spend their time responding to the numerous requests that come from client computers, such as requests for files, network authentication, and access to shared hardware resources. Network administration—including network security, backups, and network monitoring—is done from the server.

To perform their functions, server computers require additional resources and computing power. Server systems often use specialized hardware and software in fault-tolerant configurations to ensure that they remain operational. When a server fails and goes offline, it cannot respond to requests from client systems, and its functions are unavailable. This situation can be frustrating for users and costly for an organization.

In addition to requiring specific hardware, servers also require a network operating system. A network operating system stands above ordinary desktop operating systems; it has unique features and functions that allow an administrator to manage, monitor, and administer the data and resources of the server as well as the users who connect to it. In addition, network operating systems are designed to be resilient in case of the kind of downtime discussed earlier. The most common network operating systems used today are the Microsoft Windows network operating systems, Windows 2000/2003, Unix, Linux, Mac OS X servers, and Novell NetWare. Knowledge of these operating systems is an important element of the Network+ exam, so detailed coverage of them is provided in Chapter 9, "Network Operating Systems and Clients."

A network may have a single server that offers more than one network service or hundreds of servers, each performing a dedicated task. For example, one server might be used only to authenticate users, and another might be used to store an applications database. Some of the most common roles for dedicated servers include acting as file and print servers, application servers, web servers, database servers, firewall servers, and proxy servers.

Client Computers

Client computers are the other half of the client/server model. Client computers connect to the network and access the resources of the server. Software is needed to allow the client to connect to the network, although the need for networking has become so fundamental that the client software functionality is now built in to desktop operating systems.

Advantages of Client/Server Networking

The following are some of the advantages of the client/server networking model:

- ▶ **Centralized management and security**—The capability to manage the network from a single location is the biggest advantage of the client/server model. From a server, you can perform backups of all data, share resources and control access to those resources, manage user accounts, and monitor network activity.

- ▶ **Scalability**—In a server-based network administrators can easily add computers and devices. In addition, the network is not restricted to a small number of computers. In a client/server network, the number of clients is limited by factors such as licensing and network capacity rather than by the operating system's capability to support them.

- ▶ **Simplified backups**—On server-based networks, files and folders typically reside in a single location or a small number of locations and are therefore easier to back up than the files on a peer-to-peer network. Scheduling backups to occur at regular intervals is simple.

Disadvantages of Client/Server Networking

The following are some of the disadvantages of the client/server networking model:

- ▶ **High cost**—A server-based network requires additional hardware and software, so it can be a costly venture. The costs of the client/server model include the costs of the network operating system and at least one server system, replete with specialized server hardware. Also, because the client/server model can support far more systems than the peer-to-peer model, networking devices such as hubs, routers, and switches are often needed.

- ▶ **Administration requirements**—Client/server networks require additional administrative skills over those required on a peer-to-peer network. In particular, the technical capabilities of the administrator need to be greater. Organizations that use the server-based model often need technically skilled people to manage and maintain the network and the servers.

▶ **Single points of failure**—In a client/server model, the client systems depend on servers to provide network services. If the server fails, the clients can't access the services that reside on the server. Great effort and expense are needed to ensure the high availability of network servers.

Given the limitations of the peer-to-peer network design, such networks are used in only a few situations. On the other hand, the client/server networking model is versatile, and its shortcomings are overshadowed by its capabilities and advantages. You will spend most of your time working with server-based networks of all shapes and sizes.

> **NOTE**
>
> **Combination Networks** The distinction between networks that use a peer-to-peer design and those that use a client/server design is not always clear. Today's operating systems let client computers share resources with other systems in a peer-to-peer configuration and also be connected to a server. Such an arrangement is sometimes referred to as a *combination network*. Although this model takes advantage of the benefits of both network models, it is also susceptible to their combined shortcomings.

Distributed and Centralized Computing

Although they're less of an issue than in the past, you need to be familiar with two important networking concepts: distributed and centralized computing. These concepts are not directly related to the server-based/peer-to-peer discussion, although by definition a peer-to-peer and server-based network model are examples of a distributed computing model.

The terms *distributed* and *centralized computing* describe the location on a network where the processing takes place. In an environment such as a mainframe, the processing is performed on a centralized system that also stores all the data. In such a model, no data processing or data storage occurs on the client terminal. In contrast, in a distributed processing environment, processing is performed in more than one place. If a network has servers and workstations, processing can take place on the server or on the client.

It is relatively unusual for a company to have just a centralized computing environment. A company is far more likely to have a server-based network, which would fall under the banner of distributed computing, and perhaps a mainframe that is accessed from the same PCs as the server-based network, which would fall under the banner of centralized computing. A good example of such an environment might be a company that books hotel reservations for customers, in which the booking system is held on a mainframe, but the email system used to correspond with clients is held on a PC-based server and accessed through client software on the PCs.

LANs, WANs, MANs, and PANs

Networks are categorized according to how many locations they span. A network confined to a single location is known as a LAN. Networks that span multiple geographic locations are known as WANs. There is also another category, called a MAN, which is used to classify networks that fall somewhere between LANs and WANs. The following sections examine the characteristics of these types of networks.

LANs

A LAN is confined to a single geographic location, such as a single building, office, or school. LANs are created with networking media that are very fast but that can cover a limited distance. Figure 1.4 shows an example of a LAN.

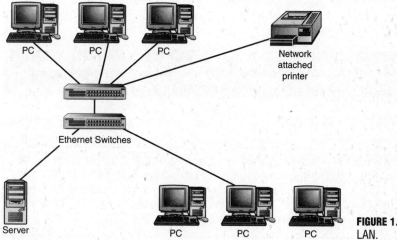

FIGURE 1.4 An example of a LAN.

WANs

A WAN is a network that spans multiple geographic locations. WANs are generally slower than LANs and are considerably more expensive to run. WANs are all about data throughput, and the more need, the more you spend. WANs connect LANs together to create an *internetwork*. Figure 1.5 shows an example of a WAN.

WANs often use different technologies from LANs. WAN technologies are discussed in Chapter 7, "WAN and Internet Access Technologies."

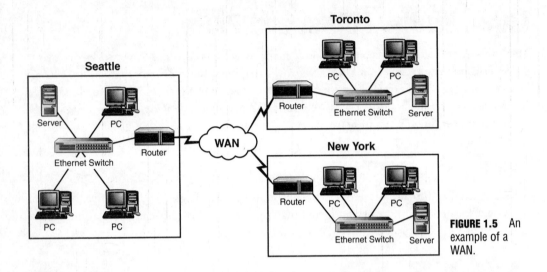

FIGURE 1.5 An example of a WAN.

NOTE

When Does a LAN Become a WAN? Technically, a LAN never becomes a WAN. If the definitions of LAN and WAN were taken literally and applied to a working model that had three connected sites, the portions of the network confined within each site would be LANs, and the network elements connecting the sites together would be called the WAN. Avoid the temptation to refer to the entire internetwork as a WAN because WANs and LANs employ some very different technologies.

MANs

A MAN is confined to a certain geographic area such as a university campus or a city. No formal guidelines dictate the differences between a MAN and a WAN; technically, a MAN is a WAN. Perhaps for this reason, the term *MAN* is used less frequently than *WAN*. If any distinction exists, it's that a MAN is smaller than a WAN. A MAN is almost always bigger than a LAN and usually smaller than or equal to a WAN. MANs utilize an ISP or Telco provider.

NOTE

CANs You might hear the term *campus area network* (CAN) in discussions of network layouts. A CAN is a network that spans a defined single location (such as an office complex with multiple buildings or a college campus) but is not large enough to be considered a WAN.

PANs

A Personal Area Network (PAN) is a small network design typically associated with a single person. A common implementation of a PAN is using wireless technologies. Wireless developments have introduced a new term—*Wireless Personal Area Networks (WPAN)*. WPAN refers to the technologies involved in connecting devices in close proximity to exchange data or resources. An example might be connecting a laptop with a PDA to synchronize an address book. Due to their small size and the nature of the data exchange, WPAN devices lend themselves well to ad-hoc networking. *Ad-hoc networks* have devices that connect to each other directly and not through a wireless access point. Ad-hoc wireless networks are discussed later in this chapter.

Because of the close proximity of WPAN networking, short-range wireless technologies are typically used. This includes Bluetooth and infrared. The key WPAN technology supported in Windows XP Professional, for example, is Infrared Data Association (IrDA). In addition, the IEEE wireless standards including 802.11b/g can be used to create a WPAN.

Having established the purpose and function of networks and how networks are classified based on size, the following section looks at the specific features of a network, beginning with LAN topologies.

LAN Topologies

Objective:

1.1 Recognize the following logical or physical network topologies given a diagram, schematic, or description:

▶ Star

▶ Bus

▶ Mesh

▶ Ring

▶ Wireless

The term *network topology* refers to the layout of a network. The type of topology affects what networking method is used, as well as what media types and network devices are required. Topologies are very important, and they serve as the foundation for the information you'll learn in the following sections. You will likely be asked about topologies on the Network+ exam.

Before we look at the different types of topologies, we must first examine one of the most confusing networking principles: the difference between physical and logical topologies. Then we'll examine the specific physical LAN topologies in use today: bus, star, ring, mesh, and wireless.

Physical and Logical Topologies

Network topologies can be defined on a physical level or on a logical level. The *physical topology* refers to how a network is physically constructed—that is, how it actually looks. The *logical topology* refers to how a network looks to the devices that use it—in other words, how it actually functions. In a number of commonly implemented network models, the physical topology differs from the logical topology. It can be difficult to appreciate what that means, so let's use an example.

The most commonly implemented network model is a physical star/logical bus topology. In this configuration, computers are connected to a central device, called a *hub* or *switch*, which gives the network the appearance of a star (or a reasonable facsimile thereof). However, the devices attached to the star see the network as a linear bus topology and use the topology based on its logical characteristics.

EXAM ALERT

Network Topologies Understanding network topologies and their characteristics is an objective for the Network+ exam. Therefore, you should make sure that you understand the concept of topologies.

NOTE

How Did We Get Here? The physical/logical topology discussion can be confusing, so let's examine its background. When networks were first created, they followed a simple path. For example, the first Ethernet network was a physical and logical bus (single length of cable). As you will see in upcoming sections, however, this physical bus approach has a number of disadvantages; therefore, alternatives were sought. In this case, the solution was to move away from the single cable segment approach and instead use different types of cable on a physical star. The media access method and the networking system remained the same, however, resulting in a physical star/logical bus topology.

The Bus Topology

The bus network topology is also known as a *linear bus* because the computers in such a network are linked together using a single cable called a *trunk*, or *backbone*. Computers are connected to this backbone as shown in Figure 1.6.

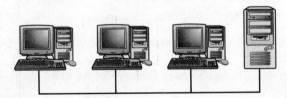

FIGURE 1.6 An example of the bus topology.

The computers can be connected to the backbone by a cable, known as a *drop cable*, or, more commonly, directly to the backbone, via T connectors. At each end of the cable, terminators prevent the signal from bouncing back down the cable. In addition, one end of the cable should be grounded. More information on the specific connectors and connections used in different networks is provided in Chapter 2, "Cabling Standards, Media, and Connectors."

NOTE

Ethernet Standards The most common implementation of a linear bus is the Institute of Electrical and Electronics Engineers (IEEE) 802.3 standard, 10Base2, which is an Ethernet standard. Ethernet standards are covered later in this chapter.

Bus topologies are easy and inexpensive to implement because a single-segment bus topology doesn't require any special networking equipment. However, they are notoriously difficult to troubleshoot, and a single break in the network cable renders the entire segment useless. For this and a number other reasons, such as limited speed capacity, bus topologies have been largely replaced with the physical star topology. Table 1.1 lists the main features, advantages, and disadvantages of bus topologies.

TABLE 1.1 Features, Advantages, and Disadvantages of the Linear Bus Topology

Features	Advantages	Disadvantages
Uses a single length of cable.	It is inexpensive and easy to implement.	It cannot be expanded easily. Doing so may render the network inaccessible while the expansion is performed.
Devices connect directly to the cable.	It doesn't require special equipment.	A break in the cable renders the entire segment unusable.
The cable must be terminated at both ends.	It requires less cable than other topologies.	It is difficult to troubleshoot.

The Star Topology

In a star topology, each device on the network connects to a centralized device via a single cable. This arrangement creates a point-to-point network connection between the two devices and overall gives the appearance of a star. Figure 1.7 shows an example of the star topology.

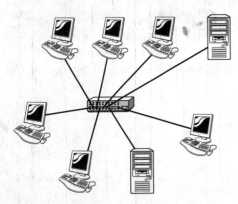

FIGURE 1.7 An example of the star topology.

EXAM ALERT

Star Topology   Be prepared to identify the star topology on the Network+ exam.

Because each device must have its own cable, a star topology requires far more cable than other topologies such as a physical linear bus. In addition, special equipment is required to create the star layout, adding to the cost of implementing a star topology. (Chapter 3, "Networking Components and Devices," explains the function of network devices such as hubs and switches that are used in a star topology.)

Multiple stars can be combined into a treelike structure known as a *hierarchical star*. The hierarchical star allows for high levels of flexibility and expandability. Depending on the networking equipment used, it also makes it possible to manage traffic and isolate high-traffic areas of the network. Figure 1.8 shows an example of a hierarchical star topology.

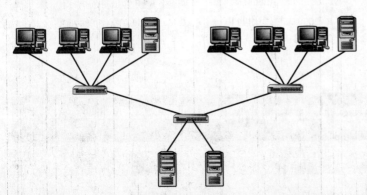

FIGURE 1.8 An example of the hierarchical star topology.

EXAM ALERT

Hierarchical Star Topology Be prepared to identify a hierarchical star topology on the Network+ exam.

One of the biggest advantages of the star topology is that computers can be connected to and disconnected from the network without affecting any other systems. Thus it's easy to add systems to or remove systems from the network. In addition, the failure of a system or the cable it uses to attach likewise generally has no effect on other stations on the network. However, in the star topology, all devices on the network connect to a central device, and this central device creates a single point of failure on the network.

NOTE

The Ethernet 10BaseT Standard The most common implementation of the physical star topology is the Ethernet 100 BaseT standard.

The star topology is the most widely implemented network design in use today; you will definitely encounter it in the real world. Working with and troubleshooting a star topology can be tricky, however, and you need to know what to look for and where to look. For more information on troubleshooting star networks and other specific network topology errors, see Chapter 15, "Troubleshooting Procedures and Best Practices."

Table 1.2 provides the features, advantages, and disadvantages of the physical star topology.

TABLE 1.2 Features, Advantages, and Disadvantages of the Physical Star Topology

Features	Advantages	Disadvantages
Devices connect to a central point.	It can be easily expanded without disruption to existing systems.	It requires additional networking equipment to create the network layout.
Each system uses an individual cable to attach.	A cable failure affects only a single system.	It requires considerably more cable than other topologies, such as the linear bus.
Multiple stars can be combined to create a hierarchical star.	It is easy to troubleshoot.	Centralized devices create a single point of failure.

EXAM ALERT

Star Topology Advantages/Disadvantages For the Network+ exam, make sure that you understand the advantages and disadvantages of the star topology.

The Ring Topology

In the ring topology, the network layout forms a complete ring. Computers connect to the network cable directly or, far more commonly, through a specialized network device.

On a ring network, data travels in one direction, passing from one computer to the next until it reaches the intended destination. Figure 1.9 shows an example of the ring topology.

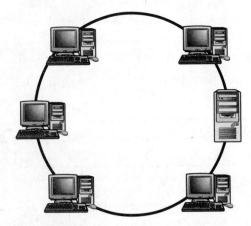

FIGURE 1.9 An example of the ring topology.

EXAM ALERT

Ring Topology   Be prepared to identify the ring topology on the Network+ exam.

Ring topologies are more difficult to install and configure than other topologies because breaking the loop disrupts the entire network. Even if network devices are used to create the ring, the ring must still be broken if a fault occurs or the network needs to be expanded.

NOTE

Dual Rings   To negate the problem of a broken ring making the network unavailable, you can configure dual rings so that one ring can be used if the other fails. One ring topology that employs this strategy is FDDI, which is discussed in Chapter 7.

Ring topologies are relatively uncommon; the physical star layout is by far the most popular topology. For this reason, you are unlikely to actually install a ring topology. Table 1.3 shows the features, advantages, and disadvantages of the ring topology.

TABLE 1.3   Features, Advantages, and Disadvantages of the Ring Topology

Features	Advantages	Disadvantages
Devices are connected in a closed loop or ring.	It is easy to troubleshoot.	A cable break can disrupt the entire network
Dual-ring configuration can be used for fault tolerance.	Can be implemented in a fault-tolerant configuration.	Network expansion creates network disruption.

EXAM ALERT

Ring Topology Advantages/Disadvantages   For the Network+ exam, make sure that you understand the advantages and disadvantages of the ring topology.

Mesh Topology

The mesh topology is unique: It requires each computer on the network to be individually connected to every other device. This configuration provides maximum reliability and redundancy for the network. If one cable or link fails, the data can use an alternate path to get to its destination. Figure 1.10 shows an example of the mesh topology.

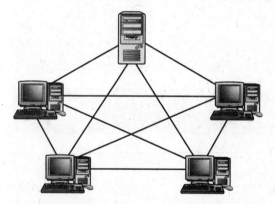

FIGURE 1.10   An example of the mesh topology.

EXAM ALERT

Mesh Topology   Be prepared to identify the mesh topology on the Network+ exam.

NOTE

Fault Tolerance   Although it is impractical to implement, the mesh layout is the most fault tolerant of all the network topologies. Redundant links exist between all nodes, and the failure of a single link does not affect the overall functionality of the network.

Given the relative ease with which the other topologies can be created and the complexity of the mesh layout, you should not be surprised to learn that networks using the mesh layout are few and far between. In fact, you are unlikely to see a mesh layout in a LAN setting. The mesh topology is sometimes adopted in WAN configurations that require direct connections between each and every geographic site.

> **NOTE**
>
> **Hybrid Mesh Networks**   The term *hybrid mesh* is sometimes used to refer to a mesh network that has direct links between some systems but not all. Again, such a configuration is more likely to be seen in a WAN configuration than in a LAN but is becoming more popular with the advent of Windows 2003.

Table 1.4 lists the features, advantages, and disadvantages of the mesh topology.

TABLE 1.4   Features, Advantages, and Disadvantages of the Mesh Topology

Features	Advantages	Disadvantages
A true mesh uses point-to-point connectivity between all devices.	Multiple links provide fault tolerance and redundancy.	It is difficult to implement.
A hybrid mesh uses point-to-point connectivity between certain devices, but not all of them.	The network can be expanded with minimal or no disruption.	It can be expensive because it requires specialized hardware and cable.

> **EXAM ALERT**
>
> **Mesh Topology Advantages/Disadvantages**   For the Network+ exam, make sure that you understand the advantages and disadvantages of the mesh topology.

Wireless Topologies

The widespread interest in networks without wires and the push toward obtaining "anywhere, anytime" Internet access has encouraged rapid growth in wireless standards and related technologies. The IEEE 802.11 wireless standards in particular have experienced considerable success. Several wireless standards fall under the 802.11 banner each with its own speeds, radio frequencies, and transmission ranges. These standards create the possibility for wireless local area networking (WLAN) and puts the possibility of complete mobile computing within reach.

The 802.11 wireless standards use two main types of network topologies: the infrastructure, or managed, wireless topology and the ad-hoc, or unmanaged, wireless topology.

Infrastructure Wireless Topology

The infrastructure wireless topology is commonly used to extend a wired LAN to include wireless devices. Wireless devices communicate with the wired LAN through a base station known as an access point (AP) or Wireless Access Point (WAP). The AP forms a bridge between a wireless and wired LAN, and all transmissions between wireless stations or between a system and a wired network client go through the AP. APs are not mobile and have to stay connected to the wired network and therefore become part of the wired network infrastructure, thus the name. In infrastructure wireless networks, several access points may provide wireless coverage for a large area, or only a single access point may provide coverage for a small area such as a single home or small building. Figure 1.11 shows an example of an infrastructure wireless network using a single AP and one using multiple APs.

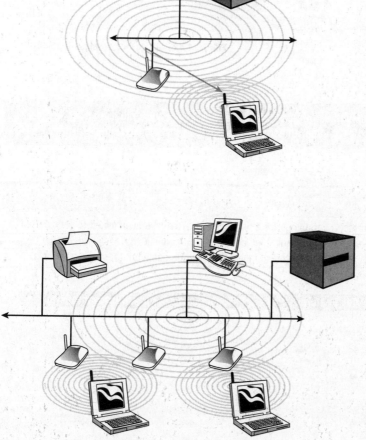

FIGURE 1.11 Wireless infrastructure topologies.

Ad-Hoc Wireless Networking

In a wireless ad-hoc topology, devices communicate directly between themselves without using an access point. This peer-to-peer network design is commonly used to connect a small number of computers or wireless devices. For example, an ad-hoc wireless network may be set up temporarily between laptops in a boardroom or to connect to systems in a home instead of a wired solution. The ad-hoc wireless design provides a quick method to share files and resources between a small number of systems. Figure 1.12 shows and example of an ad-hoc network design.

FIGURE 1.12 An ad-hoc wireless topology.

EXAM ALERT

Ad-hoc Wireless Topology The ad-hoc, or unmanaged, network design does not use an AP. All wireless devices connect directly to each other. Underlying technologies include Bluetooth or IrDA.

Challenge

You have been asked to recommend a topology for a new network. You have been asked to consider all options and prepare a document that shows how they compare. To complete your task, you decide to create a chart showing the advantages and disadvantages of the various network topologies. For this exercise, complete the following chart:

Topology Type	Key Features	Advantages	Disadvantges
Star			
Bus			
Mesh			
Ring			
Wireless infrastructure			

The IEEE and Networking Standards

Objective:

1.2 Specify the main features of 802.2 (Logical Link Control), 802.3 (Ethernet), 802.5 (Token Ring), 802.11 (wireless), and FDDI (Fiber Distributed Data Interface) networking technologies, including:

▶ Speed

▶ Access method (CSMA/CA [Carrier Sense Multiple Access/Collision Avoidance] and CSMA/CD [Carrier Sense Multiple Access/Collision Detection])

▶ Topology

▶ Media

Whereas a topology defines the structure of a network, network standards define how it works. As early as the 1970s, it was apparent that networks were going to play a large role in future corporate environments. Many manufacturers saw the computing and network trend and became increasingly active in network component development. These companies realized that for their products to work together, standards would be necessary to ensure compatibility. The task of producing the standards fell to an international body called the Institute of Electrical and Electronics Engineers (IEEE).

The IEEE developed a set of standards called the 802 project. These standards are still used today, although there have been many changes and additions along the way. By using the standards defined by the IEEE, manufacturers can be sure that their products will work with products from other companies that adhere to the standards.

Some of the IEEE 802 standards define only certain technologies, whereas others, such as the 802.3 standard, define entire networking systems. The following are some of the most important IEEE 802 standards:

▶ **802.1, bridging and management**—Defines the systems for managing networks. 802.1 specifies technologies for making sure that the network is available to users and responding to requests. It defines internetwork communications standards between devices and includes specifications for routing and bridging.

▶ **802.2, the LLC sublayer**—Defines specifications for the Logical Link Control (LLC) sublayer in the 802 standard series.

▶ **802.3, CSMA/CD**—Defines the carrier-sense multiple-access with collision detection (CSMA/CD) media access method used in Ethernet networks. This is the most popular networking standard used today.

▶ **802.4, a token passing bus (rarely used)**—Defines the use of a token-passing system on a linear bus topology.

- **802.5, Token Ring networks**—Defines Token Ring networking, also known as Token Ring Access.

- **802.6, metropolitan area network (MAN)**—Defines a data transmission method called distributed queue dual bus (DQDB), which is designed to carry voice and data on a single link.

- **802.7, Broadband Technical Advisory**—Defines the standards and specifications of broadband communications methods.

- **802.8, Fiber-Optic Technical Advisory**—Provides assistance to other IEEE 802 committees on subjects related to the use of fiber-optics.

- **802.9, Integrated Voice and Data Networks**—Works on the advancement of integrated voice and data networks.

- **802.10, network security**—Defines security standards that make it possible to safely and securely transmit and exchange data.

- **802.11, wireless networks**—Defines standards for wireless LAN communication.

- **802.12, 100BaseVG-AnyLAN**—Defines standards for high-speed LAN technologies.

For the Network+ exam and day-to-day real-life networking, some of these standards are more important than others. The Network+ exam focuses on the LAN standards: 802.2, 802.3, 802.5, and 802.11. These IEEE standards specify the characteristics of the networking systems, including the cable types used, access methods, speeds, and topologies. Although you don't need detailed knowledge of all these IEEE standards in real-world applications, a general understanding of these standards will be an asset.

Characteristics Specified in the IEEE 802 Standards

Let's review some of the characteristics specified within each standard: speed, access methods, topology, and media.

Speed

Many factors contribute to the speed of a network. The standard defines the maximum speed of a networking system. The speed normally is measured in megabits per second (Mbps), although some faster network systems use gigabits per second (that is, Gbps, where 1Gbps is equivalent to 1000Mbps).

> **NOTE**
>
> **Bandwidth** The term *bandwidth* has become a gray area in the network world. In everyday use it is sometimes used to describe the amount of data that can travel over a network connection in a given time period. This is technically not accurate; that more closely defines *data throughput*.

Some networks are faster than others. For example, a Token Ring (802.5) network has a maximum speed of 16Mbps. Many Ethernet networks (802.3 variants) now operate at 100Mbps. As you will see later in this chapter, when we discuss networking components, it is possible to further increase these figures. However, the maximum speed attainable on a network can be affected by many factors. Networks that achieve 100% of their potential bandwidth are few and far between.

Access Methods

Access methods govern the way in which systems access the network media and send data. Access methods are necessary to ensure that systems on the network can communicate with each other. Without an access method, it would be possible for two systems to communicate at the exclusion of every other system. Access methods ensure that everyone gets an opportunity to use the network.

Several access methods are used in networks; the most popular are CSMA/CD, CSMA/CA, and token passing. Other methods, such as demand priority, are also used. We'll look at each of these access methods separately.

CSMA/CD

CSMA/CD, which is defined in the IEEE 802.3 standard, is the most popular media access method because it is associated with Ethernet networking, which is by far the most popular networking system.

On a network that uses CSMA/CD, when a system wants to send data to another system, it first checks to see whether the network media is free. It must do this because each piece of network media used in a LAN can carry only one signal at a time. If the sending node detects that the media is free, it transmits, and the data is sent to the destination. It seems simple.

> **NOTE**
>
> **Nodes** A *node* is any device connected to the network. A node might be a client computer, server computer, printer, router, or gateway.

Now, if it always worked like this, you wouldn't need the CD part of CSMA/CD. Unfortunately, in networking, as in life, things do not always go as a planned. The problem arises when two systems attempt to transmit at exactly the same time. It might seem like a long shot that two systems will pick the same moment to send data, but we are dealing with communications that occur many times in a single second—and most networks have more than two machines. Imagine that 200 people are in a room. The room is silent, but then two people decide to say something at exactly the same time. Before they start to speak, they check (listen) to see whether someone else is speaking; because no one else is speaking, they begin to talk. The result is two people speaking at the same time, which is similar to a network collision.

Collision detection works by detecting fragments of the transmission on the network media that result when two systems try to talk at the same time. The two systems wait for a randomly calculated amount of time before attempting to transmit again. This amount of time—a matter of milliseconds—is known as the *backoff*.

When the backoff period has elapsed, the system attempts to transmit again. If the system doesn't succeed on the second attempt, it keeps retrying until it gives up and reports an error.

> **NOTE**
>
> **Contention**   CSMA/CD is known as a *contention media access method* because systems contend for access to the media.

The upside of CSMA/CD is that it has relatively low overhead, meaning that not much is involved in the workings of the system. The downside is that as more systems are added to the network, more collisions occur, and the network becomes slower. The performance of a network that uses CSMA/CD degrades exponentially as more systems are added. Its low overhead means that CSMA/CD systems theoretically can achieve greater speeds than high-overhead systems, such as token passing. However, because collisions take place, the chances of all that speed translating into usable bandwidth are relatively low.

> **NOTE**
>
> **Equal Access**   On a network that uses CSMA/CD, every node has equal access to the network media.

Despite its problems, CSMA/CD is an efficient system. As a result, rather than replace it with some other technology, workarounds have been created that reduce the likelihood of collisions. One such strategy is the use of network switches that create multiple collision domains and therefore reduce the impact of collisions on performance. Chapter 3 provides more information about using switches.

Table 1.5 summarizes the advantages and disadvantages of the CSMA/CD access method.

TABLE 1.5   Advantages and Disadvantages of CSMA/CD

Advantages	Disadvantages
It has low overhead.	Collisions degrade network performance.
Utilizes all available bandwidth when possible.	Priorities cannot be assigned to certain nodes. Performance degrades exponentially as devices are added.

CSMA/CA

Instead of collision detection as with CSMA/CD, the carrier-sense multiple access with collision avoidance (CSMA/CA) access method uses signal avoidance rather than detection. In a networked environment, CSMA/CA is the access mechanism used in Apple's LocalTalk network and with the 802.11 wireless standards.

On CSMA/CA networks, each computer signals its intent to transmit data signals before any data is actually sent. When a networked system detects a potential collision, it waits before sending out the transmission allowing systems to avoid transmission collisions. The CSMA/CA access method uses a random backoff time that determines how long to wait before trying to send data on the network. When the backoff time expires, the system will again "listen" to verify a clear channel on which to transmit. If the media is still busy, another backoff interval is initiated that is less than the first. The process continues until the wait time reaches zero, and the media is clear.

CSMA/CA uses a broadcast method to notify its intention to transmit data. Network broadcasts create a considerable amount of network traffic and can cause network congestion, which could slow down the entire network. Because CSMA/CD and CSMA/CA differ only in terms of detection and avoidance, they share similar advantages and disadvantages as shown previously in Table 1.5.

EXAM ALERT

CSMA/CA The CSMA/CA access method uses a "listen before talking" strategy. Any system wanting to transmit data must first verify that the channel is clear before transmitting, thereby avoiding potential collisions.

Token Passing

Although token passing, which is specified in IEEE 802.5, is the second most popular media access method, the domination of Ethernet networking makes it second by a considerable margin. However, it might not be popular, but it is clever.

On a token-passing network, a special packet called a *token* is passed among the systems on the network. The network has only one token, and a system can send data only when it has possession of the token.

When the data arrives, the receiving computer sends a verification message to the sending computer. The sender then creates a new token, and the process begins again. Standards dictate how long a system can have control over the token. Figure 1.13 shows how data is sent on a token-passing network.

One of the big advantages of the token-passing access method is the lack of collisions. Because a system can transmit only when it has the token, there is no contention. Even under heavy load conditions, the speed of a token-passing system does not degrade in the same way as a contention-based method such as CSMA/CD. In a practical scenario, this fact makes token passing more suitable than other access methods for applications such as videoconferencing.

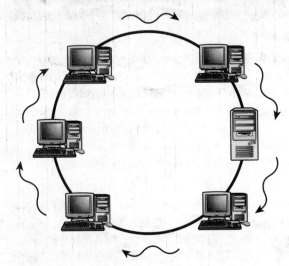

FIGURE 1.13   Data travel on a token-passing network.

However, token passing does have drawbacks. The creation and passing of the token generate overhead on the network, which reduces the maximum speed. In addition, the software and hardware requirements of token-passing network technologies are more complex—and therefore more costly—than those of other media access methods.

Token Bus

Token passing is most commonly associated with Token Ring networks. However, the IEEE's 802.4 standard defines a token-passing system implemented on a physical bus rather than a ring. Given that Token Ring is not one of the most commonly used LAN technologies and that token bus didn't catch on even as well as Token Ring, you probably won't ever see a token bus network. Still, it's nice to know that such networks exist—you never know when someone might challenge your networking knowledge.

You might have difficulty grasping the difference between the physical and the logical topologies of ring networks. For example, a common implementation of the token-passing method is Token Ring. A Token Ring network operates and passes data around the network in a logical ring, as shown previously in Figure 1.13. The physical layout of a ring network is altogether different from this. Ring networks are most commonly implemented in a star configuration. In a Token Ring network, a multistation access unit (MSAU) is equivalent to a hub or switch on an Ethernet network. The MSAU performs the token circulation internally. To create the complete ring, the Ring In (RI) port on each MSAU is connected to the Ring Out (RO) port on another MSAU. The last MSAU in the ring is then connected to the first, to complete the ring. Figure 1.14 shows how this works.

EXAM ALERT

RI and RO Ports on MSAU   Make sure that you understand the function and purpose of the RI and RO ports on an MSAU for the Network+ exam. Also make sure that you understand how the cables should be connected between MSAUs and the consequences of not connecting them correctly (that is, most likely none of the systems on the ring will be able to communicate).

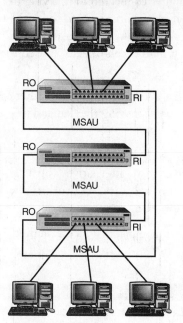

FIGURE 1.14   The physical topology of a Token Ring network.

Table 1.6 summarizes the advantages and disadvantages of the token-passing access method.

TABLE 1.6   Advantages and Disadvantages of Token Passing

Advantages	Disadvantages
No collisions means more consistent performance in high-load configurations.	The generation of a token creates network overhead.
Performance is consistently making it suitable for time-sensitive applications.	Network hardware is more complex and expensive than that used with other access methods.
	The maximum speed is limited due to the overhead of passing and token regeneration.

Demand Priority

Demand priority was developed for use on an Ethernet standard known as 100VG-AnyLAN.

> **NOTE**
>
> **100VG-AnyLAN**   Even though 100VG-AnyLAN is based on an Ethernet standard, it is defined in its own IEEE standard (802.12) because it uses demand priority as an access method instead of CSMA/CD.

On a demand priority network, a special hub queries each computer connected to it, trying to find one that has data to send. When a computer is found that has information to send, the hub opens a connection for that computer, and no other computer is allowed to transmit. This eliminates the possibility of collisions and so provides for very high access speeds and controlled media access.

Demand priority lets the administrator assign a priority to requests for media access. If there is contention for media access, the link with the highest priority wins, making the demand priority system good for time-sensitive applications.

Networks that use demand priority require specialized network devices to manage access. Thus demand priority implementations are more expensive than alternatives such as CSMA/CD. The polling process and evaluation of priorities also add to the network traffic and so create more overhead than is experienced with other networking systems.

Table 1.7 summarizes the advantages and disadvantages of the demand priority access method.

TABLE 1.7   Advantages and Disadvantages of Demand Priority

Advantages	Disadvantages
Applications can be assigned higher priorities, resulting in faster access to the network.	It has more overhead than other access methods.
No collisions means 100% access to the network bandwidth.	Extra overhead results from determination of priority.
Centralized access makes for easier network management.	Demand priority equipment is expensive compared to the equipment used with other access methods.

Topology

As discussed earlier in this chapter, topologies dictate both the physical and logical layouts of the network. Remember that topologies include bus, star, ring, mesh, and wireless. Each of the IEEE LAN standards can be implemented by using the topology specified within the standard. Some standards, such as 802.3 (Ethernet), have multiple physical topologies but always use the same logical topology. Token Ring has two possible physical topologies and a single logical topology. We'll talk more about the different topologies in the sections about their respective standards, which is discussed in the next section.

Media

Each IEEE specification defines what media are available to transport the signal around the network. The term *media*, which is the plural of *medium*, generically describes the methods by which data is transported from one point to another. Common network media types include twisted-pair cable, coaxial cable, infrared, radio frequency, and fiber-optic cable. Chapter 2 provides a detailed discussion of media types.

The IEEE 802 Standards

Now that we have looked at some of the characteristics defined by the IEEE standards, let's examine the standards themselves. Make sure that you are completely familiar with the information provided in each of the following sections before you take the Network+ exam.

802.2: The LLC Sublayer

The IEEE 802.2 standard, often referred to as LLC sublayer, is different from the other IEEE 802 networking standards because it does not define a complete networking model. Instead, it defines the standards for controlling the data received and sent by a system. It specifies protocols and technologies that perform data flow control and error-checking functions. These control functions form the foundation for the other IEEE 802 networking standards. You can think of 802.2 as an enabler for the other standards. More information on the function of the 802.2 standard can be found in Chapter 4, "The OSI Model."

802.3: Ethernet

The Ethernet standard, IEEE 802.3, is by far the most common networking standard in use today, due in part to its flexibility and ease of implementation. Similar to the other IEEE standards, the 802.3 standard specifies the key characteristics of the network model. In addition to the original standard, a number of other standards are based on 802.3. These standards are assigned a designator, such as 802.3u for Fast Ethernet.

> **EXAM ALERT**
>
> **Ethernet** Ethernet is far and away the most popular LAN networking system, and its coverage in the Network+ objectives is much more detailed than the coverage of the other networking systems. The information presented here is intended as a means for comparison with the other networking standards rather than a full tutorial on the subject.

Different implementations of Ethernet accommodate different physical topologies. For example, the 802.3 standard accommodates physical bus and physical star configurations. Other Ethernet standards support only the physical star topology. The logical topology for Ethernet is the linear bus, regardless of the physical topology used.

Table 1.8 provides a summary of the original Ethernet (802.3) standard.

TABLE 1.8   Characteristics of Ethernet

Characteristic	Description
Specification	IEEE 802.3
Physical topologies	Bus, star
Access method	CSMA/CD
Media	Twisted-pair cable, thick coaxial cable, thin coaxial cable, fiber-optic cable
Speed	10Mbps

802.3u: Fast Ethernet

In networking, speed is everything. At 10Mbps, the original Ethernet standard is too slow for modern implementations. An improved version of the standard, known as 100BaseT, or Fast Ethernet, transmits data at 100Mbps and higher. Fast Ethernet, which is defined in IEEE 802.3u, is available only over twisted-pair and fiber-optic cable.

Table 1.9 summarizes the characteristics of Fast Ethernet (100BaseT).

TABLE 1.9   Characteristics of Fast Ethernet (100BaseT)

Characteristic	Description
Specification	IEEE 802.3u
Physical topology	Star
Access method	CSMA/CD
Media	Twisted-pair cable, fiber-optic cable
Speed	100Mbps and higher

802.3z: Gigabit Ethernet

Gigabit Ethernet (1000BaseX) is another extension of the 802.3 Ethernet standard. Gigabit Ethernet, which is defined in IEEE 802.3z, can transmit data at 1Gbps (that is 1000Mbps) and can be used with Ethernet and Fast Ethernet devices. Gigabit Ethernet has the same general characteristics. Table 1.10 summarizes the characteristics of Gigabit Ethernet.

TABLE 1.10   Characteristics of Gigabit Ethernet

Characteristic	Description
Specification	IEEE 802.3z
Topology	Star
Access method	CSMA/CD
Media	Twisted-pair cable, fiber-optic cable
Speed	1Gbps

> **NOTE**
>
> **100VG-AnyLAN**   As mentioned earlier in this chapter, the 100VG-AnyLAN standard is based on the Ethernet standard but uses the demand priority access method instead of CSMA/CD. The 100VG-AnyLAN standard defines a physical star networking system over twisted-pair or fiber-optic cable at 100Mbps. 100VG-AnyLAN is defined by the IEEE 802.12 standard.

802.3ae: 10-Gigabit Ethernet

The IEEE 802.3ae standard defines a 10-Gigabit Ethernet networking standard. 802.3ae is the fastest of the Ethernet standards and as such is often used to interconnect LANS, WANS, or MANS.

Despite it being an Ethernet standard, the 802.3ae standard does have some significant differences to its predecessors. 10-Gigabit Ethernet uses full duplex modes exclusively and does not support half-duplex transmissions. Unlike other Ethernet standards, 802.3ae does not need to use the CSMA/CD access method. Finally, 10-Gigabit Ethernet can be implemented only over fiber media; however, 10-Gigabit over copper, 10GBASET, is being developed and will likely use Category 6 or 7 UTP cable.

> **EXAM ALERT**
>
> **Full Duplex and 10 Gig**   10-Gigabit Ethernet is the first Ethernet technology to become entirely full duplex and therefore does not support CSMA/CD.

These 10-Gigabit Ethernet technologies are discussed in Chapter 2.

802.5: Token Ring

Token Ring was introduced by IBM in the mid-1980s and quickly became the network topology of choice—that is, until the rise in popularity of Ethernet. Token Ring is defined for physical and logical ring topologies as well as the physical star topology. Token Ring is defined in the 802.5 specification. Table 1.11 summarizes the characteristics of the Token Ring standard.

> **NOTE**
>
> **Ethernet Versus Token Ring**   Some people compare Token Ring and Ethernet to Betamax and VHS. Although this comparison may be a little too harsh, it's not far from the truth. Some sources put the ratio of Ethernet networks to Token Ring networks as high as 99 to 1.

TABLE 1.11   Characteristics of Token Ring

Characteristic	Description
Specification	IEEE 802.5
Topology	Physical star, physical ring logical ring*
Access method	Token passing
Media	Twisted-pair cable*
Speed	4Mbps or 16Mbps

*The 802.5 standard does not mandate these characteristics, but Token Ring networks are most commonly implemented using these specifications.

As you can see from Table 1.11, Token Ring networks can operate at 4Mbps *or* 16Mbps. The key word here is *or*. All devices on the ring must operate at the same speed. Placing a system on the network without configuring the speed correctly will make it unable to participate on the ring. The maximum length of the ring depends on the cable type being used.

Although Token Ring is a good networking system, the simplicity of Ethernet networking and the low cost of Ethernet equipment has all but eliminated Token Ring from the networking market. Some organizations still use it, mainly for historical reasons, but you are unlikely to see new Token Ring implementations.

EXAM ALERT

Token Ring   This is the one and only section of the Network+ objectives that mentions Token Ring. Concentrate on the basic information provided here, and you should be able to tackle any Token Ring–related questions on the exam.

802.11: Wireless

802.11 represents the IEEE designation for wireless networking. There are four primary wireless networking specifications under the 802.11 banner: 802.11, 802.11a, 802.11b, and 802.11g. All four use the Ethernet protocol and the CSMA/CA access method.

These wireless standards can differ in terms of speed, transmission ranges, and frequency used, but in terms of actual implementation are similar. All standards can use either an infrastructure or ad-hoc network design, and each can use the same security protocols. The following list summarizes the 802.11 wireless standards:

▶ **IEEE 802.11**—There were actually two variations on the initial 802.11 standard. Both offered 1 or 2Mbps transmission speeds and the same Radio Frequency (RF) of 2.4GHz. The difference between the two was in the way in which data traveled through the RF media. One used frequency hopping spread spectrum (FHSS), and the other used direct sequence spread spectrum (DSSS). These technologies are discussed in the next section.

▸ **IEEE 802.11a**—In terms of speed, the 802.11a standard was far ahead of the original standards. 802.11a specified speeds of up to 54Mbps in the 5GHz band; but most commonly, communications takes place at 6Mbps, 12Mbps, or 24Mbps. 802.11a is not compatible with other wireless standards 802.11b and 802.11g. These standards are heavily favored to the 802.11a standard.

▸ **IEEE 802.11b**—The 802.11b standard provides for a maximum transmission speed of 11Mbps. However, devices are designed to be backward compatible with previous standards that provided for speeds of 1, 2, and 5.5Mbps. 802.11b uses a 2.4GHz RF range and is compatible with 802.11g.

▸ **IEEE 802.11g**—802.11g is a popular wireless standard today. 802.11g offers wireless transmission over distances of 150 feet and speeds up to 54Mbps compared with the 11 megabits per second of the 802.11b standard. Like 802.11b, 802.11g operates in the 2.4GHz range and is thus compatible with it.

Table 1.12 highlights the characteristics of the various 802.11 wireless standards.

TABLE 1.12   802.11 Wireless Standards

IEEE Standard	Frequency/ Media	Speed	Topology	Transmission Range	Access Method
802.11	2.4GHz RF	1 to 2Mbps	Ad hoc/ infrastructure		CSMA/CA
802.11	2.4GHz RF	1 to 2Mbps	Ad hoc/ infrastructure		CSMA/CA
802.11a	5GHz	Up to 54Mbps	Ad hoc/ infrastructure	25 to 75 feet indoors; range can be affected by building materials.	CSMA/CA
802.11b	2.4GHz	Up to 11Mbps	Ad hoc/ infrastructure	Up to 150 feet indoors; range can be affected by building materials.	CSMA/CA
802.11g	2.4GHz	Up to 54Mbps	Ad hoc/ infrastructure	Up to 150 feet indoors; range can be affected by building materials.	CSMA/CA

Data Rate Versus Throughput

When talking about wireless transmissions, it is important to distinguish between *throughput* and *data rate*. From time to time these terms are used interchangeably, but technically speaking, they are different. As shown in Table 1.12, each wireless standard has an associated speed. For instance, 802.11g lists a speed of up to 54Mbps. This represents the speed at which devices using this standard can send and receive data. However, in network data transmissions, many factors prevent the actual speeds from reaching this end-to-end theoretical maximum. For instance, data packets include overhead such as routing information, checksums, and error recovery data. Although this may all be necessary, it can impact overall speed.

The number of clients on the network can also impact the data rate; the more clients, the more collisions. Depending on the network layout, collisions can have a significant impact on end-to-end transmission speeds. Wireless network signals degrade as they pass through obstructions such as walls or doors; the signal speed deteriorates with each obstruction.

All these factors leave us with the actual throughput of wireless data transmissions. Throughput represents the actual speed to expect from wireless transmissions. In practical application, wireless transmissions will be approximately one-half or less of the data rate. This means that we could hope for about 20–25Mbps for 802.11g. Depending on the wireless setup, the transmission rate could be much less.

Want More Wireless?

As an emerging technology, wireless developments continue at a rapid pace. IEEE 802.15 and IEEE 802.16 are other wireless standards worth mentioning. 802.15 is a wireless standard specifying characteristics for wireless personal area networks (WPANs). The original 802.15 version specified the Bluetooth wireless standard. Bluetooth is often used to provide wireless links between portable digital devices, including notebook computers, peripherals, cellular telephones, beepers, and consumer electronic devices.

802.16 specifies standards for broadband wireless communications using metropolitan area networks (MANs). The original 802.16 standard identified a fixed point-to-multipoint broadband wireless systems operating in the 10–66GHz licensed spectrum. The 802.16a specified non-line-of-sight extensions in the 2–11GHz spectrum, delivering up to 70Mbps at distances up to 31 miles. Known as the *WirelessMAN specification*, 802.16 standards with faster speeds can accommodate bandwidth demanding applications. Further, the increased range of up to 30 miles provides a true end-to-end solution.

802.16 standards are in a position to take wireless to the next level. Imagine using high-speed wireless links to establish a connection backbone between geographically separate locations. This could replace cumbersome and expensive solutions used today such as T1 or T3 links. Another version of 802.16, 802.16e, is expected to enable connections for mobile devices.

> **NOTE**
>
> **War Driving**   The advent of wireless networking has led to a new phenomenon: *war driving*. Armed with a Global Positioning System (GPS) receiver and a laptop with an 802.11b wireless NIC, it is possible to drive around metropolitan areas seeking out wireless networks. When one is found, users can attempt to gain access to the network just as if they were connected to the network through a physical link. Such practices are illegal, although little can be done to prevent them other than using the built-in security features of 802.11. The problem is, not many installations use these features. If you are responsible for a network that has a wireless element, be sure to implement all the security features available. Not doing so is tantamount to letting anyone into your building and letting him use one of your PCs to access the server.

FDDI

FDDI was developed by the American National Standards Institute (ANSI) in the mid-1980s, to meet the growing need for reliable, fast network transmissions to accommodate distributed applications. In particular, FDDI was intended for use in specific applications such as backbones.

FDDI is a 100Mbps token-passing network standard. FDDI uses fiber-optic cable as its main transmission media, but it can also work over copper wire (in which case it is called Copper Distributed Data Interface [CDDI]).

Although FDDI is a ring topology, it does not suffer from the fault-tolerance issues inherent in the IEEE 802.5 standard. To avoid a single break in the ring that could disrupt network connectivity, FDDI uses a dual-ring configuration. If one computer or cable is damaged, the other ring will form a single ring topology, and the data signals can continue to travel around the network. Devices that must remain available in the event of a media failure can be attached to both rings. Less important systems can be connected to just the primary ring. Figure 1.15 shows the dual-ring configuration of FDDI.

> **NOTE**
>
> **CDDI**   It is possible to use the FDDI protocols over copper wire; this is called CDDI. Like FDDI, CDDI uses a dual-ring configuration and has transfer rates of 100Mbps.

In many ways, FDDI is similar to Token Ring. It uses a logical ring and a physical star topology, and it uses token passing as a media access method. However, FDDI has much faster data transmission rates than Token Ring, so is better suited to today's high-bandwidth applications. Table 1.13 summarizes the characteristics of FDDI.

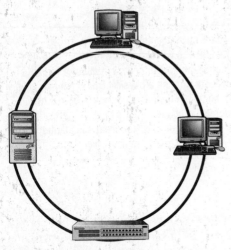

FIGURE 1.15   An example of an FDDI dual-ring configuration.

TABLE 1.13   Characteristics of FDDI

Characteristic	Description
Specification	ANSI X3T9.5
Topology	Dual ring
Access method	Token passing
Media	Fiber-optic (Shielded Twisted Pair [STP] or Unshielded Twisted Pair [UTP] is CDDI)
Speed	100Mbps

For more information on FDDI, see Chapter 7.

Introduction to Wireless Networks

Objective:

1.7 Specify the general characteristics (for example, carrier speed, frequency, transmission type, and topology) of the following wireless technologies:

▶ 802.11 (Frequency hopping spread spectrum)

▶ 802.11*x* (Direct sequence spread spectrum)

▶ Infrared

▶ Bluetooth

Over the last few years, wireless communications have made significant advances to become an integral part of business and personal operations. Today, Wireless Local Area Networks (WLANs) provide a flexible and secure data communications system to be used to augment an

Ethernet LAN or in some cases to replace it altogether. Wireless transmissions send and receive data using RF signals, freeing us from wired solutions.

In a common wireless implementation, a wireless transceiver (transmitter/receiver), known as an access point, connects to the wired network from a fixed location using standard cabling. The wireless access point receives and then transmits data between the wireless LAN and the wired network infrastructure.

Client systems communicate with a wireless access point using wireless LAN adapters. Such adapters are built into, or added to, devices such as PC cards in laptops, PDAs, or desktop computers. Wireless LAN adapters provide the communication point between the client system and the airwaves via an antenna.

Establishing Communications Between Wireless Devices

To work with wireless networks, it is important to have a basic understanding of the communication that occurs between wireless devices. If using an infrastructure wireless network design, there two key parts to the network, the wireless client, also known as the station (STA), and the AP. The AP acts as a bridge between the STA and the wired network.

> **NOTE**
>
> **Wireless Terms**   When a single AP is connected to the wired network and to a set of wireless stations, it is referred to as a *Basic Service Set (BSS)*. An *Extended Service Set (ESS)* describes the use of multiple BSSs that form a single subnetwork. Ad-hoc mode is sometimes referred to as an *Independent Basic Service Set (IBSS)*.

As with other forms of network communication, before transmissions between devices can occur, the wireless access point and the client must first begin to talk to each other. In the wireless world, this is a two-step process involving *association* and *authentication*.

The association process occurs when a wireless adapter is first turned on. The client adapter immediately begins to scan across the wireless frequencies for wireless APs or if using ad-hoc mode, other wireless devices. When the wireless client is configured to operate in infrastructure mode, the user can choose a wireless AP with which to connect. This process may also be automatic with the AP selection based on the SSID, signal strength, and frame error rate. Finally, the wireless adapter switches to the assigned channel of the selected wireless AP and negotiates the use of a port.

If at any point, the signal between the devices drops below an acceptable level or if the signal becomes unavailable for any reason, the wireless adapter initiates another scan looking for an AP with stronger signals. When the new AP is located, the wireless adapter selects the new AP and associates with it. This is known as *reassociation*.

> **NOTE**
>
> **Roaming Around** The 802.11 standard allows a wireless client to roam between multiple APs. An AP transmits a beacon signal every so many milliseconds and includes a time stamp for client synchronization and an indication of supported data rates. A client system uses the beacon message to identify the strength of the existing connection to an AP. If the connection is too weak, the roaming client attempts to associate itself with a new AP. This allows the client system to roam between distances and APs.

With the association process complete, the authentication process begins. After the devices associate, keyed security measures are applied before communication can take place. On many APs, authentication can be set to either *shared key authentication* or *open authentication*. The default setting is typically open authentication. Open authentication enables access with only the SSID and/or the correct WEP key for the AP. The problem with open authentication is that if you don't have other protection or authentication mechanisms in place, your wireless network is totally open to intruders. When set to shared key mode, the client must meet security requirements before communication with the AP can occur. Wireless security is discussed in detail in Chapter 8, "Remote Access and Security Protocols."

After security requirements are met, you have established IP level communication. This means that wireless standard requirements have been met, and Ethernet networking takes over. There is basically a switch between 802.11 to 802.3 standards. The wireless standards create the physical link to the network, allowing regular networking standards and protocols to use the link. This is how the physical cable is replaced, but to the networking technologies there is no difference between regular cable media or wireless media.

Several components combine to enable wireless communications between devices. Each of these must be configured on both the client and the AP:

- ▶ **Service Set Identifier (SSID)**—Whether your wireless network is using infrastructure mode or ad-hoc mode, an SSID is required. The SSID is a configurable client identification that allows clients to communicate to a particular base station. Only client systems configured with the same SSID as the AP can communicate with it. SSIDs provide a simple password arrangement between base stations and clients.

- ▶ **Wireless channel**—RF channels are important parts of wireless communications. A *channel* refers to the band of frequency used for the wireless communication. Each standard specifies the channels that can be used. The 802.11a standard specifies radio frequency ranges between 5.15 and 5.875GHz. In contrast, 802.11b and 802.11g standards operate between the 2.4 to 2.497GHz ranges. Fourteen channels are defined in the IEEE 802.11b/g channel set, 11 of which are available in North America. More information on working with wireless channels can be found in Chapter 15.

- ▶ **Security Features**—IEEE 802.11 provides for security using two methods, authentication and encryption. Authentication refers to the verification of the client system. In the infrastructure mode, authentication is established between an AP and each station. Wireless encryption services must be the same on the client and the AP for communication to occur.

> **NOTE**
>
> **Default Settings** Wireless devices ship with default SSIDs, security settings, channels, passwords, and usernames. To protect yourself, it is strongly recommended that you change these default settings. Today, many Internet sites list the default settings used by manufacturers with their wireless devices. This information us used by people who want gain unauthorized access to your wireless devices.

Spread Spectrum Technology

Spread spectrum refers to the manner in which data signals travel through a radio frequency. With spread spectrum, data does not travel straight through a single RF band; this type of transmission is known as *narrowband transmission*. Spread spectrum on the other hand requires that data signals either alternate between carrier frequencies or constantly change their data pattern. Although the shortest distance between two points is a straight line (narrowband), spread spectrum is designed to trade off bandwidth efficiency for reliability, integrity, and security. Spread spectrum signal strategies use more bandwidth than in the case of narrowband transmission, but the trade-off is a data signal that is clearer and easier to detect. There are two types of spread spectrum radio: *frequency hopping* and *direct sequence*.

Frequency-Hopping Spread Spectrum (FHSS) Technology

FHSS requires the use of narrowband signals that change frequencies in a predictable pattern. The term *frequency hopping* refers to hopping of data signals between narrow channels. For example, consider the 2.4GHz frequency band used by 802.11b/g. This range is divided into 70 narrow channels of 1MHz each. Somewhere between 20 and several hundred milliseconds, the signal hops to a new channel following a predetermined cyclical pattern.

Because data signals using FHSS switch between RF bands, they have a strong resistance to interference and environmental factors. The FHSS signal strategy makes it well suited for installations designed to cover a large geographical area and where the use of directional antennas to minimize the influence of environmental factors is not possible.

FHSS is not the preferred spread spectrum technology for today's wireless standards. However, FHSS is used for some lesser-used standards and for cellular deployments for fixed Broadband Wireless Access (BWA), where the use of DSSS is virtually impossible because of its limitations.

Direct-Sequence Spread Spectrum (DSSS) Technology

With DSSS transmissions, the signal is spread over a full transmission frequency spectrum. For every bit of data that is sent, a redundant bit pattern is also sent. This 32-bit pattern is called a *chip*. These redundant bits of data provide for both security and delivery assurance. The reason transmissions are so safe and reliable is simply because the system sends so many redundant copies of the data, and only a single copy is required to have complete transmission of the data or information. DSSS can minimize the effects of interference and background noise.

As for a comparison between the two, DSSS has the advantage of providing higher security and signal delivery than FHSS, but it is a sensitive technology, affected by many environmental factors.

NOTE

OFDM and 802.11a Lesser known than DSSS and FHSS RF technologies is OFDM. OFDM is associated with 802.11a wireless networks and is a method of modulation in which a signal is split into several narrowband channels at different frequencies.

FHSS, DSSS, and 802.11 Standards

The original 802.11 standard had two variations, both offering the same speeds but differing in the RF spread spectrum used. One of the 802.11 standards used FHSS. This 802.11 variant used the 2.4GHz radio frequency band and operated with at 1 or 2Mbps data rate. Since this original standard, wireless implementations have favored DSSS.

The second 802.11 variation uses DSSS and specifies a 2Mbps peak data rate with optional fallback to 1Mbps in very noisy environments. 802.11, 802.11b, and 802.11g use the DSSS spread spectrum. This means that the underlying modulation scheme is similar between each standard allowing all DSSS systems to coexist with 2, 11, and 54Mbps 802.11 standards. As a comparison, it is like the migration from the older 10Mbps Ethernet networking to the more commonly implemented 100Mbps standard. The speed was different, but the underlying technologies were similar allowing for an easier upgrade.

Table 1.14 provides a comparison of wireless standards and spread spectrum used.

TABLE 1.14   Comparison of IEEE 802.11 Standards

IEEE Standard	RF Used	Spread Spectrum	Data Rate (Mbps)
802.11	2.4GHz	DSSS	1/2
802.11	2.4GHz	FHSS	1/2
802.11a	5GHz	OFDM	54
802.11b	2.4GHz	DSSS	11
802.11g	2.4Ghz	DSSS	54

Infrared Wireless Networking

Infrared has been around for a long time; perhaps our first experience with it was the TV remote. The commands entered onto the remote control travel over an infrared lightwave to the receiver on the TV. Infrared technology has progressed, and today infrared development in networking is managed by the Infrared Data Association (IrDA).

Infrared wireless networking uses infrared beams to send data transmissions between devices. Infrared wireless networking offers higher transmission rates reaching 10Mbps to 16Mbps.

As expected, the infrared light beams cannot penetrate objects; therefore, the signal is disrupted when something blocks the light. Infrared can either be a directed (line-of-sight) or diffuse technology. A directed infrared system provides a limited range of approximately three feet and typically is used for personal area networks. Diffused infrared can travel farther and is more difficult to block with a signal object. Diffused infrared wireless LAN systems do not require line-of-sight, but usable distance is limited to room distances.

Infrared provides a secure, low-cost, convenient cable replacement technology. It is well suited for many specific applications and environments. Some key infrared points are as follows:

- ▶ Provides adequate speeds, up to 16Mbps.
- ▶ Infrared devices use less power and a decreased drain on batteries.
- ▶ Is a secure medium. Infrared signals are typically a direct line implementation in a short range and so do not travel far outside the immediate connection. This eliminates theproblem of eavesdropping or signal tampering.
- ▶ Is a proven technology. Infrared devices have been available for some time and as such are a proven, nonproprietary technology with an established user and support base.
- ▶ Has no radio frequency interference issues or signal conflicts.
- ▶ Replaces cables for many devices such as keyboards, mice, and other peripherals.
- ▶ Uses a dispersed mode or a direct line-of-sight transmission.
- ▶ Transmissions travel over short distances.

NOTE

Lazy Bones   Infrared is certainly an established technology. Apparently, the first TV remote came from Zenith in the 1950s and was named Lazy Bones.

Bluetooth

Bluetooth is a wireless standard used for many purposes, including connecting peripheral devices to a system. Bluetooth uses a low-cost, short-range radio link to create a link to replace many of the cords that used to connect devices.

Bluetooth is an easily configured technology. When Bluetooth-enabled devices are within 10 or so meters of each other, they can establish a connection. Bluetooth establishes the link using an RF-based link and therefore does not require a direct line-of-sight connection. The Bluetooth Standard defines a short RF link capable of voice or data transmission up to a maximum capacity of 720Kb/s per channel.

Bluetooth operates at 2.4 to 2.48GHz and uses a spread spectrum, frequency hopping technology. The signal hops can hop between 79 frequencies at 1MHz intervals to give a high degree of interference immunity.

> **NOTE**
>
> **Bluetooth** For implementation purposes, Bluetooth provides solutions for three primary areas: cable replacement, ad hoc networking, and data and access points.

As an established technology, Bluetooth has many advantages, but the speed of 720Kbps is limiting. The newest version of Bluetooth, Bluetooth 2.0, increases overall speed to a data rate of 3Mbps. This speed may still be significantly slower than 802.11b or g, but for an easily configured cable replacement technology, it is an attractive option. Table 1.15 highlights the advantages of the Bluetooth standard.

TABLE 1.15   Bluetooth Characteristics

Characteristic	Description
Specification	Bluetooth
Topology	Ad-hoc
Spread spectrum	FHSS
Media	2.4GHz RF
Speed	720Kbps
Range	10 meters in optimal conditions

Factors Affecting Wireless Signals

Objective:

1.8 Identify factors that affect the range and speed of wireless service (for example, interference, antenna type, and environmental factors).

Because wireless signals travel through the atmosphere, they are susceptible to different types of interference than standard wire networks. Interference weakens wireless signals and is therefore an important consideration when working with wireless networking.

Interference Types

Wireless interference is an important consideration when planning a wireless network. Interference is unfortunately inevitable, but the trick is to minimize the levels of interference. Wireless LAN communications are typically based on radio frequency signals that require a clear and unobstructed transmission path.

The following are some factors that cause interference:

▶ **Physical objects**—Trees, masonry, buildings, and other physical structures are some of the most common sources of interference. The density of the materials used in a building's construction determines the number of walls the RF signal can pass through and still maintain adequate coverage. Concrete and steel walls are particularly difficult for a signal to pass through. These structures will weaken or at times completely prevent wireless signals.

▶ **Radio frequency interference**—Wireless technologies such as 802.11b/g use an RF range of 2.4GHz, and so do many other devices, such as cordless phones, microwaves, and so on. Devices that share the channel can cause noise and weaken the signals.

▶ **Electrical interference**—Electrical interference comes from devices such as computers, refrigerators, fans, lighting fixtures, or any other motorized devices. The impact that electrical interference has on the signal depends on the proximity of the electrical device to the wireless access point. Advances in wireless technologies and in electrical devices have reduced the impact these types of devices have on wireless transmissions.

▶ **Environmental factors**—Weather conditions can have a huge impact on wireless signal integrity. Lightning, for example, can cause electrical interference, and fog can weaken signals as they pass through.

Many wireless implementations are found in the office or at home. Even when outside interference such as weather is not a problem, there are plenty of wireless obstacles around the office. More information on wireless interference and on troubleshooting wireless connections can be found in Chapter 15. Table 1.16 highlights a few examples to be aware of when implementing a wireless network indoors.

TABLE 1.16   Wireless Obstacles Found Indoors

Obstruction	Obstacle Severity	Example Use
Wood/wood paneling	Low	Inside wall or hollow doors
Drywall	Low	Inside walls
Furniture	Low	Couches or office partitions
Clear glass	Low	Windows

(continues)

TABLE 1.16 *Continued*

Obstruction	Obstacle Severity	Example Use
Tinted glass	Medium	Windows
People	Medium	High volume traffic areas where there is considerable pedestrian traffic
Ceramic Tile	Medium	Walls
Concrete blocks	Medium/high	Outer wall construction
Mirrors	High	Mirror or reflective glass
Metals	High	Metal office partitions, doors, metal-based office furniture
Water	High	Aquariums, rain, fountains

> **NOTE**
>
> **Wireless and Water**   Water is a major interference factor for 2.4GHz wireless networks because water molecules resonate at the frequency in the 2.4GHz band. Interestingly, microwaves cause water molecules to resonate during cooking, which interferes with 2.4GHz RF.

Wireless Antennas

A wireless antenna is an integral part of overall wireless communication. Antennas come in many different shapes and sizes, with each one designed for a specific purpose. Selecting the right antenna for a particular network implementation is a critical consideration and one that could ultimately decide how successful a wireless implementation will be. In addition, using the right antennas can save money on networking costs because you'll need fewer antennas and access points.

Many small home network adapters and access points come with a nonupgradable antenna, but higher grade wireless devices require a decision on the antenna that will be used. Determining which antenna to use takes careful planning and requires an understanding of what range and speed you need for a network. The antenna is designed to help wireless networks to

- ▶ Work around obstacles
- ▶ Minimize the effects of interference
- ▶ Increase signal strength
- ▶ Focus the transmission, which can increase signal speed

The following sections explore some of the characteristics of wireless antennas.

Antenna Ratings

When a wirelesssignal is low and being influenced by heavy interference, it may be possible to upgrade the antennas to create a more solid wireless connection. To determine the strength of an antenna, we refer to its *gain value*. But how do we determine the gain value?

Suppose that there was a huge wireless tower emanating circular waves in all directions. If we could see these waves, we would see the data waves forming a sphere around the tower. The signals around the antenna flow equally in all directions (including up and down). An antenna that does this has a 0dbi gain value and is referred to as an *isotropic antenna*. The isotropic antenna rating provides a base point for measuring actual antenna strength.

An antenna's gain value represents the difference between the 0dbi isotropic and the power of the antenna. For example, a wireless antenna advertised as a 15dbi antenna is 15 times stronger than the hypothetical isotropic antenna. The higher the decibel figure, the higher the gain.

> **NOTE**
>
> **db** The *db* in the designation stands for *decibels*, and the *i* references the hypothetical isotropic antenna.

When looking at wireless antennas, remember that a higher gain value means stronger send and receive signals. In terms of performance, the rule of thumb is that every 3dB of gain added doubles the effective power output of an antenna.

Antenna Coverage

When selectingan antenna for a particular wireless implementation, it is necessary to determine the type of coverage used by an antenna. In a typical configuration, a wireless antenna can be either *omnidirectional* or *directional*. The choice between the two depends on the wireless environment.

An omnidirectional antenna is designed to provide a 360-degree dispersed wave pattern. This type of antenna is used when coverage in all directions from the antenna is required. Omnidirectional antennas are good to use when a broad-based signal is required. For example, by providing an even signal in all directions, clients can access the antenna and associated access point from various locations. Because of the dispersed nature of omnidirectional antennas, the signal is weaker overall and therefore accommodates shorter signal distances. Omnidirectional antennas are great in an environment where there is a clear line of path between the senders and receivers. The power is evenly spread to all points making omnidirectional antennas well suited for home and small office applications.

EXAM ALERT

Directional Differences   Omnidirectional antennas provide wide coverage but weaker signal strength in any one direction than a directional antenna.

Directional antennas are designed to focus the signal in a particular direction. This focused signal allows for greater distances and a stronger signal between two points. The greater distances enabled by directional antennas allow a viable alternative for connecting locations, such as two offices, in a point-to-point configuration.

Directional antennas are also used when you need to tunnel or thread a signal through a series of obstacles. This concentrates the signal power in a specific direction and allows you to use less power for a greater distance than an omnidirectional antenna. Figure 1.16 shows an example of a directional antenna beam.

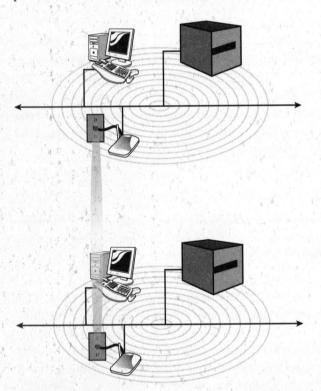

FIGURE 1.16   Directional antenna signal.

NOTE

Polarization   In the wireless world, *polarization* refers to the direction that the antenna radiates wavelengths. This direction can either be vertical, horizontal, or circular. Today, vertical antennas are perhaps the most common. As far as configuration is concerned, both the sending and receiving antennas should be set to the same polarization.

Chapter Summary

This chapter provides an overview of the functions and purposes of computer networks. Key among the functions of the network are increased communication, both in real-time and via email, sharing of hardware between multiple users, reduction in overall cost and support of multiple devices, and the capability to share files.

Two network models are identified in this chapter: peer-to-peer networking and client/server networking. Peer-to-peer networking is restricted to networks with few users and does not use a centralized server. Peer-to-peer networks are most commonly seen in home network environments and in small offices.

The client/server model is more common and familiar than the peer-to-peer model, especially in larger networks. The client/server model uses a dedicated server and offers many advantages over the peer-to-peer network model. Perhaps most notable of these advantages is the ability to centrally manage the network, although the cost and administration requirements are higher than those of peer-to-peer networks.

Networks have both physical and logical topologies. The physical topology refers to the way the network is physically laid out, including media, computers, and other networking devices such as hubs or MSAUs. The logical topology refers to how data is transmitted around the network. Common network topologies include star, ring, bus, and mesh. Each of these topologies offers distinct advantages and disadvantages and various levels of fault tolerance.

Access methods are the methods by which data is sent onto the network. The most common access methods are CSMA/CD, which uses a collision detection and contention method, CSMA/CA, and token passing.

The IEEE defines several LAN standards, including 802.2 (the LLC layer), 802.3 (Ethernet), 802.5 (Token Ring), and 802.11 (wireless). Each of these standards identifies specific characteristics, including the network's media, speed, access method, and topology.

There are several wireless standards under the 802.11 banner, including 802.11a, 802.11b, and 802.11g. Each of these standards has different characteristics including speed, range, and RF used. Wireless networks are typically implemented using ad-hoc or infrastructure network design. Many types of interference can weaken the wireless signals including weather, obstructions such as trees or walls, and RF interference.

Key Terms

- 802.11 wireless
- 802.x standards
- bus topology
- centralized computing
- client/server networking
- CSMA/CA
- CSMA/CD
- decibels
- demand priority
- directional antenna
- distributed computing
- Fast Ethernet
- FDDI
- Gigabit Ethernet
- IEEE

- LAN
- logical topology
- media
- mesh topology
- MSAU
- omnidirectional antenna
- peer-to-peer networking
- physical topology
- ring topology
- star topology
- token passing
- Token Ring
- WAN
- wireless interference
- wireless topology

Apply Your Knowledge

Exercises

1.1 Configuring Infrared Networking in Windows XP

You want to manage infrared communications on your Windows XP systems. On one computer you need to prevent other computers from sending files to your computer, and on the other computer, you need to verify that infrared is available on the system.

This exercise assumes that you are using Windows XP and have infrared networking capability.

Estimated time: 10 minutes

To enable or prevent receiving files over infrared links, perform the following steps:

1. From the Start menu, select the Control Panel option and then double-click the Wireless Link applet.

2. To allow your Windows XP system to receive files over an infrared link, select the Allow Others to Send Files to Your Computer Using Infrared Communications option.

3. To prevent your Windows XP system from receiving files, make sure that the Allow Others to Send Files to Your Computer Using Infrared Communications option is cleared.

To verify infrared support on a computer, follow these steps:

1. Verify that the computer has an infrared transceiver. The transceiver is located somewhere on the outside of the computer and looks like a small dark red window.

2. To verify infrared functionality within Windows XP, open the Device Manager and double-click on Infrared Devices.

3. If you have located an infrared transceiver on the outside and the infrared device option is not displayed in Device Manager, no infrared devices are recognized by the system.

4. Verify that infrared support is enabled in the BIOS. Enter your systems BIOS configuration screen to verify whether IrDA devices are enabled. If the infrared device is disabled in BIOS, you might be able to use your computer's BIOS setup to enable it.

5. If infrared devices are listed in the Device Manager but not enabled, verify that the infrared devices are installed correctly on your computer.

1.2 Configuring a Windows XP System to Exclusively Use a Wireless Infrastructure Connection

Configuring and managing wireless connections is an increasing part of the network administrator's role. Windows XP has built-in wizards and features to make working with wireless as easy as possible. In this exercise, we identify the setting used to determine whether a wireless connection is to be configured as an ad-hoc connection or an infrastructure connection.

This exercise assumes that the system has a wireless adapter installed.

Estimated time: 5 minutes

1. In Windows XP, choose Start and then Control Panel.

2. From within the Control Panel, double-click the Network Connections Applet to open the Network Connections dialog box.

3. Right-click on the wireless connection and select Properties from the menu screen. This Wireless Network Connection Properties dialog box opens.

4. Select the Wireless Networks tab and then click the Advanced button on the lower right-hand side of the dialog box.

5. This displays a small dialog box with three options:

> ▶ Any Available Network (Access Point Preferred)

> ▶ Access Point (Infrastructure) Networks Only

> ▶ Computer-to-Computer (Ad Hoc) Networks Only

6. To configure the XP system to use only an infrastructure wirless connection, select the radio button next to the Access Point (Infrastructure) Networks Only option.

Exam Questions

1. Which of the following is a disadvantage of the physical bus topology?

   ○ **a.** Has complex cabling requirements

   ○ **b.** Is prone to cable faults

   ○ **c.** Requires a dedicated server

   ○ **d.** Requires a dedicated hub

2. Which of the following are IEEE standards that define LAN networking systems? (Choose the three best answers.)

   ○ **a.** 802.3

   ○ **b.** 802.4

   ○ **c.** 802.5

   ○ **d.** 802.10

3. Which of the following IEEE standards provides the specifications for a Token Ring LAN?

   ○ **a.** 802.3

   ○ **b.** 802.4

   ○ **c.** 803.3

   ○ **d.** 802.5

4. Which of the following topologies offers the greatest level of redundancy?

   ○ **a.** Mesh

   ○ **b.** Star

   ○ **c.** Bus

   ○ **d.** Ring

5. Which of the following IEEE specifications does CSMA/CD relate to?

    ○ **a.** 802.2

    ○ **b.** 802.3

    ○ **c.** 802.4

    ○ **d.** 802.5

6. As a network administrator, you have been called to replace a NIC on a computer in a Token Ring network. After you replace the NIC and connect the cable, the computer cannot communicate on the network. Which of the following is the most likely problem?

    ○ **a.** The NIC is configured for the wrong speed.

    ○ **b.** A token must be created for the newly installed card.

    ○ **c.** The card's address must be added to the token list.

    ○ **d.** The computer must be inserted into the ring.

7. Which of the following IEEE standards specifies a physical star/logical ring topology and a token-passing access method?

    ○ **a.** 802.1

    ○ **b.** 803.2

    ○ **c.** 802.5

    ○ **d.** 802.2

8. Which network topology is represented in the following diagram?

    ○ **a.** Bus

    ○ **b.** Star

    ○ **c.** Logical ring

    ○ **d.** Mesh

9. Part of your responsibility as network administrator is to design your company's new network. You have been asked to implement a network in which each computer must have guaranteed and equal access to the network. Which of the following would best suit your company's needs?

   ○ **a.** Token Ring

   ○ **b.** Mesh topology

   ○ **c.** Ethernet

   ○ **d.** CSMA/CD

10. Which of the following topologies has a single connection between each node on the network and a centralized device?

   ○ **a.** Ring

   ○ **b.** Mesh

   ○ **c.** Star

   ○ **d.** Bus

11. Which of the following devices is associated with a Token Ring network?

   ○ **a.** Switch

   ○ **b.** Hub

   ○ **c.** MSAU

   ○ **d.** CSMA/CD

12. As a network administrator, you are called in to correct a problem associated with the network's MSAU. What physical topology are you troubleshooting?

   ○ **a.** Star topology

   ○ **b.** Ring topology

   ○ **c.** Mesh topology

   ○ **d.** Bus topology

13. What is the name for a network that connects two geographic locations?

   ○ **a.** PAN

   ○ **b.** LAN

   ○ **c.** DAN

   ○ **d.** WAN

14. Which network topology is represented in the following diagram?

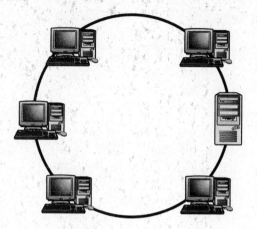

   ○ **a.** Bus

   ○ **b.** Star

   ○ **c.** Mesh

   ○ **d.** Ring

15. Which of the following is a feature of the physical star topology?

   ○ **a.** It requires less cable than other physical topologies.

   ○ **b.** The network is very easy to expand.

   ○ **c.** Apart from the cable and connectors, no other equipment is required to create the network.

   ○ **d.** There is no single point of failure.

16. The 802.11b standard describes what kind of network?

   ○ **a.** Token passing

   ○ **b.** Contention

   ○ **c.** Wireless

   ○ **d.** Token bus

17. A mainframe is an example of what computing model?

○ **a.** Segregated

○ **b.** Distributed

○ **c.** Centralized

○ **d.** Decentralized

18. What kind of access method is CSMA/CD?

○ **a.** Contention

○ **b.** Demand priority

○ **c.** Collision avoidance

○ **d.** Token passing

19. Which network topology is represented in the following diagram?

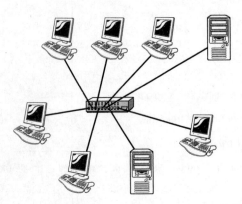

○ **a.** Star

○ **b.** Bus

○ **c.** Mesh

○ **d.** Ring

20. What is the maximum network speed defined by the 802.11b standard?

○ **a.** 100Mbps

○ **b.** 5.5Mbps

○ **c.** 11Mbps

○ **d.** 10Mbps

Answers to Exam Questions

1. **b.** One of the disadvantages of the physical bus topology is that it's ~~tion~~, a fault on the cable can render the entire network unusable. Th bus topology are that the cabling is simple, and no additional netw(ate the network. For more information, see the section "LAN Topolc

2. **a, b, c.** The IEEE 802.3 standard defines Ethernet, the 802.4 standard defines token bus, and the 802.5 standard defines Token Ring. The IEEE 802.10 defines security standards that make it possible to safely and securely transmit and exchange data. For more information, see the section "The IEEE 802 Standards," in this chapter.

3. **d.** The IEEE 802.5 standard defines Token Ring networking. The 802.3 standard defines Ethernet. The 802.4 defines the use of a token-passing system on a linear bus topology. 803.3 is not a LAN standard. For more information, see the section "The IEEE 802 Standards," in this chapter.

4. **a.** In a mesh topology, each device is connected directly to every other device. If there is a break in the connection between two devices, alternate paths between the two systems are available. None of the other topologies provide this level of redundancy. For more information, see the section "LAN Topologies," in this chapter.

5. **b.** The IEEE 802.3 standard defines the Ethernet networking system, which uses CSMA/CD as its media access method. 802.2 defines specifications for the LLC sublayer of the 802 standard series. 802.4 defines the use of a token-passing system on a linear bus topology. 802.5 defines Token Ring networking. For more information, see the section "The IEEE 802 Standards," in this chapter.

6. **a.** On a Token Ring network, all devices must be configured to run at the same speed. If a device is connected to the network and not configured for the correct speed, it will not work. None of the other answers are valid. For more information, see the section "The IEEE 802 Standards," in this chapter.

7. **c.** The IEEE 802.5 standard defines Token Ring, a physical star/logical ring topology that uses token passing as a media access method. The 802.1 standard defines internetwork communications standards between devices and includes specifications for routing and bridging. 803.2 is not a LAN standard. 802.2 defines specifications for the LLC sublayer of the 802 standard series. For more information, see the section "The IEEE 802 Standards," in this chapter.

8. **a.** The diagram shows the physical bus topology. None of the other answers are valid. For more information, see the section "LAN Topologies," in this chapter.

9. **a.** Token Ring uses a token-passing media access method that provides guaranteed and equal access to the network media. Ethernet, the only other reasonable answer, uses CSMA/CD to govern media access. For more information, see the section "The IEEE and Networking Standards," in this chapter.

10. **c.** A star topology is created when each node on the network is connected to a central device. None of the other answers are valid. For more information, see the section "LAN Topologies," in this chapter.

. An MSAU is used on Token Ring networks to connect systems to the network. Switches and hubs are used on Ethernet networks. CSMA/CD is a media access method, not a networking device. For more information, see the section "The IEEE 802 Standards," in this chapter.

12. **a.** Because MSAUs are being used, the network system in use is Token Ring. The use of MSAUs on a Token Ring network creates a physical star configuration. Star topologies are most commonly associated with Ethernet networks. Mesh topologies do not use MSAUs. Token passing, not Token Ring, can be implemented on a bus network, per the IEEE 802.4 standard, though such a configuration would not use MSAUs; therefore, Answer d is incorrect. For more information, see the section "The IEEE 802 Standards," in this chapter.

13. **d.** The term *WAN* describes a network that spans more than one geographic location. The only other valid term for a type of network is *LAN*, but a LAN is a network confined to a single location. None of the other answers are recognized terms for describing a network. For more information, see the section "LANs, WANs, MANs, and PANs" in this chapter.

14. **d.** The diagram shows a physical ring topology. All the other answers are incorrect. For more information, see the section "LAN Topologies," in this chapter.

15. **b.** Physical star networks use centralized devices to connect nodes on the network. Because devices can be plugged and unplugged from these devices without affecting any other systems on the network, star configurations are easy to expand. The disadvantages of a physical star network are that they require more cable than other topologies, require additional networking equipment, and create a single point of failure. For more information, see the section "LAN Topologies," in this chapter.

16. **c.** The IEEE 802.11b standard defines wireless networking architectures. Token passing and contention are media access methods, and token bus is an implementation of token-passing media access on a physical bus topology. For more information, see the section "The IEEE and Networking Standards," in this chapter.

17. **c.** A mainframe is an example of a centralized computing model. All the other answers are incorrect. For more information, see the section "Peer-to-Peer Versus Client/Server Networks," in this chapter.

18. **a.** CSMA/CD is described as a contention-based media access method because devices contend for access. All the other answers are incorrect. For more information, see the section "The IEEE and Networking Standards," in this chapter.

19. **a.** A star topology is shown in the diagram. All the other answers are incorrect. For more information, see the section "LAN Topologies," in this chapter.

20. **c.** The IEEE 802.11b standard for wireless networks defines a maximum speed of 11Mbps. 100Mbps is the defined speed for Fast Ethernet. 5.5Mbps is the speed specified in earlier wireless networking standards. 10Mbps is the maximum speed of standard Ethernet. For more information, see the section "The IEEE and Networking Standards," in this chapter.

Suggested Readings and Resources

1. Groth, David, Jim McBee. *Cabling: The Complete Guide to Network Wiring*. Sybex, 2001.

2. Habraken, Joe. *Absolute Beginner's Guide to Networking*, fourth edition. Que Publishing, 2003.

3. Davis, Harold. *Absolute Beginner's Guide to Wi-Fi Wireless Networking*. Que Publishing, 2004.

4. Ogletree, Terry William. *Upgrading and Repairing Networks, Fourth Edition*. Que Publishing, 2003.

5. Network cable information, www.techfest.com/networking/cabling.htm.

6. Updated technology information, http://www.wikipedia.org/.

7. Computer networking tutorials and advice, compnetworking.about.com.

8. "TechEncyclopedia," www.techencyclopedia.com.

9. Networking technology information from Cisco, www.cisco.com/public/products_tech.shtml.

10. "Network Cabling Help," www.datacottage.com.

Cabling Standards, Media, and Connectors

Objectives

This chapter covers the following CompTIA-specified objectives for the "Media and Topologies" section of the Network+ certification exam:

1.3 Specify the characteristics (for example: speed, length, topology, and cable type) of the following cable standards:

- ▶ 10BaseT and 10BaseFL
- ▶ 100BaseTX and 100BaseFX

- ▶ 1000BaseTX, 1000BaseCX, 1000BaseSX, and 1000BaseLX
- ▶ 10GBaseSR, 10GBaseLR, and 10GBaseER

- ▶ Networking standards define a number of criteria, including the transmission speed and the physical media in use. Network administrators must be able to correctly identify commonly used standards in order to support and troubleshoot a network.

1.4 Recognize the following media connectors and describe their uses:

- ▶ RJ-11 (Registered Jack)
- ▶ RJ-45 (Registered Jack)
- ▶ F-Type
- ▶ ST (Straight Tip)
- ▶ SC (Standard Connector)

- ▶ IEEE 1394 (FireWire)
- ▶ Fiber LC (Local Connector)
- ▶ MTRJ (Mechanical Transfer Registered Jack)
- ▶ USB (Universal Serial Bus)

- ▶ Specific cable types use one or more types of connectors. Being able to identify which connector is associated with which cable is an important skill for a network administrator.

1.5 Recognize the following media types and describe their uses:

- ▶ Category 3, 5, 5e, and 6
- ▶ UTP (Unshielded Twisted Pair)
- ▶ STP (Shielded Twisted Pair)

- ▶ Coaxial cable
- ▶ SMF (Single-Mode Fiber) optic cable
- ▶ MMF (Multimode Fiber) optic cable

- ▶ A wide variety of media are used in networking. To pass the Network+ exam, you need to understand the various media types and their characteristics.

Outline

Study Strategies

▶ Review the objectives covered in this chapter.

▶ Read through the material provided, paying extra attention to the Exam Alerts. They point out some specific information that you will find helpful when taking the Network+ exam.

▶ Be sure that you can identify what cables and connectors are used with what networking standards.

▶ Practice identifying network standards by their name. For example, you should be able to determine the speed and cable type from the name, as in 100BaseT (100Mbps, twisted-pair cable).

▶ Review the tables included in the chapter. They focus on specific information that you will find useful when taking the exam.

▶ Use the Internet to look up cabling and connector data from manufacturers. Be sure that you are familiar with the physical appearance of commonly used connectors.

▶ Complete the exercises and review questions at the end of the chapter.

Introduction

To provide effective technical support, administrators must have a solid understanding of the logical standards and physical media used on today's networks. *Logical standards* define characteristics such as the configuration of the network, the speed at which the network operates, and how devices access the network. *Physical media* refers to the cabling and connectors used to create the network.

Although you might think that knowledge of such things would be relevant only when designing or building a new network, you would be surprised at how frequently existing networks are expanded, upgraded, or reconfigured. When performing any of these tasks, your knowledge of standards and media will come into play. This is because the standards and media define and dictate criteria such as the maximum distance between devices, the capability of media to withstand outside interference, and even how much space is required in wiring closets and equipment cabinets.

We'll begin our discussion by looking at some of the more common standards used on today's networks.

Features and Characteristics of Ethernet 802.3 Standards

Objective:

1.3 Specify the characteristics (for example: speed, length, topology, and cable type) of the following cable standards:

▶ 10BaseT and 10BaseFL

▶ 100BaseTX and 100BaseFX

▶ 1000BaseTX, 1000BaseCX, 1000BaseSX, and 1000BaseLX

▶ 10GBaseSR, 10GBaseLR, and 10GBaseER

As outlined in Chapter 1, "Introduction to Networking," the IEEE 802 standards specify the characteristics of LAN systems. Of all the standards detailed by the IEEE, 802.3 is the most widely implemented. Since the introduction of the original 802.3 standard, many derivatives of this standard have been developed, each of which has its own specifications.

EXAM ALERT

What's in a Name? Understanding the naming format of standards in the 802.3 suite is important when taking the Network+ exam. The first part of the name, the number, defines the speed of the standard. The second part defines whether the standard uses broadband or baseband transmissions. All the 802.3 standards discussed in this chapter use baseband transmissions. The last part of the name defines the cable type used, or the variation of a cable type. So, with this information, you can deduce that the 10BaseT standard is a 10Mbps networking technology that uses baseband transmissions over twisted-pair cable. Likewise, 1000BaseFX is a 1Gbps networking standard that uses fiber-optic cable.

Each 802.3 standard specifies the signaling mode (baseband or broadband), topology, data rates, and media type used. The following sections describe the characteristics of the 802.3 standards.

EXAM ALERT

The 802.3 Standards Pay special attention to the 802.3 standards. You can expect a question regarding the characteristics of the various standards on the Network+ exam.

NOTE

Even though it is not specifically stated in the CompTIA Network+ objectives, we have included coverage on 10Base2 because there is still a chance that you will encounter it in the real world. Also, you never know when CompTIA might choose to include 10Base2 as a wrong answer for a question related to one of the other networking standards discussed in this section. When taking an exam, knowing what something isn't can be as useful as knowing what it is!

10Base2

10Base2, which is defined as part of the IEEE 802.3a standard, specifies data transmission speeds of 10Mbps and a total segment length of 185 meters using RG-58 coaxial cable. The 10Base2 standard specifies a physical bus topology and uses Bayonet Neill Concelman (BNC) connectors with 50-ohm terminators at each end of the cable. One of the physical ends of each segment must be grounded.

NOTE

When discussing network standards, the word *base*, as in 10Base2, defines that the media can only carry one data signal per wire, or channel, at one time.

10Base2 networks allow a maximum of five segments with only three of those segments populated. Each of the three populated segments can have a maximum of 30 nodes attached. 10Base2 requires that there is a minimum of .5 meters between nodes. For the network to function properly, the segment must be complete. With this in mind, the addition or removal of systems on a 10Base2 network might make the entire network unusable.

> **TIP**
>
> The coax cable used in 10Base2 networks is prone to cable breaks. A break anywhere in the cable makes the entire network inaccessible.

Coaxial and the 5-4-3 Rule

When working with Ethernet networks that use coaxial media, the 5-4-3 rule applies. The rule specifies that the network is limited to a total of five cable segments. These five segments can be connected using no more than four repeaters, and only three segments on the network can be populated.

10BaseT

The 10BaseT LAN standard specifies an Ethernet network that commonly uses unshielded twisted-pair cable; however, in some implementations that require a greater resistance to interference and attenuation, shielded twisted pair (STP) can be used. STP has extra shielding to combat interference.

> **NOTE**
>
> **Cable Types**   For more information on the cables used in each of the 802.3 specifications, refer to the section later in this chapter titled "Common Network Cable."

10BaseT uses baseband transmission and has a maximum physical segment length of 100 meters. Baseband transmissions are discussed later in this chapter, in the section titled "Common Network Cable." As with the coaxial cabling standards, repeaters are sometimes used to extend the maximum segment length, although the repeating capability is now often built into networking devices used in twisted-pair networks. 10BaseT specifies transmission speeds of 10Mbps and can use several categories of UTP cable, including Categories 3, 4, and 5 (all of which use RJ-45 connectors). 10BaseT takes advantage of the multiple wires inside twisted-pair cable to create independent transmit and receive paths, which means that a full-duplex mode can be optionally supported. The maximum number of computers supported on a 10BaseT network is 1,024.

All 10BaseT networks use a point-to-point network design, with one end of the connection attaching to the network card and the other to a hub or switch. These point-to-point connections result in a physical star topology. Chapter 3, "Networking Components and Devices," provides more information on the devices used in twisted-pair networks.

> **NOTE**
>
> **Crossover Cable** You can link two 10BaseT computer systems directly, without the use of a hub, by using a specially constructed crossover cable. Crossover cables are also sometimes used to establish other same device connections, such as when connecting two hubs or two switches together to create a larger network.

Table 2.1 summarizes the characteristics of the 10BaseT standard.

TABLE 2.1 Summary of 10BaseT Characteristics

Characteristic	Description
Transmission method	Baseband
Speed	10Mbps
Total distance/segment	100 meters
Cable type	Category 3, 4, or 5 UTP or STP
Connector	RJ-45

Make or Buy?

During your networking career, you will most certainly encounter the debate about whether to crimp your own twisted-pair network cables or buy them. The arguments for making cables always seem to hinge on cost savings. The arguments against crimping cables are often much more solid. Purchasing cables from a reputable maker ensures that the cables you install will work every time. The same cannot be said of homemade cables. In addition, when you factor in the time it takes to make a cable or troubleshoot a poorly made one, the cost savings are lessened. However, in some instances you'll have no choice but to make cables—for example, when special-distance cables are required.

10BaseFL

10BaseFL is an .implementation of 10Mbps Ethernet over fiber-optic cabling. 10BaseFL's primary advantage, over 10BaseT, is that it can be used over distances up to 2km. However, given the availability of other faster networking standards, such as 100BaseFX (discussed next), you are unlikely to encounter many 10BaseFL implementations.

Fast Ethernet

There was a time when 10Mbps networks were considered fast enough, but those days are long gone. Today, companies and home users alike demand more bandwidth than is available with 10Mbps network solutions. For such networks, Fast Ethernet is the most commonly used network design. Fast Ethernet standards are specified in the IEEE 802.3u standard. Three standards are defined by 802.3u: 100BaseTX, 100BaseT4, and 100BaseFX.

> **TIP**
>
> **Fast Ethernet Lingo**   Fast Ethernet is often referred to as 100BaseX, which also refers collectively to the 100BaseTX, 100BaseT4, and 100BaseFX standards.

100BaseTX

100BaseTX is a Fast Ethernet networking design and is one of three 802.3u standards. As its name suggests, 100BaseTX transmits network data at speed up to 100Mbps, the speeds at which most LANs operate today. 100BaseTX is most often implemented with UTP cable, but it can use STP; therefore, it suffers from the same 100 meter distance limitations as other UTP-based networks. 100BaseTX uses Category 5 UTP cable, and, like 10BaseT, it uses independent transmit and receive paths and can therefore support full-duplex operation. 100BaseTX is without question the most common Fast Ethernet standard.

100BaseT4

100BaseT4 is the second Fast Ethernet standard specified under 802.3u. It can use Category 3, 4, and 5 UTP cable, and it uses all four of the available pairs of wires within the cable, limiting full-duplex transfer. 100BaseT4 is similar in other respects to 100BaseTX: Its cable distance is limited to 100 meters, and its maximum transfer speed is 100Mbps. 100BaseT4 is not widely implemented, but it is sometimes used in environments where existing cable, such as Category 3 cable, exists. In such a situation, you can use 100BaseT4 instead of replacing the Category 3 cable with Category 5 UTP.

> **NOTE**
>
> **Limited Implementation**   100BaseT4 is not a common implementation of Fast Ethernet. As a result, it is not included in the CompTIA objectives for the Network+ exam.

> **TIP**
>
> **Repeaters**   Fast Ethernet repeaters are sometimes needed when you connect segments that use 100BaseTX, 100BaseT4, or 100BaseFX.

100BaseFX

100BaseFX is the IEEE standard for running Fast Ethernet over fiber-optic cable. Due to the expense of fiber implementations, 100BaseFX is largely limited to use as a network backbone. 100BaseFX can use two-strand multimode fiber or single-mode fiber media. The maximum segment length for half-duplex multimode fiber is 412 meters, but this maximum increases to an impressive 10,000 meters for full-duplex single-mode fiber. 100BaseFX often uses SC or ST fiber connectors. To see where 100BaseFX compares with other 100Base technologies, see Table 2.2.

> **NOTE**
>
> **100BaseVG-AnyLAN**   Another member of the 100Mbps club is the 100BaseVG-AnyLAN IEEE 802.12 specification. 100BaseVG-AnyLAN allows data transmissions of up to 100Mbps over Category 3 UTP cable, using four pairs of wires, but it can also use Category 4 and 5 with two pairs of wires. 100BaseVG-AnyLAN is not included in the 802.3 specification because it does not use the CSMA/CD access method; instead, it uses a demand priority access method. For more information on CSMA/CD, refer to Chapter 1.

REVIEW BREAK

Fast Ethernet Comparison

Table 2.2 summarizes the characteristics of the 802.3u Fast Ethernet specifications.

TABLE 2.2   Summary of 802.3u Fast Ethernet Characteristics

Characteristic	100BaseTX	100BaseT4	100BaseFX
Transmission method	Baseband	Baseband	Baseband
Speed	100Mbps	100Mbps	100Mbps
Distance	100 meters	100 meters	412 meters (multimode, half-duplex); 10,000 meters (single-mode, full-duplex)
Cable type	Category 5 or greater UTP, STP	Category 3, 4, 5	Fiber-optic
Connector type	RJ-45	RJ-45	SC, ST

Gigabit Ethernet: 1000BaseX

Gigabit Ethernet, 1000BaseX, is another variation on the 802.3 standard and is given its own identifier: 802.3z. Gigabit Ethernet offers transfer rates of up to 1000Mbps and is most often associated with fiber cable. 1000BaseX refers collectively to three distinct standards: 1000BaseLX, 1000BaseSX, and 1000BaseCX.

Both 1000BaseSX and 1000BaseLX are laser standards used over fiber. *LX* refers to *long wavelength laser*, and *SX* refers to *short wavelength laser*. Both the SX and LX wave lasers can be supported over two types of multimode fiber-optic cable: fibers of 62.5 micron and 50 micron diameters. Only LX wave lasers support the use of single-mode fiber. More information on the difference between the types of fiber-optic cable is given in the section titled "Common Network Cable " later in this chapter.

At the end of the day, the differences between 1000BaseLX and the 1000BaseSX have to do with cost and transmission distance. 1000BaseLX can transmit over 316 meters in half-duplex for both multimode fiber and single-mode fiber, 550 meters for full-duplex multimode fiber, and 5,000 meters for full-duplex single-mode fiber. Although 1000BaseSX is less expensive than 1000BaseLX, it cannot match the distances achieved by 1000BaseLX.

1000BaseCX moves away from the fiber cable and uses shielded copper wire. Segment lengths in 1000BaseCX are severely restricted; the maximum cable distance is 25 meters. Because of the restricted cable lengths, 1000BaseCX networks are not widely implemented. Table 2.3 summarizes the characteristics of Gigabit Ethernet 802.3z standards.

TABLE 2.3 Summary of IEEE 802.3z Gigabit Ethernet Characteristics

Characteristic	1000BaseSX	1000BaseLX	1000BaseCX
Transmission method	Baseband	Baseband	Baseband
Speed	1000Mbps	1000Mbps	1000Mbps
Distance	Half-duplex 275 (62.5 micron multimode fiber); half-duplex 316 (50 micron multimode fiber); full-duplex 275 (62.5 micron multimode fiber); full-duplex 550 (50 micron multimode fiber)	Half-duplex 316 (multimode and single-mode fiber); full-duplex 550 (mulitmode fiber); full-duplex 5000 (single-mode fiber)	25 meters for both full-duplex and half-duplex operations
Cable type	62.5/125 and 50/125 multimode fiber	62.5/125 and 50/125 multimode fiber; two 10-micron single-mode optical fibers	Shielded copper cable
Connector type	Fiber Connectors	Fiber Connectors	9-pin shielded connector

1000BaseT

1000BaseT, sometimes referred to as 1000BaseTX, is another Gigabit Ethernet standard, and it is given the IEEE 802.3ab designation. The 802.3ab standard specifies Gigabit Ethernet over Category 5 UTP cable. The standard allows for full-duplex transmission using the four pairs of twisted cable. To reach speeds of 1000Mbps over copper, a data transmission speed of 250Mbps is achieved over each pair of twisted-pair cable. Table 2.4 summarizes the characteristics of 1000BaseT.

TABLE 2.4   Summary of 1000BaseT Characteristics

Characteristic	Description
Transmission method	Baseband
Speed	1000Mbps
Total distance/segment	75 meters
Cable type	Category 5 or better
Connector type	RJ-45

10 Gigabit Ethernet

In the never-ending quest for faster data transmission rates, network standards are always being pushed to the next level. In today's networking environments, that level is 10 Gigabit Ethernet, also referred to as 10GbE. As the name suggests, 10GbE has the capability to provide data transmission rates of up to 10 Gigabits per second. That's 10,000 Mbps, or 100 times faster than most modern LAN implementations. There are a number of 10GbE implementations, though CompTIA chooses to focus on 10GBaseSR, 10GBaseLR, and 10GBaseER for the Network+ exam.

Designed primarily as a WAN and MAN connectivity medium, 10GbE was ratified as the IEEE 802.3ae standard in June 2002. Many networking hardware manufacturers now market 10GbE equipment. Although 10GbE network implementations are very expensive, companies such as Internet service providers (ISPs) that require extremely high-speed networks have been relatively quick to implement 10GbE.

Of the three 10GbE standards discussed here, 10GBaseSR is designed for LAN or MAN implementations, with a maximum distance of 300 meters using 50 micron multimode fiber cabling. 10BaseSR can also be implemented with 62.5 micron multimode fiber cabling but is limited to 33 meters.

10GBaseLR and 10GBaseER are designed for use in MAN and WAN implementations and are implemented using single-mode fiber-optic cabling. 10GBaseLR has a maximum distance of 10km, whereas 10GBaseER has a maximum distance of 40km. Table 2.5 summarizes the characteristics of 10 Gigabit Ethernet.

TIP
IEEE Standards   10 Gigabit Ethernet is defined in the IEEE 802.3ae standard.

88

Chapter 2: Cabling Standards, Media, and Connectors

TABLE 2.5   Summary of IEEE 802.3ae 10 Gigabit Ethernet Characteristics

Characteristic	10GbaseSR	10GbaseLR	10GbaseER
Transmission method	Baseband	Baseband	Baseband
Speed	10000Mbps	10000Mbps	10000Mbps
Distance	33m/300m	10,000m	40,000m
Cable type	62.5 micron Multimode Fiber/50 Micron Multimode fiber	Single Mode Fiber	Single Mode Fiber
Connector type	Fiber Connectors	Fiber Connectors	Fiber Connectors

Challenge

Understanding the commonly used IEEE 802.3 networking standards is an important part of a network administrator's knowledge. In the following table, many of the common standards are listed, but various pieces of information are missing. Your task is to complete the table so that all the boxes are complete. You can check your answers against the information provided in the solution table.

Standard	Speed	Baseband or Broadband	Media	Maximum Distance
	1000Mbps		UTP	75 meters
10Base2				
			50 Micron Multimode Fiber	300 meters
1000BaseSX			Single mode fiber	
				40,000 meters
	100Mbps		UTP	100 meters

Solution Table

Standard	Speed	Baseband or Broadband	Media	Maximum Distance
1000BaseT	1000Mbps	Base	UTP	75 meters
10Base2	10Mbps	Base	Thin Coax	185 meters
10GbaseSR	10Gbps	Base	50 Micron Multimode Fiber	300 meters
1000BaseSX	1000Mbps	Base	Single mode fiber	5000 Meters
10GbaseER	10Gbps	Base	Single Mode fiber	40,000 meters
100BaseTX	100Mbps	Base	UTP	100 meters

Media Connectors

Objective:

1.4 Recognize the following media connectors and describe their uses:

▶ RJ-11 (Registered Jack)

▶ RJ-45 (Registered Jack)

▶ F-Type

▶ ST (Straight Tip)

▶ SC (Standard Connector)

▶ IEEE1394 (FireWire)

▶ Fiber LC (Local Connector)

▶ MTRJ (Mechanical Transfer Registered Jack)

▶ USB (Universal Serial Bus)

All forms of network media need to be physically attached to the networked devices in some way. Media connectors provide the interface between the cables and the devices to which they attach (similar to the way an electrical cord connects a television and an electrical outlet). This section explores the common connectors you are likely to encounter in your work and, perhaps more importantly, on the Network+ exam.

EXAM ALERT

Know the Connectors You will be expected to identify the various media connectors and know which connectors are associated with which cable.

RJ Connectors

The connector you are most likely to encounter on modern networks is the RJ-45 (registered jack) connector. RJ-45 connectors bear a passing resemblance to the familiar RJ-11 connectors used with common telephone connections. The difference between the two connectors is that the RJ-11 connector supports six wires, whereas the RJ-45 network connector supports eight. Both RJ-11 and RJ-45 connectors are associated with twisted-pair cable. Figure 2.1 shows RJ-45 connectors, whereas Figure 2.2 shows RJ-11 connectors.

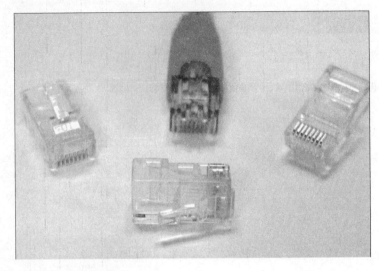

FIGURE 2.1   RJ-45 connectors.

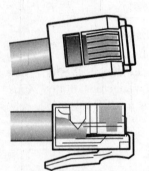

FIGURE 2.2   RJ-11 connectors.

F-Type Connectors

F-Type connectors are used for attaching coaxial cable to devices. In the world of modern networking, F-Type connectors are most commonly associated with connecting Internet modems to cable or satellite Internet providers' equipment. However, they are also used for connecting to some proprietary peripherals.

EXAM ALERT

'F' Is Not for Fiber   Because of its name, people often mistakenly assume that an F-Type connector is used with fiber-optic cabling. It is not. The F-Type connector is used only with coaxial or copper-based cables.

F-Type connectors screw into place, ensuring a firm contact between the cable and device. Hand tightening is all that should be required to make the contact, and the use of tools such as pliers to tighten connections is not recommended. Should a connector prove difficult to remove, however, you can use a pair of pliers or grips with a light pressure. F-Type connectors have a "nut" on the connection to assist this process. Figure 2.3 shows an example of an F-Type connector.

FIGURE 2.3   An F-Type connector.

Fiber Connectors

Several types of connectors are associated with fiber-optic cable. Which one is used is determined by the fiber implementation. Figure 2.4 shows some of the different fiber connectors you might encounter when working with fiber networks.

EXAM ALERT

Fiber-Optic Connectors   You will be expected to identify the various fiber-optic connectors for the Network+ exam. Specifically, the CompTIA Network+ exam objectives refer to the SC, ST, MTRJ, and LC connectors.

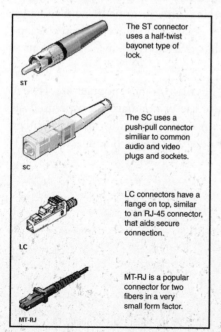

The ST connector uses a half-twist bayonet type of lock.

ST

The SC uses a push-pull connector similiar to common audio and video plugs and sockets.

SC

LC connectors have a flange on top, similar to an RJ-45 connector, that aids secure connection.

LC

MT-RJ is a popular connector for two fibers in a very small form factor.

MT-RJ

FIGURE 2.4   Fiber connectors. (Reproduced with permission from Computer Desktop Encyclopedia© 1981–2001 The Computer Language Co. Inc., www.computerlanguage.com.)

IEEE 1394 (FireWire)

The IEEE 1394 interface, also known as FireWire, is more commonly associated with the attachment of peripheral devices such as digital cameras or printers than network connections. However, it is possible to create small networks with IEEE 1394 cables, which is why discussion of the connectors is included here.

The IEEE 1394 interface comes in a 4- or 6-pin version, both of which are shown in Figure 2.5.

FIGURE 2.5 4-pin (left) and 6-pin (right) IEEE 1394 (FireWire) connectors.

Universal Serial Bus (USB)

Universal Serial Bus ports (USB) are now a common sight on both desktop and laptop computer systems. Like IEEE 1394, USB is associated more with connecting consumer peripherals such as MP3 players and digital cameras than networking. However, many manufacturers now make wireless network cards that plug directly into a USB port. Most desktop and laptop computers have between two and four USB ports, but USB hubs are available that provide additional ports if required.

A number of connectors are associated with USB ports, but the two most popular are Type A and Type B. Type A connectors are the more common of the two and are the type used on PCs. Although many peripheral devices also use a Type A connector, an increasing number now use a Type B. Figure 2.6 shows a Type A connector (left) and a Type B connector (right).

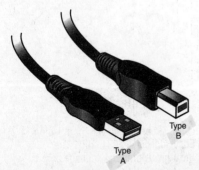

Type
B

Type
A

Figure 2.6 Type A (left) and Type B (right) USB connectors.

Objective:

1.5 Recognize the following media types and describe their uses:

▶ Category 3, 5, 5e, and 6

▶ UTP (Unshielded Twisted Pair)

▶ STP (Shielded Twisted Pair)

▶ Coaxial cable

▶ SMF (Single Mode Fiber) optic cable

▶ MMF (Multimode Fiber) optic cable

Networking Media

As identified in Chapter 1, "Introduction to Networking," a *network* is simply a group of connected computers. The computers on a traditional local area network (LAN) are connected by physical network media. Many types of media are used to connect network devices, and each type offers unique characteristics that you must understand to determine the media's suitability for a given network environment.

Before discussing the various network media, this section identifies some of the terms and general considerations relevant to network media.

> **NOTE**
>
> **Media** Because not all networks use traditional cable, the term *media* is used. This term encompasses copper-based and fiber-optic cable as well as wireless media types.

Choosing the correct network media is an important consideration because the media forms the foundation for the entire network. When you're working with any media, you must be aware of the factors that influence its suitability for a given network implementation. Some of the most common media considerations are discussed in the following sections.

Media Interference

As a data signal travels through a specific media, it may be subjected to a type of interference known as *electromagnetic interference (EMI)*. Many different things cause EMI; common sources include computer monitors and fluorescent lighting fixtures—basically, anything that creates an electromagnetic field. If a network cable is too close to such devices, the signal within the cable can become corrupted. As you might expect, some network media are more susceptible than others to the effects of EMI. Copper-based media are prone to EMI, whereas fiber-optic cable is completely resistant to it.

In most networks, standard cable provides sufficient resistance so that EMI isn't a problem. However, you might work in some environments in which interference is a concern. In such environments, it becomes important to understand which media offer the greatest resistance to EMI.

> **NOTE**
>
> **EMI-Resistant Cable Cost** Cables designed for greater resistance to EMI cost more than those that aren't.

EMI is just one of the threats to network transmissions. Data signals may also be subjected to something commonly referred to as *crosstalk*, which occurs when signals from two cables in close proximity to one another interfere with each other. As a result, the signals on both cables may become corrupted. When you're troubleshooting intermittent network problems, it might be worth your time to confirm that crosstalk or EMI is not at the root of your problems.

> **EXAM ALERT**
>
> **Jitter** Although EMI and crosstalk can be the cause of network problems, the condition that they result in is often referred to as *jitter*. Jitter is the destabilization of a signal as it travels across the media. Too much jitter and the signals become unusable, which is why so much effort is expended in protecting against jitter-causing conditions such as EMI and crosstalk.

Transmission Speed

One of the more important media considerations is the supported data transmission rate or speed. Different media types are rated to certain maximum speeds, but whether they are used to this maximum depends on the networking standard being used and the network devices connected to the network.

> **NOTE**
>
> The transmission rate of media is sometimes referred to incorrectly as the *bandwidth* In truth, the term bandwidth refers to the width of the range of electrical frequencies, or amount of channels that the media can support. Bandwidth correlates to the amount of data that can traverse the media at one time, but other factors determine what the maximum speed supported by a cable will be.

Transmission rates are normally measured by the number of data bits that can traverse the media in a single second. In the early days of data communications this measurement was expressed as bits per second (bps), but today's networks are measured in Mbps (megabits per second) and Gbps (gigabits per second).

The different types of network media vary in the transmission rates they can accommodate. If you're working on a network that accommodates huge amounts of data, transmission rates are a crucial consideration. In contrast, many older networks in small offices may only occasionally share files and maybe a printer. In such an environment, transmission rate is not a big issue.

Media Length

Not all networks have the same design. Some are isolated to a single office building, and others span large distances. For large network implementations, *media length* (that is, the maximum distance over which a certain type of media can be used) may be a factor in the network administrator's choice of network media. Each media has a recommended maximum length, and surpassing these recommendations can cause unusual network problems that are often difficult to troubleshoot. In some cases, the network simply will not work.

Media have maximum lengths because a signal weakens as it travels farther from its point of origin. If the signal travels far enough, it can weaken so much that it becomes unusable. The weakening of data signals as they traverse the media is referred to as *attenuation*.

Copper-based media is susceptible to attenuation, although different types of cable offer varying degrees of resistance to weakening signals. Some media, such as Shielded Twisted Pair (STP) use a special shielding inside the cable, which increases the distance the signal travels. Another strategy commonly employed to compensate for attenuation is *signal regeneration*. The cable itself does not perform the regeneration process; rather, network devices such as switches or repeaters handle signal regeneration. These devices strengthen the signal as it passes, and in doing so, they increase the distance the signal can travel. Network devices, such as hubs, routers, and switches, are covered in Chapter 3.

Fiber-optic cable does not suffer from attenuation. Instead, it suffers from a condition called "chromatic dispersion." Chromatic dispersion refers to the weakening of the light strength as it travels over distance. Although the scientific processes behind chromatic dispersion and attenuation are different, the end result is the same. Signals get weaker and at some point become unusable unless they are regenerated.

Some cable types, such as fiber-optic, offer support for very long distances; other types, such as twisted-pair, offer support for much shorter distances (a fraction of the distance of fiber). Some unbound media (wireless media) don't have an exact figure for the allowable distance because so many variables can limit the effective range.

EXAM ALERT

Attenuation   For the Network+ exam, you will be expected to know what attenuation is and how it affects a network.

Secure Transmission and Physical Media

Physical media provides a relatively secure transmission medium, because to gain access to the signal on the cable, a person must be able to physically access it—that is, he or she must be able to tap into the cable. Fiber-optic cable is more secure than copper-based media because the light transmissions and glass or plastic construction make it particularly hard to tap into. When it comes to security, wireless media is another topic entirely.

Installation and Repair

Some network media are easier to manage and install than others. This might seem like a minor consideration, but in real-world applications, it can be important. For example, fiber-optic cable is far more complex to install and troubleshoot than twisted-pair. It's so complicated, in fact, that special tools and training are often needed to install a fiber-optic based network.

It is important to be aware of what you are in for when it's time to implement or repair the network media.

NOTE

Plenum Cables   *Plenum* is the mysterious space that resides between the false, or drop, ceiling and the true ceiling. This space is typically used for the air conditioning or heating ducts. It might also hold a myriad of cables, including telephone, electrical, and network cables. The cables that occupy this space must be plenum rated. Plenum cables are coated with a nonflammable material, often Teflon or Kynar, and do not give off toxic fumes if they catch fire. As you might imagine, plenum-rated cables cost more than regular cables, but they are mandatory when cables are not run through a conduit. As an added bonus, plenum-rated cables suffer from less attenuation than non-plenum cables.

In addition to the factors already discussed, you need to understand some important concepts before we examine the specific media types; you need to understand baseband and broadband signaling, physical media terminology, and duplexing.

Baseband Versus Broadband Signaling

Two types of signaling methods are used to transmit information over network media: baseband and broadband.

Baseband

Baseband transmissions typically use digital signaling over a single wire; the transmissions themselves take the form of either electrical pulses or light. The digital signal used in baseband transmission occupies the entire bandwidth of the network media to transmit a single data signal. Baseband communication is bidirectional, allowing computers to both send and receive data using a single cable; however, the sending and receiving cannot occur on the same wire at the same time.

NOTE

Ethernet and Baseband   Ethernet networks use baseband transmissions.

Using baseband transmissions, it is possible to transmit multiple signals on a single cable by using a process known as *multiplexing*. Baseband uses Time-Division Multiplexing (TDM), which divides a single channel into time slots. The key thing about TDM is that it doesn't change how baseband transmission works—only the way data is placed on the cable.

Broadband

Whereas baseband uses digital signaling, broadband uses analog signals in the form of optical or electromagnetic waves over multiple transmission frequencies. For signals to be both sent and received, the transmission media must be split into two channels. Alternatively, two cables can be used—one to send and one to receive transmissions.

Multiple channels are created in a broadband system by using a multiplexing technique known as *Frequency-Division Multiplexing (FDM)*. FDM allows broadband media to accommodate traffic going in different directions on a single media at the same time.

Simplex, Half-Duplex, and Full-Duplex

Those who do not know about duplexing might assume that network transmissions travel in any direction through the media. In fact, specific dialog control modes determine the direction in which data can flow through the network media. The three dialog modes are simplex, half-duplex, and full-duplex.

The *simplex* mode allows only one-way communication through the media. A good example of simplex is a radio or television signal: There is only one transmitting device, and all other devices are receiving devices. A simplex dialog mode uses the full bandwidth of the media for transmitting the signal. The advantages of the simplex dialog mode can be seen in many applications, but networks are not among them.

> **EXAM ALERT**
>
> **Simplex Transmission** A broadcast message—that is, one that is sent to all nodes on the network—is a good example of a simplex transmission. Remember this for the exam.

Half-duplex allows each device to both transmit and receive, but only one of these processes can occur at one time. Many networks are configured for and support only half-duplex communication. A good example of half-duplex transmission is a modem that can either transmit or receive but not do both simultaneously. The transmitting device can use the entire bandwidth of the media.

> **EXAM ALERT**
>
> **Know the Difference** Half-duplex allows two-way communication over a single channel. Full-duplex provides two-way communication by using different channels for sending and receiving signals. For the exam, know the difference.

If at all possible, the preferred method of communication on networks is full-duplex mode. *Full-duplex* allows devices to receive and transmit simultaneously. On a network, devices that can use full-duplexing can double their transfer rates provided the devices they are connected to will also support the higher speed. For instance, a 100Mbps network card connected to a switch in full-duplex mode can operate at 200Mbps and therefore significantly increase the transmission speed. An example of full-duplex is a telephone conversation, where both parties are able to talk (send) and listen (receive) simultaneously.

> **Networking Terminology**
>
> The term *segment* is used extensively in discussions of network media. However, what *segment* means appears to be open to some interpretation. Technically speaking, a segment is simply a section of a larger entity. In networking, a segment is a part of the network or a single length of cable. You can just as easily say that one computer is on the same segment as another as you can say that each computer is on its own segment. In this case, the cable type affects the definition of *segment*. The first statement is correct if you're using coaxial cable; the second is correct if you're using twisted-pair.

Common Network Cable

Having now examined some of the general considerations that surround network media, the next step is to look at the different types of media available. The network media are not the most glamorous part of computer networking, but they are important both for the Network+ exam and the real world. Besides, who said networking was glamorous?

Network media can be divided into two distinct categories: cable and wireless, sometimes referred to as *bound* and *unbound* media. Cable media come in three common types: twisted-pair, coaxial, and fiber-optic. Wireless media have another range. The following sections identify the characteristic of each type of media.

Cable Media

Even with the rapid growth of wireless networking, you are still far more likely to work with cable media than with any wireless alternative. Cable media provide a physical connection between networked devices—for example, a copper cable running from a desktop computer to a hub or switch in the server room. Data transmissions pass through the cable to their destination.

There are three types of cable media: metal (normally copper), glass, or plastic. Copper-based cable is widely used to connect LANs and wide area networks (WANs), and optical cable, which uses glass or plastic, is mainly used for large-scale network implementations or over long distances. The following sections review the various types of cable media and the networks on which they are used.

Twisted-Pair

Now and for the foreseeable future, twisted-pair cable is the network media of choice. It is relatively inexpensive, easy to work with, and well suited to the needs of the modern network. There are two distinct types of twisted-pair cable: unshielded twisted pair (UTP) and shielded twisted pair (STP). UTP is the by far the most common implementation of twisted-pair cable, and it is used for both telephone systems and computer networks.

EXAM ALERT

Another Name for STP   STP cable is sometimes called *IBM-type cable*. You should know this for the exam.

STP, as its name implies, adds extra shielding within the casing, so it copes with interference and attenuation better than regular UTP. Because of this shielding, cable distances for STP can be greater than for UTP; but, unfortunately, the additional shielding also makes STP considerably more costly than regular UTP.

NOTE

What's with the Twist? Ever wonder why twisted-pair wiring is twisted? In the ongoing battle with interference and attenuation, it was discovered that twisting the wires within a cable resulted in greater signal integrity than running the wires parallel to one another. UTP cable is particularly susceptible to crosstalk, and increasing the number of twists per foot in the wire achieves greater resistance against interference. The technique of twisting wires together is not limited to network cable; some internal and external SCSI cables employ a similar strategy.

The Electronic Industries Association/Telecommunications Industry Association (EIA/TIA) has specified a number of categories of twisted-pair cable:

- **Category 1**—Voice-grade UTP telephone cable. Due to its susceptibility to interference and attenuation and its low bandwidth capability, Category 1 UTP is not practical for network applications.

- **Category 2**—Data-grade cable capable of transmitting data up to 4Mbps. Category 2 cable is, of course, too slow for networks. It is unlikely that you will encounter Category 2 used on any network today.

- **Category 3**—Data-grade cable capable of transmitting data up to 10Mbps. A few years ago, Category 3 was the cable of choice for twisted-pair networks. As network speeds pushed the 100Mbps speed limit, Category 3 became ineffective.

- **Category 4**—Data-grade cable that has potential data throughput of 16Mbps. Category 4 cable was often implemented in the IBM Token Ring networks.

- **Category 5**—Data-grade cable capable of transmitting data at 100Mbps. Category 5 is the cable of choice on twisted-pair networks and is associated with Fast Ethernet technologies.

- **Category 5e**—Data-grade cable used on networks that run at up to 1000Mbps. Category 5e cabling can be used up to 350 meters, depending on the implementation.

- **Category 6**—High performance UTP cable capable of transmitting data at over 1000Mbps. Category 6 cabling is rated up to 550 meters depending on the implementation. The only reason not to use Category 6 cabling in all new implementations is that it is marginally more expensive than Category 5e cable.

It should be noted that although these are the categories of twisted-pair cabling currently in use, other categories, such as category 6e, 7, and 8 are already available or in development. However, they have not become ratified standards as yet.

Determining Cable Categories   If you're working on an existing network that is a few years old, you might need to determine which category of cable is used on the network. The easiest way to do this is to simply read the cable. The category number should be clearly printed on it.

Cable's Don't Have Speeds   For the Network+ exam, be aware of the speeds at which commonly implemented network standards operate, rather than what the maximum speed supported by a cable might be. It is the networking equipment, manufactured to meet certain IEEE standards, that defines what speed the network will operate at, not the network cabling. All the network cabling needs to do is support that speed as a minimum.

It should be noted that the figures provided for each of the cabling categories refer to speeds that these cables are commonly used to support. Ratified standards for these cabling categories may actually specify lower speeds than those listed, but cable and network component manufacturers are always pushing the performance envelope in the quest for greater speeds. The ratified standards define minimum specifications. For more information on cabling standards, visit the TIA website at http://www.tiaonline.org/.

Coaxial Cable

At one time, almost all networks used coaxial cable. Times have changed, and coax has fallen out of favor, giving way to faster and more durable cable options. That is not to say that you won't be working with coax at some point. Many environments have been using coax and continue to do so because their network needs do not require an upgrade to another media—at least not yet. Many small offices continue to use coax on their networks, so we'll include it in our discussion.

Coaxial cable resembles standard TV cable and is constructed using an outside insulation cover, braided metal shielding, and a copper wire at the center. The shielding and insulation help combat attenuation, crosstalk, and EMI. Some coax is available with dual and even quad shielding.

Two types of coax are used in networking: thin coax and thick coax. Neither is particularly popular anymore, but you are most likely to encounter thin coax. Figure 2.7 shows the construction of a typical coaxial cable.

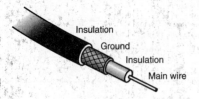

FIGURE 2.7   Coaxial cable construction.

Thin Coax

Even though thin coax is by far the most widely used type of coax, you are unlikely to be encounter it unless you are supporting an older network. As the name suggests, it is thin—at least compared to other forms of available coax. Thin coax, also called Thinnet, is only .25 inches in diameter, making it fairly easy to install. In networking uses, it has a maximum cable length of 185 meters (that is, just over 600 feet). If longer lengths of thin coax are used, data signals sent along the cable will suffer from attenuation, compromising data integrity. Table 2.6 summarizes the types of thin coax cable.

TABLE 2.6   Thin Coax Types

Cable Type	Description
RG-58 /U	Has a solid copper core
RG-58 A/U	Has a stranded wire core
RG-58 C/U	Used for military specifications
RG-6	Often used for cable TV and cable modems

In network implementations, thin coax typically runs from computer to computer and uses Bayonet Neill Concelman (BNCs) to connect to network devices. Figure 2.8 shows BNC T connectors and terminators, which are often used with thin coax.

> **NOTE**
>
> **BNC Connectors**   BNC connectors are also sometimes referred to as British Naval Connectors. Fortunately, CompTIA just uses the acronym, so you don't need to worry about this for the Network+ exam.

> **NOTE**
>
> **Cable and Standards**   Thin coax cable is used for the Institute of Electrical and Electronics Engineers (IEEE) 10Base2 network standard.

Figure 2.8 BNC T connectors
and terminators.

Fiber-Optic Cable

Fiber-optic cable is a newcomer on the networking scene compared to the other network cable media, and it is perhaps the most interesting. Unlike standard networking cables, which use electric signals to send data transmissions, fiber uses light. As a result, fiber-optic transmissions are not susceptible to EMI or crosstalk, giving fiber cable an obvious advantage over copper-based media. In addition, fiber-optic cable is highly resistant to the signal weakening, referred to as chromatic dispersion, which was mentioned earlier. All this allows data signals on a fiber-optic cable to travel distances measured in kilometers rather than meters, as with copper-based media. Further advantages of fiber cable include the facts that it's small in diameter, it's lightweight, and it offers significantly faster transmission speeds than other cable media. Quite simply, fiber beats twisted-pair from almost every angle. So, why aren't all networks using fiber cable? The same reason we don't all drive Porsches: cost.

A few things will continue to ensure that there is room for twisted-pair and copper-based media in network environments. First, a fiber solution is costly in comparison to UTP-based cable implementations, eliminating it from many small- to mid-sized companies that simply do not have the budget to support a fiber-optic solution. The second drawback of fiber is that it can be more complex to install than UTP. Creating custom lengths of fiber-optic cable requires trained professionals and specialized tools. In contrast, custom lengths of UTP cabling can be created easily with commonly available tools. Third, fiber technology is incompatible with much of the existing electronic network infrastructure, meaning that to use fiber-optic cable, much of the current network hardware needs to be retrofitted or upgraded, and that can be a costly commitment.

A fiber-optic cable consists of several components, including the optic core at the center, an optic cladding, insulation, and an outer jacket. The optic core is responsible for carrying the light signal and is commonly constructed of plastic or glass. Figure 2.9 shows an example of the components of a fiber-optic cable.

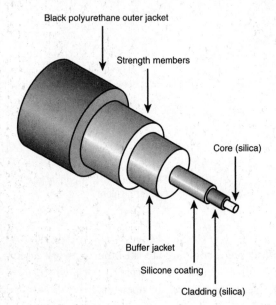

Black polyurethane outer jacket

Strength members

Core (silica)

Buffer jacket

Silicone coating

Cladding (silica)

Figure 2.9   Fiber-optic cable.

Two types of optical fiber are commonly available: single-mode and multimode. Multimode fiber (MMF) has a larger core than single-mode. This larger core allows hundreds of light rays to flow through the fiber simultaneously. Single-mode fiber (SMF), on the other hand, has a small core that allows only a single light beam to pass. The light transmissions in single-mode fiber pass through the core in a direct line, like a flashlight beam. The numerous light beams in multimode fiber bounce around inside the core, inching toward their destination. Because light beams bounce within the core, the light beams slow down, reduce in strength, and take some time to travel along the cable. For this reason, single-mode fiber's speed and distance are superior to those of multimode.

Fiber cable can also have a variety of internal compositions (glass or plastic core), and the size of the core inside the cable, measured in microns, can vary. Some of the common types of fiber-optic cable include the following:

▸ 62.5 micron core/125 micron cladding multimode

▸ 50 micron core/125 micron cladding multimode

▸ 8.3 micron core/125 micron cladding single mode

> **NOTE**
>
> **Fiber-Optic Cable Transmission Rates**   The rate at which fiber-optic cable can transmit data is determined by the mode used and whether the fiber core is glass or plastic.

REVIEW BREAK

Cable Summary

Be prepared: The CompTIA Network+ exam will require you to identify the basic characteristics of each cable type discussed in this section. In particular, you will be expected to know which cables offer the greatest resistance to interference and attenuation, and you must be able to identify which type of cable is best suited for a particular network environment. Table 2.7 summarizes the characteristics of the various cable media.

TABLE 2.7   Cable Media Characteristics

Media	Resistance to Attenuation	Resistance to EMI/ Crosstalk	Cost of Implementation	Difficulty of Implementation
UTP	Low	Low	Low	Low
STP	Moderate	Moderate	Moderate	Low
Thin coax	Moderate	Moderate	Low	Low
Fiber-optic	Very high*	Perfect	Very high	Moderate

*Technically, the weakening of signals as they travel along a fiber-optic cable is considered chromatic dispersion and not attenuation.

Chapter Summary

Networks are often complex in design, maintenance, and implementation, and the basics—such as network standards, media, and connectors—are often forgotten. But these elements are the foundation blocks of a network.

The IEEE 802.3 standard specifies Ethernet networking and uses the various cable media discussed in this chapter. The 802.3 LAN standards include 10Mbps, 100Mbps, 1000Mbps, 1Gbps, and 10Gbps network standards. Each of these standards specifies numerous networking characteristics, including network speed, cable type, topology, transmission method, and cable distance.

Several different types of cable are used on modern networks, including coaxial, twisted-pair, and fiber-optic cable. Each cable has different strengths and weaknesses, making some types of cable more suitable than others in a given network environment. Part of the role of the network administrator is to be able to identify the characteristics of the various cable types and to know how to troubleshoot them when required.

Each of these different cable types requires the appropriate connector. By far the most commonly used connector type today is the RJ-45 connector, which is used with twisted-pair cable. Other connector types include SC and MIC connectors for fiber-optic cable and BNCs for thin coax cable.

To be able to add clients to an existing network, you need to identify the connectors and cables already in use on the network. By using observation techniques—examining the cables and connectors already in use—you can find out what you need to know to correctly add computers to the network.

Several key characteristics and considerations determine a media's suitability for a specific network environment. These considerations include crosstalk, attenuation, EMI, bandwidth, installation and repair, and security. You need to understand each of these to determine the appropriate media for a network.

Networks use dialog modes to determine the direction that transmissions flow over the network media. Three dialog modes are used: simplex, half-duplex, and full-duplex. Simplex allows only one-way communication; half-duplex allows two-way communication, but devices cannot send and receive simultaneously; and full-duplex allows devices to simultaneously receive and transmit.

Key Terms

- 10BaseFL
- 10BaseT
- 10GBaseER
- 10GBaseLR
- 10GBaseSR
- 100BaseFX
- 100BaseTX
- 802.3
- 1000BaseCX
- 1000BaseLX
- 1000BaseSX
- 1000BaseTX
- coaxial

- F-Type
- IEEE1394
- LC
- media
- MMF
- MTRJ
- RJ-11
- RJ-45
- SC
- SMF
- ST
- STP
- UTP

Apply Your Knowledge

Exercises

2.1 Identifying Cable Costs

In this project, you use the Internet to identify cable characteristics and associated costs.

In this chapter we looked at the network media, connectors, and standards—all of which are essential to networks. As a network administrator, you need to have a detailed knowledge of network media and their associated connectors. When you are called on to troubleshoot or implement a network, this knowledge will prove invaluable.

A common task for network administrators is to source out the costs of cable and connectors. Consider the following scenario: You have been contracted by BootCo, a maker of snowshoes and toques, to begin the process of implementing a network. BootCo requires a network of 25 systems and needs to know the costs associated with the media for the network. The network cable lengths are as follows:

6×22 meters

10×18 meters

4×9 meters

5×72 meters

In this exercise, you will determine the difference in cost of using Category 5e cable or Category 6 cable. You will also determine the cost difference in buying pre-made cables or making your own.

Estimated time: 20 minutes

1. Get on the Internet and from a search engine, look for a company that sells network cable. The search is likely to return many results, and it may be necessary to restrict your search to local vendors.

2. Browse a vendor's website and locate UTP Category 5e and Category 6 cable.

3. You will need to price out the cables based on the lengths stated above. Also remember that you will need 50 connectors, and a special tool called a "crimper" if you are going to make the cables yourself.

4. Continue to search the site for the costs for the Category 5e and Category 6 cable. To get a better idea of costs, it might be necessary to find information from several vendors.

5. Compare the cost of buying bulk cable and connectors to the cost of buying premade cables and connectors.

Exam Questions

1. Which of the following 10 Gigabit Ethernet standards has the greatest maximum transmission distance?

   ○ **a.** 10GBaseSR

   ○ **b.** 10GBaseER

   ○ **c.** 10GBaseLR

   ○ **d.** 10GBaseXR

2. You have been asked to support a network installation, and you are required to identify a network media that can connect two remote servers that are 1.5 km apart. The network cable should not be dependent on network devices to help regenerate the signal. Which of the following cables best suits the company's needs?

   ○ **a.** Fiber-optic

   ○ **b.** Category 3

   ○ **c.** Category 6 UTP

   ○ **d.** Category 5e UTP

3. You are connecting some equipment at a client's home. You notice that one of the cables provided with the equipment has an F-type connector on it. Which of the following tasks are you most likely performing?

   ○ **a.** Connecting a printer to a FireWire port.

   ○ **b.** Creating a peer-to-peer network using IEEE1394 cables.

   ○ **c.** Connecting a cable Internet modem.

   ○ **d.** Creating a peer-to-peer network with STP cabling.

4. You need to connect two servers located 600 meters apart. You require a direct connection without the use of signal regeneration. Which of the following Ethernet standards would you employ?

   ○ **a.** 10BaseT with Category 5e cable.

   ○ **b.** 100BaseT with Category 6 cable.

   ○ **c.** 100BaseT with Category 5e cable.

   ○ **d.** 100BaseFX

5. You are working on an older network and are required to add a client. The network is using Category 5 UTP cable. Which connector should you use?

   ○ **a.** MTRJ
   ○ **b.** Transceiver
   ○ **c.** RJ-45
   ○ **d.** RJ-11

6. You have been asked to develop the specifications for a new storage wide area network. The new link will provide a direct connection between two office blocks, 3,200 meters apart. The specifications call for the fastest connection possible using currently ratified standards. Which of the following 802.3 standards are you most likely to recommend?

   ○ **a.** 1000BaseFX
   ○ **b.** 10GBaseER
   ○ **c.** 10GBaseSR
   ○ **d.** 10GBaseWR

7. While reviewing the specifications for a new network installation, you notice that the design calls for RJ-45 and MTRJ connectors. The network is a high-speed design capable of supporting speeds up to 1000Mbps. What two types of network cable will the specifications call for?

   ○ **a.** Thin coax and UTP

   ○ **b.** RJ-11 and fiber optic

   ○ **c.** Cat 6 UTP and fiber optic

   ○ **d.** Cat 5 UTP and fiber optic

8. Which of the following terms is used to describe interference created by individual wires within a network cable such as UTP?

   ○ **a.** Attenuation

   ○ **b.** Crosstalk

   ○ **c.** FDM

   ○ **d.** Disruption

9. As a network administrator, you have been asked to recommend a networking standard that can support data transfers of up to 100Mbps, using the existing Category 3 cable and the CSMA/CD access method. Which of the following best suits your needs?

   ○ **a.** 100BaseTX

   ○ **b.** 100BaseFX

   ○ **c.** 100BaseVG-AnyLAN

   ○ **d.** 100BaseT4

10. What is the maximum distance a signal can travel over multimode fiber?

   ○ **a.** 10,000 meters

   ○ **b.** 412 meters

   ○ **c.** 500 meters

   ○ **d.** 100 meters

11. Which of the following are associated with IEEE 802.3z? (Choose the three best answers.)

   ○ **a.** 1000BaseLX

   ○ **b.** 1000BaseCX

   ○ **c.** 1000BaseBX

   ○ **d.** 1000BaseSX

12. Which of the following media types offers the greatest resistance to interference?

○ **a.** STP

○ **b.** MTRJ

○ **c.** Fiber-optic

○ **d.** UTP

13. What is the maximum transfer distance defined by the 1000BaseT standard?

○ **a.** 100 meters

○ **b.** 75 meters

○ **c.** 1,000 meters

○ **d.** 550 meters

14. Which of the following is an advantage of 100BaseFX over 100BaseTX

○ **a.** 100BaseFX is faster than 100BaseTX.

○ **b.** 100BaseFX implementations are cheaper than 100BaseTX implementations.

○ **c.** 100BaseFX can be implemented over existing Category 3 or 4 UTP cabling.

○ **d.** 100BaseFX can be implemented over greater distances than 100BaseTX.

15. Which of the following connectors is *not* associated with fiber-optic cabling?

○ **a.** F-Type

○ **b.** SC

○ **c.** ST

○ **d.** LC

16. Which of the following terms identifies the loss in signal strength as a signal travels through a media?

○ **a.** Crosstalk

○ **b.** EMI

○ **c.** Plenum

○ **d.** Attenuation

17. You are a network administrator for a large company. Transfer speeds have been too slow, and you have been asked to recommend a 1000Mbps network solution. The network requires a transfer distance of 3,500 meters. Which of the following would you recommend?

- ○ **a.** 1000BaseCX
- ○ **b.** 1000BaseLX
- ○ **c.** 1000BaseBX
- ○ **d.** 1000BaseSX

18. Which fiber-optic mode allows the fastest transfer rates?

- ○ **a.** SC
- ○ **b.** ST
- ○ **c.** Single-mode
- ○ **d.** Multimode

19. A company that transfers sensitive data has asked you to install a media that is highly resistant to eavesdropping and signal tampering. Which of the following media would you recommend?

- ○ **a.** STP
- ○ **b.** UTP
- ○ **c.** FTP
- ○ **d.** Fiber

20. Baseband sends transmissions in which of the following forms?

- ○ **a.** Digital
- ○ **b.** Analog
- ○ **c.** Digital and analog
- ○ **d.** RF

Answers to Exam Questions

1. **b.** The 10GBaseER standard specifies a maximum transmission distance of 40,000m. The 10GBaseSR standard specifies a maximum transmission distance of 300 meters, whereas 10GBaseLR specifies a maximum transmission distance of 10,000 meters. 10GBaseXR is not a recognized 10 Gigabit Ethernet standard. For more information, see the section "Features and Characteristics of Ethernet 802.3 Standards," in this chapter.

2. **a.** Fiber-optic cable uses light transmission, making it less susceptible to interference and attenuation. Therefore, data signals can travel significant distances. In this case, only fiber-optic cable meets the distance requirements. All the other cables listed in the answer are limited to much shorter distances than fiber-optic. For more information, see the section "Common Network Cable," in this chapter.

3. **c.** F-Type connectors are most commonly associated with the coaxial cable used to connect with cable Internet modems. F-Type connectors are not used on cables with IEEE1394 or FireWire connectors, nor are they used with STP cabling. For more information, see the section "Media Connectors" in this chapter.

4. **d.** 100BaseFX has the potential to transmit distances that exceed 600 meters. However, to reach distances of 600 meters, you'd need to use single-mode fiber. Of the other standards, 100BaseT can reach only 550 meters when using Category 5e or Category 6 cabling. For more information, see the section "Features and Characteristics of Ethernet 802.3 Standards," in this chapter.

5. **c.** To add a client to an existing network that is using Category 5 UTP, you would work with RJ-45 connectors. MTRJ connectors are used with fiber-optic cable, and RJ-11 is the connector type associated with telephone cable. For more information, see the section "Media Connectors," in this chapter.

6. **b.** The 10GBaseER standard provides 1GBps transmission speeds over distances up to 10,000 meters. It is a currently ratified IEEE 802.3 standard. 1000BaseFX only runs at 1Gbps, which makes it the slowest of the technologies listed in the answer. 10GBaseSR can be used only over distances up to 330 meters. 10GBaseWR is not a recognized 10Gbps standard. For more information, see the section "Features and Characteristics of Ethernet 802.3 Standards," in this chapter.

7. **c.** RJ-45 connectors are associated with UTP cabling, whereas MTRJ connectors are associated with fiber-optic cabling. Because the network design is high speed (1000Mbps), you would need to use Category 5e cabling or higher. All fiber-optic cable is capable of speeds in excess of 1000Mbps. For more information, see the section "Media Connectors," in this chapter.

8. **b.** The interference created between wires in a cable is called *crosstalk*. *Attenuation* is the term given to the loss of strength in a signal as it travels over the media. Frequency Division Multiplexing (FDM) is a technology that allows more than one signal to be transmitted across a cable at one time. *Disruption* is not a term used to describe the interference created between wires in a cable. For more information, see the section "Networking Media," in this chapter.

9. **d.** 100BaseT4 is a Fast Ethernet standard that can use existing Category 3 cable and have transmission speeds of up to 100Mbps. 100BaseVG-AnyLAN can also use Category 3 cable, but it uses a demand priority access method. 100Base- requires Category 5 cable, and 100BaseFX uses fiber-optic cable. For more information, see the section "Features and Characteristics of Ethernet 802.3 Standards," in this chapter.

10. **b.** The maximum distance for multimode fiber is 412 meters. Single-mode fiber increases the distance to 10,000 meters. Answers c and d are not valid. For more information, see the section "Features and Characteristics of Ethernet 802.3 Standards," in this chapter.

11. **a, b, d.** Three standards are associated with 802.3z: 1000BaseLX, 1000BaseSX, and 1000BaseCX. 100BaseBX is not a valid standard. For more information, see the section "Features and Characteristics of Ethernet 802.3 Standards," in this chapter.

12. **c.** Because fiber uses light to transmit data, it is not susceptible to EMI and crosstalk. It is the media of choice in high-interference network environments. All the other cable types mentioned are copper based and are therefore susceptible, to varying degrees, to EMI and crosstalk. MTRJ is a type of connector used with fiber-optic cabling. It is not a type of network media. For more information, see the section "Common Network Cable," in this chapter.

13. **b.** The 1000BaseT standard uses copper cable and specifies a segment maximum of 75 meters. For more information, see the section "Features and Characteristics of Ethernet 802.3 Standards," in this chapter.

14. **d.** 100BaseFX is a Fast Ethernet standard implemented on fiber-optic cabling. It is more expensive and more difficult to install than 100BaseTX, which uses twisted-pair cabling. Both standards have a maximum speed of 100Mbps; however, 100BaseFX can be used over greater distance than 100BaseTX. For more information, see the section "Features and Characteristics of Ethernet 802.3 Standards," in this chapter.

15. **a.** F-Type connectors are used with coaxial cabling. They are not used with fiber-optic cable. All the other connector types are used with fiber-optic cabling. For more information, see the section "Media Connectors," in this chapter.

16. **d.** *Attenuation* refers to signal degradation as it travels through media. *Crosstalk* is the term used to refer to interference from other cables; *EMI* is a condition created by electronic or mechanical equipment. *Plenum* is not a type of interference; it is the term used to classify cables suitable for installation in suspended ceilings and other enclosed areas. For more information, see the section "Networking Media," in this chapter.

17. **b.** 1000BaseLX can transmit up to 5,000 meters, using single-mode fiber. The other standards listed operate over much shorter distances. For more information, see the section "Features and Characteristics of Ethernet 802.3 Standards," in this chapter.

18. **c.** Single-mode fiber allows faster transfer rates than multimode fiber and supports longer data transmissions. SC and ST are types of fiber connectors, not types of cable. For more information, see the section "Common Network Cable," in this chapter.

19. **d.** Because of the construction of fiber cable and the fact that it uses light transmission rather than electronic signals, it is very resistant to tampering and eavesdropping. All the other cable types listed are copper based and are therefore less secure than fiber-based media. FTP is a protocol used for transferring files between systems on a network. It is not a type of network media. For more information, see the section "Common Network Cable," in this chapter.

20. **a.** Baseband transmissions use digital signaling. Analog signaling is associated with broadband. For more information, see the section "Baseband Versus Broadband Signaling," in this chapter.

Suggested Readings and Resources

1. Groth, David, Jim McBee. *Cabling: The Complete Guide to Network Wiring*. Sybex, 2001.

2. Habraken, Joe. *Absolute Beginner's Guide to Networking*, fourth edition. Que Publishing, 2003.

3. Ogletree, Terry William. *Upgrading and Repairing Networks, Fourth Edition*. Que Publishing, 2003.

4. Network Cabling Information, www.techfest.com/networking/cabling.htm.

5. "TechEncyclopedia," www.techencyclopedia.com.

6. Networking technology information, www.cisco.com/public/products_tech.shtml.

7. "Network Cabling Help," www.datacottage.com.

CHAPTER 3

Networking Components and Devices

Objectives

This chapter covers the following CompTIA-specified objectives for the "Media and Topologies" and "Protocols and Standards" sections of the Network+ exam:

1.6 Identify the purpose, features, and functions of the following network components:

- ▶ **Hubs**
- ▶ **Switches**
- ▶ **Bridges**
- ▶ **Routers**
- ▶ **Gateways**
- ▶ **CSU/DSU**
- ▶ **Network interface cards (NICs)**
- ▶ **ISDN adapters**
- ▶ **Wireless access points (WAPs)**
- ▶ **Modems**
- ▶ **Transceivers (media converters)**
- ▶ **Firewalls**

- ▶ A wide range of devices is used in modern networking. As a Network+ certified technician, you need to have a good understanding of commonly used devices.

2.1 Identify a MAC (Media Access Control) address and its parts.

- ▶ MAC addresses are the means by which systems communicate at a base level. As a network administrator, you need to understand the purpose, function, and expression of MAC addresses.

Outline

Study Strategies

▶ Review the purpose, function, and key characteristics of the various networking components.

▶ Review the component summary provided in Table 3.3.

▶ Review the types of routing protocols, link state and distance vector.

▶ Distinguish between RIP and OSPF as routing protocols.

▶ Identify the protocols used within TCP/IP, IPX/SPX, and AppleTalk that provide routing functionality.

▶ Practice identifying the MAC address of a network card using the appropriate utility.

▶ Remember to review the Notes, Tips, Tables, and Exam Alerts in this chapter. Make sure that you understand the information in the Exam Alerts. If you don't understand the topic referenced in an Exam Alert, refer to the information in the chapter text and then read the Exam Alert again.

Introduction

So far this book has examined topologies, media access methods, networking standards, and cable types and connectors. To complete our examination of networking on a physical level, this chapter looks at the network devices used to create networks.

Objective:

1.6 Identify the purpose, features, and functions of the following network components:

▶ Hubs

▶ Switches

▶ Bridges

▶ Routers

▶ Gateways

▶ CSU/DSU

▶ Wireless access points (WAPs)

▶ Modems

▶ Network interface cards (NICs)

▶ ISDN adapters

▶ Transceivers

▶ Firewalls

Each of these devices fulfills a specific role in a network; however, only the largest and most complex environments use all of them. We'll begin our discussion of networking devices with perhaps the most simple and common network device used today: the hub.

NOTE

Repeaters Traditionally, any discussion of networking components would include repeaters, but today repeaters are a little outdated. Repeaters were once used to increase the usable length of the cable, and they were most commonly associated with coaxial network configurations. Because coaxial networks have now fallen out of favor, and because the functionality of repeaters has been built in to other devices, such as hubs and switches, repeaters are rarely used. For this reason, CompTIA has elected to leave them out of the required knowledge for the Network+ exam.

Hubs

Hubs are simple network devices, and their simplicity is reflected in their low cost. Small hubs with four or five ports (often referred to as *workgroup hubs*) cost less than $50; with the requisite cables, they provide everything needed to create a small network. Hubs with more ports are available for networks that require greater capacity. Figure 3.1 shows an example of a workgroup hub, and Figure 3.2 shows an example of the type of hub you might see on a corporate network.

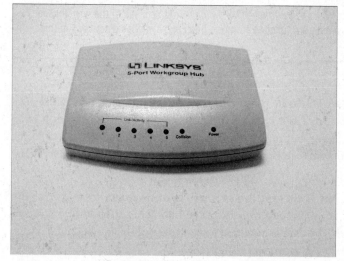

FIGURE 3.1 A workgroup hub.

FIGURE 3.2 A high-capacity, or high-density, hub.

Computers connect to a hub via a length of twisted-pair cabling. In addition to ports for connecting computers, even an inexpensive hub generally has a port designated as an uplink port that enables the hub to be connected to another hub to create larger networks. The "Working with Hubs and Switches" section later in this chapter presents a detailed discussion of this feature.

> **NOTE**
>
> **Token Ring and MSAUs** Both hubs and switches are used in Ethernet networks. Token Ring networks, which are few and far between, use special devices called *multistation access units (MSAUs)* to create the network. In some cases, MSAUs are referred to as *Token Ring switches*; but because of the way Token Ring operates, these devices perform a different function from the hubs and switches discussed in this section.

Most hubs are referred to as either active or passive. *Active* regenerate a signal before forwarding it to all the ports on the device and requires a power supply. Small workgroup hubs normally use an external power adapter, but on larger units the power supply is built in. *Passive* hubs, which today are seen only on older networks, do not need power and they don't regenerate the data signal.

Regeneration of the signal aside, the basic function of a hub is to take data from one of the connected devices and forward it to all the other ports on the hub. This method of operation is inefficient because, in most cases, the data is intended for only one of the connected devices. You can see a representation of how a hub works in Figure 3.3.

> **NOTE**
>
> **Broadcasting** The method of sending data to all systems regardless of the intended recipient is referred to as *broadcasting*. On busy networks, broadcast communications can have a significant impact on overall network performance.

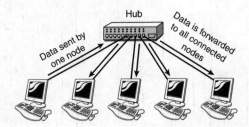

FIGURE 3.3 How a hub works.

Due to the inefficiencies of the hub system and the constantly increasing demand for more bandwidth, hubs are slowly but surely being replaced with switches. As you will see in the next section, switches offer distinct advantages over hubs.

Switches

On the surface, a *switch* looks much like a hub. Despite their similar appearance, switches are far more efficient than hubs and are far more desirable for today's network environments. Figure 3.4 shows an example of a 32-port Ethernet switch. If you refer to Figure 3.2, you'll notice few differences in the appearance of the high-density hub and this switch.

FIGURE 3.4 A 32-port Ethernet switch. (Photo courtesy TRENDware International, www.trendware.com.)

As with a hub, computers connect to a switch via a length of twisted-pair cable. Multiple switches are often interconnected to create larger networks. Despite their similarity in appearance and their identical physical connections to computers, switches offer significant operational advantages over hubs.

As discussed earlier in the chapter, a hub forwards data to all ports, regardless of whether the data is intended for the system connected to the port. This arrangement is inefficient; however, it requires little intelligence on the part of the hub, which is why hubs are inexpensive.

Rather than forwarding data to all the connected ports, a switch forwards data only to the port on which the destination system is connected. It looks at the Media Access Control (MAC) addresses of the devices connected to it to determine the correct port. A *MAC address* is a unique number that is stamped into every NIC. By forwarding data only to the system to which the data is addressed, the switch decreases the amount of traffic on each network link dramatically. In effect, the switch literally channels (or *switches*, if you prefer) data between the ports. Figure 3.5 illustrates how a switch works.

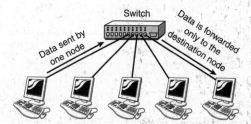

FIGURE 3.5 How a switch works.

You might recall from the discussions of Ethernet networking in Chapter 2, "Cabling Standards, Media, and Connectors," that collisions occur on the network when two devices attempt to transmit at the same time. Such collisions cause the performance of the network to degrade. By channeling data only to the connections that should receive it, switches reduce the number of collisions that occur on the network. As a result, switches provide significant performance improvements over hubs.

Switches can also further improve performance over the performance of hubs by using a mechanism called *full-duplex*. On a standard network connection, the communication between the system and the switch or hub is said to be *half-duplex*. In a half-duplex connection, data can be either sent or received on the wire but not at the same time. Because switches manage the data flow on the connection, a switch can operate in full-duplex mode—it can send and receive data on the connection at the same time. In a full-duplex connection, the maximum data throughput is double that for a half-duplex connection—for example, 10Mbps becomes 20Mbps, and 100Mbps becomes 200Mbps. As you can imagine, the difference in performance between a 100Mbps network connection and a 200Mbps connection is considerable.

> **EXAM ALERT**
>
> **Half-Duplex** It's important to remember that a full-duplex connection has a maximum data rate of double the standard speed, and a half-duplex connection *is* the standard speed. The term *half-duplex* can sometimes lead people to believe that the connection speed is half of the standard, which is not the case. To remember this, think of the half-duplex figure as half the full-duplex figure, not half the standard figure.

The secret of full-duplex lies in the switch. As discussed previously in this section, switches can isolate each port and effectively create a single segment for each port on the switch. Because only two devices are on each segment (the system and the switch), and because the switch is calling the shots, there are no collisions. No collisions means no need to detect collisions—thus, a collision-detection system is not needed with switches. The switch drops the conventional carrier-sense multiple-access with collision detection (CSMA/CD) media access method and adopts a far more selfish (and therefore efficient) communication method.

> **NOTE**
>
> **Microsegmentation** The process that switches perform is referred to as *microsegmentation*.

To use a full-duplex connection, you basically need three things: a switch, the appropriate cable, and a NIC (and driver) that supports full-duplex communication. Given these requirements, and the fact that most modern NICs are full-duplex-ready, you might think everyone would be using full-duplex connections. However, the reality is a little different. In some cases, the NIC is simply not configured to use the driver.

TIP

Troubleshooting Network Connection Speed   Most NICs can automatically detect the speed of the network connection they are connected to. However, although the detection process is normally reliable, on some occasions it may not work correctly. If you are troubleshooting a network connection and the autodetect feature is turned on, try setting the speed manually (preferably to a low speed) and then give it another go. If you are using a managed switch you might have to do the same thing at the switch end of the connection.

All Switches Are Not Created Equal

Having learned the advantages of using a switch and looked at the speeds associated with the network connections on the switch, you could assume that one switch is just as good as another. This is not the case. Switches are rated by the number of packets per second (pps) they can handle. When you're buying network switches, it may be necessary to look at the pps figures before making a decision.

Switching Methods

Switches use three methods to deal with data as it arrives:

- ▸ **Cut-through**—In a cut-through configuration, the switch begins to forward the packet as soon as it is received. No error checking is performed on the packet, so the packet is moved through quickly. The downside of cut-through is that because the integrity of the packet is not checked, the switch can propagate errors.

- ▸ **Store-and-forward**—In a store-and-forward configuration, the switch waits to receive the entire packet before beginning to forward it. It also performs basic error checking.

- ▸ **Fragment-free**—Building on the speed advantages of cut-through switching, fragment-free switching works by reading only the part of the packet that enables it to identify fragments of a transmission.

As you might expect, the store-and-forward process takes longer than the cut-through method, but it is more reliable. In addition, the delay caused by store-and-forward switching increases with the packet size. The delay caused by cut-through switching is always the same—only the address portion of the packet is read, and this is always the same size, regardless of the size of the data packet. The difference in delay between the two protocols is high. On average, cut-through switching is 30 times faster than store-and-forward switching.

It might seem that cut-through switching is the obvious choice, but today's switches are fast enough to be able to use store-and-forward switching and still deliver high performance levels. On some managed switches, you can select the switching method you want to use.

> **NOTE**
>
> **Latency** The time it takes for data to travel between two locations is known as the *latency*. The higher the latency, the bigger the delay in sending the data.

Working with Hubs and Switches

Despite the advantages of switches over hubs, hubs are still widely used in older networks. Whether working with hubs or switches, it is important to be aware of some of their characteristics to troubleshoot a network. For instance, if performance-monitoring tools show network bottlenecks or a congested network, the hubs may need to be replaced with switches for increased performance. This is especially important when working with both hubs and switches in a production environment.

> **NOTE**
>
> **Production Environments** The term *production* is used to describe a working, or live, computing environment.

Hub and Switch Ports

Hubs and switches have two types of ports: medium dependent interface (MDI) and medium dependent interface crossed (MDI-X). The two types of ports differ in their wiring. As the *X* implies, an MDI-X port's wiring is crossed; this is because the transmit wire from the connected device must be wired to the receive line on the other. Rather than use a crossover cable (which is discussed in the next section, "Cables Connecting Hubs and Switches"), you can use the more simple straight-through cable (also discussed in the next section) to connect systems to the switch or hub.

On most modern hubs and switches, a special port called the *uplink port* allows you to connect two hubs and switches to create larger networks. Because the aim of this type of network connection is to make each hub or switch think that it is simply part of a larger network, the connection for the port is not crossed; a straight-through network cable is used to connect the two hubs or switches together. Figure 3.6 shows the uplink port on an Ethernet switch.

In the absence of an uplink port, you can connect two hubs or switches together by using MDI-X ports, but you must use a crossover cable to do so.

> **NOTE**
>
> **Hub Ports** Instead of having a dedicated uplink port, some switches and hubs have a port that you can change between MDI and MDI-X by pushing a button. If you are using the port to connect a computer, make sure that it is set to MDI-X. If you're connecting to another hub or switch, make sure that it's set to MDI.

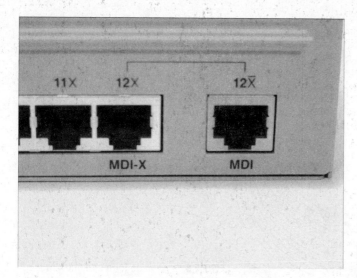

FIGURE 3.6 The uplink port on an Ethernet switch.

Cables Connecting Hubs and Switches

Two types of cables are used to connect devices to hubs and switches: crossover cables and straight-through cables. The difference between the two types is that in a crossover cable, two of the wires are crossed; in a straight-through cable, all the wires run straight through.

Specifically, in a crossover cable, Wires 1 and 3 and Wires 2 and 6 are crossed: Wire 1 at one end becomes Wire 3 at the other end, Wire 2 at one end becomes Wire 6 at the other end, and vice versa in both cases. You can see the differences between the two cables in Figures 3.7 and 3.8. Figure 3.7 shows the pinouts for a straight-through cable, and Figure 3.8 shows the pinouts for a crossover cable.

How Many Is Too Many?

Although Ethernet standards state that you can have as many as 1,024 nodes on a network, the practical maximum may be much lower. The number of nodes you can accommodate depends on a number of factors. Using switches instead of hubs makes a *huge* difference, particularly if you are using the full-duplex features of these devices. The amount of traffic generated by clients also has a significant effect, as does the type of traffic. On a more subtle level, you must consider the quality of the networking components and devices you use.

NOTE

Switches—Read the Label   Switches are often labeled as being 10/100 switches. This label normally means that the ports on the switch are capable of operating at 10Mbps or 100Mbps. Don't take it for granted, though. Some older switches have 10Mbps ports for connecting systems and 100Mbps ports for uplinking. Because there are no guidelines for labeling devices, some of those older switches are referred to as 10/100 switches. Always check the specifications before buying a switch.

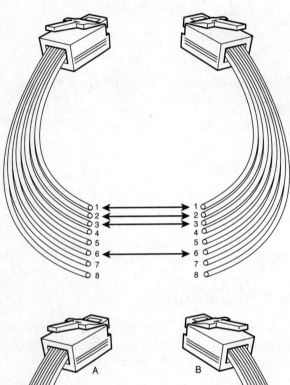

FIGURE 3.7 Pinouts for a straight-through twisted-pair cable.

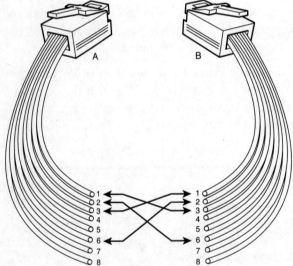

FIGURE 3.8 Pinouts for a crossover twisted-pair cable.

Hubs and switches are sometimes equipped with a network connection for another cable type, such as coaxial. Such switches that accommodate different media types such as fiber-optic cable and UTP, are referred to as *hybrid switches*. Other higher-end devices simply have empty sockets into which you can plug connectivity modules of choice. This approach lets you create very fast networks. For example, three 24-port 10/100 Ethernet switches could be connected to each other by a Gigabit Ethernet fiber-optic connection. This would create a very fast network structure in which switch-to-system communication can occur at 200Mbps (in full-duplex mode) and switch-to-switch communication can occur at Gigabit Ethernet speeds. The result is a very fast local area network (LAN).

Hub and Switch Indicator Lights

Both hubs and switches use light-emitting diodes (LEDs) to indicate certain connection conditions. At the very least, a link light on the hub will indicate the existence of a live connection. On higher-end devices, additional lights might indicate activity, the speed of the connection, whether the connection is at half- or full-duplex, and sometimes errors or collisions. The LEDs provide an immediate visual indicator about the status of the device, so familiarizing yourself with their function is a worthwhile exercise. A further discussion of hub and switch LEDs is provided in Chapter 13, "Troubleshooting Tools and Utilities."

Rack-Mount, Stackable, and Freestanding Devices

Some hubs and switches, as well as many other networking devices, are designed to be placed in a rack, whereas others are labeled as stackable or freestanding. Rack-mount devices are designed for placement into equipment racks, which are a common sight in computer rooms. The racks are approximately 19 inches wide; devices designed to be rack-mounted are slightly smaller than freestanding devices, so they can fit in the racks. Small metal brackets are screwed to the sides of the devices to allow them to be fitted into the racks.

If you don't have racks, you need to use stackable or freestanding devices. These devices can literally be placed on top of one another. Many network equipment manufacturers realize that not everyone has racks, and so they make their equipment usable in either a rack or a freestanding configuration.

Managed Hubs and Switches

Both hubs and switches come in managed and unmanaged versions. A managed device has an interface through which it can be configured to perform certain special functions. For example, it may allow for port mirroring, which can be useful for network monitoring, or allow ports to be specified to operate at a certain speed. Because of the extra functionality of a managed device, and because of the additional components required to achieve it, managed devices are considerably more expensive than unmanaged devices. When you're specifying switches or hubs, consider the need for manageability carefully. If a switch will be used to connect servers to the network, a managed device might make the most sense—the extra functionality might come in handy. On parts of the network that accommodate client computers, unmanaged devices generally suffice.

> **NOTE**
>
> **Port Density** Excluding the small workgroup hubs, hubs and switches normally have 8, 16, 24, or 32 ports each, although variations are available. To help you compare prices between devices, manufacturers often quote a price per port. In some cases, a higher-density device with more ports may cost significantly less per port than a device with fewer ports. Typically, the more ports on a device, the lower the price per port.

At the time of this writing, switches are still quite a bit more expensive than hubs with equivalent capacity, but the gap is narrowing quickly. Some manufacturers have stopped producing hubs and instead are putting all their efforts into developing switches. This would seem to be a sound strategy. In all but the smallest networks or companies with the most restrictive budgets, hubs are rapidly being replaced by switches. In new implementations, hubs are unlikely to be specified and installed.

Bridges

Bridges are networking devices that connect networks. Sometimes it is necessary to divide networks into subnets to reduce the amount of traffic on each larger subnet or for security reasons. Once divided, the bridge connects the two subnets and manages the traffic flow between them. Today, network switches have largely replaced bridges.

A bridge functions by blocking or forwarding data, based on the destination MAC address written into each frame of data. If the bridge believes the destination address is on a network other than that from which the data was received, it can forward the data to the other networks to which it is connected. If the address is not on the other side of the bridge, the data is blocked from passing. Bridges "learn" the MAC addresses of devices on connected networks by "listening" to network traffic and recording the network from which the traffic originates. Figure 3.9 shows a representation of a bridge.

> **NOTE**
>
> **Manual Bridge Configuration** Some early bridge implementations required you to enter the information for each device on the network manually. Fortunately, bridges are now of the learning variety, and manual configuration is no longer necessary.

The advantages of bridges are simple and significant. By preventing unnecessary traffic from crossing onto other network segments, a bridge can dramatically reduce the amount of network traffic on a segment. Bridges also make it possible to isolate a busy network from a not-so-busy one, thereby preventing pollution from busy nodes.

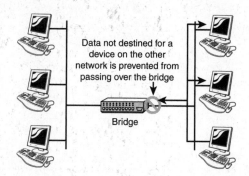

Data not destined for a device on the other network is prevented from passing over the bridge

Bridge

FIGURE 3.9 How a bridge works.

Bridge Implementation Considerations

Although implementing bridges can offer huge improvements in performance, you must factor in a number of considerations. The first is bridge placement. Generally, you should follow the 80/20 rule for bridge placement: 80% of the traffic should not cross the bridge, and 20% of the traffic should be on the other side of the bridge. The rule is easy to understand, but accurately determining the correct location for the bridge to accommodate the rule is another matter.

Another, potentially more serious, consideration is bridging loops, which can be created when more than one bridge is used on a network. Multiple bridges can provide fault tolerance or improve performance. Bridging loops occur when multiple bridges become confused about where devices are on the network.

As an example of bridging loops, imagine that you have a network with two bridges, as depicted in Figure 3.10. During the learning process, the north bridge receives a packet from Interface A (step 1 in Figure 3.11) and determines that it is for a system that is not on Network Z; therefore, the bridge forwards the packet to Network X (step 2 in Figure 3.11). Now, the south bridge sees a packet originating on Network X on Interface C (step 3 in Figure 3.11); because it thinks the destination system is not on Network X, it forwards the packet to Network Z (step 4 in Figure 3.11), where the north bridge picks it up (step 5 in Figure 3.11). The north bridge determines that the destination system is not on Network Z, so it forwards the packet to Network X—and the whole process begins again.

You can work around the looping problem by using the Spanning Tree Algorithm (STA). When STA is used, each interface on a bridge is assigned a value. As the bridge forwards the data, the value is attached to the packet. When another bridge sees the data, if the STA value for the interface is higher than that assigned to its interfaces, the bridge doesn't forward the data, thus eliminating the possibility of a bridging loop. STA eliminates the bridging loop but still provides the fault tolerance of having more than one bridge in place. If the bridge with the higher STA value (sometimes referred to as the *primary bridge*) fails, the other bridge continues functioning because it becomes the bridge with the higher STA value. All this is achieved by the Spanning Tree Protocol (STP).

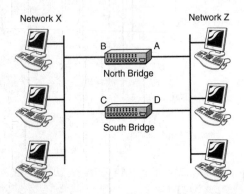

FIGURE 3.10 A network with two bridges.

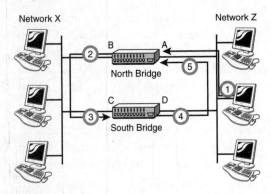

FIGURE 3.11 A bridging loop.

> **NOTE**
>
> **STP** STP is defined in the IEEE 802.1d standard.

Types of Bridges

Three types of bridges are used in networks. You don't need detailed knowledge of how each bridge works, but you should have an overview:

▶ **Transparent bridge**—A transparent bridge is invisible to the other devices on the network. Transparent bridges perform only the function of blocking or forwarding data based on the MAC address; the devices on the network are oblivious to these bridges' existence. Transparent bridges are by far the most popular types of bridges.

▶ **Translational bridge**—A translational bridge can convert from one networking system to another. As you might have guessed, it translates the data it receives. Translational bridges are useful for connecting two different networks, such as Ethernet and Token Ring networks. Depending on the direction of travel, a translational bridge can add or remove information and fields from the frame as needed.

▶ **Source-route bridge**—Source-route bridges were designed by IBM for use on Token Ring networks. The source-route bridge derives its name from the fact that the entire route of the frame is embedded within the frame. This allows the bridge to make specific decisions about how the frame should be forwarded through the network. The diminishing popularity of Token Ring makes the chances that you'll work with a source-route bridge very slim.

EXAM ALERT

Identify the Bridge   On the Network+ exam, you might be asked to identify the purpose of a certain type of bridge.

As switches become ever cheaper, bridges have been overtaken by switches in terms of both functionality and performance. Expect to be working with switches more often than with bridges.

Routers

Routers are an increasingly common sight in any network environment, from a small home office that uses one to connect to an Internet service provider (ISP) to a corporate IT environment where racks of routers manage data communication with disparate remote sites. Routers make internetworking possible, and in view of this, they warrant detailed attention.

Routers are network devices that literally route data around the network. By examining data as it arrives, the router can determine the destination address for the data; then, by using tables of defined routes, the router determines the best way for the data to continue its journey. Unlike bridges and switches, which use the hardware-configured MAC address to determine the destination of the data, routers use the software-configured network address to make decisions. This approach makes routers more functional than bridges or switches, and it also makes them more complex because they have to work harder to determine the information. Figure 3.12 shows basically how a router functions.

The basic requirement for a router is that it must have at least two network interfaces. If they are LAN interfaces, the router can manage and route the information between two LAN segments. More commonly, a router is used to provide connectivity across wide area network (WAN) links. Figure 3.13 shows a router with two LAN ports (marked AUI 0 and AUI 1) and two WAN ports (marked Serial 0 and Serial 1). This router is capable of routing data between two LAN segments and two WAN segments.

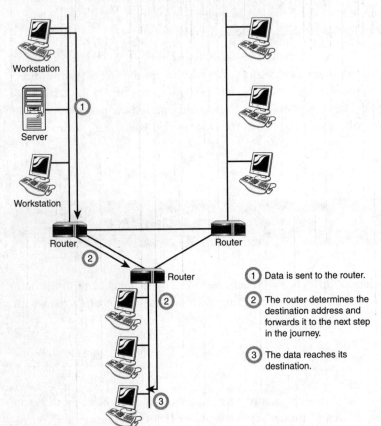

Workstation

1

Server

Workstation

Router

Router

2

Router

1 Data is sent to the router.

2 The router determines the destination address and forwards it to the next step in the journey.

3 The data reaches its destination.

FIGURE 3.12   The basic function of a router.

Routable Protocols and Routing Protocols

Routers rely on two types of network protocols to make the routing magic happen: routable protocols and routing protocols. We'll examine them separately in the next sections.

Routable Protocols

Large internetworks need protocols that allow systems to be identified by the address of the network to which they are attached and by an address that uniquely identifies them on that network. Network protocols that provide both of these features are said to be *routable*. Three routable LAN network protocols are used today:

- **Transmission Control Protocol/Internet Protocol (TCP/IP)**—TCP/IP was developed in the 1970s by the Department of Defense, which needed a protocol to use on its WAN. TCP/IP's flexibility, durability, and functionality meant that it soon became the WAN protocol of choice and also became the standard for LANs. Today, most networks use TCP/IP in some fashion, even if the main LAN protocol is something other than TCP/IP. TCP/IP is a huge topic, and anyone in networking must understand it. The Network+ exam dedicates an entire exam objective to it. Chapter 6, "Working with TCP/IP," provides complete coverage of TCP/IP.

  TCP/IP is a protocol suite comprised of numerous individual protocols. Within TCP/IP, the two routing protocols used are the Routing Information Protocol (RIP) and Open Shortest Path First (OSPF). RIP is a distance-vector routing protocol, and OSPF is a link-state routing protocol.

- **Internetwork Packet Exchange/Sequenced Packet Exchange (IPX/SPX)**— Created by Novell for use on NetWare networks, IPX/SPX is a routable protocol that was popular for many years. Today, even Novell acknowledges that TCP/IP is the network protocol of choice and so has moved away from IPX/SPX and toward a pure TCP/IP environment. In fact, the last few versions of Novell NetWare have used TCP/IP as the default protocol and allowed IPX/SPX to be enabled if needed.

  Like TCP/IP, IPX/SPX is also a protocol suite. Within IPX/SPX, the NetWare Link State Protocol (NLSP) and the Routing Information Protocol (RIP) manage routing. RIP uses a distance-vector route-discovery method, which calculates routes based on the number of hops. NLSP uses a link-state route discovery method to build routing tables.

▶ **AppleTalk**—AppleTalk is a full-featured protocol designed to be used with the Macintosh computer systems. AppleTalk has been around since the early 1980s and widely deployed in Apple networks. Like TCP/IP and IPX/SPX, AppleTalk is a protocol suite. Within the suite, the Routing Table Maintenance Protocol (RTMP) provides routing functionality. RTMP is a distance-vector routing protocol similar to the RIP, which is used by IPX/SPX and TCP/IP.

Some routers are capable of routing more than one protocol at a time, a feature known as *multiprotocol routing*. Multiprotocol routing brings with it a number of considerations, not the least of which is the fact that a multiprotocol router may have to work considerably harder than a router working with only a single protocol. This is the case not only because there is more than one protocol but because there may also be multiple routing protocols.

Routing Protocols

Routing protocols are the means by which routers communicate with each other. This communication is necessary so that routers can learn the network topology and changes that occur in it.

NOTE

Static Routing   The alternative to using routing protocols is *static routing*, which means that route information must be manually entered by the administrator. There are two main disadvantages of this approach: First, manually entering routes is time-consuming and susceptible to human error. Second, if the topology of the network changes, the routers must be manually reconfigured. Therefore, static routing is generally used only in the smallest of environments. In environments with more than a handful of routers, dynamic routing is the preferred option.

NOTE

Metrics   In routing, the term *metric* describes the "cost" of a certain route. The metric can be a combination of factors, including the number of routers between a router's position and the destination, the time it takes to complete the journey, and even a value that can be assigned by an administrator to discourage use of a certain route. Under normal circumstances, routers choose the route with the lowest metric.

The two types of routing protocols are *distance-vector* and *link-state protocols*. Each has a different strategy for dealing with router-to-router communication.

Distance-Vector Protocols

With distance-vector routing protocols, each router communicates all the routes it knows about to all other routers to which it is directly attached (that is, its *neighbors*). Because each router in the network knows only about the routers to which it is attached, it doesn't know how to complete the entire journey; instead, it only knows how to make the next hop. *Hops* are the means by which distance-vector routing protocols determine the shortest way to reach a given destination. Each router constitutes one hop; so if a router is four hops away from another router, there are three routers, or hops, between itself and the destination. Distance-vector protocols can also use a time value known as a *tick*, which enables the router to make a decision about which path is quickest if given the choice of more than one (a common situation on networks with redundant links).

The frequency with which routers send route updates depends on the routing protocol being used, but it is usually between 10 and 60 seconds. At each update, the entire routing table of the sender is sent to the other connected routers. When the other routers receive the information, they check it against the existing information; if there are any changes, they alter their routing tables accordingly.

This constant update cycle is one of the problems of distance-vector routing protocols because it can lead to large amounts of network traffic. Furthermore, after the initial learning period, the updates should (hopefully) be irrelevant—the chances of the network topology changing every 30 seconds or so are slim, and if you do have such a network, some troubleshooting may be in order.

When a change does occur on the network, it may take some time for all the routers to learn of the change. The process of each router learning about the change and updating its routing tables is known as *convergence*. In a small network, convergence might not take long; but in larger networks, those with, say, more than 20 routers, it might take some time to complete. Rather than cause the routers to wait for the updates, you can configure *triggered updates*, which are sent when a topology change is detected. Using triggered updates can significantly improve the convergence speed of distance-vector–based networks.

You can also use *hold-down timers* to improve convergence. A hold-down timer prevents a router from trying to make too many changes too quickly. When a router receives a change about a route, it makes the change and then applies a hold-down timer to the change. The hold-down timer prevents further changes from being made to that route within the defined time period. Hold-down timers are particularly useful when an unreliable router keeps going on and off the network. If hold-down timers are not applied, updates to the routing tables on routers would continually be changing, and the network might never converge.

In some configurations, distance-vector routing protocols can lead to routing loops. *Routing loops* occur when a router tells another router about a route that it heard about from the same router. For example, consider the router layout in Figure 3.14. If Router C becomes unable to access Router D through Network 1, it removes the route from its table and sends the update to Router B; Router B removes the route. But if Router B receives an update from Router A before it sends an update to Router A, the route is reinstated because according to Router A, it can still access Network 1. Now Router B begins to send anything destined for Network 1 back to Router A, which duly sends it back to Router B, and so on, thus creating a routing loop.

Each time the route is added to the table, the hop count for the route increases—a problem known as the *count to infinity*.

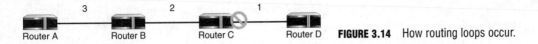

FIGURE 3.14 How routing loops occur.

You can use two strategies to prevent routing loops when using distance-vector routing protocols:

▸ **Split horizon**—The split horizon algorithm addresses the problem of routing loops by not advertising routes back on the interface from which they are learned. In other words, using Figure 3.14 as an example, Router C would not advertise back to Router B any route that it learned from Router B. Basically, Router C figures that, because it learned about the route from Router B, Router B must be nearer to the destination than it is.

▸ **Split horizon with poison reverse**—With this strategy, also known simply as poison reverse, routers do advertise routes back on the interfaces from which they were learned, but they do so with a hop count of infinity. The value used for infinity (which seems like an impossible situation) depends on the routing protocol being used. Again using the example from Figure 3.14, Router C would advertise to Router B the routes it learned from Router B, but it would also add the infinite hop count. In other words, Router C would say, "I know about Router A, but I can't reach it myself." This way, Router B would never try to add the route to Router A through Router C, because according to Router C, it can't reach Router A.

The most popular distance-vector routing protocols are both called Routing Information Protocol (RIP). The distance-vector routing protocol for TCP/IP is called RIP, as is the one for IPX/SPX. To set the two apart, the IPX version is often called IPX RIP.

Link-State Protocols

A router that uses a link-state protocol differs from a router that uses a distance-vector protocol because it builds a map of the entire network and then holds that map in memory. On a network that uses a link-state protocol, routers send out link-state advertisements (LSAs) that contain information about what networks they are connected to. The LSAs are sent to every router on the network, thus enabling the routers to build their network maps.

When the network maps on each router are complete, the routers update each other at a given time, just like with a distance-vector protocol, but the updates occur much less frequently with link-state protocols than with distance-vector protocols. The only other circumstance under which updates are sent is if a change in the topology is detected, at which point the routers use LSAs to detect the change and update their routing tables. This mechanism, combined with the fact that routers hold maps of the entire network, makes convergence on a link-state–based network occur very quickly.

Although it might seem like link-state protocols are an obvious choice over distance-vector protocols, routers on a link-state–based network require more powerful hardware and more RAM than those on a distance-vector–based network. Not only do the routing tables have to be calculated, but they must also be stored. A router that uses distance-vector protocols need only maintain a small database of the routes accessible by the routers to which it is directly connected. A router that uses link-state protocols must maintain a database of the routers in the entire network.

Two of the most popular link-state routing protocols are Open Shortest Path First (OSPF) and NetWare Link State Protocol (A.K.A NetWare Link Services Protocol) (NLSP). The former is used on TCP/IP networks, and the latter is used on networks that use IPX/SPX.

> **EXAM ALERT**
>
> **Identify the Protocols**   Be prepared to identify both the link-state and distance-vector routing protocols used on both TCP/IP and IPX/SPX networks.

> **NOTE**
>
> **Multiprotocol Routing**   In this section and the previous section, we discussed routing protocols as they apply to single protocols. But remember that one router may be routing more than one protocol; it may, for example, use OSPF and NLSP.

Dedicated Hardware Versus Server-Based Routers

A router can be either a dedicated hardware device or a server system that has at least two network interfaces installed in it. All common network operating systems offer the capability to act as routers as part of their functionality.

Dedicated hardware routers offer greater performance levels than server-based solutions, but they have the disadvantage of offering a limited range of features for their cost. However, the attraction of a dedicated hardware device often outweighs this factor.

The following are some of the advantages of dedicated hardware routers:

- ▶ Typically faster than server-based routers
- ▶ Generally more reliable than server-based routers
- ▶ Easier to harden against attacks than server-based routing solutions

The following are some of the disadvantages of dedicated hardware routers:

▶ More expensive than server-based router solutions; extra functionality may have to be purchased

▶ Often require specialized skills and knowledge to manage them

▶ Limited to a small range of possible uses

The capabilities of a router depend on the features it has. A basic router may route only one protocol between two network interfaces of the same type. A more advanced router may act as a gateway between two networks and two protocols. In addition, it may offer firewall services, security and authentication, or remote access functionality such as virtual private networking.

> **NOTE**
>
> **Brouters**   A *brouter* is a device that can route traffic that can be routed and bridge anything that cannot be routed. As bridges have been replaced by the more flexible routers, brouters have also fallen out of favor. In today's networking world, routers rule. Just ask Cisco.

The topic of routing is complex, and the routing information provided in this chapter is the most basic of tutorials. Although we've told you what you need to know for the exam, if you're working with routers on a daily basis, you will want to seek out further sources of information—and there is no shortage of such sources (including the Cisco Press and *Exam Cram* titles you'll find at www.informit.com).

Gateways

The term *gateway* is applied to any device, system, or software application that can perform the function of translating data from one format to another. The key feature of a gateway is that it converts the format of the data, not the data itself.

> **NOTE**
>
> **Gateways Versus Default Gateways**   Don't confuse gateways, which are networking devices, with default gateways, which are discussed in Chapter 6, "Working with TCP/IP." The two perform different roles on a network.

You can use gateway functionality in many ways. For example, a router that can route data from an IPX network to an IP network is, technically, a gateway. The same can be said of a translational bridge that, as described earlier in this chapter, converts from an Ethernet network to a Token Ring network and back again.

Software gateways can be found everywhere. Many companies use an email system such as Microsoft Exchange or Novell GroupWise. These systems transmit mail internally in a certain format. When email needs to be sent across the Internet to users using a different email system, the email must be converted to another format, usually to Simple Mail Transfer Protocol (SMTP). This conversion process is performed by a software gateway.

Another good (and often used) example of a gateway involves the Systems Network Architecture (SNA) gateway, which converts the data format used on a PC to that used on an IBM mainframe or minicomputer. A system that acts as an SNA gateway sits between the client PC and the mainframe and translates requests and replies from both directions. Figure 3.15 shows how this would work in a practical implementation.

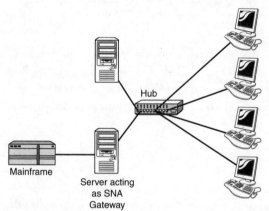

Hub

Mainframe

Server acting
as SNA
Gateway

FIGURE 3.15   An SNA gateway.

If it seems from the text in this section that we are being vague about what a gateway is, it's because there is no definite answer. The function of a gateway is very specific, but how the gateway functionality is implemented is not.

No matter what their use, gateways slow the flow of data and can therefore potentially become bottlenecks. The conversion from one data format to another takes time, and so the flow of data through a gateway is always slower than the flow of data without one.

CSUs/DSUs

A Channel Service Unit/Data Service Unit (CSU/DSU) acts as a translator between the LAN data format and the WAN data format. Such a conversion is necessary because the technologies used on WAN links are different from those used on LANs. Some consider a CSU/DSU as a type of digital modem; but unlike a normal modem, which changes the signal from digital to analog, a CSU/DSU changes the signal from one digital format to another. Figure 3.16 shows how a CSU/DSU might fit into a network.

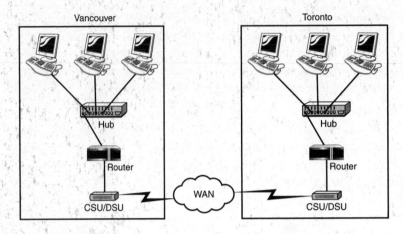

FIGURE 3.16 How a CSU/DSU is used in a network.

A CSU/DSU has physical connections for the LAN equipment, normally via a serial interface, and another connection for a WAN. Traditionally, the CSU/DSU has been in a separate box from other networking equipment; however, the increasing use of WAN links means that some router manufacturers are now including the CSU/DSU functionality in routers or are providing the expansion capability to do so.

Modems

Modem is a contraction of the terms *modulator* and *demodulator*. Modems perform a simple function: They translate digital signals from a computer into analog signals that can travel across conventional phone lines. The modem modulates the signal at the sending end and demodulates at the receiving end.

Modems provide a relatively slow method of communication. In fact, the fastest modem available on the market today has a maximum speed of 56Kbps. Compare that to the speed of a 10Mbps network connection, and you'll find that the modem is approximately 180 times slower. That makes modems okay for browsing web pages or occasionally downloading small files but wholly unsuitable for downloading large files. As a result, many people prefer to use other remote access methods, including ISDN (which is discussed later in this chapter, in the section "ISDN Terminal Adapters") and cable/DSL access.

Modems are available as internal devices that plug into expansion slots in a system; external devices that plug into serial or USB ports; PCMCIA cards designed for use in laptops; and specialized devices designed for use in systems such as handheld computers. In addition, many laptops now come with integrated modems. For large-scale modem implementations, such as at an ISP, rack-mounted modems are also available. Figure 3.17 shows an internal modem and a PCMCIA modem.

FIGURE 3.17 An internal modem (left) and a PCMCIA modem (right).

Modems are controlled through a series of commands known as the Hayes AT command set. Hayes was a company that, for many years, led the field in the development of modems and modem technology. The AT commands allow you to control a modem as well as configure and diagnose it. Table 3.1 lists some of the most commonly used AT commands.

EXAM ALERT

Know the AT Command On the Network+ exam, you might be asked to identify the correct AT command to be used in a given situation.

TABLE 3.1   Commonly Used AT Modem Commands

Command	Result
ATA	Answers an incoming call
ATH	Hangs up the current connection
ATZ	Resets the modem
ATI3	Displays modem identification information

Modem Connection Speeds

The actual speed you obtain on a modem connection depends on a variety of factors, including the quality of the line you are using and the speed of the modem. For example, you might find (as we often do) that even with a 56Kbps modem, the most you can get on a certain connection is 49Kbps. If you try the same connection again on a different phone line, you might get a higher or lower rate. Quality of the connection aside, two factors govern the maximum speed attainable by your modem: the speed of the Universal Asynchronous Receiver/Transmitter (UART) chip in your system (which controls the serial ports) and the speed of the modem itself.

In older systems, the UART chips were capable of only slow speeds, making them unable to keep up with fast modems. Today, most systems have UART chips capable of speeds well in excess of those offered by modems. Now the modem, not the UART chip, is the bottleneck. Table 3.2 lists the types of commonly used UART chips and their associated speeds.

TABLE 3.2   UART Chips and Their Associated Speeds

UART Chip	Speed (bps)
8250	9,600
16450	115,200
16550	115,200
16650	430,800
16750	921,600
16950	921,600

EXAM ALERT

Know the UART Speed   On the Network+ exam, you might be asked to identify the maximum speed of a given UART chip.

Modem speeds can be expressed in either baud rate or bits per second (bps). The *baud rate* refers to the number of times a signal changes in each second, and the *bps rate* is the number of bits of data that can be sent or received in a second. Although the figures are identical in some modems, in others the bps rate is higher than the baud rate. The baud rate is actually not as important, and the higher the bps figure, the better. Most modern modems offer bps rates far greater than the baud rate.

To make it easier to compare modems, standards have been created that define the data throughput of the modem and what features it provides. These are sometimes referred to as the *V standards*, and you can use them when buying a modem to determine the modem's capabilities.

Network Interface Cards (NICs)

NICs—sometimes called network cards—are the mechanisms by which computers connect to a network. NICs come in all shapes and sizes, and they come in prices to suit all budgets. Consider the following when buying a NIC:

> **NOTE**
>
> **NIC Terminology**   Many different terms are used to refer to NICs, such as *network card*, *network adapter*, and *LAN adapter*. All refer to the same thing.

▶ **Network compatibility**—Perhaps this is a little obvious, but sometimes people order the wrong type of NIC for the network. Given the prevalence of Ethernet networks, you are likely to have to specify network compatibility only when buying a NIC for another networking system.

▶ **Bus compatibility**—Newly purchased NICs will almost certainly use the Peripheral Component Interconnect (PCI) bus, although if you are replacing a card in an older system, you might have to specify an Industry Standard Architecture (ISA) bus card instead. If the card you are buying is PCI, check to see what kind of PCI interface is being used. Many high-end server systems now come with 64-bit PCI slots; if you have them, it is definitely worth taking advantage of the extra performance they offer. Such 64-bit PCI slots can be easily identified because they are the same color and width as 32-bit PCI slots but are longer. 64-bit slots are referred to as PCI-X and are backward compatible with 32-bit PCI. Figure 3.18 shows 32-bit PCI slots on a system board.

▶ **Port compatibility**—Generally a NIC has only one port, for twisted-pair cabling. If you want some other connectivity, you need to be sure to specify your card accordingly; for example, you might need a fiber-optic or coaxial cable port.

> **NOTE**
>
> **Combo Cards**   Sometimes a NIC has a twisted-pair socket, a coaxial connector, and an attachment unit interface (AUI) port. These cards are referred to as *combo* cards. Today, the dominance of twisted-pair cabling means that most NICs have only a twisted-pair connection.

▶ **Hardware compatibility**—Before installing a network card into a system, you must verify compatibility between the network card and the operating system on the PC in which you are installing the NIC. If you are using good-quality network cards from a recognized manufacturer, such verification should be little more than a formality.

FIGURE 3.18 32-bit PCI slots on a system board. (Photo copyright © Intel Corporation.)

Types of Network Interfaces

Network interfaces come as add-in expansion cards or as PCMCIA cards used in laptop systems. In some cases, rather than have an add-in NIC, the network interface is embedded into the motherboard. Figure 3.19 shows an example of an add-in NIC, Figure 3.20 shows a PCMCIA network card, and Figure 3.21 shows a built-in network interface in a laptop system.

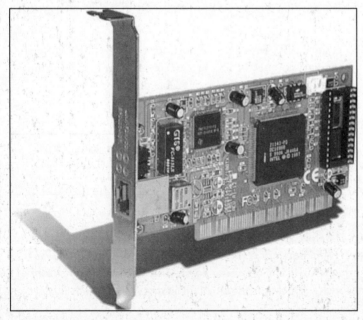

FIGURE 3.19 An expansion NIC.

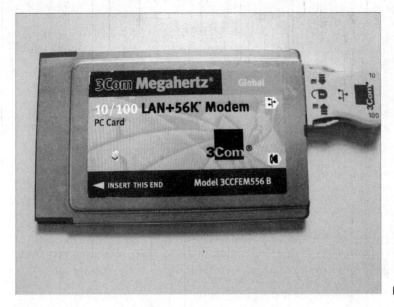

FIGURE 3.20   A PCMCIA NIC.

FIGURE 3.21   A built-in network interface on a laptop system.

The False Economy of NICs

The difference between an inexpensive network card and an expensive one is less than you might think; but even so, people are tempted to go for the low-cost option. In many cases, this turns out to be a false economy. Not only do higher-end cards tend to be easier to install, they are generally easier to

(continues)

(continued)

> troubleshoot as well. An hour trying to troubleshoot a misbehaving inexpensive network card can negate any cost savings from the purchase. This is particularly relevant on server systems, where a problem network card will not only cause you frustration but also will most likely cause the users of the server problems. In fact, if you are working on server systems, it's worth investigating fault-tolerant network card configurations, such as adapter teaming.

A network interface typically has at least two LEDs that indicate certain conditions:

- ▶ **Link light**—This LED indicates whether a network connection exists between the card and the network. An unlit link light is an indicator that something is awry with the network cable or connection.

- ▶ **Activity light**—This LED indicates network activity. Under normal conditions, the light should flicker sporadically and often. Constant flickering may indicate a very busy network or a problem somewhere on the network that is worth investigating.

- ▶ **Speed light**—This LED indicates that the interface is connected at a certain speed. This feature is normally found on Ethernet NICs that operate at 10Mbps/100Mbps— and then only on certain cards.

Some network cards combine the functions of certain lights by using dual-color LEDs. PCM-CIA cards sometimes have no lights, or the lights are incorporated into the media adapter that comes with the card. You can see an example in Figure 3.22.

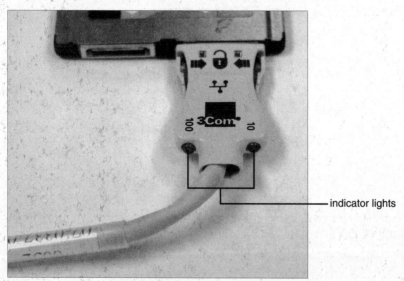

indicator lights

FIGURE 3.22 Indicator lights on a media adapter for a PCMCIA NIC.

Installing Network Cards

At some point in your networking career, it is likely that you will have to install a NIC into a system. For that reason, an understanding of the procedures and considerations related to NIC installations is useful. Here are some of the main things to consider:

▶ **Drivers**—Almost every NIC is supplied with a driver disk, but the likelihood of the drivers on the disk being the latest drivers is slim. Always make sure that you have the latest drivers by visiting the website of the NIC manufacturer. The drivers play an important role in the correct functioning of the NIC, so spend a few extra minutes to make sure that the drivers are installed and configured correctly.

▶ **NIC configuration utilities**—In days gone by, NICs were configured with small groups of pins known as *jumpers*, or with small plastic blocks of switches known as *dip switches*. Figure 3.23 shows an example of jumpers. Unless you are working with very old equipment, you are unlikely to encounter dip switches.

FIGURE 3.23   A block of jumpers.

Although these methods were efficient and easy to use, they have now largely been abandoned in favor of software configuration utilities, which allow you to configure the settings for the card (if any) and to test whether the card is working properly. Other utilities can be used through the operating system to obtain statistical information, help, and a range of other features.

▶ **System resources**—To function correctly, NICs must have certain system resources allocated to them: the interrupt request (IRQ) and memory addresses. In some cases, you might need to assign the values for these manually. In most cases, you can rely on plug-and-play, which assigns resources for devices automatically.

▶ **Physical slot availability**—Most modern PCs have at least three or four usable expansion slots. Not only that, but the increasing trend toward component integration on the motherboard means that devices such as serial and parallel ports and sound cards are now built in to the system board and therefore don't use up valuable slots. If you're working on older systems or systems that have a lot of add-in hardware, you might be short of slots. Check to make sure that a slot is available before you begin.

▶ **Built-in network interfaces**—A built-in network interface is a double-edged sword. The upsides are that it doesn't occupy an expansion slot, and hardware compatibility with the rest of the system is almost guaranteed. The downside is that a built-in component is not upgradeable. For this reason, you might find yourself installing an add-in NIC and at the same time disabling the on-board network interface. Disabling the on-board interface is normally a straightforward process, achieved by going into the BIOS setup screen or, on some systems, a system configuration utility. In either case, consult the documentation that came with the system or look for information on the manufacturer's website.

As time goes on, NIC and operating system manufacturers are making it increasingly easy to install NICs in systems of all sorts and sizes. By understanding the requirements of the card and the correct installation procedure, you should be able to install cards simply and efficiently.

ISDN Terminal Adapters

When the speed provided by a modem just isn't enough, you must seek alternatives. One of the speedier options available is an ISDN link. ISDN is a digital communication method that can be used over a conventional phone line, although certain criteria must be met for an ISDN line to be available (such as the availability of the service and the proximity of your location to the telco's site). (The information in this section is intended to cover only ISDN terminal adapters, not ISDN as a system. Detailed coverage of ISDN is provided in Chapter 7, "WAN and Internet Access Technologies," which covers WAN topics.)

To use ISDN, you need a device called an *ISDN terminal adapter*. ISDN terminal adapters are available as add-in expansion cards installed into computers, external devices that connect to the serial interfaces of PC systems, or modules in a router. You can think of an ISDN terminal adapter as a kind of digital modem. (Remember that a modem converts a signal from digital to analog and vice versa. An ISDN terminal adapter translates the signal between two digital formats.) Figure 3.24 shows an external ISDN terminal adapter, and Figure 3.25 shows an example of an internal ISDN adapter. Notice that an ISDN terminal adapter is similar in appearance to a standard NIC.

FIGURE 3.24 An external ISDN adapter.

FIGURE 3.25 An internal ISDN adapter.

Installing an external ISDN adapter is simple because, like an external modem, an external ISDN adapter plugs in to the serial port of the system and thus uses its resources. You need drivers for an ISDN terminal adapter, so be sure to visit the manufacturer's website and download the latest available drivers. An internal ISDN terminal adapter requires a little more effort: You must make sure that you have physical and logical system resources to accommodate it.

Wireless Access Point (WAP)

Wireless access points, referred to as either *WAPs* or *wireless APs*, are a transmitter and receiver (*transceiver*) device used for wireless LAN (WLAN) radio signals. A WAP is typically a separate network device with a built-in antenna, transmitter, and adapter. WAPs use the wireless infrastructure network mode to provide a connection point between WLANs and a wired Ethernet LAN. WAPs also typically have several ports allowing a way to expand the network to support additional clients.

Depending on the size of the network, one or more WAPs may be required. Additional WAPs are used to allow access to more wireless clients and to expand the range of the wireless network. Each WAP is limited by a transmissions range, the distance a client can be from a WAP and still get a useable signal. The actual distance depends on the wireless standard being used and the obstructions and environmental conditions between the client and the WAP. Figure 3.26 shows an example of a WAP in a network configuration.

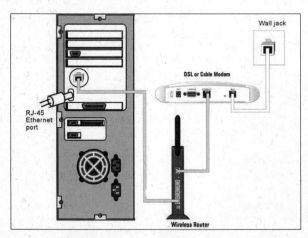

FIGURE 3.26 WAPs connect WLANs and a wired Ethernet LAN.

NOTE

Wireless Access Points—A WAP can operate as a bridge connecting a standard wired network to wireless devices or as a router passing data transmissions from one access point to another.

As mentioned, a WAP is used in an infrastructure wireless network design. Used in the infrastructure mode, the WAP receives transmissions from wireless devices within a specific range and transmits those signals to the network beyond. This network may be a private Ethernet network or the Internet. The transmission range a WAP can support and number of wireless devices that can connect to it depends on the wireless standard being used and the signal interference between the two devices. In infrastructure wireless networking, there may be multiple access points to cover a large area or only a single access point for a small area such as a single home or small building.

Figure 3.27 shows an example of an infrastructure wireless network using a WAP.

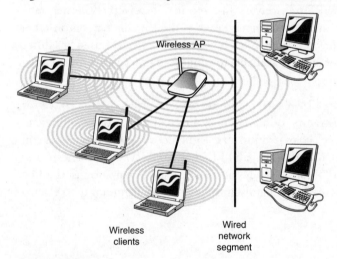

Wireless AP

Wireless
clients

Wired
network
segment

FIGURE 3.27   An infrastructure wireless network uses a WAP.

Transceivers

The term *transceiver* does not necessarily describe a separate network device but rather an integrated technology embedded in devices such as network cards. In a network environment, a transceiver gets its name from being both a transmitter and a receiver of signals, such as analog or digital. Technically, on a LAN the transceiver is responsible to place signals onto the network media and also detecting incoming signals traveling through the same cable. Given the description of the function of a transceiver, it makes sense that that technology would be found with network cards.

Although transceivers are found in network cards, they can be external devices as well. As far as networking is concerned, transceivers can ship as a module or chip type. *Chip transceivers* are small and are inserted into a system board or wired directly on a circuit board. *Module transceivers* are external to the network and are installed and function similarly to other computer peripherals, or they may function as standalone devices.

There are many types of transceivers: RF transceivers, fiber-optic transceivers, Ethernet transceivers, wireless (WAP) transceivers, and more. Though each of these media types is different, the function of the transceiver remains the same. Each type of the transceiver used has different characteristics such as the number of ports available to connect to the network and whether full-duplex communication is supported.

Listed with transceivers in the CompTIA objectives are media converters. Media converters are a technology that allows administrators to interconnect different media types—for example, twisted pair, fiber, and thin or thick coax—within an existing network. Using a media converter, it is possible to connect newer 100Mbps, Gigabit Ethernet, or ATM equipment to existing networks such as 10Base-T or 100Base-T. They can also be used in pairs to insert a fiber segment into copper networks to increase cabling distances and enhance immunity to electromagnetic interference (EMI).

Firewalls

Today, firewalls are an essential part of a network's design. A *firewall* is a networking device, either hardware or software based, that controls access to your organization's network. This controlled access is designed to protect data and resources from outside threat. To do this, firewalls are typically placed at entry/exit points of a network. For example, a firewall might be placed between an internal network and the Internet. After the firewall is in place, it can control access in and out of that point.

Although firewalls typically protect internal networks from public networks, they are also used to control access between specific network segments within a network. For example, you might place a firewall between the Accounts Department and the Sales Department.

As mentioned, firewalls can be implemented through software or through a dedicated hardware device. Organizations implement software firewalls through network operating systems (NOS) such as Linux/Unix, Windows servers, and Mac OS servers. The firewall is configured on the server to allow or permit certain types of network traffic. In small offices and for regular home use, a firewall is commonly installed on the local system and configured to control traffic. Many third-party firewalls are available.

Hardware firewalls are used in networks of all sizes today. Hardware firewalls are often dedicated network devices and can be implemented with very little configuration and protect all system behind it from outside sources. Hardware firewalls are readily available and often combined with other devices today. For example, many broadband routers and wireless access points have firewall functionality built in. In such a case, the router or WAP may have a number of ports available to plug systems into.

> **NOTE**
>
> **More on Firewalls**   A complete discussion of firewalls is provided in Chapter 11, "Securing the Network."

Network Devices Summary

The information in this chapter is important for the Network+ exam. To summarize our coverage of network devices, we have placed some of the key points about each device in Table 3.3. You should learn this information well.

REVIEW BREAK

TABLE 3.3   Network Devices Summary

Device	Function/Purpose	Key Points
Hub	Connects devices on a Ethernet twisted-pair network.	A hub does not perform any tasks besides signal regeneration.
Switch	Connects devices on a twisted-pair network.	A switch forwards data to its destination by using the MAC address embedded in each packet.
Bridge	Connects LANs to reduce overall network traffic.	A bridge allows or prevents data from passing through it by reading the MAC address.
Router	Connects networks together.	A router uses the software-configured network address to make forwarding decisions.
Gateway	Translates from one data format to another.	Gateways can be hardware or software based. Any device that translates data formats is called a gateway.

(continues)

TABLE 3.3 *Continued*

Device	Function/Purpose	Key Points
CSU/DSU	Translates digital signals used on a LAN to those used on a WAN.	CSU/DSU functionality is sometimes incorporated into other devices, such as a router with a WAN connection.
Network card	Enables systems to connect to the network.	Network interfaces can be add-in expansion cards, PCMCIA cards, or built-in interfaces.
ISDN terminal adapter	Connects devices to ISDN lines.	ISDN is a digital WAN technology often used in place of slower modem links. ISDN terminal adapters are required to reformat the data format for transmission on ISDN links.
WAP	Provides network capabilities to wireless network devices.	A WAP is often used to connect to a wired network, thereby acting as a link between wired and wireless portions of the network.
Modem	Provides serial communication capabilities across phone lines.	Modems modulate the digital signal into analog at the sending end and perform the reverse function at the receiving end.
Transceiver	A device that can be both a transmitter and a receiver of signals.	A transceiver is a device that functions as a transmitter and a receiver of signals such as analog or digital.
Firewall	Provides controlled data access between networks.	Firewalls can be hardware or software based and are an essential part of a network's security strategy.

Identifying MAC Addresses

Objective:

2.1 Identify a MAC (Media Access Control) address and its parts.

This chapter many times refers to MAC addresses and how certain devices use them. However, it has not yet discussed why MAC addresses exist, how they are assigned, and what they consist of. Let's do that now.

> **TIP**
>
> **A MAC Address Is the Physical Address**   A MAC address is sometimes referred to as a *physical address* because it is physically embedded in the interface. Sometimes it is also referred to as a *network address*, which is incorrect. A *network address* is the logical protocol address assigned to the network to which the interface is connected.

A MAC address is a 6-byte hexadecimal address that allows a NIC to be uniquely identified on the network. The MAC address forms the basis of network communication, regardless of the protocol used to achieve network connection. Because the MAC address is so fundamental to network communication, mechanisms are in place to ensure that there is no possibility of duplicate addresses being used.

To combat the possibility of duplicate MAC addresses being assigned, the Institute of Electrical and Electronics Engineers (IEEE) took over the assignment of MAC addresses. But rather than be burdened with assigning individual addresses, the IEEE instead decided to assign each manufacturer an ID and then let the manufacturer further allocate IDs. The result is that in a MAC address, the first three bytes define the manufacturer, and the last three are assigned by the manufacturer.

For example, consider the MAC address of the computer on which this book is being written: 00:D0:59:09:07:51. The first three bytes (00:D0:59) identify the manufacturer of the card; because only this manufacturer can use this address, it is known as the *Organizational Unique Identifier (OUI)*. The last three bytes (09:07:51) are then referred to as the *Universal LAN MAC address*: They make this interface unique. You can find a complete listing of organizational MAC address assignments at `http://standards.ieee.org/regauth/oui/oui.txt`.

> **EXAM ALERT**
>
> **MAC Address Tip**   Because MAC addresses are expressed in hexadecimal, only the numbers 0 through 9 and the letters A through F can be used in them. If you get a Network+ exam question about identifying a MAC address and some of the answers contain letters and numbers other than 0 through 9 and the letters A through F, you can discount those answers immediately.

You can discover the MAC address of the NIC in various ways, depending on what system or platform you are working on. Table 3.4 defines various platforms and the method you can use to view the MAC address of an interface.

TABLE 3.4   Methods of Viewing the MAC Addresses of NICs

Platform	Method
Windows 95/98/Me	Run the `winipcfg` utility
Windows 2000/2003/XP	Run `ipconfig /all` from a command prompt
Linux/some Unix	Run the `ifconfig -a` command
Novell NetWare	Run the `config` command
Cisco router	Run the `sh int <interface name>` command

Figure 3.28 shows the `ipconfig /all` command run on a Windows 2000 system. The MAC address is defined on the Physical Address line of the output.

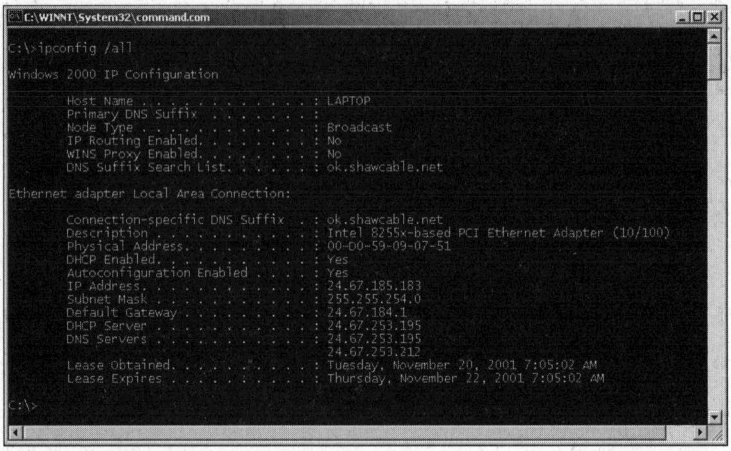

```
C:\WINNT\System32\command.com                                          _|□|×|
C:\>ipconfig /all

Windows 2000 IP Configuration

        Host Name . . . . . . . . . . . . : LAPTOP
        Primary DNS Suffix  . . . . . . . :
        Node Type . . . . . . . . . . . . : Broadcast
        IP Routing Enabled. . . . . . . . : No
        WINS Proxy Enabled. . . . . . . . : No
        DNS Suffix Search List. . . . . . : ok.shawcable.net

Ethernet adapter Local Area Connection:

        Connection-specific DNS Suffix  . : ok.shawcable.net
        Description . . . . . . . . . . . : Intel 8255x-based PCI Ethernet Adapter (10/100)
        Physical Address. . . . . . . . . : 00-D0-59-09-07-51
        DHCP Enabled. . . . . . . . . . . : Yes
        Autoconfiguration Enabled . . . . : Yes
        IP Address. . . . . . . . . . . . : 24.67.185.183
        Subnet Mask . . . . . . . . . . . : 255.255.254.0
        Default Gateway . . . . . . . . . : 24.67.184.1
        DHCP Server . . . . . . . . . . . : 24.67.253.195
        DNS Servers . . . . . . . . . . . : 24.67.253.195
                                            24.67.253.212
        Lease Obtained. . . . . . . . . . : Tuesday, November 20, 2001 7:05:02 AM
        Lease Expires . . . . . . . . . . : Thursday, November 22, 2001 7:05:02 AM

C:\>
```

FIGURE 3.28   The output from the ipconfig /all command on a Windows 2000 system.

Challenge

You are concerned about security on your new wireless connection. As a result you decide to implant MAC level security on the wireless AP. You want to allow both of your client systems, one Linux and one Windows XP, to access the Internet through the wireless AP. Identify the procedures and command for obtaining the MAC address on both a Linux and Windows XP system.

Chapter Summary

Many devices are used to create networks. Every network except the simplest, single-segment coaxial networks uses one or more of these devices. Knowledge of the purpose of the devices discussed in this chapter is vital for the Network+ exam, as well as for the real world.

Hubs and switches provide a mechanism to connect devices to a network created with twisted-pair cabling. Switches offer a speed advantage over hubs because they can use full-duplex communications. They also create dedicated paths between devices, reducing the number of collisions that occur. Both hubs and switches are available in managed and unmanaged varieties.

Bridges allow network traffic to be confined to certain network segments, thereby reducing the amount of network traffic. On Ethernet networks, an additional benefit is reduced collisions.

Routers are devices that connect networks and thereby create internetworks. Because routers use software-configured network addresses instead of hardware-defined MAC addresses, they can provide more functionality than bridges. Routers either can be dedicated hardware devices or can be implemented through software on server systems.

A gateway is a device that translates from one data format to another; it can be a hardware device or a software application. A CSU/DSU is an example of a gateway: CSUs/DSUs translate from the data format used on LANs to that used on WANs. A modem, which translates a signal from digital to analog so that it can be transmitted across a conventional phone line, is another example of a gateway.

WAPs are a relative newcomer to the networking equipment field. Wireless network clients use WAPs to connect to the network. WAPs also generally have a connection point that lets them connect to a wired network infrastructure.

NICs are the point of connectivity between devices and the network. NICs can be add-in expansion cards, PCMCIA devices for laptops, or devices built in to the system board. When you install NICs, you must observe ESD best practices and also pay attention to hardware compatibility and bus compatibility issues.

In addition to NICs used to connect to a LAN, ISDN terminal adapters are sometimes used for remote connectivity.

When you're using clustering, a special system-area NIC is applied to network interfaces used to communicate clustering information between servers.

On a network, each NIC is identified by a unique MAC address. MAC addresses are assigned by the manufacturers that produce the devices, although the high-level assignment of addresses is managed and carried out by the IEEE.

If you get a chance to use all the hardware devices discussed in this chapter, count yourself lucky. Almost every environment will use some of them, but few use them all.

Key Terms

- 80/20 rule
- AT modem commands
- bridge
- CSU/DSU
- cut-through
- distance-vector protocols
- fragment-free
- gateway
- hub
- IPX/SPX
- ISDN adapter
- link-state protocol
- MAC address
- MDI
- MDI-X
- modem
- multiprotocol routing
- NIC
- rack mounting
- RIP
- router
- source-route bridge
- split horizon
- split horizon with poison reverse
- STA
- store-and-forward
- STP
- switch
- TCP/IP
- translational bridge
- transparent bridge
- UART chips
- uplink port
- WAP

Apply Your Knowledge

Exercises

3.1 Determining MAC Addresses for Network Cards

This chapter identifies the characteristics and functions of network devices. In an ideal world, this project would require hands-on experience with these devices, but this is not an ideal world, and access to this equipment is not always easy. Therefore, we will include two exercises that you might be required to perform if such devices are used on your network.

This project assumes that you are using Windows 2000 Server or Professional. You will need an installed NIC with a working driver.

Estimated time: 20 minutes

1. Open a command window by selecting Start, Run. In the command box, type **cmd** and then click OK.

2. At the command prompt, type **ipconfig /all**. The MAC address of your NIC is displayed in the Physical Address line.

3. Open a web browser and go to the following website: http://standards.ieee.org/regauth/ oui/oui.txt.

4. Using the Find functionality in your Web browser, locate the entry that corresponds with the address of your NIC. Is the manufacturer of your NIC the company you expected it to be? Some NIC manufacturers re-brand cards manufactured by another company. For that reason, the MAC address may correspond to a manufacturer that is different from the brand name of the card.

3.2 Using the `tracert` Utility to View the Path to an Internet Destination

One of the tools network administrators have at their disposal is the `tracert` utility. `tracert` allows you to see the hops a network packet takes to get to its destination. At each point along the way, the packet gives information about the route it is taking, along with details of the routers it crosses. More information on the `tracert` utility is provided in Chapter 14, "Troubleshooting Network Connectivity."

> **NOTE**
>
> **Firewalls**   If you are using a system protected by a firewall system, this exercise might not work because firewalls are commonly configured to block `tracert` traffic.

In this exercise, you use the `tracert` utility to view the path to an Internet destination. This project assumes that you are using Windows 2000/2003 or Windows XP with a working Internet connection.

Estimated time: 5 minutes

1. Open a command window by selecting Start, Run. In the command box, type **cmd.exe** and then click OK.

2. At the command prompt, type **tracert www.novell.com**. The route to the Novell web server is displayed.

3. How many hops are you from the destination?

In addition to performing a `tracert` on a remote location, you can use the command on your internal network. If you have a small network set up with a wireless AP or a hub/switch, try doing this exercise using these network devices.

Exam Questions

1. You have configured a 100Mbps network connection between your computer and the switch as half-duplex. What will be the maximum speed of the connection?

    ○ **a.** 50Mbps

    ○ **b.** 100Mbps

    ○ **c.** 100MBps

    ○ **d.** 200Mbps

2. You want to create a larger network by connecting two switches together. One of the switches has a port that can be switched from MDI to MDI-X as needed. The other switch doesn't have such a port or a dedicated uplink port. Which type of cable should you use, and how should you configure the switchable port to create the larger network?

    ○ **a.** Use a straight-through cable and set the port to MIDI

    ○ **b.** Use a crossover cable and set the port to MDI-X

    ○ **c.** Use a straight-through cable and set the port to MDI-X

    ○ **d.** Use a crossover cable and set the port to MDI

3. Of the following, which represents a valid MAC address?

    ○ **a.** 00:D0:59:09:07:51

    ○ **b.** 000:D00:599:099:071:512

    ○ **c.** 00:D0:59:09:07:51:C4:56

    ○ **d.** 00:H0:59:09:07:51

4. A bridge makes forwarding decisions based on what information?

    ○ **a.** IP address

    ○ **b.** MAC address

    ○ **c.** Binary address

    ○ **d.** IRQ address

5. What information does a switch use to determine the port to which data should be sent?

    ○ **a.** The IP address of the connected device

    ○ **b.** The priority of the connected device

    ○ **c.** The MAC address of the connected device

    ○ **d.** The Ethernet address of the connected device

6. Which of the following is a link-state routing protocol used on TCP/IP networks?

  ○ **a.** RIP

  ○ **b.** ARP

  ○ **c.** OSPF

  ○ **d.** NLSP

7. On a Windows 2000 system, what command would you use to view the MAC address?

  ○ **a.** `ifconfig -a`

  ○ **b.** `ipconfig /all`

  ○ **c.** `ipconfig`

  ○ **d.** `config /all`

8. What is the purpose of the uplink port on a hub or switch?

  ○ **a.** It allows for satellite connections.

  ○ **b.** It allows hubs or switches to be connected together.

  ○ **c.** It allows computers to connect to the device.

  ○ **d.** It provides a spare port, which can be used if another port fails.

9. By what method does a router determine the destination address for a packet?

  ○ **a.** It looks at the MAC address of the sender.

  ○ **b.** It looks for the MAC address of the destination.

  ○ **c.** It looks for the software-configured network address for the destination.

  ○ **d.** It looks at the FCS field of the packet.

10. Which of the following statements best describes split horizon?

  ○ **a.** Routes are advertised back on the interface from which they were learned, with a metric of 16.

  ○ **b.** Routes are advertised back on the interface from which they were learned, with a metric of 0.

  ○ **c.** Routes are not advertised back on the interface from which they were learned.

  ○ **d.** Routes are advertised back on the interface from which they were learned, with a metric of 16, and on all other interfaces they are advertised back on the interface from which they were learned, with a metric of 0.

11. In a network that uses distance-vector routing protocols, what information is included in the update sent out by each router?

   ○ **a.** Details of the routers to which it is directly managed by

   ○ **b.** A map of the entire network, with hop counts valued from its current position

   ○ **c.** Details of all the routers it knows about

   ○ **d.** Details of its own configuration

12. What is the difference between an active hub and a passive hub?

   ○ **a.** An active hub has management capabilities.

   ○ **b.** An active hub forwards the data only to the ports that need it.

   ○ **c.** An active hub channels bandwidth to a given connection if the connection becomes too slow.

   ○ **d.** An active hub regenerates the signal before forwarding it.

13. What condition can arise if routers advertise a route back to the router from which it was learned?

   ○ **a.** Count to infinity

   ○ **b.** Road to nowhere

   ○ **c.** Loop de loop

   ○ **d.** Count to 16

14. What term is used by routers to describe each step necessary to reach a destination?

   ○ **a.** Hop

   ○ **b.** Jump

   ○ **c.** Skip

   ○ **d.** Leap

15. What is the maximum speed of a 16550 UART chip?

   ○ **a.** 64,000bps

   ○ **b.** 115,200bps

   ○ **c.** 430,800bps

   ○ **d.** 921,600bps

16. What is the name of the bridging method used to segregate Ethernet networks?

   ○ **a.** Source-route

   ○ **b.** Invisible

   ○ **c.** Cut-through

   ○ **d.** Transparent

17. Which of the following is a distance-vector routing protocol used on TCP/IP networks?

   ○ **a.** ARP

   ○ **b.** NLSP

   ○ **c.** OSPF

   ○ **d.** RIP

18. A CSU/DSU is used in which of the following network configurations?

   ○ **a.** When converting from a Token Ring network to an Ethernet network

   ○ **b.** When converting a digital signal to an analog signal

   ○ **c.** When converting from the digital signals used on a LAN to the digital signals used on a WAN

   ○ **d.** When converting from the digital signal format used on a LAN to the analog signal format used on a WAN

19. A router makes its forwarding decisions based on which of the following information?

   ○ **a.** IP address

   ○ **b.** ARP address

   ○ **c.** Binary address

   ○ **d.** Frame address

20. You are tasked with upgrading a new NIC in the company file and print server. Which of the following should you determine before buying a replacement card? (Choose the three best answers.)

   ○ **a.** Bus compatibility

   ○ **b.** Network compatibility

   ○ **c.** Hardware compatibility

   ○ **d.** Cooling requirements

Answers to Exam Questions

1. **b.** A half-duplex connection operates at the normal speed of the link. Thus, a 100Mbps network connection in a half-duplex configuration would operate at a maximum of 100Mbps. All the other answers are invalid. For more information, see the section "Working with Hubs and Switches" in this chapter.

2. **b.** Because one of the switches does not have MDI capability, the switchable port should be set to MDI-X. Then, a crossover cable should be used to cancel out the crossing between the two devices. None of the other options would result in a successful connection. For more information, see the section "Working with Hubs and Switches" in this chapter.

3. **a.** A MAC address comprises 6 bytes presented in a hexadecimal format. The letters A through F and numbers 0 through 9 are the only valid characters. Therefore, all the other answers provided are incorrect. For more information, see the section "Identifying MAC Addresses" in this chapter.

4. **b.** Bridges make forwarding decisions based on the destination MAC address embedded in each packet. Routers use software addresses, such as IP addresses, to make forwarding decisions. Answers c and d are not valid options. For more information, see the section "Bridges" in this chapter.

5. **c.** A switch uses the MAC address of the connected device to determine the port to which data is forwarded. Routers use software addresses, such as IP addresses, to make forwarding decisions. Answer b is not valid. Although there are many addressing schemes used on networks, *Ethernet address* is not a valid term. Therefore, Answer d is incorrect. For more information, see the section "Switches" in this chapter.

6. **c.** OSPF is a link-state routing protocol used on TCP/IP networks. RIP is a distance-vector routing protocol used on both TCP/IP and IPX/SPX networks; ARP is a component of the TCP/IP protocol suite. NLSP is a link-state routing protocol used on IPX/SPX networks. For more information, see the section "Routers" in this chapter.

7. **b.** The `ipconfig /all` command shows a range of network-related information, including the MAC addresses of any installed NICs. Answers a and d are valid, and using the `ipconfig` command without the `/all` switch shows limited information. For more information, see the section "Identifying MAC Addresses" in this chapter.

8. **b.** The uplink port can be used to connect hubs and switches together, using a standard twisted-pair cable. All the other answers are invalid. For more information, see the section "Working with Hubs and Switches" in this chapter.

9. **c.** Routers use the software-configured network address to make routing decisions. Bridges use MAC addresses to make decisions. Answer d is not valid. The FCS (that is, frame checksum) field is used for error detection. For more information, see the section "Routers" in this chapter.

10. **c.** Split horizon is a routing algorithm that dictates that routes are not advertised back on the interface from which they were learned. Answer a describes the operation of the split horizon with poison reverse algorithm. None of the other answers are valid. For more information, see the section "Routers" in this chapter.

11. **c.** In a network that uses distance-vector routing protocols, routers advertise details of the routers they know about. These updates are sent to all the neighbor routers. Answer a describes the actions on a link-state-based network. Answers b and d are invalid. For more information, see the section "Routers" in this chapter.

12. **d.** An active hub regenerates the data signal before forwarding it to all connected devices. Active hubs come in both managed and unmanaged varieties. Answer b describes the action of a switch. Answer c is invalid. For more information, see the section "Hubs" in this chapter.

13. **a.** A count to infinity occurs when two routers provide information on the same destination and so create a routing loop. All the other answers are invalid. For more information, see the section "Routers" in this chapter.

14. **a.** Each step in the path between a router and its destination is called a hop. The other terms are not used in networking. For more information, see the section "Routers" in this chapter.

15. **b.** A 16550 UART chip is capable of speeds up to 115,200bps. None of the other answers represent the speed for the 16550 UART chip. For more information, see the section "Modems" in this chapter.

16. **d.** The bridging method used on Ethernet networks is called *transparent* because the other network devices are unaware of the existence of the bridge. Source-route bridges are used on Token Ring networks, invisible is not a type of bridge, and cut-through is a switching method, not a type of bridge. For more information, see the section "Bridges" in this chapter.

17. **d.** RIP is a distance-vector routing protocol used on TCP/IP networks. ARP is a component of the TCP/IP protocol suite. NLSP is a link-state routing protocol used on IPX networks, and OSPF is a link-state routing protocol used on TCP/IP networks. For more information, see the section "Routers" in this chapter.

18. **c.** CSUs/DSUs are used to convert the digital signals used on a LAN to the digital signals used on a WAN. The process described in Answer a would be performed by a gateway, and the process described in Answer b would be performed by a modem. Answer d is not valid because WANs commonly use digital signals. For more information, see the section "CSU/DSU" in this chapter.

19. **a.** Routers make routing decisions based on the software-configured network address, which is protocol dependent. There is no such thing as an ARP address. Answers c and d are invalid. For more information, see the section "Routers" in this chapter.

20. **a, b, c.** You should verify bus compatibility, network compatibility, and hardware compatibility before you buy a new NIC. You do not typically need to concern yourself with cooling requirements of a component. For more information, see the section "Network Interface Cards (NICs)" in this chapter.

Suggested Readings and Resources

1. Olexa, Ron. *Implementing 802.11, 802.16, and 802.20 Wireless Networks: Planning, Troubleshooting, and Operations* (Communications Engineering). Newnes Publishing, 2004.

2. Computer networking products and information, www.alliedtelesyn.com.

3. Computer networking device information, www.3com.com.

4. "Computer Networking Tutorials and Advice," compnetworking.about.com.

5. "TechEncyclopedia," www.techencyclopedia.com.

6. "Networking Technology Information from Cisco," www.cisco.com/public/products_tech.shtml.

CHAPTER FOUR

The OSI Model

Objectives

This chapter covers the following CompTIA-specified objectives for the "Protocols and Standards" section of the Network+ exam:

2.2 Identify the seven layers of the OSI (Open Systems Interconnect) model and their functions.

▶ The OSI reference model provides a theoretical framework used to describe the processes and technologies associated with networking.

2.3 Identify the OSI (Open Systems Interconnect) layers at which the following network components operate:

▶ **Hubs**

▶ **Switches**

▶ **Bridges**

▶ **Routers**

▶ **NICs (Network Interface Card)**

▶ **WAPs (Wireless Access Point)**

▶ Understanding how devices' functions relate to the OSI model can provide a greater understanding of networking principles.

Outline

Study Strategies

▶ Read the objectives at the beginning of the chapter.

▶ Read through the description of the OSI model, paying attention to the functions that occur at each level.

▶ Develop a personal mnemonic to help you remember the order of the OSI model layers.

▶ Review the information on what layers of the OSI model various common network devices operate.

▶ Have a friend ask you questions about the OSI model, using Tables 4.2 and 4.3 as a guide.

▶ On a blank piece of paper, draw the OSI model, labeling each layer and providing a brief description of what processes occur at that layer.

▶ Work through the review questions at the end of the chapter and the exercise on matching the layers of the OSI model.

Introduction

One of the most important networking concepts to understand is the Open Systems Interconnect (OSI) reference model. This conceptual model, created by the International Organization for Standardization (ISO) in 1978 and revised in 1984, describes a network architecture that allows data to be passed between computer systems. Even though the OSI model is conceptual, an appreciation of its purpose and function can help you better understand how protocol suites and network architectures work in practical applications.

This chapter takes a detailed look at the OSI model and describes how it relates to real-world networking. It also examines how common network devices relate to the OSI model.

Why Do We Need a Network Model?

Because we are about to spend some of your valuable time discussing a theoretical model, it is only reasonable that we first discuss why we have such a model in the first place and how it can help us.

In simple terms, the OSI model provides a structure that helps us work with networks. By relating services and devices to a certain layer of the model, you can get a better idea of their function and purpose. For example, recall from Chapter 3, "Networking Components and Devices," that switches use the Media Access Control (MAC) address of the attached devices to make forwarding decisions. In the OSI model, MAC addresses are defined in the MAC sublayer of the data-link layer (Layer 2). If you knew that a bridge was also a data-link layer device, you could reasonably draw the conclusion that it, too, works with MAC addresses—and you would be right. This example is perhaps one of the simplest that we could have used, but it serves the purpose well: It shows how the theoretical model can be translated into actual scenarios.

OSI Reference Model 101

Objective:

Identify the seven layers of the OSI (Open Systems Interconnect) model and their functions.

The OSI model consists of seven layers, which is why it is sometimes called the OSI seven-layer model. In diagram form, as shown in Figure 4.1, the model is drawn from bottom to top in the following order: physical, data-link, network, transport, session, presentation, and application layers. The physical layer is classified as Layer 1, and the application layer is classified as Layer 7. In many cases, devices are referred to in relationship to the numbered layers at which they operate. For example, a router is said to be a Layer 3 (network layer) device.

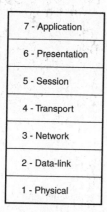

7 - Application
6 - Presentation
5 - Session
4 - Transport
3 - Network
2 - Data-link
1 - Physical

FIGURE 4.1 The OSI reference model.

EXAM ALERT

OSI Mnemonics Many people find it helps to use a mnemonic device to remember the order of the OSI model. Plenty are available, and they range from the surreal to the obscene. Two that we particularly like are Please Do Not Throw Sausage Pizza Away and All People Seem To Need Data Processing. If you prefer, you can make up your own or even search the Internet to find some of the alternatives. If a mnemonic device helps you remember the model and the appropriate functions at each layer, it is worth using.

The model is used to relate the transport of data from one host to another. If the data were being sent from an application, such as a web browser, to a web server, it would travel down through all the layers on the sending device, across the network media, and up through all the layers on the receiving device. Figure 4.2 shows a representation of how this works.

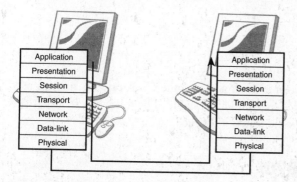

FIGURE 4.2 How data travels between two devices.

As data is passed up or down through the OSI model structure, headers are added (going down) or removed (going up) at each layer—a process called *encapsulation* (addition) or *decapsulation* (removal). Figure 4.3 shows how this works.

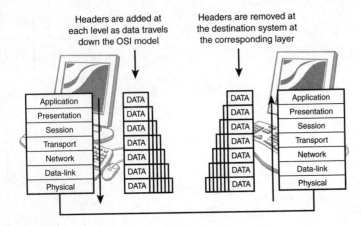

FIGURE 4.3 Encapsulation and decapsulation.

The corresponding layer at the receiving end removes the information added by each device at the sending end. Each layer defines a certain aspect of the communication process, and as data travels up and down the model, the information is sorted into logical groups of bits. The exact term used to refer to the logical group of bits depends on the layer. Table 4.1 contains the terminology used at each layer of the OSI model.

TABLE 4.1 Terminology Used for Logical Groups of Bits at the Layers of the OSI Model

Layer	Terms Used
Application	Packets and messages
Presentation	Packets
Session	Packets
Transport	Packets, segments, and datagrams
Network	Packets and datagrams
Data-link	Packets and frames
Physical	Packets and bits

As you can see, at every layer the term *packet* is used, and in some cases, other terms are used as well. Each layer of the OSI model defines specific functionality. The following sections look at each of the layers separately and discuss the function of each.

Layer 1: The Physical Layer

The physical layer (sometimes referred to incorrectly as the hardware layer) is the layer of the OSI model that defines the physical characteristics of the network. The physical characteristics can include the cable and connector type, the format for pinouts for cables, and so on. It also defines how the data actually travels across the network.

The physical layer also defines the voltage used on the cable and the frequency at which the signals that carry the data are transitioned from one state to another. Such characteristics directly affect the speed of a given media as well as the maximum distance over which a certain media type can be used.

Because the physical layer defines the physical connection to the network, it also defines the physical topology of the network. Recall that there are a number of common physical topologies, including star, ring, bus, mesh, and hybrid, with star being the most common.

> **NOTE**
>
> **OSI Numbering**   Some discussions of the OSI model examine it from top to bottom, and others examine it in reverse. Both methods are valid, but remember that the numbering starts from the bottom and works up. Therefore, it seems most logical to us to explain the model starting at Layer 1 and working up.

Various standards are defined at the physical layer—for example, the Institute of Electrical and Electronics Engineers (IEEE) 802.3 Ethernet standard and the 802.5 Token Ring standard. If you think about it, this is reasonable: An Ethernet network card has different physical characteristics than a Token Ring network card. However, you should know that some of these standards overlap more than one layer of the OSI model. For example, the Ethernet standard also defines the media access method, which is a function of the data-link layer.

Layer 2: The Data-Link Layer

The data-link layer is responsible for sending data to the physical layer so that it can be transmitted across the network. The data-link layer can perform *checksums* and *error detection* on the data to make sure that the data sent is the same as the data received.

The data-link layer is different from the other layers of the OSI model because it has two distinct sublayers—the Logical Link Control (LLC) sublayer and the Media Access Control (MAC) sublayer. Each has a specific role:

▶ **LLC**—The LLC sublayer, which is defined by the IEEE 802.2 standard, controls the access of the media, allowing multiple high-level protocols to use a single network link.

▶ **MAC**—The MAC sublayer manages and controls access to the network media for the protocols trying to use it. The MAC address is defined at this layer.

As discussed in Chapter 1, "Introduction to Networking," there is a difference between the physical topology (how a network looks) and the logical topology (how the network works). Whereas the physical layer sees it from a physical topology perspective, the data-link layer sees the network from a logical topology perspective.

Layer 3: The Network Layer

The network layer of the OSI model is primarily concerned with providing a mechanism by which data can be moved between two networks or systems. The network layer does not define how the data is moved; rather, it is concerned with providing the mechanism that can be used for that purpose. The mechanisms that can be used include defining network addressing and conducting route discovery and maintenance. Common network layer protocols include

▶ **IPX**—Part of Novell's IPX/SPX protocol suite, IPX provides a connectionless transport mechanism.

> **EXAM ALERT**
>
> **Watch IPX** IPX actually operates at both the network and transport layers of the OSI model, but for the purposes on the Network+ exam, consider it a network layer protocol.

▶ **IP**—IP performs much the same function as IPX, but IP is part of TCP/IP protocol suite.

When a system attempts to communicate with another device on the network, network layer protocols attempt to identify that device on the network. When the target system has been identified, it is then necessary to identify the service to be accessed. This is achieved by using a *service identifier*. On Transmission Control Protocol/Internet Protocol (TCP/IP) networks, service identifiers are commonly referred to as *ports*, and on Internetwork Packet Exchange/Sequenced Packet Exchange (IPX/SPX) networks they are called *sockets*, although technically the terms can be used interchangeably.

Switching Methods

An important concept related to the network layer is switching methods. The switching method describes how the data sent from one node reaches another. Three types of switching are used on networks:

> **EXAM ALERT**
>
> **Know the Switching Methods** Be prepared to identify switching methods on the Network+ exam.

▶ **Circuit switching**—The best example of circuit switching is a telephone call. The link between caller and receiver is created, after which there is a dedicated communications link between the two points (hence the term *circuit*). The circuit cannot be broken, which is good because it means that no one else can use the line. In a data communications environment, however, this is a disadvantage because the data often originates from various sources.

▶ **Message switching**—In a message-switching environment, transmissions are broken down into messages that can traverse the network by the fastest means available. It might be that all messages travel over the same path, or it might be that messages travel on different paths. At each point in the journey, a node stores the message before it is forwarded to the next hop on the journey. Such a mechanism gives rise to the phrase *store and forward*. The message-switching system works well in environments in which the amount of data being moved around varies at different times, but it also causes problems such as where to store the data before it is forwarded.

▶ **Packet switching**—Although both circuit switching and message switching can get the job done, both have some serious drawbacks that make them unsuitable for use in a modern network environment. Today, most networks use packet switching, which includes the good points of both circuit and message switching and does not include the bad points. In a packet-switched network, data is broken down into packets that can then be transported around the network. Most modern networks use packet switching as the switching method.

NOTE

More on Switching   A more comprehensive discussion of switching methods, in particular how they relate to wide area networks, is included in Chapter 7, " WAN and Internet Access Technologies."

Network Layer Addressing

From a network administrator's perspective, one of the most important aspects of the network layer is addressing. Network addresses allow a system to be identified on the network by a *logically assigned address*. This is in contrast to the physically assigned MAC addresses used on the data-link layer. The logical assignment of addresses means that schemes can be created that allow a more hierarchical approach to addressing than MAC addresses provide. By using a hierarchy, it is possible to assign a certain address to logical groups of systems as well as to the systems themselves. The result is that network addressing can be used to create portions of the network called *subnets*.

Hierarchical addressing systems are possible only with *routable* network protocols. The most common routable protocol in use today is TCP/IP, although IPX/SPX can still be found on some networks. Other routable protocols, such as AppleTalk, have all but been replaced with TCP/IP.

Of course, you don't have to use a routable protocol. Other nonroutable protocols, such as NetBEUI, can be used, although they are of limited use in today's modern networking environments, where routable protocols are the order of the day. A more detailed discussion of networking protocols is included in Chapter 5, "Overview of Network Protocols."

Another function of the network layer is *route selection*, which refers to determining the best path for the data to take throughout the network. Recall from Chapter 3 that there are two ways in which routes can be configured: *statically* and *dynamically*. In a static routing environment, the network administrator must manually add routes to the routing tables. In a dynamic routing environment, routing protocols such as Routing Information Protocol (RIP) and Open Shortest Path First (OSPF) are used. These protocols work by automatically communicating routing information between devices on the network.

Layer 4: The Transport Layer

The basic function of the transport layer is, as its name suggests, to transport data from one host to another. The transport layer handles the actual processing of data between devices. This includes functions such as segmenting data so that it can be sent over the network and then reassembling the segmented data on the receiving end. The transport layer also deals with some of the errors that can occur in a stream of data, such as dropped and duplicated packets. In addition, the transport layer deals with some of the problems that can be produced by the fragmentation and reassembly process performed by the network layer.

The protocols that operate at the transport layer are those directly concerned with the transporting of data across the network. The following are some of the most commonly used transport-layer protocols:

▶ **TCP**—Part of the TCP/IP protocol suite, TCP provides a connection-oriented transport mechanism.

▶ **User Datagram Protocol (UDP)**—Part of the TCP/IP protocol suite, UDP provides a connectionless transport mechanism.

▶ **SPX**—Part of Novell's IPX/SPX protocol suite, SPX provides a connection-oriented transport mechanism.

Connection-Oriented Protocols

As you can see from the descriptions of the protocols in the preceding section, some are connection oriented and others are connectionless. In a connection-oriented session, the communication dialog between two systems is established, maintained, and then broken when the communication is complete. In technical jargon, this is often referred to as the *setting up* and *tearing down* of a session. While we are on the subject of sessions, we should make something clear: The session layer is also responsible for setting up, maintaining, and closing sessions with other hosts, but it does so at the application level rather than the network level. TCP and other transport-layer protocols maintain the sessions at the network level.

Connection-oriented protocols, such as TCP, enable the delivery of data to be guaranteed because the receipt of each packet that is sent must be acknowledged by the receiving system. Any packet not received is re-sent. This makes for a reliable communication system, though the additional steps necessary to guarantee delivery mean that connection-oriented protocols have higher overhead than do connectionless protocols.

Connectionless Protocols

In contrast to connection-oriented communication, connectionless protocols offer only a *best-effort* delivery mechanism. A connectionless communication is a "fire and forget" mechanism in which data is sent, but no acknowledgments of receipt are sent. This mechanism has a far lower overhead than the connection-oriented method, and it places the onus of ensuring complete delivery on a higher layer, such as the session layer.

Flow Control

Flow control also occurs at the transport layer. As the name suggests, flow control deals with the acceptance of data. It controls the data flow in such a way that the receiving system can accept the data at an adequate rate. Two methods of flow control are commonly used:

▶ **Buffering**—In a buffering system, data is stored in a holding area and waits for the destination device to become available. A system that uses this strategy encounters problems if the sending device can send data much faster than the receiving device can accept it.

▶ **Windowing**—Windowing is a more sophisticated approach to flow control than buffering. In a windowing environment, data is sent in groups of segments that require only one acknowledgment. The size of the window (that is, how many segments can be sent for one acknowledgment) is defined at the time the session between the two devices is established. As you can imagine, the need to have only one acknowledgment for every, say, five segments can greatly reduce overhead.

Layer 5: The Session Layer

The session layer is responsible for managing and controlling the synchronization of data between applications on two devices. It does this by establishing, maintaining, and breaking sessions. Whereas the transport layer is responsible for setting up and maintaining the connection between the two devices, the session layer performs much the same function on behalf of the application.

> **EXAM ALERT**
>
> **About the OSI Layers**   The Network+ exam touches lightly on the upper layers of the OSI model; therefore, only a basic explanation of them is provided here.

Layer 6: The Presentation Layer

The presentation layer's basic function is to convert the data intended for or received from the application layer into another format. Such conversion is necessary because the way in which data is formatted so that it can be transported across the network is not necessarily readable by applications. Some common data formats handled by the presentation layer include the following:

- **Graphics files**—JPEG, TIFF, GIF, and so on are graphics file formats that require the data be formatted in a certain way.

- **Text and data**—The presentation layer can translate data into different formats such as American Standard Code for Information Interchange (ASCII) and Extended Binary Coded Decimal Interchange Code (EBCDIC).

- **Sound/video**—MPEGs, QuickTime video, and MIDI files all have their own data formats to and from which data must be converted.

Another important function of the presentation layer is encryption. *Encryption* is the scrambling of data so that it cannot be read by anything or anyone other than the intended destination. Data encryption is performed at the sending system, and *decryption* (that is, the unscrambling of data at the receiving end) is performed at the destination. Given the basic role of the presentation layer—that of data format translator—it is the obvious place for encryption and decryption to take place.

Layer 7: The Application Layer

The most common misconception about the application layer, the topmost layer of the OSI model, is that it represents applications used on a system such as a word processor or a spreadsheet. This is not correct. Instead, the application layer defines the processes that allow applications to use network services. For example, if an application needs to open a file from a network drive, the functionality is provided by components that reside at the application layer.

In simple terms, the function of the application layer is to take requests and data from the user and pass them to the lower layers of the OSI model. Incoming information is passed to the application layer, which then displays the information to the user. Some of the most basic application-layer services include file and print capabilities.

REVIEW BREAK

OSI Model Summary

Now that we have discussed the functions of each layer of the OSI model, it's time for a quick review. Table 4.2 lists the seven layers of the OSI model and describes some of the most significant points of each layer.

TABLE 4.2   OSI Model Summary

OSI Layer	Major Functions
Application	Provides access to the network for applications and certain end-user functions.
	Displays incoming information and prepares outgoing information for network access.
Presentation	Converts data from the application layer into a format that can be sent over the network.
	Converts data from the session layer into a format that can be understood by the application layer.
	Handles encryption and decryption of data. Provides compression and decompression functionality.
Session	Synchronizes the data exchange between applications on separate devices.
	Handles error detection and notification to the peer layer on the other device.
Transport	Establishes, maintains, and breaks connections between two devices.
	Determines the ordering and priorities of data.
	Performs error checking and verification and handles retransmissions if necessary.
Network	Provides mechanisms for the routing of data between devices across single or multiple network segments.
	Handles the discovery of destination systems and addressing.
Data-link	Has two distinct sublayers: LLC and MAC.
	Performs error detection and handling for the transmitted signals.
	Defines the method by which the media is accessed.
	Defines hardware addressing through the MAC sublayer.
Physical	Defines the physical structure of the network.
	Defines voltage/signal rates and the physical connection methods.
	Defines the physical topology.

EXAM ALERT

Know Table 4.2 For the Network+ exam, as well as for your real-world experience, the information supplied in Table 4.2 should be sufficient.

The Layers at Which Devices Operate

Objective:

Identify the OSI (Open Systems Interconnect) layers at which the following network components operate:

▶ **Hubs**

▶ **Switches**

▶ **Bridges**

▶ **Routers**

▶ **NICs (Network Interface Card)**

▶ **WAPs (Wireless Access Point)**

Now that we have examined the OSI network layer in some detail, we can look at how it relates to the network connectivity devices discussed in Chapter 3: hubs, switches, bridges, routers, and network interface cards (NICs). These devices are said to operate at certain layers of the OSI model based on their functions and roles in the network. Because these devices are covered in Chapter 3, this chapter does not describe them in detail. Instead, this chapter contains a brief description of each device, to jog your memory.

Hubs

Hubs act as the connectivity points of the network on systems that use twisted-pair cabling. There are two types of hubs: active and passive. Each performs the same basic function; they both provide a pathway along which the electrical signals that carry the data can travel. The difference between the two types of hubs is that an active hub has power, and a passive hub does not. Even an active hub does nothing with a signal except regenerate it. Therefore, it is said to be a physical-layer device. Recall that the physical layer deals with placing signals on the media.

Switches

In Chapter 3 you learned that, like hubs, switches act as the connectivity points of the network on systems that use twisted-pair cable. You also learned that a switch offers performance benefits over a hub because it forwards data only to the port on which the destination device is connected. This has the benefit of reducing network traffic because data isn't forwarded to all the ports on a switch. The switch does this by examining the MAC address of the devices connected to it. The use of the MAC address as an identifier places the switch at Layer 2 of the OSI model. Therefore, it is a data-link layer device.

> **TIP**
>
> **Layer 3 Switches and Layer 4 Switches**   For the Network+ exam consider switches as Layer 2 devices. In the real world, devices that are called Layer 3 switches and Layer 4 switches are available. These devices "switch" data but do so using other mechanisms.

Bridges

Bridges are used to divide a network into smaller areas through a process known as *segmentation*. Then, by learning which devices are located on which interface, a bridge can block or forward traffic between the interfaces. It does this by using the MAC address of the attached devices. The use of the MAC address makes a bridge a Layer 2 (that is, data-link layer) device.

Routers

Routers are more complex and more functional than either bridges or switches because they are used to connect networks and then manage the flow of data between the networks. Unlike switches and bridges, routers use software-configured logical network addresses. Because the routing function is implemented at the network layer of the OSI model, routers are referred to as Layer 3 devices.

> **NOTE**
>
> **Brouters**   Chapter 2, "Cabling Standards, Media, and Connectors," briefly discusses a device called a brouter. A *brouter* can route data that can be routed or bridge data that cannot be routed. Such a device is said to be both a Layer 2 device and a Layer 3 device.

NICs

A NIC provides the physical connectivity point to the network for a computer system. But although NICs are physical components, they are defined as data-link layer devices because they are used in physical media access (which is handled at the MAC sublayer) and the logical access of the network media (which is handled at the LLC sublayer).

> **NOTE**
>
> There is some debate as to whether a NIC is in fact just a Layer 2 device, or whether it is both a Layer 1 and Layer 2 device. This is because although it provides addressing and media access functions (Layer 2 roles), it is also responsible for placing the signal on the network media, which is a layer 1 task. For the purposes of the Network+ exam, CompTIA considers the NIC to be just a Layer 2 device, which is why we have classified it as such here.

Wireless Access Points (WAPs)

Wireless Access Points are devices that provide connectivity between wireless portions of a network and wired portions of a network. WAPs are considered data-link layer devices because their primary function is to provide connectivity to the network. This connectivity is independent of the network communications protocol. Like a NIC, WAPs are involved in both the physical access of the network (which is handled at the MAC sublayer) and the logical access of the network (which is handled at the LLC sublayer).

REVIEW BREAK

Summary of the Layers at Which Devices Operate

Table 4.3 summarizes the devices discussed in the previous sections and the corresponding layers at which they operate.

> **EXAM ALERT**
>
> **Know Where a Device Operates**   In the Network+ exam you might be asked to identify the layer at which a given device operates.

TABLE 4.3   The OSI Model Layers at Which Various Devices Operate

Device	OSI Layer at Which the Device Operates
Hub	Physical (Layer 1)
Switch	Data-link (Layer 2)
Bridge	Data-link (Layer 2)
Router	Network (Layer 3)
NIC	Data-link (Layer 2)
WAP	Data-link (Layer 2)

Chapter Summary

The OSI model is a conceptual model that defines seven layers. Each of these layers performs a specific function that plays an important part in the end-to-end communication between two devices. The model allows us to relate the function of a certain protocol or service to a specific function of the model. For example, IP is responsible for the discovery and establishment of routes through the network. Therefore, it is reasonable to assume that IP is a network-layer protocol because such functions are performed at the network layer. The ability to draw parallels like this can be a useful aid to understanding networking from both conceptual and practical levels.

Because the OSI model defines the functions performed at various layers, it can be said that network devices operate at certain layers of the OSI model. The layer at which a device operates is defined by the function of the device and the information the device uses to complete its task. Of the commonly used network devices, hubs operate at the physical layer; network cards, bridges, and switches operate at the data-link layer; and routers operate at the network layer.

Understanding the OSI model is important for networking. Even though it can sometimes be difficult to see how the OSI model is relevant in day-to-day tasks, it helps to reinforce networking theory and provides a framework in which to work.

Key Terms

- application layer
- buffering
- circuit switching
- connectionless protocols
- connection-oriented protocols
- data-link layer
- dynamic routing
- encapsulation
- LLC
- MAC
- message switching
- network layer
- OSI
- packet switching
- physical layer
- presentation layer
- segmentation
- session layer
- SPX
- static routing
- TCP
- transport layer
- UDP
- windowing

Apply Your Knowledge

Exercises

4.1 Identifying OSI Layers

Developing an exercise for a chapter focusing on the OSI model is almost an impossible task. For the Network+ exam, you will need to be able to identify the various layers of the OSI model and the network devices that correspond to each level. With that in mind, in lieu of a hands-on project, this chapter provides a practical exercise to reinforce the concepts discussed in this chapter. Your ability to correctly complete this exercise will show sufficient knowledge of the OSI model to get you through any questions on it in the exam.

Estimated time: 10 minutes

1. Refer to the worksheet in Figure 4.4 and identify two functions for each layer of the OSI model.

2. Check your responses against the information in Table 4.2.

7
Layer Name _____
Purpose/Function _____
Purpose/Function _____

6
Layer Name _____
Purpose/Function _____
Purpose/Function _____

5
Layer Name _____
Purpose/Function _____
Purpose/Function _____

4
Layer Name _____
Purpose/Function _____
Purpose/Function _____

3
Layer Name _____
Purpose/Function _____
Purpose/Function _____

2
Layer Name _____
Purpose/Function _____
Purpose/Function _____

1
Layer Name _____
Purpose/Function _____
Purpose/Function _____

FIGURE 4.4 A hands-on OSI model project.

Exam Questions

1. At which layer of the OSI model does a switch operate?

   ○ **a.** Physical

   ○ **b.** Data-link

   ○ **c.** Network

   ○ **d.** Session

2. Which of the following devices operate at Layer 2 of the OSI model? (Choose the three best answers.)

   ○ **a.** Switch

   ○ **b.** Network card

   ○ **c.** Hub

   ○ **d.** Bridge

3. Which layer of the OSI model is responsible for synchronizing the exchange of data between two devices at the application level?

   ○ **a.** Transport

   ○ **b.** Session

   ○ **c.** Presentation

   ○ **d.** Data-link

4. Which of the following transport-layer protocols offer guaranteed delivery? (Choose the two best answers.)

   ○ **a.** SPX

   ○ **b.** UDP

   ○ **c.** IPX

   ○ **d.** TCP

5. Which layer of the OSI model is responsible for route discovery?

   ○ **a.** Session

   ○ **b.** Data-link

   ○ **c.** Network

   ○ **d.** Transport

6. What are the two sublayers of the data-link layer?

○ **a.** Logical link control

○ **b.** Logical loop control

○ **c.** Media access control

○ **d.** Multiple access control

7. Which of the following are responsibilities of the transport layer? (Choose the two best answers.)

○ **a.** Performs error detection and handling for the transmitted signals

○ **b.** Synchronizes data exchange between two applications

○ **c.** Performs error checking and verification

○ **d.** Establishes, maintains, and breaks connections between devices

8. Which layer of the OSI model defines the method by which the network media are accessed on a logical level?

○ **a.** Data-link

○ **b.** Physical

○ **c.** Session

○ **d.** Presentation

9. At which layer of the OSI model does a hub operate?

○ **a.** Application

○ **b.** Network

○ **c.** Physical

○ **d.** Data-link

10. Which of the following terms is *not* used to describe a logical grouping of bits?

○ **a.** Datagram

○ **b.** Segment

○ **c.** Package

○ **d.** Packet

11. Which layer of the OSI model defines the signal rates and voltages that are used?

- ○ **a.** Data-link
- ○ **b.** Physical
- ○ **c.** Session
- ○ **d.** Presentation

12. At which layer of the OSI model does a WAP operate?

- ○ **a.** Physical
- ○ **b.** Data-link
- ○ **c.** Network
- ○ **d.** Transport

13. At which layer of the OSI model does a NIC operate?

- ○ **a.** Physical
- ○ **b.** Data-link
- ○ **c.** Network
- ○ **d.** Transport

14. At which layer of the OSI model do encryption and decryption take place?

- ○ **a.** Physical
- ○ **b.** Session
- ○ **c.** Application
- ○ **d.** Presentation

15. Which of the following are commonly used flow control strategies? (Choose the two best answers.)

- ○ **a.** Buffering
- ○ **b.** Segmentation
- ○ **c.** Windowing
- ○ **d.** Direct flow management

16. You have been called in to troubleshoot a 10Base2 network that is experiencing problems. After performing some tests, you determine that the problem lies with one of the terminators on the network. At which layer of the OSI model does the problem exist?

    ○ **a.** Physical

    ○ **b.** Data-link

    ○ **c.** Network

    ○ **d.** Session

17. Which of the following OSI layers is responsible for establishing connections between two devices?

    ○ **a.** Session

    ○ **b.** Network

    ○ **c.** Transport

    ○ **d.** Data-link

18. At which layer do the protocols that handle route discovery reside?

    ○ **a.** Transport

    ○ **b.** Network

    ○ **c.** Session

    ○ **d.** Application

19. At the transport layer, two types of protocols are used for sending data to a remote system. What terms are used to describe these protocols? (Choose the two best answers.)

    ○ **a.** Connection oriented

    ○ **b.** Connection reliant

    ○ **c.** Connection dependent

    ○ **d.** Connectionless

20. At which layer of the OSI model does a router operate?

    ○ **a.** Application

    ○ **b.** Session

    ○ **c.** Network

    ○ **d.** Transport

Answers to Exam Questions

1. **b.** A switch uses the MAC addresses of connected devices to make forwarding decisions and therefore operates at the data-link layer of the OSI model. Components at the physical layer define the actual connection to the network. Physical layer components include cabling and connectors. Protocols at the network layer handle addressing and route discovery. Protocols at the session layer deal with establishment and termination between systems or applications on the network. None of the other answers apply. For more information, see the section "The Layers at Which Devices Operate," in this chapter.

2. **a, b, d.** Switches, bridges, and NICs operate at the data-link layer of the OSI model, which is also known as Layer 2. A hub is defined as a physical layer (that is, Layer 1) device. For more information, see the section "The Layers at Which Devices Operate," in this chapter.

3. **b.** The synchronization of data between applications is performed at the session layer of the OSI model. Protocols at the transport layer establish, maintain, and break connections between two devices. Protocols at the presentation layer convert data so that it can be received from or sent to the network. Devices at the data-link layer define the media access method and hardware addressing. For more information, see the section "OSI Reference Model 101," in this chapter.

4. **a, d.** Both SPX and TCP are connection-oriented protocols that offer guaranteed delivery of data. UDP and IPX are both connectionless protocols. For more information, see the section "OSI Reference Model 101," in this chapter.

5. **c.** Route discovery is performed by protocols that operate at the network layer of the OSI model. Devices at the data-link layer define the media access method and hardware addressing. Protocols at the network layer handle addressing and route discovery. Protocols at the transport layer establish, maintain, and break connections between two devices. For more information, see the section "OSI Reference Model 101," in this chapter.

6. **a, c.** The data-link layer of the OSI model is divided into two distinct sublayers: the LLC sublayer and the MAC sublayer. None of the other answers are valid. For more information, see the section "OSI Reference Model 101," in this chapter.

7. **c, d.** The network layer is responsible for, among other things, performing error checking and verification, and establishing, maintaining, and breaking connections between devices. Synchronizing data exchange between applications occurs at the session layer. Error detection and handling for the transmitted signals occur at the data-link layer. For more information, see the section "OSI Reference Model 101," in this chapter.

8. **a.** Standards at the data-link layer define how the network is accessed on a logical level. Do not confuse the function of the data-link layer with that of the physical layer, which performs similar functions but at a physical rather than a logical level. The session layer handles the synchronization of data between applications on networked devices. Protocols at the presentation layer prepare data for transmission on the network, or prepare data from the network to be passed to the application layer. For more information, see the section "OSI Reference Model 101," in this chapter.

9. **c.** A hub operates at the physical layer of the OSI model. Components at the application layer are software based. A router is an example of a network layer device. A switch is an example of a data-link layer device. For more information, see the section "The Layers at Which Devices Operate," in this chapter.

10. **c.** The term *package* is not valid when referring to a logical grouping of bits. All the other answers are valid terms. For more information, see the section "OSI Reference Model 101," in this chapter.

11. **b.** The physical layer of the OSI model defines the physical characteristics of the network, including voltages and signaling rates. The data-link layer performs error detection and handling for transmitted signals. It also defines the method by which the media is accessed. The session layer handles the synchronization of data between applications on networked devices. Protocols at the presentation layer prepare data for transmission on the network, or prepare data from the network to be passed to the application layer For more information, see the section "OSI Reference Model 101," in this chapter.

12. **b.** WAPs provide connectivity between wireless and wired portions of a network. They are classified as data-link layer devices because they provide logical connectivity but are protocol independent. Components at the physical layer define the actual connection to the network. Physical layer components include cabling and connectors. A router is an example of a network layer device. Protocols at the transport layer establish, maintain, and break connections between two devices. For more information, see the section "The Layers at Which Devices Operate," in this chapter.

13. **b.** NICs operate at the data-link layer of the OSI model. Physical layer components include cabling and connectors. A router is an example of a network layer device. Transport layer components are typically software. For more information, see the section "The Layers at Which Devices Operate," in this chapter.

14. **d.** Encryption is a function that takes place at the presentation layer of the OSI model. Components at the physical layer define the actual connection to the network. Physical layer components include cabling and connectors. The session layer handles the synchronization of data between applications on networked devices. Protocols at the presentation layer prepare data for transmission on the network, or prepare data from the network to be passed to the application layer. For more information, see the section "OSI Reference Model 101," in this chapter.

15. **a, c.** Windowing and buffering are commonly used flow control strategies. *Segmentation* is the term used to describe the division of packets to enable them to be transported across the network. Answer d is not valid. For more information, see the section "OSI Reference Model 101," in this chapter.

16. **a.** Cable and connectors are physical elements of the network, so they relate to the physical layer of the OSI model. The data-link layer performs error detection and handling for transmitted signals. It also defines the method by which the media is accessed. Protocols at the network layer handle addressing and route discovery. The session layer handles the synchronization of data between applications on networked devices. For more information, see the section "The Layers at Which Devices Operate," in this chapter.

17. **c.** The transport layer is responsible for establishing connections between two devices. The session layer handles the synchronization of data between applications on networked devices. Protocols at the network layer handle addressing and route discovery. The data-link layer performs error detection and handling for transmitted signals. It also defines the method by which the media is accessed. For more information, see the section "OSI Reference Model 101," in this chapter.

18. **b.** Protocols at the network layer are responsible for route discovery. Protocols at the transport layer establish, maintain, and break connections between two devices. The session layer handles the synchronization of data between applications on networked devices. Protocols at the application layer provide access to network functions. For more information, see the section "OSI Reference Model 101," in this chapter.

19. **a, d.** The two terms used to describe protocols at the transport layer are *connection oriented* and *connectionless*. The terms in Answers b and c are not used. For more information, see the section "OSI Reference Model 101," in this chapter.

20. **c.** A router uses the logical network address to make decisions and is therefore a network layer device. Application, session, and transport level components are software based. For more information, see the section "The Layers at Which Devices Operate," in this chapter.

Suggested Readings and Resources

1. Habraken, Joe. *Absolute Beginner's Guide to Networking, Fourth Edition.* Que Publishing, 2003.

2. Ogletree, Terry William. *Upgrading and Repairing Networks, Fourth Edition.* Que Publishing, 2003.

3. "TechEncyclopedia," www.techencyclopedia.com.

4. "OSI Technical Information," www.cisco.com/univercd/cc/td/doc/cisintwk/ito_doc/osi_prot.htm.

5. "OSI Model Tutorial," www.itp-journals.com/search/ t04124.htm.

6. Computer networking tutorials and advice, compnetworking.about.com.

CHAPTER FIVE

Overview of Network Protocols

Objectives

This chapter covers the following CompTIA-specified objectives for the "Protocols and Standards" section of the Network+ exam:

2.4 Differentiate between the following network protocols in terms of routing, addressing schemes, interoperability, and naming conventions:

▶ **IPX/SPX (Internetwork Packet Exchange/Sequence Packet Exchange)**

▶ **NetBEUI (Network Basic Input/Output System Extended User Interface)**

▶ **AppleTalk/AppleTalk over IP (Internet Protocol)**

▶ **TCP/IP (Transmission Control Protocol/Internet Protocol)**

▶ For the Network+ exam, you will be expected to demonstrate an understanding of commonly used network protocols.

Outline

Study Strategies

▶ Review the objectives covered in this chapter.

▶ Read the material presented in this chapter, paying special attention to Exam Alerts and tables.

▶ If you have a Windows, Mac, or Linux system to use as a server, investigate what is involved in installing and configuring support for IPX/SPX or AppleTalk.

▶ Visit the websites provided in the readings and resources sections at the end of the chapter. Review the information they provide about the protocols discussed in this chapter.

▶ Confine your inquiry and investigations to IPX/SPX, AppleTalk, and NetBEUI. Chapter 6, "Working with TCP/IP," is devoted to a further discussion of TCP/IP.

▶ Complete the exercise and review questions at the end of the chapter.

Introduction

In networks, as in everyday life, rules and procedures govern communication. The rules and procedures that allow devices on a network to communicate with each other are referred to as *protocols*. Some protocols deal specifically with the process of transferring data from one system to another, and others are responsible for things such as route discovery and providing client functionality.

This chapter identifies the protocols used on today's networks and the environments in which you are likely to see them. It also examines some of the characteristics of each protocol. Understanding these characteristics is important for the Network+ exam.

> **NOTE**
>
> **Protocols**   The term *protocol* refers to any set of instructions that governs communication between two devices.

Introduction to Protocols

Objective:

2.4 Differentiate between the following network protocols in terms of routing, addressing schemes, interoperability, and naming conventions:

▶ IPX/SPX (Internetwork Packet Exchange/Sequence Packet Exchange)

▶ NetBEUI (Network Basic Input/Output System Extended User Interface)

▶ AppleTalk/AppleTalk over IP (Internet Protocol)

▶ TCP/IP (Transmission Control Protocol/Internet Protocol)

When computers were restricted to standalone systems there was little need for mechanisms to communicate between them. However, it wasn't long before the need to connect computers for the purpose of sharing files and printers became a necessity. Establishing communication between network devices required more than a length of cabling; a method or a set of rules was needed to establish how systems would communicate. Protocols provide that method.

It would be nice if a single protocol facilitated communication between all devices, but this is not the case. A number of protocols can be used on a network, each of which has its own features, advantages, and disadvantages. What protocol you choose can have a significant impact on the functioning and performance of the network.

Protocols are grouped together into *protocol suites*. Each protocol suite defines a complete set of protocols that allow the devices to communicate. Within each protocol suite are a variety of different protocols, which can be broken down into three distinct categories:

▶ **Application protocols**—Application protocols deal with providing client functionality.

▶ **Transport protocols**—Transport protocols provide mechanisms for moving data around the network.

▶ **Network protocols**—Network protocols perform the underlying tasks that enable the movement of data.

Three main protocol suites are used today:

▶ **Transmission Control Protocol/Internet Protocol (TCP/IP)**—By far the most prevalent of all the protocols discussed in this chapter, the TCP/IP protocol suite is a comprehensive set of protocols, and versions of it are available for all common platforms.

▶ **Internetwork Packet Exchange/Sequenced Packet Exchange (IPX/SPX)**— Developed by Novell, IPX/SPX is a set of protocols originally designed for use on Novell networks. It is now less popular than it once was, due to the impact of TCP/IP.

▶ **AppleTalk**—Designed for use on networks that use Macintosh systems, AppleTalk is an advanced suite of protocols that provides high levels of functionality.

In addition to these protocol suites, certain other protocols, such as NetBIOS Extended User Interface (NetBEUI), are used on smaller networks. This chapter describes NetBEUI, but it mainly focuses on the three major suites.

The Function of Protocols

To get an idea of exactly how protocols facilitate communication between devices, let's look at the role protocols play at the sending and receiving computers. In the data communication process, the information that passes between computers on a network goes through certain steps at both the sending and receiving devices. The following sections discuss what takes place at each end of the communication process.

Protocols from the Sending Device

For a computer to send data, the following steps must be performed; keep in mind that these are general steps—the actual processes taken at the sending device are far more complex:

1. The protocol is responsible for breaking the data into smaller parts, called *packets*.

2. Addressing information is assigned to each of the individual packets. This addressing information is used to locate the destination computer on the network.

3. The data is prepared for transmission and sent through the network interface card (NIC) and on to the network.

You can match steps 1 through 3 to the OSI model, starting with the application layer and ending with the physical layer, where the data is passed through the NIC and onto the network media. This process is discussed in greater detail later in this chapter.

Protocols on the Receiving Device

The steps for the receiving device are pretty much the same as those for the sending device, but they occur in the opposite order:

1. When data reaches the destination computer, the data packets are taken off the network media and in through the system's NIC.

2. The addressing information added by the sending computer is stripped from the packets.

3. The data packets are reassembled.

4. The reassembled packets are passed to the specific application for use.

To accomplish these steps, the same protocol must be used on the sending and receiving devices. It is possible for two devices that use different protocols to communicate with each other, but a *gateway*—an intermediary device that has the capability to translate between two formats—is needed. For more information on gateways, refer to Chapter 3, "Networking Components and Devices."

Mapping Protocols to the OSI Model

As discussed previously in this chapter, three categories of protocols are used on networks: application protocols, transport protocols, and network protocols. These protocols can be matched to the OSI model, as shown in Figure 5.1.

Understanding how protocols map to OSI layers can be useful as an aid in understanding how protocols within a suite work together. The following sections look more specifically at some of the protocols that reside at each level. First, let's look at application protocols.

Application Protocols

As shown in Figure 5.1, the application protocols work in the upper layers of the OSI seven-layer model: Application protocols map to the application, presentation, and session layers of the OSI model. The following are some examples of the specific application protocols from the various protocol suites:

▶ **AppleTalk File Protocol (AFP)**—AFP is the protocol used by Macintosh systems for remote file access and management. It is part of the AppleTalk protocol suite.

▶ **File Transfer Protocol (FTP)**—FTP is one of the protocols that make up the TCP/IP protocol suite. It is used for transferring files between systems on a network.

▶ **NetWare Core Protocol (NCP)**—NCP is a protocol in the IPX/SPX suite that provides application-level functionality to client systems.

▶ **Simple Network Management Protocol (SNMP)**—SNMP is used to monitor network devices. Like FTP, SNMP is part of the TCP/IP protocol suite.

▶ **Simple Mail Transfer Protocol (SMTP)**—SMTP is the protocol used in the transporting of email. It is part of the TCP/IP protocol suite.

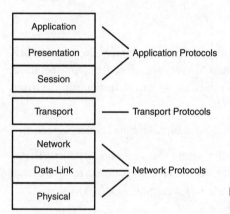

FIGURE 5.1 Matching protocol types to layers of the OSI model.

Although application protocols provide clients access to functionality, the transport protocols, which are described in the following section, actually move the data across the network.

Transport Protocols

Transport protocols map to the transport layer of the OSI model and are responsible for the transporting of data across the network. The following are some examples of transport protocols from the commonly used protocol suites:

▶ **AppleTalk Transaction Protocol (ATP)**—ATP is a connectionless protocol used with the AppleTalk protocol suite.

▶ **NetBEUI**—NetBEUI is a simple and fast network protocol used with NetBIOS.

▶ **SPX**—SPX is the NetWare communications protocol used to transport data across the network. It is a connection-oriented protocol.

▶ **TCP**—One of the protocols in the TCP/IP protocol stack, TCP is a connection-oriented protocol, and is responsible for establishing connections between systems.

▶ **User Datagram Protocol (UDP)**—Part of the TCP/IP protocol suite, UDP is used instead of TCP when guaranteed data delivery is not required.

EXAM ALERT

The Two Categories of Transport Protocols   Transport protocols fall into two basic categories: connection-oriented and connectionless protocols. Connection-oriented protocols offer guaranteed delivery, and connectionless protocols don't. You will be required to know this for the Network+ exam.

Although transport protocols are concerned with moving data around the network, they rely on network protocols, described in the following section, to provide the underlying services that enable the process.

Network Protocols

The network protocols provide the rules for communication between devices on the network. Network protocols are responsible for providing the addressing and routing information, error checking, and such things as retransmission requests for incomplete communications. The following are some examples of network protocols:

▶ **IP**—Part of the TCP/IP protocol suite, IP is used for addressing and route selection.

▶ **IPX**—IPX is a communications protocol used for routing messages on networks that use the IPX/SPX protocol suite. Strictly speaking, IPX is also considered to operate at the Transport layer of the OSI model, but is commonly accepted as a Network layer protocol.

▶ **Datagram Delivery Protocol (DDP)**—DDP provides connectionless service on AppleTalk networks.

Now that you have seen how protocols are used on a network and some of the protocols used at the various layers, let's look at the specific protocols used in today's networks. In the following sections we look in more detail at each of the commonly used protocol suites.

Internetwork Packet Exchange/Sequenced Packet Exchange (IPX/SPX)

IPX/SPX is the native protocol used, until recently, on Novell networks. Today even Novell, creator of IPX/SPX, has started using TCP/IP as the default protocol.

IPX/SPX was developed by Novell with a bit of help from Xerox. (IPX was based on an early protocol called Xerox Network System [XNS], and SPX was based on another Xerox protocol, Sequenced Packet Protocol [SPP].) During the reign of the Novell operating system, those working with networks would certainly have had to be familiar with IPX/SPX. Today, however, you might never come in contact with it.

Despite its fading use, IPX offers certain distinct advantages: Addressing is almost completely automatic, IPX is a routable protocol, and, on small networks, IPX provides an excellent alternative to TCP/IP.

NOTE

NWLink   Many of today's networking environments are not restricted to a single server platform but instead use different servers on the same network. To accommodate this, Microsoft developed the NWLink protocol to allow interoperability between Novell NetWare networks and servers running Windows server platforms.

NWLink is a Windows implementation of the IPX/SPX protocol that lets Windows systems access applications running on a NetWare server. In turn, NetWare clients can use the NWLink protocol to access services running on Windows-based servers.

When IPX/SPX was a popular protocol for networks, such interoperability was mandatory. As the popularity of NetWare and the IPX/SPX protocol have diminished in recent years, the need for a means of interoperability has decreased. Windows 2000 and Windows Server 2003 still include the NWLink protocol, but it is not widely used. As NetWare itself moves away from IPX/SPX, the need for the NWLink protocol is all but gone.

The IPX/SPX Protocol Suite

Like TCP/IP, IPX/SPX is a protocol suite made up of a variety of separate protocols, each of which has a different function and purpose. The individual protocols that form the IPX/SPX protocol suite include the following:

- Internetwork Packet Exchange (IPX)
- Sequenced Packet Exchange (SPX)
- Routing Information Protocol (RIP)
- NetWare Link State Protocol (NLSP)
- Service Advertising Protocol (SAP)
- NetWare Core Protocol (NCP)

Although a detailed understanding of each of these protocols is not required for the Network+ exam, the following sections briefly examine each of them and identify their purposes and functions.

Internetwork Packet Exchange (IPX)

IPX provides connectionless communication and is used to route messages from one node to another. Essentially, IPX is responsible for logical network addressing, route selections, and connection services. IPX operates at both the Network and Transport layer of the OSI model. The route selections used are determined by tables created with another of the IPX/SPX protocols: RIP or OSPF. Because IPX is a connectionless protocol, it is unsuitable for some network applications. For this reason, it is used in conjunction with SPX.

Sequenced Packet Exchange (SPX)

SPX adds reliability to IPX. SPX is a connection-oriented protocol used when guaranteed message delivery is required on the network. Protocols that provide connection-oriented service are inherently slower than those that do not because they are concerned with error control. Within the IPX/SPX protocol suite, SPX is responsible for fragmenting the packets into data, sequencing this data to ensure that the receiving device knows the correct order for the data, and reassembling the data.

Routing Information Protocol (RIP)

RIP is responsible for the routing of packets on an IPX/SPX network. RIP uses the distance-vector route-discovery method; it calculates routes based on the number of hops (that is, routers) that must be crossed to reach a particular device.

NetWare Link Services Protocol (NLSP)

Both RIP and SAP are relatively old broadcast-based protocols that can function inefficiently in some network environments. To reduce broadcast traffic, you can use NLSP. NLSP uses a link-state route discovery method to build routing tables. Link-state protocols do not broadcast routing information periodically; rather, they broadcast routing information only when changes have been made to the routing information or at extended intervals. This process is more efficient than RIP.

Service Advertising Protocol (SAP)

NetWare uses SAP to allow systems providing services to the network, such as file and print services, to announce their services and addresses to the network. SAP lets NetWare clients know the location of the systems providing network resources. To let clients know whether a service is available to them, a SAP packet is broadcast every 60 seconds.

NetWare Core Protocol (NCP)

NCP is responsible for providing services to client applications. NCP is a connection-oriented protocol that provides the connection between clients and services.

IPX Addressing

Addressing for the IPX/SPX protocol suite is the responsibility of IPX. IPX addressing is somewhat simpler than TCP/IP addressing because instead of making up an addressing scheme and applying it to a network segment, IPX uses the Media Access Control (MAC) address assigned to each network interface. By combining this MAC address with an eight-character hexadecimal address, which is used to refer to the network segment, IPX creates a hierarchical addressing system that is routable.

An example of an IPX address is 0BAD33CE:0003FE7C06EC. The 0BAD33CE portion represents the IPX address for the network segment; 0003FE7C06EC is the MAC address of the node, derived from the network interface for that system, which is used for the second part of the address. In addition to this format, IPX addresses can also be written with each group of four hexadecimal characters separated by colons (:)—for example, 0000:0007:003C:7F53:04CF. In some cases, any leading 0s on the network address portion are dropped. For example, 00000007 can be expressed simply as 7. The address would then be 7:003C:7F53:04CF.

NOTE

Hexadecimal IPX Addresses   Because IPX addresses are expressed in hexadecimal, they can only contain the letters A through F and the numbers 0 through 9. There can be a maximum of 8 characters in the segment portion and 12 characters in the MAC address portion.

Figure 5.2 shows how IPX addressing works in a sample network.

The IPX segment, or network, address is defined by the first server that comes up on a network. If another system that has a different number is subsequently brought onto the network, errors are generated. When a workstation system is brought onto the network, the IPX segment address is normally detected automatically. Alternatively, in some configurations it is possible to manually configure the address, although you don't need to do so under normal circumstances.

EXAM ALERT

Identify Network Addresses   For the Network+ exam, make sure that you can identify network addresses for all the protocols discussed in this chapter.

Mapping IPX/SPX to the OSI Model

Mapping the IPX/SPX protocol suite to the OSI model is not an easy task. As shown in Figure 5.3, the core protocols of the suite map to the network and transport layers of the OSI model.

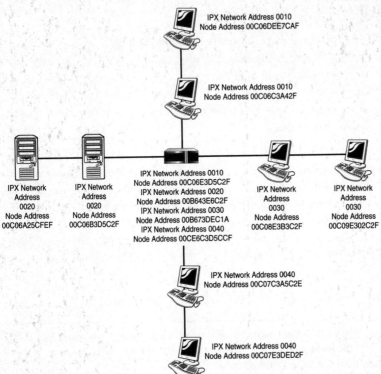

FIGURE 5.2 IPX addressing in a sample network.

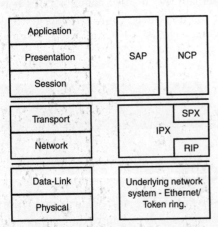

FIGURE 5.3   The OSI model and the IPX/SPX protocol suite.

IPX/SPX Interoperability

The IPX/SPX protocol suite is supported by Novell NetWare and by the Microsoft Windows platforms. Microsoft created its own implementation of the IPX/SPX protocol suite, called NWLink, which can be used with the Microsoft Client Services for NetWare (CSNW) to allow Windows systems to connect to a NetWare server. Even on a network with only Windows systems, some people prefer to use NWLink because it offers easier addressing of other protocols such as TCP/IP.

IPX/SPX Naming

As already mentioned, IPX addressing is essentially automatic. Naming also is not an issue with IPX/SPX because servers are normally the only parts of a network assigned a name. These names can be up to 47 characters (in current versions of NetWare). Workstations do not need such addresses and instead just use IPX addressing.

For a time, IPX/SPX was the king of the network protocols, but over time it has given way to TCP/IP. Even Novell has, for many years, used TCP/IP as the default protocol with its network operating systems. Within a short time, we may we be bidding farewell to IPX/SPX for good.

Challenge

You have been tasked with installing NWLink on a Windows Server 2003 system, so that you can migrate some files from an old NetWare 3.12 server. Attempt to do this on your own, but if you have difficulty, follow these steps to add the new protocol to your server.

1. On the Windows Server 2003 system, click Start, Control Panel, Network Connections, and then choose the first Local Area Connection for your system.

2. On the Local Area Connection Status dialog, click the Properties button. The Local Area Connection Properties dialog will be displayed. Click Install.

3. In the Select Network Component Type dialog, select Protocol and then click the Add button.

4. In the Select Network Protocol dialog, highlight the entry for NWLink IPX/SPX/NetBIOS Compatible Transport Protocol and then click OK. The protocol is installed, and you are returned to the Local Area Connection Properties dialog box.

5. Scroll through the This Connection Uses the Following Items field. You will see that two new items have been added to the list: NWlink NetBIOS and NWLink IPX/SPX/NetBios Compatible Transport Protocol.

NetBEUI

Despite the prominence of TCP/IP, you may still encounter other protocols, particularly on legacy networks. One protocol that was once popular, but has since fallen out of favor is NetBEUI. NetBEUI is a simple but fast protocol designed by Microsoft and IBM in the mid-1980s. The speed of NetBEUI can be attributed to the fact that it has very little overhead, but this in turn means that NetBEUI has limited functionality. Although it is now not commonly implemented, NetBEUI is still sometimes used on small networks, such as those in home offices and small businesses.

The biggest limitation of the NetBEUI protocol is that it is not routable. Thus, an organization that requires more than a single segment cannot use NetBEUI. Bridges can be used to divide up a network that uses NetBEUI, but in reality few people bother to do this anymore and instead just use a protocol such as TCP/IP.

Mapping NetBEUI to the OSI Model

NetBEUI is a simplistic network protocol and as such does not map to many layers of the OSI model. Specifically, the NetBEUI protocol operates only at the transport and network layers of the OSI model. Because NetBEUI operates at only two layers, other protocols are needed to help in the network communication process. NetBEUI requires NetBIOS, which maps to the session layer of the OSI model, to establish a connection between two network devices; it needs a redirector to allow client systems to see network resources; and it needs the Server Message Block (SMB) protocol, which maps to the presentation layer of the OSI model, to provide communication between client redirectors and network services.

NetBEUI Addressing

Compared to the addressing schemes of IPX/SPX and TCP/IP, NetBEUI's is very simple. NetBEUI allows the computers on a network to be identified by *NetBIOS name*. In older implementations, such as on Windows NT4 and Windows 95/98 the NetBIOS name must be no more than 15 characters in length, and it must be unique to the network. A NetBIOS name can be made up of any combination of characters, with the exclusion of certain special characters such as spaces.

NOTE

FQDN With the introduction of Windows 2000, Microsoft moved away from the NetBEUI addressing scheme described here. Instead of the 15-character naming, Windows 2000 uses the fully qualified domain name (FQDN) of the system.

You can create NetBEUI names such as *workstation1* and *fileserver*. As you can imagine, such a scheme works well in small environments that don't have many systems; in the few cases where you come across NetBEUI, they will be in exactly these kinds of environments.

NetBEUI was designed and is well suited for small networks that have no need for routing. Its ease of configuration and maintenance also make it suitable for network environments in which administrative support is not always accessible. At the end of the day, however, its limitations exclude it from most networking environments, and therefore it is becoming extinct.

AppleTalk/AppleTalk over IP (Internet Protocol)

As you might have surmised, AppleTalk is the name given to the protocol used on Apple networks. The roots of the AppleTalk protocol can be traced back to the early 1980s. The first implementation of AppleTalk was limited and not suitable for internetworks. Late in the 1980s, however, significant improvements were made to the protocol; it then allowed for support of internetworking by supporting network addresses. Although you may still encounter AppleTalk networks in your travels, AppleTalk is slowly being phased out, and TCP/IP is being used as its replacement.

> **NOTE**
>
> **AppleTalk over IP** The CompTIA objective for this topic cites AppleTalk over IP under the same heading as AppleTalk. In reality, AppleTalk over IP, or AppleShare over IP, refers to the use of the AppleTalk Filing Protocol (AFP) over a TCP/IP connection. AFP is a presentation layer protocol that provides file-sharing capabilities on Apple networks. Working with the understanding of the OSI model that was gained in Chapter 4, "The OSI Model," it is easy to see how a presentation layer protocol from one protocol suite (AppleTalk) can run using the rest of the OSI layers from another protocol suite (TCP/IP).

Like the IPX/SPX and TCP/IP protocol suites, the AppleTalk protocol suite is comprised of several protocols. The following are the AppleTalk protocols:

▶ **AppleShare**—AppleShare provides application-layer services. It comprises three different protocols: AppleShare File Server, AppleShare Print Server, and AppleShare PC.

▶ **AppleTalk Address Resolution Protocol (AARP)**—AARP maps the AppleTalk addresses to both Ethernet and Token Ring physical addresses.

▶ **AppleTalk Data Stream Protocol (ADSP)**—ADSP is a session-layer protocol that also performs transport-layer functions. At the session layer, ADSP establishes and releases connections. At the transport layer, it provides sequencing and handles flow control.

- **AppleTalk Filing Protocol (AFP)**—AFP manages file sharing on a network.

- **AppleTalk Session Protocol (ASP)**—Like ADSP, ASP works at the session layer and is used to establish and release connections between devices.

- **AppleTalk Transaction Protocol (ATP)**—ATP is a transport layer connectionless protocol used to establish connections between computers.

- **Datagram Delivery Protocol (DDP)**—DDP provides connectionless service on an AppleTalk network.

- **EtherTalk Link Access Protocol (ELAP)**—ELAP is an implementation of the AppleTalk protocol that is compatible with the Ethernet protocol.

- **Name Binding Protocol (NBP)**—NBP maps computer hostnames to network layer addresses.

- **Printer Access Protocol (PAP)**—PAP is a session-layer protocol used to facilitate printing on an AppleTalk network. PAP also allows connections between file servers and workstations.

- **Routing Table Maintenance Protocol (RTMP)**—RTMP is a distance-vector routing protocol similar to the RIP, which is used by IPX/SPX and TCP/IP. RTMP maintains routing tables for a network.

- **TokenTalk Link Access Protocol (TLAP)**—TLAP is an implementation of the AppleTalk protocol that is compatible with the Token Ring protocol.

- **Zone Information Protocol (ZIP)**—ZIP divides network devices into logical groups called *zones*.

> **EXAM ALERT**
>
> **Know the Functions of the Protocols**   For the Network+ exam, make sure that you understand the functions of the protocols in the AppleTalk protocol suite.

AppleTalk Addressing

Like TCP/IP and IPX/SPX, AppleTalk requires two parts in the addressing system: the network part of the address and the node part. To get a node address, a system must simply be booted on an AppleTalk network. When the system is first brought up on the network, it generates a random node number that is then broadcast to the entire network. If by some unusual circumstance this number is already assigned to another system, a different node number is generated and broadcast to the network.

> **NOTE**
>
> **LocalTalk** AppleTalk is a complete networking protocol that can be made compatible with both Token Ring and Ethernet; LocalTalk was developed for AppleTalk in Apple-only networks. LocalTalk uses carrier-sense multiple-access with collision avoidance (CSMA/CA) as an access method. A LocalTalk network uses shielded twisted pair (STP) media but can be configured to use regular unshielded twisted pair (UTP) or fiber-based media. LocalTalk uses a bus topology and can support up to 32 devices.

The node number must be used in conjunction with a network number, which is assigned by the administrator. When these numbers are used together, they form the network address of the computer.

AppleTalk addresses are 24 bits long; 16 of the bits are used for the network address, and 8 are used for the node address. Having only 8 bits available for node addresses means that there can be a maximum of 254 nodes on each network. However, you can use a strategy called *Extended AppleTalk Network* to get around this limitation. To use this technique, you assign a network a range of addresses rather than a single address.

AppleTalk addresses are expressed in decimal format, with the network and node addresses separated by a period. An example of an AppleTalk address might be 4.67. The four represents the network number, and 67 is the node number.

Another feature of AppleTalk networking that is worthy of note is the *zone*. Zones allow an administrator to divide an AppleTalk network into logical areas to simplify administration and make it easier for users to find network resources.

Mapping AppleTalk to the OSI Model

Like the other protocol suites, AppleTalk can be mapped to the OSI model. Table 5.1 shows the various AppleTalk protocols and the corresponding OSI levels.

TABLE 5.1 AppleTalk Protocols Mapped to the OSI Model

OSI Layer	AppleTalk Protocols
Application	AppleTalk, AppleShare, AFP
Presentation	AFP
Session	ADSP, ZIP, PAP, ASP
Transport	ATP, NBP, RTMP
Network	DDP, AARP
Data-link	LocalTalk,
Physical	LocalTalk, Ethertalk, TokenTalk

AppleTalk Interoperability

Of the three protocol suites discussed in this chapter, AppleTalk is the least interoperable; only Macintosh systems use it as the default protocol. AppleTalk support can be provided on certain other platforms, such as Microsoft Windows, but additional software is required to enable it.

AppleTalk Routing

AppleTalk is a routable protocol (although early versions were not). The routing functionality is enabled by RTMP. Like RIP, which is used on IP- and IPX-based networks, RTMP is a distance-vector routing protocol.

AppleTalk Naming

Systems on an AppleTalk network are assigned names so that users can locate resources more easily than by using network addresses. This functionality is provided by the NBP, which handles the resolution of computer names to network addresses.

Transmission Control Protocol/Internet Protocol (TCP/IP)

Not many technologies have survived the test of time, but TCP/IP can make this claim and then some. In the dynamic IT industry, technologies come and go; new and improved methods, procedures, and equipment replace the old at a staggering pace. TCP/IP is one of the few exceptions to the rule. Not only has it survived in a state similar to its original, but also as other networking protocols have fallen away, networks' dependency on TCP/IP has increased. There may have been pretenders to the protocol crown, but TCP/IP is truly the champion.

A Brief History of TCP/IP

In the late 1970s and early 1980s, the U.S. Department of Defense Advanced Research Projects Agency (ARPA) needed a system that would allow it to share the resources of its expensive mainframe computer systems. From this the ARPANET—the forerunner of today's Internet—was developed.

The original ARPANET network used a communication protocol known as NCP, but limitations were soon discovered, and a new protocol was needed to meet the new networking demands. That new protocol was TCP/IP. TCP/IP soon became the unquestioned leader in the protocol arena; increasingly, networks of all shapes and sizes were using it.

The history of the Internet and the development of TCP/IP have been closely linked and continue to be so today. ARPANET itself was retired in 1989, but its functions were steadily improved, and today we have the Internet. TCP/IP has always been at the root of the Internet; if you are working in network environments that require Internet access, you can expect to be using the TCP/IP protocol. All the major network operating systems include support for TCP/IP.

The TCP/IP Protocol Suite

Although TCP/IP is often referred to as a single protocol, the TCP/IP suite comprises many protocols, many of which have been mentioned already in this chapter. Each of the protocols in the TCP/IP suite provides a different function, and together they provide the functionality we know as TCP/IP.

The TCP/IP protocol suite got its name from the two main protocols in the suite: TCP and the IP. TCP is responsible for providing reliable transmissions from one system to another, and IP is responsible for addressing and route selection. The following are some of the other protocols in the TCP/IP protocol suite:

▶ Address Resolution Protocol (ARP)

▶ File Transfer Protocol (FTP)

▶ Internet Control Message Protocol (ICMP)

▶ Internet Protocol (IP)

▶ Reverse Address Resolution Protocol (RARP)

▶ Simple Mail Transfer Protocol (SMTP)

▶ Transmission Control Protocol (TCP)

Chapter 6, "Working with TCP/IP," is dedicated to explaining the TCP/IP protocol suite. Therefore, the various protocols used in the suite are only listed here. For a complete discussion of the TCP/IP protocol suite and the specific protocols, see Chapter 6.

TCP/IP Standards

Unlike protocols such as AppleTalk and IPX, TCP/IP is not owned by any one party and is not licensed. As a result, anyone can develop TCP/IP compatibility for their products. This open approach has done much to advance TCP/IP as the protocol of choice across platforms and products.

Because of TCP/IP's open nature, development of TCP/IP is performed under a unique system. Standards pertaining to the TCP/IP protocol suite are published in documents known as

Requests for Comments (RFCs). Any proposed idea for new standards or changes to old ones can be found in an RFC. The Internet Engineering Task Force (IETF) is responsible for maintaining and managing the list of RFCs, and any individual, company, or group can submit a new RFC or review and comment on an existing one. Information on the IETF can be found at www.ietf.org. This site also includes a complete list of the RFCs.

TCP/IP Addressing

Addressing in TCP/IP networks is a major topic, and it can take some getting used to. This section explores only the most basic principles of TCP/IP addressing. For a full discussion, see Chapter 6.

In TCP/IP networks, each node is identified by a unique address, as is each network segment. The IP address consists of four sets of 8 bits, referred to as *octets*, which are expressed in numbers and separated by periods. An example of an IP address is 192.168.1.1. This format is commonly referred to as *dotted decimal notation*.

> **EXAM ALERT**
>
> **IANA** The assignment of IP addresses is handled by suborganizations of a global organization called the Internet Assigned Numbers Authority (IANA). To find out more about IANA, go to www.iana.org.

Because a single IP address represents both the IP address of the host and the IP address of the network to which the host is attached, a mechanism is needed to let the system know what part of the address refers to what. That mechanism is the *subnet mask*. The system uses the subnet mask to determine what part of the address refers to the network and what part refers to the node. If part of the address refers to the network, it is assigned a binary value of 1. If it is the node address, it's assigned a binary value of 0. So, if the subnet mask is 255.255.0.0, the first two parts of the address refer to the network, and the last two refer to the node. Using our original address example (192.168.1.1) and a subnet mask of 255.255.0.0, the system is on a network called 192.168, and the node address is 1.1. Figure 5.4 shows how IP addressing works in a simple network.

IP addressing is a complex subject that warrants more than just the basic discussion included here. Chapter 6 provides extensive coverage of the topic.

TCP/IP Interoperability

Of all the protocols discussed in this chapter, TCP/IP is by far the most interoperable—that is, TCP/IP is supported by all the popular operating systems. Over the years, TCP/IP has become the networking protocol of choice for almost all applications. The generic nature of TCP/IP means that systems using it can communicate with each other no matter what operating system is being used. This fact also allows TCP/IP-based services to be platform independent. For example, you might use a Windows 98 workstation on your desktop, but the server that resolves your Internet requests might be a Linux server, and the server that provides file and print services might be a NetWare server. TCP/IP even transcends platforms; it is available in versions for minicomputers and mainframes as well.

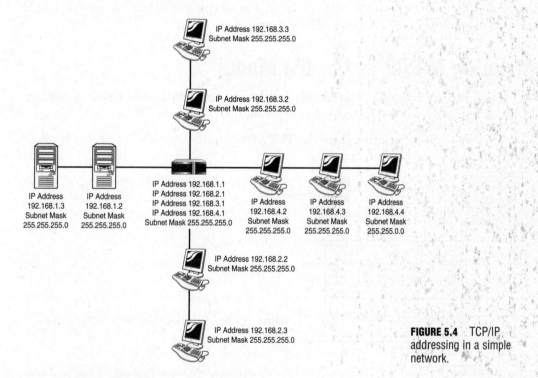

FIGURE 5.4 TCP/IP addressing in a simple network.

TCP/IP Naming

Hosts that run the TCP/IP protocol can be referred to either by their IP address, such as 192.168.4.3, or by a hostname, which can be a more human-readable name such as *server*. Other systems can then communicate by using the IP address or the hostname, although the latter must be resolved before it can be used. This resolution can be performed manually, through a text file, or dynamically, through a server running the Domain Name Server (DNS) service. Again, Chapter 6 provides more information.

TCP/IP Routing Protocols

TCP/IP is a fully routable protocol, making it suitable for use on large networks. Routers on a TCP/IP network can communicate with each other using special protocols called *routing protocols*.

Two routing protocols are commonly used on TCP/IP-based networks: Routing Information Protocol (RIP) and Open Shortest Path First (OSPF). RIP is a distance-vector routing protocol, and OSPF is a link-state routing protocol. For more information on the differences between these two types of protocols, refer to Chapter 3.

Mapping TCP/IP to the OSI Model

As we discussed in Chapter,the OSI model provides a structure by which you can relate how protocols fit together to facilitate network communication.

Figure 5.5 shows the core protocols of the TCP/IP suite and how they map to the layers of the OSI model.

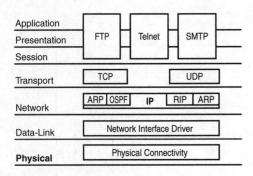

FIGURE 5.5   The OSI model and the TCP/IP protocol suite.

REVIEW BREAK

Protocol Overview and Comparison

As you've seen in this chapter, a number of protocols are used in modern networks, but TCP/IP is by far the most widely implemented of them. Each network protocol has unique characteristics—some good and some not so good. Table 5.2 compares the characteristics of the major protocols.

TABLE 5.2 Protocol Comparison

Protocol	Network Operating System	Routable?	Configuration	Primary Use
IPX/SPX	Used to be the default protocol for NetWare, but now TCP/IP is preferred: can also be used with Linux; Windows supports NWLink, a version of the IPX/SPX protocol suite that was created by Microsoft for cross-platform compatibility	Yes	Very easy to configure because most information is autoconfigured	Primarily used on legacy NetWare networks
NetBEUI	Used by Windows	No	Easy network configuration, requiring only the computer's NetBIOS name	Primarily used on smaller networks where routing is not required
AppleTalk	Used by Macintosh, with some support on other platforms	Yes	Minimal configuration difficulty; required a node address (automatically assigned when systems boot) and a network address	Used on legacy Macintosh networks
TCP/IP	Used by default with Unix, Linux, NetWare, and Windows systems; supported by Macintosh and just about every other computing platform available	Yes	Comparatively difficult to configure; has a number of different configuration requirements	Used on many networks of all shapes and sizes; is the protocol of the Internet

Chapter Summary

This chapter introduces the various protocols commonly found in modern network environments. A protocol is a set of rules that govern how communication and the exchange of data take place between devices on a network.

Several protocols are used today, including, IPX/SPX, NetBEUI, AppleTalk, and TCP/IP. Each offers unique features, advantages, and disadvantages, so certain protocols are more suitable for some network implementations than others. Protocols such as TCP/IP, IPX/SPX, and AppleTalk are in fact protocol suites that consist of several other protocols. Each individual protocol provides a different function for the protocol suite.

TCP/IP is the protocol used for the Internet and is the most widely implemented protocol today. IPX/SPX has lost ground in recent years, and now even Novell NetWare uses TCP/IP as the default protocol. AppleTalk is a protocol suite used for Macintosh networks. On smaller networks, the largely self-configuring NetBEUI can be used, but it has limitations that make it unsuitable for many of today's networked environments.

Key Terms

- AppleTalk
- application protocol
- ATP
- FTP
- IP
- IPX
- LocalTalk
- NetBEUI
- network protocol
- NWLink
- packet
- protocol suite
- RIP
- routing protocols
- SMTP
- SNMP
- SPX
- TCP
- TCP/IP addressing
- transport protocol
- UDP

Apply Your Knowledge

Exercises

5.1 Installing AppleTalk on a Windows 2003 Server

In this exercise, you learn how to install the AppleTalk protocol on a Windows Server 2003 system.

Estimated time: 10 minutes

1. Click Start, Control Panel, Network Connections, and choose the first network interface for your system. If you have only one network interface, choose that. The default name for the first or only network connection is Local Area Connection.

2. The Local Area Network Connection (or whatever your network connection is called) Status dialog box appears. Click the Properties button, which causes the Properties dialog box to be displayed, as shown in Figure 5.6

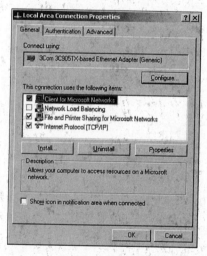

FIGURE 5.6   The Local Area Connection Properties dialog box.

3. Click the Install button, and then from the Select Network Component Type dialog box, choose protocol. Then click Add. The Select Network Protocol dialog box, as shown in Figure 5.7 is displayed.

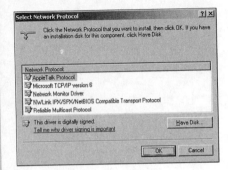

FIGURE 5.7 The Select Network Protocol dialog box.

4. Select AppleTalk Protocol from the list of available options, and click OK. If you are asked to do so, insert the Windows Server 2003 distribution CD or provide a path to the setup files.

5. When you are returned to the Local Area Connection Properties dialog box, the AppleTalk protocol will be listed in the This Connection Uses the Following Items area of the screen as shown in Figure 5.8.

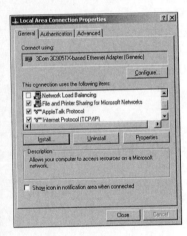

FIGURE 5.8 The Local Area Connection Properties Dialog box with the AppleTalk protocol installed.

6. To configure the AppleTalk protocol, you can select it and then click the Properties button.

Exam Questions

1. At what layer of the OSI model does SPX operate?

   ○ **a.** Physical

   ○ **b.** Transport

   ○ **c.** Network

   ○ **d.** Session

2. Which of the following protocols is not routable?

   ○ **a.** AppleTalk

   ○ **b.** IPX/SPX

   ○ **c.** NetBEUI

   ○ **d.** TCP/IP

3. Which of the following are considered transport protocols? (Choose the two best answers.)

   ○ **a.** TCP

   ○ **b.** IP

   ○ **c.** UDP

   ○ **d.** NCP

4. Which of the following is an example of a NetBIOS name?

   ○ **a.** 192.168.1.1

   ○ **b.** workstation

   ○ **c.** 00-23-F3-C8-5A-06

   ○ **d.** 0C0E:0832:33EC:AE2C:11AC

5. Which of the following routing protocols has a version for both the TCP/IP and IPX/SPX protocol suites?

   ○ **a.** RIP

   ○ **b.** RTMP

   ○ **c.** NLSP

   ○ **d.** OSPF

6. Which of the following protocols is responsible for connectionless service on an AppleTalk network?

   ○ **a.** DCP

   ○ **b.** DLC

   ○ **c.** DDP

   ○ **d.** CCP

7. Which of the following are routing protocols used with the IPX/SPX protocol suite? (Choose the two best answers.)

○ **a.** NLSP

○ **b.** RIP

○ **c.** NCP

○ **d.** IPX

8. Which of the following protocol suites uses ZIP?

○ **a.** AppleTalk

○ **b.** NetBEUI

○ **c.** TCP/IP

○ **d.** IPX/SPX

9. Which of the following is an example of an IPX address?

○ **a.** 0C0E:0832:33EC:AE2C:11AC

○ **b.** 00-23-F3-C8-5A-06

○ **c.** 192.168.1.1

○ **d.** 0C0K:0832:33EC:AH2C:11AC

10. At which layer of the OSI model does the IPX protocol function?

○ **a.** Network

○ **b.** Session

○ **c.** Application

○ **d.** Data-link

11. You have been tasked with specifying a network for a customer. The network consists of three segments connected by two routers. When it is first installed, the network will have two Windows 2000 systems, one Linux server, and a NetWare server. In the near future, the client will be adding an IBM minicomputer running OS/400. Which of the following network protocols would you recommend for the installation?

○ **a.** IPX/SPX

○ **b.** AppleTalk

○ **c.** NetBEUI

○ **d.** TCP/IP

12. Which of the following protocols are distance-vector routing protocols? (Choose the two best answers.)

   ○ **a.** RTMP

   ○ **b.** ARP

   ○ **c.** RIP

   ○ **d.** RARP

13. Which of the following are considered application protocols? (Choose the two best answers.)

   ○ **a.** TCP

   ○ **b.** IP

   ○ **c.** AFP

   ○ **d.** FTP

14. Which of the following protocols is used by the IPX/SPX protocol suite to advertise the availability of resources on the network?

   ○ **a.** RIP

   ○ **b.** SAP

   ○ **c.** NLSP

   ○ **d.** NCP

15. NWLink is a version of what protocol suite?

   ○ **a.** TCP/IP

   ○ **b.** IPX/SPX

   ○ **c.** NetBEUI

   ○ **d.** AppleTalk

16. You are designing a new network installation for a client. The network consists of three segments separated by routers. The client wants to make sure that configuration of the workstation addresses is as simple as possible. Which of the following protocols are you most likely to recommend?

   ○ **a.** TCP/IP

   ○ **b.** AppleTalk

   ○ **c.** NetBEUI

   ○ **d.** IPX/SPX

17. In an AppleTalk network, what is the function of a zone?

    ○ **a.** It defines physical boundaries on the network.

    ○ **b.** It allows administrators to manage systems based on a system-generated zone ID.

    ○ **c.** It creates a password system that is common across a group of computers.

    ○ **d.** It allows the network to be broken up into logical administrative units.

18. Which of the following protocols is not part of the IPX/SPX protocol suite?

    ○ **a.** NCP

    ○ **b.** NLSP

    ○ **c.** UDP

    ○ **d.** RIP

19. TCP is an example of what kind of transport protocol?

    ○ **a.** Connection-oriented

    ○ **b.** Connection-reliant

    ○ **c.** Connection-dependent

    ○ **d.** Connectionless

20. In the IPX/SPX protocol suite, what is the function of NCP?

    ○ **a.** It is used to advertise services on the network.

    ○ **b.** It is a connectionless transport protocol.

    ○ **c.** It provides application-level functionality to clients.

    ○ **d.** It is a link-state routing protocol.

Answers to Exam Questions

1. **b.** SPX operates at the transport layer of the OSI model. None of the other answers are valid. For more information, see the section "Internetwork Packet Exchange/Sequenced Packet Exchange (IPX/SPX)," in this chapter.

2. **c.** NetBEUI is not a routable protocol. All the protocols listed are routable. For more information, see the section "NetBEUI," in this chapter.

3. **a, c.** Both UDP and TCP are transport protocols. IP is a network protocol, and NCP is an application protocol. For more information, see the section "Transport Protocols," in this chapter.

4. **b.** NetBIOS addresses are typically descriptive words such as *workstation*. Answer a is an IP address, Answer c is a MAC address, and Answer d is an example of an IPv6 address. For more information, see the section "NetBEUI," in this chapter.

5. **a.** Versions of RIP are available for both TCP/IP and IPX/SPX. RTMP is a routing protocol associated with AppleTalk, NLSP is a link-state routing protocol associated with the IPX/SPX protocol suite, and OSPF is a link-state routing protocol associated with TCP/IP. For more information, see the section "Transmission Control Protocol/Internet Protocol (TCP/IP)," in this chapter.

6. **c.** DDP provides connectionless communication on AppleTalk networks. None of the other answers are valid. For more information, see the section "AppleTalk/AppleTalk over IP (Internet Protocol)," in this chapter.

7. **a, b.** NLSP and RIP are routing protocols used on IPX/SPX networks. NCP is an application protocol used on IPX/SPX networks, and IPX is a network protocol. For more information, see the section "Internetwork Packet Exchange/Sequenced Packet Exchange (IPX/SPX)," in this chapter.

8. **a.** AppleTalk uses ZIP. None of the other answers are valid. For more information, see the section "AppleTalk/AppleTalk over IP (Internet Protocol)," in this chapter.

9. **a.** IPX addresses are expressed in hexadecimal format, and so can only include the numbers and the letters A through F. Answer b is a MAC address, Answer c is an IP address, and Answer d is not a valid network address. For more information, see the section "Internetwork Packet Exchange/Sequenced Packet Exchange (IPX/SPX)," in this chapter.

10. **a.** IPX functions at both the network layer of the OSI model and the transport layer. It does not operate at the session, application, or data-link layers of the OSI model. For more information, see the section "Internetwork Packet Exchange/Sequenced Packet Exchange (IPX/SPX)," in this chapter.

11. **d.** The only protocol suitable for this environment is TCP/IP. None of the other protocols accommodate all the computing platforms listed in the question. For more information, see the section "Transmission Control Protocol/Internet Protocol (TCP/IP)," in this chapter.

12. **a, c.** Both RTMP and RIP are distance-vector routing protocols. ARP is not a routing protocol; like RARP, it is an address resolution protocol. For more information, see the section "Transmission Control Protocol/Internet Protocol (TCP/IP)," in this chapter.

13. **c, d.** Both AFP and FTP are application protocols. TCP is a transport protocol, and IP is a network protocol. For more information, see the section "Transmission Control Protocol/Internet Protocol (TCP/IP)," in this chapter.

14. **b.** SAP is used by systems to advertise services on the network. RIP and NLSP are both routing protocols, and NCP is an application protocol. For more information, see the section "Transmission Control Protocol/Internet Protocol (TCP/IP)," in this chapter.

15. **b.** NWLink is a version of IPX/SPX created by Microsoft to allow for cross-platform compatibility. TCP/IP is supported natively on Windows platforms, as are NetBEUI and AppleTalk. For more information, see the section "Internetwork Packet Exchange/Sequenced Packet Exchange (IPX/SPX)," in this chapter.

16. **d.** Of the routable and widely supported protocols, IPX/SPX is the most suitable in this environment. TCP is a routable protocol, but the addressing of a TCP/IP network is more involved than IPX/SPX. NetBEUI is not routable and so could not be used in this configuration. For more information, see the sections "Transmission Control Protocol/Internet Protocol (TCP/IP)" and "Internetwork Packet Exchange/Sequenced Packet Exchange (IPX/SPX)," in this chapter.

17. **d.** A zone enables a network to be broken into logical administrative units. None of the other answers are valid. For more information, see the section "AppleTalk/AppleTalk over IP (Internet Protocol)," in this chapter.

18. **c.** UDP is part of the TCP/IP protocol suite. All the other protocols are part of the IPX/SPX protocol suite. For more information, see the section "Transmission Control Protocol/Internet Protocol (TCP/IP)," in this chapter.

19. **a.** TCP is an example of connection-oriented transport protocol. UDP is an example of a connectionless protocol. Connection-reliant and connection-dependent are not terms commonly associated with protocols. For more information, see the section "Transmission Control Protocol/Internet Protocol (TCP/IP)," in this chapter.

20. **c.** NCP provides application-level functionality to clients. It is not used as a connectionless transport protocol. In the IPX/SPX protocol suite that function is performed by IPX. SAP is a protocol in the IPX/SPX protocol suite used to advertise services on the network. NLSP is a link-state routing protocol associated with the IPX/SPX protocol suite. For more information, see the section "Internetwork Packet Exchange/Sequenced Packet Exchange (IPX/SPX)," in this chapter.

Suggested Readings and Resources

1. Habraken, Joe. *Absolute Beginner's Guide to Networking*, fourth edition. Que Publishing, 2003.

2. Ogletree, Terry William. *Upgrading and Repairing Networks, Fourth Edition*. Que Publishing, 2003.

3. "TechEncyclopedia," www.techencyclopedia.com.

4. Information on a wide range of data communications protocols, http://www.protocols.com/.

5. Network+ network protocol tutorial, www.learnthat.com/courses/computer/networkplus/network11.shtml.

CHAPTER SIX

Working with TCP/IP

Objectives

This chapter covers the following CompTIA-specified objectives for the "Protocols and Standards" section of the Network+ exam.

2.5 Identify the components and structure of IP (Internet Protocol) addresses (IPv4, IPv6) and the required setting for connections across the Internet.

▶ IP addressing is perhaps one of the most complex principles in TCP/IP networking. This chapter introduces you to TCP/IP addressing as it relates to real-world networking scenarios.

2.6 Identify classful IP (Internet Protocol) ranges and their subnet masks (for example: Class A, B, and C).

▶ The IP address space is divided into logical parts called *classes*. Understanding the default classes is foundational knowledge for understanding TCP/IP addressing.

2.7 Identify the purpose of subnetting.

▶ Subnetting allows you to maniupulate an assigned IP network address to create more network IDs. It is an important principle of TCP/IP networking.

2.8 Identify the differences between private and public network addressing schemes.

▶ Private network address ranges are now commonly used as a means to provide flexible TCP/IP addressing schemes within organizations. You are very likely to encounter private network addressing in the real world.

2.9 Identify and differentiate between the following IP addressing methods: Static, Dynamic, and Self-assigned (APIPA).

▶ You can assign IP addresses to systems on the network in a number of ways. Understanding the best method to use in a given situation is critical.

2.10 Define the purpose, function, and use of the following protocols used in the TCP/IP protocol suite: TCP, UDP, FTP, SFTP, TFTP, SMTP, HTTP, HTTPS, POP3/IMAP4, Telnet, SSH, ICMP, ARP, RARP, NTP, NNTP, SCP, LDAP, IGMP, and LPR.

▶ The TCP/IP protocol suite is composed of many different protocols. As a network administrator, you need to be able to identify the various protocols and their purposes.

2.11 Define the function of TCP/UDP (Transmission Control Protocol/User Datagram Protocol ports).

▶ Understanding the function and role of ports in TCP/IP networking is a key skill for a network administrator.

2.12 Identify the well-known ports associated with the following commonly used services and protocols: FTP, SSH, Telnet, SMTP, DNS, TFTP, HTTP, POP3, NNTP, NTP, IMAP4, and HTTPS.

▶ Knowing the ports associated with commonly used services and protocols is vital when configuring network connectivity and security.

2.13 Identify the purpose of the network services and protocols: DNS, NAT, ICS, WINS, SNMP, NFS, Zeroconf, SMB, AFP, and LPD.

▶ Many different TCP/IP-related services are used on networks. Understanding the services available and their functions is a key skill in network administration.

Outline

Study Strategies

▶ This chapter contains a great deal of information, so take time to read carefully the information presented.

▶ Complete the challenge exercises provided in this chapter. They serve to reinforce some of the key points taught in this chapter.

▶ To ensure that you understand IP address classes completely, have a friend pick random numbers from the range of 1 to 255 and then identify what class of IP address starts with that number. You can check your answers against Table 6.2.

▶ Have a friend test you using the information provided in Tables 6.3, 6.6, 6.8, 6.9, and 6.12. These tables contain a great deal of information directly relevant to the Network+ exam.

▶ Using the links in the "Suggested Readings and Resources" section at the end of this chapter, research TCP/IP addressing and read information from the different sources.

▶ Complete the practice questions at the end of the chapter.

Introduction

Transmission Control Protocol/Internet Protocol (TCP/IP) is so dominant that it warrants its own chapter. In fact, numerous chapters in this book in addition to this one also provide coverage of the many aspects of TCP/IP. This chapter deals with TCP/IP as a protocol suite, and Chapter 13, "Troubleshooting Tools and Utilities," deals mainly with the troubleshooting aspects of TCP/IP. There is a great deal of ground to cover, so let's get started.

IP Addressing

Objective:

2.5 Identify the components and structure of IP (Internet Protocol) addresses (IPv4, IPv6) and the required setting for connections across the Internet.

Addressing is perhaps the most challenging aspect of TCP/IP. It's certainly a topic that often has many people scratching their heads for a while. The following sections look at how IP addressing works for both IPv4 and the newest version of the IP, IPv6. In today's IT environment, and certainly in the immediate future, IPv4 will remain the protocol of choice for networking. For that reason, this chapter dedicates considerably more time to it.

General IP Addressing Principles

To communicate on a network using the TCP/IP protocol, each system has to be assigned a unique address. The address defines both the number of the network to which the device is attached and the address of the node on that network. In other words, the IP address provides two pieces of information. It's a bit like a street name and a house number of a person's home address.

> **NOTE**
>
> **IP Terminology** Two important phrases in IP addressing are *network address* and *node address*. The IP address defines both, but you must understand that the network address and the node address are different from one another. You need to be aware, also, that some people call the network address the *network ID* and the host address the *host ID*.

Each device on a logical network segment must have the same network address as all the other devices on the segment. All the devices must have different node addresses.

So how does the system know which part of the address is the network part and which is the node part? That is the function of a *subnet mask*. On its own, an IP address is no good to the system because it is simply a set of four numbers. The subnet mask is used in concert with the IP address to determine which portion of the IP address refers to the network address and which refers to the node address.

IPv4

An IPv4 address (which we just call an *IP address* from now on) is comprised of four sets of 8 bits, or octets. The result is that IP addresses are 32 bits in length. Each bit in the octet is assigned a decimal value. The leftmost bit has a value of 128, followed by 64, 32, 16, 8, 4, 2, and 1, left to right.

Each bit in the octet can be either a 1 or a 0. This numbering system is called *binary*. If the value is 1, it is counted as its decimal value, and if it is 0, it is ignored. If all the bits are 0, the value of the octet is 0. If all the bits in the octet are 1, the value is 255, which is 128+64+32+16+8+4+2+1. Figure 6.1 shows a chart representing the binary-to-decimal conversion. In Figure 6.1, the chart is used to derive the decimal of 195.

128	64	32	16	8	4	2	1
1	1	0	0	0	0	1	1

FIGURE 6.1 A binary-to-decimal conversion chart showing how 195 is derived.

By using the set of 8 bits and manipulating the 1s and 0s, any value between 0 and 255 can be obtained for each octet. Table 6.1 shows a few examples of this.

TABLE 6.1 Examples of Numbers Derived Through Binary

Decimal Value	Binary Value	Decimal Calculation
10	00001010	8+2=10
192	11000000	128+64=192
205	11001101	128+64+8+4+1=205
223	11011111	128+64+16+8+4+2+1=223

As mentioned earlier, the IP address is composed of four sets of these bits, each of which is separated by a period. For this reason, an IP address is said to be expressed in dotted-decimal format.

Subnet Mask Assignment

Like an IP address, a subnet mask is a 32-bit address expressed in dotted-decimal format. Unlike an IP address, though, a subnet mask performs just one function: It defines which parts of the IP address refer to the network address and which refer to the node address. For systems to be on the same network, they must have the same subnet mask. Even a 1-bit difference in the subnet mask means that the systems are on different networks.

Broadcast Addresses and "This Network"

Two important concepts to keep in mind when working with TCP/IP are broadcast addresses and the addresses used to refer to "this network." When referring to "this network," the host ID portion of the address is expressed as 0s. So, for network number 192.168, the reference would be 192.168.0.0. For a Class A network number 12, it would be 12.0.0.0.

Broadcast addresses work much the same way as "this network" addresses, except that the host ID portion of the address is set to 255, to reflect that the message is going to be sent to all the hosts on that network. Using the preceding examples, the broadcast addresses would be 192.168.255.255 and 12.255.255.255.

Classless Interdomain Routing (CIDR)

Classless interdomain routing (CIDR) is a method of assigning addresses outside the standard Class A, B, and C structure. By specifying the number of bits in the subnet mask as a specific number, there is more flexibility than with the three standard class definitions.

Using CIDR, addresses are assigned using a value known as the *slash*. The actual value of the slash depends on how many bits of the subnet mask are used to express the network portion of the address. For example, a subnet mask that uses all 8 bits from the first octet and 4 from the second would be described as /12, or "slash 12." A subnet mask that uses all the bits from the first three octets would be called /24. Why the slash? In actual addressing terms, the CIDR value is expressed after the address, using a slash. So the address 192.168.2.1/24 means that the IP address of the node is 192.168.2.1, and the subnet mask is 255.255.255.0.

IPv6

IPv4 has served faithfully for many years, and it seems that it is still not yet ready to yield to the next version of IP, IPv6. However, sooner or later we will be moved to IPv6, so an understanding of what is involved in IPv6 and its addressing is both useful and required for the Network+ exam.

IPv6 Addressing

By far the most significant aspect of IPv6 is its addressing capability. The address range of IPv4 is nearly depleted, and it is widely acknowledged that we are at just the beginning of the digital era. Therefore, we need an addressing scheme that offers more addresses than could possibly be used in the foreseeable future. IPv6 delivers exactly that. Whereas IPv4 uses a 32-bit address, IPv6 uses a 128-bit address that yields a staggering 340,282,366,920,938,463,463,374,607,431,768,211,456 possible addresses. And no, the numeric pad on the PC didn't go nuts; that is actually the number.

IPv6 addresses are expressed in a different format from those used in IPv4. An IPv6 address is composed of eight octet pairs in hexadecimal, separated by colons. The following is an example of an IPv6 address:

42DE:7E55:63F2:21AA:CBD4:D773:CC21:554F

Notice that the format of this address is similar to that used to express a MAC address, although it is longer. Because the address is expressed in hexadecimal format, only numbers and the letters A through F are used in IPv6 addresses.

Other Benefits of IPv6

Although addressing is the biggest change in IPv6, the new version of the protocol will bring a number of other features, including the following:

- ▶ **Smaller header**—Some of the fields included in the IPv4 packet header format have been dropped or made optional. The upshot of this is that IPv6 has lower overhead than IPv4.

- ▶ **Packet labeling**—Packets can be labeled in such a way that they are recognized by a router as being special. This makes it possible for the router to prioritize data.

- ▶ **Improved authentication/security**—Realizing our increasing need for more security and authentication capabilities, the IPv6 specification includes extensions to support features such as IPSec (see Chapter 8, "Remote Access and Security Protocols," for more information).

Most manufacturers are building IPv6 support into their products now, to get ready for the time when we move to the new system. In the meantime, we will continue to use IPv4.

Default Gateways

Default gateways are the means by which a device can access hosts on other networks for which it does not have a specifically configured route. Most workstation configurations actually default to just using default gateways rather than having any static routes configured. This allows workstations to communicate with other network segments, or with other networks, such as the Internet.

> **EXAM ALERT**
>
> **Default Gateways**   For the Network+ exam, you will be expected to identify the purpose and function of a default gateway.

When a system wants to communicate with another device, it first determines whether the host is on the local network or a remote network. If the host is on a remote network, the system looks in the routing table to determine whether it has an entry for the network on which the remote host resides. If it does, it uses that route. If it does not, the data is sent to the default gateway.

NOTE

Default Gateway Must Be Local   Although it might seem obvious, it's worth mentioning that the default gateway must be on the same network as the nodes that use it.

In essence, the default gateway is simply the path out of the network for a given device. Figure 6.2 shows an example of how a default gateway fits into a network infrastructure.

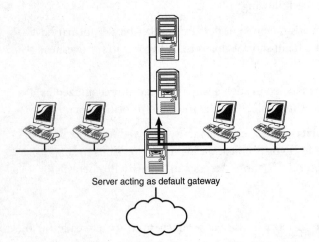

Server acting as default gateway

FIGURE 6.2   The role of a default gateway.

If a system is not configured with any static routes or a default gateway, it is limited to operating on its own network segment.

IP Address Classes

Objective:

2.6 Identify classful IP (Internet Protocol) ranges and their subnet masks (for example: Class A, B, and C).

IP addresses are grouped into logical divisions called *classes*. In the IPv4 address space, there are five address classes (A through E), although only three are used for assigning addresses to clients. Class D is reserved for multicast addressing, and Class E is reserved for future development.

Of the three classes available for address assignments, each uses a fixed-length subnet mask to define the separation between the network and the node address. A Class A address uses only the first octet to represent the network portion, a Class B address uses two octets, and a Class C address uses three octets. The upshot of this system is that Class A has a small number of network addresses but a large number of possible host addresses. Class B has a larger number of networks but a smaller number of hosts, and Class C has an even larger number of networks, as well as an even smaller number of hosts. The exact figures are provided in Table 6.2.

TABLE 6.2 IPv4 Address Classes and the Number of Available Network/Host Addresses

Address Class	Range	Number of Networks	Number of Hosts per Network	Binary Value of First Octet
A	1–126	126	16,777,214	0xxxxxxx
B	128–191	16384	65,534	10xxxxxx
C	192–223	2,097,152	254	110xxxxx
D	224–239	NA	NA	1110xxxx
E	240–255	NA	NA	1111xxxx

Notice in Table 6.2 that the network number 127 is not included in any of the ranges. The 127 network ID is reserved for the local loopback. The local loopback is a function that is built in to the TCP/IP protocol suite and can be used for troubleshooting purposes.

Subnet Masks

Each of the classes of IP address used for address assignment has a standard subnet mask associated with it. Table 6.3 lists the default subnet masks.

TABLE 6.3 Default Subnet Masks Associated with IP Address Classes

Address Class	Default Subnet Mask
A	255.0.0.0
B	255.255.0.0
C	255.255.255.0

EXAM ALERT

Address Classes For the Network+ exam, be prepared to identify into which class a given address falls, as well as the default subnet mask for a given class.

Challenge

In the following table you see six IP addresses. For each line, identify what class the IP address falls into and also provide the default subnet mask for that class. You can compare your answers with the solution table. The first entry is completed as an example.

IP Address	Class	Subnet Mask
151.76.24.77	B	255.255.0.0
129.43.202.105		
65.231.78.101		
207.19.113.72		
192.168.43.102		
7.15.104.24		

Solution Table

IP Address	Class	Subnet Mask
151.76.24.77	B	255.255.0.0
129.43.202.105	B	255.255.0.0
65.231.78.101	A	255.0.0.0
207.19.113.72	C	255.255.255.0
192.168.43.102	C	255.255.255.0
7.15.104.24	A	255.0.0.0

Understanding Subnetting

Objective:

2.7 Identify the purpose of subnetting.

Now that we have looked at how IP addresses are used, we can discuss the process of subnetting. *Subnetting* is a process by which bits from the node portion of an address are used to create more networks than you would have if you used the default subnet mask.

EXAM ALERT

IP Subnetting   IP subnetting is a complex task, and it is difficult to explain fully in the space available in this book. The information provided in this section is more than sufficient to answer any subnetting-related questions you might see on the Network+ exam. In fact, this material goes into more detail than is required. In the real world, subnetting is an important skill.

To illustrate subnetting, let's use an example. Suppose that you have been assigned the Class B address 150.150.0.0. Using this address and the default subnet mask, you could have a single network (150.150) and can use the rest of the address as node addresses. This would give you many possible node addresses, which in reality is probably not very useful. So, what you can do is "borrow" bits from the node portion of the address to use as network addresses. This reduces the number of nodes per network, but chances are, you will still have more than enough.

The simplest use of subnetting in this example would be to use a subnet mask of 255.255.255.0 instead of the default Class B subnet mask of 255.255.0.0. This would give you 254 networks (150.150.1 through .0150.150.254.0), and 254 nodes on each of those networks. The only problem arises if you need more than 254 nodes on each network. You then have to use a process sometimes referred to as *partial-octet* or *fractional subnetting*.

In partial-octet/fractional subnetting, only part of the octet is used to create more networks, and the rest of the octet is still available for assigning as node addresses. Here's how it works. Using the example of 150.150.0.0, let's say that you want to create six networks. To do that, you need to take enough bits from the third octet to create six network addresses, and at the same time, you need to preserve as many node addresses as possible. If you take the first 3 bits, you can use combinations of the bits to create values as the network addresses. Table 6.4 shows the values.

TABLE 6.4   Values of Subnets When Using 3 Bits from an Octet

Binary Value	Decimal Value
000	0
001	32
010	64
011	96
100	128
101	160
110	192
111	224

Because no portion of the address can be all 0s or all 1s, you can't use the 000 and 111 combinations. Therefore, you lose the network assignments of 0 and 224. You are conveniently left with six possible networks.

The bits you are taking are from the left side of the octet. To take this a step further, imagine that you use 5 bits of the octet instead of 3, as in the previous example. Using 5 bits, you would be taking the 128, 64, 32, 16, and 8 binary positions. The network numbers you could use would be 8, 16, 24, 32, 40, 48, 56, 64, and so on up to 248, in multiples of 8, which is the lowest number of the set that was used. In each instance, the available network IDs can be derived by taking the lowest number used, which in the first example is 32 and in this example is 8, and then multiplying up from there.

> **NOTE**
>
> **A Little Subnet Math**   You can use a calculation to work out how many networks you'll get from a number of bits. For example, 2 to the power of the number of masked bits minus 2 equals the number of networks, and 2 to the power of the number of unmasked bits minus 2 gives you the number of nodes on the network. You have to subtract 2 from the total in each case because you can't have a portion of the address as all 1s or all 0s.

Let's look at another example. Imagine that you have been assigned the address 211.106.15.0. You need to have at least four networks. What would the subnet mask be, and what are the network IDs that you could use?

The subnet mask would be 255.255.255.224. To create four networks, you would need to use 3 bits (128, 64, and 32). This would give you six possible networks (32, 64, 96, 128, 160, and 192). It's simple! Remember that, as was discussed earlier, you can't use the values that correspond to all 0s or all 1s when working with subnets, which is why the network numbers 0 and 224 are not included.

The network addresses that can be derived from an address of 211.106.15.0 and a subnet mask of 255.255.255.224 are shown in Table 6.5, along with the usable address ranges for each network.

TABLE 6.5   Subnetted Network Addresses from the Address 211.106.15.0

Network Address	Usable Address Range
211.106.15.32	211.106.15.33–211.106.15.63
211.106.15.64	211.106.15.65–211.106.15.95
211.106.15.96	211.106.15.97–211.106.15.127
211.106.15.128	211.106.15.129–211.106.15.159
211.106.15.160	211.106.15.161–211.106.15.191
211.106.15.192	211.106.15.193–211.106.15.223

The question normally on people's minds is "Okay, but how does this work in the real world?" Using the 211.105.15.0 example as a base, let's look at how the addressing would occur on the client systems. A system with the address 211.106.15.122 would be on the network 211.106.15.96, and the host ID would be 26 (96+26=122). The value of the third octet is the combination of the network address and the host ID.

As you can see, the use of subnetting makes addressing seem more complex, but when you are used to the calculations involved, it's really straightforward.

Reasons to Subnet

There are two main reasons for subnetting. First, it allows you to use IP address ranges more effectively. Second, it provides increased security and manageability to IP networking by providing a mechanism to create multiple networks rather than having just one. Using multiple networks confines traffic to only the network that it needs to be on, which reduces overall network traffic levels. Multiple subnets also create more broadcast domains, which in turn reduces networkwide broadcast traffic.

Public and Private IP Address Schemes

Objective:
2.8 Identify the differences between private and public network addressing schemes.

IP addressing involves many considerations, not least important of which are public and private networks. A *public network* is a network to which anyone can connect. The best, and perhaps only pure example of such a network is the Internet. A *private network* is any network to which access is restricted. A corporate, school, or home network would be considered a private network.

The main difference between public and private networks, apart from the fact that access to a private network is tightly controlled and access to a public network is not, is that the addressing of devices on a public network must be considered carefully, whereas addressing on a private network has a little more latitude.

As we have already discussed, for hosts on a network to communicate by using TCP/IP, they must have unique addresses. The address defines the logical network each host belongs to and the host's address on that network. On a private internetwork with, say, three logical networks and 100 nodes on each network, addressing is not a particularly complex task. On a network on the scale of the Internet, however, addressing is more involved.

Each device on the Internet must be assigned a unique address, often referred to as a *registered address*, in light of the fact that it is assigned to a specific party. If two devices have the same address, chances are that neither will be able to communicate. Therefore, the assignment of addresses is carefully controlled by various organizations. Originally, the organization responsible for address assignments was the IANA, but it has since devolved some of the addressing responsibility to other organizations. Around the world, three organizations shoulder the responsibility for assigning IP addresses. In the Americas and parts of the Caribbean, address assignments are the responsibility of the American Registry for Internet Numbers (ARIN); in the Asia Pacific region, it is the Asia Pacific Network Information Centre (APNIC); and in Europe, the Middle East, and parts of Africa, it is Réseaux IP Européens Network Coordination Centre (RIPE NCC).

NOTE

IPv4 Assignments   You can view the IP address range assignments for IPv4 at www.iana.org/assignments/ipv4-address-space.

Between them, these organizations ensure that there are no IP address space conflicts and that the assignment of addresses is carefully managed.

If you are connecting a system directly to the Internet, you need to get a valid registered IP address from one of these organizations. Alternatively, you can obtain an address from an ISP. Because of the nature of their business, ISPs have large blocks of IP addresses that they can then use to assign to their clients. If you need a registered IP address, getting one from an ISP will almost certainly be a simpler process than going through a regional numbers authority. In fact, getting a number from an ISP is the way most people get addresses. Some ISPs' plans actually include blocks of registered IP addresses, working on the principle that businesses are going to want some kind of permanent presence on the Internet. Of course, if you discontinue your service with the ISP, you will no longer be able to use the IP address the ISP provided.

Private Address Ranges

To provide flexibility in addressing, and to prevent an incorrectly configured network from polluting the Internet, certain address ranges are set aside for private use. These address ranges are called *private ranges* because they are designated for use only on private networks. These addresses are special because Internet routers are configured to ignore any packets they see marked with these addresses. This means that if a network "leaks" onto the Internet, it won't make it any further than the first router it encounters.

Three private address ranges are defined in RFC 1918, one each from Classes A, B, and C. You can use whichever range you want, although the Class A and Class B address ranges offer more addressing options than does Class C. Table 6.6 defines the address ranges.

TABLE 6.6   Private Address Ranges

Class	Address Range	Default Subnet Mask
A	10.0.0.0–10.255.255.255	255.0.0.0
B	172.16.0.0–172.31.255.255	255.255.0.0
C	192.168.0.0–192.168.255.255	255.255.255.0

As you can see, the ranges offer a myriad of addressing possibilities. Even the Class C range offers 254 networks, with 254 nodes on each network, which is more than sufficient for the majority of network installations.

There is no requirement to use these addresses. In fact, many organizations choose not to use them and instead use an addressing scheme of another range. Such a strategy is fine if there is no chance the data from the network will find its way on to a public network. Given that the private ranges are created for this reason and are flexible in terms of accommodating addresses, there is no reason not to use them.

Practical Uses of Public and Private IP Addressing

Having established the purpose of both public and private networks, and of public and private IP addressing, we can now look at how these fit into a practical scenario. It is common practice for a company to have only a handful of registered IP addresses and to configure the internal, private network by using one of the private addressing schemes. Figure 6.3 shows the most basic example of this.

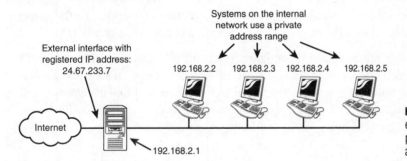

FIGURE 6.3   A basic example of public and private network address assignments.

The network in Figure 6.3 could provide Internet access to clients through the proxy server system. The external interface of the proxy server would have a registered IP address, and all the systems on the internal network would use one of the private ranges.

In this example, the external interface of the proxy server could use an ISP-assigned DHCP address. But what if the company wanted to have the same address all the time for a web server or a web access gateway for its email system? Then you would need to consider how you would assign IP addresses to the systems so that they could be accessed by an outside source.

Assigning IP Addresses

Objective:

2.9 Identify and differentiate between the following IP addressing methods: Static, Dynamic, and Self-assigned (APIPA).

Having established the need for each system on a TCP/IP-based network to have a unique address, we can now go on to look at how those systems receive their addresses. There are two basic ways in which a system can receive an address—*static* and *dynamic*. Microsoft Windows systems also provide an additional feature, called *automatic* or *self-addressing*, but in essence this is a variation of dynamic addressing so we will examine it under that heading.

Static Addressing

Static addressing refers to the manual assignment of IP addresses to a system. In other words, a person has to physically configure the system with the correct IP address. There are problems with this approach, most notably that of human error. Configuring one system with the correct address is simple, but in the course of configuring, say, a few hundred systems, mistakes are likely to be made. If the IP addresses are entered incorrectly, the system will most likely not be able to connect to other systems on the network. If a client system were misconfigured with the IP address of a server, it could even prevent anyone from connecting to the server because both systems may disable their network interfaces as a result of the conflict.

Another drawback of static addressing is reconfiguration. If the IP addressing scheme for the organization changes, each system must again be manually reconfigured. In a large organization with hundreds or thousands of systems, such a reconfiguration could take a considerable amount of time and manpower even if it only occurs infrequently. These drawbacks to static addressing are so significant that nearly all networks use dynamic IP addressing.

> **NOTE**
>
> **Sometimes You Need Static** Some systems such as web servers should always be configured with static IP addresses.

Dynamic Addressing

Dynamic addressing refers to the assignment of IP addresses automatically. On modern networks the mechanism used to do this is the Dynamic Host Configuration Protocol (DHCP). DHCP is a protocol, part of the TCP/IP protocol suite, that allows a central system to provide client systems with IP addresses. Assigning addresses automatically with DHCP alleviates the burden of address configuration and reconfiguration that occurs with static IP addressing.

Dynamic Host Configuration Protocol (DHCP)

DHCP, which is defined in RFC 2131, allows ranges of IP addresses, known as *scopes*, to be defined on a system running a DHCP server application. When another system configured as a DHCP client is initialized, it asks the server for an address. If all things are as they should be, the server assigns an address from the scope to the client for a predetermined amount of time, known as the *lease*. Figure 6.4 shows a representation of DHCP.

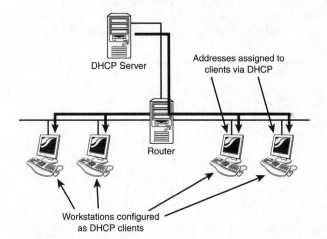

FIGURE 6.4   An example of DHCP.

At various points during the lease (normally the 50% and 85% points), the client attempts to renew the lease from the server. If the server cannot perform a renewal, the lease expires at 100%, and the client stops using the address.

In addition to an IP address and the subnet mask, the DHCP server can supply many other pieces of information, although exactly what can be provided depends on the DHCP server implementation. In addition to the address information, the default gateway is often supplied, along with Domain Name Service (DNS) information.

As well as having DHCP supply a random address from the scope, it's also possible to configure it to supply a specific address to a client. Such an arrangement is known as a *reservation*. Reservations are a means by which you can still use DHCP for a system but at the same time guarantee that it will always have the same IP address.

The advantages of using DHCP are numerous. First, administrators do not have to manually configure each system. Second, human error such as the assignment of duplicate IP addresses is eliminated. Third, DHCP removes the need to reconfigure systems if they move from one subnet to another, or if you decide to make a wholesale change of the IP addressing structure. The downsides are that DHCP traffic is broadcast based, and thus generates network traffic, albeit a small amount. Finally, the DHCP server software must be installed and configured on a server, which can place additional processor load (again, minimal) on that system.

From an administrative perspective, after the initial configuration, DHCP is about as maintenance free as a service can get, with only occasional monitoring normally required.

> **NOTE**
>
> **Platform Independence** DHCP is a protocol-dependent service, and it is not platform dependent. This means that you can use, say, a Linux DHCP server for a network with Windows clients or a Novell DHCP server with Linux clients. Although the DHCP server offerings in the various network operating systems might differ slightly, the basic functionality is the same across the board. Likewise, the client configuration for DHCP servers running on a different operating system platform is the same as for DHCP servers running on the same base operating system platform.

The DHCP Process

To better understand how DHCP works, it is worth spending a few minutes looking at the processes that occur when a DHCP-enabled client connects to the network. When a system configured to use DHCP comes onto the network, it broadcasts a special packet that looks for a DHCP server. This packet is known as the DHCPDISCOVER packet. The DHCP server, which is always on the lookout for DHCPDISCOVER broadcasts, picks up the packet and compares the request with the scopes that it has defined. If it finds that it has a scope for the network from which the packet originated, it chooses an address from the scope, reserves it, and sends the address, along with any other information, such as the lease duration, to the client. This is known as the DHCPOFFER packet. Because the client still does not have an IP address, this communication is also achieved via broadcast.

When the client receives the offer, it looks at the offer to determine whether it is suitable. If more than one offer is received, which can happen if more than one DHCP server is configured, the offers are compared to see which is best. *Best* in this context can involve a variety of criteria but is normally the length of the lease. When the selection process is complete, the client notifies the server that the offer has been accepted, through a packet called a DHCPREQUEST packet, at which point the server finalizes the offer and sends the client an acknowledgment. This last message, which is sent as a broadcast, is known as a DHCPACK packet. When the client system has received the DHCPACK, it initializes the TCP/IP suite and can communicate on the network. Figure 6.5 shows a representation of the DHCP process between a server and a client.

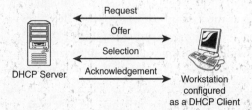

DHCP Server

Request
Offer
Selection
Acknowledgement

Workstation
configured
as a DHCP Client

FIGURE 6.5 The DHCP process.

NOTE

What If the DHCP Server Is on a Different Subnet from the Client? A common question about DHCP is "What happens if the DHCP server is on a different subnet from the client?" Normally, a router is configured not to forward a broadcast, but if the router is configured appropriately, it recognizes that the broadcast packet is a DHCP discovery packet, and it therefore forwards the packet. When it does, however, it embeds in the packet information about which network the packet originated from. This allows the DHCP server to match the source network address with one of its ranges. This strategy allows a single DHCP server to serve the entire internetwork. If the router doesn't accommodate DHCP forwarding, a special service called a DHCP relay agent can be configured on a server. The DHCP relay agent forwards DHCP packets directly to the DHCP server instead of using broadcasts, allowing packets to traverse the routers.

NOTE

Configuring Systems with DHCP Addresses In some configurations, it might not be possible to configure a system with a DHCP address. In other cases, as with a server system, it might be possible but not recommended. This is because certain systems, such as web servers, should always have the same IP address.

Fault-Tolerant DHCP Configurations

It is prudent to have more than one DHCP server to provide fault tolerance; however, you need to consider a number of factors when you use this approach. If multiple servers are used, the scopes defined on each server must not overlap, or else it is highly likely that systems will be assigned duplicate addresses from the different scopes. If you don't have enough addresses to create multiple, non-overlapping scopes, consider configuring the DHCP server functionality on an additional server but not actually enabling the service. That way, if one of the DHCP servers goes down, the other system can be enabled quickly. Thanks to the lease renewal system, having the server down for a short amount of time is unlikely to cause too many problems. This, combined with a robust monitoring system, should ensure that the DHCP service is always available.

Should You Use DHCP?

Given the simplicity of DHCP's setup, the fact that all common network operating systems include a DHCP server free of charge, and the fact that running a DHCP server consumes very little server resources, it's difficult to think of an environment in which a DHCP server is not a good idea. Unless you have a small number of systems (fewer than, say, 10), a DHCP server is a good idea indeed.

BOOT Protocol (BOOTP)

BOOTP was originally created so that diskless workstations could obtain information—such as the TCP/IP address, subnet mask, and default gateway—needed to connect to the network.

Such a system was necessary because diskless workstations had no way of storing the information.

When a system configured to use BOOTP is powered up, it broadcasts for a BOOTP server on the network. If there is such a server, it compares the MAC address of the system issuing the BOOTP request with a database of entries. From this database, it supplies the system with the appropriate information. It can also notify the workstation of a file that it must run on BOOTP.

In the unlikely event that you find yourself using BOOTP, you should be aware that, like DHCP, it is a broadcast-based system. Therefore, routers must be configured to forward BOOTP broadcasts.

APIPA

Automatic Private IP addressing (APIPA) is a feature introduced with Windows 98, and included in all subsequent Windows versions. The function of APIPA is that a system can provide itself with an IP address in the event that it is unable to receive an address dynamically from a DHCP server. In such an event, APIPA assigns the system an address from the 169.254.0.0 address range and configures an appropriate subnet mask (255.255.0.0). However, it doesn't configure the system with a default gateway address. As a result, communication is limited to the local network.

EXAM ALERT

Inability to Obtain an Address from a DHCP Server   If a system that does not support APIPA cannot get an address from a DHCP server, the default action is to configure itself with an IP address of 0.0.0.0. Keep this in mind when troubleshooting IP addressing problems on non-APIPA platforms.

The idea behind APIPA is that systems on a segment can communicate with each other in the event of DHCP server failure. In reality, the limited usability of APIPA makes it little more than a measure of last resort. For example, imagine that a system is powered on while the DHCP server is operational and receives an IP address of 192.168.100.2. Then the DHCP server fails. Now, if the other systems on the segment are powered on and cannot get an address from the DHCP server because it is down, they would self-assign addresses in the 169.254.0.0 address range via APIPA. The systems with APIPA addresses can talk to each other, but they cannot talk to a system that received an address from the DHCP server. Likewise, any system that received an IP address via DHCP would be unable to talk to systems with APIPA assigned addresses. This, and the absence of a default gateway, is why APIPA is of limited use in real-world environments.

> **NOTE**
>
> **APIPA—Smarter Than It Looks** How does APIPA know what address to assign to the system? Before assigning an address, it broadcasts that address on the network. The default action of TCP/IP is to generate an error if it hears from another system with the same address. If APIPA hears this error, it broadcasts another address, and another, from the 169.254.0.0 range until it receives no errors. It then assigns that address to the system. All this occurs invisibly in the background on the computer.

Common TCP/IP Protocols

know 4 next week!!

Objective:

2.10 Define the purpose, function, and use of the following protocols used in the TCP/IP protocol suite: TCP, UDP, FTP, SFTP, TFTP, SMTP, HTTP, HTTPS, POP3/IMAP4, Telnet, SSH, ICMP, ARP, RARP, NTP, NNTP, SCP, LDAP, IGMP, and LPR.

As discussed in Chapter 5, "Overview of Network Protocols," the TCP/IP protocol suite is made up of many different protocols, each of which performs a specific task or function. The Network+ exam focuses on the following, which are some of the most commonly used and encountered protocols.

The following sections look at the functions of these protocols and their purposes.

Internet Protocol (IP)

IP, which is defined in RFC 791, is the protocol used to transport data from one node on a network to another. IP is connectionless, which means that it doesn't guarantee the delivery of data; it simply makes a best effort to do so. To ensure that transmissions sent via IP are completed, a higher-level protocol such as TCP is required.

> **NOTE**
>
> **IP and the OSI Model** IP operates at the network layer of the OSI model.

In addition to providing best-effort delivery, IP also performs fragmentation and reassembly tasks for network transmissions. Fragmentation is necessary because the maximum transmission unit (MTU) size is limited in IP. In other words, network transmissions that are too big to traverse the network in a single packet have to be broken up into smaller chunks and reassembled at the other end. Another function of IP is addressing. IP addressing is a complex subject, so a more detailed discussion of it occurs earlier in this chapter, in the section "IP Addressing."

Transmission Control Protocol (TCP)

TCP, which is defined in RFC 793, is a connection-oriented protocol that uses IP as its transport protocol. Being connection-oriented means that TCP establishes a mutually acknowledged session between two hosts before communication takes place. TCP provides reliability to IP communications. Specifically, TCP adds features such as flow control, sequencing, and error detection and correction. For this reason, higher-level applications that need guaranteed delivery use TCP rather than its lightweight and connectionless brother, UDP.

How TCP Works

When TCP wants to open a connection with another host, it follows this procedure:

1. It sends a message called a *SYN* to the target host.

2. The target host opens a connection for the request and sends back an acknowledgment message called an *ACK* (or SYN ACK).

3. The host that originated the request sends back another acknowledgment, saying that it has received the ACK message and that the session is ready to be used to transfer data.

When the data session is completed, a similar process is used to close the session. This three-step session establishment and acknowledgment process is referred to as the *TCP three-way handshake*.

> **NOTE**
>
> **TCP and the OSI Model**   TCP operates at the transport layer of the OSI model.

TCP is a reliable protocol because it has mechanisms that can accommodate and handle errors. These mechanisms include *timeouts*, which cause the sending host to automatically retransmit data if its receipt is not acknowledged within a given time period.

> **NOTE**
>
> **SYN Flooding**   A problem with the TCP SYN/ACK system is that the TCP/IP protocol stack assumes that each of the SYN requests it receives is genuine. Although this is normally the case, hackers can also exploit this trust as a weakness by using an attack known as a *SYN flood*. In a SYN flood, large numbers of SYN requests are directed at a host, but the source address to which the system attempts to send an ACK is false, and therefore there is no acknowledgement of the ACK. The host, assuming that the lack of response is attributable to a network problem, keeps the SYN connections open for a period of time as a "just in case" precaution, and during this time, the connection cannot be used by another host. If enough false SYN requests are directed at a server, the result is that there aren't any connections left to service legitimate requests. To guard against this occurrence, some applications and operating systems have strategies that determine when a false connection is made, which helps prevent SYN flooding.

User Datagram Protocol (UDP)

UDP, which is defined in RFC 768, is the brother of TCP. Like TCP, UDP uses IP as its transport protocol, but the big difference is that UDP does not guarantee delivery like TCP does. In a sense, UDP is a "fire and forget" protocol; it assumes that the data sent will reach its destination intact. In fact, the checking of whether data is delivered is left to upper-layer protocols.

> **NOTE**
>
> **UDP and the OSI Model**   UDP operates at the transport layer of the OSI model.

Unlike with TCP, with UDP there is no establishment of a session between the sending and receiving hosts, which is why UDP is referred to as a connectionless protocol. The upshot of this is that UDP has a much lower overhead than TCP. In fact, a TCP packet header has 14 fields. A UDP packet header has 4. Therefore, UDP is much more efficient than TCP. In applications that don't need the added features of TCP, UDP is much more economical in terms of bandwidth and processing effort.

File Transfer Protocol (FTP)

As its name suggests, FTP provides for the uploading and downloading of files from a remote host running FTP server software. As well as uploading and downloading files, FTP allows you to view the contents of folders on an FTP server and rename and delete files and directories if you have the necessary permissions. FTP, which is defined in RFC 959, uses TCP as a transport protocol to guarantee delivery of packets.

FTP has security mechanisms used to authenticate users. However, rather than create a user account for every user, you can configure FTP server software to accept anonymous logons. When you do this, the username is anonymous, and the password is normally the user's email address. Most FTP servers that offer files to the general public operate in this way.

In addition to being popular as a mechanism for distributing files to the general public over networks such as the Internet, FTP is also popular with organizations that need to frequently exchange large files with other people or organizations. For example, the chapters in this book were sent between the authors and Que Publishing using FTP. Such a system is necessary because the files we exchange are larger than can be accommodated using email.

> **NOTE**
>
> **FTP and the OSI Model**   FTP is an application layer protocol.

All the common network operating systems offer FTP server capabilities, although whether you use them depends on whether you need FTP services. All popular workstation operating systems offer FTP client functionality, although it is common to use third-party utilities such as CuteFTP and SmartFTP instead. Figure 6.6 shows an FTP session with the site ftp.red-hat.com, from the FTP command-line client included with Windows 2000. Notice that this is an anonymous logon.

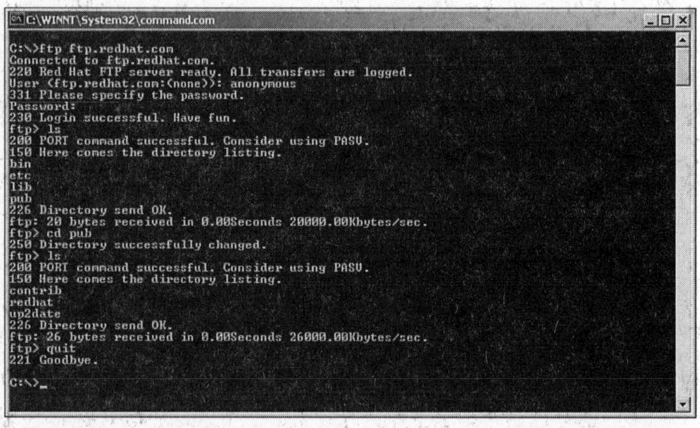

FIGURE 6.6 An FTP session, using the Windows 2000 FTP client.

FTP assumes that files being uploaded or downloaded are straight text (that is, ASCII) files. If the files are not text, which is likely, the transfer mode has to be changed to binary. With sophisticated FTP clients, such as CuteFTP, the transition between transfer modes is automatic. With more basic utilities, you have to perform the mode switch manually.

Unlike some of the other protocols discussed in this chapter that perform tasks transparently to the user, FTP is an application layer service that is called upon frequently. Therefore, it can be useful to know some of the commands supported by FTP. If you are using a client such as CuteFTP, you might never need to use these commands, but they are useful to know in case you find yourself using a command-line FTP client. Table 6.7 lists some of the most commonly used FTP commands.

EXAM ALERT

FTP Commands On the Network+ exam, you might be asked to identify the appropriate FTP command to use in a given situation.

TABLE 6.7 Commonly Used FTP Commands

Command	Purpose
ls	Lists the files in the current directory on the remote system
cd	Changes working directory on the remote host

TABLE 6.7 *Continued*

Command	Purpose
lcd	Changes working directory on the local host
put	Uploads a single file to the remote host
get	Downloads a single file from the remote host
mput	Uploads multiple files to the remote host
mget	Downloads multiple files from the remote host
binary	Switches transfers into binary mode
ascii	Switches transfers into ASCII mode (the default)

Secure File Transfer Protocol (SFTP)

One of the big problems associated with FTP is that it is considered insecure. Even though simple authentication methods are associated with FTP, it is still susceptible to relatively simple hacking approaches. In addition, FTP transmits data between sender and receiver in an unencrypted format. By using a packet sniffer, a hacker could easily copy packets from the network and read the contents. In today's high-security computing environments, a more robust solution is needed.

That solution is the Secure File Transfer Protocol, which, based on the Secure Shell (SSH) technology, provides robust authentication between sender and receiver. It also provides encryption capabilities, which means that even if packets are copied from the network, their contents will remain hidden from prying eyes.

SFTP is implemented through client and server software available for all commonly used computing platforms.

> **NOTE**
>
> **Which SFTP Is It?** In an industry dominated by acronyms, it should come as no surprise that eventually there will be two protocols with the same acronym. In this case, the SFTP acronym is used to describe both the Secure File Transfer Protocol and the Simple File Transfer Protocol. If you are researching additional information for the Network+ exam, make sure that you are reading about the right protocol.

Trivial File Transfer Protocol (TFTP)

A variation on FTP is TFTP, which is also a file transfer mechanism. However, TFTP does not have either the security capability or the level of functionality that FTP has. TFTP, which is defined in RFC 1350, is most often associated with simple downloads, such as those associated with transferring firmware to a device such as a router and booting diskless workstations.

Another feature that TFTP does not offer is directory navigation. Whereas in FTP, commands can be executed to navigate around and manage the file system, TFTP offers no such capability. TFTP requires that you request not only exactly what you want but also the particular location. Unlike FTP, which uses TCP as its transport protocol to guarantee delivery, TFTP uses UDP.

> **NOTE**
>
> **TFTP and the OSI Model**   TFTP is an application layer protocol that uses UDP, which is a connectionless transport layer protocol. For this reason, TFTP is referred to as a connectionless file transfer method.

Simple Mail Transfer Protocol (SMTP)

SMTP, which is defined in RFC 821, is a protocol that defines how mail messages are sent between hosts. SMTP uses TCP connections to guarantee error-free delivery of messages. SMTP is not overly sophisticated, and it requires that the destination host always be available. For this reason, mail systems spool incoming mail so that users can read later. How the user then reads the mail depends on how the client accesses the SMTP server.

> **NOTE**
>
> **Sending and Receiving Mail**   SMTP can be used for both sending and receiving mail. POP and IMAP can be used only for receiving mail.

Hypertext Transfer Protocol (HTTP)

HTTP, which is defined in RFC 2068, is the protocol that allows text, graphics, multimedia, and other material to be downloaded from an HTTP server. HTTP defines what actions can be requested by clients and how servers should answer those requests.

In a practical implementation, HTTP clients (that is, web browsers) make requests in an HTTP format to servers running HTTP server applications (that is, web servers). Files created in a special language such as Hypertext Markup Language (HTML) are returned to the client, and the connection is closed.

> **EXAM ALERT**
>
> **HTTP and TCP**   HTTP is connection-oriented protocol that uses TCP as a transport protocol. You should know this for the exam.

HTTP uses a uniform resource locator (URL) to determine what page should be downloaded from the remote server. The URL contains the type of request (for example, http://), the name of the server being contacted (for example, www.novell.com), and optionally the page being requested (for example, /support). The result is the syntax that Internet-savvy people are familiar with: http://www.novell.com/support.

Hypertext Transfer Protocol Secure (HTTPS)

One of the downsides of using HTTP is that HTTP requests are sent in clear text. For some applications, such as e-commerce, this method of exchanging information is not suitable—a more secure method is needed. The solution is HTTPS. HTTPS uses a system known as Secure Sockets Layer (SSL), which encrypts the information sent between the client and the host.

For HTTPS to be used, both the client and server must support it. All popular browsers now support HTTPS, as do web server products, such as Microsoft Internet Information Server (IIS), Apache, and almost all other web server applications that provide sensitive applications. When you are accessing an application that uses HTTPS, the URL starts with https rather than http—for example, https://www.mybankonline.com.

Post Office Protocol Version 3/Internet Message Access Protocol Version 4 (POP3/IMAP4)

Both POP3, which is defined in RFC 1939, and IMAP4, the latest version of which is defined in RFC 1731, are mechanisms for downloading, or pulling, email from a server. They are necessary because, although the mail is transported around the network via SMTP, users cannot always read it immediately, so it must be stored in a central location. From this location, it needs to be downloaded, which is what POP and IMAP allow you to do.

POP and IMAP are popular, and many people now access email through applications such as Microsoft Outlook, Netscape Communicator, and Eudora, which are POP and IMAP clients.

One of the problems with POP is that the password used to access a mailbox is transmitted across the network in clear text. This means that if someone wanted to, he could determine your POP password with relative ease. This is an area in which IMAP offers an advantage over POP. It uses a more sophisticated authentication system, which makes it more difficult for someone to determine a password.

EXAM ALERT

POP and IMAP   POP and IMAP can be used to download, or pull, email from a server, but they cannot be used to send mail. That function is left to SMTP, which can both send and receive.

> **NOTE**
>
> **Web-Based Mail—The Other, Other Email**   Although there are many good points about accessing email by using POP and IMAP, such systems rely on servers to hold the mail until it is downloaded to the client system. In today's world, a more sophisticated solution to anytime/anywhere email access is needed. For many people, that solution is web-based mail. Having an Internet-based email account allows you to access your mail from anywhere and from any device that supports a web browser. Recognizing the obvious advantages of such a system, all the major email systems have, for some time, included web access gateway products.

Telnet

Telnet, which is defined in RFC 854, is a virtual terminal protocol. It allows sessions to be opened on a remote host, and then for commands to be executed on that remote host. For many years, Telnet was the method by which multiuser systems such as mainframes and minicomputers were accessed by clients. It was also the connection method of choice for Unix systems. Today, Telnet is still commonly used for accessing routers and other managed network devices.

One of the problems with Telnet is that it is not secure. As a result, remote session functionality is now almost always achieved by using alternatives such as Secure Shell (SSH).

> **EXAM ALERT**
>
> **Telnet and Unix/Linux**   Telnet is used to access Unix and Linux systems.

Secure Shell (SSH)

Created by students at the Helsinki University of Technology, Secure Shell (SSH) is a secure alternative to Telnet. SSH provides security by encrypting data as it travels between systems. This makes it difficult for hackers using packet sniffers and other traffic detection systems. It also provides more robust authentication systems than Telnet.

Two versions of SSH are available, referred to as SSH1 and SSH2. Of the two, SSH2 is considered more secure. It should also be noted that the two versions are not compatible. So, if you are using an SSH client program, the server implementation of SSH that you are connecting to must be the same version.

Although SSH, like Telnet, is primarily associated with Unix and Linux systems, implementations of SSH are available for all commonly used computing platforms including Windows and Macintosh. As discussed earlier, SSH is the foundational technology for the Secure File Transfer Protocol (SFTP).

Internet Control Message Protocol (ICMP)

ICMP, which is defined in RFC 792, is a protocol that works with the IP layer to provide error checking and reporting functionality. In effect, ICMP is a tool that IP uses in its quest to provide best-effort delivery.

ICMP can be used for a number of functions. Its most common function is probably the widely used and incredibly useful `ping` utility. `ping` sends a stream of ICMP echo requests to a remote host. If the host is able to respond, it does so by sending echo reply messages back to the sending host. In that one simple process, ICMP enables the verification of the protocol suite configuration of both the sending and receiving nodes and any intermediate networking devices.

However, ICMP's functionality is not limited to just the use of the `ping` utility. ICMP also can return error messages such as Destination Unreachable and Time Exceeded messages. (The former message is reported when a destination cannot be contacted and the latter when the time to live (TTL) of a datagram has been exceeded.)

In addition to these and other functions, ICMP performs *source quench*. In a source quench scenario, the receiving host cannot handle the influx of data at the same rate as the data is being sent. To slow down the sending host, the receiving host sends ICMP source quench messages, telling the sender to slow down. This action prevents packets from being dropped and having to be re-sent.

ICMP is a useful protocol. Although ICMP operates largely in the background, the `ping` utility alone makes it one of the most valuable of the protocols discussed in this chapter.

Address Resolution Protocol (ARP)/Reverse Address Resolution Protocol (RARP)

ARP, which is defined in RFC 826, is responsible for resolving IP addresses to Media Access Control (MAC) addresses. When a system attempts to contact another host, IP first determines whether the other host is on the same network it is on, by looking at the IP address. If IP determines that the destination is on the local network, it consults the ARP cache to see whether it has a corresponding entry.

If there is not an entry for the host in the ARP cache, a broadcast on the local network asks the host with the target IP address to send back its MAC address. The communication is sent as a broadcast because without the target system's MAC address, the source system cannot communicate directly with the target system.

Because the communication is a broadcast, every system on the network picks it up. However, only the target system replies because it is the only device whose IP address matches the request. The target system, recognizing that the ARP request is targeted at it, replies directly to the source system. It can do this because the ARP request contains the MAC address of the system that sent it. If the destination host is determined to be on a different subnet than the sending host, the ARP process is performed against the default gateway and then repeated for each step of the journey between the sending and receiving hosts.

The Reverse Address Resolution Protocol (RARP) performs the same function as ARP, but in reverse. In other words, it resolves MAC addresses to IP addresses. RARP makes it possible for applications or systems to learn their own IP address from a router or DNS server. Such a resolution is useful for tasks such as performing reverse lookups in DNS. RARP is defined in RFC 903.

TIP

ARP Functions   The function of ARP is to resolve the IP address of a system to the MAC address of the interface on that system. Do not confuse ARP with DNS or WINS, which also perform resolution functions, but for different things.

Network Time Protocol (NTP)

NTP, which is defined in RFC 958, is the part of the TCP/IP protocol suite that facilitates the communication of time between systems. The idea is that one system configured as a time provider transmits time information to other systems that can be both the time receivers and the time providers to other systems.

Time synchronization is important in today's IT environment because of the distributed nature of applications. Two good examples of situations where time synchronization is important are email and directory services systems. In each of these cases, having time synchronized between devices is important because without it there would be no way of keeping track of changes to data and applications.

In many environments, external time sources such as radio clocks, global positioning system (GPS) devices, and Internet-based timeservers are used as sources for NTP time. In others, the BIOS clock of the system is used. Regardless of what source is used, the time information is communicated between devices by using NTP.

> **NOTE**
>
> **NTP Rules**   Specific guidelines dictate how NTP should be used. These "rules of engagement" can be found at www.eecis.udel.edu/~mills/ntp/servers.htm.

NTP server and client software is available for a wide variety of platforms and devices. If you are looking for a way to ensure time synchronization between devices, look to NTP as a solution.

Network News Transfer Protocol (NNTP)

The Network News Transfer Protocol (NNTP) is a protocol associated with the posting and retrieval of messages from newsgroups. A *newsgroup* is the name given to a discussion forum hosted on a remote system. By using NNTP client software, like that included with many common email clients, users can post, reply, and retrieve messages.

Although web-based discussion forums are slowly replacing newsgroups, demand for newsgroup access remains high. The distinction between web-based discussion forums and NNTP newsgroups is in the fact that messages are retrieved from the server to be read. In contrast, on a web-based discussion forum the messages are not downloaded. They are simply viewed from a remote location.

NNTP, which is defined in RFC977, is an application layer protocol that uses TCP as its transport mechanism.

Secure Copy Protocol (SCP)

The Secure Copy Protocol (SCP) is another protocol based on Secure Shell (SSH) technology. SCP provides a secure means to copy files between systems on a network. By using SSH technology, it encrypts data as it travels across the network, thereby securing it from eavesdropping. It is intended as a more secure substitute for the Remote Copy Protocol (RCP). SCP is available as a command-line utility, or as part of application software for most commonly used computing platforms.

Lightweight Directory Access Protocol (LDAP)

The Lightweight Directory Access Protocol (LDAP) is a protocol that provides a mechanism to access and query directory services systems. In the context of the Network+ exam, these directory services systems are most likely to be Novell Directory Services (NDS) and Microsoft's Active Directory. Although LDAP supports command-line queries executed directly against the directory database, most LDAP interactions will be via utilities such as an authentication program (network logon) or locating a resource in the directory through a search utility.

Internet Group Management Protocol (IGMP)

As the name suggests, the IGMP protocol is associated with the process of multicasting. *Multicasting* is a mechanism by which groups of network devices can send and receive data between the members of the group at one time, instead of sending messages to each device in the group separately. The multicast grouping is established by each device being configured with the same multicast IP address. These multicast IP addresses are from the 224.0.0.0 address range and are separate from the standard IP address assigned to that device.

The IGMP protocol is used to register devices into a multicast group, as well as to discover what other devices on the network are members of the same multicast group. Common applications for multicasting include groups of routers on an internetwork and videoconferencing clients.

Line Printer Remote (LPR)

Line Printer Remote (LPR) is a protocol that provides a means to connect to print servers across the network. It is a generic printing protocol supported by all commonly used operating systems including Unix, Windows, and Linux.

To use LPR, client software is installed on a system. When a file is sent to print, it is channeled over the network by LPR to a print server or printer. That server or printer runs a print server program, normally the Line Printer Daemon (LPD), which accepts the LPR information and adds that job to the print queue.

REVIEW BREAK

TCP/IP Protocol Suite Summary

Table 6.8 summarizes the details of each of the protocols discussed in the preceding sections. You can use this table for review before you take the Network+ exam.

TABLE 6.8   TCP/IP Protocol Suite Summary

Protocol	Full Name	Description
IP	Internet Protocol	Connectionless protocol used for moving data around a network.
TCP	Transmission Control Protocol	Connection-oriented protocol that offers flow control, sequencing, and retransmission of dropped packets.
UDP	User Datagram Protocol	Connectionless alternative to TCP used for applications that do not require the functions offered by TCP.

TABLE 6.8 *Continued*

Protocol	Full Name	Description
FTP	File Transfer Protocol	Protocol for uploading and downloading files to and from a remote host; also accommodates basic file management tasks.
SFTP	Secure File Transfer Protocol	Protocol for securely uploading and downloading files to and from a remote host. Based on SSH security.
TFTP	Trivial File Transfer Protocol	File transfer protocol that does not have the security or error checking of FTP. TFTP uses UDP as a transport protocol and is therefore connectionless.
SMTP	Simple Mail Transfer Protocol	Mechanism for transporting email across networks.
HTTP	Hypertext Transfer Protocol	Protocol for retrieving files from a web server.
HTTPS	Hypertext Transfer Protocol Secure	Secure protocol for retrieving files from a web server.
POP3/IMAP4	Post Office Protocol version 3/ Internet Message Access Protocol version 4	Used for retrieving email from a server on which the email is stored. Can only be used to retrieve mail. IMAP and POP cannot be used to send mail.
Telnet	Telnet	Allows sessions to be opened on a remote host.
SSH	Secure Shell	Allows secure sessions to be opened on a remote host.
ICMP	Internet Control Message Protocol	Used on IP-based networks for error reporting, flow control, and route testing.
ARP	Address Resolution Protocol	Resolves IP addresses to MAC addresses, to enable communication between devices.
RARP	Reverse Address Resolution Protocol	Resolves MAC addresses to IP addresses.
NTP	Network Time Protocol	Used to communicate time synchronization information between devices.
NNTP	Network News Transport Protocol	Facilitates the access and downloading of messages from newsgroup servers.
SCP	Secure Copy Protocol	Allows files to be copied securely between two systems. Uses Secure Shell (SSH) technology to provide encryption services.
LDAP	Lightweight Directory Access Protocol	Protocol used to access and query directory services systems such as Novell Directory Services and Microsoft Active Directory.
IGMP	Internet Group Management Protocol	Provides a mechanism for systems within the same multicast group to register and communicate with each other.
LPR	Line Printer Remote	Used to connect to and send print tasks to printers and print servers.

TCP/UDP Ports

Objective:

2.11 Define the function of TCP/UDP (Transmission Control Protocol/User Datagram Protocol ports).

The TCP/IP protocol suite offers so many services and applications that a mechanism is needed to identify to which protocol the incoming communications should be sent. That mechanism is a TCP/IP port.

> **NOTE**
>
> **TCP and UDP Ports** CompTIA's objective for this section states, "Describe the functions of TCP/UDP ports," which leaves you wondering whether there is a difference between TCP and UDP ports. In reality there isn't. It's simply that some protocols use UDP, and others use TCP.

Each TCP/IP protocol or application has a port associated with it. When a communication is received, the target port number is checked to see what protocol or service it is destined for. The request is then forwarded to that protocol or service. Take, for example, HTTP, whose assigned port number is 80. When a web browser forms a request for a web page, the request is sent to port 80 on the target system. When the target system receives the request, it examines the port number, and when it sees that the port is 80, it forwards the request to the web server application.

You can understand ports by thinking about the phone system of a large company. You can dial a central number (analogous to the IP address) to reach the switchboard, or you can append an extension number to get to a specific department directly (analogous to the port number). Another analogy is an apartment block. An apartment block has a single street address, but each apartment in the building has its own apartment number. And no, we are not going to suggest a poor comparison between an apartment suite and the TCP/IP protocol suite. Oops, too late!

TCP/IP has 65,535 ports available, but they are broken down into three designations:

- **Well-known ports**—The port numbers range from 0 to 1023. When CompTIA states "identify the well-known ports," as in Objective 2.12, this is what it is referring to.

- **Registered ports**—The port numbers range from 1024 to 49151. Registered ports are used by applications or services that need to have consistent port assignments.

- **Dynamic or private ports**—The port numbers range from 49152 to 65535. These ports are not assigned to any protocol or service in particular and can be used for any service or application.

It is common for protocols to establish communication on one of the well-known ports and then move to a port in the dynamic range for the rest of the conversation. It's a bit like using a CB radio, in that you try to get a "breaker" on Channel 19, but then you go to another channel to have a conversation, leaving 19 open for others.

> **NOTE**
>
> **IANA** You can obtain a list of port numbers from Internet Assigned Numbers Authority (IANA), at www.iana.org/assignments/port-numbers.

Identifying Common TCP/IP Port Numbers

Objective:

2.12 Identify the well-known ports associated with the following commonly used services and protocols: FTP, SSH, Telnet, SMTP, DNS, TFTP, HTTP, POP3, NNTP, NTP, IMAP4, and HTTPS.

Understanding some of the most common TCP/IP port assignments is important because administrators are often required to specify port assignments when working with applications and configuring security for a network. Table 6.9 shows some of the most well-known port assignments. For the Network+ exam, concentrate on the information provided in Table 6.9, and you should be able to answer any port-related questions you might receive.

TABLE 6.9   Some of the Most Common TCP/IP Suite Protocols and Their Port Assignments

Protocol	Port Assignment	TCP/UDP Service
FTP	20	TCP
FTP	21	TCP
SSH	22	TCP
Telnet	23	TCP
SMTP	25	TCP
DNS	53	UDP
TFTP	69	UDP
HTTP	80	TCP/UDP
POP3	110	TCP
NNTP	119	TCP
NTP	123	TCP
IMAP4	143	TCP
SNMP	161	UDP
HTTPS	443	TCP

EXAM ALERT

Port Numbers   Expect to know what port numbers are used for each protocol for the Network+ exam.

NOTE

You may have noticed in Table 6.9 that FTP has two ports associated with it. Port 20 is considered the Data port, whereas Port 21 is considered the Control port. In practical use, FTP connections use Port 21. Port 20 is rarely used in modern implementations.

Although these are the standard ports for each of these protocols, in some cases it's possible to assign other port numbers to services. For example, you might choose to have one web server application listen to the default port 80 while another listens to a different port. The result would be that if a user accesses the server but specifies a different port number, the user would be directed to the other web server application running on the server.

Challenge

You are an engineer for a systems implementation company. A new client calls to ask whether you can provide some guidance on how to configure a new firewall he wants to implement. The client has a relatively small network with only 16 client systems and two file servers. The client provides the following summary of the services that he wants to allow through the firewall:

▶ Users should be able to send and receive email from Microsoft Outlook. An ISP hosts the users' mailboxes.

▶ Users should be able to browse both nonsecure and secure web pages. The company uses the ISP's DNS servers.

▶ Users should be able to access remote servers to download files via FTP.

▶ A timing device in one of the servers maintains time for the entire network, but that server needs access to a time source hosted on the Internet.

▶ Users should be able to access Internet-based newsgroups.

Based on the information provided, what protocols would you inform the client to allow through the firewall, and what port numbers are associated with those protocols?

Challenge Exercise Answer

Based on the information provided, you would likely recommend configuring the firewall to allow SMTP (Port 80) traffic for sending email and POP3 (110) for receiving email. Nonsecure browsing would require HTTP (80), and secure browsing would require HTTPS (443). Name resolutions would be performed via DNS (53). FTP access would require port 20 and 21 to be opened. Time information is transmitted using the NTP protocol (123). Newsgroup access is facilitated through the NNTP protocol on port 119.

TCP/IP-Based Network Services

Objective:

2.13 Identify the purpose of the network services and protocols: DNS, NAT, ICS, WINS, SNMP, NFS, Zeroconf, SMB, AFP, and LPD.

On its own, TCP/IP provides devices with a means to communicate, but combined with other services, such as the following, it can do even more:

- Dynamic Host Configuration Protocol (DHCP)

- BOOT Protocol (BOOTP)

- Domain Name System (DNS)

- Network Address Translation (NAT) and Internet Connection Sharing (ICS)

- Windows Internet Name Service (WINS)

- Simple Network Management Protocol (SNMP)

- Network File System (NFS)

- Zeroconf

- Server Message Block

- AppleTalk Filing Protocol

- Line Printer Daemon

Services such as the ones discussed in the following sections provide functionality far beyond the basics of network communication. They provide a means to manage, administer, and make the most use of a TCP/IP-based network. Today, it is likely that a network of any size uses one or all of the services discussed in the following sections. The first service we'll look at is the Domain Name Service, or DNS.

Domain Name System (DNS)

DNS performs an important function on TCP/IP-based networks. It resolves hostnames, such as www.quepublishing.com, to IP addresses, such as 24.67.164.63. Such a resolution system makes it possible for people to remember the names of, and refer to frequently used hosts, using the easy-to-remember hostnames rather than the hard-to-remember IP addresses.

> **NOTE**
>
> **Platform Independent**   Like other TCP/IP-based services, DNS is a platform-independent protocol. Therefore, it can be used on Linux, Unix, Windows, NetWare, and almost every other platform.

In the days before the Internet, the network that was to become the Internet used a text file called HOSTS to perform name resolutions. The file was regularly updated with changes and distributed to other servers. The following is a sample of some entries from a HOSTS file:

```
192.168.3.45    server1  s1          #The main
                                      file and
                                      print server
192.168.3.223   mail     mailserver  #The email server
```

> **EXAM ALERT**
>
> **The HOSTS File**   On the Network+ exam, you might be asked to identify the purpose and function of a DNS HOSTS file.

> **EXAM ALERT**
>
> **Comments in a HOSTS File**   A comment in a HOSTS file is preceded by a hash symbol (#).

As you can see, the IP address of the host is listed, along with the corresponding hostname. It is possible to add to a HOSTS file aliases of the server names, which in this example are s1 and mailserver. All the entries have to be added manually, and each system to perform resolutions has to have a copy of the file.

Even when the Internet was growing at a relatively slow pace, such a mechanism was both cumbersome and prone to error. It was obvious that as the network grew, a more automated and dynamic method of performing name resolution was needed. DNS became that method.

> **NOTE**
>
> **Resolution Via the HOSTS File**   HOSTS file resolution is still supported by practically every platform. If you need to resolve just a few hosts that will not change often or at all, you can still use the HOSTS file for this.

DNS solves the problem of name resolution by offering resolution through servers configured to act as name servers. The name servers run DNS server software, which allows them to receive, process, and reply to requests from systems that want to resolve hostnames to IP addresses. Systems that ask DNS servers for a hostname-to-IP address mapping are referred to as *resolvers*. Figure 6.7 shows an example of the DNS resolution process.

Because the DNS namespace, which is discussed in the following section, is large, a single server cannot hold all the records for the entire namespace. As a result, there is a good chance that a given DNS server might not be able to resolve the request for a certain entry. In this case, the DNS server asks another DNS server whether it has an entry for the host.

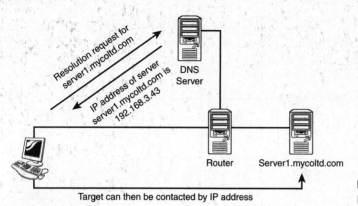

FIGURE 6.7 The DNS resolution process.

> **NOTE**
>
> **DDNS** One of the problems with DNS is that despite all its automatic resolution capabilities, entries and changes to those entries must still be performed manually. A strategy to solve this problem is to use Dynamic DNS (DDNS), a newer system that allows hosts to be automatically registered with the DNS server.

The DNS Namespace

DNS operates in what is referred to as the *DNS namespace*. This space has logical divisions organized in a hierarchical structure. At the top level are domains such as .com and .edu, as well as domains for countries, such as .uk (United Kingdom) and .de (Germany). Below the top level are subdomains associated with organizations or commercial companies, such as Red Hat and Microsoft. Within these domains, hosts or other subdomains can be assigned. For example, the server ftp.redhat.com would be in the redhat.com domain, or another domain called, say, development, could be created, and hosts could be placed in that (that is, ftp.development.redhat.com). Figure 6.8 shows a graphical representation of a DNS hierarchical namespace.

> **NOTE**
>
> **FQDNs** The domain name, along with any subdomains, is referred to as the fully qualified domain name (FQDN) because it includes all the components from the top of the DNS namespace to the host. For this reason, many people refer to DNS as *resolving FQDNs to IP addresses*.

The lower domains are largely open to use in whatever way the domain name holder sees fit. However, the top-level domains are relatively closely controlled. Table 6.10 lists a selection of the most widely used top-level DNS domain names. Recently, a number of top-level domains were added, mainly to accommodate the increasing need for hostnames.

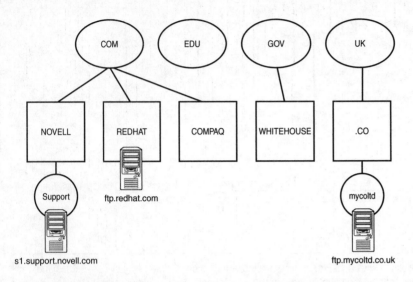

FIGURE 6.8 An example of a DNS hierarchical name-space.

s1.support.novell.com

ftp.mycoltd.co.uk

TABLE 6.10 Selected Top-Level Domains in the DNS Namespace

Top-Level Domain Name	Intended Purpose
com	Commercial organizations
edu	Educational organizations/establishments
gov	U.S. government organizations/establishments
net	Network providers/centers
org	Not-for-profit/other organizations
mil	Military
arpa	Reverse lookup
de	A country-specific domain, in this case Germany*

*In addition to country-specific domains, many countries have created subdomains that follow roughly the same principles as the original top-level domains (for example, co.uk, .gov.nz).

It should be noted that although the assignment of domain names is supposed to conform to the structure in Table 6.10, the assignment of names is not as closely controlled as you might think. It's not uncommon for some domain names to be used for other purposes. In particular, the .net and .org namespaces have been used for purposes other than what was intended.

> **NOTE**
>
> **Reverse Lookup** Although the primary function of DNS is to resolve hostnames to IP addresses, it is also possible to have DNS perform an IP address-to-hostname resolution. This process is called *reverse lookup*.

Types of DNS Entries

Although the most common entry in a DNS database is an A (ADDRESS) record, which maps a hostname to an IP address, DNS can hold numerous other types of entries, as well. Some of particular note are the MX record, which is used to map entries that correspond to mail exchanger systems; and CNAME, or canonical record name, which can be used to create alias records for a system. A system can have an A record and then multiple CNAME entries for its aliases. A DNS table with all these types of entries might look like this:

```
fileserve.mycoltd.com  IN   A     192.168.33.2
email.mycoltd.com      IN   A     192.168.33.7
fileprint.mycoltd.com  IN CNAME fileserver.mycoltd.com
mailer.mycoltd.com     IN   MX  10    email.mycoltd.com
```

As you can see, rather than map to an actual IP address, the CNAME and MX record entries map to another host, which DNS in turn can resolve to an IP address.

DNS in a Practical Implementation

In a real-world scenario, whether you use DNS is almost a non-issue. If you have Internet access, you will most certainly use DNS, but you are likely to use the DNS facilities of your Internet service provider (ISP) rather than have your own internal DNS server. However, if you operate a large, complex, multiplatform network, you might find that internal DNS servers are necessary. The major network operating system vendors are conscious of the fact that you might need DNS facilities in your organization, so they include DNS server applications with their offerings. It should also be noted that Microsoft Active Directory (see Chapter 9, "Networking Operating Systems and Clients") requires DNS to operate.

It is common practice for workstations to be configured with the IP addresses of two DNS servers for fault-tolerance. Figure 6.9 shows an example of this.

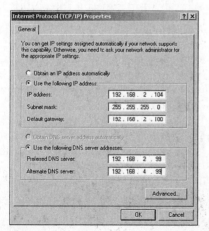

FIGURE 6.9 The DNS entries on a Windows 2000 Professional system.

The importance of DNS, particularly in environments where the Internet is heavily used, cannot be overstated. If DNS facilities are not accessible, the Internet effectively becomes unusable, unless you can remember the IP addresses of all your favorite sites.

Network Address Translation (NAT)

The basic principle of NAT is that many computers can "hide" behind a single IP address. The main reason we need to do this (as you will see earlier in this chapter, in the section "IP Addressing") is because there simply aren't enough IP addresses to go around. Using NAT means that only one registered IP address is needed on the external interface of the system acting as the gateway between the internal and external networks.

NOTE

NAT and Proxy Servers Don't confuse NAT with proxy servers, which are discussed in Chapter 11, "Securing the Network." The proxy service is different from NAT, but many proxy server applications do include NAT functionality.

NAT allows you to use whatever addressing scheme you like on your internal networks, although it is common practice to use the private address ranges, which were discussed earlier in the chapter.

How NAT Works

When a system is performing NAT service, it funnels the requests given to it to the Internet. To the remote host, the request looks like it is originating from a single address. The system performing the NAT function keeps track of who asked for what and makes sure that when the data is returned, it is directed to the correct system. Servers that provide NAT functionality do so in different ways. For example, it is possible to statically map a specific internal IP address to a specific external one (known as the *one-to-one NAT method*), so that outgoing requests are always tagged with the same IP address. Alternatively, if you have a group of public IP addresses, you can have the NAT system assign addresses to devices on a first-come, first-served basis. Either way, the basic function of NAT is the same. Figure 6.10 shows a representation of NAT.

Internet Connection Sharing (ICS)

Although ICS is discussed separately from NAT, it is nothing more than an implementation of NAT on Windows platforms. More specifically, Windows versions since Millennium Edition include the ICS feature, which makes it simple for users to create shared Internet connections.

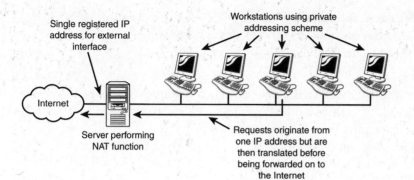

Single registered IP
address for external
interface

Workstations using private
addressing scheme

Internet

Server performing
NAT function

Requests originate from
one IP address but are
then translated before
being forwarded on to
the Internet

FIGURE 6.10 An
example of NAT.

Because ICS was intended as a simple mechanism for a small office network or a home network to share a single Internet connection, configuration is simple. However, simplicity is also the potential downfall of ICS. ICS provides no security, and the system providing the shared connection is not secure against outside attacks. For that reason, ICS should be used only when no other facilities are available.

Windows Internet Name Service (WINS)

On Windows networks, a system called WINS enables Network Basic Input/Output System (NetBIOS) names to be resolved to IP addresses.

> **NOTE**
>
> **NBNS**   WINS is also referred to as the NetBIOS Name Service (NBNS).

NetBIOS name resolution is necessary on Windows networks so that systems can locate and access each other by using the NetBIOS computer name rather than the IP address. It's a lot easier for a person to remember that Mary's PC is called Mary than to remember its IP address, 192.168.2.34. However, even though the system can be accessed, from the user's perspective using the NetBIOS's computer name, this name still needs to be resolved to an IP address and subsequently to a MAC address (by ARP).

A system can perform NetBIOS name resolution in three ways:

▶ **Statically**—A file called LMHOSTS can be manually updated with NetBIOS machine name-to-IP address mappings. It's also possible to make an entry in the file that points to a centrally located LMHOSTS file.

▶ **Via broadcast**—When a resolution is needed, the system can broadcast on the local network for the target host. The broadcast is picked up by all the devices on the local network, and each device looks at the target NetBIOS name to determine whether it is the target system. Only the intended target replies to the request.

▶ **By using dynamic name resolution**—When a WINS server is installed, WINS clients called *resolvers* can pass requests directly to the WINS server and have those requests answered from a database of records.

Of these three methods, the first requires that you manually configure at least one file with the entries. As you can imagine, this can be a time-consuming process, particularly if the systems on the network change frequently. You can forget using DHCP with static resolution. Unless you make reservations for each and every system on the network, the LMHOSTS file is likely to fall out of sync with the network fairly quickly.

EXAM ALERT

Resolving NetBIOS Names In a network that does not use WINS, there are two methods by which NetBIOS names can be resolved: via broadcasts or in the LMHOSTS file.

The second method, broadcasts, works well in a small network environment, but if many devices are on the network, the broadcast traffic can quickly become a problem. Add to that the fact that you can't browse across network segments (which is discussed shortly), and you'll see that the broadcast method is limited in its applications.

There are two basic reasons you might use a WINS server:

▶ **To reduce broadcasts**—In a network that does not have a WINS server, a system uses broadcasts to locate another system. On a large segment, these broadcasts can have a significant impact on network traffic.

▶ **To communicate across routers**—Because NetBIOS resolutions are broadcast based, they are not forwarded by routers. This makes it impossible for a NetBIOS name to be resolved from one segment to another. Although you can configure routers to forward these broadcasts, a more common practice is simply to use WINS. Because systems are configured with the address of the WINS server, it is possible for the client systems to query the server directly for name resolutions.

WINS in the Real World

WINS is a dynamic system. Each time a system is brought on to the network, it registers itself with a WINS server. When the system is taken off the network (that is, when it is powered down), it deregisters itself with the WINS server to make sure that the WINS database is kept up-to-date. For this and many other reasons, it is important that Windows systems are powered down correctly.

It is possible to tune the NetBIOS name resolution by configuring the resolvers to use a specific order of resolution. For example, you can direct them to attempt a broadcast first and then contact a WINS server. Or you can direct them to use only a WINS server and dispense with the broadcast resolution methods completely.

Although you'll find WINS servers implemented in many environments, Microsoft has moved away from WINS as a resolution method and has now standardized on DNS. Windows server versions since Windows 2000 have offered DDNS, which basically eliminates the need for WINS.

Simple Network Management Protocol (SNMP)

SNMP allows network devices to communicate information about their state to a central system. It also allows the central system to pass configuration parameters to the devices.

> **NOTE**
>
> **SNMP Is Not an NMS** SNMP is a protocol that facilitates network management functionality. It is not, in itself, a network management system (NMS).

Components of SNMP

In an SNMP configuration, a central system known as a *manager* acts as the central communication point for all the SNMP-enabled devices on the network. On each device that is to be managed and monitored via SNMP, software called an SNMP agent is set up and configured with the IP address of the manager. Depending on the configuration, the SNMP manager then communicates with and retrieves information from the devices running the SNMP agent software. In addition, the agent can communicate the occurrence of certain events to the SNMP manager as they happen. These messages are known as *traps*. Figure 6.11 shows how an SNMP system works.

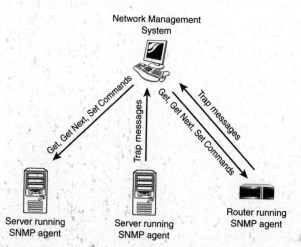

FIGURE 6.11 How SNMP works.

SNMP Management Systems

An SNMP management system is a computer running a special piece of software called a Network Management System (NMS). These software applications can be free, or they can cost thousands of dollars. The difference between the free applications and those that cost a great deal of money normally boils down to functionality and support. All NMS systems, regardless of cost, offer the same basic functionality. Today, most NMS applications use graphical maps of the network to locate a device and then query it. The queries are built in to the application and are triggered by a point and click. You can actually issue SNMP requests from a command-line utility, but with so many tools available, it is simply not necessary.

> **NOTE**
>
> **Trap Managers**   Some people refer to SNMP managers or NMSs as *trap managers*. This reference is misleading because NMS can do more than just accept trap messages from agents.

Using SNMP and an NMS, it is possible to monitor all the devices on a network, including switches, hubs, routers, servers, and printers, as well as any device that supports SNMP, from a single location. Using SNMP, you can see the amount of free disk space on a server in Jakarta or reset the interface on a router in Helsinki—all from the comfort of your desk in San Jose. Such power, though, does bring with it some considerations. For example, because an NMS gives you the ability to reconfigure network devices, or at least get information from them, it is common practice to implement an NMS on a secure workstation platform such as Linux or Windows server and to place the NMS PC in a secure location.

SNMP Agents

Although the SNMP manager resides on a PC, each device that is part of the SNMP structure also needs to have SNMP functionality enabled. This is performed through a software component called an *agent*.

An SNMP agent can be any device capable of running a small software component that facilitates communication with an SNMP manager. SNMP agent functionality is supported by almost any device designed to be connected to a network.

As well as providing a mechanism for managers to communicate with them, agents also can tell SNMP managers when something happens. When a certain condition is met on a device running an SNMP agent, a trap is sent to the NMS, and the NMS then performs an action, depending on the configuration. Basic NMS systems may sound an alarm or flash a message on the screen. Other, more advanced, products may send a pager message, dial a cell phone, or send an email message.

Management Information Bases (MIBs)

Although the SNMP trap system may be the most commonly used aspect of SNMP, the manager-to-agent communication is not just a one-way street. In addition to being able to read information from a device using the SNMP commands Get and Get Next, SNMP managers can also issue the Set command. Having just three commands might make SNMP seem like a limited mechanism, but this is not the case. The secret of SNMP's power is in how it uses those three commands.

> **NOTE**
>
> **SNMP Versions** The version of SNMP in widespread use now is Version 1. Other versions of SNMP are available, but they are not generally used due to a lack of standardization. Later versions of SNMP have more than just the three commands discussed here.

To demonstrate how SNMP commands work, imagine that you and a friend each have a list on which the following four words are written: four, book, sky, and table. If you, as the manager, ask your friend for the first value, she, acting as the agent, will reply "four." This is analogous to an SNMP Get command. Now, if you ask for the next value, she would reply "book." This is analogous to an SNMP Get Next command. If you then say "set green," and your friend changes the word *book* to *green*, you will have performed the equivalent of an SNMP Set command. Sound simplistic? Well, if you can imagine expanding the list to include 100 values, you can see how you could navigate and set any parameter in the list, using just those three commands. The key, though, is to make sure that you and your friend have exactly the same list, which is where Management Information Bases (MIBs) come in.

SNMP uses databases of information called MIBs to define what parameters are accessible, which of the parameters are read-only, and which are capable of being set. MIBs are available for thousands of devices and services, covering every imaginable need.

> **TIP**
>
> **Finding a MIB** Do you want to find a MIB for a device on your network? MIB Central (www.mibcentral.com) provides a searchable database of nearly 2,400 MIBs for a wide range of equipment.

To ensure that SNMP systems offer cross-platform compatibility, MIB creation is controlled by the International Organization for Standardization (ISO). An organization that wants to create a MIB can apply to the ISO. The ISO then assigns the organization an ID under which it can create MIBs as it sees fit. The assignment of numbers is structured within a conceptual model called the *hierarchical name tree*. Figure 6.12 shows an example of the MIB hierarchical name tree.

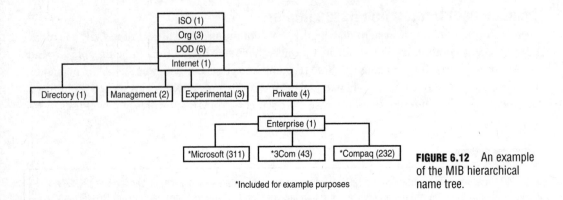

FIGURE 6.12 An example of the MIB hierarchical name tree.

*Included for example purposes

Table 6.11 extends the hierarchical tree further, to show the MIB entry on a Windows NT server, which corresponds to the number of DHCP offers that have been made by that server.

TABLE 6.11 Extending MIB Identifiers to Their Conclusion

Designator	Identifier
International Standards Organization	1
Organization	3
Department of Defense	6
Internet	1
Private	4
Enterprise	1
Microsoft	311
Software	1
DHCP	3
DHCPPar	1
ParDhcpTotalNoOfOffers	5.0

EXAM ALERT

MIB Identifiers Understanding how MIBs work is one thing, and trying to remember MIB designations is another. On the Network+ exam you won't be expected to know what the MIB identifier is for a certain parameter, so don't spend time trying to remember them.

SNMP Communities

Another feature of SNMP that allows for manageability is communities. *SNMP communities* are logical groupings of systems. When a system is configured as part of a community, it communicates only with other devices that have the same community name. In addition, it accepts `Get`, `Get Next`, or `Set` commands only from an SNMP manager with a community name it recognizes. Typically, two communities are defined by default: a public community intended for read-only use and a private community intended for read and write operations.

Whether you use SNMP depends on how many devices you have and how distributed your network infrastructure is. Even in environments that have just a few devices, SNMP can be useful because it can act as your eyes and ears, notifying you in the event of a problem on the network.

Network File System (NFS)

The network File System (NFS) is a protocol and network service that allows you to access file systems on remote computers across the network. Once connected to these remote file systems, they appear to the user as if they were on the local system. NFS is most commonly associated with Unix and Linux operating system platforms, but as an open source protocol implementation, versions of NFS are available for a wide range of server operating systems including Microsoft Windows. From a client perspective, Unix and Linux implementations use NFS as the default file system access mechanism. However, versions of NFS client software are also available for most commonly deployed operating systems.

Zero Configuration (Zeroconf)

Zero Configuration (Zeroconf) answers the call for a means of networking computer systems without requiring configuration time or technical know-how. This approach is becoming increasingly necessary as we use a larger number and wider variety of computing devices in a networked scenario. In fact, although zero configuration networking is obviously of use in creating small ad-hoc networks with computers, its real purpose is to provide a simple means of connecting other "noncomputer" type devices—for example, the garage door opener and the house lights.

There are three basic requirements for a system to support Zeroconf. First, the system must be able to assign itself an IP address without the need for a DHCP server. Second, the system must be able to resolve the hostname of another system to an IP address without the use of a DNS server. Finally, a system must be able to locate or advertise services on the network without a directory services system like Microsoft's Active Directory or Novell Directory Services. Currently, Zero Configuration is supported by Mac and Windows operating systems, as well as by Linux and Unix.

NOTE

Zeroconf and Rendezvous   Although the use of Zero Configuration networking has started to gain ground, Apple has taken the initiative and created its own open standards[en]based Zero Configuration networking system called Rendezvous. A version of the software is available for Microsoft Windows XP, 2000, and Server 2003, as well as for the Mac operating systems. Although Apple created Rendezvous, it has submitted the technology to the IETF for approval in a move that may eventually create an open and widely adopted standard for Zero Configuration networking.

Server Message Block (SMB)

Server Message Block (SMB) is an application and presentation layer protocol that provides a mechanism to access shared network resources such as files or printers on network servers. SMB is the default file access method used on Windows networks. Today, SMB is more commonly referred to as the Common Internet File System (CIFS), though the functionality remains the same. On a network that uses Windows servers and clients, administrators access the functionality of SMB through utilities such as Windows Explorer and the command-line NET utility.

> **NOTE**
>
> **SMB and Samba**   Although Microsoft Windows continues to be the dominant server operating system platform, other operating systems such as Unix and Linux are rapidly gaining ground. To allow Windows clients to more easily use these other server platforms for file and print services, an open source SMB server application called Samba can be implemented. Samba allows Unix and Linux servers to provide file and print services to Windows clients. No additional client configuration is required. For more information on Samba, visit www.samba.org.

Apple File Protocol (AFP)

The Apple File Protocol (AFP), more correctly called the AppleTalk Filing Protocol, is to Apple systems what NFS is to Linux/Unix systems, and SMB or CIFS is to Windows Systems. It is a protocol through which the file system on remote computers can be accessed. AFP is not widely used outside Apple networks, and unless you are working on networks that use Apple Macintosh systems, you are unlikely to encounter AFP.

Line Printer Daemon (LPD)

The Line Printer Daemon (LPD) protocol, which is defined in RFC 1179, provides print services on both client and server systems. The most common use of LPD is as a print server and client on Unix and Linux systems. As well as providing the basic print mechanisms, LPD supports a set of commands that allow the print queue to be controlled. It also provides commands for controlling print jobs after they have been placed in the print queue.

REVIEW BREAK

Table 6.12 helps you quickly identify the purpose and function of each of the TCP/IP services covered in the previous sections.

TABLE 6.12   **Summary of TCP/IP Services**

Service	Purpose/Function
DHCP/BOOTP	Automatically assigns IP addressing information.
DNS	Resolves hostnames to IP addresses.
NAT	Translates private network addresses into public network addresses.
ICS	Allows a single Internet connection to be shared among multiple systems on the network.
WINS	Resolves NetBIOS names to IP addresses.
SNMP	Provides network management facilities on TCP/IP-based networks.
NFS	Provides file sharing between server and client. Typically associated with Unix and Linux operating systems, but versions are available for most commonly deployed operating systems.
Zero Configuration	Provides a system by which devices can communicate with no network configuration or setup.
SMB	Application and presentation layer protocol that provides access to file and print services on server platforms that provide SMB access.
AFP	Provides remote file system access on Apple networks.
LPD	Printing service that provides both server and client printing functions.

Chapter Summary

This chapter discusses some of the aspects of the TCP/IP protocol suite. It looks at some of the most commonly used protocols in the suite, as well as the function of ports and the port assignments for some of the most common protocols. Understanding the functions of the protocols and their associated port assignments is important when you're working with security products and reconfiguring services.

IP addressing is a major topic, and it is important for network administrators to understand it. Of particular importance are the structure of the addresses and the classes in which they fit. Understanding subnetting allows network administrators to use the allocated IP address space in the most efficient way possible.

An important component of configuring TCP/IP addressing on a system is the default gateway. Without a default gateway address, a system can communicate only with other systems on the same subnet.

This chapter also examines the purpose of private and public networks and their role in a TCP/IP network environment. As the IP address space continues to be depleted, such concepts will become increasingly important.

A network that uses TCP/IP has a number of services that offer needed functionality. Services such as DHCP and NAT offer a solution to the time-consuming and sometimes problematic task of IP addressing. DNS and WINS offer name resolution services that can allow users to access hosts by using easy-to-remember names rather than TCP/IP addressing. Another TCP/IP-based service, SNMP, allows a network to be managed from a central location.

Key Terms

- AFP
- ARP
- BOOTP
- default gateways
- DHCP
- DNS
- FTP
- HOSTS file
- HTTP
- HTTPS
- ICMP
- ICS
- IMAP
- IP
- IP addressing
- IPv4
- IPv6
- LMHOSTS file

- ▶ LPD
- ▶ NAT
- ▶ NFS
- ▶ NTP
- ▶ POP
- ▶ private network
- ▶ public network
- ▶ SMB
- ▶ SMTP

- ▶ SNMP
- ▶ subnet mask
- ▶ subnetting
- ▶ TCP
- ▶ Telnet
- ▶ TFTP
- ▶ UDP
- ▶ WINS
- ▶ Zeroconf

Apply Your Knowledge

Exercises

6.1 Installing the DHCP Server Service and Configuring a DHCP Scope

In most networks, clients obtain TCP/IP information from a DHCP server. Therefore, most network administrators are required to both install and manage a DHCP server.

In this exercise, you walk through the steps involved in installing DHCP server software on a Windows Server 2003 system. You also configure and activate DHCP scopes.

NOTE

Authorizing DHCP Servers in Active Directory In an Active Directory environment, DHCP servers must be authorized in the directory before they can issue IP addresses to DHCP clients. Authorization of DHCP servers in Active Directory is beyond the scope of this exercise, but it must be understood in production environments.

Estimated time: 20 minutes

1. Select Start, Control Panel, Add or Remove Programs. The Add or Remove Programs dialog box appears.

2. In the left column of the dialog, click Add/Remove Windows Components. The Windows Components Wizard dialog box, shown in Figure 6.13, appears.

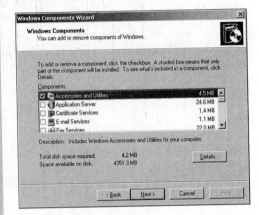

FIGURE 6.13 The Windows Components Wizard dialog box.

3. Scroll down in the Components area of the dialog until you reach the Networking Services entry. Highlight the entry, and click the Details button. The Networking Services dialog, shown in Figure 6.14 appears.

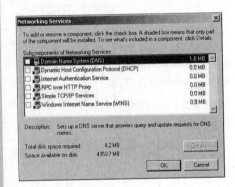

FIGURE 6.14 The Networking Services dialog box.

4. From the Networking Services dialog box, it is possible to install a number of Windows 2000 network services. Select the Dynamic Host Configuration Protocol option and click OK. You are returned to the Windows Component Wizard dialog. Click Next, and the DHCP server software is installed.

5. If your system is already configured to use DHCP—for example, if you use a DHCP address from your ISP—you need to enter a static IP address. For this exercise, you can use one of the private IP addresses discussed in this chapter. An example is 192.168.1.150.

6. After the DHCP server software is installed, the Completing the Windows Component Wizard dialog appears. A shortcut for the DHCP Management Console, shown in Figure 6.15, is added to the Start, Administrative Tools menu.

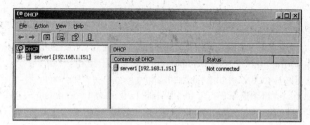

FIGURE 6.15 The DHCP management console.

7. To create a DHCP scope, first open the DHCP Management Console. Then, highlight the server object in the left pane of the utility. Next, from the Action menu, click New Scope. The New Scope Wizard is displayed.

8. From the front page of the New Scope Wizard, click Next. In the Scope Name screen, type a name and description for this scope. In a real-world environment, you would typically choose a meaningful name such as "Head Office" or "Sales." For the purposes of this exercise, use Head Office and then add a description. Click Next when you are finished. The IP Address Range page of the wizard is displayed.

9. On the IP Address Range page, enter the starting and ending IP address of the range you want to include in your DHCP scope. For the purposes of this exercise, use a Start IP Address of 192.168.1.50, and an End IP Address of 192.168.1.100. As you will see, the default subnet mask is generated when the Start IP Address field is completed. This default subnet mask can be altered as needed by using the Length field. The completed page should look like that shown in Figure 6.16.

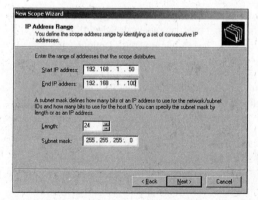

FIGURE 6.16 The IP Address Range page of the New Scope Wizard with Start and End IP addresses configured.

After you check your settings, click Next. The Add Exclusions page of the New Scope Wizard is displayed.

10. The Add Exclusions page allows you to define one or more IP addresses in the defined scope that will not be assigned to systems via DHCP. You can add a single address by entering the same address in both the Start IP Address and End IP Address fields, or define a range of addresses by using the first IP address of the range in the Start IP Address field, and the last IP address of the range in the End IP Address field. For the purposes of this exercise, add a single address exclusion of 192.168.1.63, and a range exclusion of 192.168.1.70 to 192.168.1.75. When you finish, the Add Exclusions screen should look like the example provided in Figure 6.17.

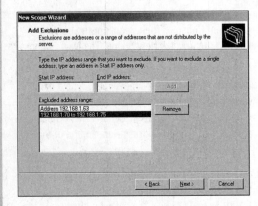

FIGURE 6.17 A single address exclusion and a range exclusion.

When you finish your configurations, click Next. The Lease Duration screen of the New Scope Wizard is displayed.

11. The Lease Duration screen of the New Scope Wizard allows you to define the maximum amount of time an IP address can be kept by a client system before it must be renewed. Select the desired duration, or leave at the default of 8 days, and click Next. The Configure DHCP Options page is displayed.

12. In the Configure DHCP Options screen, select No, I Will Configure These Options Later, and click Next. The final screen in the wizard indicates that you have successfully completed the New Scope Wizard.

13. You are returned to the DHCP Configuration screen, where the newly created scope appears. Notice in Figure 6.18 that beside the scope is a red arrow that points down. This lets you know that the scope is not yet active and cannot give IP addresses to clients. To activate the scope, right-click on the new scope and select Activate from the menu that appears.

14. When the scope has been activated, the red "deactivated" arrow is removed. Figure 6.19 shows an activated DHCP scope.

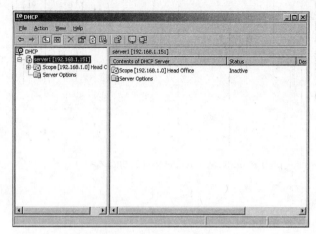

FIGURE 6.18 A deactivated DHCP scope.

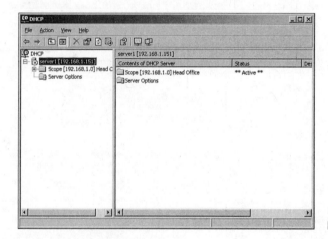

FIGURE 6.19 An activated DHCP scope.

Exam Questions

1. What is the function of HTTP?

   ○ **a.** It allows files to be retrieved from web servers.

   ○ **b.** It provides a mechanism for time synchronization information to be communicated between hosts.

   ○ **c.** It allows virtual terminal sessions to be opened on a remote host.

   ○ **d.** It resolves NetBIOS names to IP addresses.

2. On a DHCP system, what term is given to the period of time for which a system is assigned an address?

  ○ **a.** Rent

  ○ **b.** Sublet

  ○ **c.** Lease

  ○ **d.** Assignment time

3. When using FTP, which command would you use to upload multiple files at once?

  ○ **a.** mget

  ○ **b.** put

  ○ **c.** mput

  ○ **d.** get

4. During a discussion with your ISP's technical support representative, he mentions that you might have been using the wrong FQDN. Which TCP/IP-based network service is he referring to?

  ○ **a.** DHCP

  ○ **b.** WINS

  ○ **c.** SNMP

  ○ **d.** DNS

5. What is the function of ARP?

  ○ **a.** It resolves MAC addresses to IP addresses.

  ○ **b.** It resolves NetBIOS names to IP addresses.

  ○ **c.** It resolves IP addresses to MAC addresses.

  ○ **d.** It resolves hostnames to IP addresses.

6. What is the function of NTP?

  ○ **a.** It provides a mechanism for the sharing of authentication information.

  ○ **b.** It is used to access shared folders on a Linux system.

  ○ **c.** It is used to communicate utilization information to a central manager.

  ○ **d.** It is used to communicate time synchronization information between systems.

7. Which port is assigned to the POP3 protocol?

   ○ **a.** 21

   ○ **b.** 123

   ○ **c.** 443

   ○ **d.** 110

8. You decide to move your network from NetBEUI to TCP/IP. For the external interfaces, you decide to obtain registered IP addresses from your ISP, but for the internal network, you choose to configure systems by using one of the private address ranges. Of the following address ranges, which one would you *not* consider?

   ○ **a.** 192.168.0.0 to 192.168.255.255

   ○ **b.** 131.16.0.0 to 131.16.255.255

   ○ **c.** 10.0.0.0 to 10.255.255.255

   ○ **d.** 172.16.0.0 to 172.31.255.255?

9. Which of the following addresses is a Class B address?

   ○ **a.** 129.16.12.200

   ○ **b.** 126.15.16.122

   ○ **c.** 211.244.212.5

   ○ **d.** 193.17.101.27

10. Consider the IP address 195.16.17.8. Assuming that the default subnet mask is being used, which part of the address would be considered the network address?

   ○ **a.** 195.16

   ○ **b.** 195.16.17

   ○ **c.** 16.17.8

   ○ **d.** 17.8

11. When you are configuring a new server application, the manual tells you to enable access through port 443. What kind of application are you configuring?

   ○ **a.** A virtual terminal application

   ○ **b.** A web-based email application

   ○ **c.** An FTP server

   ○ **d.** A secure website

12. Which of the following is the correct broadcast address for the Class A network 14?

   ○ **a.** 14.255.255.0

   ○ **b.** 14.0.0.0

   ○ **c.** 255.255.255.255

   ○ **d.** 14.255.255.255

13. What is the purpose of a reverse lookup in DNS?

   ○ **a.** It resolves IP addresses to hostnames.

   ○ **b.** It resolves NetBIOS names to IP addresses.

   ○ **c.** It resolves hostnames to IP addresses.

   ○ **d.** It allows you to see who owns a particular domain name.

14. You ask your ISP to assign a public IP address for the external interface of your Windows 2000 server, which is running a proxy server application. In the email message you get that contains the information, the ISP tells you that you have been assigned the IP address 203.15.226.12/24. When you fill out the subnet mask field on the IP configuration dialog box on your system, what subnet mask should you use?

   ○ **a.** 255.255.255.255

   ○ **b.** 255.255.255.0

   ○ **c.** 255.255.240.0

   ○ **d.** 255.255.255.240

15. You are the administrator for a small network of 25 PCs. All the workstations are Windows XP Professional systems, and the server is a Windows Server 2003 system. Presently, the only Internet access is from a single PC that uses a modem, but your manager has asked you to get cable Internet access and share the connection with all the other workstations on the network. Which of the following services might you use to accomplish this?

   ○ **a.** SNMP

   ○ **b.** ICS

   ○ **c.** DNS

   ○ **d.** WINS

16. You are troubleshooting a problem with a system: A single workstation is unable to communicate with a server on another network; however, it can communicate with the other systems on its own subnet. All the other workstations on the subnet can contact the server on the remote network. Which of the following is most likely the cause of the problem?

- ○ **a.** The problem workstation has some faulty cabling.
- ○ **b.** The IP address on the workstation is not configured correctly.
- ○ **c.** There is an incorrectly configured or missing default gateway on the problem system.
- ○ **d.** The remote server is unavailable.

17. Which of the following addresses is a valid IPv6 address?

- ○ **a.** 211.16.233.17.12.148.201.226
- ○ **b.** 42DE:7E55:63F2:21AA:CBD4:D773:CC21:554F
- ○ **c.** 42DE:7E55:63G2:21AT:CBD4:D773:CC21:554F
- ○ **d.** 42DE:7E55:63F2:21AA

18. You are the administrator for a network that uses a Windows Server 2003 system and 45 Windows XP Professional systems. Recently, a new Linux system was installed as a managed web server. None of the users in your organization need access to the Linux system, but you personally need the ability to periodically upload files to the web server. Which of the following strategies are you most likely to employ to do this?

- ○ **a.** Implement SMB functionality on the Linux server.
- ○ **b.** Implement NFS functionality on your Windows XP Professional workstation.
- ○ **c.** Implement LPD functionality on your Windows XP Professional workstation.
- ○ **d.** Implement SMB functionality on your Windows XP Professional workstation.

19. In SNMP, what message is sent by a system in the event of a threshold being triggered?

- ○ **a.** Alert
- ○ **b.** Trap
- ○ **c.** Catch
- ○ **d.** Signal

20. Which of the following port ranges is described as "well known"?

- ○ **a.** 0 to 1023

- ○ **b.** 1024 to 49151

- ○ **c.** 49152 to 65535

- ○ **d.** 65535 to 78446

Answers to Exam Questions

1. a. Web browsers use HTTP to retrieve text and graphics files from web servers. Answer b describes NTP, Answer c describes SSH or Telnet, and Answer d describes the function of WINS. For more information, see the section "Common TCP/IP Protocols," in this chapter.

2. c. The term *lease* is used to describe the amount of time a DHCP client is assigned an address. All the other terms are invalid. For more information, see the section "TCP/IP-Based Network Services," in this chapter.

3. c. The mput command, which is an abbreviation for *multiple put*, allows more than one file to be uploaded at a time. mget is used to download multiple files in a single command, put is used to upload a single file, and get is used to download a single file. For more information, see the section "Common TCP/IP Protocols," in this chapter.

4. d. DNS is a system that resolves hostnames to IP addresses. The term *FQDN* is used to describe the entire hostname. None of the other services use FQDNs. For more information, see the section "TCP/IP-Based Network Services," in this chapter.

5. c. ARP resolves IP addresses to MAC addresses. Answer a describes the function of RARP, Answer b describes the process of WINS, and Answer d describes the process of DNS resolution. For more information, see the section "Common TCP/IP Protocols," in this chapter.

6. d. NTP is used to communicate time synchronization information between devices. NFS is typically associated with accessing shared folders on a Linux system. Utilization information is communicated to a central management system most commonly by using the SNMP protocol. For more information, see the section "Common TCP/IP Protocols," in this chapter.

7. d. POP3 uses port 110 for network communication. Port 21 is used for FTP, port 123 is used by NTP, and port 443 is used by HTTPS. For more information, see the section "TCP/UDP Ports," in this chapter.

8. b. The 131.16 range is from the Class B range and is not one of the recognized private IP address ranges. All the other address ranges are valid private IP address ranges. For more information, see the section "Public and Private IP Address Schemes," in this chapter.

9. a. Class B addresses fall into the range 128 to 191. Therefore, Answer a is the only one of the addresses listed that falls into that range. Answer b is a Class A address, and Answers c and d are both Class C IP addresses. For more information, see the section "IP Addressing," in this chapter.

10. b. The address given is a Class C address and therefore, if you are using the default subnet mask, the first three octets represent the network address. None of the other answers are valid. For more information, see the section "IP Addressing," in this chapter.

11. d. Port 443 is used by HTTPS. Therefore, the application you are configuring is likely to be a secure website application. A virtual terminal application is most likely to use Telnet on TCP/IP port 23, or SSH on port 22. A web-based email application is most likely to use the HTTP protocol on TCP/IP port 80. An FTP server would need access to the TCP/IP port for the FTP protocol, which is 20 and 21. For more information, see the section "TCP/UDP Ports," in this chapter.

12. d. The broadcast address for a network uses the network ID, and all other octets in the address are set to all nodes, to indicate that every system should receive the message. Therefore, with a network address of 14, the broadcast address is 14.255.255.255. None of the other answers are valid. For more information, see the section "IP Addressing," in this chapter.

13. a. A reverse lookup resolves an IP address to a hostname rather than the hostname-to-IP address resolution normally performed by DNS. Answer b describes the functions of WINS, Answer c describes the process of a standard DNS resolution, and Answer d is not a valid answer. For more information, see the section "TCP/IP-Based Network Services," in this chapter.

14. b. In CIDR terminology, the number of bits to be included in the subnet mask is expressed as a slash value. If the slash value is 24, the first three entire octets form the subnet mask, so the value is 255.255.255.0. None of the other answers are correct. For more information, see the section "IP Addressing," in this chapter.

15. b. As its name implies, ICS allows a single Internet connection to be shared among multiple computers. SNMP is a protocol associated with network management systems. DNS is a TCP/IP-based service that performs hostname to IP address resolutions. WINS is a service that performs NetBIOS name to IP address resolutions. For more information, see the section "TCP/IP-Based Network Services," in this chapter.

16. c. The symptoms described indicate that the default gateway configuration on the system in question is likely incorrect. If Answer a or Answer b were correct, you would not be able to connect to other systems on the same subnet. If Answer d were correct, other systems would not be able to access the remote server, which, according to the question, you are able to do. For more information, see the section "Default Gateways," in this chapter.

17. b. IPv6 addresses are expressed in hexadecimal format and can therefore use only the letters A through F and numbers. They are also expressed in eight parts. None of the other answers fit these criteria. For more information, see the section "IP Addressing," in this chapter.

18. b. Installing NFS client software on your Windows XP Professional workstation would allow you to upload files to the Linux server. You are unlikely to install SMB functionality on the Linux server because only one person, you, needs access to the Linux system. LPD is a service related to printing. It is not used to upload files to a server. Windows XP Professional already has SMB functionality because this is the default file access service for Windows platforms. However, it would not allow you to upload files to a Linux server unless an SMB service such as Samba has been installed on the Linux server. For more information, see the section "TCP/IP-Based Network Services," in this chapter.

19. **b.** The term used to refer to a message sent by an SNMP agent when a condition is met is *trap message*. None of the other terms are used to describe the message sent by SNMP. For more information, see the section "TCP/IP-Based Network Services," in this chapter.

20. **a.** Well-known ports are defined in the range 0 to 1023. Answer b describes the range known as registered ports 1024 to 49151. Answer c describes the dynamic, or private, ports, which range from 49152 to 65535. Answer d is not a valid answer. For more information, see the section "TCP/UDP Ports," in this chapter.

Suggested Readings and Resources

1. Habraken, Joe. *Absolute Beginner's Guide to Networking*, fourth edition. Que Publishing, 2003.

2. Sportack, Mark. *TCP/IP First-Step*. Cisco Press, 2004.

3. Shivendra S. Panwar, Shiwen Mao, Jeong-dong Ryoo, Yihan Li. *TCP/IP Essentials : A Lab-Based Approach*. Cambridge University Press, 2004.

4. Hunt, Craig. *TCP/IP Network Administration*, third edition. O'Reilly & Associates, 2002.

5. Subnetting information, www.howtosubnet.com.

6. General TCP/IP and networking information, www.cisco.com.

7. "TechEncyclopedia," www.techencyclopedia.com.

8. Links to various TCP/IP resources, www.private.org.il/tcpip_rl.html.

7

CHAPTER SEVEN

WAN and Internet Access Technologies

Objectives

This chapter covers the following CompTIA-specified objectives for the "Protocols and Standards" section of the Network+ exam.

2.14 Identify the basic characteristics (for example, speed, capacity, and media) of the following WAN (wide area network) technologies:

- ▶ **Packet switching**

- ▶ **Circuit switching**

- ▶ **ISDN (Integrated Services Digital Network)**

- ▶ **FDDI (Fiber Distributed Data Interface)**

- ▶ **T1 (T Carrier level 1)/E1/J1**

- ▶ **T3 (T Carrier level 3)/E3/J3**

- ▶ **OCx (Optical Carrier)**

- ▶ **X.25**

- ▶ Wide area networking is one of the most interesting aspects of a network. Although for the Network+ exam, you will not be expected to understand detailed information about WANs, you will be expected to demonstrate a basic knowledge of the most commonly used WAN technologies.

2.15 Identify the basic characteristics of the following Internet access technologies:

- ▶ **xDSL (Digital Subscriber Line)**

- ▶ **Broadband Cable (Cable modem)**

- ▶ **POTS/PSTN (Plain Old Telephone Service/Public Switched Telephone Network)**

- ▶ **Satellite**

- ▶ **Wireless**

- ▶ The Internet has become an integral component of modern business. Many different methods are used to configure Internet access. Businesses and home users alike must decide which method best suits their needs.

Outline

Study Strategies

▶ Review and compare the various switching methods used.

▶ Identify the main characteristics of WAN technologies including information presented in Table 7.5.

▶ Review xDSL variants and characteristics. Review Table 7.6.

▶ Review the characteristics of wireless Internet access technologies.

▶ Compare and contrast DSL and cable Internet access.

▶ Review the Notes, Tips, and Exam Alerts in this chapter. Be sure that you understand the information in the Exam Alerts. If you don't understand the topic referenced in an Exam Alert, refer to the information in the chapter text and then read the Exam Alert again.

Introduction

In the beginning, there was a single computer. Soon it connected to other computers and became a local area network (LAN). LANs allowed files, printers, and applications to be shared freely and securely throughout an organization. For a short time, a LAN was sufficient in many organizations, but the need arose to interconnect LANs to provide enterprisewide data availability.

As you might imagine, connecting LANs together provided a challenge primarily because of the distances separating them. Some were across town, and some were thousands of miles apart, a long way to run a segment of coaxial cable.

New technologies such as X.25 were introduced that could span these distances, and the wide area network (WAN) was born. Some technologies used by WANs are different from those used by LANs; essentially WANs use different wires and different protocols. In addition, WANs can be far more complex to implement. As far as functionality is concerned, a WAN does exactly what a LAN does: It provides connectivity between computers.

> **EXAM ALERT**
>
> **Be Familiar with WAN** The Network+ exam covers a number of WAN technologies. To answer the WAN-related questions, you need to be very familiar with WAN technologies.

Introduction to Wide Area Networking

Objective:

2.14 Identify the basic characteristics (for example: speed, capacity, and media) of the following WAN (wide area network) technologies:

▶ Packet switching

▶ Circuit switching

▶ ISDN (Integrated Services Digital Network)

▶ FDDI (Fiber Distributed Data Interface)

▶ T1 (T Carrier level 1)/E1/J1

▶ T3 (T Carrier level 3)/E3/J3

▶ OCx (Optical Carrier)

▶ X.25

To implement a WAN there needs to be a way to connect two geographically separated networks. Depending on the financial resources of an organization, a WAN can use a dedicated link between networks to establish communication. Or, the WAN can be created using a larger public network such as the Internet. Before looking at the various WAN technologies available, we'll start our examination of WANs by looking at perhaps the most significant consideration facing anyone who is implementing a WAN: whether to use a public or a private network as a means of connectivity. Both the private and public WAN network services have their advantages and disadvantages, and knowing the difference between them is a good place to start.

Public Networks

The bottom line for many decisions made in networking often has to do with money. This is often true when choosing a WAN networking method. To save money and a certain amount of administrative effort, you can choose to set up a WAN using an existing transmission infrastructure. Two key public networks can be used to establish a WAN: the public switched telephone network (PSTN) and the Internet. Each of these is discussed in the following sections.

The Public Switched Telephone Network (PSTN)

The *PSTN*, often called *plain old telephone system (POTS)*, is the entire collection of interconnected telephone wires throughout the world. Discussions of the PSTN include all the equipment that goes into connecting two points together, such as the cable, the networking equipment, and the telephone exchanges.

EXAM ALERT

Use PSTN to Save Money   If financial cost is a major concern, PSTN is the method of choice for creating a WAN.

The modern PSTN is largely digital, with analog connections existing primarily between homes and the local phone exchanges. Modems are used to convert the computer system's digital signals to analog, so they can be sent out over the analog connection.

Using the PSTN to establish WAN connections is a popular choice, although the significant drawback is the limited transfer speeds. Transfer on the PSTN is limited to 56Kbps with a modem and 128Kbps with an Integrated Services Digital Network (ISDN) connection, and it's difficult to share large files or videoconferencing at such speeds. However, companies that need to send only small amounts of data remotely can use the PSTN as an inexpensive alternative for remote access, particularly when other resources such as the Internet are not available.

The Internet

The Internet has become popular for establishing WAN connections. Using the Internet to provide remote access creates a cost-effective and reliable solution for interconnecting LANs. One of the most common methods of using the Internet for connecting LANs is through the use of *virtual private networks (VPNs)*. Essentially, a VPN uses a public network, such as the Internet, to create a communication tunnel between two points. Unlike private networks, VPNs can be used on an as-needed basis. A connection can be established to a remote location and then dropped when no transmissions are required. Many organizations use VPNs as dedicated links that permanently connect private LANs. The security available for VPNs further makes them an attractive option. Figure 7.1 shows a VPN connection over a public network.

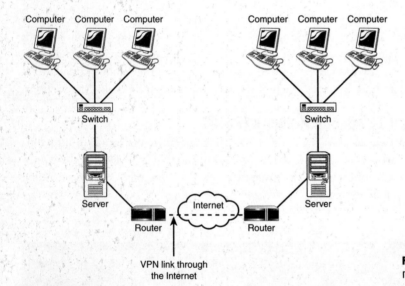

FIGURE 7.1 A VPN connecting two private LANs.

> **NOTE**
>
> **Cable and DSL** The increasing availability of cable and Digital Subscriber Line (DSL) services has meant that companies are increasingly looking toward these technologies as a means to establish VPN connections. Cable and DSL are particularly suited for such a purpose because they offer high speeds for comparatively low cost. They are also available 24/7 for an inclusive cost, which is a bonus over other methods such as ISDN, which may be billed on a usage basis. Cable and DSL, in concert with VPNs, are making it possible for companies to establish low-cost, secure WAN links. Previously, many companies would not have been able to afford a solution that offers this kind of speed, availability, and security.

Public Networks: Advantages and Disadvantages

The biggest advantages of a public network such as the PSTN and the Internet are accessibility and availability. Public network access is everywhere, and perhaps more importantly, it is inexpensive. In addition, the technologies required to use public networks, such as VPNs, are typically easy to configure and can be implemented in a short amount of time. All major client operating systems today ship with the software necessary to create a VPN.

You are most likely to see public networks being utilized by small organizations, where the money for a private network is simply not available or needed. For many small organizations, the capabilities that the Internet provides are sufficient.

As you might have already surmised, there are some drawbacks in using a public network to interconnect LANs. First and foremost is security. When you establish a link over a public network, there is a risk that another user on that network may compromise your data. Technologies such as VPNs put a lot of emphasis on security measures such as encryption and authentication that are aimed at reducing the security risk. Commonly a security protocol called IPSec is used on the connection to ensure that data sent over the link is encrypted and that strict authentication requirements are met. However, if you are sending sensitive data over a public network, there is always a risk. Discussions about the degree of risk are best left to hackers, crackers, and security experts, and that debate is sure to go on for a long time.

In addition to the security risks, there are numerous other considerations concerning public lines, such as disconnections, logon troubles for modems, Internet failures, and a host of other likely and unlikely circumstances. Keep in mind that with a public network you are getting something for nothing—or at least very little—and you will have to make concessions. If you can't live with the drawbacks, you can always switch to a private network.

Private Networks

If we all had unlimited IT budgets, most of us would be using private networking to connect LANs together. Private networks provide a solid way to maintain connectivity between LANs, at least for those who can afford them.

A private network does not suffer from the same considerations of a public network. Many technologies are used to create private networks, and they vary in cost and implementation difficulty. The specific technologies used to create WANs over private networks are discussed in detail in this chapter.

A private network can be designed and implemented from scratch based on an organization's specific needs. The network can be as complex or simple, expensive or inexpensive, secure or insecure as allowed by the budget, location, utilization, and data usage demands. The network can also be designed around the security needs of the data being carried over the network. For instance, fiber-based networks are more secure and more expensive than copper-based networks or wireless networks. A private network can employ various protocols based on security or performance needs. Basically, a private network gives the designer an opportunity to correct most of the problems presented by public networks.

Probably the biggest single disadvantage of a private network is the cost. Whereas the PSTN is yours for the asking at a nominal monthly fee, a private network requires that you purchase or lease every piece of cable, all the network cards, hubs, routers, switches, and so on, until you have enough equipment to go live.

Because of the required networking equipment, private networks often require more administrative effort than public networks, where the networking infrastructure is maintained by outside administrators. Often, a hidden cost associated with private networks is the need for qualified people to manage and maintain them. As the network grows—and it will—it becomes increasingly complex and requires more attention. Good administration is a must, or inefficiencies and lack of dependability will quickly consume the value of the private network. A company needs to carefully weigh administrative issues before getting into private networking.

Using a private WAN need not be a total do-it-yourself approach. In fact, most telephone companies provide managed WAN services, which include all the equipment you need to create a WAN. They also monitor and manage the connection for you, making sure that everything operates as it is supposed to. There is, of course, a price attached to such a service, but for many companies, a managed solution is money well spent.

Switching Methods

Before we go on to discuss the specific WAN technologies, we must first look at an important element of the WAN technologies—the switching methods. For systems to communicate on a network, there has to be a communication path between them on which the data can travel. To communicate with another entity, you need to establish a path that can be used to move the information from one location to another and back. This is the function of *switching*: It provides a path between two communication endpoints and switches the data, to make sure that it follows the correct path. Three types of switching are used most often in networks today:

▶ Packet switching

▶ Circuit switching

▶ Message switching

EXAM ALERT

Know the Differences   For the Network+ exam, you will be expected to identify the differences between the various switching methods.

Packet Switching

In packet switching, messages are broken down into smaller pieces called *packets*. Each packet is assigned source, destination, and intermediate node addresses. Packets are required to have this information because they do not always use the same path or route to get to their intended destination. Referred to as *independent routing*, this is one of the advantages of packet switching. Independent routing allows for a better use of available bandwidth by letting packets travel different routes, to avoid high-traffic areas. Independent routing also allows packets to take an alternate route if a particular route is unavailable for some reason. Figure 7.2 shows how packets can travel in a packet-switching environment.

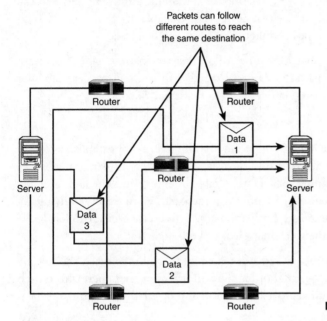

FIGURE 7.2 An example of packet switching.

NOTE

Packet Switching   Packet switching is the most popular switching method for networks and is used on most LANs.

In a packet-switching system, when packets are sent onto the network, the sending device is responsible for choosing the best path for the packet. This path might change in transit, and it is possible for the receiving device to receive the packets in a random or nonsequential order. When this happens, the receiving device waits until all the data packets are received, and then it reconstructs them according to their built-in sequence numbers.

NOTE

Packet Size Restrictions   The packet size is restricted in a packet-switching network, to ensure that the packets can be stored in RAM instead of on a hard disk. The benefit of this size restriction is faster access because retrieving data from RAM is faster than retrieving data from a hard disk.

Two types of packet-switching methods are used on networks: *virtual-circuit packet switching* and *datagram packet switching*. Each of these methods is described in the following sections.

Virtual-Circuit Packet Switching

When virtual-circuit switching is used, a logical connection is established between the source and the destination device. This logical connection is established when the sending device initiates a conversation with the receiving device. The logical communication path between the two devices can remain active for as long as the two devices are available or can be used to send packets once. After the sending process has completed, the line can be closed.

All the packets in virtual-circuit packet switching must follow the same path. That is, they travel through the logical communication path that is established. Virtual-circuit packet switching is commonly used for connection-oriented services such as real-time video.

Datagram Packet Switching

Unlike virtual-circuit packet switching, datagram packet switching does not establish a logical connection between the sending and transmitting devices. The packets in datagram packet switching are independently sent, meaning that they can take different paths through the network to reach their intended destination. To do this, each packet must be individually addressed, to determine where its source and destination are. This method ensures that packets take the easiest possible routes to their destination and avoid high-traffic areas.

Because in datagram packet switching the packets can take multiple paths to reach their destination, they can be received in a nonsequential order. The information contained within each packet header is used to reconstruct all the packets, and so the original message is received intact.

NOTE

Datagram Packet Sizes   The data packet size used with datagram packet switching is kept small in case of error, which would cause the packets to be re-sent.

Circuit Switching

In contrast to the packet-switching method, *circuit switching* requires a dedicated physical connection between the sending and receiving devices. The most commonly used analogy to represent circuit switching is a telephone conversation, in which the parties involved have a dedicated link between them for the duration of the conversation. When either party disconnects, the circuit is broken, and the data path is lost. This is an accurate representation of how circuit switching works with network and data transmissions. The sending system establishes a physical connection, the data is transmitted between the two, and when the transmission is complete, the channel is closed.

Some clear advantages to the circuit-switching technology make it well suited for certain applications. The primary advantage is that after a connection is established, there is a consistent and reliable connection between the sending and receiving device. This allows for transmissions at a guaranteed rate of transfer.

Like all technologies, circuit switching has downsides. As you might imagine, a dedicated communication line can be inefficient. After the physical connection is established, it is unavailable to any other sessions until the transmission is complete. Again using the phone call analogy, this would be like a caller trying to reach another caller and getting a busy signal. Circuit switching can therefore be fraught with long connection delays. Figure 7.3 shows an example of circuit switching.

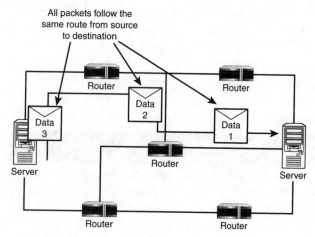

FIGURE 7.3 An example of circuit switching.

Message Switching

In some respects, *message switching* is similar to packet switching, but instead of using and sending packets, message switching divides data transmissions into messages. Like packets, each of these messages contains the destination address. Devices on the network that forward the message use this destination address. Each intermediate device in the message's path stores the message momentarily and then forwards it to the next device in the network, until it finally reaches its destination. Message switching is therefore often referred to as the *store-and-forward* method.

NOTE

Email and the Store-and-Forward Method   The store-and-forward method used by message switching makes it well suited for certain applications, including email.

Message switching offers many advantages over circuit switching. Because message switching doesn't require a dedicated connection as does circuit switching, a larger number of devices can share the bandwidth of the network. A message-switching system also has the capability of storing messages, which allows the traffic on the network to clear. This strategy can significantly reduce the traffic congestion on the network.

The main drawbacks of the message-switching method are that the store-and-forward method makes it a poor choice for real-time applications, such as videoconferencing, in which the temporary storing of data would be disruptive to the message. A second drawback is that the intermediate devices, often PC systems, must be capable of temporarily storing messages by using their hard disk space.

REVIEW BREAK

Switching Methods Comparison

Table 7.1 summarizes the characteristics of the various switching methods.

TABLE 7.1 Comparison of Switching Methods

Switching Method	Pros	Cons	Key Features
Packet switching	Packets can be routed around network congestion. Packet switching makes efficient use of network bandwidth.	Packets can become lost while taking alternate routes to the destination. Messages are divided into packets that contain source and destination information.	Packets can travel the network independently, looking for the best route to the destination system. There are two types of packet switching: datagram and virtual-circuit packet switching.
Circuit switching	Offers a dedicated transmission channel that is reserved until disconnected.	Dedicated channels can cause delays because a channel is unavailable until one side disconnects.	Offers the capability of storing messages temporarily to reduce network congestion.

TABLE 7.1 *Continued*

Switching			
		Uses a dedicated physical link between the sending and receiving devices.	
Message switching	Multiple devices have the capability to share bandwidth.	The store-and-forward system makes message switching impractical for many real-time applications.	Entire messages are sent during transmissions. Intermediate devices temporarily store and then forward messages.

WAN Technologies

Having looked at the differences between the various switching methods, we can now take a better look at the technologies used to create WANs. Several technologies, including the following, can be used to implement WANs:

- ISDN (Integrated Services Digital Network)
- FDDI (Fiber Distributed Data Interface)
- T1 (T Carrier level 1)/E1/J1
- T3 (T Carrier level 3)/E3/J3
- OCx (Optical Carrier)
- X.25

These technologies vary in terms of cost, complexity, and switching methods. We'll start our discussion by looking at perhaps the simplest of WAN technologies—the modem.

Dial-up Modem Connections

Today, people are more likely to associate a modem with a dial-up Internet service provider (ISP) account than with a WAN technology. But the reality is that for many years, and still today, modems have been used to provide WAN capabilities.

The biggest drawback of a modem connection is the speed, which is limited to 56Kbps. There are, however, a few advantages to modem connections. The cost of a modem link depends on the distance covered. In parts of the world such as North America, where local calls are free, modem links can provide an inexpensive WAN solution where there would otherwise be no WAN connectivity at all. All that is needed to create the modem WAN link is a phone line and a modem at each end of the link. You also need software to enable, support, and configure the link, but all modern network operating systems include this functionality, so this is not a problem.

Integrated Services Digital Network (ISDN)

ISDN is a dial-up technology capable of transmitting voice and data simultaneously over the same physical connection. Using ISDN, users are able to access digital communication channels via both packet- and circuit-switching connections. ISDN is much faster than a regular modem connection. To access ISDN, a special phone line is required, and this line is usually paid for through a monthly subscription. You can expect these monthly costs to be significantly higher than those for a dial-up modem account.

To establish an ISDN connection, you dial the number for the end of the connection, much as you would with a conventional phone call or modem dial-up connection. A conversation between the sending and receiving devices is then established. The connection is dropped when one end disconnects or hangs up. The line pickup of ISDN is very fast, allowing a connection to be established, or brought up, very quickly—much more quickly than a conventional phone line.

> **NOTE**
>
> **B-ISDN**   Broadband ISDN (B-ISDN) is an enhanced version of ISDN and is capable of faster transmission rates than ISDN. It is implemented with fiber-optic media.

ISDN has two defined interface standards—Basic Rate Interface (BRI) and Primary Rate Interface (PRI)—which are discussed in the following sections.

Basic Rate Interface (BRI)

BRI defines a communication line that utilizes three separate channels. There are two B (that is, bearer) channels of 64Kbps each and one D (that is, delta) channel of 16Kbps. The two B channels are used to carry digital information, which can be either voice or data. The B channels can be used independently to provide 64Kbps access or combined to utilize the entire 128Kbps. The D channel is used for out-of-band signaling.

> **TIP**
>
> **2B+D**   BRI ISDN is sometimes referred to as 2B+D. This abbreviation simply refers to the available channels.

To use BRI ISDN, the connection point must be within 5,486 meters (18,000 feet) of the ISDN provider's BRI service center. In addition, to use BRI ISDN, special equipment is needed, such as ISDN routers and ISDN terminal adapters. Figure 7.4 shows a standard ISDN router.

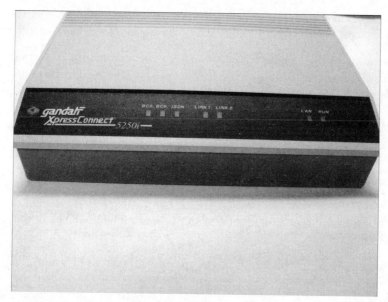

FIGURE 7.4   An ISDN router.

Primary Rate Interface (PRI)

PRI is a form of ISDN that is generally carried over a T1 line (called E1 in Europe) and can handle transmission rates of up to 1.544Mbps. PRI is composed of 23 B channels (30 in Europe), each providing 64Kbps for data/voice, and one 64Kbps D channel.

> **NOTE**
>
> **Leased Lines**   ISDN is considered a *leased line* because access to ISDN is leased from a service provider.

REVIEW BREAK

BRI and PRI ISDN Comparison

Table 7.2 compares BRI and PRI ISDN.

TABLE 7.2   BRI and PRI ISDN Comparison

Characteristic	BRI	PRI
Speed	128Kbps	1.544M
Channels	2B+D	23B+D
Transmission carrier	PSTN	T1

T-carrier Lines

T-carrier lines are high-speed lines that can be leased from telephone companies. T-carrier lines can support both voice and data transmissions and are often used to create point-to-point private networks. Four types of T-carrier lines are available:

- **T1**—T1 lines offer transmission speeds of 1.544Mbps, and they can be used to create point-to-point dedicated digital communication paths. T1 lines have commonly been used for connecting LANs.

- **T2**—T2 leased lines offer transmission speeds of 6.312Mbps. T2 lines accomplishes this by using 96 64Kbps B channels.

- **T3**—T3 lines offer transmission speeds of up to 44.736Mbps, using 672 64Kbps B channels.

- **T4**—T4 lines offer impressive transmission speeds of up to 274.176Mbps by using 4,032 64Kbps B channels.

Of these T-carrier lines, the ones commonly associated with networks are T1 and T3 lines, which are discussed further in the following sections.

T1/E1/J1 Lines

T1 (also known as a *leased line*) is actually a dedicated digital circuit leased from the telephone company. This creates an always-open, always-available line between you and whomever you choose to connect to when you establish the service. T1 lines also eliminate the "one call per wire" limitation by using a method called *multiplexing*, or *muxing*. Using a device called a *multiplexer*, the signal is broken into smaller pieces and assigned identifiers. Multiple transmissions are divided by the multiplexer and transmitted across the wire simultaneously. When the signals reach their destination, they are put back in the proper order and converted back into the proper form.

Having T1 service used to be the way to show someone you were serious about your particular communication needs. T1 lines were expensive; however, their prices have fallen in the past few years, as other technologies have begun to rival their transmission rates. T1 offers speeds up to 1.544Mbps. The obvious advantages of a T1 line are its constant connection—no dial-up or other connection is required because it is always on—and it can easily be budgeted because it has a fixed monthly cost. In addition, the transfer rate is guaranteed because it, like a telephone call, is a private circuit. Many companies use T1 lines as their pipelines to the Internet.

It is important to point out that T-carrier is the designation to the technology used in the United States and Canada. In Europe, they are referred to as E-carriers and in Japan, J-carriers. Table 7.3 shows the T/E/J carriers.

REVIEW BREAK

TABLE 7.3   Comparing T/E/J Carriers

Name	Transmission Speed	Voice Channels
T-1	1.544Mbps	24
T-1C	3.152Mbps	48
T-2	6.312Mbps	96
T-3	44.736Mbps	672
T-4	274.176Mbps	4032
J-0	64Kbps	1
J-1	1.544Mbps	24
J-1C	3.152Mbps	48
J-2	6.312Mbps	96
J-3	32.064Mbps	480
J-3C	97.728Mbps	1440
J-4	397.200Mbps	5760
E-0	64Kbps	1
E-1	2.048Mbps	30
E-2	8.448Mbps	120
E-3	34.368Mbps	480
E-4	139.264Mbps	1920
E-5	565.148Mbps	7680

T3 Lines

For a time, the speeds offered by T1 lines were sufficient for all but a few organizations. As networks and the data they support expanded, T1 lines did not provide enough speed for many organizations. T3 service answered the call by providing transmission speeds of 44.736Mbps.

T3 lines are dedicated circuits that provide very high capacity and are generally used by large companies, ISPs, or long-distance companies. T3 service offers all the strengths of a T1 service (just a whole lot more), but the costs associated with T3 limits its use to the few organizations that have the money to pay for it.

> **NOTE**
>
> **Fractional T** Due to the cost of a T-carrier solution, it is possible to lease portions of a T-carrier service. Known as *fractional T*, you can subscribe and pay for service based on 64Kbps channels.

Fiber Distributed Data Interface (FDDI)

FDDI was introduced in the mid-1980s. FDDI is an American National Standards Institute (ANSI) topology standard that uses fiber-optic cable and token-passing media access. Recall from Chapter 1, "Introduction to Networking," that the token-passing method requires systems that are sending data on the network to have access to a token. The data is attached to the token and transported throughout the network.

FDDI can be used over both multimode and single-mode fiber cable and can reach transmissions speeds of up to 100Mbps. FDDI combines the strengths of Token Ring, the speed of Fast Ethernet, and the security of fiber-optic cable. Although not widely deployed, FDDI is used for creating network backbones and connecting private LANs to create WANs.

FDDI Versus IEEE 802.5

FDDI and the IEEE 802.5 standard share some common features. For instance, both standards use a token-passing access method, and both can use fiber-optic media. However, despite their surface similarities, if you dig a little deeper, there are some significant differences.

As mentioned previously, the FDDI standard uses a token-passing access method similar to that of the IEEE 802.5 standard, with one notable difference. The original 802.5 standard specifies that only a single data frame can be attached to a token. However, a computer in an FDDI network can transmit as much data on the token as possible within a specified period. When the specified time has expired, the computer releases the token to the ring, and then it must wait until the token returns before it can send more data.

CDDI The Copper Distributed Data Interface (CDDI) standard defines FDDI over copper cable rather than fiber-optic cable. CDDI has an even lower level of popularity than FDDI.

Another key difference between standards 802.5 and FDDI is that FDDI uses a dual-ring configuration. The first, or primary, ring is used to transfer the data around the network, and the secondary ring is used for redundancy and fault tolerance; the secondary ring waits to take over if the primary ring fails. If the primary ring fails, the secondary ring kicks in automatically, with no disruption to network users. Figure 7.5 shows an FDDI dual-ring configuration.

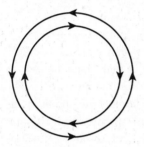

FIGURE 7.5 An example of an FDDI configuration.

Even though the second ring sits dormant, you can connect network devices to both rings. Network devices that attach to both rings are referred to as *Class A stations*, or *dual attached stations (DASs)*. Network devices that connect to a single ring are called *Class B stations*, or *single attached stations (SASs)*. Class A stations are the more reliable of the two because they continue to function in the event that one of the rings fails—a technique known as *wrapping*. SASs, on the other hand, are not fault tolerant; if the ring attached to the device fails, the device becomes isolated from the network. Figure 7.6 shows an example of DASs and SASs on an FDDI network.

Wrapping In the FDDI topology, *wrapping* refers to the capability of a network device to continue to operate if one of the rings fails.

Implementing FDDI

If you are implementing or troubleshooting an FDDI network, keep in mind a few factors. The practical limitations of an FDDI network are 500 workstations and a maximum of 100 kilometers of cable. The FDDI specification calls for multimode fiber-optic cable with a 62.5-micrometer core. Two kilometers (6,561 feet) is the maximum cable segment length; to cover a longer distance with FDDI, a repeating device is needed every 2 kilometers (6,561 feet).

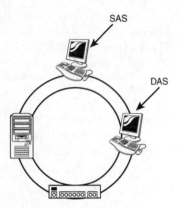

FIGURE 7.6   An FDDI ring with both a SAS and a DAS.

FDDI Fault Detection

The FDDI standard uses a technique called *beaconing* to detect faults on a network. When a computer on an FDDI network detects an error, it sends a continual signal called a *beacon* to its immediately upstream neighbor until it hears a beacon response from the upstream neighbor. This process continues until the only computer system still beaconing is the one immediately downstream from the one with the fault. Of course, the upstream system cannot respond to the beacon because there is a fault between it and the sending computer, disabling the connection between the two devices. To identify the location of the cable break, the network administrator looks for the computer sending the beacons and then looks upstream for the problem.

Advantages and Disadvantages of FDDI

FDDI has a few significant advantages, some of which stem directly from the fact that it uses fiber-optic cable as its transmission media. The following list contains some of the advantages associated with FDDI:

▶ **Immune to electromagnetic interference (EMI)**—Fiber is not susceptible to the influences of EMI.

▶ **Secure**—Fiber is more secure than copper-based media. Eavesdropping and tapping into the line are far more difficult with fiber-optic cable than with copper-based cable.

▶ **Long cable distances**—Fiber-optic cable has a transmission range of more than 2 kilometers (6,561 feet).

In addition to the advantages provided by the fiber-optic cable, FDDI itself has a few strong points:

▶ **Fault-tolerant design**—By using a dual-ring configuration, FDDI provides some fault tolerance. If one cable fails, the other can be used to transmit the data throughout the network.

- ▶ **Speed due to the use of multiple tokens**—Unlike the IEEE 802.5 standard, FDDI uses multiple tokens, which increases the overall network speed.

- ▶ **Beaconing**—FDDI uses beaconing as a built-in error-detection method, making finding faults such as cable breaks a lot easier.

FDDI also has a few key drawbacks, including the following:

- ▶ **High cost**—The costs associated with FDDI and the devices and cable needed to implement an FDDI solution are high—too high for many small organizations.

- ▶ **Implementation difficulty**—FDDI setup and management can be complex, requiring trained professionals with significant experience to manage and maintain the cable and infrastructure.

Because of the cost, FDDI is implemented in only a limited number of environments. As a result, your chances of encountering FDDI in the real world are relatively low.

X.25

X.25 was one of the original packet-switching technologies, but today it has been replaced in many applications by Frame Relay. Various telephone companies, along with network providers, developed X.25 in the mid-1970s to transmit digital data over analog signals on copper lines. Because so many different entities had their hands in the development and implementation of X.25, it works well on many different kinds of networks with different types of traffic. X.25 is one of the oldest standards, and therein lie both its greatest advantage and its greatest disadvantage. On the upside, X.25 is a global standard that can be found all over the world. On the downside, its maximum transfer speed is 56Kbps—which is reasonable when compared to other technologies in the mid-1970s but slow and cumbersome today. However, in the 1980s a digital version of X.25 was released, increasing throughput to a maximum of 64Kbps. This too is slow by today's standards.

Because X.25 is a packet-switching technology, it uses different routes to get the best possible connection between the sending and receiving device at a given time. As conditions on the network change, such as increased network traffic, so do the routes that the packets take. Consequently, each packet is likely to take a different route to reach its destination during a single communication session. The devices that make it possible to use X.25 service are called *packet assemblers/disassemblers (PADs)*. A PAD is required at each end of the X.25 connection.

SONET/OCx Levels

In 1984 the U.S. Department of Justice and AT&T reached an agreement stating that AT&T was a monopoly that needed to be divided into smaller, directly competitive companies. This created a challenge for local telephone companies, which were then faced with the task of connecting to an ever-growing number of independent long-distance carriers, each of which had a different interfacing mechanism. Bell Communications Research answered the challenge by developing SONET, a fiber-optic WAN technology that delivers voice, data, and video at speeds in multiples of 51.84Mbps. Bell's main goals in creating SONET were to create a standardized access method for all carriers within the newly competitive U.S. market and to unify different standards around the world. SONET is capable of transmission speeds between 51.84Mbps and 2.488Gbps.

One of Bell's biggest accomplishments with SONET was that it created a new system that defined data rates in terms of Optical Carrier (OCx) levels. Table 7.4 contains the OC levels you should be familiar with.

TABLE 7.4   OCx Levels and Transmission Rates

OC Level	Transmission Rate
OC-1	51.84Mbps
OC-3	155.52Mbps
OC-12	622.08Mbps
OC-24	1.244Gbps
OC-48	2.488Gbps

NOTE

SDH   Synchronous Digital Hierarchy (SDH) is the European counterpart to SONET.

Asynchronous Transfer Mode (ATM) and Frame Relay

Though not identified in the CompTIA objectives, two other WAN technologies deserve a mention, ATM and Frame Relay. Most of us got our first look at ATM in the early 1990s, when it was introduced. ATM was heralded as a breakthrough technology for networking because it was an end-to-end solution, ranging in use from a desktop to a remote system. Though promoted as both a LAN and WAN solution, ATM did not live up to its hype due to associated implementation costs and a lack of standards. The introduction of Gigabit Ethernet, which offered great transmissions speeds and compatibility with existing network infrastructure, further dampened the momentum of the ATM bandwagon. ATM has, however, found a niche with some ISPs and is also commonly used as a network backbone.

ATM is a packet-switching technology that provides transfer speeds ranging from 1.544Mbps to 622Mbps. It is well suited for a variety of data types, such as voice, data, and video. Using fixed-length packets, or cells, that are 53 bytes long, ATM can operate much more efficiently than variable-length-packet packet-switching technologies such as Frame Relay. Having a fixed-length packet allows ATM to be concerned only with the header information of each packet. It does not need to read every bit of a packet to determine the beginning and end of the packet. ATM's fixed cell length also makes it easily adaptable to other technologies as they develop. Each cell has 48 bytes available for data, with 5 bytes reserved for the ATM header.

ATM is a circuit-based network technology because it uses a virtual circuit to connect two networked devices. Two types of circuits are used in an ATM network:

▶ **Switched virtual circuits (SVCs)**—SVCs are set up only for the duration of a conversation or data transmission. An SVC is a temporary connection that is dropped when the transmission is complete.

▶ **Permanent virtual circuits (PVCs)**—PVCs are permanently established virtual circuits between two devices.

ATM is compatible with the most widely used and implemented networking media types available today, including single-mode and multimode fiber, coaxial cable, unshielded twisted pair, and shielded twisted pair. Although it can be used over various media, the limitations of some of the media types make them impractical choices. ATM can also operate over other media, including FDDI, T1, T3, SONET, OC-3, and Fiber Channel.

Frame Relay was designed to provide standards for transmitting data packets in high-speed bursts over digital networks, using a public data network service. Frame Relay is a packet-switching technology that uses variable-length packets. Essentially, Frame Relay is a streamlined version of X.25. It uses smaller packet sizes and fewer error-checking mechanisms than X.25, and consequently it has less overhead than X.25.

A Frame Relay connection is built by using PVCs that establish end-to-end circuits. This means that Frame Relay is not dependent on the best-route method of X.25. Frame Relay can be implemented on 56Kbps, T1, T3, and ISDN lines.

REVIEW BREAK

WAN Technology Summary

Table 7.5 summarizes the main characteristics of the various WAN technologies discussed in this chapter. You can use this table as an aid in reviewing before you take the Network+ exam.

Table 7.5   WAN Technology Overview

WAN Technology	Speed	Supported Media	Switching Method Used	Key Characteristics
ISDN	BRI: 64Kbps to 128Kbps PRI: 64Kbps to 1.5Mbps	Copper/ fiber-optic	Can be used for circuit-switching or packet-switching connections	ISDN can be used to transmit all types of traffic, including voice, video, and data. BRI uses 2B+D channels, PRI uses 23B+D channels. B channels are 64Kbps. ISDN uses the public network and requires dial-in access.
T-carrier (T1, T3)	T1: 1.544Mbps T3: 44.736Mbps	Copper/ fiber-optic	Circuit switching	T-carrier is used to create point-to-point network connections for private networks.
FDDI	100Mbps	Fiber-optic	N/A	Uses a dual-ring configuration for fault tolerance. Uses a token-passing media-access method. Uses beaconing for error detection.
ATM	1.544Mbps to 622Mbps	Copper/ fiber-optic	Cell switching	ATM uses fixed cells that are 53 bytes long.
X.25	56Kbps/ 64Kbps	Copper/ fiber-optic	Packet switching	X.25 is limited to 56Kbps. X.25 provides a packet-switching network over standard phone lines.
Frame Relay	56Kbps to 1.544Mbps	Copper/ fiber-optic	PVCs and SVCs	Frame Relay is a packet-oriented protocol, and it uses variable-length packets.
SONET/OCx	51.8Mbps to 2.4Gbps	Fiber-optic	N/A	SONET defines synchronous data transfer over optical cable.

Objective:

2.15 Identify the basic characteristics of the following Internet access technologies:

- ▶ xDSL (Digital Subscriber Line)

- ▶ Broadband Cable (Cable modem)

- ▶ POTS/PSTN (Plain Old Telephone Service / Public Switched Telephone Network)

- ► Satellite

- ► Wireless

Internet access has become an integral part of modern business. We rely on the Internet to provide business and personal communication through such technologies as email and video-conferencing. Organizations depend on the Internet to provide up-to-date and reliable information on a range of topics. It is used as a key element in a company's marketing strategy and often provides the first impression of a business. If that wasn't enough, it enables easy remote access for offsite clients. These are just a few of the services that the Internet provides and the reason why organizations give careful thought to the technologies they use to provide their Internet access.

There are several ways to obtain Internet access. The type chosen often depends on the cost as well as what technologies are available in the area you are located. This section explores some of the more common methods of obtaining Internet access.

> **NOTE**
>
> **Broadband**   The term *broadband* refers to high-speed Internet access. Both DSL and cable modem are common broadband Internet technologies. Broadband routers and broadband modems are network devices that support both DSL and cable.

xDSL Internet Access

DSL is an Internet access method that uses a standard phone line to provide high-speed Internet access. DSL is available only in certain areas, although as the telephone companies try to cash in on the broadband Internet access market, the areas of coverage are likely to increase.

DSL offers phone and data transmissions over a standard phone connection. DSL is most commonly associated with high-speed Internet access; because it is less expensive than technologies such as ISDN, it is often used in homes and small businesses. With DSL a different frequency can be used for digital and analog signals, which means that you can talk to a friend on the phone while you're uploading data.

DSL arrived on the scene in the late 1990s, and it brought with it a staggering number of flavors. Together, all these variations are known as xDSL:

- ► **Asymmetric DSL (ADSL)**—Probably the most common of the DSL varieties is ADSL. The word *asymmetric* describes different channels on the line: One channel is used for POTS and is responsible for analog traffic, the second channel is used to provide upload access, and the third channel is used for downloads. With ADSL, downloads are faster than uploads.

- **Symmetric DSL (SDSL)**—SDSL offers the same speeds for uploads and for downloads, making it most suitable for business applications such as web hosting, intranets, and ecommerce. It is not widely implemented in the home/small business environment and cannot share a phone line.

- **ISDN DSL (IDSL)**—ISDN DSL is a symmetric type of DSL commonly used in environments where SDSL and ADSL are unavailable. IDSL does not support analog phones.

- **Rate Adaptive DSL (RADSL)**—RADSL is a variation on ADSL that can modify its transmission speeds based on the signal quality. RADSL supports line sharing.

- **Very High Bit Rate DSL (VHDSL)**—VHDSL is an asymmetric version of DSL and, as such, can share a telephone line.

- **High Bit Rate DSL (HDSL)**—HDSL is a symmetric technology that offers identical transmission rates in both directions. HDSL does not allow line sharing with analog phones.

Why are there are so many DSL variations? The answer is simply that each flavor of DSL is aimed at a different user, business, or application. Businesses with high bandwidth needs are more likely to choose a symmetric form of DSL, whereas budget-conscious environments such as home offices are likely to choose an option that allows phone line sharing at the expense of bandwidth. When you're working in a home/small office environment, you should expect to work with an ADSL system.

What is the difference? DSL options can be a shared or dedicated link. ADSL for instance is a shared DSL connection. The shared connection means that a single telephone line can support both voice and Internet service. This is possible because a telephone cable uses two frequencies—high and low. The low frequency is used for DSL Internet, whereas the high frequency is used for voice.

If you see the term *Rate Adaptive* used with a DSL technology, it means that the speed of the connection fluctuates. This fluctuation is caused by several factors, including the distance between the DSL provider and the Internet system, the condition of the physical line used by the DSL connection, or interference on the line. This makes technologies such as ADSL inconsistent in terms of speed, but for most day-to-day applications, these speed fluctuations will go largely unnoticed.

If there are shared DSL links, there must be dedicated DSL links. A dedicated DSL link is a more costly Internet solution but provides some clear advantages. Business DSL solutions such as SDSL provide a dedicated DSL link over copper from the service provider to the Internet system. A dedicated DSL line is not used for regular voice transmissions.

Table 7.6 summarizes the expected speeds of the various DSL options.

TABLE 7.6   Expected DSL Speeds

DSL Variation	Upload Speed	Download Speed
ADSL	1Mbps	8Mbps
SDSL	1.5Mbps	1.5Mbps
IDSL	144Kbps	144Kbps
RADSL	1Mbps	7Mbps
VHDSL	1.6Mbps	13Mbps
HDSL	768Kbps	768Kbps

Cable Internet Access

Cable Internet access is an always-on Internet access method available in areas that have digital cable television. Not all cable TV providers offer Internet access, but an increasing number are taking advantage of the relatively simple jump from being cable providers to being ISPs.

Cable Internet access is attractive to many small businesses and home office users because it is both inexpensive and reliable. Most cable providers do not restrict how much use is made of the access. Connectivity is achieved by using a device called a *cable modem*; it has a coaxial connection for connecting to the provider's outlet and an unshielded twisted-pair (UTP) connection for connection directly to a system or to a hub or switch.

Cable providers often supply a cable modem free of charge, although of course you are paying for the rental of the modem in a monthly service fee. Many cable providers offer free or low-cost installation of cable Internet service, which includes installing a network card in a PC. Some providers also do not charge for the network card. Cable Internet costs are comparable to a DSL subscription at about $30 to $50 a month.

Most cable modems supply a 10Mbps Ethernet connection for the home LAN, although you wouldn't expect the actual Internet connection to reach these speeds. The actual speed of the connection can vary somewhat depending on the utilization of the shared cable line in your area. In day-to-day application, data rates range from 1.5Mbps to 3Mbps.

> **NOTE**
>
> **MDI-X Ports**   A cable modem is generally equipped with a medium-dependent interface crossed (MDI-X) port, so a straight-through UTP cable can be used to connect the modem to a system.

One of the biggest disadvantages of cable access is cited (by DSL providers at least) as the fact that you share the available bandwidth with everyone else in your cable area. As a result, during peak times, performance of a cable link might be poorer than in low-use periods. In residential areas, busy times are evenings and weekends, and particularly right after school. In general, though, performance with cable systems is good, and in low-usage periods it can be very fast.

Cable Versus DSL

There is an ongoing debate as to which broadband option is the best. In truth, DSL and cable are actually quite similar, and the choice between them often comes down to availability in your area. Some areas offer only cable or DSL, so the choice is simple. Still, there are a few differences that might make the decision easier.

Cable Internet will likely win the raw speed battle between the two if the theoretical speeds are compared. In real-world application, the performance of DSL and cable can fluctuate depending on Internet congestion and other factors. This makes the actual usable speeds of each technology similar. Rarely would either technology reach its theoretical maximum speed. Table 7.7 provides a quick comparison between the two technologies.

TABLE 7.7 Comparing DSL and Cable Internet

Feature	Cable Internet	DSL Internet
Bandwidth/speed	The theoretical maximum cable speed of 30Mbps downstream, aside, in practical use the rate is somewhere between 300 and 700Kbps downstream and a 128 connection.	DSL lists speeds from to 384Kbps to 6.0Mbps depending on the type of DSL used and whom you ask. DSL offers 128Kbps upstream transfers.
Connection type	Cable Internet uses a shared connection. You share the connection with others in your area. This can affect bandwidth performance during peak usage times.	DSL bandwidth is dedicated and not shared.
Distance factors	With cable Internet distance is not a concern. Subscribers maintain the same speeds regardless of the distance from the Internet provider.	DSL speeds degrade as the distance from the ISP increases. The farther you are, the more overall speed deteriorates.
Security	Some believe that the shared nature of cable Internet make it an increased security risk. Security risks include eavesdropping, tampering, service theft and more.	Some consider DSL more secure because it offers a dedicated link to the ISP. The dedicated link helps protect against attacks associated with a shared connection.

> **NOTE**
>
> **The Choice Is Yours** Although the debate between cable and DSL goes on, for us regular users it really won't make that much difference which one we choose. Although cable modem technology delivers *shared bandwidth* within the local neighborhood, its speeds are marginally higher but influenced by this shared bandwidth. DSL delivers *dedicated local bandwidth* but is sensitive to distance, which impacts overall performance. With the monthly costs about the same, it really is too close to call.

Broadband Considerations

Whether you are using DSL or cable Internet access, keep a few things in mind. First, each of these technologies offers always-on service. This means that even when you are away from your computer, it is still on the Internet. As you can imagine, this creates a security risk. The longer you are online, the more chance someone has of remotely accessing your system.

The operating systems we use today all have some security holes through which some people are waiting to exploit. These attacks often focus on technologies such as email or open TCP/UDP ports. Combining OS security holes with an always-on Internet technology is certainly a dangerous mix.

Today, DSL and cable Internet connections have to use mechanisms such as firewalls to protect the system. The firewall system offers features such as packet filtering and network address translation (NAT). The firewall can be a third-party software application installed on the system, or it can be a hardware device.

In addition to a firewall, it is equally important to ensure that the operating system you are using is completely up-to-date in terms of service packs and security updates. Today's client systems typically offer automatic update features that alert you when a new security update is available.

If you follow a few safety rules, both DSL and cable Internet can provide safe Internet access. You just have to be security diligent.

Satellite Internet Access

Many of us take DSL and cable Internet access for granted, but these technologies are not offered everywhere. For areas where cheaper broadband options are not available, there are a limited number of Internet options. One of the primary ones is Internet via satellite.

Satellite access provides a viable Internet access solution for those who cannot get other methods of broadband. Satellite Internet offers an always-on connection with theoretical speeds advertised anywhere from 512Kbps upload speeds to 2048Kbps download speeds, considerably faster than a 56K dial-up connection. One primary drawback to satellite Internet is the cost, and even with the high price tag, it is not as fast as DSL or cable modem.

Although satellite Internet is slower and more costly than DSL or cable, it offers some attractive features, first of which has to be its portability. Quite literally, wherever you go you have

Internet access with no phone lines or other cables. For businesses with remote users and clients, the benefit to this is clear. But the technology has a far-reaching impact; it is not uncommon to see RVs with a satellite dish on the roof. They have 24/7 unlimited access to the Internet as they travel.

Many companies offer satellite Internet services, and a quick Internet search reveals many. These Internet providers offer different Internet packages that vary greatly in terms of price, access speeds, and service. Some target business, whereas others aim for the private market.

Two different types of broadband Internet satellite services are deployed: one-way and two-way systems. A *one-way satellite system* requires a satellite card and a satellite dish installed at the end user's site; this system works by sending outgoing requests on one link using a phone line, with inbound traffic returning on the satellite link. A *two-way satellite system*, on the other hand, provides data paths for both upstream and downstream data. Like a one-way system, a two-way system also uses a satellite card and a satellite dish installed at the end user's site; bidirectional communication occurs directly between the end user's node and the satellite.

Home satellite systems are asymmetric; that is, download speeds are faster than upload speeds. In fact, a home satellite system is likely to use a modem for the uplink traffic, with downloads coming over the satellite link. The exact speeds you can expect with satellite Internet depend on many factors. As with other wireless technologies, atmospheric conditions can significantly affect the performance of satellite Internet access. One additional consideration for satellite Internet is increased *propagation time*—the time it takes for the signal to travel back and forth from the satellite. In networking terms, this time is high and an important consideration for business applications.

Challenge

Assume that you are the network administrator tasked with implementing an Internet solution for your company. Your boss is always searching for cutting-edge technologies and therefore has asked you to research and provide a report on satellite Internet access. The completed report must include the following:

▶ The name of two satellite service providers

▶ A cost comparison of monthly service between the two providers

▶ A comparison of the speeds advertised by the two providers

▶ Area coverage supported by their service

▶ Key features of the connection

Wireless Internet Access

Not too long ago, it would have been inconceivable to walk into your local coffee shop with your laptop under your arm and surf the Web while drinking a latte. But today, it is becoming increasingly common to see people surfing the Web in many different public places. This is made possible by subscribing to a wireless Internet service provider (WISP) or connecting to a company's local wireless router.

A WISP provides public wireless Internet access known as *hotspots*. Hotspots provide Internet access for mobile network devices such as laptops, handheld computers, and cell phones in airports, coffee shops, conference rooms, and so on. A hotspot is created using one or many wireless access points near the hotspot location.

Client systems might need to install special application software for billing and security purposes; others require no configuration other than obtaining the network name (SSID). Hotspots are not always a pay-for service because companies use them as a marketing tool to lure Internet users to their businesses.

As of today, hotspots are not everywhere, but finding them is not difficult. Typically, airports, hotels, and coffee shops will advertise that they offer Internet access for customers or clients. In addition, WISP providers list their hotspot sites online so that they are easily found.

Establishing a connection to a wireless hotspot is a straightforward process. If not equipped with built-in wireless capability, laptops will require an external wireless adapter card. With the physical requirements of the wireless card taken care of, the steps to connect are as follows:

1. When you arrive at the hotspot site, power up your laptop. In some instances, you might need to reboot your system if it was on standby to clear out old configuration settings.

2. The card might detect the network automatically. If this is the case, configuration settings, such as the SSID, will be automatically detected, and the wireless Internet will be available. If Internet access is free, there is little else to do; if it is a paid-for service, you will need to enter a method of payment. One thing to remember is to verify that you are using encryption for secure data transfer.

3. If for some reason the wireless settings are not automatically detected, you will need to open up your wireless NIC's configuration utility and manually set the configurations. These settings can include setting the mode to infrastructure, inputting the correct SSID, and setting the level of encryption used.

In addition to using a WISP, some companies such as hotels, cafes, and so on will provide wireless Internet access by connecting a wireless router to a DSL or cable Internet connection. The router becomes the wireless access point to which the users connect, and it allows clients to connect to the Internet through the broadband connection. The technology is based on the 802.11 standards, typically 802.11b/g, and client systems require only an internal or external wireless adapter.

Challenge

You were previously tasked with researching satellite Internet options but are convinced there is a better solution for your company. In addition to the satellite research, you decide to provide your boss with a report on other wireless Internet technologies. Your additional report must include the following:

▶ The name of two WISP service providers

▶ A cost comparison of monthly service between the two providers

▶ A comparison of the speeds advertised by the two providers

▶ Area coverage supported by their service

▶ Key features of the connection

NOTE

Troubleshooting Wireless Connectivity   There will be times when the Internet connection just fails to work. Troubleshooting a wireless connectivity issue is covered in Chapter 15, "Troubleshooting Procedures and Best Practices."

POTS Internet Access

The most popular means of connecting to the Internet or a remote network may still be the good old telephone line and modem. Because the same line used for a household phone is used for dial-up access, it is referred to as the POTS method of access. Although many parts of the world are served by broadband providers offering services such as those discussed so far in this chapter, many people still connect with a modem.

Internet access through a phone system requires two things: a modem and a dial-up access account through an ISP. As you might recall from Chapter 2, "Cabling Standards, Media, and Connectors," modems are devices that convert the digital signals generated by a computer system into analog signals that can travel across a phone line. A computer can have either an internal or external modem. External modems tend to be less problematic to install and troubleshoot because they don't require reconfiguration of the host system. Internal modems use one of the serial port assignments (that is, a COM port) and must therefore be configured not to conflict with other devices.

The second piece of the puzzle, the dial-up ISP account, can easily be obtained by contacting one of the many local, regional, or national ISPs. Most ISPs offer a range of plans normally priced based on the amount of time the user is allowed to spend online. Almost without exception, ISPs offer 56Kbps access, the maximum possible under current standards. Most ISPs also provide email accounts, access to newsgroup servers, and often small amounts of web space.

It is a good idea to research an ISP choice carefully. Free services exist, but they generally restrict users to a certain number of online hours per month or use extensive banner advertising to pay for the services. Normally, you pay a monthly service fee for an ISP; doing so provides a degree of reassurance because the ISP can be held accountable. Paid-for service also tends to provide a higher level of support.

Another big consideration for dial-up Internet access is how many lines the ISP has. ISPs never have the same number of lines as subscribers; instead, they work on a first-come, first-served basis for dial-up clients. This means that on occasion, users get busy signals when they try to connect. Before signing up for a dial-up Internet access account, ask the company what its ratio of lines to subscribers is and use that figure as part of your comparison criteria.

With a modem and an ISP account, you are ready to get connected. But what happens if things do not run as planned? Welcome to the interesting and sometimes challenging world of troubleshooting dial-up connections.

Chapter Summary

This chapter outlines the technologies used to create WANs and various Internet access technologies. Each WAN technology has advantages and disadvantages, making some of them well suited for certain environments and completely impractical in others. Each of the technologies varies in terms of media, speed, availability, and cost.

Public networks such as the PSTN and the Internet are the most widely used methods of establishing WANs due in part to their availability, accessibility, and perhaps most importantly, their cost. The downsides of using these networks are security and speed issues.

Private networks allow secure communications between devices; however, the costs of dedicated private networks make them unattainable for many small companies. In addition, the implementation and management of private networks can often be more complex than that of public networks.

Several switching methods are used to establish communication between devices. With packet switching, messages are broken down into smaller pieces, with each packet assigned source, destination, and intermediate node addresses. These packets are independently routed toward the destination address. Circuit switching, on the other hand, requires a dedicated physical connection between the sending and receiving devices. Data transmissions follow the dedicated path to the receiving device. Message switching sends the entire message via intermediate devices, such as computers, temporarily storing and then forwarding the messages.

There are several methods of accessing the Internet all varying in terms of speeds, range, cost, and complexity. Cable and DSL Internet are a popular Internet access solution for home users and small business. They are a cost-effective solution offering broadband speeds and always-on service. Satellite and wireless Internet access take availability outside the home to practically anywhere. Dial-up Internet access, although slow, remains readily available and a viable solution for many situations.

Key Terms

- 802.11
- ATM
- Beaconing
- BRI
- circuit switching
- datagram packet switching
- FDDI

- Frame Relay
- hotspot
- independent routing
- ISDN
- message switching
- modem
- packet switching

▶ PRI

▶ private network

▶ PSTN

▶ public network

▶ PVC

▶ Satellite Internet

▶ SONET/OCx

▶ SVC

▶ T1/E1

▶ T3/E3

▶ T-carrier

▶ virtual circuit packet

▶ WAP

▶ wireless

▶ WISP

▶ X.25

Apply Your Knowledge

Exercises

7.1 Investigating WAN Options

Estimated time: 30 minutes

Because you are unlikely to have the equipment or facilities to create your own WAN, this exercise requires that you investigate the WAN options that would be available to you if you were to create a WAN from your location to another.

Your research should include visiting the website of a local telecommunications provider and ascertaining the options open to you. Given that financial considerations are generally a major factor in a decision such as this, you should look at the lower-cost options such as cable, DSL, or ISDN in preference to leased-line circuits, such as T1 lines. From your research you should be able to answer the following questions:

▶ Which services are available in your location?

▶ Which services offer the best value for the money, based on available bandwidth, cost of installation, ongoing costs (line/equipment rental), maintenance, and call charges, if applicable?

▶ Which of the available services would you choose, and what would the estimated annual cost be for that service?

Although you should not sign up for any of the services during the course of this exercise, through this exercise you will gain valuable information because this is exactly the kind of project you are likely to be assigned when working in a real-world situation as an administrator. Evaluation and recommendation of products is an important element of a network administrator's role.

Exam Questions

1. Your company currently uses a standard PSTN communication link to transfer files between LANs. Until now, the transfer speeds have been sufficient for the amount of data that needs to be transferred. Recently, a new application was purchased that requires a minimum transmission speed of 1.5Mbps. You have been given the task of finding the most cost-effective solution to accommodate the new application. Which of the following technologies would you use?

   ○ **a.** T3

   ○ **b.** X.25

   ○ **c.** T1

   ○ **d.** BRI ISDN

2. Which of the following terms is used to describe a station on an FDDI network that is attached to both rings?

   ○ **a.** DUS

   ○ **b.** SAS

   ○ **c.** DAS

   ○ **d.** DRS

3. Which of the following statements are true of ISDN? (Choose the two best answers.)

   ○ **a.** BRI ISDN uses 2B+1D channels.

   ○ **b.** BRI ISDN uses 23B+1D channels.

   ○ **c.** PRI ISDN uses 2B+1 D channels.

   ○ **d.** PRI ISDN uses 23B+1D channels.

4. You have been hired to establish a WAN connection between two offices—one in Vancouver and one in Seattle. The transmission speed can be no less than 2Mbps. Which of the following technologies could you choose?

   ○ **a.** T1

   ○ **b.** PSTN

   ○ **c.** T3

   ○ **d.** ISDN

5. A customer calls you and wants information on FDDI. Which of the following are true of FDDI? (Choose the two best answers.)

- ○ **a.** DASs are linked to both rings on FDDI.
- ○ **b.** SASs are linked to both rings on FDDI.
- ○ **c.** FDDI uses fiber-based media.
- ○ **d.** FDDI uses copper-based media.

6. Which of the following technologies use exclusively fiber-based media? (Choose the two best answers.)

- ○ **a.** FDDI
- ○ **b.** T1
- ○ **c.** SONET
- ○ **d.** ISDN

7. Due to recent cutbacks, your boss approaches you, demanding an alternative to the company's costly dedicated T1 line. Only small amounts of data will require transfer over the line. Which of the following are you likely to recommend?

- ○ **a.** ISDN
- ○ **b.** FDDI
- ○ **c.** The PSTN
- ○ **d.** X.25

8. Which of the following technologies requires a logical connection between the sending and receiving devices?

- ○ **a.** Circuit switching
- ○ **b.** Virtual-circuit packet switching
- ○ **c.** Message switching
- ○ **d.** High-density circuit switching

9. Which of the following technologies requires dial-up access? (Choose the two best answers.)

- ○ **a.** FDDI
- ○ **b.** ISDN
- ○ **c.** Packet switching
- ○ **d.** The PSTN

10. Which of the following is an advantage of ISDN over the PSTN?

    ◯ **a.** ISDN is more reliable.

    ◯ **b.** ISDN is cheaper.

    ◯ **c.** ISDN is faster.

    ◯ **d.** ISDN uses 53Kbps fixed-length packets.

11. Which of the following best describes the process of creating a dedicated circuit between two communication endpoints and directing traffic between those two points?

    ◯ **a.** Multiplexing

    ◯ **b.** Directional addressing

    ◯ **c.** Addressing

    ◯ **d.** Circuit switching

12. Which of the following technologies uses fixed-length packets, or cells, that are 53 bytes in length?

    ◯ **a.** ATM

    ◯ **b.** ISDN

    ◯ **c.** VPN

    ◯ **d.** FDDI

13. You need to implement a low-cost WAN implementation. Which of the following are considered public networks? (Choose the two best answers.)

    ◯ **a.** ATM

    ◯ **b.** The Internet

    ◯ **c.** FDDI

    ◯ **d.** The PSTN

14. Which of the following switching methods is associated with the store-and-forward technique?

    ◯ **a.** Packet switching

    ◯ **b.** Message switching

    ◯ **c.** Circuit switching

    ◯ **d.** Virtual-circuit packet switching

15. Which of the following are packet-switching technologies? (Choose the two best answers.)

    ○ **a.** ATM

    ○ **b.** X.25

    ○ **c.** FDDI

    ○ **d.** Frame Relay

16. Which of the following are disadvantages of a public network? -

    ○ **a.** Security

    ○ **b.** Accessibility

    ○ **c.** Availability

    ○ **d.** Cost

17. Which of the following circuit-switching strategies are used by ATM? (Choose the two best answers.)

    ○ **a.** SVC

    ○ **b.** VCD

    ○ **c.** PVC

    ○ **d.** PCV

18. On an ISDN connection, what is the purpose of the D channel?

    ○ **a.** It carries the data signals.

    ○ **b.** It carries signaling information.

    ○ **c.** It allows multiple channels to be combined, to provide greater bandwidth.

    ○ **d.** It provides a temporary overflow capacity for the other channels.

19. Which of the following technologies uses a PAD?

    ○ **a.** ISDN

    ○ **b.** ATM

    ○ **c.** X.25

    ○ **d.** OC-3

20. Of the following technologies, which are limited to 56Kbps? (Choose the two best answers.)

- ○ **a.** Modem

- ○ **b.** ISDN

- ○ **c.** X.25

- ○ **d.** Frame Relay

Answers to Exam Questions

1. c. A T1 line has a transmission capability of 1.544Mbps and is considerably cheaper than a T3 line. X.25 and BRI ISDN cannot provide the required transmission speed. For more information, see the "WAN Technologies" section in this chapter.

2. c. DAS describes a device that occupies both rings on an FDDI network. None of the other answers are valid. For more information, see the "WAN Technologies" section in this chapter.

3. a, d. BRI ISDN uses 2B+1D channels, which are two 64Kbps data channels, and PRI-ISDN uses 23B+1D channels. The other answers are not valid. For more information, see the "WAN Technologies" section in this chapter.

4. c. The only technology in this question capable of transfer speeds above 2Mbps is a T3 line. None of the other technologies listed can provide the transmission speed required. For more information, see the "WAN Technologies" section in this chapter.

5. a, c. DASs in an FDDI network connect to both rings, creating a fault-tolerant measure for the Class A device. FDDI is implemented over a fiber-based media. Answer b is incorrect because an SAS is connected to only one ring. Answer d is incorrect because FDDI can be implemented only over fiber-optic cable. For more information, see the "WAN Technologies" section in this chapter.

6. a, c. FDDI is implemented as two counter-rotating rings using fiber-based media. SONET is a fiber-based standard developed by Bell Communications Research, following the AT&T breakup in 1984. T1 and ISDN can both be implemented over copper-based cable. For more information, see the "WAN Technologies" section in this chapter.

7. c. When very little traffic will be sent over a line, the PSTN is the most cost-effective solution, although it is limited to 56Kbps. All the other WAN connectivity methods accommodate large amounts of data and are expensive in comparison to the PSTN. For more information, see the "WAN Technologies" section in this chapter.

8. b. When virtual circuit switching is used, a logical connection is established between the source and the destination device. None of the other answers are valid. For more information, see the "Introduction to Wide Area Networking" section in this chapter.

9. **b, d.** Both the PSTN and ISDN require dial-up connections to establish communication sessions. The other answers are not valid. For more information, see the "WAN Technologies" section in this chapter.

10. **c.** One clear advantage that ISDN has over the PSTN is its speed. ISDN can combine 64Kbps channels for faster transmission speeds than the PSTN can provide. ISDN is no more or less reliable than the PSTN. ISDN is more expensive than the PSTN. Answer d describes ATM. For more information, see the "WAN Technologies" section in this chapter.

11. **d.** Circuit switching is the process of creating a dedicated circuit between two communications endpoints and directing traffic between those two points. None of the other answers are valid types of switching. For more information, see the "Introduction to Wide Area Networking" section in this chapter.

12. **a.** ATM uses fixed packets, or cells, with lengths of 53 bytes—48 bytes for data information and 5 bytes for the header. None of the other technologies listed use this cell format. For more information, see the "WAN Technologies" section in this chapter.

13. **b, d.** The Internet and the PSTN are considered public networks and are therefore the most cost-effective data transmission solutions. ATM and FDDI are examples of private networking technologies. For more information, see the "Introduction to Wide Area Networking" section in this chapter.

14. **b.** Message switching uses a store-and-forward switching method. This method is impractical for real-time data transmissions but well suited for other applications, such as email. None of the other switching methods are associated with store-and-forward. For more information, see the "Introduction to Wide Area Networking" section in this chapter.

15. **b, d.** X.25 and Frame Relay are both packet-switching technologies. ATM and FDDI are not considered packet-switching technologies. For more information, see the "WAN Technologies" section in this chapter.

16. **a.** There are many advantages of a public network, but security is a concern because data transmissions can be intercepted. All the other answers are advantages of using a public network. For more information, see the "Introduction to Wide Area Networking" section in this chapter.

17. **a, c.** ATM uses two types of circuit switching—PVC and SVC. VCD and PCV are not the names of switching methods. For more information, see the "WAN Technologies" section in this chapter.

18. **b.** The D channel on an ISDN link carries signaling information, whereas the B, or bearer, channels carry the data. The other answers are not valid. For more information, see the "WAN Technologies" section in this chapter.

19. **c.** A PAD is associated with X.25 networks. None of the other technologies listed use PADs. For more information, see the "WAN Technologies" section in this chapter.

20. **a, c.** Both modem links and X.25 are limited to 56Kbps. ISDN and Frame Relay are both capable of greater speeds than either X.25 or modems. For more information, see the "WAN Technologies" section in this chapter.

Suggested Readings and Resources

1. Alexander, Bruce. *802.11 Wireless Network Site Surveying and Installation*. Cisco Press, 2004.

2. WAN technology information from Cisco, www.cisco.com/univercd/cc/td/doc/cisin-twk/ito_doc/introwan.htm.

3. General WAN info and links, www.techfest.com/networking/wan.htm.

4. Computer Networking Tutorials and Advice, compnetworking.about.com.

5. "TechEncyclopedia," www.techencyclopedia.com.

CHAPTER EIGHT

Remote Access and Security Protocols

Objectives

This chapter covers the following CompTIA-specified objectives for the "Protocols and Standards" section of the Network+ exam:

2.16 Define the function of the following remote access protocols and services:

- ▶ **RAS (Remote Access Service)**
- ▶ **PPP (Point-to-Point Protocol)**
- ▶ **SLIP (Serial Line Internet Protocol)**
- ▶ **PPPoE (Point-to-Point Protocol over Ethernet)**
- ▶ **PPTP (Point-to-Point Tunneling Protocol)**
- ▶ **VPN (Virtual Private Network)**
- ▶ **RDP (Remote Desktop Protocol)**

- ▶ Remote access is a common feature of today's networks. An understanding of the common remote access protocols and services is a must for any network administrator.

2.17 Identify the following security protocols and describe their purpose and function:

- ▶ **IPSec (Internet Protocol Security)**
- ▶ **L2TP (Layer 2 Tunneling Protocol)**
- ▶ **SSL (Secure Sockets Layer)**
- ▶ **WEP (Wired Equivalent Privacy)**
- ▶ **WPA (Wi-Fi Protected Access)**
- ▶ **802.1x**

- ▶ Providing remote access facilities for a network brings with it a multitude of security concerns. To address these concerns, security protocols are available to ensure that only the intended users can access the network and the data transmitted to it.

2.18 Identify authentication protocols (for example, CHAP [Challenge Handshake Authentication Protocol], MS-CHAP [Microsoft Challenge Handshake Authentication Protocol], PAP [Password Authentication Protocol], RADIUS [Remote Authentication Dial-In User Service], Kerberos, and EAP [Extensible Authentication Protocol]).

- ▶ Authentication protocols play an important part in a network's security strategy. Authentication protocols verify that the user has the right to the server or resource to which he is attempting to access.

Outline

Study Strategies

► Review the various remote access protocols and their uses.

► Identify the features of security protocols including encryption and authentication services.

► Identify and compare wireless security protocols.

► Review the protocols used to provide authentication.

► Ensure that you can identify the protocols discussed in this chapter from both their acronym and full name.

► Review the Notes, Tips, and Exam Alerts in this chapter. Make sure that you understand the information in the Exam Alerts.

Introduction

Networks are no longer restricted to the confines of a single location or even a small group of locations. Users can, and do, connect to remote networks from virtually anywhere. The ability to remotely access networks has changed the way we work and do business. Today, anywhere/anytime access to computer networks is an expectation rather than a bonus. Whether a user is working from home, his car, or a branch office, the ability to access the corporate network has become a critical requirement.

Modern network and workstation operating systems facilitate remote access by providing the means and methods to do it. By using remote access capabilities, it's possible to create a secure, transparent connection that lets remote corporate users feel as if they were operating from the local network.

Traditionally, remote access has been achieved by using a modem and a dial-up connection. Although this method is still widely used and is by far the most popular method of remote connectivity, new technologies continue to emerge, increasing the variety of ways that networks can be accessed remotely. Technologies such as fixed wireless, Internet access using cable, and Digital Subscriber Line (DSL) have opened up new possibilities for remote access through their increased speed and reduced costs. These high-speed remote access methods mean that instead of just using the connection to transfer a file or two, remote workers can use a variety of modern technologies such as videoconferencing.

Regardless of the technique used for remote access or the speed at which access is achieved, certain technologies need to be in place to facilitate a remote connection. These technologies include the protocols both to allow the access to the server and to secure the data transfer after the connection is established. Security protocols are also required that ensure that only authorized users can access the network remotely.

All the major operating systems provide built-in support for the remote access strategies we use today. This includes support for interoperable access protocols and security features required to establish and secure a remote connection. This chapter focuses on the protocols and services used to create a remote link. It begins by looking at the remote access protocols and the protocols used for security. Finally, the chapter examines two remote access methods—dial-in access and virtual private networks (VPNs)—and the protocols they use to establish and secure remote connections.

Remote Access Protocols and Services

Objective:

2.16 Define the function of the following remote access protocols and services:

- ▶ RAS (Remote Access Service)

- ▶ PPP (Point-to-Point Protocol)

- ▶ SLIP (Serial Line Internet Protocol)

- ▶ PPPoE (Point-to-Point Protocol over Ethernet)

- ▶ PPTP (Point-to-Point Tunneling Protocol)

- ▶ VPN (Virtual Private Network)

- ▶ RDP (Remote Desktop Protocol)

In addition to the actual physical requirements to make a remote connection, establishing a remote connection requires various protocols and services. Many types of protocols and services are associated with remote networking, some of which include

- ▶ RAS (Remote Access Service)

- ▶ PPP (Point-to-Point Protocol)

- ▶ SLIP (Serial Line Internet Protocol)

- ▶ PPPoE (Point-to-Point Protocol over Ethernet)

- ▶ PPTP (Point-to-Point Tunneling Protocol)

- ▶ VPN (Virtual Private Network)

- ▶ RDP (Remote Desktop Protocol)

Each of these protocols and services has advantages, disadvantages, and limitations, but each has a place in establishing remote connectivity.

This chapter begins its discussion of remote access technologies by looking at the remote access mechanism used on Windows Server platforms: the RAS, which is the most popular form of remote connectivity.

Remote Access Service (RAS)

RAS is a full-featured remote access solution included with Windows Server products. The popularity of RAS has a lot to do with the popularity of Windows, but RAS is also feature rich, easy to configure, and easy to use. As a result of this ease of use, many companies that previously had not used remote access now embrace it. (The fact that RAS is included with Windows has probably also had something to do with its popularity.)

> **NOTE**
>
> **RRAS** In Windows 2000 Microsoft renamed the RAS service to Routing and Remote Access Service (RRAS). The basic RAS functionality, however, is the same as in previous versions of Windows.

Any system that supports the appropriate dial-in protocols can connect to a RAS server. Most commonly, the clients are Windows systems that use the dial-up networking feature; but any operating system that supports dial-up client software will work. Connection to a RAS server can be made over a standard phone line, using a modem, over a network, or via an Integrated Services Digital Network (ISDN) connection.

> **NOTE**
>
> **RAS Server Callbacks**   RAS includes a feature called *callback* that allows for an extra degree of security. When a call is placed to a RAS server, the server hangs up and calls back either a predetermined number or a number that can be input by the remote user. When a predetermined number is used, only calls that originate from that number will be serviced, which is more secure than allowing calls from any number.

When a connection is made to the RAS server, the client is authenticated, and the system that is dialing in becomes a part of the network, although it is connected over a slow link. Depending on the configuration of the RAS server, the client is then able to access just the RAS server or the entire network. The number of RAS connections is normally limited by the number of dial-in connections the system can physically accommodate, but there are also some limits built in to the software. Windows 2000 Server, for example, supports up to 256 remote connections, whereas workstation products such as Windows XP Professional and Windows 2000 Professional support only a single RAS connection. Figure 8.1 shows an example of remote access through a RAS server.

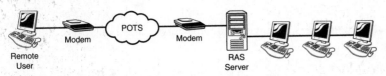

Remote
User

Modem   POTS   Modem

RAS
Server

FIGURE 8.1   Remote access through a RAS server.

RAS Client Support

RAS supports remote connectivity from all the major client operating systems from the old to the new, including

- ▶ Windows 95/98/Me–based clients
- ▶ Windows NT Workstation–based clients
- ▶ Windows 2000/XP Professional–based clients
- ▶ Unix-based/Linux clients
- ▶ Macintosh-based clients

The RAS service relies on remote access protocols to establish and secure a remote connection.

Point-to-Point Protocol (PPP)

PPP, which is described in RFC 1661, is the standard remote access protocol in use today. PPP is actually a family of protocols that work together to provide connection services. PPP provides solutions to most of SLIP's shortcomings.

Because PPP is an industry standard, it offers interoperability between different software vendors in various remote access implementations. PPP provides a number of security enhancements compared to SLIP, the most important being the encryption of usernames and passwords during the authentication process. PPP allows remote clients and servers to negotiate data encryption methods and authentication methods and support new technologies. PPP even gives administrators the ability to choose which particular local area network (LAN) protocol to use over a remote link. Administrators can choose from among NetBIOS Extended User Interface (NetBEUI), NWLink (Internetwork Packet Exchange/Sequenced Packet Exchange [IPX/SPX]), AppleTalk, or TCP/IP.

PPP Authentication Protocols

During the establishment of a PPP connection between the remote system and the server, the remote server needs to authenticate the remote user and does so by using the PPP authentication protocols. PPP accommodates a number of authentication protocols; the protocol used in the authentication process depends on the security configurations established between the remote user and the server. Some of the common authentication protocols used by PPP include the Challenge Handshake Authentication Protocol (CHAP), Microsoft Challenge Handshake Authentication Protocol (MS-CHAP), Password Authentication Protocol (PAP), Extensible Authentication Protocol (EAP), and Shiva Password Authentication Protocol (SPAP). Each of these is described later in this chapter in the "Authentication Protocols" section.

NOTE

ATCP Macintosh users can dial in to a Windows 2000/2003 server by using PPP over AppleTalk Control Protocol (ATCP). ATCP is installed when the AppleTalk protocol is installed, or it can be installed separately.

The PPP Dial-up Sequence

The following specific steps are performed when a remote connection is established:

1. To allow communication between devices to occur, framing rules are established between the client and the server.

2. The remote client system is authenticated by the authentication server, using one of the PPP authentication protocols: CHAP, MS-CHAP, EAP, or PAP.

3. Network control protocols (NCPs) configure the remote client for the correct LAN protocols, TCP/IP, and so on.

After these steps are successfully completed, the server and the client can begin to exchange data.

> **TIP**
>
> **SLIP and PPP**   If you are working on a network that uses SLIP, try to move to PPP as soon as possible because it is more flexible and secure than PPP.

Serial Line Internet Protocol (SLIP)

In the 1970s, students at the University of California, Berkeley, developed SLIP. SLIP was designed to allow data to be transmitted via Transmission Control Protocol/Internet Protocol (TCP/IP) over serial connections in a Unix environment. SLIP did an excellent job, but time proved to be its enemy. SLIP was developed in an atmosphere in which security was not an overriding concern; consequently, SLIP does not support encryption or authentication. It transmits all the data used to establish a connection (username and password) in clear text, which is, of course, dangerous in today's insecure world.

> **EXAM ALERT**
>
> **SLIP**   SLIP is an older remote access protocol, and, although still widely supported, it is replaced with PPP in most environments.

SLIP also does not provide error checking or packet addressing, so it can be used only in serial communications. It supports only TCP/IP, and logon is accomplished through a terminal window. You can avoid the terminal window logon by utilizing scripts, but doing so can be difficult as well. SLIP does also not provide support for dynamic address assignment, link testing, or multiplexing different protocols over a single link.

Is SLIP a bad protocol? No; in its day, it performed its intended duties perfectly. It is just not a match for today's computing environment or the new dial-up protocols that are available.

Many operating systems still provide at least minimal SLIP support for backward capability to older environments, but SLIP has been replaced by a newer and more secure alternative: PPP. SLIP is still used by some government agencies and large corporations in Unix remote access applications, so you might come across it from time to time.

Point-to-Point Protocol over Ethernet (PPPoE)

PPPoE (Point-to-Point Protocol over Ethernet) is a protocol used for connecting multiple network users on an Ethernet local area network to a remote site through a common device. For example, using PPPoE, it is possible to have all users on a network share the same link such as a DSL, cable modem, or wireless connection to the Internet. PPPoE gets its name because it is a combination of PPP and the Ethernet protocol, which supports multiple users in a local area network. The PPP protocol information is encapsulated within an Ethernet frame.

With PPPoE, a number of different users can share the same physical connection to the Internet, and in the process, PPPoE provides a way to keep track of individual user Internet access times. Because PPPoE allows for individual authenticated access to high-speed data networks, it is an efficient way to create a separate connection to a remote server for each user. This strategy allows Internet access and billing on a per-user basis rather than a per-site basis.

Users accessing PPPoE connections require the same information as required with standard dial-up phone accounts, including a username and password combination. As with a dial-up PPP service, an Internet service provider (ISP) will most likely automatically assign configuration information such as the IP address, subnet mask, default gateway, and DNS server.

There are two distinct stages in the PPPoE communication process: the discovery stage and the PPP session stage. The discovery stage completes four steps to establish the PPPoE connection: initiation, offer, request, and session confirmation. These steps represent back-and-forth communication between the client and the PPPoE server. After these steps have been negotiated, the PPP session can be established using familiar PPP authentication protocols.

Challenge

You have been asked to implement a broadband connection solution that requires each user to sign in with a username and password. You are unfamiliar with the process of setting up such a connection, so you refer to Microsoft's Knowledge Base. From this resource, identify the protocol and procedures required to configure your system to create a high-speed connection that requires you to sign in.

Point-to-Point Tunneling Protocol (PPTP)

PPTP, which is documented in RFC 2637, is often mentioned together with PPP. Although it's used in dial-up connections as PPP is, PPTP provides different functionality: It creates a secure *tunnel* between two points on a network, over which other connectivity protocols, such as PPP, can be used. This tunneling functionality is the basis for VPNs, which are discussed later in this chapter.

VPNs are created and managed by using the PPTP protocol, which builds on the functionality of PPP, making it possible to create dedicated point-to-point tunnels through a public network such as the Internet. Figure 8.2 shows an example of a PPTP connection through a public network.

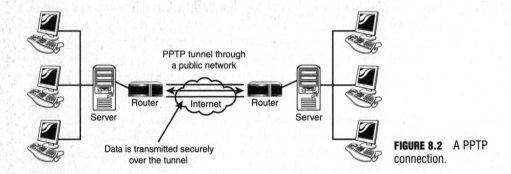

PPTP tunnel through
a public network

Router   Internet   Router

Server   Server

Data is transmitted securely
over the tunnel

FIGURE 8.2   A PPTP connection.

To establish a PPTP session between a client and server, a TCP connection known as a *PPTP control connection* is required to create and maintain the communication tunnel. The PPTP control connection exists between the IP address of the PPTP client and the IP address of the PPTP server, using TCP port 1723 on the server and a dynamic port on the client. It is the function of the PPTP control connection to pass the PPTP control and management messages used to maintain the PPTP communication tunnel between the remote system and the server. PPTP provides authenticated and encrypted communications between two end points such as a client and a server. PPTP does not use a public key infrastructure but does use a user ID and password. Table 8.1 provides examples of these control and management messages.

TABLE 8.1   PPTP Call Control and Management Messages

PPTP Control Message	Function
Start Control Connection Request	The initial message sent by the client to create the PPTP control connection. To establish a PPTP tunnel, this control connection must be initiated before any other PPTP messages can be sent.
Start Control Connection Reply	The response sent by the server, acknowledging the client's request.
Outgoing Call Request	The request sent by the client to establish the PPTP tunnel.
Outgoing Call Reply	The server's reply to the Outgoing Call Request message.
Call Clear Request	The request sent by the PPTP client, indicating the termination of the tunnel.
Call Disconnect Notify	The message sent by the server in response to the Call Clear Request message.
Stop Control Connection Request	The request sent by either the PPTP client or the PPTP server to indicate that the control connection is being terminated.

PPTP uses the same authentication methods as PPP, including MS-CHAP, CHAP, PAP, and EAP.

Virtual Private Networks (VPN)

In the mid-1990s, Microsoft, IBM, and Cisco began working on a technology called *tunneling*. By 1996, more companies had become interested and involved in the work, and the project soon produced two new virtual private networking solutions: PPTP and L2TP. Ascend, 3Com, Microsoft, and U.S. Robotics had developed PPTP, and Cisco Systems had introduced L2F.

From these developments, virtual private networks (VPNs) became one of the most popular methods of remote access. Essentially, a VPN extends a LAN by establishing a remote connection, using a public network such as the Internet. A VPN provides a point-to-point dedicated link between two points over a public IP network.

VPN encapsulates encrypted data inside another datagram that contains routing information. The connection between two computers establishes a switched connection dedicated to the two computers. The encrypted data is encapsulated inside PPP, and that connection is used to deliver the data.

A VPN allows anyone with an Internet connection to use the infrastructure of the public network to dial in to the main network and access resources as if she were logged on to the network locally. It also allows two networks to be connected to each other securely.

Many elements are involved in establishing a VPN connection, including the following:

▶ **A VPN client**—The VPN client is the computer that initiates the connection to the VPN server.

▶ **A VPN server**—The VPN server authenticates connections from VPN clients.

▶ **An access method**—As mentioned, a VPN is most often established over a public network such as the Internet; however, some VPN implementations use a private intranet. The network used must be IP based.

▶ **VPN protocols**—Protocols are required to establish, manage, and secure the data over the VPN connection. PPTP and L2TP are commonly associated with VPN connections.

VPNs have become popular because they allow the public Internet to be safely utilized as a wide area network (WAN) connectivity solution. (A complete discussion of VPNs would easily fill another book and goes beyond the scope of the Network+ objectives.)

EXAM ALERT

VPN Connections   VPNs support analog modems and ISDN as well as dedicated broadband connections such as cable and DSL. You should remember this for the exam.

Remote Desktop Protocol (RDP)

In a Windows environment, Terminal Services provides a way for a client system to connect to a server, such as Windows Server 2000/2003, and by using the Remote Desktop Protocol (RDP) run programs on the server as if they were local client applications. Such a configuration is known as *thin client computing*, whereby client systems use the resources of the server instead of their local processing power.

Originally, Terminal Services was available in remote administration mode or application server mode. Today, in Windows 2003, Terminal Services remote administration mode is no more; it has been replaced with the Remote Desktop feature.

Windows Server 2003 and XP Professional have built-in support for Remote Desktop connections. The underlying protocol used to manage the connection is RDP. RDP is a low-overhead protocol used to send mouse movements, keystrokes, and bitmap images of the screen on the server to the client computer. RDP does not actually send data over the connection only screenshots and client keystrokes. In application, what the client sees on his local screen is actually the functions occurring on the remote server and viewing the computing over RDP.

Security Protocols

Objective:

2.17 Identify the following security protocols and describe their purpose and function:

► IPSec (Internet Protocol Security)

► L2TP (Layer 2 Tunneling Protocol)

► SSL (Secure Sockets Layer)

► WEP (Wired Equivalent Privacy)

► WPA (Wi-Fi Protected Access)

► 802.1x

Any discussion of remote access is sure to include security, and for a good reason: As its name implies, remote access literally opens your network to remote users. Although you'd like to think that only authorized users would try to connect from remote locations, the reality is that an equal number of illegitimate users will probably attempt to connect. Because many of the methods used to establish remote access are over public networks, securing the data you send and the points at which you connect is an important consideration. Significant elements of this security are encryption and authentication.

As a quick overview, *encryption* is the process of encoding the data sent over remote connections, and it involves scrambling the usernames and passwords used to gain access to the remote network. Encryption is simply the process of encoding data using a mathematical algorithm that makes it difficult for unauthorized users to read the data if they are able to intercept it. The algorithm is actually a mathematical value known as a *key*. The key is required to read the encrypted data. Encryption techniques use public and private keys; public keys can be shared, and private keys cannot.

A *key* is a binary number that has a large number of bits. As you might imagine, the bigger the number or key, the more difficult it is to guess. Today, simple encryption strategies use 40 to 56 bits. On a 40-bit encryption, there are 2^{40} possible keys; 56-bit encryption has 2^{56} possible keys—that's a lot of keys. Remember that without the correct key, the data cannot be accessed. Although the number of keys associated with lower-grade encryption may seem amazing, they have been cracked by some very high-end, specialized systems. That makes necessary higher-grade encryption: Many online transactions require 128-bit encryption, and other applications support encryption as high as 1,024 bits. (If you have time, try to calculate the key combinations for these higher-grade encryption strategies.)

Using and managing remote access connections requires knowledge of security protocols and what they are designed to do. The following sections examine several different security protocols:

- ▶ IPSec (Internet Protocol Security)
- ▶ L2TP (Layer 2 Tunneling Protocol)
- ▶ SSL (Secure Sockets Layer)
- ▶ WEP (Wired Equivalent Privacy)
- ▶ WPA (Wi-Fi Protected Access)
- ▶ 802.1x

IPSec

The IP Security (IPSec) protocol is designed to provide secure communications between systems. This includes system-to-system communication in the same network as well as communication to systems on external networks. IPSec is an IP layer security protocol that can both encrypt and authenticate network transmissions. In a nutshell, IPSec is comprised of two separate protocols, Authentication Headers (AH) and Encapsulating Security Payloads (ESP). AH provides the authentication and integrity checking for data packets, and ESP provides encryption services.

Using both AH and ESP, data traveling between systems can be secured ensuring that transmissions cannot be viewed, accessed, or modified by those who should not have access to it. It might seem that protection on an internal network is less necessary than on an external network; however, much of the data you send across networks has little or no protection, allowing unwanted eyes to access it.

> **NOTE**
>
> **Using IPSec**   IPSec was created by the Internet Engineering Task Force (IETF) and can be used on both IPv4 and IPv6 networks.

IPSec provides three key security services:

- ▶ **Data verification**—It verifies that the data received is from the intended source.

- ▶ **Protection from data tampering**—It ensures that the data has not been tampered with and changed between the sending and receiving devices.

- ▶ **Private transactions**—It ensures that the data sent between the sending and receiving devices is unreadable by any other devices.

IPSec operates at the network layer of the Open Systems Interconnect (OSI) model and provides security for protocols that operate at the higher layers. Thus, by using IPSec, you can secure practically all TCP/IP-related communications.

> **TIP**
>
> **IPSec and TCP/IP**   IPSec can be used only on TCP/IP networks. If you are using another network protocol, you need to use a security protocol such as L2TP.

Layer Two Tunneling Protocol (L2TP)

L2TP is a combination of PPTP and Cisco's L2F technology. L2TP, as the name suggests, utilizes tunneling to deliver data. It authenticates the client in a two-phase process: It first authenticates the computer and then the user. By authenticating the computer, it prevents the data from being intercepted, changed, and returned to the user in what is known as a *man-in-the-middle attack*. L2TP assures both parties that the data they are receiving is exactly the data sent by the originator.

> **NOTE**
>
> **L2TP Tunneling Without Encryption**   It is possible to create an L2TP tunnel without using encryption, but this is not a true VPN and, obviously, lacks a certain amount of security.

> **TIP**
>
> **L2TP and the Data-Link Layer**   Unlike IPSec, which operates at the network layer of the OSI model, L2TP operates at the data-link layer, making it protocol independent. This means that an L2TP connection can support protocols such as IPX and AppleTalk.

L2TP and PPTP are both tunneling protocols, so you might be wondering which you should use. Here is a quick list of some of the advantages of each, starting with PPTP:

- PPTP has been around the longest; it offers more interoperability than L2TP.
- PPTP is an industry standard.
- PPTP is easier to configure than L2TP because L2TP uses digital certificates.
- PPTP has less overhead than L2TP.

The following are some of the advantages of L2TP:

- L2TP offers greater security than PPTP.
- L2TP supports common public key infrastructure technology.
- L2TP provides support for header compression.

NOTE

L2TP and NAT   L2TP cannot be used if Network Address Translation (NAT) is being used.

Secure Sockets Layer (SSL)

SSL is a security protocol used on the Internet. Originally developed by Netscape for use with its Navigator browser, SSL uses public key encryption to establish secure connections over the Internet. SSL provides three key services:

- **Server authentication**—SSL allows a user to confirm a server's identity. For example, you can use this capability when you are purchasing something online with a credit card but first want to verify the server's identity.
- **Client authentication**—SSL allows a server to confirm a user's identity. This functionality is often used when a server is sending sensitive information—such as banking information or sensitive documents—to a client system and wants to verify the client's identity.
- **Encrypted connections**—It is possible to configure SSL to require all information sent between a client and a server to be encrypted by the sending software and decrypted by the receiving software. Doing this establishes private and secure communication between two devices. In addition, SSL has a mechanism to determine whether the data sent has been tampered with or altered in transit.

You can see SSL security on the Web when you access a secure universal resource locator (URL). Secure websites begin with https:// instead of http://. Hypertext Transfer Protocol over SSL (HTTPS) connections require a browser to establish a secure connection.

EXAM ALERT

SSL and Port 443 For the exam, don't forget that SSL connections for web pages are made through port 443 by default.

Secure Shell (SSH)

Because Unix- and Linux-based systems are prominent in modern network environments, network administrators face huge security interoperability concerns. Windows-based clients often use Telnet to remotely access Unix/Linux servers. Unfortunately, Telnet is a very insecure remote access method; it sends the entire session—including passwords and login information—in clear text. (*Clear text* simply means that the information is sent unencrypted, and anyone can intercept with a packet capture program and read the data with his favorite word processor.)

SSH provides a secure multiplatform replacement for Telnet. SSH allows users to connect to a remote server, and it encrypts the entire session. SSH has become an IETF standard, and development for SSH now includes a number of operating systems besides Linux and Unix. Using SSH, Windows 2000/XP as well as Macintosh systems can securely access remote servers.

To download and try SSH, go to www.freessh.org and download the client software.

Securing Wireless Networks

As mentioned throughout this book, many different strategies and protocols are used to secure LAN and WAN transmissions. What about those network transmissions that travel over the airwaves?

In the last few years wireless networking has changed the look of modern networks, bringing with it an unparalleled level of mobility and a host of new security concerns.

Wireless LANs (WLANs) require new protocols and standards to handle security for radio communications. As it stands today, wireless communications represent a significant security concern. There are a few wireless security standards to be aware of when working with wireless, including Wired Equivalent Privacy (WEP), Wi-Fi Protected Access (WPA), and 802.1x.

Wired Equivalent Privacy (WEP)

Wired equivalent privacy (WEP) was the first attempt to keep wireless networks safe. WEP was designed to be easy to configure and implement, and originally it was hoped that WEP would provide the same level of security to wireless networks as was available to wired. For a time it was the best and only option for securing wireless networks.

WEP is an IEEE standard introduced in 1997 designed for securing 802.11 networks. With WEP enabled, each data packet transmitted over the wireless connection would be encrypted. Originally, the data packet was combined with a secret 40-bit number key as it passed through an encryption algorithm known as RC4. The packet was scrambled and sent across the airwaves. On the receiving end, the data packet passed through the RC4 backward, and the host received the data as it was intended. WEP originally used a 40-bit number key, but later specified 128-bit encryption, making WEP that much more robust.

WEP was designed to provide security by encrypting data from the sending and receiving devices. In a short period of time, however, it was discovered that WEP encryption was not nearly as secure as hoped. Part of the problem was that when the 802.11 standards were being written, security was not the major concern it is today. As a result, WEP security was easy to crack with freely available hacking tools. From this point, wireless communication was regarded as a potentially insecure transmission media.

There are two types of WEP security: static and dynamic WEP. The primary security risks are associated with static WEP, which uses a shared password to protect communications. Security weaknesses discovered in static WEP means that WLANs protected by it are vulnerable to several types of threats. Freely available hacking tools make breaking into static WEP-protected wireless networks a trivial task. Unsecured WLANs are obviously exposed to these same threats as well; the difference being that less expertise, time, and resources are required to carry out the attacks.

Wi-Fi Protected Access (WPA)

Security weaknesses associated with WEP provided administrators with a valid reason to be concerned with wireless security. The need for increased wireless security was important for wireless networking to reach its potential and to bring a sense of confidence for those with sensitive data to use wireless communications. In response, the Wi-Fi Protected Access (WPA) was created. WPA was designed to improve on the security weaknesses of WEP and to be backward compatible with older devices using the WEP standard. WPA addressed two main security concerns:

- **Enhanced data encryption**—WPA uses a *temporal key integrity protocol (TKIP)*, which scrambles encryption keys using a hashing algorithm. Then the keys are issued an integrity check to verify that they have not been modified or tampered with during transit.

- **Authentication**—Using the extensible authentication protocol (EAP). WEP regulates access to a wireless network based on a computer's hardware-specific MAC address, which is relatively simple to be sniffed out and stolen. EAP is built on a more secure public-key encryption system to ensure that only authorized network users can access the network.

802.1x

802.1x is an IEEE standard specifying port-based network access control. 802.1x was not specifically designed for wireless networks, rather it provides authenticated access for both wired and wireless networks. Port-based network access control uses the physical characteristics of a switched local area network (LAN) infrastructure to authenticate devices attached to a LAN port and to prevent access to that port in cases where the authentication process fails.

During a port-based network access control interaction, a LAN port adopts one of two roles: authenticator or supplicant. In the role of *authenticator*, a LAN port enforces authentication before it allows user access to the services that can be accessed through that port. In the role of *supplicant*, a LAN port requests access to the services that can be accessed through the authenticator's port. An authentication server, which can either be a separate entity or co-located with the authenticator, checks the supplicant's credentials on behalf of the authenticator. The authentication server then responds to the authenticator, indicating whether the supplicant is authorized to access the authenticator's services.

The authenticator's port-based network access control defines two logical access points to the LAN through one physical LAN port. The first logical access point, the *uncontrolled port*, allows data exchange between the authenticator and other computers on the LAN, regardless of the computer's authorization state. The second logical access point, the *controlled port*, allows data exchange between an authenticated LAN user and the authenticator.

Authentication Protocols

Objective:

2.18 Identify authentication protocols (for example, CHAP [Challenge Handshake Authentication Protocol], MS-CHAP [Microsoft Challenge Handshake Authentication Protocol], PAP [Password Authentication Protocol], RADIUS [Remote Authentication Dial-In User Service], Kerberos, and EAP [Extensible Authentication Protocol]).

Two primary technologies are required for securing data transmissions: encryption and authentication. Encryption was discussed earlier; this section reviews authentication protocols.

When designing a remote connection strategy, it is critical to consider how remote users will be authenticated. Authentication defines the way in which a remote client and server negotiate on a user's credentials when the user is trying to gain access to the network. Depending on the operating system used and the type of remote access involved, several different protocols are used to authenticate a user. The following are authentication protocols used with various technologies including PPP.

Microsoft Challenge Handshake Authentication Protocol (MS-CHAP)/(MS-CHAP v2)

MS-CHAP is a protocol used to authenticate incoming connections from remote Windows workstations. MS-CHAP works with remote connection strategies including PPP, PPTP, and L2TP. MS-CHAP uses a challenge-response mechanism and prevents client passwords from being sent during the authentication process. MS-CHAP uses something called the Message Digest 5 (MD5) hashing algorithm and the Data Encryption Standard (3DES) encryption algorithm to generate the challenge and response and provides mechanisms for reporting connection errors and for changing the user's password.

On the heels of MS-CHAP is the updated MS-CHAP2. As with any second version, MS-CHAP introduces enhancements over its predecessor. A key improvement includes support for two-way authentication or mutual authentication. Two-way authentication confirms the identity of both sides of the connection. The remote access client authenticates against the remote access server, and the remote access server authenticates against the remote access client. Mutual authentication provides protection against remote server impersonation. MS-CHAP2 also includes a few changes in which the cryptographic key is analyzed. As far as authentication methods are concerned, MS-CHAP v2 is the most secure. MS-CHAP v2 also supports PPP, PPTP, and L2TP network connections.

Challenge Handshake Protocol (CHAP)

CHAP is a widely supported authentication method and works much the same way as MS-CHAP. A key difference between the two is that CHAP supports non-Microsoft remote access clients. CHAP allows for authentication without actually having the user send his password over the network, and because it's an industry standard, it allows Windows Server 2003 to behave as a remote client of almost any third-party PPP server.

Like the Microsoft varieties, CHAP is a challenge-response authentication protocol. CHAP authentication uses the MD5 encryption scheme to secure authentication responses. CHAP is a commonly used protocol, and as the name suggests, anyone trying to connect is challenged for authentication information. When the correct information is supplied, the systems "shake hands," and the connection is established.

> **EXAM ALERT**
>
> **CHAP** CHAP is used to authenticate non-Microsoft clients.

Extensible Authentication Protocol (EAP)

EAP is an extension of the Point-to-Point Protocol (PPP) that supports authentication methods that go beyond the simple submission of a username and password. EAP was developed in response to an increasing demand for authentication methods that use other types of security devices such as smartcards or digital certificates.

Password Authentication Protocol (PAP)

Password Authentication Protocol (PAP) is not a widely used security method due to some insecurities. PAP is a simple authentication protocol in which the username and password are sent to the remote access server in unencrypted text, making it possible for anyone listening to network traffic to steal both. PAP is typically used only when connecting to older Unix-based remote access servers that do not support any additional authentication protocols.

Remote Authentication Dial-In User Service (RADIUS)

Among the potential issues network administrators face when implementing remote access are utilization and the load on the remote access server. As a network's remote access implementation grows, reliance on a single remote access server might be impossible, and additional servers might be required. RADIUS can help in this scenario.

RADIUS is a protocol that allows a single server to become responsible for all remote access authentication, authorization, and auditing (or accounting) services. The RADIUS protocol can be implemented as a vendor-specific product such as Microsoft's Internet Authentication Server (IAS).

RADIUS functions as a client/server system. The remote user dials in to the remote access server, which acts as a RADIUS client, or network access server (NAS), and connects to a RADIUS server. The RADIUS server performs authentication, authorization, and auditing (or accounting) functions and returns the information to the RADIUS client (which is a remote access server running RADIUS client software); the connection is either established or rejected based on the information received.

RADIUS can also be configured in a fault-tolerant architecture that provides backup servers that process requests when other RADIUS servers fail. Because RADIUS is actually a set of protocols based on RFCs, it works with many remote access servers—it is not a Microsoft-only implementation.

Kerberos

Seasoned administrators can tell you about the risks of sending clear-text, unencrypted passwords across any network. The Kerberos network authentication protocol is designed to ensure that the data sent across networks is safe from attack. Its purpose is to provide authentication for client/server applications.

Kerberos authentication works by assigning a unique key (called a *ticket*), to each client that successfully authenticates to a server. The ticket is encrypted and contains the password of the user, which is used to verify the user's identity when a particular network service is requested.

Kerberos was created at Massachusetts Institute of Technology to provide a solution to network security issues. With Kerberos, the client must prove its identity to the server, and the server must also prove its identity to the client. Kerberos provides a method to verify the identity of a computer system over an insecure network connection.

EXAM ALERT

Tickets For the exam, you should know that the security tokens used in Kerberos are known as *tickets*.

Kerberos is distributed freely, as is its source code, allowing anyone interested to view the source code directly. Kerberos is also available from many different vendors that provide additional support for its use.

Chapter Summary

Remote access has become an important part of modern business, and companies have come to depend on the ability to access network applications and services from a remote location. To facilitate remote access, all major operating systems offer the protocols necessary to connect a remote client to a server system. Some of the most common remote access protocols are SLIP, PPP, PPTP, RAS, L2TP, and RDP.

Implementing remote access for an organization introduces another issue for the network administrator: security. You must understand and use security protocols to ensure that data is not compromised. The common security protocols include IPSec, SSL, WEP, WPA, 802.1x, and Kerberos.

Key Terms

- ▶ 802.1x
- ▶ CHAP
- ▶ EAP
- ▶ encryption
- ▶ IPSec
- ▶ Kerberos
- ▶ L2TP
- ▶ MS-CHAP
- ▶ PAP
- ▶ PPP
- ▶ PPTP

- ▶ RADIUS
- ▶ RAS
- ▶ RDP
- ▶ security protocol
- ▶ SLIP
- ▶ SPAP
- ▶ SSL
- ▶ VPN
- ▶ WEP
- ▶ WPA

Apply Your Knowledge

Exercises

8.1   Enabling the Remote Access Service on a Computer Running Windows 2000 Server

Whether through a RAS, VPN, or some other method, the ability to configure remote access methods has become an important consideration for network administrators. In this exercise, you configure a server to allow incoming remote access.

Estimated time: 15 minutes

1. Select Start, Programs, Administrative Tools, Routing and Remote Access. The Routing and Remote Access window shown in Figure 8.3 appears.

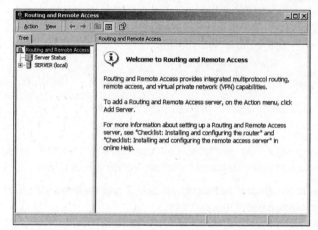

FIGURE 8.3 The Routing and Remote Access window.

2. To make the system a RAS server, select the Add Server option from the Action menu. The Add Server dialog box appears. Select the This Computer radio button, as shown in Figure 8.4.

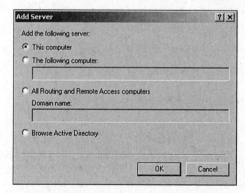

FIGURE 8.4 The Add Server dialog box.

3. In the left pane of the Routing and Remote Access window, right-click on your server and choose Configure and Enable Routing and Remote Access. The Routing and Remote Access Server Setup Wizard opens. Click Next to start the wizard.

4. Select the Remote Access Server radio button, as shown in Figure 8.5, and then click Next.

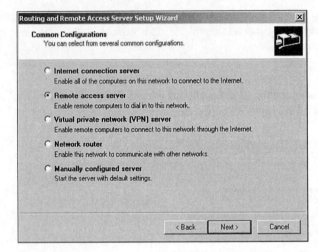

FIGURE 8.5 The Routing and Remote Access Server Setup Wizard.

5. The next screen in the wizard requires you to choose which protocols your clients will be able to use to connect to the remote access server. Accept the default, TCP/IP, and click Next.

6. You need to decide how to handle client IP addressing. For now, accept the default setting of Automatically, as shown in Figure 8.6, and then click Next.

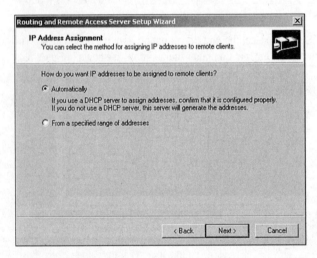

FIGURE 8.6 Configuring automatic IP addressing for remote clients.

7. In the next wizard screen, you have the option to set up a RADIUS server. Choose not to do so at this time and click Next.

8. The final wizard screen acknowledges the successful configuration of a Windows RAS server. Click Next, and the RAS service attempts to start automatically. Figure 8.7 shows the Routing and Remote Access window, with a successfully installed RAS server.

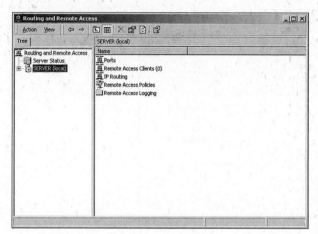

FIGURE 8.7 The Routing and Remote Access window with an installed RAS server.

8.2 Configuring a Client System to Access a Remote Server

After you have the server side of a remote access connection configured, you can configure the client side. To create a dial-up connection in Windows 2000 that allows a user to connect to a resource as a dial-up client, follow the steps in this exercise.

Estimated time: 15 minutes

1. Select Start, Settings, Network and Dial Up Connections. The Network and Dial-up Connections window shown in Figure 8.8 appears.

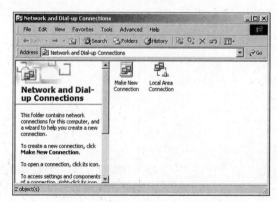

FIGURE 8.8 The Network and Dial-up Connections window.

2. Double-click the Make New Connection icon to start the Network Connection Wizard. Click Next to configure the connection.

3. The first screen of the Network Connection Wizard allows you to choose the type of network connection you want to create. Select the Dial-up to Private Network option, as shown in Figure 8.9, and then click Next. The Phone Number to Dial dialog box appears.

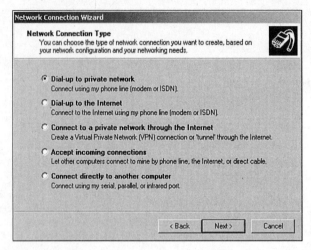

FIGURE 8.9 The Network Connection Type dialog box.

4. Enter the telephone number of the remote access server (a line that the remote access server will use to accept incoming calls). For this exercise, enter your personal telephone number. Click Next, and the Connection Availability screen appears. It allows you to limit the use of this dial-up connection to your personal logon or to anyone who logs on to this computer.

5. Make sure that For All Users is selected, as shown in Figure 8.10, and then click Next.

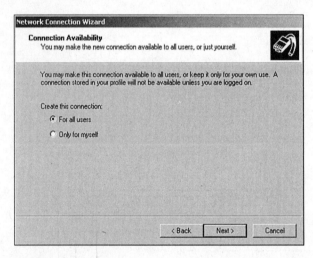

FIGURE 8.10 The Connection Availability dialog box.

6. The next screen lets you choose whether you will let other users access resources through this connection. For this exercise, leave the Internet Connection Sharing box unchecked. Click Next.

7. The Completing the Network Connection Wizard dialog box appears. You need to enter a descriptive name for the connection you are creating, so for this connection, enter **Real World Project Test**. Select Add a Shortcut to My Desktop, and then click Finish. A shortcut icon appears on your desktop.

8. In a real-world scenario, you can now establish a connection to a remote access server by double-clicking the shortcut icon.

Exam Questions

1. Which of the following statements best describes a VPN?

   ○ **a.** It is any protocol that allows remote clients to log in to a server over a network such as the Internet.

   ○ **b.** It provides a system whereby only screen display and keyboard and mouse input travel across the link.

   ○ **c.** It is a secure communication channel across a public network such as the Internet.

   ○ **d.** It is a protocol used for encryption of user IDs and passwords.

2. Which of the following is a disadvantage of SLIP?

   ○ **a.** It transmits passwords and usernames in clear text.

   ○ **b.** It can be used only on Linux systems.

   ○ **c.** It can be used only on Microsoft Windows systems.

   ○ **d.** It is not a Network Driver Interface Specification (NDIS)–compliant protocol.

3. What is the function of SSL?

   ○ **a.** It provides a mechanism for data downloaded from and information uploaded to a website to be secured against unauthorized viewing.

   ○ **b.** It allows a secure remote connection to be established to a remote host for the purpose of opening a session on the remote host.

   ○ **c.** It allows an insecure remote connection to be established to a remote host for the purpose of opening a session on the remote host.

   ○ **d.** It allows a remote system to dial in to a server and uses the resources of that server as a gateway to the network.

4. What is the function of RAS?

   ○ **a.** It allows an insecure remote connection to be established to a remote host for the purpose of opening a session on the remote host.

   ○ **b.** It provides a mechanism for data downloaded from and information uploaded to a website to be secured against unauthorized viewing.

   ○ **c.** It allows a secure remote connection to be established to a remote host for the purpose of opening a session on the remote host.

   ○ **d.** It allows a remote system to dial in to a server and uses the resources of that server as a gateway to the network.

5. In a remote access scenario, what function does PPP serve?

    ○ **a.** It is a secure technology that allows information to be securely downloaded from a website.

    ○ **b.** It is a dial-up protocol used over serial links.

    ○ **c.** It is a technology that allows a secure tunnel to be created through a public network.

    ○ **d.** It provides a public key/private key exchange mechanism.

6. At what layer of the OSI model does IPSec operate?

    ○ **a.** Physical

    ○ **b.** Data-link

    ○ **c.** Network

    ○ **d.** Transport

7. Which of the following are PPP authentication methods? (Choose the two best answers.)

    ○ **a.** SLAP

    ○ **b.** CHAP

    ○ **c.** MS-CHAP

    ○ **d.** POP

8. Which of the following protocols is used in thin-client computing?

    ○ **a.** RDP

    ○ **b.** PPP

    ○ **c.** PPTP

    ○ **d.** RAS

9. SSH is a secure alternative to which of the following?

    ○ **a.** Telnet

    ○ **b.** DHCP

    ○ **c.** PPTP

    ○ **d.** Kerberos

10. Kerberos is an authentication system that can be used on what operating systems?

○ **a.** Windows 2000

○ **b.** Linux

○ **c.** Unix

○ **d.** All of the above

11. What encryption method does CHAP use when replying to an authentication request?

○ **a.** Kerberos

○ **b.** MDA

○ **c.** MD5

○ **d.** PPTP

12. How does the callback feature work in RAS?

○ **a.** It allows the RAS server to call a preset number any time it receives a connection.

○ **b.** It allows the RAS server to call a user-defined number any time it receives a connection.

○ **c.** It allows the RAS server to call a preset or user-defined number any time it receives a connection.

○ **d.** It allows the RAS server to generate a random number to call each time it receives a connection.

13. Which of the following URLs is using SSL?

○ **a.** http:ssl//www.comptia.org

○ **b.** http://www.comptia.org

○ **c.** httpssl://www.comptia.org

○ **d.** https://www.comptia.org

14. Which of the following is not an authentication protocol?

○ **a.** IPSec

○ **b.** CHAP

○ **c.** PAP

○ **d.** EAP

15. In a thin-client scenario, what information is propagated across the communications link between the client and the server?

    ○ a. Any data retrieved by the client from websites

    ○ b. Screen updates and keyboard and mouse input

    ○ c. Any file opened by the client during the session

    ○ d. Only the graphics files used to create the user's desktop, screen updates, and keyboard and mouse input

16. Which of the following is a reason to use L2TP rather than IPSec to create a VPN connection?

    ○ a. You need to have a secure connection.

    ○ b. You are a using a protocol other than TCP/IP.

    ○ c. You are using Microsoft Windows systems.

    ○ d. You are using public key/private key encryption.

17. You are onsite as a consultant. The client's many remote access users are experiencing connection problems. Basically, when users try to connect, the system is unable to service their authentication requests. What kind of server might you recommend to alleviate this problem?

    ○ a. RADIUS server

    ○ b. IPSec server

    ○ c. Proxy server

    ○ d. Kerberos server

18. Your company wants to create a secure link between two networks over the Internet. Which of the following protocols would you use to do this?

    ○ a. PPP

    ○ b. VPN

    ○ c. PPTP

    ○ d. SLIP

19. Which of the following protocols does PPTP use to establish connections?

    ○ a. DHCP

    ○ b. FTP

    ○ c. SSH

    ○ d. TCP

20. You are working for a client on a remote access connectivity solution. The client wants to use the RAS service for up to 10 clients at the lowest possible cost. Which of the following operating systems would you recommend to the client?

    ○ **a.** Samba

    ○ **b.** Novell NetWare 5.x

    ○ **c.** Windows 2000 Professional

    ○ **d.** Windows 2000 Server

Answers to Exam Questions

1. **c.** A VPN provides a secure communication path between devices over a public network such as the Internet. None of the other answers describes a VPN. For more information, see the section "Remote Access Protocols and Services" in this chapter.

2. **a.** SLIP transmits passwords and usernames in clear text and is therefore insecure. SLIP is usable across all platforms that support it, including Linux and Windows. Answer d is not valid. For more information, see the section "Remote Access Protocols and Services" in this chapter.

3. **a.** SSL provides a mechanism for securing data across a network. Answer b describes SSH, and Answer d describes RAS. Answer c is not valid. For more information, see the section "Security Protocols" in this chapter.

4. **d.** RAS allows a remote system to dial in to a network and use the resources of the network. All the other answers are not valid. For more information, see the section "Remote Access Protocols and Services" in this chapter.

5. **b.** PPP is a protocol that allows for dial-up connections over serial links. Answer a describes SSL, Answer c describes a VPN, and Answer d describes PKI. For more information, see the section "Remote Access Protocols and Services" in this chapter.

6. **c.** IPSec operates at the network layer of the OSI model. All the other answers are incorrect. For more information, see the section "Security Protocols" in this chapter.

7. **b, c.** Both CHAP and MS-CHAP are PPP authentication methods. The other answers are not valid authentication protocols. For more information, see the section "Remote Access Protocols and Services" in this chapter.

8. **a.** The RDP protocol is used in thin-client networking, where only screen, keyboard, and mouse inputs are sent across the line. RDP has been used for Windows Terminal Services and now is used with the Remote Desktop feature with Windows XP. PPP is a dial-up protocol used over serial links, PPTP is a technology used in VPNs, and RAS is a remote access service. For more information, see the section "Remote Access Protocols and Services" in this chapter.

9. **a.** SSH is a secure alternative to Telnet. None of the other answers are valid. For more information, see the section "Security Protocols" in this chapter.

10. **d.** Kerberos is available for all the major operating systems. For more information, see the section "Security Protocols" in this chapter.

11. **c.** CHAP uses the MD5 encryption method. None of the other answers are correct. For more information, see the section "Remote Access Protocols and Services" in this chapter.

12. **c.** The callback feature in RAS allows it to call a preset or user-defined number when it receives a connection. None of the other answers are valid. For more information, see the section "Remote Access Protocols and Services" in this chapter.

13. **d.** You can identify when SSL is used by the s in the URL (in this case https://www.comptia.org). Answer b is a valid HTTP URL, but it is not secure. None of the other answers are valid URLs. For more information, see the section "Security Protocols" in this chapter.

14. **a.** IPSec is not an authentication protocol. All the other protocols listed are classed as authentication protocols. For more information, see the section "Security Protocols" in this chapter.

15. **b.** Only screen, keyboard, and mouse inputs are sent across the communications link in a thin-client scenario. This allows the processing to be handled by the server. None of the other answers are valid. For more information, see the section "Remote Access Protocols and Services" in this chapter.

16. **b.** You need to use L2TP instead of IPSec when you are using a protocol other than TCP/IP. IPSec can be used only with TCP/IP. None of the other answers are valid. For more information, see the section "Security Protocols" in this chapter.

17. **a.** By installing a RADIUS server, it is possible to move the workload associated with authentication to a dedicated server. A proxy server would not improve the dial-up connection's performance. There is no such thing as a Kerberos server or an IPSec server. For more information, see the section "Security Protocols" in this chapter.

18. **c.** To establish the VPN connection between the two networks, use PPTP. PPP is a protocol used on dial-up links. A VPN is a type of network, not a protocol. SLIP is a nonsecure dial-up protocol. For more information, see the section "Remote Access Protocols and Services" in this chapter.

19. **d.** PPTP uses TCP. None of the other answers are valid. For more information, see the section "Remote Access Protocols and Services" in this chapter.

20. **d.** Windows 2000 Server supports more than 10 remote clients. Windows Me is not capable of being a RAS server. Novell NetWare does not include RAS server capability because RAS is a Microsoft product. Windows 2000 Professional supports only a single dial-in RAS connection. For more information, see the section "Remote Access Protocols and Services" in this chapter.

Suggested Readings and Resources

1. Ogletree, Terry William. *Upgrading and Repairing Networks, Fourth Edition*. Que Publishing, 2003.

2. Habraken, Joe. *Absolute Beginner's Guide to Networking*, fourth edition. Que Publishing, 2003.

3. Sugano, Alan. *The Real-world Network Troubleshooting Manual: Tools, Techniques, and Scenarios (Administrator's Advantage Series)*. Charles River Media, 2004.

4. Hunt, Craig. *TCP/IP Network Administration*, third edition. O'Reilly & Associates, 2002.

5. "Computer Networking Tutorials and Advice," compnetworking.about.com.

6. "TechEncyclopedia," www.techencyclopedia.com.

7. Network+ network protocol tutorial, www.learnthat.com/courses/computer/network-plus/network11.shtml.

8. Information on VPNs, including security protocols, www.vpnc.org.

CHAPTER NINE

Network Operating Systems and Clients

Objectives

This chapter covers the following CompTIA-specified objectives for the "Network Implementation" section of the Network+ exam:

3.1 Identify the basic capabilities (for example, client support, interoperability, authentication, file and print services, application support, and security) of the following server operating systems to access network resources:

▶ **Unix/Linux/Mac OS X Server**

▶ **NetWare**

▶ **Windows**

▶ **AppleShare IP (Internet Protocol)**

▶ Network operating systems are the means by which functionality is provided on a net-work. Each of the common operating systems has specific features and characteristics, and a capable network administrator must be familiar with them.

Outline

Study Strategies

▶ Compare and contrast the main features and characteristics of the server operating systems discussed in this chapter.

▶ Identify the file sharing protocols used with the various operating systems.

▶ Review the main features and components of the Windows operating systems.

▶ Identify the interoperability capabilities and configuration requirements for the various client operating systems.

▶ When reviewing the operating systems, take time to familiarize yourself with the tools and utilities discussed.

▶ Review the Notes, Tips, and Exam Alerts in this chapter. Make sure that you understand the information in the Exam Alerts. If you don't understand the topic referenced in an Exam Alert, refer to the information in the chapter text and then read the Exam Alert again.

Introduction

Network operating systems (NOS) are some of the most powerful and complex software products available today. This chapter looks at a number of operating systems that are widely used in today's network environments.

Each network operating system featured in this chapter has unique strengths and weaknesses, and each has its share of the increasingly competitive network operating system market. As a network administrator, it is your responsibility to maintain and manage these operating systems and ensure that they provide the required network services to users.

Even though the Network+ exam does not require that you be an expert or have an in-depth knowledge of the operating systems discussed in this chapter, a basic understanding of the common network operating system offerings is required. For those who find themselves working with operating systems, further study is certainly warranted.

A network requires both a network operating system and client operating systems. In this chapter we look at the steps involved in configuring common client operating systems for connection to the network.

The information described in this chapter is not intended to provide a tutorial on any of the operating systems discussed. Rather, this chapter provides overview information along with the basic commands used for setting up, installing, and configuring each operating system.

> **EXAM ALERT**
>
> **Operating Systems** The information included in this chapter is intended to provide the information necessary to answer any related question on the Network+ exam. Apart from studying the information provided, you should research and learn more about each of these operating systems for your own interest.

Introduction to Network Operating Systems

Objective:

3.1 Identify the basic capabilities (for example, client support, interoperability, authentication, file and print services, application support, and security) of the following server operating systems to access network resources:

▶ Unix/Linux/Mac OS X Server

▶ NetWare

▶ Windows

▶ AppleShare IP (Internet Protocol)

Early network operating systems provided just a few network services, such as file and printer sharing. Today's network operating systems offer a far broader range of services. Some of these services are used in almost every network environment, and others are used in only a few.

Despite the complexity of operating systems, the basic function and purpose of a network operating system is straightforward: to provide services to the network. Network operating systems provide several types of service for the client systems on the network. Some of the most common include:

- Authentication

- File sharing services

- Printer sharing services

- Web server services

- Firewall and proxy services

- Dynamic Host Configuration Protocol (DHCP) and Domain Name System (DNS) services

These are just a few of many services that a network operating system can provide. When you take the time to list all the different aspects of network operating systems, you gain an appreciation for their complexity and the many functions they are designed to perform.

Choosing a Network Operating System

When it comes to choosing a network operating system, you have a few choices. Which system you choose depends on a number of factors including what operating systems you are already running and, to a lesser extent, what applications you want to host. It may be that, for example, you want to run an application that is available for Windows Server 2003 but not available for Novell NetWare. More likely, though, is that your organization has decided that either one NOS is to be deployed for all server installations, or that a specific NOS is to be deployed for a given circumstance. As a network administrator, it is your responsibility to ensure that you recommend the most appropriate server platform for the intended purpose. As per the CompTIA Network+ objectives, this chapter discusses the following network operating systems, which together represent pretty much the entire installed base of PC-based NOSs:

- **Unix and Linux**—Some people might think that Linux is the new kid on the block, but in fact, Linux has been around for quite some time, and the operating system it is based on, Unix, has been around for decades. Linux is a free, open-source operating system and has found considerable popularity as a server operating system. Although Unix is not free, it has been the network operating system of choice for many large organizations. Be prepared, however; although they are powerful, these network operating systems are not as pretty and graphically intensive as what you might be used to.

Working with both Unix and Linux requires some command-line input and a better understanding of the underlying technologies than you need when you use some of the other network operating systems.

▶ **Novell NetWare**—Novell NetWare has long been one of the most widely used network operating systems. In the past, NetWare was viewed primarily as a file and print platform, but in reality, it can do much more. NetWare can be implemented in small networks, but it truly shines in a large corporate environment. Novell NetWare has lost a great deal of ground to the Windows and Linux platforms, although it still has a solid base of users, particularly in governmental and educational environments.

▶ **Windows 2000 Server/Windows Server 2003**—Windows is the most popular network operating system in use today. With the introduction of the latest version, Windows Server 2003, it continues its push to become the network operating system of choice in organizations of all sizes. Many people like the Windows-based network operating systems because of their familiar and easy-to-navigate graphical interfaces, even though these same graphical utilities and menus place increased demands on a server's hardware resources.

▶ **Macintosh**—Although not nearly as prevalent as the other network operating systems discussed in this list, Apple Macintosh OS X Server is aimed squarely at capturing some of the NOS market share. It's too early to tell at this point whether Apple's foray into the NOS market place will be successful, but as with its desktop operating systems it is sure to gain a loyal following.

▶ **ApplesShare IP**—AppleShare is a system that enables data and resource sharing on the network. AppleShare works in a client/server configuration, which means that client software is required to access resources on an AppleShare server. Once installed, the AppleShare server can share network resources and network-based services to new and older Macintosh systems ranging from the early Apple IIe systems to the Mac OS X systems.

Which Network Operating System Is Best?

The debate over which is the *best* network operating system is ongoing and will not be resolved in the pages of this book. All network operating systems have good and bad points, and each provides a solid choice for most modern network environments. Over time, services, features, and tools have been added to each of the operating systems, and today there is little difference in functionality between the offerings. However, similarity in service offerings aside, several points will influence an organization's choice of network operating system. The following are some of the factors to consider when choosing a network operating system:

▶ **Hardware compatibility**—Maintaining a network involves maintaining the hardware on the server. If you intend to use existing hardware in a server, verify that the network operating system supports that hardware. Some network operating systems support a wider range of hardware than others, although the best hardware from the mainstream manufacturers is supported by all the major network operating systems. Network operating system manufacturers have a vested interest in supporting the broadest range of hardware possible, and unless you are using some weird and wonderful hardware device, you should not encounter any problems. If you have a selection of unusual hardware, make sure that your chosen operating system will support it. Manufacturers publish lists of hardware devices verified as compatible, so be sure to check these lists if you intend to use unusual hardware. These *hardware compatibility lists* are available on the network operating system vendors' websites.

▶ **Technical capabilities**—Small organizations often have server administrators who double as teachers, secretaries, or data entry clerks. In environments where a dedicated server administrator is nonexistent and available technical skills are few, choosing the most user-friendly network operating system might be an important consideration. It might be easier for the administrator/data entry clerk to add a new user to a Windows 2000 Server from a graphical screen than to enter a cryptic command at a command prompt. The inability of existing personnel to support a product would almost certainly cause more problems than it would cure. There are of course alternatives: Training can bridge the knowledge gap where necessary.

▶ **Application support**—Most software manufacturers go to great lengths to ensure that the software they are designing is available to all network operating system platforms. Sometimes, however, a manufacturer cannot or does not ensure that its software will work on every network operating system, so it is important that you check. For example, if your company is using an application database not supported by Linux, this would make the installation of a Linux server out of the question for that purpose.

▶ **Budget**—Many choices in IT boil down to the money available, and choosing a network operating system is no exception. If a Linux server provides all the functionality and services your organization needs and does it for very little money, why pay for Windows? For those used to paying the price for a desktop operating system, the cost of a network operating system can be surprising because it is considerably higher.

▶ **Technical support**—An important factor in choosing a network operating system is technical support. Each network operating system manufacturer offers support for its product(s); however, the cost and the usefulness of this support might not be in line with what you need. One thing is for sure: Support and network management go hand in hand. Of the network operating systems we have discussed, Novell, Microsoft, and Unix have very defined support structures. Linux has a less well-defined support structure, although some Linux distributors offer comprehensive technical support programs. Other Linux distributors take a more hands-off approach, leaving you to rely on Internet newsgroups and your own savvy.

Now that we have looked at some of the considerations when selecting a network operating system, we'll take a more detailed look at common NOSs and some of the utilities and procedures associated with them. We will also look at each of the CompTIA-prescribed criteria related to network operating systems:

▶ **Authentication**—Authentication is a fundamental security-related consideration for networks. Authentication is essentially the process of verifying the identity of the person trying to access a resource on the system. The most common use of authentication is the logon process, in which a user's identity is validated. A detailed discussion of authentication methods used by the various network operating systems is not required for the Network+ exam; however, a basic knowledge of how each of the network operating systems handles authentication is an asset in real-world network administration.

▶ **File and print services**—A fundamental and commonly used network service is file and print services. Each of the network operating systems is fully capable of providing these services to network users, but each provides these services in its own way and with a unique set of features.

▶ **Application support**—What applications are supported by a network operating system plays a major part in how the network operating system is used and in its popularity.

NOTE

Third-Party Vendors   The term *third-party* is used to refer to an entity besides the original manufacturer or your own organization that creates a product. In this context, a third-party application is one not created by the network operating system manufacturer or you.

▶ **Security**—A discussion of network operating system security is difficult to capture in a single chapter. In fact, you will find volumes of books dedicated to discussions on how to establish security and how to work around it. This chapter provides only a brief introduction to the security measures taken in network operating systems. Security is a major consideration on networks, and the skills and strategies needed to properly secure a network against inside and outside threats are valuable skills for network administrators to have.

NOTE

Resource Security Models   Two ways are commonly used to secure files shared over a network: user-level security and share-level security. Networks that use user-level security apply rights to user accounts for specific resources such as files, directories, or printers. Networks that use share-level security require that passwords be assigned to individual files or network resources; users who need access to a specific printer, for example, would require a password to access it.

Unix/Linux

Providing a summary of any operating system can be difficult; Linux is particularly challenging. Linux has many different distributions, each offering a slightly different approach. Some of the most common Linux distributions include Red Hat, SuSE, Debian, and Caldera. In light of the many versions of Linux, if a command or an approach is listed in this section and is not available in the version of Linux you are using, you can look for an equivalent command or approach in your version, and you will very likely find one.

The history of Linux can be traced back to 1991, when Linus Torvalds, then a student at the University of Helsinki, set out to make a Unix-like operating system. After developing the original Linux kernel, the core of the operating system, he distributed it on the Internet and asked anyone who was interested to develop it. Many eager developers jumped on the programming bandwagon, and in a few short years, Linux had progressed into a viable alternative to the commercially available network operating systems.

Today, the development of Linux continues in much the same way as it always has: Anyone who wants to can develop Linux to further enhance its capabilities. To ensure that this is always the case, the Linux kernel is protected under a licensing agreement, which implies that the source code will always be available to anyone who wants access. More information on Linux licensing and development can be found at www.gnu.org.

Linux is based on Unix, which predates Linux by several years. In 1965 Bell Laboratories hooked up with MIT and General Electric in the development effort for the new operating system, Multics. The new OS was ahead of its time and designed to provide a multiuser, multiprocessor, and hierarchical file system.

Development was slow, and in 1969 AT&T decided to quit the Multics project. Development focus shifted, the project was renamed, and the Unix OS was on its way. In the early 1970s Unix was becoming increasingly popular among programmers offering features such as

- Simple user interface
- Numerous and simple utilities
- Hierarchical file system
- Simple interface to devices consistent with file format
- Multiuser, multiprocess system
- Architecture independent and transparent to the user

At the core of Unix/Linux is the kernel, which communicates directly with the hardware and provides the services to the user programs. These user programs don't need to know anything about the hardware. They just need to know how to interact with the kernel, and it's up to the kernel to provide the desired service.

On a basic level, Unix and Linux function similarly in terms of basic commands and administrative procedures. Therefore, for the depth required in this book the two operating systems are combined. The following are some of the key features of the Unix and Linux operating systems:

▶ **Multitasking**—Unix/Linux supports multitasking, which is the capability for several programs to run simultaneously.

▶ **Multiplatform**—Unix/Linux operates on a number of different platforms, not just on Intel machines.

▶ **Multiprocessor support**—Unix/Linux supports multiple processors, meaning that it recognizes multiple processors in a system.

▶ **Development**—In all the noncommercial programs available for Unix/Linux, the source code is available. This allows you to customize and further develop Linux.

▶ **Virtual consoles**—Unix/Linux supports virtual consoles, which are essentially independent logon sessions.

▶ **File system support**—In addition to the Unix/Linux native file systems, such as EXT2, both OSes support a wide range of file systems, including FAT, HFS+ (for Macintosh), VFAT, CDFS (for CD-ROMs), and more.

▶ **Network support**—Both Unix and Linux have the capability to connect to a variety of network environments. They include TCP/IP networking such as FTP, Telnet, and NFS; support for AppleTalk server; and Internetwork Packet Exchange/Sequenced Packet Exchange (IPX/SPX) and NetWare connectivity software.

NOTE

Comparing Linux and Unix   Because Linux is based on Unix, their basic functioning is similar. There are, however, differences between versions and distributions. The following section focuses on Linux, however, the technologies and tools discussed are relevant for both Unix and Linux.

System Requirements

Unix and Linux are dynamic and diverse network operating systems, and, therefore, it is almost impossible to make a blanket statement about the hardware needed to get a Unix or Linux server up and running. You can be reasonably sure, however, that the minimum hardware requirements are lower than those for any other operating system. Linux users are particularly quick to point out the limited hardware required for a Linux system, and it really is amazing. One reason that Linux has the capability to run on limited hardware is because, although it offers familiar graphical utilities, it is primarily a command-line operating system.

Windows, on the other hand, is a graphical operating system that offers some command-line utilities. It is the graphical nature of the operating systems that increases the need for faster and more expensive hardware.

You can find the minimum hardware requirements for each of the different Linux distributions at the distributors' respective websites, but they are all fairly similar.

Unix/Linux File Systems

The number of file systems supported by Unix/Linux is really remarkable. The default Linux file system is called EXT2, but to coexist on the same partition as a Windows operating system, Linux also supports file systems used by Windows. The EXT2 file system is the most widely used on Linux systems and provides support for large hard disks.

Hardware Verification

Verifying the hardware that goes into a Linux server is important—perhaps more important than with any of the other network operating systems. Linux has had compatibility issues with certain hardware configurations, and verifying hardware support before purchasing hardware for a Linux system is a good idea. Each of the various Linux distributors offers hardware compatibility lists on its website (although these lists can be difficult to find). In addition to a hardware compatibility list, many server administrators turn to newsgroups to post questions about hardware compatibility. The Linux hardware compatibility lists are not as comprehensive as Novell's or Microsoft's, and they sometimes require some additional digging.

Monitoring and Performance Tools

Network administrators who are used to the slick graphical performance tools of the Windows server environments might be taken aback by the visual presentation of some of the Linux utilities used to monitor performance. Many Linux distributions do provide graphical tools, but many Linux servers are command-line driven and do not provide a graphical interfaces.

When you get past the appearance of the utilities, you will find that the actual performance and monitoring that these tools provide is second to none. Performance tools vary somewhat among Linux distributions, but they all offer a variety of performance-monitoring tools. The following sections discuss a few ways to view system resources and usage.

The Top Utility

Top is a command-line utility that displays the processes currently being run on the system, and how much of the system's resources these processes are using. Similar information is provided in Windows 2000 on the Processes tab in the Task Manager utility.

Also included in the display are various counters that show how physical memory is being used, the amount of swap space in use, and the total number of processes in use. One of the best features about the Top utility is that it is dynamic, and every few seconds, the information is updated, to give you the most current picture of your system.

Process File System

A Linux system has a /proc directory, which is a virtual directory used to view just about any aspect of a Linux system. All the mainstream Linux distributions include /proc directories, and as a network administrator, you can expect to be spending some time looking in this directory when working on Linux machines.

The components that can be viewed with the proc command are listed in the /proc directory. The most useful switches for the proc command include the following:

- ▶ **/proc/dma**—Provides information on the Direct Memory Access (DMA) channels in use

- ▶ **/proc/cpuinfo**—Lists complete information about the CPU

- ▶ **/proc/apm**—Includes information on power management, if it is supported

- ▶ **/proc/meminfo**—Includes information on physical memory and the swap file

- ▶ **/proc/net**—Provides networking information

- ▶ **/proc/pci**—Provides information on the Peripheral Component Interconnect (PCI) devices within the system

Graphical Utilities

The two most common Linux graphical interfaces, GNOME and the K Desktop Environment (KDE), provide a number of easy-to-use performance-monitoring utilities.

Managing Linux Disk Drives

Linux partitions are usually managed through the Fdisk utility. Administrators used to the cleaner Microsoft Disk Management utility might have to take some time to get used to Linux Fdisk. In inexperienced hands, Fdisk can be a dangerous utility; it should be used only by server administrators who are comfortable with it.

TIP

Command-Line Case-Sensitivity   Unlike Windows and NetWare, command-line utilities in Linux are case-sensitive. This means that Fdisk is different from fdisk. When you first start working with Linux, this can be frustrating, but you soon get the hang of it.

In addition to Fdisk, many of the major Linux distributions also have their own disk-management utilities. Red Hat uses Disk Druid, Mandrake Linux uses Disk Drake, and Caldera Linux uses LIZARD. Each of these utilities does essentially the same thing: partition and manage the hard disks.

Linux User Management Basics

At first, the management of users' accounts in Linux might seem awkward, and compared to user management in other network operating systems, it is. You typically add users on a Linux system by using the useradd command from the command line, with the following syntax:

useradd <USERNAME>

The next step is to set a password for the user account that was created; to do this, you use the passwd command. After you type the command, Linux prompts you to enter the password and then to enter it again for confirmation. Various graphical utilities are available that can also be used for adding user accounts. If you prefer, you can use one of them instead of the command-line utilities.

> **NOTE**
>
> **Linux Graphical Utilities**   Although many Linux administrators prefer to use command-line utilities for tasks such as adding users, a number of graphical utilities are available.

User account information is stored in a file called passwd in the /etc directory. This is a text file, and in a standard configuration, passwords are also stored in this file, in plain text. Because this represents a security issue, it is common to use a process called *password shadowing* in which the password is stored and encrypted in a separate file, called /etc/shadow. Group accounts are created in much the same way as user accounts, except that the command used is groupadd.

Linux has a more distributed method of security than either NetWare or Windows, in that it relies more heavily on the security capabilities of applications than on the core user accounts. This is one of the features that make Linux the most customizable of the operating systems described in this chapter.

Verifying Linux Network Settings

Network settings, much like anything else in Linux, are stored in text files normally are located in the /etc/ directory or subdirectories of this directory. Network settings can be configured through a variety of command-line and graphical utilities.

The following are the commands most commonly used to verify and test network connectivity in a Linux environment:

- ▶ **ifconfig**—ifconfig shows detailed information—including TCP/IP address, default gateway, and subnet mask—about all network interfaces. It also provides basic usage statistics for each interface.

- ▶ **ping**—ping works the same way as with the other network operating system server platforms: It tests network connectivity between two devices. The ping command in Linux uses a simple syntax: ping *<IP address>*.

- ▶ **traceroute**—traceroute displays the network path between two nodes. At each hop, information about the hop, including the response time and IP address, is shown. The syntax for the traceroute command is traceroute *<IP address>*.

TIP

Linux Help   You can access help for most Linux commands by using the *<command>* --help command.

Linux Authentication

People used to working on a Windows-based system will no doubt discover that administration on a Linux system is different from what they are used to. For example, authentication information such as a list of users is kept in a text file. This file, /etc/passwd, controls who can and cannot log on to the system.

NOTE

Linux Authentication   Linux supports Kerberos authentication.

For a user to log on to the system, a valid username and password combination must be supplied. Both of these pieces of information are case-sensitive.

Linux File and Print Services

Although it is not the most obvious choice for a file and print server platform, Linux can perform the role of a file and print server admirably. In a base configuration, the volumes on a Linux server are not available to network clients. To make them available, one of two file sharing services is commonly used:

▶ **NFS**—NFS is the original file-sharing system used with Linux. NFS makes it possible for areas of the hard disk on a Linux system to be shared with other clients on the network. After the share has been established from the client side, the fact that the drive is on another system is transparent to the user.

▶ **Samba**—Samba provides Server Message Block functionality so that areas of the Linux server disks can be made available to Windows clients. In much the same way as on Windows servers, Samba facilitates the sharing of folders that can then be accessed by Windows client computers. Samba also makes it possible for Linux printer resources to be shared with Windows clients.

As with Windows and NetWare, Linux has a file system permission structure that makes it possible to restrict access to files or directories. In Linux, each file or directory can be assigned a basic set of file rights that dictate the actions that can be performed on the file. The basic rights are Read, Write, and Execute. The rights can be expressed in an alphabetic format (that is, RWX) or a numeric format (777). The rights to a file can be derived from the file ownership, from a group object, or from an "everyone" designator, which covers all users who are authenticated on the server. The Linux file permission structure might not be as sophisticated as those found in other network operating systems, but it is still more than sufficient in many environments.

Printing on a Linux system occurs through a service called the Line Printer daemon. The Line Printer functionality can be accessed by any user on the network who is properly authorized and connected. Some distributions of Linux have started to provide a more enhanced printing system called the Common Unix Printing System (CUPS). Many people, however, still prefer to use the traditional Line Printer system because of its simplicity and efficiency.

Linux Application Support

If you can think of an application that you might need, chances are that it is available for Linux in some form. As well as highly sophisticated commercial applications produced by large software companies, you can find software for the Linux platform that is written by an equally enthusiastic army of small software development companies and individuals. This means that application support for Linux is on par with, if not greater than, that in other network operating systems, such as NetWare, even if it has not yet reached the levels achieved by Windows server platforms.

In a sense, all applications created for Linux are third-party applications in that Linux itself is only an operating system kernel. The applications that run on this kernel provide Linux with functionality.

On the assumption that a network server will have a number of requirements, it is common practice for the Linux kernel to be bundled with various applications and provided to customers as a package, which, as we discussed earlier, are called *distributions*.

One respect in which Linux certainly has the edge over the other operating systems discussed is that many Linux applications are free of charge. Developed in the same spirit as Linux itself, and in many cases governed by the same licensing types, these free applications can seriously reduce the cost of maintaining a network server. Although it can be said that there are also free server-type applications for Windows and NetWare, there are certainly not as many of them as there are for Linux. (Note that we are referring to server applications, not workstation or end-user applications.)

Linux Security

Considerable effort has been put into making Linux a secure network operating system, and those efforts are evident. When configured correctly, Linux is a secure operating system, and therefore it is often chosen to be used as a company's firewall server. The following are a few highlights of Linux security:

- ▶ **Resource access**—As in the other network operating systems, access to resources on a Linux network is controlled through permissions. Access control lists identifying which systems and who can access what resources are held in text files such as `hosts.deny` and `hosts.allow`. Permissions for network resources and services can be assigned to an individual user or to a group of users.

- ▶ **User authentication**—To access the local system resources or any network resources, user authentication, in the form of a username and a password, is required. The user account information is kept in a text file known as the `/etc/passwd` file in the Linux system.

> **EXAM ALERT**
>
> **Logging on to Linux Servers**   To log on to a Linux server, the user must supply a valid username and password. Both of these values are case sensitive. You should know this for the exam.

- ▶ **File and directory security**—The default file system used by Linux is the EXT2 file system. Like NTFS, which is used with Windows servers, EXT2 allows administrators to assign permissions to individual files and folders. These permissions are used to control who is allowed access to specific data on the server. A secure server should have permissions set on the important data in the system.

As Linux continues to grow in popularity, it will become an increasingly common sight in server rooms of organizations of all sizes. As a network administrator, prepare yourself for *when* you encounter a Linux system—not *if*.

Mac OS X Server

Mac OS is the operating system created for Apple Computer's line of personal computers. The Mac OS has a long history, with the original version being released in 1984 to run on the original Macintosh computer. In 1999 Apple released its last major revision to its aging "Classic" operating system, Mac OS 9.

The successor to the Classic Mac OS was Mac OS X, a Unix-like operating system with a friendly and familiar user interface. Successive versions of Mac OS X have a decimal numeral—for example, Mac OS X.1, X.2, and so on. Because Mac OS X uses Linux/Unix technology, most of the previous section on Linux applies to Mac OS X server. This includes many of the same command-line utilities and file permissions.

> **NOTE**
>
> **OS Identity**   To identify a version of an operating system installed on any Macintosh computer, click on the Apple menu, and choose About This Mac or About This Computer. You see a screen listing the version number of the operating system as well as the amount of RAM installed.

Mac OS Basics

Mac OS X is a Unix-like operating system made up of different layers or components that interact with each other. The layers are as follows:

► **Core OS**—The first layer of the operating system, the core operating system contains the kernel (or more accurately, the microkernel). The kernel itself is one of the more remarkable aspects of the operating system because it integrates features from both FreeBSD and the Mach Kernel from the GNU project. The result of the integration is a hybrid kernel that supports FreeBSD's advanced memory management, task management and process communication facilities, and virtual memory technology. The GNU portions of the kernel provide a plug-in architecture for adding functionality.

► **Core services**—This next layer provides essential services to the system, including networking services, memory management, process management, and other functionality required by higher levels of the system to function.

► **Application and multimedia services**—Application services provide features consumed by other applications, such as HTML rendering, disc recording services, an LDAP address book, font management, and speech recognition.

A developer can take advantage of these services by inserting components into his program. For example, instead of writing software to display an image on the screen, the author could just call the QuickTime service. This saves the author from having to be an expert in image formats just to display an image on the screen.

▶ **Application environments**—Runtime environments such as Classic, Carbon, Cocoa, Java, Perl, Ruby, Python, XFree86, and others reside here. Each environment provides different services and is useful in different ways.

Cocoa is Apple's name for the application environment native to Mac OS X. Developers wanting access to Mac OS's modern object-oriented frameworks on which to build applications use this environment. However, a developer might choose Java if portability is more of a concern.

▶ **User experience**—For most users, this is the only part of Mac OS X they ever experience. They have no interest in how or why their applications work, or how their computer manages files on their disks. Applications reach down through the various layers of the system to access services and features, returning the result back to the user.

Each layer in the operating system functions independently of the others, essentially abstracting users, programs, core services, and computer management from each other. One program crashing on the system, therefore, has no effect on other running programs or services. A web browser crashing, for example, has no effect on a web or file server running on the same system.

To learn more about how these different layers work together, visit Apple's developer website at http://developer.apple.com/.

Mac OS X File Systems and File and Print Services

As you might expect, the file systems used on Windows-based PCs are different from those used in an Apple system. Instead of the FAT or FAT32 file system, the original Mac file system was Apple's Macintosh File System (MFS). MFS was used with earlier Mac versions, including Mac OS 1-3.

Mac OS 4 introduced Apple's Hierarchical File System (HFS). HFS was the primary file system format used on the Macintosh Plus and later models, until Mac OS 8.1, when HFS was replaced by HFS+.

HFS+ is the file system most commonly associated with Mac OS X. Like NTFS, HFS+ includes many enhanced features. HFS+ supports disk quotas, byte-range locking, finder information in metadata, support for hiding file extensions on a per-file basis, and more. One of the more publicized features of HFS+ is journaling. In a journaled file system, the system keeps a log of the hard disk's main data activity. In case of a crash or other system failure, the file system can retrieve lost data by consulting the "journal" log, restoring the system to its previous state instead of having to go through the lengthy process of rebuilding the data.

> **NOTE**
>
> **Choosing the File System** When installing the Mac OS on a computer, always choose an HFS+ or HFS+ (Journaled) file system type. Other file systems do not properly support metadata and permissions used by the OS.

The following is a list of other file systems supported by Mac OS X:

▶ **ISO9660**—Mac supports the ISO9660 file system standard. This is a system-independent file system for read-only data CDs.

▶ **MSDOS**—Mac OS X includes support for MSDOS file systems (FAT12, FAT16, and FAT32).

▶ **NTFS**—Mac OS X includes read-only support for NTFS.

▶ **UDF**—UDF (Universal Disk Format) is the file system used by DVD-ROM (including DVD-video and DVD-audio) discs, and by many CD-R/RW packet-writing programs.

When working in a heterogeneous network environment (one that uses different OS platforms), Mac OS X offers a wide range of support for network file and print services supporting various file sharing protocols. A file sharing protocol is a high-level network protocol that provides the structure and language for file requests between clients and servers. It provides the commands for opening, reading, writing, and closing files across the network. Each OS uses a different protocol as the file sharing protocol.

For a client to have access to multiple servers running different operating systems, either the client supports the file sharing protocol of each operating system or the server supports the file sharing protocol of each client. Software that adds this capability is common and allows interoperability between Windows, Macintosh, NetWare, and Unix platforms. The following is a list of file sharing protocols supported by Mac OS X.

▶ **Apple Filing Protocol (AFP)**—The Apple Filing Protocol (AFP) is an Apple proprietary protocol for file sharing over the network using TCP/IP. If you have a Windows NT or Windows 2000\2003 server, you can turn on Apple File Protocol (AFP). AFP is the native Macintosh file sharing protocol and when enabled, Macs will be able to see the server.

▶ **Server Message Blocks/Common Internet File System(SMB/CIFS)**—Mac OS 10 includes cross-platform support for SMB/CIFS, the protocols that allow file sharing between network nodes in a Windows environment. Using Mac OS X, Macintosh clients can connect directly to Windows servers thanks to the SMB client built into the Mac OS. Support for SMB/CIFS is supplied by the Samba software package, installed on all versions of Mac OS X by default. Samba is a networking tool originally designed to integrate the Windows file sharing protocol (SMB/CIFS) and Unix systems on a network. Running on a Unix system, it allows Windows to share files and printers on the Unix host, and it also allows Unix users to access resources shared by Windows systems. Whenever possible, use Mac OS 10.2 or greater to ensure the best compatibility with Windows file servers. When using the SMB protocol to connect to a Windows 2000 or 2003 file server, make sure that SMB signing (packet signing) is disabled on that server.

▶ **Network Filing System (NFS)**—NFS is a file sharing protocol associated with Unix/Linux systems. Clients using Mac OS X can connect to Linux/Unix servers using NFS, just like the other Unix stations on the network. NFS can be problematic because file permissions are applied to newly created files and folders on the server based on the user ID and group ID from the client computer, unless otherwise specified by the server administrator.

Mac OS X Security

As with any other OS, Mac OS X has been designed to meet the security needs of today's businesses. This includes security measures in the local network and security protocols to be used on remote networks.

The most fundamental level of security lies within the operating system itself. Any interaction with the system requires some form of authentication. The first level is *user authentication*. Mac OS X implements role-based user accounts. Three account types are available on Mac OS X client machines (machines not a part of a Windows domain or Mac OS X Server infrastructure), whose options can be configured in the Accounts area in the System Preferences application. The three accounts types are as follows:

▶ **Limited**—The most restricted type of account, limited users may only be able to see certain parts of the file system, and only run applications approved by an administrative user. As of Mac OS 10.4, system administrators can also restrict network access to lists of approved websites and email addresses.

▶ **Standard**—Most users on a machine fall into this category. A standard user is allowed to run any applications installed in directories they have access to but can only write to their home directories and directories that have been set up for them by a system administrator. Standard users are also restricted from making any configuration changes that affect anything beyond their user account (such as network settings).

▶ **Administrator**—This account type allows the user to make systemwide changes to the machine, change permissions of files and directories they do not directly own, and manage accounts. Every Mac OS X computer must have at least one administrative account.

Being a Unix-like operating system, Mac OS X naturally inherits a Unix-style file system permission system. Every file and folder on the machine has three levels of access with three possible settings each. The three main file permissions include read, write and execute. Persons familiar with Unix, Linux, and BSD systems will feel right at home with this environment. Fortunately for those not familiar with the chmod and chown GNU commands, the MAC Finder provides an interface for managing permissions.

In the Info window for any file or folder on the computer is an Ownership & Permissions area listing all possible permissions variables for the given object. The three levels of access for each file and folder are Owner, Group, and Everyone (or Other). The owner is usually the user who created the object on the system. Groups are logical collections of users on a machine. On Mac OS X client machines, groups cannot be created or modified; however, two key groups are automatically created and maintained to assist with machine administration:

▶ **Admin**—All administrator level users automatically belong to the Admin group.

▶ **Staff**—All other users belong to the Staff group.

One other important thing to note about Mac OS X is how system level changes are implemented. Before installing software or changing system level directives (such as file or folder permissions), a user is required to enter a password. This activity is called a *privilege escalation*. Although this may be a minor inconvenience to the user, it prevents malicious software from making unauthorized changes to a system beyond the scope of the user's account. For example, if a user of a Mac OS X computer downloads and executes an application that contains malicious code, the rogue application will be unable to affect any parts of the system that the user does not have access to unless it asks the user for the name and password of an administrative account. This prevents rogue applications from performing such actions as terminating background processes not directly owned by the user (such as a web server), modifying files or folders outside the user's home directory to which the user hasn't been given read and write access, and executing any code that could halt the system (either by executing a shutdown command, or executing code that could cause the system to crash).

This is even true for administrator level accounts; even a system administrator is required to enter a username and password before making changes that affect system settings beyond her user account. The entire privilege escalation is handled by the Mac OS; the username and password pair are never seen or recorded by any individual application. In some instances, a user can request that the system grant privilege escalations to applications without requesting intervention from the user. Again, this is handled by the Mac OS, not the application itself.

Novell NetWare

Once the network operating system of choice for all but a few networks, NetWare's popularity has declined significantly over recent years. However, NetWare is still widely used in many environments, including government and education. The latest version of NetWare, version 6.5, continues Novell's tradition of providing feature-rich enterprise class network operating systems.

> **NOTE**
>
> **NetWare Versions**   The information this chapter provides on Novell NetWare is intended to apply to NetWare 6 and 6.5. If you find yourself working on an older version of NetWare, you might find that some of the commands and utilities are different from those discussed here.

One feature that really put NetWare on the networking map was Novell Directory Services (NDS). Like Microsoft's Active Directory, NDS (which has been around since 1994) is a directory services system that allows network objects to be stored in a database. This database can then be divided up and distributed among different servers on the network. These processes are known as *partitioning* (the dividing up) and *replication* (the distribution among servers on the network). Although introduced as NDS with NetWare 4.x, Novell renamed the product eDirectory when NetWare 6 was released.

> **EXAM ALERT**
>
> **eDirectory**   Although a detailed understanding of eDirectory is not required for the Network+ exam, working with a NetWare server will most certainly require a thorough knowledge of this product.

> **NOTE**
>
> **eDirectory Versions**   eDirectory, or NDS, was originally created for NetWare, but versions are now available for other platforms, including Linux, Windows server, and various versions of Unix.

Like the other network operating systems discussed in this chapter, NetWare is a full-featured operating system that offers all the functions required by an organization, including file and print services, DNS and DHCP servers, and FTP and web servers. NetWare also supports a wide range of third-party hardware and software.

NetWare System Requirements

In terms of hardware, NetWare system requirements are modest, and even moderately powered servers can provide adequate levels of performance to a relatively large numbers of users. Table 9.1 shows the minimum hardware requirements for a NetWare 6.5 server, but generally you would use a far more powerful server than this.

TABLE 9.1   Minimum Server Requirements for NetWare 6.5

Hardware	Minimum Requirement
Processor	Pentium II or better
RAM	512MB
Hard disk space	Approximately 2.5GB

NetWare File Systems

Unlike Windows server platforms that use share points to make disk resources available to users, NetWare has a more versatile approach in which all areas of the disk are available to all users who have permissions. There is no concept of share points, although it is possible for a user to connect to a specific folder on the server if necessary. Instead, users can map a drive to an area of a disk called a *volume*. Only the areas of the volume to which the user has been assigned permissions are available to that user.

> **NOTE**
>
> **NSS**   In versions of NetWare since 5.1, Novell has offered a service called Novell Storage Services (NSS). NSS allows for larger volume sizes and improves the performance of file serving.

Novell offers compatibility with client operating systems by using special software drivers known as *name spaces* to make drives available to clients. Different name space drivers are available, depending on which clients are being used. Most commonly, the driver that mimics the file properties of Windows clients, which is called "long," is used, though NFS is also enabled by default in NetWare 6.x.

> **NOTE**
>
> **Viewing Name Spaces**   You can quickly and easily see the volumes "mounted" on a NetWare server along with name spaces added to those volumes by issuing the **VOLUMES** command at the server console.

Part of NetWare's reputation as a high-performance file server is related to the way it handles file caching. When a volume is initialized, the file allocation table is copied into memory, as are parts of another table, called the *directory entry table*. When a file is requested, the tables are searched for the location of the file, and the file is read from the disk. The holding of tables in memory makes this process fast, and the caching of files in memory helps to increase the speed of the process. In fact, any memory available on a NetWare server after the server modules and workspace are loaded is assigned to the caching of files.

NetWare Performance-Monitoring Tools

As with other common server platforms, NetWare includes utilities that enable you to gauge the performance of the server system. The main tool, NetWare Monitor, which is shown in Figure 9.1, provides an exhaustive range of information. The following are some of the most commonly used performance indicators in NetWare Monitor:

▶ **Processor utilization**—This indicates how busy the processor is at any given time. If the counter is consistently high, the processor is unable to keep up with the load.

▶ **Total cache buffers**—This is the amount of memory available for file caching. Make sure that this counter does not run too low (below 40%). Insufficient RAM for caching degrades server performance considerably.

▶ **Dirty cache buffers**—A dirty cache buffer is an area of memory that holds data waiting to be written to disk. Excessively high numbers of dirty cache buffers can indicate that the disk channel is unable to keep up with disk demands.

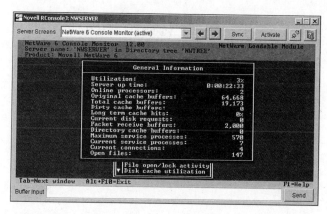

FIGURE 9.1 The Monitor screen from a NetWare 6 server.

NetWare User Administration

One of the differences between working with Windows servers and working with NetWare servers is that with NetWare much of the configuration of the server is actually performed from a workstation, not from the server itself, although Novell is moving toward a more server-centric model in this respect. Performing administrative tasks from the workstation is a good practice because fewer server resources are used for administration, and more are available for carrying out user requests.

Two basic tools are used for administering NetWare: NetWare Administrator and ConsoleOne. Both utilities are Windows based, but ConsoleOne is a Java-based application, whereas NetWare Administrator is a standard 32-bit Windows application. NetWare Administrator and ConsoleOne can be used to manage practically all network objects, including users, groups, printing, and the server file system. With NetWare 6.5, Novell has also introduced a browser-based administration tool called iManager.

A range of other browser-based management tools can be used on the NetWare server console as well as a server-based version of ConsoleOne. Figure 9.2 shows an example of a screen from the NetWare Administrator utility, and Figure 9.3 shows an example of the workstation version of ConsoleOne.

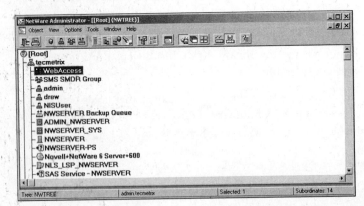

FIGURE 9.2 The NetWare Administrator utility.

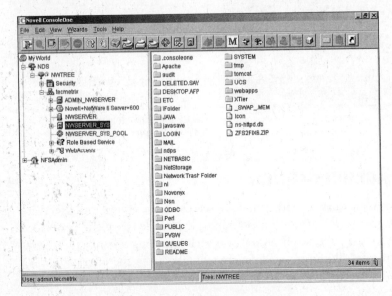

FIGURE 9.3 The NetWare ConsoleOne utility.

NetWare Server Configuration

On a NetWare server, network and user administration is typically performed from a workstation; however, some tasks such as network configuration are often performed directly on the server. Various utilities are available, including ones for networking configuration (inetcfg) and for working with the NDS structure (dsrepair).

NOTE

NetWare Administration As of NetWare 6, some disk-management tasks have been moved from the nwconfig utility to ConsoleOne and iManager.

Although they are not configuration tools per se, there are a number of other useful NetWare server console commands. Table 9.2 lists some of these.

TABLE 9.2   Useful NetWare Server Commands

Command	Function
config	Displays network configuration information, including network addresses and protocol information.
version	Displays the NetWare version currently installed on the server.
Volumes	Displays a list of the currently mounted volumes as well as the name space modules loaded for each volume.
Down	Tells the server to shut down. A prompt follows that asks for confirmation before the shutdown process runs.

NOTE

Ctrl+Esc Pressing Ctrl+Esc on a NetWare server brings up a list of the currently loaded "screens."

Viewing and Testing NetWare Network Configuration

From a NetWare server, the primary tool for configuring network settings is the Internetworking Configuration utility (inetcfg). Figure 9.4 shows a sample screen from the inetcfg utility, which is similar to many of the NetWare server utilities that use a menu-based format.

In addition, you can use a number of command-line tools from the console to view and test the network configuration of a NetWare server. Table 9.3 summarizes some of the tools commonly used for this purpose.

FIGURE 9.4 A sample screen from the `inetcfg` utility.

TABLE 9.3 NetWare Network Configuration Commands

Command	Function
inetcfg	Configures network settings.
config	Displays network configuration and other information, such as the NDS context of the server.
ping	Simultaneously tests connectivity to multiple TCP/IP hosts.
ipxping	Tests connectivity between two hosts running Internetwork Packet Exchange (IPX).
tcpcon	Displays TCP/IP statistics and configuration in the familiar menu-based format.
iptrace	Verifies the route to a remote system.

NetWare Authentication

As with all the other network operating systems discussed in this chapter, by default NetWare authentication is performed by using a username and password combination. As well as supplying this information, users also need to tell client software which NDS tree to authenticate to and the location of the user object in the NDS tree. Like the other operating systems discussed in this chapter, NetWare also supports numerous other authentication mechanisms such as smartcards and biometrics.

> **NOTE**
>
> **NetWare Passwords** By default, passwords in NetWare are not case-sensitive.

After a user has been validated, an assortment of restrictions is verified, including allowed logon times and station restrictions. These prevent users from logging on during restricted times and from certain workstations.

Information about the user account and what the user can and cannot access is stored in the NDS. For this reason, a copy of the NDS must be available for the user to be able to log on. Also, each time a user attempts to access a resource, the authentication status is checked in the NDS to make sure that the user is who she says she is and that she is allowed to access the resource.

NetWare File and Print Services

For many years, NetWare was considered *the* operating system of choice for providing file and print services. Although that might no longer be the case, many people in the IT industry still see NetWare as primarily a file and print server platform.

Of all the network operating systems discussed in this chapter, NetWare has by far the most comprehensive (and complex) file system security structure. In addition to allowing an administrator to assign a comprehensive set of rights to users and groups, NetWare provides file permission inheritance systems, as well as the capability to block the inherited rights if needed. All this adds up to a sophisticated file system security method that can take some getting used to.

EXAM ALERT

eDirectory—It Wasn't Always Like That   Any discussion of Novell NetWare now invariably involves eDirectory, or NDS. The functionality provided by the directory services system is so ingrained in NetWare that without it the system is little more than a collection of software programs. It wasn't always like this, though. In versions of NetWare up to and including 3.x, NetWare used a system called the *Bindery* to store user, group, and printing information. The Bindery was actually a group of three files stored on each server and not shared between servers in the same way that directory services databases are shared. If a user needed access to more than one server, the user's account needed to be created on each server. Although numerous strategies and products eased the administrative burden that this created, Novell realized that a more dynamic approach was needed, hence the introduction of NDS and subsequently eDirectory.

In addition to file permission rights, on a NetWare server files can also be assigned a range of attributes. These attributes work the same as file attributes in DOS and Windows. However, whereas Windows file permissions are limited to attributes such as read-only and hidden, the NetWare file attributes include such possibilities as rename inhibit and delete inhibit.

Printing with NetWare can be implemented in a variety of ways. Traditionally, printers were defined on the server, and print queues were associated with those printers. In NetWare 6, a feature called Novell Distributed Print Services was introduced, which allows a more dynamic printing environment to be created. NetWare 6 also introduced a new feature called iPrint, which allows users to see graphical maps of the network and point and click to access network devices.

To access a printer on NetWare, clients capture the output that would normally be directed to a local printer port and send it to the network printer. In early versions of NetWare, this was a process performed by using a command-line utility, called `capture`. Today, the process has been hidden behind the graphical interface of the client software and is largely unnoticed.

NetWare Application Support

Although application support will always be a topic of much debate, the reality is that third-party application support for NetWare is not nearly at the same level as it is for the Windows server platforms. In terms of third-party application support, NetWare would even have a hard time competing against Linux. However, many applications are available for NetWare, and you are likely to have a choice of applications for any given purpose.

> **EXAM ALERT**
>
> **NLMs**   On a NetWare server, console utilities and drivers are implemented through pieces of software called NetWare Loadable Modules (NLMs). Most NLMs can be loaded and unloaded as needed.

Even though third-party support might be lacking, the applications included with the NetWare package provide many of the commonly desired network services. This includes a DHCP server, a DNS server, and a web server application, as well as a range of other services.

NetWare Security

Like the other network operating systems, NetWare has many security features to help secure the server and the network. The key areas of NetWare security include the following:

▶ **Resource access**—Resource access in NetWare is controlled, as is everything else related to security, through directory services. For a user to gain access to a network resource—whether it be a file, directory, printer, or server—the appropriate permissions must be applied through the directory. Permissions can be granted to the user, to a group to which the user belongs, or to an NDS container object in which the user resides. Rights to objects can be inherited or gained from other user IDs through a process called *security equivalence*.

▶ **User authentication**—As with the other network operating systems, accessing a NetWare server and network resources requires a username and password combination. To log on to a NetWare server, the context of the user must also be specified and, in some instances, the name of the NDS tree must also be provided. *Context* is a term used to refer to the location of the container that holds an object in the NDS tree. Without the correct context, the security subsystem cannot identify the correct user ID and does not grant access to the server. Because the context can be complex and because the tree name is generally not used except at the point of logon, it's common practice to configure users' workstations to default to a certain tree and context so that users do not need to supply that information. This way, a user needs to provide only a username and password.

▶ **File and directory security**—NetWare provides a comprehensive file and directory permissions system, which allows rights to be assigned to users, groups, and other directory services objects. Rights are inheritable, which means that rights assigned at one file system level flow down through the structure until they reach the end of the file system tree, unless they are countered by an inherited rights mask or by an explicit trustee assignment. Much the same process is used to manage and assign rights within the eDirectory tree, although the actual set of rights that can be assigned is different.

Like the Windows console, the NetWare console can and should be locked for security purposes. You can lock the NetWare console by using a utility called `scrsaver`, which you run from the server command line.

TIP

Headless Operation As an extra security precaution, NetWare supports *headless* operation, which means that the NetWare server can run without a keyboard, mouse, and monitor. It is safe to plug these devices back in while the system is running if you want to gain access.

NetWare Summary

With the proliferation of Microsoft Windows server platforms, you might not actually get to work with a NetWare server. But if you do, you'll find that there is good reason why NetWare was king of the network operating system hill for so long.

Windows 2000 and Windows Server 2003

Windows 2000 was the follow-up to the popular Windows NT 4 network operating system, and it quickly established itself as a reliable and robust operating system. Windows 2000 built on the success of its predecessor and offered many improvements and advancements. In 2003,

Microsoft released the latest version of its Windows server family of products—the aptly named Windows Server 2003. Microsoft still currently supports Windows 2000, and many organizations still have many Windows 2000 Server systems deployed.

Three different versions of Windows 2000 are available for server platforms: *Windows 2000 Server*, *Advanced Server*, and *Datacenter Server*. There are some subtle and not-so-subtle differences between these respective offerings, such as processor support and cost. Windows 2000 is also available as a workstation operating system: Windows 2000 Professional. Windows 2000 Professional has the majority of features, capabilities, and strengths of Windows 2000 Server products but omits the server-type network services and capabilities.

Like Windows 2000, there are also a number of versions of Windows Server 2003, each intended to fulfill a given role or function. Windows Server 2003 Standard Edition is intended as a general-purpose operating system, whereas Windows Server 2003 Enterprise and Datacenter Editions are intended for large-scale, high-availability environments. Windows Server 2003 Web Edition is designed as a platform for web-based applications and services. Although all editions of Windows Server 2003 provide basic features such as file and print serving, remote access and Active Directory support, you'll want to examine the features provided by each edition before making a purchase. The good news is that Microsoft fully expects that you will mix and match editions on a network, so interoperability between the editions is seamless.

NOTE

Server Versions   To make things easier, from this point on we'll refer to both Windows 2000 Server and Windows Server 2003 simply as *Windows servers*, unless there is a need to identify differences between the two.

Microsoft Active Directory

Active Directory is a directory services system that allows network objects such as users and groups to be placed into logical areas of a database. This database can then be distributed among various servers, all of which participate in the Active Directory structure. Because all the network object information is placed in a single database, albeit a distributed one, it can be used by any network application or subsystem, eliminating the need for duplicate information to be held on each server of the network. In the case of Microsoft server operating systems, Windows 2000 was the first network operating system to take this approach. Previous to this, user accounts were stored on each server, and special relationships called *trusts* had to be set up to allow users on one server to access resources in another. In Active Directory, trusts still exist, though their role is somewhat different.

Windows servers on a network can either be domain controllers or member servers. Domain controllers are servers that have Active Directory installed and hold a copy of the Active Directory database. The term *domain* is used to describe a logical section of the Active Directory database. Domain controllers store user account information and so can provide network authentication. An Active Directory domain can have several domain controllers, with each one having a read/write copy of the Active Directory database. In fact, for fault-tolerant reasons, this is a good strategy to employ.

EXAM ALERT

Active Directory Active Directory is a complex subject, and much of the information in this section is not needed for the Network+ exam. For further information on Active Directory, refer to Microsoft's website (www.microsoft.com).

Member servers are not involved in the authentication of network users and do not take part in the Active Directory replication process. Member servers are commonly employed as file and print servers, or with additional software, as database servers, web servers, firewalls, or servers for other important network services such as DHCP and DNS.

Windows Server System Requirements

By today's standards, the minimum requirements for running both Windows 2000 Server and Windows Server 2003 are considered low. Table 9.4 lists the minimum recommended hardware requirements, but keep in mind that these are only enough to install the product and get it running. In a practical scenario, the hardware specifications should be significantly higher.

NOTE

Windows OS Requirements The figures identified in Table 9.4 show the requirements for Windows 2000 Server and Windows Server 2003 Standard Edition. The hardware requirements for other Windows server products such as Windows 2000 Advanced Server or Windows Server 2003 Datacenter Edition are considerably higher.

TABLE 9.4 Minimum Server Requirements for Windows 2000 Server and Windows Server 2003 Standard Edition

Hardware	Minimum Requirement
Processor	Pentium at 133MHz
RAM	128MB
Hard disk space	1GB (2GB during installation)

Windows Server File Systems

Windows server systems support the FAT, FAT32, and NTFS file systems. However, if you are configuring a server, you are unlikely to use FAT or FAT32 because they do not offer any file level security. Also, you need NTFS if you want to take advantage of features such as file compression, encryption, or auditing.

> **NOTE**
>
> **FAT32** Windows client systems often use the FAT32 file system, but on a server you should always use NTFS unless you have a good reason not to.

> **TIP**
>
> **NTFS** Although it is possible to convert a partition formatted with FAT or FAT32, it is recommended that you format a drive as NTFS when you are creating partitions rather than converting at a later date. Drives originally formatted with NTFS have less fragmentation and better performance than those converted from FAT. If you do need to convert a partition, you can use the CONVERT utility, but the process is one-way. After you have converted from FAT, you can never go back. The syntax for the command is `convert e:/fs:ntfs /v`. This example assumes that you are converting the "e" drive.

Windows Server Performance Monitoring Tools

Windows server systems offer a variety of performance monitoring tools.

Since Windows 2000, Microsoft has used an application called the Microsoft Management Console (MMC) to centralize the location of administrative tools. These tools, referred to as *snap-ins*, can be added to the MMC to manage the hardware, software, and networking components of the server. Some of the most common tools used as snap-ins are Event Viewer, Device Manager, Computer Management and Performance Logs and Alerts, and Services.

Event Viewer

On a Windows server system, as with the other operating systems discussed in this chapter, events and occurrences are logged to files for later review. On Windows servers, the key logs in which these are stored can be viewed with an MMC snap-in called Event Viewer. The logs in Event Viewer can be used to find information on, for example, an error on the system or a security incident. Information is recorded into three main log files, though you will also see additional log files under certain conditions, such as if the system is a domain controller or is running a DHCP server application. The three main log files and their purpose are as follows:

▶ **Security log**—This log contains events related to security incidents such as successful and unsuccessful logon attempts and failed resource access.

► **Application log**—This log contains information logged by applications that run on a Windows server system rather than the server operating system itself. Vendors of third-party applications can use the Application log as a destination for error messages generated by their applications.

► **System log**—This log records information about components or drivers in the server. This is the place to look when you're troubleshooting a problem with a hardware device on your system or a problem with network connectivity. For example, messages related to the client element of DHCP appear in this log. The System log is also the place to look for hardware device errors, time synchronization issues, or service startup problems.

Figure 9.5 shows the Windows 2000 Event Viewer.

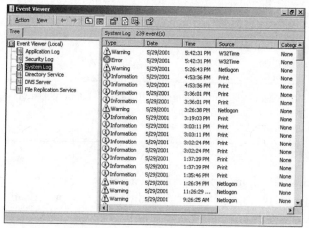

FIGURE 9.5   The Windows 2000 Event Viewer.

NOTE

Log Files   Application logs and System logs can be viewed by any user. Security logs can be viewed only by users who are using accounts with administrative privileges.

Challenge: Reviewing Event Viewer Logs

In this exercise, you locate an event from the System Log in Event Viewer and then look for information on that event on the Microsoft website.

1. Click Start, Administrative Tools, Event Viewer. The Event Viewer opens.

2. In the left pane of Event Viewer, select the System Log. The events in the System Log are displayed in the right-hand pane.

(continues)

(continued)

3. In the right pane, double-click an event to view the details. Note the number from the Event ID field. In the unlikely event that no items are in the System Log, check the Application, Security, or Directory Services log.

4. Log on to the Microsoft website at support.microsoft.com. In the Search the Knowledge Base field, type the Event ID you recorded from step 3. Review the information provided about that Event ID.

5. Repeat the process for another, different type of event.

The Performance Console

The Performance Console is a tool used to view the current performance statistics of a Windows server system. Using the Performance Console, you can analyze a single piece of hardware, such as memory, or view the impact a particular application is having on the system. Performance Console can also be used to determine whether a system is experiencing bottle-necks due to insufficient or malfunctioning hardware.

> **NOTE**
>
> **Baselines** Baselining is the process of taking measurements of system performance for the purposes of future comparison. Taking baselines under normal, medium, and high network usage conditions allows you to determine whether the system is behaving abnormally at a later date.

The Performance console, shown in Figure 9.6, provides two snap-ins: System Monitor and Performance Logs and Alerts. These tools are responsible for providing different but equally critical system performance-related information:

▶ **System Monitor**—System Monitor allows you to monitor the components within the server and determine whether they are causing bottlenecks. Many counters can be viewed, and the graphical interface allows you to view the state of the system in real-time. Literally hundreds of performance counters can be added to the System Monitor display, providing a versatile and effective way to monitor the operation of the system.

▶ **Performance Logs and Alerts**—This tool is designed to capture performance-related statistics from the local computer or a remote system over an extended time period. The information gathered can then be viewed through System Monitor. A key feature in Performance Logs and Alerts is the capability to set alerts. By right-clicking on the Alerts icon and choosing New Alert Settings, you can set thresholds; when these thresholds are exceeded, an alert message can be sent. For example, if a hard disk is reaching its capacity, an alert message can be sent to the administrator, warning him of the situation before it becomes a problem.

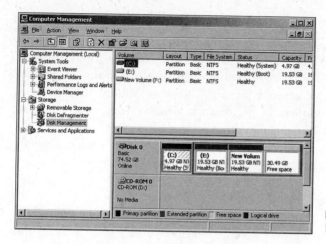

FIGURE 9.6 The Windows 2000 Performance console.

Of the many different items that can be viewed with the Performance Console, some of the most commonly viewed counters are the following:

▸ **Memory - Available Bytes**—This counter identifies the amount of physical memory that is free. If this counter is low, there might be a RAM shortage.

▸ **Memory - Pages/Sec**—This counter shows the number of pages requested from virtual memory. For this counter, a number above 10 indicates a potential problem and means that more memory might be required.

▸ **Processor - % Processor Time**—This counter shows the amount of processor usage. If this counter indicates that the processor usage is consistently at 100%, the processor might not be able to handle the load. Keep in mind, however, that a processor might surge to a high count and then drop again. To be a true indicator of a processor bottleneck, the processor count would have to remain high for an extended period of time.

▸ **Physical Disk - % Disk Time**—If this counter is consistently over 65% to 70%, the server probably has a performance problem. This counter indicates the number of hard disk read and write requests. Installing more memory might solve a problem indicated by this counter.

▸ **Physical Disk – Avg. Disk Queue Length**—If the average disk queue length is consistently over 2, there is disk performance degradation, and you will may need to upgrade to improve performance.

In addition to these counters, literally hundreds of others allow you to monitor almost every aspect of your Windows server systems.

Network Monitor

One of the tasks that network administrators are most frequently responsible for is monitoring what the network is doing. On Windows server platforms, the Network Monitor tool is used to capture and analyze a range of network-related statistics. It is one of the key utilities to use for network troubleshooting and capacity planning. Network Monitor can help you identify whether and where there are bottlenecks in a network. Windows server operating systems come with a basic version of the Network Monitor tool that allows you to view the network information only for the system on which it is running. An enhanced version available separately allows you to view information from other nodes on the network as well.

The System Information Console

The System Information console is used to view a wealth of information about your Windows server. The System Information console provides a comprehensive look at the hardware and operating system software components used in the system. It is an invaluable tool for troubleshooting hardware-related problems. Figure 9.7 shows the System Information console on a Windows Server 2003 system.

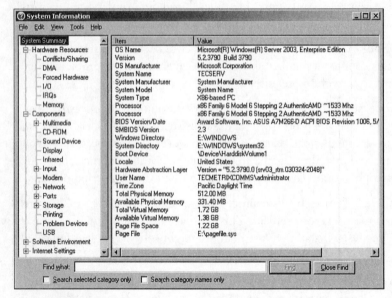

FIGURE 9.7 The System Information console on a Windows Server 2003 system.

Task Manager

Task Manager has been a perennial favorite of Windows server administrators since the early days of Windows NT. It can be used to view the system resources in use, or end processes or applications that have stopped responding. It can also be used to view statistical information on what applications are hogging CPU time or memory space, which can be invaluable for identifying misbehaving applications.

Task Manager is accessed by pressing Ctrl+Alt+Del and then selecting Task Manager from the Windows Security Dialog box. Figure 9.8 Shows the Performance tab from Task Manager on a Windows Server 2003 system.

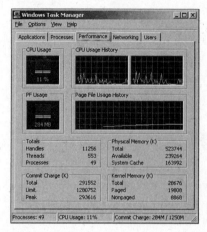

FIGURE 9.8 The Performance tab of Task Manager on a Windows Server 2003 system.

The Recovery Console

Introduced with Windows 2000, the Recovery console is a set of command-line utilities that allow you to attempt a repair on a Windows server that is experiencing problems on boot up.

If a server refuses to boot, you can start the Recovery console from the Windows server CD, or from the system itself if the utility is installed. (If the Recovery console is installed, it appears as a boot option on the startup menu screen.) Because this utility consumes only a small amount of hard disk space, it's worthwhile to have it installed before a problem arises, instead of having to spend time installing it during the process of repairing a failed server.

Viewing Network Configurations and Testing Connectivity

The configuration of network settings on a Windows server platform is done through the Network Connections applet in the Control Panel. Most network-related tasks can be performed from here, including installing and configuring protocols, managing network interface cards (NICs), and installing additional services.

To test network connectivity from a Windows server system, you can use several utilities. The following are some of the utilities used on Windows server platforms:

▸ **ping**—Perhaps the mostly widely used Transmission Control Protocol/Internet Protocol (TCP/IP) utility, the `ping` utility tests connectivity between networked devices.

▸ **ipconfig**—The `ipconfig` utility displays all the TCP/IP configurations for a server. The most common command syntax used with this utility is `ipconfig /all`, which displays information on all NICs in the system, including the gateway and the subnet mask. `ipconfig` can also be used to release and renew addresses obtained via DHCP.

▸ **tracert**—This utility verifies the route to a remote system. `tracert` is often used after a failed `ping` request, to see where packets were dropped.

The utilities used to troubleshoot connectivity in a TCP/IP network are covered in greater detail in Chapter 13, "Troubleshooting Tools and Utilities."

Managing Windows Server Storage

Storage devices on a Windows server system are managed through the Disk Management MMC snap-in. This easy-to-use tool makes it simple to see what storage devices are installed in a system, and how those devices are being used. It also provides statistical information on free space, which is a commonly sought statistic by network administrators.

The Disk Management snap-in can be accessed through the Computer Management application, or it can be added as a snap-in to a blank MMC. Figure 9.9 shows the Disk Administrator tools as viewed through the Computer Management application on a Windows Server 2003 system.

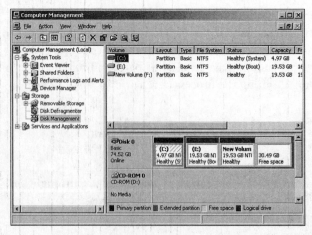

FIGURE 9.9 The Disk Management snap-in viewed through Computer Management on a Windows Server 2003 system.

Windows Server User Management Basics

User account management, like many other administration tasks on a Windows server, is accomplished through the Active Directory Users and Computers MMC snap-in. A shortcut to this application is added to the Administrative Tools menu when a Windows server becomes a domain controller.

TIP

Local User Administration   If a server is installed without Active Directory, local user administration is performed through the Computer Management application, which is found in the Administrative Tools applet of the Control Panel.

EXAM ALERT

Using the Administrator Account   To perform your role as a network administrator in a Windows server environment, it is necessary to have access to an Administrator account. For security reasons, network users should never be given access to the Administrator account. Server administrators should log on with a regular user account, and only use the Administrator account when necessary. As an additional security measure, the administrator account should be given a complex password.

Active Directory Users and Computers is straightforward to use, though you must have a strong understanding of the Active Directory structure before you begin creating or editing user accounts. Figure 9.10 shows an example of Active Directory Users and Computers on a Windows Server 2003 system.

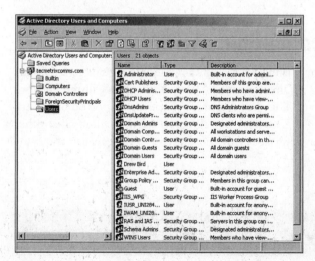

FIGURE 9.10   The Active Directory Users and Computers MMC snap-in on a Windows Server 2003 system.

In addition to user account management, Active Directory Users and Computers is also used for other administrative tasks such as the configuration of Group Policy. Group Policy is a system in Active Directory that allows groups of configuration settings to be deployed to users or computers that connect to the Active Directory. Group Policy is a powerful tool, and although a discussion of its capabilities is outside the scope of Network+, in most organizations with Windows servers, administrations will need to develop a deep understanding of Group Policy and what it can offer.

Challenge: Creating User Accounts in Active Directory

You are the network administrator for a small insurance company in Boise, Idaho. The network is comprised of 2 Windows Server 2003 systems and 65 Windows XP Professional workstations. In this exercise, you create two user accounts for new users joining the company in the middle of next week. The users' names are Andrew Wiseman and Sally Ridge.

1. Click Start, Administrative Tools, Active Directory Users and Computers.

2. If it is not already open, double-click the Users folder in the left pane of the MMC.

3. With the Users folder highlighted, right-click and select New; then click User.

4. Complete the first and last name fields for the user using the names provided in the introduction to this exercise. For the User Logon Name field, use a format of firstname.lastname. Click Next when you have completed the required fields.

5. Provide and confirm a strong password for the user. The User Must Change Password at Next Logon box will be checked automatically. Also check the option for Account is Disabled. This is standard practice for a new user account that will not be accessed immediately.

6. Repeat steps 3 through 5 to create the account for the second user named in the introduction.

Windows Server Authentication

The authentication process facilitated by a Windows server allows users logging on to the network to identify themselves to the Active Directory, and subsequently access all the network resources to which they have permissions. This means that it is necessary to log on only once to access all the resources on the network. The nature of directory services means that other applications, such as a web server, can interface with the directory and can use the same authentication information.

EXAM ALERT

Active Directory and Kerberos Microsoft Active Directory uses Kerberos as its native authentication protocol.

EXAM ALERT

Case Sensitivity Passwords on Windows server operating systems are case sensitive.

In addition to the standard authentication mechanism of usernames and passwords, Windows server platforms also support other authentication systems such as smartcards and biometrics. Implementation of these methods requires additional hardware and software.

Windows Server File and Print Services

The provision of file and print sharing services is a mainstay of any network operating systems, and Windows server is no exception. Windows server systems use a principle called *shares* to make areas of a disk available to users. These shares can be secured by file permissions if they are resident on NTFS partitions, as well as share permissions that can be used on any file system.

EXAM ALERT

File Level Permissions To use file level permissions on a Windows server system, the disk must be formatted with the NTFS file system. FAT or FAT32 partitions do not support file level permissions and must rely solely on share permissions to provide security.

In addition to the basic file sharing and permission systems, Windows server systems also include some advanced features to further enhance the file and serving capabilities. These features include the following:

▶ **Disk quotas**—The amount of disk space available to a user can be restricted and managed through disk quotas. This is a useful element of control over disk usage.

▶ **Encrypting File System (EFS)**—EFS allows files to be encrypted while on the disk, preventing unauthorized access.

▶ **Distributed File System (DFS)**—DFS allows multiple directories on distributed servers to be represented through a single share point, simplifying access for users and administration.

All these features combine to make Windows server operating systems a solid choice for a file server.

Windows server has always provided comprehensive print server functionality, and the latest versions are no exception. Clients can connect to printers across the network without the need for locally installed printer drivers. The drivers are stored on the server and downloaded when the user connects to the printer, making it easy to ensure that users are using the latest version of the correct driver.

Printing on a Windows server can be controlled through a permission mechanism similar to that used in file system security, though it is less complex. Preconfigured groups also allow you to delegate the management of printing functions, which can be a good idea in large environments.

Windows Server Application Support

Of all the network operating systems discussed in this chapter, Windows server platforms have the best overall level of support by third-party applications. Why is Windows so well supported? If you were a software developer, wouldn't you rather develop a program for the most popular operating system than for one of the others? The answer is probably yes, and this is perhaps the largest factor that influences application development for Windows. Another factor is that many applications provided for Windows server platforms also work on Windows XP Professional desktop operating systems, which only serves to further expand the available market for application developers.

In addition to having superb third-party application support, Windows server operating systems come with a complete set of tools and services that satisfy almost every need a company could have from a network operating system. These applications include DNS and DHCP server services, performance-monitoring tools, web server applications, remote access capabilities, and network monitoring tools.

Windows Server Security

Windows server operating systems provide a full range of security features that make for very secure network operating systems. Windows Server 2003 is considered more secure than Windows 2000 because it employs a "secure by default" strategy through which unnecessary applications, services, and security configurations are disabled by default. Administrators can then enable applications and services on an as-needed basis.

NOTE

Make Sure You Are Updated   As with any other network operating system, make sure that Windows servers are updated with the latest operating systems service packs, patches, and security updates. Without them, your systems my be vulnerable to a range of threats and attacks that might compromise your network.

Authentication security is provided on Windows servers through Kerberos version 5. File system security and encryption are provided through NTFS permissions and EFS. Network communication can be protected by a range of security and authentication protocols, although

IPSec (discussed in Chapter 8, "Remote Access and Security Protocols") is most commonly used on Windows server networks to provide both encryption and authentication for network data.

Windows Summary

Although it has its detractors, Windows provides a robust, secure, and feature-rich operating system that is easy to deploy, administer, and manage. The familiarity of the graphical interface provides a "head start" for new network administrators who can find their way around a Windows server within a few minutes. However, the beauty of a Windows server is more than skin deep, and as Microsoft continues to add more features and functionality in each Windows server release, it looks set to remain atop the network operating system pile for some considerable time to come.

AppleShare IP

AppleShare is a technology that enables data and resource sharing on the network. AppleShare works in a client/server configuration, which means that client software is required to access resources on a AppleShare server. Once installed, the AppleShare server can share network resources and network-based services to new and older Macintosh systems ranging from the early Apple IIe systems to the Mac OS X systems.

After an AppleShare server has been installed in the network and has configured shared resources, the server provides three primary application services:

- ▶ **File sharing**—Using AFP, users store and access files on the network. It logs in users and associates them with network volumes and directories.

- ▶ **Print sharing**—The AppleShare Print Server performs print spooling and manages printing on networked printers.

- ▶ **Interaction with Windows clients**—The AppleShare PC enables PCs using Windows-based clients to access AppleShare services by running an AppleShare PC program.

Mac OS-based computers usually can be counted on to rely on the AppleShare IP protocol. When connecting Macintosh clients to a server of a different platform, it is often necessary to enable AppleShare services to provide backward compatibility to older workstations, or to provide effective security.

In the classic versions of the Mac OS, AppleShare functionality was provided by a suite of extensions and control panels providing configuration and core services for this networking protocol. As always, when integrating computers using older software onto a newer network, download and install the latest versions of the AppleShare software from Apple Computer's website and make sure that the operating system is up-to-date. Mac OS X computers should be kept up-to-date with the Software Update utility accessible via System Preferences.

Although AppleShare IP provides a secure way for a user and server to exchange names and passwords, it is not an encrypted protocol. It is theoretically possible for an IP packet to be intercepted by a third party and its contents read. Therefore, be careful when exchanging sensitive data. Fortunately, AppleShare IP is a pure TCP/IP protocol, so it may be "tunneled" using any variety of encryption methods. The Mac OS itself supports L2TP over IPSec and PPTP, which are capable of encrypting network packets to prevent anyone from reading intercepted packets.

AppleShare Authentication

The most important task to be accomplished between the client and server using the AppleShare protocol is authentication. How is the server to know that the user can be trusted to perform operations on files and folders? What if the user is attempting to connect to a non-Apple file server that supports a unique authentication standard?

On connecting to any AppleShare service on any server, the first thing the client does is try to determine what method of authentication the server supports. Can an Apple protocol be used? What about Kerberos, or the Microsoft authentication protocol? If the server supports more than one authentication method, the user is asked to choose one. The exception is the plain-text method. If the server and client don't have compatible authentication software installed, a username and password can be exchanged via plain text, if the server has been allowed to support it. However, if another more secure method is available, the plain text option won't be given.

Because various software vendors sell servers that support AppleShare IP, clients need to be able to add authentication methods. Recent versions of AppleShare support user authentication modules, which are simple plug-ins that add authentication methods to a client.

The most common plug-in is the Microsoft UAM, required to connect to Windows 2000 and 2003 servers. This software comes with the server and is also available for download from Microsoft's support website. This module allows AppleShare IP clients to use Microsoft's native Windows authentication protocol, allowing administrators to provide enhanced security by using SMB services with packet signing turned on, as well as providing secure access to Macintosh clients.

Operating System Interoperability

Rather than use the same network operating system on all servers, modern networks often work in multivendor environments, meaning that you might encounter more than one of the major network operating systems functioning on the same network. In such a scenario, you might, for example, have a NetWare server that handles authentication as well as file and print services, a Windows 2000 server that hosts the corporate email system, and two Linux systems—one acting as a database server while the other provides firewall services. Although it is completely possible to use a single operating system for all these tasks, in some situations a more flexible approach is required.

To facilitate such environments, network operating system manufacturers build in features and services that allow their operating systems to coexist on networks with other vendors' operating systems. In some cases, the manufacturers appear to do so grudgingly, but in the IT environment of the 21st century, it would be a bold move indeed not to provide such services.

The following sections take a brief look at how well some of the major network operating systems "play" with each other.

Using Windows with NetWare

In some environments, you may find that both Windows and NetWare servers are deployed. Unfortunately for Novell, an increasing number of these environments are in place to facilitate migration to a completely Windows-based network.

In some other environments, organizations leverage the power of eDirectory and NetWare for file and print services and use a Windows server product for application hosting. Because it realizes that there will be such environments, Microsoft supplies a range of tools, including the following, to help in the communication between Windows server products and NetWare:

▶ **Client Services for NetWare (CSNW)**—CSNW is designed to allow Windows client systems to access file and print services on a NetWare server. CSNW is installed on a client system and allows only that client to connect to the NetWare server. In effect, CSNW is a Microsoft provided client for NetWare.

▶ **Gateway Services for NetWare (GSNW)**—GSNW is used on Windows 2000 systems to allow Windows client systems to access resources on a NetWare server. GSNW is installed on the server and allows Windows clients to connect to the NetWare server through it. As the name suggests, the service allows a Windows server to act as a gateway to the NetWare server. Clients do not need to authenticate against the Novell server directly. Authentication is performed on behalf of all users through the GSNW software. GSNW is not included with Windows Server 2003.

> **NOTE**
>
> **Windows Services For NetWare** For Windows Server 2003, Microsoft provides Windows Services for NetWare. This free download is geared more toward facilitating the migration from a NetWare/eDirectory environment to Active Directory than as a tool for providing long-term integration.

> **EXAM ALERT**
>
> **CSNW and GSNW** You should understand the functions of CSNW and GSNW for the Network+ exam. You should also understand where they are installed.

Using Windows and Linux/Unix Servers

In today's environments, Linux and Windows servers are commonly used together, and therefore, the servers themselves must be able to communicate. That said, most of that communication is likely to take place with industry standard protocols such as FTP and HTTP, so no additional client software is necessary to communicate between servers under these conditions.

Microsoft provides some degree of integration for Unix systems via a special add-on pack called Windows Services for Unix. This add-on pack provides compatibility with the Unix NFS and a variety of Unix utilities.

Although the name might suggest otherwise, the add-on pack can also be used on Linux servers. However, Microsoft states clearly that it has tested Windows Services for Unix only on a limited number of versions of Unix, and only one version of Linux—Red Hat 8.

Using NetWare and Linux Servers

NetWare and Linux servers are fully interoperable and are often found together in network environments. For example, a NetWare file and print server might coexist with a Linux firewall and proxy server. In addition, it is possible, by using eDirectory, to integrate the management of Linux servers into the directory services system to streamline administration.

To make these scenarios possible, Linux supports both IPX/SPX, which is required for NetWare 3.x and 4.x, and TCP/IP, which is used in the later NetWare versions. However, many of the Linux distributions do not natively support IPX/SPX. If you use one of those distributions, you need to download extra software and perform additional configuration.

Network Operating System Client Support

Because many different client operating systems—including Linux, Windows, and Macintosh—are used in today's networks, network operating systems need to provide support for these clients to connect to the network. Of the three client systems mentioned, Microsoft Windows is by far the most popular. However, in recent years, other platforms have experienced a surge in popularity.

Windows Server Client Support

Windows-based servers support all the client software used on networks today. Microsoft provides client software for all previous versions of Windows allowing for easy client connectivity. In the latest client operating systems, such as Windows 2000 Professional and Windows XP Professional, network functionality is tightly integrated into the operating system. On older versions of Windows, additional software might have to be installed to gain the full benefits of network connectivity.

> **EXAM ALERT**
>
> **Windows XP Home Edition** Although you can use a system running Windows XP Home Edition to connect to network resources, you cannot join a domain or log on to Active Directory.

To support Macintosh clients, Windows server platforms include a File Services for Macintosh service, as well as a Print Services for Macintosh service. These allow Macintosh clients to use access shared resources on a Windows server. The aforementioned Windows Services for Unix provides some client functionality for Unix and Linux clients connecting to Windows client platforms.

NetWare Server Client Support

As a major player in the network operating system world, NetWare provides support for a variety of clients. When connecting Windows systems to a NetWare environment, consider the following:

▶ To connect a Windows client system to a Novell network, you can use Novell-supplied client software or CSNW. Novell makes itsclient software available for download from its website. The client software for current versions of Windows operating systems is called Novell Client for Windows XP/2000.

> **NOTE**
>
> **NetWare 6.x Client Access** NetWare 6.x provides a number of mechanisms that allow files to be accessed from a NetWare server without client software.

▶ Using a Windows 2000 server system to act as a gateway to a NetWare server requires GSNW. As stated previously, GSNW is not provided with Windows Server 2003.

▶ To connect Windows desktop systems to a NetWare 3.x or 4.x network, Microsoft NWLink is required on the workstation, as is CSNW or the Novell client software. NetWare 5.x does not specifically require that clients use NWLink because it also supports TCP/IP. NetWare 6 does not necessarily require client-side software.

Linux Client Support

Because a Linux workstation uses the same operating system that is running on the server, client support is both integrated and seamless. Linux client systems can access all the resources offered by a Linux server with ease. The most common resources are file sharing, which is normally facilitated through NFS, and printing, which is made available through the Line Printer daemon (LPD).

One of the programs used to increase interoperability between Linux and Windows clients is Samba. Samba is a software application that allows Linux servers to easily share resources with Windows workstations. Samba is available free of charge and is commonly installed by default during a Linux installation. Connection to a Samba server requires the use of the Microsoft network client, which is installed by default with most Windows client operating systems.

EXAM ALERT

Samba You might be asked to identify the function and purpose of Samba for the Network+ exam. Samba is an implementation of the Server Message Block (SMB)/Common Internet File System (CIFS) file sharing and access protocols.

Chapter Summary

Network operating systems are specialized and complex software packages used to provide network services such as authentication and file and print services to client computers.

A few key network operating systems are used in modern network environments, each with a unique share of the market. These operating systems include Linux, Unix, Novell NetWare, Mac OS X Server, and Windows server platforms. As a network administrator, you will be required to know how each of these operating systems functions to adequately manage a network. Each of these network operating systems has certain characteristics and deals with network functionality in its own way.

Workstation operating systems provide the interface that allows clients to access network resources and facilities. Therefore, an awareness of the connectivity capabilities of network operating systems and common client operating systems is necessary for any network administrator.

Key Terms

- ▶ Active Directory
- ▶ authentication
- ▶ config
- ▶ CSNW
- ▶ FAT
- ▶ FAT32
- ▶ file and print services
- ▶ Group Policy
- ▶ GSNW
- ▶ ifconfig
- ▶ inetcfg
- ▶ ipconfig
- ▶ ipxping
- ▶ Kerberos

- ▶ Linux
- ▶ Mac OS X
- ▶ multitasking
- ▶ NDS
- ▶ NFS
- ▶ NLM
- ▶ Novell NetWare
- ▶ NTFS
- ▶ ping
- ▶ Samba
- ▶ traceroute
- ▶ tracert
- ▶ Unix
- ▶ web server services

Apply Your Knowledge

Exercises

Working with Windows Server 2003

> **NOTE**
>
> **System Requirements** For this exercise, you need a Windows Server 2003 system. You should *not* use a live server for these exercises. Instead, use a server on a test network, or install Windows Server 2003 on a system specifically for the purposes of experimentation. You can order or download an evaluation version of Windows Server 2003 from http://www.microsoft.com/windowsserver2003/evaluation/trial/ evalkit.mspx. Alternatively, you can use Windows 2000 Server, Windows 2000 Professional, or Windows XP Professional, though the steps may not be exactly as described here.

9.1 Using the Performance Console

One of the best ways to understand the different tools available on a network operating system is to try out some of the utilities and perform tasks similar to those that you would likely do during a normal day's work. In the following three exercises, you do exactly this on a Windows Server 2003 system.

Estimated time: 60 minutes

1. From the Start menu, click Administrative Tools and then choose Performance. The Performance console opens as shown in Figure 9.11.

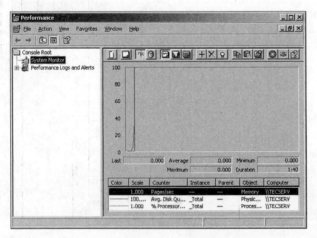

FIGURE 9.11 The Performance Console.

2. Spend a few moments observing the statistics provided in the default screen. If there is little or no activity, open a utility such as Computer Management to generate activity.

3. In the Graph pane of the Performance Console, locate and click the Add counter button. This is represented by a menu button with a "+" symbol on it. The Add Counters dialog appears as shown in Figure 9.12.

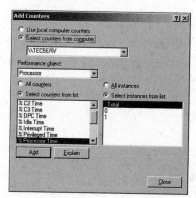

FIGURE 9.12 The Add Counters dialog of the Performance Console.

4. Click the drop-down arrow on the Performance Object field and take a moment to review the range of objects available for monitoring. When you have finished reviewing the list, select Memory. A list of the available counters for the memory object is displayed in the counters field directly below.

5. In the counters field, pick any entry you want and click it once. Now click the Explain button at the bottom of the Add Counters dialog box. Take a moment to read the explanation provided.

6. When you have finished reading the explanation, click the Add button in the Add Counters dialog box. The counter is added to the System Monitor screen. Click Close to return to the Performance Console.

7. Repeat steps 3 through 6 as many times as you want, adding counters and reviewing their purpose. You may need to open applications or generate disk activity to see noticeable results in the System Monitor graph.

8. When you have finished, close the Performance Console.

9.2 Ending a Failed Program in Task Manager

This exercise simulates an unwanted, but often necessary task of ending a failed program or application. On a server, failed programs can use up available memory or processing power robbing it from other applications. In this exercise, we use the Microsoft Paint application as a "volunteer." The application will not have hung, but we will treat it as if it has.

1. From the Start menu, click All Programs, Accessories. Then open the Paint program from the menu. Leave the Paint program open.

2. Press Ctrl+Alt+Del to open the Windows Security dialog. Click the Task Manager button. The Task Manager opens.

3. Click the Processes tab and then, In the Mem Usage column, click on the column heading to sort the running processes by the amount of memory they are using. Notice how you can now identify which applications are using the most memory. Do the same for the CPU column to determine what applications are using the most CPU time.

4. Click the Applications tab and select the entry for Untitled – Paint. Click End Task. The application closes, and the entry disappears from the list of running applications. Leave the Task Manager open.

   In some cases, an application may appear to close, but the processes associated with it may continue to run in the background. In this case, it is necessary to end the process. However, it should be noted that this is a last resort. Halting processes may affect other running applications or, in rare cases, crash the host system. Be aware of this possibility when performing this task in a live environment.

5. Open the Paint program again and then switch back to Task Manager.

6. Select the Processes tab of Task Manager and locate the mspaint.exe executable in the Image Name column. Select the mspaint.exe entry and click End Process. A warning appears similar to that shown in Figure 9.13.

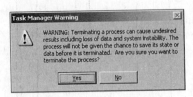

FIGURE 9.13   The End Process warning from Task Manager.

7. Click Yes on the warning dialog box. Microsoft Paint closes automatically. Close Task Manager.

9.3   Creating a Customized MMC Console

As discussed in the chapter, the Microsoft Management Console is a tool used as a shell for many of the administration utilities on a Windows Server system. In this exercise, you create a customized MMC console with two commonly used applications.

1. From the Start menu, click Run. In the Open field, type **MMC** and click OK. A blank MMC opens.

2. From the File menu, click Add/Remove Snap-in. The Add/Remove snap-in dialog box is displayed. Click the Add button. A list of the available snap-ins is displayed in the Add Standalone Snap-in dialog box.

3. From the list of available snap-ins, double-click the entry for Computer Management. A dialog box appears asking you to specify what computer you are creating this snap-in for. Leave as Local Computer, and click Finish. You are returned to the Add Standalone Snap-in dialog. Perform the same procedure for the Disk Manager and Shared Folders snap-ins. Then make a choice of your own.

4. After you complete your selections, click Close. You are returned to the Add/Remove snap-in dialog. Click OK. You are returned to the MMC screen, which should look similar to that shown in Figure 9.14.

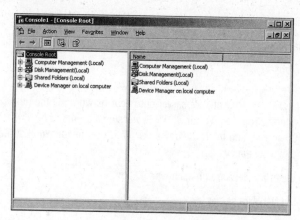

FIGURE 9.14 An example of a customized MMC.

5. To save your customized MMC console for later use, click the File menu and then select Save. Provide a name for your console and save it to the Desktop.

6. Close the console, and then reopen it by locating the .msc icon for the console you created in step 5. You can now use this to access your customized MMC at any time.

Exam Questions

1. Which of the following commands can you use on a Windows Server 2003 system to display detailed network configuration information?

   ○ **a.** `ipconfig`

   ○ **b.** `ipconfig /all`

   ○ **c.** `ifconfig`

   ○ **d.** `config`

2. Which of the following commands would you use to display the network configuration on a NetWare server?

   ○ **a.** `ifconfig`

   ○ **b.** `config`

   ○ **c.** `ipconfig`

   ○ **d.** `ping`

3. Which of the following should you consider when selecting a network operating system? (Choose the three best answers.)

◯   **a.** Application support

◯   **b.** Technical capabilities

◯   **c.** Distribution media

◯   **d.** Existing infrastructure

4. You have been instructed to install a Novell NetWare server onto your network. All the other servers are Windows 2000 systems. You want Windows XP Professional clients to be able to access both the Windows 2000 servers and the NetWare server. Which of the following strategies could you adopt? (Choose the two best answers.)

◯   **a.** Install the Novell Client for NetWare on each workstation.

◯   **b.** Install GSNW on the NetWare server.

◯   **c.** Install GSNW on the Windows XP Professional clients.

◯   **d.** Install GSNW on one of the Windows 2000 servers.

5. What is the name of the Java-based utility that can be used on a NetWare server or on a workstation to manage NDS objects?

◯   **a.** NetWare Administrator

◯   **b.** NetWare Console

◯   **c.** nwadmin

◯   **d.** ConsoleOne

6. You are troubleshooting a hardware problem on a server, and you use the top command to get detailed hardware information. Which operating system are you running on your server?

◯   **a.** Novell NetWare

◯   **b.** Linux

◯   **c.** Windows 2000

◯   **d.** Windows Me

7. Which of the following security systems is the default authentication method used with Microsoft Active Directory?

○ **a.** IPSec

○ **b.** Shadow passwords

○ **c.** Bindery

○ **d.** Kerberos

8. Which of the following services can be installed on a Windows 2000 server to enable Windows clients to access the resources on a NetWare server?

○ **a.** IPSec

○ **b.** eDirectory

○ **c.** CSNW

○ **d.** GSNW

9. On a Linux system, which file holds user account information?

○ **a.** /etc/users

○ **b.** /etc/shadow

○ **c.** /etc/passwd

○ **d.** /etc/userinfo

10. How many domain controllers can be placed in a single Active Directory domain?

○ **a.** 1

○ **b.** 3

○ **c.** 10

○ **d.** Unlimited

11. Which of the following is a common disk-management tool used in a Linux environment?

○ **a.** nwconfig

○ **b.** partmgr

○ **c.** Fdisk

○ **d.** Disk Administrator

12. Which of the following file systems are supported by Windows server operating systems? (Choose the three best answers.)

   ○ a. FAT

   ○ b. FAT32

   ○ c. NTFS

   ○ d. NSS

   ○ e. EXT2

13. Which of the following file permissions is not available in Mac OS X?

   ○ a. Read

   ○ b. Write

   ○ c. Modify

   ○ d. Execute

14. You are given the task of installing a DHCP server system on your network. You currently run Windows NT, Windows 2000, Novell NetWare 5, and Linux servers. On which of the server platforms could you implement DHCP server functionality?

   ○ a. Novell NetWare

   ○ b. Linux

   ○ c. Windows 2000/2003

   ○ d. Any of the above

15. Which of the following utilities would you use to configure the network settings on a NetWare 6.x server?

   ○ a. ipconfig

   ○ b. config

   ○ c. inetcfg

   ○ d. ifconfig

16. Which of the following services would you install on a Windows 2000 system to enable Macintosh clients to use the resources on the server?

    ○ **a.** Services for Macintosh

    ○ **b.** MacGW

    ○ **c.** GSNW

    ○ **d.** MacGate

17. You are given the task of specifying an operating system for use as a file and print server platform. Security is a priority, as are very broad hardware and application support. Which of the following operating systems are you most likely to consider? (Choose the three best answers.)

    ○ **a.** Linux

    ○ **b.** Macintosh

    ○ **c.** Windows Server 2003

    ○ **d.** Windows XP Professional

    ○ **e.** Novell NetWare

18. Which of the following services is required to make the file and print resources of a Linux server available to Windows clients?

    ○ **a.** Squid

    ○ **b.** GSFL

    ○ **c.** FP4Linux

    ○ **d.** Samba

19. Which of the following commands can be used to test TCP/IP network connectivity on a Windows server system?

    ○ **a.** ping

    ○ **b.** tping

    ○ **c.** ifconfig

    ○ **d.** inetcfg

20. On a Linux server, which of the following is the preferred file system?

   ○ **a.** FAT

   ○ **b.** HPFS

   ○ **c.** EXT2

   ○ **d.** NTFS

Answers to Exam Questions

1. **b.** The command `ipconfig /all` is used to show detailed network configuration information. The `ipconfig` command can be used alone, but it shows much less information when it is not used with the `/all` option. `ifconfig` is a utility used on Linux, Unix, and Macintosh systems to view configuration information for network interfaces. The `config` command does the same on a NetWare server. For more information, see the section "Windows 2000 and Windows Server 2003" in this chapter.

2. **b.** The `config` command is used to display network configuration information on a NetWare server. `ifconfig` is a utility used on Linux, Unix, and Macintosh systems to view configuration information for network interfaces. The `ipconfig` command is used to view network configuration on Windows systems. The `ping` utility is used to verify network connectivity between two devices. For more information, see the section "Novell NetWare" in this chapter.

3. **a, b, d.** Application support, technical capabilities, and existing infrastructure are all important considerations in choosing a network operating system. The distribution media would not be a concern because all modern network operating systems are available on a variety of media. For more information, see the section "Introduction to Network Operating Systems" in this chapter.

4. **a, d.** To facilitate connection to a NetWare server from Windows clients, you can install the Novell client on each workstation or install Gateway Services for NetWare on a Windows 2000 server. In addition, Microsoft supplies a client for NetWare that can be used in place of the Novell-provided client. GSNW is a server-based service and would not be installed on the client. Answer b is not valid. GSNW is a Windows server-based service. You cannot run it on a NetWare server. For more information, see the section "Operating System Interoperability" in this chapter.

5. **d.** ConsoleOne is the Java-based utility used to manage the NDS. NetWare Administrator is not a Java-based utility, and NetWare Console is a server utility. `nwadmin` is the abbreviated term used to refer to NetWare Administrator. For more information, see the section "Novell NetWare" in this chapter.

6. **b.** The Top utility is used on Linux systems to provide system information. The other operating systems do not provide or accommodate the Top utility. For more information, see the section "Unix/Linux" in this chapter.

7. **d.** Kerberos is the default authentication protocol used by Active Directory. Shadow passwords are associated with Linux. The Bindery is associated with NetWare versions up to 4. For more information, see the section "Windows 2000 and Windows Server 2003" in this chapter.

8. **d.** GSNW can be installed on the server to allow Windows clients to access a NetWare server. IPSec is a security protocol and does not provide access to a NetWare server. NDS is the directory services system provided on NetWare. CSNW is installed on the client to allow it to connect to a NetWare server. For more information, see the section "Operating System Interoperability" in this chapter.

9. **c.** The `/etc/passwd` file is where user account information is stored on a Linux-based system. The `etc/shadow` file is used for storing encrypted passwords. The other files are not valid. For more information, see the section "Unix/Linux" in this chapter.

10. **d.** There is no practical limit to the number of domain controllers that can be deployed in a single Active Directory domain. More than one should be deployed for fault-tolerant reasons, but beyond that as many can be used as is deemed necessary. The other answers are invalid. For more information, see the section "Windows 2000 and Windows Server 2003" in this chapter.

11. **c.** Fdisk is a commonly used Linux disk-management utility. None of the other utilities are available for Linux. For more information, see the section "Unix/Linux" in this chapter.

12. **a, b, c.** Windows server operating systems support the FAT, FAT32, and NTFS file systems. NSS is a file system associated with NetWare. EXT2 is a Linux/Unix file system. For more information, see the section "Windows 2000 and Windows Server 2003" in this chapter.

13. **c.** Mac OS X is based on the Unix operating system and therefore inherits the characteristics of that OS. In Mac OS X, like Unix, three file permissions are available: read, write, and execute. Modify is not a valid file permission on a Mac OS X system. For more information on file permissions for Unix, Linux, and Mac OS X, see to the section "Unix/Linux" in this chapter.

14. **d.** All these operating systems support the use of DHCP. For more information, see the sections "Windows 2000 and Windows Server 2003," "Unix/Linux," and "Novell NetWare" in this chapter.

15. **c.** The `inetcfg` utility is used on NetWare servers to configure a network. The `config` utility can be used to view but not set, the network configuration on a NetWare server. The other answers are not valid NetWare utilities or commands. For more information, see the section "Novell NetWare" in this chapter.

16. **a.** Services for Macintosh needs to be loaded on a Windows server to allow Macintosh clients to access file and print services in a Windows environment. None of the other answers are valid. For more information, see the section "Network Operating System Client Support" in this chapter.

17. **a, c, e.** When you need security, application, and hardware support, you can use Linux, Windows 2000, and NetWare. Macintosh does provide these services, but there are possible hardware compatibility issues. Windows XP Professional is a workstation operating system and is not designed for use as a server operating system. For more information, see the sections "Windows 2000 and Windows Server 2003," "Unix/Linux," and " Novell NetWare" in this chapter.

18. **d.** Samba is used to provide Windows clients with file and print services from a Linux server. None of the other options are valid. For more information, see the section "Operating System Interoperability" in this chapter.

19. **a**. The `ping` command is used to test connectivity on a Windows server system. `tping` is a NetWare-specific utility, as is `inetcfg`. `ifconfig` is used on Unix, Linux, and Macintosh systems to view and configure network interfaces. For more information, see the section "Windows 2000 and Windows Server 2003" in this chapter.

20. **c**. The native and most-used file system on Linux is the EXT2 file system. Linux supports FAT, but it is not the file system of choice, and neither is HPFS. Linux does not support NTFS. For more information, see the section "Unix/Linux" in this chapter.

Suggested Readings and Resources

1. Habraken, Joe. *Absolute Beginner's Guide to Networking*, fourth edition. Que Publishing, 2003.

2. Nemeth, Evi, Garth Snyder, Trent Hein. *Linux Administration Handbook*. Prentice Hall, 2002.

3. Williams, G. Robert, Mark Walla. *The Ultimate Windows 2000 Systems Administrators Guide*. Addison-Wesley, 2000.

4. Morimoto, Rand, et al. *Microsoft Windows Server 2003 Unleashed, 2nd Edition*. Sams Publishing, 2004.

5. Frisch, Æleen. *Essential System Administration, Third Edition*. O'Reilly & Associates, 2002.

6. Ness, Robyn, Ray, John. *Sams Teach Yourself Mac OS X Panther All In One*. Sams Publishing, 2004.

7. Harris, Jeffrey. *Novell NetWare 6.5 Administrator's Guide*. Novell Press, 2003.

8. Windows 2000 information, www.microsoft.com/windows2000.

9. Windows Server 2003 information, www.microsoft.com/windowsserver2003.

10. Novell NetWare information, www.novell.com/products/netware.

11. Unix information and links, www.unix.org.

12. Linux information and links, www.linux.org.

13. Macintosh information, http://www.apple.com/macosx.

14. Computer networking tutorials and advice, compnetworking.about.com.

15. "TechEncyclopedia," www.techencyclopedia.com.

10

Configuring Network Connectivity

Objectives

This chapter covers the following CompTIA-specified objectives for the "Network Implementation" and "Network Support" sections of the Network+ exam:

3.2 Identify the basic capabilities needed for client workstations to connect to and use network resources (for example, media, network protocols, and peer and server services).

▶ Connecting client workstations to a network is a common task for administrators. Successfully attaching a client station to the network requires many steps including connecting the physical media, configuring the protocols, and establishing user authentication and permissions.

3.3 Identify the appropriate tool for a given wiring task (for example, wire crimper, media tester/certifier, punchdown tool, or tone generator).

▶ Managing networks will from time to time require that administrators work with physical cabling. Administrators have many tools at their disposal to use with network media. Knowing what these tools are and when and where they are used is important for real-world application as well as for the Network+ exam.

3.4 Given a remote connectivity scenario comprised of a protocol, an authentication scheme, and physical connectivity, configure the connection. Includes connection to the following servers:

▶ Unix/Linux/MAC OS X Server

▶ NetWare

▶ Windows

▶ AppleShare IP (Internet Protocol)

▶ The ability to access an internal network remotely is a requirement for many networks today. As such, administrators must be aware of the physical and protocol requirements necessary to connect a remote client to the network.

Outline

Study Strategies

▶ Review the technologies required to connect a client system to the network.

▶ Identify the function and purpose of the various networking tools discussed in this chapter.

▶ Identify the physical methods for remotely connecting a remote client.

▶ Review the protocols used to establish a remote connection.

▶ Review the Notes, Tips, and Exam Alerts in this chapter. Make sure that you understand the information in the Exam Alerts. If you don't understand the topic referenced in an Exam Alert, refer to the information in the chapter text and then read the Exam Alerts again.

Introduction

Configuring network connectivity—whether on a remote network connection or with systems on a local area network (LAN)—is one of the daily responsibilities of a network administrator. Configuring network connectivity encompasses many different skills, including working with protocols, system hardware, and a variety of network services.

This chapter focuses on the network settings required for network connectivity within a LAN and connecting a remote client to the network. In addition, various tools used to manage the physical media of the network are discussed. To begin we will look at the requirements to attach a client system to the network.

Configuring Client Connectivity

Objective:

3.2 Identify the basic capabilities needed for client workstations to connect to and use network resources (for example, media, network protocols, and peer and server services).

Connecting clients to an existing network is a common task for network administrators. There are several layers to connecting a client system including establishing the physical connection, defining network protocols, assigning permissions, and accessing server services and resources. This section explores the requirements to connect a client PC to a network.

Configuring Client Physical Connections

Establishing physical connectivity requires configuring the client network card and connecting the system to the network media. The first requirement is to select the network card. Today, selecting a NIC is simple, although there are a few factors to consider.

The choice of what NIC to use depends on certain criteria, including the following:

- **Bus compatibility**—Some older systems have only Industry Standard Architecture (ISA) slots, but most modern systems have either Peripheral Component Interconnect (PCI) slots or both PCI and ISA slots. Either way, verify that an expansion slot of the correct type is available.

- **Type of network**—As mentioned in the discussion on NICs in Chapter 3, "Networking Components and Devices," unless you are using a networking system other than Ethernet, you should not need to specify another type of NIC.

- **Media compatibility**—Today although most NICs have UTP-based connections, there are some exceptions. Some older networks may require coaxial connections, other newer networks may require a NIC that can support fiber-optic cable, and still other networks may use wireless NICs.

Besides these criteria, which dictate to a certain extent which cards you can use, the choice then depends on manufacturer, cost, and requirements. The NIC might come preinstalled in the system or, as in an increasing number of cases, the network interface might be built in to the system board. In either of these situations, you do not have to install a NIC.

Connecting to Network Media

With the NIC chosen and functioning, the next step is to connect the PC to the network media. This can simple or complicated, depending on the type of network you are using. The following are some of the factors to consider when connecting a new system to an existing network:

▶ **Connecting to a coaxial network**—The biggest consideration when connecting to a coaxial network is that it might be necessary to break the coaxial segment to insert a British Naval Connector (BNC) T-connector to physically connect the PC. Recall from Chapter 1, "Introduction to Networking," that breaking a coaxial cable segment prevents any device connected to it from working. So if you are adding a computer to a coaxial segment and you need to add a length of cable and a connector, you need to either arrange with network users for a few minutes when the network will be unavailable or add the cable and connector before or after working hours. The good news is that you can leave spare BNC T-connectors in the coaxial cable segment as a just-in-case precaution. Doing so can mean that you can add a system to the coaxial segment without affecting users other than the one whose system you are connecting.

▶ **Connecting to a twisted-pair network**—Twisted-pair is the easiest of all the network types to connect to. All you need to connect is a cable (referred to as a *patch cable*) that connects the system to a hub or switch. In environments that use a structured cable system, the cable can be connected to a wall jack or a jack in a floor box. In a less structured environment, the cable can be run directly between the system and the hub or switch. One item worthy of note is that if you are using a Token Ring network, you must configure the NIC to work at the correct speed. Twisted-pair Ethernet networks can accommodate different speeds, if the networking hardware supports a speed higher than the base 10Mbps. Token Ring networks do not offer this function; all devices on the ring must operate at the same speed (4Mbps or 16Mbps). Connecting a system to the network with a NIC configured for the wrong speed prevents the system from communicating on the network, and it might even cause problems with other devices on the segment.

▶ **Connecting to a wireless network**—Wireless network connections commonly use radio frequency instead of traditional wire. Connecting a wireless client requires a wireless access point that provides a bridge between a wired network and the wireless network segment. Wireless standards use RF frequencies of 2.4GHz for 802.11b/g and 5GHz for 802.11a. The wireless client also requires the SSID of the wireless access point and the security settings to connect. Once connected, the wireless client can access the wired network through the AP.

With the network card installed and the client system connected to the media, the client is physically attached to the network. The next step is to configure the network protocols.

Configuring Protocol Settings

Setting LAN protocols on a client system is typically straightforward. A number of protocols may be used on the network, but by far the most common is TCP/IP. The following list is a summary of LAN protocols. For a complete description of the various protocols, see Chapter 5, "Overview of Network Protocols."

▶ **TCP/IP**—By far the most prevalent of network protocol suites, TCP/IP is available for almost every computing platform and has widespread industry support. The majority of LANs now use TCP/IP as the default protocol. Configuring TCP/IP connectivity requires the use of an IP address, a subnet mask, a default gateway, and possibly Domain Name Service (DNS) server information and Windows Internet Naming System (WINS) information.

▶ **IPX/SPX**—Novell invented and implemented IPX/SPX when it introduced NetWare in the 1980s. At that time, TCP/IP was for the most part an academic/military/government protocol, and Novell realized the need for a robust, routable protocol. IPX/SPX is one of the main reasons that Novell owned the networking market through the 1980s and most of the 1990s. IPX/SPX was also easy to install and configure. Today, TCP/IP has largely displaced IPX. One of the advantages of IPX is that workstation configuration is simple. Generally, the only item that might need to be configured is the frame type, which determines the format in which data is grouped into the frames placed on the network. Older versions of NetWare use a frame type called 802.3, whereas newer versions use a frame type called 802.2. Fortunately, most client software can detect the frame type automatically.

NOTE

NWLink and IPX/SPX—When Microsoft began working on adding support for interoperability with NetWare, it opted to develop its own fully compatible version of Novell's proprietary IPX/SPX. This development led to the NWLink protocol and was necessary because earlier versions of NetWare did not support authentication over TCP/IP. NWLink is not commonly used today nor is IPX/SPX.

▶ **AppleTalk**—AppleTalk is a protocol associated with Apple networks. The AppleTalk protocol is an established protocol, having been introduced in the early 1980s, and continued development toward the end of the 1980s enabled it to become a viable internetworking protocol. Like the IPX/SPX and TCP/IP protocol suites, the AppleTalk protocol suite is comprised of several protocols.

▶ **NetBEUI**—Microsoft chose IBM's NetBEUI as the protocol for its first networking implementation in the mid-1980s. One reason Microsoft chose to base its early networking efforts on NetBEUI was the protocol's simplicity and speed. Microsoft wanted to offer a simple, easy workgroup configuration. Name services and addressing are both handled automatically with NetBEUI. There are no configuration issues, other than setting up the NIC and installing NetBEUI as the protocol. Because of NetBEUI's simplicity, administrators sometimes use it to troubleshoot hard-to-find communication problems between two machines. The simplicity of NetBEUI also created problems for Microsoft as the 1980s progressed. NetBEUI is a nonroutable protocol, and as networks began to interconnect, Microsoft found its clients stranded within the confines of small LANs.

As mentioned earlier, TCP/IP is by far the most common of the networking protocols in use today. For that reason, we will take a more in-depth look at configuring client systems to use TCP/IP.

Configuring Client Systems for TCP/IP

Configuring a client for TCP/IP can be relatively complex, or it can be simple. Any complexity involved is related to the possible need to configure TCP/IP manually. The simplicity is related to the fact that TCP/IP configuration can occur automatically via DHCP or through APIPA. This section looks at some of the basic information required to make a system function on a network, using TCP/IP. At the least, a system needs an IP address and a subnet mask. The default gateway, DNS server, and WINS server are all optional, but network functionality is limited without them. The following list briefly explains the IP-related settings used to connect to a TCP/IP network:

▶ **IP address**—Each system must be assigned a unique IP address so that it can communicate on the network.

▶ **Subnet mask**—The subnet mask allows the system to determine what portion of the IP address represents the network address and what portion represents the node address.

▶ **Default gateway**—The default gateway allows the system to communicate with systems on a remote network, without the need for explicit routes to be defined.

▶ **DNS server addresses**—DNS servers allow dynamic hostname resolution to be performed. It is common practice to have two DNS server addresses defined so that if one server becomes unavailable, the other can be used.

▶ **WINS server addresses**—A WINS server enables Network Basic Input/Output System (NetBIOS) names to be resolved to IP addresses. As with DNS servers, it is common practice to enter two WINS server addresses, to provide a degree of fault tolerance.

EXAM ALERT

TCP/IP Connection Requirements At the very minimum, an IP address and a subnet mask are required to connect to a TCP/IP network. With just this minimum configuration, connectivity is limited to the local segment, and DNS and WINS resolution are not possible.

Exactly how this information is entered on the client depends on the operating system being configured. For example, Figure 10.1 shows the Internet Protocol (TCP/IP) Properties dialog box on a Windows XP system. As you can see, the system represented in Figure 10.1 is fully configured for operation on a private network.

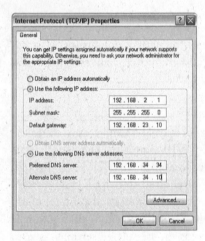

FIGURE 10.1 The Internet Protocol (TCP/IP) Properties dialog box on a Windows XP system.

The configuration screens for other systems are slightly different, but visually they are all similar regardless of the operating system used.

In any case, the parameters required need to be entered into the respective dialog boxes carefully. Entering a duplicate IP address may prevent the client system from being able to log on to the network. To view the IP settings of a client system, many utilities are used. An overview of the utilities used to configure and view current IP information is reviewed in Chapter 13, "Troubleshooting Tools and Utilities."

Accessing Server and Network Services and Resources

With the protocols configured and physical connections established, the client should be able to access the network. If not, see Chapter 14, "Troubleshooting Network Connectivity." Even when the client can access the network, the client still needs to be authenticated and have the correct permissions assigned to connect to network resources:

▶ **Authentication**—After a client system is connected and configured for a network, the user on the new client system must be authenticated. The primary function of authentication is to verify that someone is who they claim they are. This usually involves a username and a password, but can include any other method of demonstrating identity, such as a smart card, biometrics, voice recognition, fingerprints, codes and so on. By far the most common type of authentication used is the standard username and password combination. When a user account is created, it is good practice for the administrator to set a password. The user should change that password immediately so that the administrator no longer knows it. Users should be forced to change their logon passwords periodically, although that often creates the problem of users forgetting their passwords. Mechanisms should therefore be in place that allow users to get new passwords quickly.

▶ **Authorization**—Authorization is finding out if the person, once identified and authenticated, is allowed to have access to a particular resource. This is usually determined by finding out if that person is a part of a particular group that provides the correct permissions or has a particular level of security clearance. Access to programs, data, and resources across the network are often controlled by access permissions. Permissions are responsible for ensuring that only those who should have access to particular data or resources do.

Reviewing Network Connectivity

The following is a quick review of what is needed to connect a client to a network:

▶ **NIC**—From time to time, NICs fail. To confirm that a card is working, you might need to swap out the card with one that is known to be working.

▶ **Physical connections**—Check to see whether a cable has come unplugged. Correcting connectivity issues may be as simple as reconnecting a cable.

▶ **LAN protocol configuration**—It might be necessary to confirm that the network settings on the client computer have not changed.

▶ **Username/password**—Your first consideration when determining connectivity issues is to confirm that the correct username and password configuration is used. Often, this is as far as your troubleshooting needs to go.

▶ **Permissions**—Verify that the user has an active account on the network and that it has the correct permissions set. It is often a good idea to try to log on with a known working account.

Networking Tools

A large part of network administration involves having the right tools for the job and knowing when and how to use them. Selecting the correct tool for a networking job sounds like an easy task, but network administrators can choose from a mind-boggling number of tools and utilities.

Given the diverse range of tools and utilities available, it is unlikely that you will encounter all the ones available—or even all those discussed in this chapter. For the Network+ exam, however, you are required to have a general knowledge of the tools available and what they are designed to do.

Selecting the Appropriate Tool for Wiring

Objective:

3.3 Identify the appropriate tool for a given wiring task (for example, wire crimper, media tester/certifier, punchdown tool, or tone generator).

Until networks become 100% wireless, network administrators can expect to spend some of their time using a variety of media-related troubleshooting and installation tools. Some of these tools (such as the tone generator and locator) may be used for troubleshooting media connections, and others (such as wire crimpers and punchdown tools) are used to create network cables and connections.

The Basic Tools

Although many costly, specialized networking tools and devices are available to network administrators, the most widely used tools cost only a few dollars: the standard screwdrivers we use on almost a daily basis. As a network administrator, you can expect to take the case off a system to replace a network interface card (NIC) or perhaps remove the cover from a hub to replace a fan with amazing regularity. Advanced cable testers and specialized tools will not help you when you need a screwdriver.

Wire Crimpers

Wire crimpers are tools you might find yourself using regularly. Like many things, making your own cables can be fun at first, but the novelty soon wears thin. Basically, a wire crimper is a tool that you use to attach media connectors to the ends of cables. For instance, you use one type of wire crimper to attach RJ-45 connectors on unshielded twisted-pair (UTP) cable, and you use a different type of wire crimper to attach British Naval connectors (BNCs) to coaxial cabling. Figure 10.2 shows an example of a wire crimper for crimping both RJ-11 and RJ-45 connectors.

Challenge

Network administrators often are required to make their own UTP cables for a specific situation. This may be a straight-through or a reverse cable. For this exercise, search the Internet for the pinouts for both a straight-through and reverse UTP cable configuration.

Making network cables is really a hands-on experience. For those who can, using a length of UTP cable, RJ-45 connectors, and UTP wire crimpers creates both a reverse cable and a straight-through cable. When made, test the cables to verify that they work. The reverse cable can be tested by connecting two computer systems directly together or by interconnecting hubs or switches.

TIP

Cable Caveat   When making cables, always order more connectors than you need; there will probably be a few mishaps along the way.

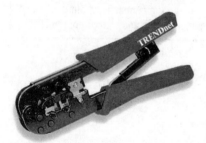

FIGURE 10.2   A wire crimper for RJ-45 and RJ-11 cables. (Photo courtesy of TRENDware International, www.trendware.com.)

In a sense, you can think of a wire crimper as a pair of special pliers. You insert the cable and connector separately into the crimper, making sure that the wires in the cable align with the appropriate connectors. Then, by squeezing the crimper's handles, you force metal connectors through the wires of the cable, making the connection between the wire and the connector.

When you crimp your own cables, you need to be sure to test them before putting them on the network. It only takes a momentary lapse to make a mistake when creating a cable, and you can waste time later trying to isolate a problem in a faulty cable. The section "Media Testers" later in this chapter includes a discussion of how you can test whether a cable is working correctly.

> **NOTE**
>
> **Make or Buy?** There is some debate about whether it is better to buy network cables from a cable manufacturer or make your own. The advantage of buying cables is simply that they are guaranteed to work because they are tested before being sent out. Homemade cables are often made incorrectly and can create hard-to-troubleshoot errors. For example, loose connectors that work when the cable is in one position may not work it's in another. Those who make cables claim that the cost savings over buying cables is a clear benefit. However, if the associated labor costs were introduced into the equation, it is a more difficult argument to make. Many network administrators take the best from both worlds, buying network cable when standard cable lengths are needed and making their own when specific cable lengths are required.

Punchdown Tools

If you have ever looked in a network closet, you have probably seen a distribution block, more commonly called a patch panel. A *patch panel* is a freestanding or wall-mounted unit with a number of port connections on the front. In a way, it looks like a wall-mounted hub without the light-emitting diodes (LEDs). The patch panel provides a connection point between network equipment such as hubs and switches and the ports to which PCs are connected, which are normally distributed throughout a building. Figure 10.3 shows three patch panels.

> **NOTE**
>
> **Direct Cable Connections** Not all environments use patch panels. In some environments, cables are run directly between systems and a hub or switch. This is an acceptable method of connectivity, but it is not as easy to make tidy as a structured cabling system that uses a patch panel system and wall or floor sockets.

FIGURE 10.3 A selection of patch panels. (Photo courtesy of TRENDware International, www.trendware.com.)

Behind each of the individual RJ-45 jacks on the patch panel are connectors to which are attached the eight wires from a piece of twisted-pair cable. These wires are commonly attached to the patch panel by using a tool called a *punchdown tool*. To use the punchdown tool, you place the wires in the tip of the tool and push it into the connector at the back of the patch panel. The insulation is stripped, and the wires are firmly embedded into the connector. Because the connector strips the insulation on the wire, it is known rather grandiosely as an *insulation displacement connector (IDC)*. (Most network administrators choose to refer to it as a *thingy*, if they call it anything at all.) Figure 10.4 shows an example of a typical punchdown tool.

FIGURE 10.4 A punchdown tool. (Photo courtesy of TRENDware International, www.trendware.com.)

Using a punchdown tool is much faster than using wire strippers to prepare each individual wire and then twisting the wire around a connection pole or tightening a screw to hold the wire in place. In many environments, cable tasks are left to a specialized cable contractor. In others, the administrator is the one with the task of connecting wires to a patch panel.

Tone Generators

A *tone generator* is a device that can save a network installer many hours of frustration. Strangely, the tone generator has a partner that goes wherever it goes but is seldom mentioned: the *tone locator*. You might hear the tone generator and the tone locator referred to as the *fox and hound*.

As you might expect, the purpose of the tone generator is to generate a signal that is transmitted on the wire you are attempting to locate. At the other end, you press the tone locator against individual wires. When it makes contact with the wire that has the signal on it, the locator emits an audible signal or tone.

The tone locator is a useful device, but it does have some drawbacks. First, it often takes two people to operate—one at each end of the cable. Of course, one person could just keep running back and forth; but if the cable is run over great distances, this can be a problem. Second, using the tone generator is time consuming because it must be attached to each cable independently.

> **NOTE**
>
> **Labeling Cables** Many problems that can be discovered with a tone generator are easy to prevent by simply taking the time to properly label cables. If the cables are labeled at both ends, you will not need to use such a tool to locate them.

Media Testers

A *media tester*, also called a *cable tester*, is used to test whether a cable is working properly. Any tool that facilitates the testing of a cable can be deemed a cable tester. One of the simplest cable-testing devices is a *multimeter*. By using the continuity setting, you can test for shorts in a length of coaxial cable; or, if you know the correct cable pinouts and have needlepoint probes, you can test twisted-pair cable. Various other single-purpose and multipurpose devices allow you to test cables. Some of these devices tell you whether the cable is working correctly and, if it's not, give you some idea why it's not. Figure 10.5 shows an example of a media tester. Note that there are two parts to the media tester: one for each end of the cable.

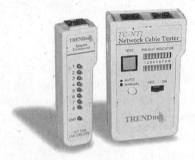

FIGURE 10.5   An example of a media tester. (Photo courtesy of TRENDware International, www.trendware.com.)

Because the majority of network cabling is copper based, most tools designed to test cabling are designed for copper-based cabling. However, when you test fiber-optic cable, you need an optical tester.

An optical cable tester performs the same basic function as a wire media tester, but on optical media. The most common problem with an optical cable is a break in the cable that prevents the signal from reaching the other end. Due to the extended distances that can be covered with fiber-optic cables, degradation is rarely an issue in a fiber-optic LAN environment.

Ascertaining whether a signal reaches the other end of a fiber-optic cable is relatively easy, but when you determine that there is a break, the problem becomes locating the break. That's when you need a tool called an *optical time-domain reflectometer (OTDR)*. By using an OTDR, you can locate how far along in the cable the break occurs. The connection on the other end of the cable might be the source of the problem, or perhaps there is a break halfway along the cable. Either way, an OTDR can pinpoint the problem.

Unless you work extensively with fiber-optic cable, you're unlikely to have an OTDR or even a fiber-optic cable tester in your toolbox. Specialized cabling contractors will have them, though, so knowing they exist is important.

Hardware Loopback Connectors

Hardware loopback connectors are simple devices that redirect outgoing transmissions from a system directly back into it. Hardware loopback connectors are used in conjunction with diagnostic software for diagnosing transmission problems. Loopback connectors are available for a number of ports, including RJ-45, serial, and parallel ports.

Specifically, a hardware loopback connector loops the outgoing data signal wires back into the system on the incoming data signal line. It in effect tricks the system into thinking that the PC is sending and receiving data on the network, when in fact the data being sent is just being rerouted back in. Note that in some cases, a hardware loopback connector is referred to as an adapter or a plug.

For the purposes of this discussion, we're interested in the hardware loopback connector used with twisted-pair network ports (10BaseT, 100BaseT, and so on). You can buy hardware loopback plugs or make your own. The wiring of a hardware loopback connector is fairly simple: Pin 1 is wired to Pin 3, and Pin 2 is wired to Pin 6. A picture is worth a thousand words in this case; Figure 10.6 shows a graphical representation of the wiring of a hardware loopback connector. The wiring pinouts for a hardware loopback connector are the same as those for a UTP crossover cable.

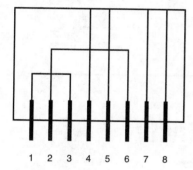

1 2 3 4 5 6 7 8   **FIGURE 10.6**   The wiring for a hardware loopback connector.

NOTE

Software Versus Hardware Loopback   Previously we discussed the local loopback address (127.0.0.1) as a means of testing the Transmission Control Protocol/Internet Protocol (TCP/IP) connectivity of a system. Although this test is an effective way of ensuring that the TCP/IP protocol suite is operating correctly, it does not ensure that the network is functional at a physical level because the software loopback functionality is built in to the protocol suite. In other words, a software loopback never makes it as far as the physical NIC or connection. A hardware loopback takes the test one step further by providing a mechanism to test the physical connectivity. The software loopback test is still a useful tool, however, because without a functioning network card, operating systems generally won't allow the protocol suite to be tested.

Wireless Detection

Wireless media requires its own types of tools. One such tool is a Wi-Fi detector. The intent of such a device is to reveal Wi-Fi hot spots and detect wireless network access with LED visual feedback. Such devices can be configured to scan specific frequencies. When working with 802.11b/g networks, you will most certainly require scanning for 2.4GHz RF signals.

Such devices can be used in the troubleshooting process to identify where and how powerful RF signals are. Given the increase in wireless technologies, RF detectors are sure to increase in popularity. Figure 10.7 shows a Wi-Fi detector.

FIGURE 10.7 Wireless RF detector.

Configuring Remote Connectivity

Objective:

3.4 Given a remote connectivity scenario comprised of a protocol, an authentication scheme, and physical connectivity, configure the connection. Includes connection to the following servers:

▶ Unix/Linux/MAC OS X Server

▶ NetWare

▶ Windows

▶ AppleShare IP (Internet Protocol)

The capability to remotely access networks has become an important part of the modern IT infrastructure. All organizations, from the smallest business to the largest corporation, are taking advantage of the potential that remote network access provides. Therefore, today's network administrators are as likely to be responsible for managing remote network access as they are for LAN access. Configuring and managing remote access requires knowledge of the protocols and procedures involved in establishing a remote connection.

The following sections explore some of the common considerations in configuring a remote connection, including a discussion of physical connections, protocols (which facilitate the connection), software (which establishes the connection), the dial-up connection method, and security.

For information on remote access protocols, see Chapter 8, "Remote Access and Security Protocols." For more information on troubleshooting remote access, see Chapter 13.

Physical Connections

There are many ways to connect to a remote network. Some, such as the plain old telephone system (POTS), offer a direct connection between you and the remote host. Others, such as cable and Digital Subscriber Lines (DSL), allow you to connect, but the connection occurs over a public network (the Internet), which can bring additional considerations such as authentication and security problems. The methods that can be used to establish a remote connection are discussed in detail in Chapter 7, "WAN and Internet Access Technologies." For that reason, only a brief recap is included in this section:

▶ **Public switched telephone network (PSTN)**—The PSTN offers by far the most popular method of remote connectivity. A modem and a POTS line allow for inexpensive and somewhat reliable, if not fast, remote access.

▶ **Integrated Services Digital Network (ISDN)**—ISDN is a dial-up technology that works much like the PSTN, but instead of using analog signals to carry the data, ISDN uses digital signals. This makes it faster than the PSTN.

▶ **Cable**—In an effort to take advantage of the increasing demand for high-speed Internet access, cable TV providers now offer broadband Internet access over the same connection used to carry cable TV signals.

▶ **DSL**—DSL services are the telecom companies' broadband offering. *x*DSL (that is, the family of DSL services) comes in many different varieties, and as with cable, you need a special modem to use it.

▶ **Satellite**—Perhaps the least popular of the connection methods discussed here, satellite provides wireless Internet access, although in some scenarios a PSTN connection is also required for upstream access. Of the technologies discussed in this section, satellite is the least suitable for remote access.

▶ **Wireless**—Wireless Internet access is provided by a Wireless Internet Service Provider (WISP). The WISP provides public wireless Internet access known as *hotspots*. Hotspots provide Internet access for mobile network devices such as laptops, handheld computers, and cell phones in airports, coffee shops, conference rooms, and so on. When connected to the Internet, it is possible to use that connection to establish a remote connection to a network.

Protocols

When you have decided on the physical aspect of the connection, the next consideration is the protocols that allow you to make a connection to the remote server.

To facilitate a connection between a remote system and a remote access server, common protocols must be used between the systems. Two types of protocols are required to establish a remote connection. You first need to have the protocols that communicate at the data-link layer, including the following:

▶ **Point-to-Point Protocol (PPP)**—PPP is actually a family of protocols that work together to provide connection services. PPP allows remote clients and servers to negotiate authentication between devices. PPP can employ a variety of encryption methods to secure transmissions.

▶ **Serial Line Internet Protocol (SLIP)**—SLIP is an older connection protocol than PPP, and it was originally designed to allow data to be transmitted via Transmission Control Protocol/Internet Protocol (TCP/IP) over serial connections in a Unix environment. Unfortunately, SLIP does not support encryption or authentication and therefore has largely fallen out of favor. If you have users that use SLIP to connect from remote systems, you should move them to PPP connections as soon as possible.

▶ **Point-to-Point Protocol over Ethernet (PPPoE)**—PPPoE is a method of using PPP connections over Ethernet. Using PPPoE and a broadband connection such as *x*DSL or cable Internet access, it is possible for individual users to have authenticated access to high-speed data networks, which provides an efficient way to create a separate connection to a remote server for each user. This strategy allows Internet access and billing on a per-user basis rather than a per-site basis. Users accessing PPPoE connections require the same information as required with standard dial-up phone accounts, including a username and password combination. As with a dial-up PPP service, an Internet service provider (ISP) will most likely automatically assign configuration information such as the IP address, subnet mask, default gateway, and DNS server information.

After a data link has been established as the connection between the devices, other network layer and transport layer protocols are required to facilitate signal transmission. Examples of these protocols include the following:

▶ **TCP/IP**—TCP/IP is the most widely used protocol today, and it is the protocol most commonly used to configure remote connectivity. As with access for systems on a LAN, remote access requires unique TCP/IP addressing. The most common way for remote clients to get IP information from the remote server is through automatic assignment from a DHCP server. However, it is possible to manually assign IP addresses from a static pool of addresses that have been assigned to the remote access server by the network administrator.

▶ **Internetwork Packet Exchange/Sequenced Packet Exchange (IPX/SPX)**—Like TCP/IP, IPX/SPX is a fully routable protocol, and it can therefore be used for connecting to a remote system. However, just as TCP/IP is replacing IPX/SPX on LANs, it is also replacing IPX/SPX on remote access links.

Generally, TCP/IP is the protocol suite to use for remote access. However, popular remote access solutions such as Microsoft Remote Access Service (RAS) can accommodate connections established using IPX/SPX, so you should be aware of the fact that IPX/SPX can be used.

> **NOTE**
>
> **Using PPPoE**   How do you know whether your ISP is using PPPoE? If you have xDSL or cable, you can just open your browser and be online. With PPPoE, authentication is required before you can access the Internet.

Software

With the physical connection and the protocols in place, you are almost ready to establish a connection. You just need some software to make the magic happen.

To establish a remote connection, the remote system typically requires software that initiates contact with the remote server. This software can take many forms: In some Windows client systems, for example, a remote connection can be configured by using dial-up networking. Figure 10.8 shows the Connect To screen on a Windows XP system.

In addition to the client-side software that initiates the remote connection, server-side software responsible for answering the request is required. The server responding to the remote access requests is referred to as the *remote access server*. On Windows server platforms, the network service responsible for handling remote client connections is RAS. Figure 10.9 shows the Routing and Remote Access Service dialog box on a Windows 2000 system.

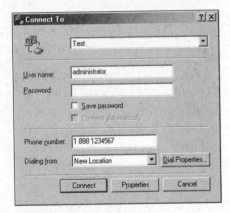

FIGURE 10.8 The Connect To screen on a Windows client system.

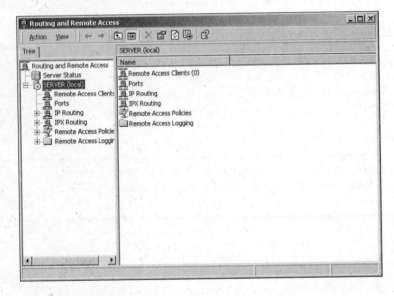

FIGURE 10.9 Routing and Remote Access configuration screen.

EXAM ALERT

Windows RAS Many remote access products are available; however, Windows RAS is the most likely of these products to appear on the Network+ exam.

Dial-up Access

As noted previously, dial-up is one of the most popular methods of gaining remote access to a LAN. There was a time when dial-up referred to using a modem on a POTS line, but today the term is applied generally to any connection that must be manually established to a remote system. For example, the establishment of a virtual private network (VPN) connection to a remote system over a cable Internet connection would be considered a dial-up connection.

The specifics of configuring dial-up access to a remote server depend on the client system being used. Linux, Macintosh, and the various Windows client systems all have different methods and means of connecting to a remote server via a dial-up connection. Instead of individually documenting the procedures for configuring each of the respective client systems, the following list identifies the configuration information and hardware required by all client systems to access a remote server using a dial-up connection:

▶ **Hardware**—To access the remote server, the client system has to have the correct hardware installed to make the connection. Most dial-up remote connections require a modem on the client and a modem on the server system.

▶ **Phone number, hostname, or IP address**—To connect to a remote access server over a dial-up connection, you need to have the phone number of the remote server, the IP address, or the hostname.

▶ **Transmission protocols**—You need to choose the compatible protocol used by the remote server—NetBIOS Extended User Interface (NetBEUI), TCP/IP, or IPX/SPX. If the server is using TCP/IP, you might need to configure the IP configuration information manually, or this information might be assigned through a remote DHCP server.

▶ **Security**—On the client system, you might need to establish security information so that it can be authenticated by the server. The security information includes a username and password combination that will be verified by the remote server, as well as data encryption options.

▶ **Client connection options**—On the client side, you can configure connection options such as redialing or disconnecting after a certain amount of time.

Dial-up Connection Troubleshooting

It would be nice if every time you dialed in to a remote server, it answered, and you were authenticated to the network. Although this usually happens most of the time, there are times when you just can't connect. If you are unable to establish the remote connection through dial-up, consider the following:

▶ **Verify that the remote access server is operational**—You might be trying to log on to a remote server that is down. This might require a call to the remote network administrator to confirm.

▶ **Verify that you have correct authentication information**—To access the remote access server, you need a valid user account for the remote network and permissions to access the server.

▶ **Confirm that you are calling the correct number or trying to connect to the correct server**—Frequently, the cause of a problem can be traced to something simple. In the case of remote connectivity, this can often be using the wrong phone number or IP address for the remote server.

▶ **Verify local settings**—To connect to the remote server, the client system needs to be correctly configured to access the server. These configuration settings include protocol information and compatible security settings.

Security

In today's world, it is necessary to establish security measures for remote network connections. In the same way users on local network systems must be authenticated to use network services and resources, remote clients must also be authenticated. The intention of remote authentication is to ensure that only users who have permission to access the remote network can access it. Most remote authentication requires at least a username and password combination, similar to that required for local network connections. More sophisticated systems use token generators or special authentication devices. Security protocols for remote and local networks are discussed in Chapter 8.

Chapter Summary

This chapter focuses on the protocols and procedures involved in establishing and configuring remote and local network connectivity. Each of the major operating systems requires configuration; however, the protocols and physical requirements are universal between operating systems.

Configuring network access involves a number of different software configurations. To access a remote network, a user must have a valid protocol, a means of accessing the remote network (such as a dial-up account), and a valid user account. Accessing a remote network requires considerable configuration on both the client and server computer systems.

To log on to a local network, a number of settings have to be configured on the client system. These settings include DNS, DHCP, WINS, NetBIOS names, and protocols. If you do not correctly configure these settings, the client system might be unable to access the network. Although the need to configure these, or similar, settings is the same for all operating systems, the method of configuring these settings in each of the operating systems varies. Network administration requires a knowledge of how each of the different client-based operating systems is configured.

A variety of networking tools can be used to manage the physical media of the network. Working with networks requires knowledge of what each of these tools is designed to do.

Key Terms

- cable Internet
- coaxial network
- default gateway
- dial-up
- IP address
- ISDN
- media testers
- NetBIOS
- PPP
- PPPoE
- PSTN
- punchdown tool
- remote connectivity
- satellite Internet
- SLIP
- subnet mask
- twisted-pair
- wire crimpers
- wireless
- xDSL

Apply Your Knowledge

Exercises

10.1 Installing a Remote ISDN Connection

In this exercise, you walk through the steps to create a client-side remote connection over an ISDN connection. The exercise assumes that you are using a Windows XP system.

Estimated time: 10 minutes

1. Select Start, Connect To, Show All Connections.

2. This opens the Network Connections dialog screen. From the left menu options, select the option to Create a New Connection.

3. The New Connection Wizard starts. Click the Next button to continue.

4. The second screen of the New Connection Wizard asks you to choose the required connection type. For this exercise, select the Connect to the Network at My Workplace button. This is used to create VPN and dial-up connections. Once selected, click Next to continue.

5. The next screen in the New Connection Wizard asks you to choose whether this connection is to be a VPN connection or an ISDN connection. Select the Dial-up Connection option and click Next to continue.

6. You are asked to specify a name for the connection. For this exercise, name the connection `remote`. Click Next.

7. Enter the phone number used to establish the connection. Because there is no actual connection point, you can enter any phone number such as 555-1234. Click Next.

8. The final screen in the New Connection Wizard is displayed indicating that the connection has been made. Click Finish. When finished, the connection dialog box for the new connection is displayed.

10.2 Setting the Remote Connection to Use the SLIP Protocol

In this exercise, we change the remote protocol being used to establish the connection made in Exercise 10.1.

Estimated time: 5 minutes

1. Choose Start, Connect To, and then remote. The remote option is the connection made in Exercise 10.1. When selected, the connection dialog box displays.

2. From the remote connection dialog box, select the Properties button. This opens the Remote Properties dialog box.

3. Select the Networking tab at the top of the dialog box.

4. The top option from the Networking tab provides a menu bar allowing the remote connection to be changed from PPP to SLIP.

Exam Questions

1. You are troubleshooting a network that uses the SLIP protocol for dial-up access. Recently, there have been many drops in communication and you are becoming increasingly concerned with remote access security. Which of the following would you recommend?

   ○ **a.** Upgrade SLIP to TCP/IP

   ○ **b.** Upgrade SLIP to PPP

   ○ **c.** Upgrade SLIP to VPN

   ○ **d.** Upgrade SLIP to IPSEC

2. You are configuring a client system and require the systems to communicate with systems on a remote network. In addition to TCP/IP and a subnet mask, which of the following pieces of information are required?

   ○ **a.** RIP

   ○ **b.** OSPF

   ○ **c.** Gateway address

   ○ **d.** IP routing address

3. Which of the following data-link layer protocols are used to establish a remote access connection? (Choose the two best answers.)

   ○ **a.** PPP

   ○ **b.** TCP

   ○ **c.** SLIP

   ○ **d.** IPX

4. Which of the following pieces of information are required to configure a system for TCP/IP connectivity? (Choose the two best answers.)

   ○ **a.** DNS server addresses

   ○ **b.** Default gateway

   ○ **c.** IP address

   ○ **d.** Subnet mask

5. What tool would you use when working with an IDC?

   ○ **a.** Wire crimper

   ○ **b.** Media tester

   ○ **c.** OTDR

   ○ **d.** Punchdown tool

6. As a network administrator, you find yourself working in a wiring closet where none of the cables have been labeled. Which of the following tools are you most likely to use to locate the physical ends of the cable?

   ○ **a.** Tone generator

   ○ **b.** Wire crimper

   ○ **c.** Punchdown tool

   ○ **d.** ping

7. Which of the following are required to connect a wireless client to a wired network? (Select two.)

   ○ **a.** SSID

   ○ **b.** Wireless access point

   ○ **c.** DHCP address

   ○ **d.** SLIP protocol

8. Which of the following must be configured to allow clients to use hostname resolution?

   ○ **a.** WINS server address

   ○ **b.** Gateway address to the WINS server

   ○ **c.** DNS server address

   ○ **d.** Gateway address to the DNS server

9. Which of the following best describes the function of authentication?

   ○ **a.** Authorizes a user to use a particular resource.

   ○ **b.** Limits access to network resources.

   ○ **c.** Authentication is any process by which you verify that users are who they claim they are.

   ○ **d.** Determines the level of access a user will have to network data.

10. You are installing a new system into an existing star network and need a cable that is 45 feet long. Your local vendor does not stock cables of this length, so you are forced to make your own. Which of the following tools will you need to complete the task?

   ○ **a.** Optical tester

   ○ **b.** Punchdown tool

   ○ **c.** Crimper

   ○ **d.** UTP splicer

11. Which of the following are required when choosing a NIC for your network? (Choose the two best answers.)

   ○ **a.** DNS compatibility

   ○ **b.** Bus compatibility

   ○ **c.** Correct authentication method

   ○ **d.** Correct type of network

12. You are troubleshooting a problem with a workstation and have managed to narrow it down to a single patch cable. What tool might you use to troubleshoot the problem further?

   ○ **a.** Tone generator/locator

   ○ **b.** OTDR

   ○ **c.** ping

   ○ **d.** Media tester

13. Which of the following are true of authorization? (Select two.)

   ○ **a.** Authorization occurs before authentication.

   ○ **b.** Authorization determines the network resources that can be accessed by a user.

   ○ **c.** Authorization occurs after authentication.

   ○ **d.** Authorization is not used for remote clients.

14. What tool can be used to find a break in a length of fiber-optic cable?

   ○ **a.** Tone generator

   ○ **b.** TDR

   ○ **c.** OTDR

   ○ **d.** Fox and hare

15. Which networking tool is reperesented in the following figure?

    ○ **a.** Punchdown tool

    ○ **b.** Fox and hound

    ○ **c.** Fiber connector

    ○ **d.** UTP wire separator

16. You are attempting to access a network printer to print out a sales document. You type in yor username and password and can successfully log on to the network. However, when you try and access the printer, you receive an error stating that you do not have permissions to use that printer. Which of the following statements are true? (Seclect two.)

    ○ **a.** The authentication process has failed.

    ○ **b.** The authorization process has failed.

    ○ **c.** The authentication process was successful.

    ○ **d.** The authorization process was successful.

17. A tone generator and locator are commonly referred to as what?

    ○ **a.** Fox and rabbit

    ○ **b.** Fox and hare

    ○ **c.** Fox and hound

    ○ **d.** Fox and dog

18. Which of the following protocols allows for an individual billing strategy?

    ○ **a.** TCP/IP

    ○ **b.** RCP

    ○ **c.** PPPoE

    ○ **d.** PPP

19. Which of the following are required to establish a remote connection? (Choose the three best answers.)

    ○ **a.** Windows Dial-Up Networking

    ○ **b.** A physical means of connection

    ○ **c.** A protocol to establish the connection

    ○ **d.** A protocol to establish the communication

20. Which of the following remote connectivity methods is least likely to be used in a network?

    ○ **a.** Satellite

    ○ **b.** PSTN

    ○ **c.** ISDN

    ○ **d.** xDSL

Answers to Exam Questions

1. **b.** In a remote connection scenario, both SLIP and PPP can be used to create a remote connection. Of the two, PPP is more robust and offers greater reliability and security. PPP includes error checking features to help maintain a reliable connection. For more information see the section "Configuring Remote Connectivity" in this chapter.

2. **c.** The default gateway allows the system to communicate with systems on a remote network, without the need for explicit routes to be defined. To allow systems to access remote networks, the default gateway address must be included with the TCP/IP information. For more information on TCP/IP addressing, see the "Configuring Client Systems for TCP/IP" section in this chapter.

3. **a, c.** PPP and SLIP are data-link layer protocols that can be used to establish remote connectivity between two devices. TCP and IPX are both transport layer protocols. For more information, see the section "Configuring Remote Connectivity" in this chapter.

4. **c, d.** To configure TCP/IP, you only need an IP address and the subnet mask. However, without a default gateway, network functionality is limited to the local network segment, and DNS or WINS resolutions are not available. For more information, see the section "Configuring Client Systems for TCP/IP" in this chapter.

5. **d.** You use a punchdown tool when working with an IDC. All the other tools are associated with making and troubleshooting cables, but they are not associated with IDCs. For more information, see the section "Selecting the Appropriate Tool for Wiring" in this chapter.

6. **a.** The tone generator tool, along with the tone locator, can be used to trace cables. Crimpers and punchdown tools are not used for locating a cable. The `ping` utility would be of no help in this situation. For more information, see the section "Selecting the Appropriate Tool for Wiring" in this chapter.

7. **a, b.** When connecting wireless clients to a wired network, a wireless access point is used to create the bridge between the wireless client and the wired network. Once connected to the access point, the wireless clients can use the resources of the wired network. The client must also use the same SSID as the access point to connect. The wireless client does not need a DHCP address because other addressing schemes can also be used. The SLIP protocol is not required to make the connection. For more information, see the section "Configuring Client Physical Connections" in this chapter.

8. **c.** The function of the DNS server is to provide hostname resolution. To allow the client to use hostname resolution, it must have the address of the DNS sever configured. The WINS service is used to resolve NetBIOS name resolution. Answers b and d are not valid. For more information, refer to the section "Configuring Protocol Settings" in this chapter.

9. **c.** Authentication is used to verify that someone is who he says he is. This usually involves a username and a password but can include any other method of demonstrating identity, such as a smartcard, biometrics, voice recognition, or fingerprints. Authentication does not determine who can access a particular resource; that is the function of authorization and permissions. Authentication is simply the user's verification. For more information, refer to the section "Accessing Server and Network Services and Resources" in this chapter.

10. **c.** When attaching RJ-45 connectors to UTP cables, the wire crimper is the tool you use. None of the other tools are used in the construction of UTP cable. For more information, see the section "Selecting the Appropriate Tool for Wiring" in this chapter.

11. **b, d.** When choosing a NIC, consider bus compatibility and the type of network to which you are going to connect. Answers a and c are not valid considerations for selecting a network card. For more information, see the section "Configuring Client Physical Connections" in this chapter.

12. **d.** If you suspect a problem with a patch cable, you can use a media tester to test it. An OTDR is used to test optical cables, and so it would not be used on UTP, which is copper-based cable. The other tools discussed in this question would not be used. For more information, see the section "Selecting the Appropriate Tool for Wiring" in this chapter.

13. **b, c.** Authentication is the process of determining whether a user is who he says he is, whereas authorization determines what a user can access after being authorized. Therefore, authorization occurs after authentication and determines what resources a user can access. For more information see the section "Accessing Server and Network Services and Resources" in this chapter.

14. **c.** An OTDR can be used to find a break in a length of fiber-optic cable. The other tools listed cannot be used to troubleshoot a break in a fiber-optic cable. For more information, see the section "Selecting the Appropriate Tool for Wiring" in this chapter.

15. **a.** The figure shows an example of a punchdown tool. The punchdown tool is used to attach wires into a patch panel. For more information on networking tools, refer to the section on "Networking Tools" in this chapter.

16. **c, d.** Because the user was able to successfully log on to the network, it indicates that the authentication process was successful. Also, because the user was unable to access the printer because of inadequate permissions, it shows that the authorization process was also working. Authentication refers to the verification of a user, confirming that the user is who he says he is. Once confirmed, the user is able to log on to the network. Authorization determines what a user can and cannot do after he accesses the network. In this scenario, the user was not authorized to use that particular printer. For more information refer to the section "Accessing Server and Network Services and Resources" in this chapter.

17. **c.** A tone generator and locator are commonly referred to as the fox and hound. None of the other answers are valid. For more information, see the section "Selecting the Appropriate Tool for Wiring" in this chapter.

18. **c.** In some cases it is necessary to have an Internet access technology that allows for individual billing for Internet users. PPPoE enables separate connections to a RAS server allowing all billing to be managed on an individual basis, rather than a per-site basis. Clients can create both dial-up and dial-on-demand connections using PPPoE. For more information see the section "Configuring Remote Connectivity" in this chapter.

19. **b, c, d.** To establish a remote connection, you need the physical connection method, a protocol to establish the connections, and a protocol to communicate with the remote system. Windows Dial-Up Networking is not necessarily required. For more information, see the section "Configuring Remote Connectivity" in this chapter.

20. **a.** Of those listed, satellite is the least suitable method for remote access because it has limited upload speeds and requires both a satellite and a dial-up connection. All the other options are valid and widely used methods of Internet access. For more information, see the section "Configuring Remote Connectivity" in this chapter.

Suggested Readings and Resources

1. Habraken, Joe. *Absolute Beginner's Guide to Networking*, fourth edition. Que Publishing, 2003.

2. Nemeth, Evi, Garth Snyder, Trent Hein. *Linux Administration Handbook*. Prentice Hall, 2002.

3. Williams, G Robert, Mark Walla. *The Ultimate Windows 2000 Systems Administrators Guide*. Addison-Wesley, 2000.

4. Morimoto, Rand, et al. *Microsoft Windows Server 2003 Unleashed, 2nd Edition*. Sams Publishing, 2004.

5. Frisch, Æleen. *Essential System Administration, Third Edition*. O'Reilly & Associates, 2002.

6. Ness, Robyn, Ray, John. *Sams Teach Yourself Mac OS X Panther All In One*. Sams Publishing, 2004.

7. Harris, Jeffrey. *Novell NetWare 6.5 Administrator's Guide*. Novell Press, 2003.

8. Windows 2000 information, www.microsoft.com/windows2000.

9. Windows Server 2003 information, www.microsoft.com/windowsserver2003.

10. Novell NetWare information, www.novell.com/products/netware.

11. Unix information and links, www.unix.org.

12. Linux information and links, www.linux.org.

13. Macintosh information, http://www.apple.com/macosx.

14. Computer networking tutorials and advice, compnetworking.about.com.

15. "TechEncyclopedia," www.techencyclopedia.com.

CHAPTER ELEVEN

Securing the Network

Objectives

This chapter covers the following CompTIA-specified objectives for the "Network Implementation" section of the Network+ exam:

3.5 Identify the purpose, benefits, and characteristics of using a firewall.

▶ Firewalls are a means by which to secure a network from outside intruders. With the proliferation of the Internet and WAN connectivity, the use of firewalls is becoming commonplace.

3.6 Identify the purpose, benefits, and characteristics of using a proxy service.

▶ The Internet provides many benefits to an organization. One of the challenges associated with being connected to the Internet, though, is providing access to all users in a controlled manner. A proxy service is a tool that allows us to do this.

3.7 Given a connectivity scenario, determine the impact on network functionality of a particular security implementation (for example, port blocking/filtering, authentication, and encryption).

▶ The measures used to protect networks also add a layer of complexity to these networks. Understanding how these measures operate and the consequences of changing or removing services are key skills for a network administrator.

3.9 Identify the main characteristics and purpose of extranets and intranets.

▶ Today's modern networks provide an ever-increasing range of services to users. These services include specialized applications and networks designed to help groups and teams to work together more efficiently, whether they are in the office or at home.

Outline

Study Strategies

▶ Read through the information provided in this chapter, paying special attention to Notes and Exam Alerts.

▶ Review the information provided on configuring strong passwords and password policies. If you have a server system available, review the password policy features provided by that system. This will serve to reinforce the purpose of password policies and some of the commonly configured options.

▶ Make sure that you understand what file permissions are associated with common operating systems. This information is provided in Tables 11.1, 11.2, and 11.3.

▶ Visit the websites cited in the "Suggested Readings and Resources" section at the end of this chapter. They provide useful additional information on network security principles and common practices.

▶ Complete the review questions at the end of the chapter.

Introduction

Today, more than ever, the security of networks is a major consideration for network administrators. Notwithstanding the risks associated with the fact that most networks are now connected by some means to the Internet, security from a more local perspective is a big issue.

For a network administrator to fully understand the security risks associated with the network, she must take a holistic view and consider every aspect, threat, and possible weakness. The network administrator must assume that someone will attempt to gain unauthorized access to the network or the systems attached to it at some point. This might sound a little dramatic, but there are plenty of network administrators who can attest to the fact that it is a reality.

There are, of course, certain environments in which security is more of a concern than in others. If you work for, say, a bank or a branch of the government, security is likely to be a high priority. For a chain of florists in Fresno, security is likely to be less of an issue, but it must still be considered.

Security today is not just about stopping corporate espionage or preventing theft of equipment. It's about protecting the physical assets and, perhaps more importantly, the data of the organization. The cracker coming in through your firewall and entering 50 bogus orders for gift hampers might think it's funny. Your boss is likely to find it less amusing.

In essence, security is about ensuring the privacy, integrity, and quality of a network's data and the systems that hold it, with the purpose of ensuring business continuity. Determining what measures are required to ensure this security is the concern of the network administrator.

Threats to Security

Before we look at the measures you can take to secure your network, let's first look at what you are trying to protect against. The following are some possible threats to a network's security:

- **Internal threats**—It is a sad fact that the most common source of security problems in an organization is from the employees of that organization. For example, a user might decide to "borrow" the apparently unused hub from the equipment cupboard on the third floor, or he might really want to know just how much money the president of the company actually earns. In more extreme cases, a user might attempt to pass valuable corporate information to an outside party. Sound far-fetched? It's not; it happens every day.

- **Deliberate data damage**—To most people, the idea of deliberately damaging someone else's property is, to say the least, distasteful. Unfortunately, not everyone operates with the same values. Whether "just for fun" or with more shady intent, some people might delight in corrupting data or deleting it completely. Either way, business continuity will almost certainly be affected.

▶ **Industrial espionage**—This dramatic sounding security threat involves the process of a person retrieving data from a server for a purpose. The intruder might want to get her hands on the latest blueprints of your new widget, or she might want financial information for a buyout bid. Either way, the integrity (and in some cases, the future viability) of the business can be affected by such events.

▶ **Physical equipment theft**—Although it is normally less of an issue than theft of data, theft of physical equipment can still affect business continuity. If an important piece of equipment is stolen (for example, the server or a backup tape), the intruder will have access to your data. Insurance normally takes care of replacing the actual equipment, but data is generally not insured, unless specified, so the cost of restructuring the data is not provided for.

You might be fortunate enough not to suffer from any of these threats. Certainly, in a small organization that performs a seemingly uninteresting (to outsiders) business, there might not be any occurrences of security threats. But as an organization grows, so too do the amount of information, the number of methods that can be used to access it, and the number of people interested in finding out about the business. Also, as the number of employees grows, the chance that a "bad apple" will find its way into the cart increases as well. Sadly, it is a fact of life.

Security Responsibilities of a Network Administrator

To combat possible security threats, what is expected of you, as a network administrator? The exact network security responsibilities you have depend on the kind of environment in which you are working. In large companies, an individual or a group might be responsible specifically for security issues. You might be part of that group or be under its direction. In small companies, the entire onus of network security might be placed on your—the network administrator's—shoulders. This chapter assumes that as a network administrator you are primarily responsible for network security. Assume that you need to do the following to ensure network security in your organization:

▶ **Ensure that a security policy is in place**—A security policy defines the security measures, how they function, what is involved in their operation, and how problems are dealt with. The security policy should be created with the support of management.

▶ **Ensure that the security policy is enforced**—There is no point in having a policy if it is not enforced. As the network administrator, you need to make sure that the security policy works and is implemented as described.

▶ **Ensure that any infractions of the security policy are dealt with**—Perhaps the most undesirable part of a network administrator's security responsibilities involves dealing with infractions of the security policy. Because the majority of security-related incidents occur with people inside the company, this can often be an unpleasant task.

> ► **Ensure that the security situation is continually evaluated, revised, and updated**—Networks change, as does the company structure. The security needs of an organization should be evaluated constantly. Any changes deemed necessary should be incorporated into the security policy, again with the cooperation of management.

This is just a brief look at the responsibilities a network administrator has in implementing security on a network. Depending on the environment you work in, you might have to consider more or fewer security-related responsibilities. Now that you have an idea of some of the basic security responsibilities, let's look at the two types of network security: physical and logical.

Physical and Logical Security

Security can be broken down into two distinct areas: physical security and logical security. *Physical security* refers to the issues related to the physical security of the equipment that comprises or is connected to the network. Physical security measures include controlling access to equipment, supervising visitors, controlling physical access to areas that contain networking equipment, and ensuring that removable media such as backup tapes are transported and stored securely.

Logical security is concerned with security of data held on devices connected to the network. Logical security involves controlling passwords and password policies, controlling access to data on servers through file system security, controlling access to backup tapes, and perhaps most importantly, preventing sources outside the network from gaining access to the network through a connection from another network, such as the Internet. Because logical security is a large and complex topic, this chapter covers only topics related to the Network+ exam and some supporting information.

Physical Security

Physical security is concerned with the prevention of unauthorized access to the physical equipment that makes up the network or the systems attached to it.

> **EXAM ALERT**
>
> **Physical Security**   The Network+ exam focuses much more on logical security than on physical security. For this reason, the discussion of physical security is confined to just the basics.

Perhaps the biggest consideration related to physical security is restricting access to networking equipment and servers. Most commonly, the people you are trying to protect against in this respect are the employees of the company rather than malicious outsiders. That said, there is always the chance that a miscreant may decide that it is easier to break in to your premises and steal a server rather than access data through a firewall.

Specific physical security considerations include the following:

▶ **Controlling access to equipment**—Networking equipment should be kept in a secure location. For example, you might have a dedicated, environmentally controlled room in which all the network servers and networking equipment are kept. Alternatively, as in many small organizations, networking equipment might be stored in a cupboard or even a rack. Wherever your equipment is located, access control systems (including locks and keys) should be in place to prevent unauthorized access.

▶ **Creating and enforcing visitor policies**—Even if you have a dedicated server room, it's highly likely that other equipment will be in the room, such as telephone systems, air-conditioning units, and fire-protection systems. Each of these systems will have a scheduled maintenance program, which will periodically require visitors to be in the server room. Procedures should be in place so that the identities of visitors are verified, and that they are supervised when in the equipment room.

▶ **Securing the area**—The physical security of the network environment should be examined from a big-picture perspective. If a dedicated room is used for the server, determine the security of the room. Are there windows in the room that might represent a security risk? Are there windows that could facilitate someone outside the building seeing in? All these aspects and more must be factored in when considering physical security.

Logical Security

Logical security is a much more involved subject than physical security. Not only are there more ways in which data can be threatened logically than physically but also the measures available to secure data are equally diverse. This section focuses on two of the most significant aspects of logical security: authentication and file system security.

> **NOTE**
>
> **Hacker or Cracker?**   The terms *hacker* and *cracker* are tossed about freely when it comes to network security, but the two terms describe very different individuals. A *hacker* is someone who attempts to disassemble or delve into a computer program with the intention of understanding how it works, normally to make it better. A *cracker*, on the other hand, is someone who attempts to gain access to a computer system or application without authorization, with the intention of using the application illegally or viewing the data. Crackers, not hackers, are the people network administrators need to be concerned with. However, over time, the term *hacker* has become synonymous with people who attempt to gain access to systems without permission, and the term *cracker* has fallen out of use.

Challenge

In this challenge exercise, you evaluate some simple scenarios to determine whether a security threat presents either a physical risk, a logical risk, or both. A table is provided for your answers. The first line of the table has been completed to provide an example. The solution table on page X also explains each correct answer.

Scenario Table

Scenario	Type of Threat
A hacker attempts to gain access to the network through a firewall.	Logical
An air conditioning repairman is left unsupervised in the room that houses your fileservers.	
A user from the Sales department attempts to access the payroll files on the accounting department server.	
You discover that one of the backup tapes has gone missing from the offsite storage location.	
During a break-in at your company premises, one of the corporate fileservers is stolen.	
A contractor from an external company damages the Ethernet switch serving the second floor.	
A user calls to report that he has lost his wallet, which contained a piece of paper with his network username and password written down on it.	

Authentication, Passwords, and Password Policies

Although there are many different methods of authentication, none have attained the level of popularity of username and password combinations. The reason is that, apart from the fact that usernames and passwords do not require any additional equipment, which practically every other method of authentication does, the username and password process is familiar to users, easy to implement, and relatively secure. Although the popularity of other authentication methods such as biometrics (for example, fingerprint recognition, retinal scans), and smartcards is growing, it appears that the username and password will be with us as the primary means of authentication for some time.

Solution Table

Scenario	Type of Threat	Explanation
A hacker attempts to gain access to the network through a firewall.	Logical	Because the hacker is attempting access through a logical security measure (the firewall), this would be considered a logical threat.
An air conditioning repairman is left unsupervised in the room that houses your fileservers.	Physical and Logical	This is considered a physical security threat because the repairman has physical access to network components—in this case the fileservers. However, there is also a logical threat because the repairman may choose to view data on the servers, or even copy data off to a removable storage device.
A user from the Sales department attempts to access the payroll files on the accounting department server.	Logical	This is considered a logical threat because the user is attempting to access files through the network.
You discover that one of the backup tapes has gone missing from the offsite storage location	Physical and Logical	This represents a physical threat because a physical object related to the network has gone missing. However, there is also a logical risk because the backup tape would likely contain data.
A contractor from an external company damages the Ethernet switch serving the second floor.	Physical	This would represent a physical threat because a physical part of the network has been damaged, which could impact network services. No data has been lost, however, so there is no logical risk.
A user calls to report that he has lost his wallet, which contained a piece. of paper with his network username and password written down on it.	Logical	This represents a logical threat. If an unauthorized person who wanted to access the network discovered the username and password, the data on the network would be at risk.

Before we talk about some of the specific considerations for working with usernames and passwords, we should perhaps answer a simple question. Why do we need usernames and passwords in the first place? The obvious answer, of course, is that they provide a mechanism for users to prove that they are entitled to access the network or a specific resource. But there is another reason: accountability. If users must prove their identity, they are made accountable for their actions. This is particularly relevant in environments in which the auditing of system events is performed because it allows events to be attributed to certain users, based on their usernames. Without some form of authentication—be it usernames and passwords or something else—users cannot be held accountable for their actions.

Passwords are a relatively simple form of authentication in that only a string of characters can be used. However, how the string of characters is used and what policies you can put in place to govern them make usernames and passwords an excellent form of authentication.

NOTE

Passphrases   In some environments, passwords are called *passphrases*.

Password Policies

All popular network operating systems include password policy systems that allow the network administrator to control how passwords are used on the system. The exact capabilities vary between network operating systems. However, a password policy generally allows the following parameters to be configured:

▶ **Minimum length of password**—Shorter passwords are easier to guess than longer ones. Setting a minimum password length does not prevent a user from creating a longer password than the minimum, although each network operating system has a limit on how long a password can be.

▶ **Password expiration**—Also known as the *maximum password age*, password expiration defines how long the user can use the same password before having to change it. A general practice is that a password is changed every month or every 30 days. In high-security environments, you might want to make this value shorter, but you generally should not make it any longer. Having passwords expire periodically is an important feature because it means that if a password is compromised, the unauthorized user will not have access indefinitely.

▶ **Prevention of password reuse**—Although a password expiration policy can cause a password to expire, many users are tempted to simply use the same password again. A process by which the system remembers the last, say, 10 passwords is most secure because it forces the user to create completely new passwords.

▶ **Prevention of easy-to-guess passwords**—Some systems have the capability to evaluate the password provided by a user to see whether it meets a required level of complexity. This prevents users from having passwords such as *password* or *12345678*.

The process of setting password policies differs between network operating systems. As an example, Figure 11.1 shows the Password Policy configuration screen on a Windows Server 2003 system. As you can see from Figure 11.1, Windows Server 2003 also provides an additional enforcement mechanism—minimum password age. This setting prevents a user from changing her password immediately over and over again so that she can then reuse the previous password.

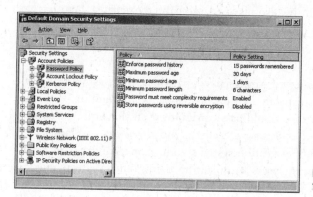

FIGURE 11.1   The Password Policy configuration screen in Windows Server 2003.

Each network operating system uses slightly different terms to describe the parameters that can be set in the password policy, although the options are similar across all network operating systems. For more information, consult the documentation for your network operating system. (Exercise 11.2 at the end of this chapter describes how to set the password policy on a Windows 2000 system.)

Understanding Password Strength

No matter how good a company's password policy, it is only as effective as the passwords created within it. A password that is difficult to guess, or *strong*, is more likely to protect the data on a system than one that is easy to guess, or *weak*.

To understand the difference between a strong password and a weak one, consider this: A password of six characters that uses only numbers and letters and is not case-sensitive has 10,314,424,798,490,535,546,171,949,056 possible combinations. That might seem like a lot, but to a password-cracking program, it's really not much security. A password that uses eight case-sensitive characters, with letters, numbers, and special characters has so many possible combinations that a standard calculator cannot display the actual number.

> **NOTE**
>
> **The Administrator's Password**   The password used to log on to an account with administrative privileges is, without question, the most valuable of all the passwords on the system. For that reason, you should treat passwords on administrative level accounts with an even greater level of respect than the passwords for normal user IDs. Administrative account passwords should, ideally, be changed more often than standard user account passwords, and they should also be as difficult to guess or crack as possible.

There has always been a debate over how long a password should be. It should be sufficiently long that it is difficult to break but sufficiently short that the user is able to easily remember it (and type it). In a normal working environment, passwords of eight characters are seen as sufficient. Certainly, they should be no fewer than six characters. In environments where security is a concern, passwords should be ten characters or more. As we will see in the following sections, what those ten characters might be also plays a large part in ensuring the effectiveness of a password.

Users, You Are the Weakest Link

For all your efforts to create and implement a strong password policy, there is normally one weak link in the chain—the user. You can specify that passwords be a minimum of 10 characters and that the user is not allowed to reuse an old password. However, that still doesn't stop the user from using a password like *peterdecember* for December and *peterjanuary* in January. As discussed earlier in this chapter, some authentication systems do have mechanisms that try to detect easy-to-guess passwords and prevent users from setting them, but its effectiveness is limited to only basic character sequences/dictionary words. For example, they would not dispute a Social Security number combined with the user's name. This might constitute a strong password in terms of characters used to create it and length, but it would still be potentially easy to guess for a password cracker.

> **NOTE**
>
> **Weak Passwords**   The Computer Emergency Response Team (CERT) Coordination Center estimates that four out of five network security incidents are caused by weak passwords.

The best way to deal with users choosing weak passwords is education. You must educate users so that they understand why passwords are used, their purpose, and what the rules are to create them. You should also tell users what are and are not considered acceptable passwords. In these days of identity theft and personal computer security alerts, you might think that users would automatically understand the need for strong and hard-to-guess passwords, but the reality is different. Users are notorious for choosing easy-to-guess passwords, such as their surname, a spouse's name, a pet's name, a home address, or a vehicle license plate number.

This is the kind of information that a password cracker will try first when attempting to crack a password.

Users should be encouraged to use a strong password. A strong password has at least eight characters; has a combination of letters, numbers, and special characters; uses mixed case; and does not form a proper word. Examples might include *3Ecc5T0h* and *e1oXPn3r*. Even though such passwords might be secure, users are likely to have problems remembering them. For that reason, a popular strategy is to use a combination of letters and numbers to deform phrases or long words. Examples include *d1eTc0La* and *tAb1eT0p*. These passwords might not be quite as secure as the preceding examples, but they are still very strong and much better than the name of the user's household pet.

Passwords: The Last Word

One last password-related topic is worth mentioning. A password is effective only if just the intended users have it. As soon as a password is passed to someone else, its effectiveness as an authentication mechanism is diminished, and as a tool for accountability, the password is almost useless. Passwords are a means of accessing a system and the data on it. Passwords known by anyone other than the intended user(s) might as well not be set at all.

Security of Backup Tapes

One of the most overlooked aspects of security is ensuring that backup tapes are made, transported, and stored securely. Backup tapes make an attractive target for anyone who wants to get hold of your data. It's much easier to steal a backup tape than a hard disk. To make sure that data is available in the event of a disaster, backup tapes are often taken offsite, away from the secure environment created just to secure the data.

To provide an extra measure of security for your backups, consider password-protecting backup media, using a registered courier service to transport the media between locations, and ensuring that the tapes are secure at the remote location. As an extra measure, if your budget allows, you could also consider using an encryption system that would scramble the data on the tape, making it very difficult to read should it fall into the wrong hands.

File System Security

Because they are the heart of the system, network operating systems are chock-full of security-related features and subsystems. All popular network operating systems have robust authentication systems that control access to the network and file system security measures, which ensure that users can view and use only the data they are supposed to. Chapter 9, "Network Operating Systems and Clients," discusses the authentication methods used by the various network operating systems, so this chapter does not cover that again. Instead, the following sections take a more in-depth look at the file system security measures available on popular network operating systems.

After logon security, file system security is perhaps the most important aspect of network system security. If you have a solid file system security structure in place, even if someone does manage to gain unauthorized access to the system, the amount of damage he may be able to do can be limited.

Novell NetWare File System Security

File system security on NetWare is the most sophisticated of any of the popular network operating systems. In addition to a full set of file permissions, NetWare also accommodates file permission inheritance and filters to cancel out that inheritance. For those unfamiliar with the various features of NetWare file system security, it can all seem a bit bewildering. When you are used to it, though, you realize that it allows an extremely high level of control over files and directories.

NOTE

Inheritance The term *inheritance* is used to describe the process of rights flowing down the folder structure. For example, rights are assigned at the top of the folder structure, and unless they are blocked at a lower level, they flow to the bottom of the structure. All common network operating systems employ file inheritance in one way or another.

At the core of NetWare file system security are the basic permissions. These permissions can be assigned to individual files or, where appropriate, folders. Table 11.1 lists the file system rights available on a NetWare server.

TABLE 11.1   File Permissions on a NetWare Server

Right	Description
Supervisor	Supervisory—implies all rights
Read	Allows the file to be read
Write	Allows the file to be written to
Create	Allows new files to be created
Erase	Allows files to be deleted
Modify	Allows the attributes of the file to be changed
Filescan	Allows the files in a folder to be viewed
Access Control	Allows the file permissions to be manipulated

Figure 11.2 shows a file permission assignment on a NetWare 6 server.

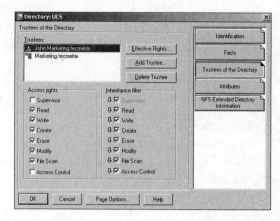

FIGURE 11.2 File permission assignment on a NetWare 6 server.

Unix/Linux File System Security

Of the platforms discussed in this chapter, Unix and Linux have the most simplistic approach to file system security, although for most environments, this approach is more than sufficient. File permissions can be assigned to either the creator of a file or directory, a group, or the entity "everyone," which includes any authenticated user.

Unix and Linux have only three rights that can be assigned, as listed in Table 11.2.

TABLE 11.2 File Permissions on Unix/Linux

Right	Description
Read	Allows files to be listed, opened, and read
Write	Allows files to be created, written to, or modified
Execute	Allows the file to be executed (that is, run)

Figure 11.3 shows a directory listing from a Linux server with the assigned permissions for each file or directory. The file permissions are listed to the right of the file. The first value specifies whether the file is a file (-) or a directory (d). The next three values specify the file rights for the user, the next three for the group, and the next three for the "everyone" assignment.

Windows 2000 and Windows Server 2003 File System Security

Both Windows 2000 Server and Windows Server 2003 use the New Technology File System (NTFS) to provide file system security. Rights can be assigned to users, groups, and some special entities, which include the "everyone" assignment. Table 11.3 describes the basic file permissions that can be used with NTFS on Windows 2000 and Windows Server 2003.

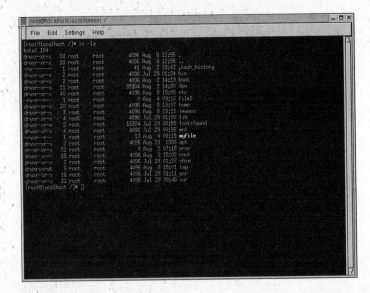

FIGURE 11.3 A directory listing from a Linux server, showing file and directory permissions.

TABLE 11.3   File Permissions with NTFS on Windows 2000 and Windows Server 2003

Right	Description
Full Control	Provides all rights
Modify	Allows files to be modified
Read & Execute	Allows files to be read and executed (that is, run)
List Folder Contents	Allows the files in a folder to be listed
Read	Allows a file to be read
Write	Allows a file to be written to

Figure 11.4 shows the Disk Properties screen, through which file permissions are assigned.

An added complexity to file system security on Windows platforms is that the shares created to allow users to access folders across the network can also be assigned a set of permissions. Although these permissions are basic (Full Control, Change, and Read), they must be considered because, when assigned, they are combined with NTFS permissions. The rule in this situation is that the most restrictive permissions assignment applies. For example, if a user connects through a share with Read permission and then tries to access a file to which he has the NTFS Full Control right, the actual permissions would be Read. The most restrictive right (in this case, Read) overrides the other permissions assignment.

EXAM ALERT

Know the File Permissions   On the Network+ exam, you might be asked to identify valid and invalid file permissions for certain platforms.

FIGURE 11.4 The Disk Properties screen, through which file permissions are assigned.

File Permissions Best Practices

In an ideal world, every file and folder would be assigned exactly the needed set of permissions that allows every user only the required level of access. If you have just a few dozen files, such an approach might be possible. But in the real world, where servers might have hundreds of thousands of files or more, it's simply not feasible.

The commonly adopted solution is to assign rights to folders rather than files and then try to group files that have a similar level of access together in one location. If such a system is implemented carefully, it can work very well. However, it requires certain considerations, such as whether there are groups of files that require the same access, and it can be implemented only in environments where file system security is not of paramount concern.

Challenge

As a network administrator you will likely be called on to determine the appropriate file system permissions that should be given to users. To prepare you for this eventuality, consider the following scenario and suggest what file permissions you would assign. The scenario is based on a Novell NetWare server.

Scenario:

You have created a folder called SALESDATA on the data volume of the NetWare server for the Sales department. There are six users in the Sales department. Four are Sales Representatives, one is the Sales Manager, and the remaining person is the Sales Support Assistant. Because the Sales Representatives all have the same access requirements, you have created a group called SalesReps and placed all the user accounts in that group. You must now determine the appropriate permissions to assign to the users in the Sales department to the SALESDATA folder.

All users in the Sales department should be able to view the files in the SALESDATA folder. The Sales Representatives also need the ability to change files in the folder, but they should not be able to delete

(continues)

(continued)

any files or create new ones. The Sales Manager should be able to read and change existing files and create new files. The Sales Manager should also be able to delete files. The Sales Support Assistant needs to be able to open files and view the contents, but he should not be able to change or delete files, nor does the Sales Support Assistant need permissions to create new files. No users in the Sales department need the ability to change the attributes of a file in the SALESDATA folder, nor should any of them be able to modify the permissions assigned to files in the SALESDATA folder.

Using the table provided, define what permissions should be assigned to the users in the Sales department for the SALESDATA folder.

User/Group	Permissions
SalesReps (Group)	
Sales Manager	
Sales Support Assistant	

Challenge Exercise Solution

User/Group	Permissions
SalesReps (Group)	Filescan, Read, Write
Sales Manager	Filescan Read, Write, Create, Erase
Sales Support Assistant	Filescan, Read

All users should be able to view the files in the SALESDATA folder, so they all need the Filescan permission. The Sales Support Assistant needs to view the contents of files, so he also needs the Read permission. The SalesReps group needs to view existing files and also make changes to those files. Therefore, they need the Read and Write permissions. The Sales Manager needs the Create and Erase permissions to create new files and delete files. No users need the Modify, Access Control, or Supervisory permissions.

Auditing

Auditing is an important part of system security. It provides a means to track events that occur on a system. Auditing increases accountability on a network by making it possible to isolate events to certain users. For example, it is possible to log failed logon attempts that might indicate that someone is trying to gain access to the network by guessing a username or password.

A network administrator might need to audit many different events on a system. Some of these events include failed/successful logons, printer access, file and directory access, and remote access. Reviewing the log files generated by auditing allows an administrator to better gauge the potential threats to the network. (Exercise 11.1 at the end of this chapter describes the procedures involved in enabling auditing on a Windows 2000 server.)

Escalation Procedures

One of the most important aspects of network security is knowing what to do when a security problem occurs. The exact actions you take depend on the circumstances surrounding the breach and what the breach actually is.

For example, your reaction to the discovery that two users are sharing the same user account would be different from your reaction if you found that a cracker had gained access to your ecommerce web server during the night. In either case, *after* an event has happened is not the time to think, "What do I do now?" Having a plan in place before a security incident occurs makes it much easier to follow the correct procedures after a security breach.

If there is one blanket rule to security breaches, it is that management should be informed of the problem as soon as is practically possible. As discussed at the beginning of the chapter, the implications of a security issue can affect the viability and continuation of the business. For such incidents to be dealt with and to ensure that the business is not affected, management participation is necessary.

Firewalls

Objective:
3.5 Identify the purpose, benefits, and characteristics of using a firewall.

Even though a firewall is considered a logical security measure, it deserves its own section because it is a specific objective for the Network+ exam.

A firewall is a system or group of systems that controls the flow of traffic between two networks. The most common use of a firewall is to protect a private network from a public network such as the Internet. However, firewalls are also used as a means to separate a sensitive area of a private network from other, less-sensitive, areas of the private network.

At its most basic, a *firewall* is a device (it could be a computer system or a dedicated hardware device) that has more than one network interface and manages the flow of network traffic between those interfaces. How it manages the flow and what it does with certain types of traffic depend on its configuration. Figure 11.5 shows the most basic firewall configuration.

Strictly speaking, a firewall performs no action on the packets it receives besides the basic functions just described. However, in a real-world implementation, a firewall is likely to offer other functionality, such as Network Address Translation (NAT) and proxy server services. Without NAT, any host on the internal network that needs to send or receive data through the firewall needs a registered IP address. Although there are such environments, most people have to settle for using a private address range on the internal network and therefore rely on the firewall system to translate the outgoing request into an acceptable public network address.

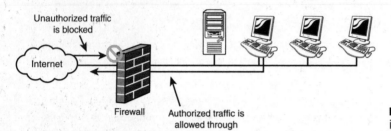

FIGURE 11.5   A basic firewall implementation.

The Purpose and Function of a Firewall

Although the fundamental purpose of a firewall is to protect one network from another, you need to configure the firewall to allow some traffic through. If you don't need to allow traffic to pass through a firewall, you can dispense with it entirely and completely separate your network from other networks.

A firewall can employ a variety of different methods to ensure security. A firewall can use just one of these methods, or it can combine different methods to produce the most appropriate and robust configuration. The following sections discuss the various firewall methods commonly used: packet filtering firewalls, circuit-level firewalls, and application gateway firewalls.

Packet-Filtering Firewalls

Of the firewall methods discussed in this chapter, *packet filtering* is the most commonly implemented. Packet filtering allows the firewall to examine each and every packet that passes through it and determine what to do with the packet, based on the configuration. A packet-filtering firewall deals with packets at the data-link and network layers of the Open Systems Interconnect (OSI) model. The following are some of the criteria by which packet filtering can be implemented:

▸ **IP address**—By using the IP address as a parameter, the firewall can allow or deny traffic, based on the source or destination IP address. For example, you can configure the firewall so that only certain hosts on the internal network can access hosts on the Internet. Alternatively, you can configure it so that only certain hosts on the Internet can gain access to a system on the internal network.

▸ **Port number**—As discussed in Chapter 6, "Working with TCP/IP," the Transmission Control Protocol/Internet Protocol (TCP/IP) protocol suite uses port numbers to identify what service a certain packet is destined for. By configuring the firewall to allow certain types of traffic, you can control the flow. You might, for example, open port 80 on the firewall to allow Hypertext Transfer Protocol (HTTP) requests from users on the Internet to reach the corporate web server. You might also, depending on the application, open the HTTP Secure (HTTPS) port, port 443, to allow access to a secure web server application.

▶ **Protocol ID**—Because each packet transmitted with IP has a protocol identifier in it, a firewall can read this value and then determine what kind of packet it is. If you are filtering based on protocol ID, you specify which protocols you will and will not allow to pass through the firewall.

▶ **MAC address**—This is perhaps the least used of the packet-filtering methods discussed, but it is possible to configure a firewall to use the hardware-configured MAC address as the determining factor in whether access to the network is granted. This is not a particularly flexible method, and it is therefore suitable only in environments where you can closely control who uses which MAC address. The Internet is not such an environment.

Circuit-Level Firewalls

Circuit-level firewalls are similar in operation to packet-filtering firewalls, but they operate at the transport and session layers of the OSI model. The biggest difference between a packet-filtering firewall and a circuit-level firewall is that a circuit-level firewall forwards all requests to the other network, using its own IP address rather than the IP address of the internal system that sent the request. This serves to "hide" the identity of the inside system, which is good from a security standpoint because outside users cannot see the internal network.

Application Gateway Firewalls

The *application gateway firewall* is the most functional of all the firewall types. As its name suggests, the application gateway firewall functionality is implemented through an application. Application gateway firewall systems can implement sophisticated rules and closely control traffic that passes through. Features of application gateway firewalls can include user authentication systems, the capability to control which systems an outside user can access on the Internal network, and even bandwidth control mechanisms. Because application gateway firewalls operate above the session layer of the OSI model, they can provide protection against any software-based network traffic that attempts to pass through them.

TIP

The Three Firewall Methods The three firewall methods described in this chapter are often combined into a single firewall application. Packet filtering is the basic firewall function. Circuit-level functionality provides NAT, and an application gateway firewall provides proxy functionality.

Demilitarized Zones

An important firewall-related concept is *demilitarized zones (DMZs)*. A DMZ is part of a network on which you place servers that must be accessible by sources both outside and inside your network. However, the DMZ is not connected directly to either network, and it must always be accessed through the firewall. The military term DMZ is used because it describes an area in which there is little or no enforcement or policing.

Using DMZs provides an extra level of flexibility, protection, and complexity to your firewall configuration. Figure 11.6 shows an example of a DMZ configuration.

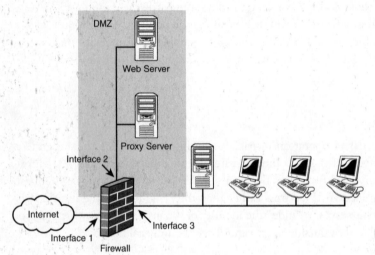

FIGURE 11.6 A DMZ configuration.

By using a DMZ, you can create an additional step that makes it more difficult for an intruder to gain access to the internal network. In Figure 11.6, for example, an intruder who tried to come in through Interface 1 would have to spoof a request from either the web server or proxy server into Interface 2 before it could be forwarded to the internal network. Although it is not impossible for an intruder to gain access to the internal network through a DMZ, it is difficult.

NOTE

Personal Firewalls   For exactly the same reasons that a firewall is implemented on a corporate network, you should protect your personal computer at home with a firewall as well. The increasing use of always-on Internet access methods such as cable and Digital Subscriber Line (DSL) means that you are just as likely to become the target of an intruder at home as you are at work. Remember that most intruders are not looking for anything in particular; they are just looking for something. If you connect to the Internet from a computer system, you are exposing yourself to millions of other users, some of whom would love to have a look at your hard drive to see whether there is anything of interest. The solution is to implement a personal firewall. All commonly used client operating systems, including Windows XP, MAC, and Linux include firewall capabilities. Alternatively, you can purchase third-party personal firewall products.

Firewalls have become a necessity for organizations of all sizes. As the Internet becomes an ever more hostile place, firewalls and the individuals who understand them are likely to become an essential part of the IT landscape.

Proxy Services

Objective:

3.6 Identify the purpose, benefits, and characteristics of using a proxy service.

A proxy service provides management and control over what is now an essential feature of any modern network—Internet access. A *proxy server*, which can be a computer or a dedicated hardware device running proxy service software, acts as an intermediary between a user on the internal network and a service on the external network (normally the Internet). The proxy server takes requests from a user and then performs those requests on behalf of the user. To the external system, the request looks as if it originated from the proxy server, not from the user on the internal network. Figure 11.7 shows how a proxy server fits into a network configuration.

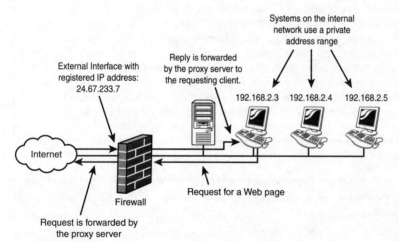

FIGURE 11.7 A proxy server in a typical network configuration.

> **NOTE**
>
> **Single IP Address Representation** A proxy server enables a network to appear to external networks as a single IP address—that of the external network interface of the proxy server.

There are a couple of excellent reasons to implement a proxy server:

▶ **To perform NAT functions**—A proxy server processes and executes commands on behalf of clients that have "private" IP addresses. This enables an organization with only one registered IP address to provide Internet access to many computers. This process is commonly referred to as *IP proxy*.

▶ **To allow Internet access to be controlled**—Having a centralized point of access allows for a great deal of control over the use of the Internet. By using the functionality of a proxy server application or by using an add-on feature, proxy servers can filter requests made by clients and either allow or disallow them. You could, for example, implement uniform resource locator (URL) filtering, which allows or denies users access to certain sites. More sophisticated products can also perform tests on retrieved material to see whether it fits acceptable criteria. Such measures are intended to prevent users from accessing inappropriate Internet web pages. As an "after the event" feature, proxy server applications also normally provide logging capabilities so that Internet usage can be monitored.

NOTE

Proxy Servers Versus Firewalls   The function of a proxy server should not be confused with the function of a firewall, even though some applications integrate the functionality of both. In basic terms, a proxy server is a centralized point of access to the Internet. It also, generally, provides caching capabilities. Strictly speaking, a proxy service does not provide protection to the internal network from outside threats, although the NAT function provided by a proxy server does provide some level of protection. That said, if you have an Internet connection to your network and want to provide access through a proxy server, you should also implement a firewall system to provide protection. Alternatively, a number of products are available that combine the security features of a firewall with the functionality of a proxy server in one application.

Although the most common function of a proxy server is to provide access to the World Wide Web for internal clients, that is not its only function. A proxy server, by definition, can be used as an intermediary for anything, not just HTTP requests. Other services can be supported by a proxy server, depending on the proxy server application being used and the configuration. For example, you might configure a proxy server to service HTTP requests (TCP port 80), Post Office Protocol 3 (POP3) email retrieval (TCP port 110), Simple Mail Transfer Protocol (SMTP) mail sending (TCP port 25), and HTTPS requests (TCP port 443).

With an understanding of what a proxy server is designed to do, you can look at one additional feature built into proxy server functionality: caching.

Caching Proxy Servers

An additional feature offered by many proxy server applications is caching; such a system is known as a *caching proxy server*. Caching allows the proxy server to store pages that it retrieves as files on disk. Consequently, if the same pages are requested again, they can be provided more quickly from the cache than if the proxy server had to go back to the web server from which the pages were originally retrieved. This approach has two benefits:

▶ **Significantly improves performance**—Performance is improved particularly in environments such as a school, where there is a great likelihood that more than one user might retrieve the same page.

▶ **Reduces demands on Internet connections**—Because there are fewer requests to the Internet when a caching proxy server is in use, there is reduced demand on the Internet connection. In some cases, this results in a general speed improvement. In extreme cases, it might even be possible to adopt a less expensive Internet connectivity method because of the lower level of demand.

> **NOTE**
>
> **Proxy Servers and Protocols**   Proxy servers are sometimes referred to as *HTTP proxies* or *HTTP proxy servers*. In reality, most proxy servers provide proxy services for multiple protocols, not just HTTP.

As with any technology, with caching proxy servers there are issues to be considered. Sometimes a sizable amount of hard disk space is required to store the cached pages. With the significant decline in the cost of hard disk space over recent years, this is not likely to be much of a problem, but it still needs to be considered.

Another factor is that it's possible for pages held in the cache to become stale. As a result, a user might retrieve a page and believe that it is the latest version when in fact it has since changed, but the new page has not been updated in the proxy server cache. To prevent this problem, caching proxy servers can implement measures such as aging of cached information so that it is removed from the cache after a certain amount of time. Some proxy applications also can check to make sure that the page stored in the cache is the same as the page currently available on the Internet. If the page in the cache is the same as the one on the Internet, it is served to the client from the cache. If the page is not the same, the newer page is retrieved, cached, and supplied to the client.

Using a Proxy Server

Before clients can use a proxy server, it is necessary to configure the client applications to use it, and in some cases, additional client software is needed. In the case of web browsers, it is sometimes necessary to manually tell the application that it needs to use a proxy server. Figure 11.8 shows the configuration screen in Microsoft Internet Explorer that allows the configuration of proxy parameters.

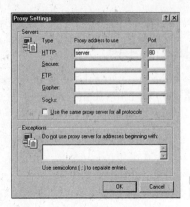

FIGURE 11.8   The Proxy Settings configuration screen in Internet Explorer.

Other applications besides web browsers might need to use the proxy server functionality. In some cases, you might need to actually load client software. In essence, this client software modifies elements of the TCP/IP software on the system, to either make it aware of or allow it to cope with the existence of a proxy server. The good news is that the use of proxy servers is now so widespread that applications that require special client software are becoming increasingly rare.

By now, you might have realized that both firewalls and proxy servers play an important part in the network infrastructure. For that reason, many applications are now available that combine the functionality of both roles. These "firewalling proxy servers" provide a convenient means for an organization to control and secure the access of its network, and at the same time provide the benefits of Internet access to users.

Understanding How Security Affects a Network

Objective:

3.7 Given a connectivity scenario, determine the impact on network functionality of a particular security implementation (for example, port blocking/filtering, authentication, and encryption).

Implementing any security measures has an effect on the network. How much of an effect it has depends on which security measures are implemented and the habits of the network users. CompTIA specifies some examples of network security measures (port blocking/filtering, authentication, and encryption) and asks that you determine what effect the implementation of those measures will have on the network. The following sections help you prepare for this part of the exam.

Port Blocking/Filtering

Port blocking or filtering is one of the most widely used security methods on networks. Port blocking is associated with firewalls and proxy servers, although in fact it can be implemented on any system that provides a means to manage network data flow, according to data type.

Essentially, when you block a port, you disable the capability for traffic to pass through that port, thereby filtering that traffic. Port blocking is typically implemented to prevent users on a public network from accessing systems on a private network, although it is equally possible to block internal users from external services, and internal users from other internal users, by using the same procedure.

Depending on the type of firewall system in use on a network, you might find that all the ports are disabled (blocked) and that the ones you need traffic to flow through must be opened. The benefit of this strategy is that it forces the administrator to choose the ports that should be unblocked rather than specify those that need to be blocked. This ensures that you allow only those services that are absolutely necessary into the network.

What ports remain open largely depends on the needs of the organization. For example, the ports associated with the services listed in Table 11.4 are commonly left open.

TABLE 11.4   Commonly Opened Port Numbers and Their Associated Uses

Port Number	Protocol	Purpose
80	HTTP	Web browsing
443	HTTPS	Secure web transactions
21	FTP	File transfers
25	SMTP	Email sending
110	POP3	Email retrieval
53	DNS	Hostname resolution

These are, of course, only a few of the services you might need on a network, and allowing traffic from other services to traverse a firewall is as easy as opening the port. Keep in mind, though, that the more ports that are open, the more vulnerable you become to outside attacks. Never open a port on a firewall unless you are absolutely sure that you need to.

NOTE

A Complete List of Ports   You can obtain a complete list of port numbers and their associated protocols from the Internet Assigned Numbers Authority (IANA), at www.iana.org/assignments/port-numbers.

Port Blocking and Network Users

Before you implement port blocking, you should have a good idea of what the port is used for. Although it is true that blocking unused ports does not have any impact on internal network users, if the wrong port is blocked, you can create connectivity issues for users on the network.

For instance, a network administrator was given the task of reducing the amount a spam emails received by his company. He decided to block port 25, the port used by the Simple Mail Transfer Protocol (SMTP). He succeeded in blocking the spam email, but in the process, he also prevented users from sending email.

Authentication

Although CompTIA lists authentication and its effect on network users in Objective 3.7, it is a topic covered in a number of other sections in this book. In this section we'll briefly explore some of the authentication methods commonly used on today's networks and discuss the things you need to be aware of when implementing them.

As a security mechanism, authentication is provided by every major network operating system and is implemented in all but the most insecure networks. Its "impact on network functionality," as stated in Objective 3.7, is that it requires users to identify themselves to the network. As discussed earlier, this process provides two benefits. It secures the network from unauthorized access and provides a degree of accountability for users after they are logged on.

Three basic categories of authentication are used on modern networks:

▶ **Passwords**—The "traditional" authentication method, passwords do a good job of providing security, but users choosing passwords that are easy to guess can negate their effectiveness. Additionally, passwords can be passed from one person to another, diminishing their role as an accountability mechanism. Although network users will likely be very comfortable with using passwords, you should make them aware of the rules governing password use in your organization. Also make sure that they understand the electronic policies that dictate conditions such as password length and expiration times.

▶ **Smartcards**—Smartcards, which are normally used in conjunction with a password or personal identification number (PIN), provide a higher level of accountability and access control than passwords. This is because the user has to be in possession of a physical item (the smartcard), as well as information (the password or PIN) to gain access. If a user loses his smartcard, it cannot be used without the user's PIN or password, and if someone else discovers the user's password or PIN, that person cannot gain access without the smartcard. Although a cost consideration is associated with smartcard implementations, it is typically much lower than the cost associated with biometric systems.

▶ **Biometrics**—Biometrics, which can mean the scanning or verification of some part of your person, is the ultimate "proof of person" authentication technique. Because it is almost impossible to fake biometric mediums such as fingerprints or retinal patterns, you can be very sure that people gaining access to the system biometrically are who they say they are. Even so, biometric systems typically also use passwords or PINs as an additional measure of security.

Each of these authentication mechanisms has advantages and disadvantages. For example, password authentication is easy to implement, but in comparison to the other methods is considered less secure. Biometrics do a great job of ensuring that the person authenticating to the system is who she says she is, but the systems, hardware, and software associated with biometrics can be very expensive. Although the cost of biometric systems is coming down quickly, the reality is that it is only practical and relevant in environments where security is paramount.

Smartcards are an interesting technology. They are more affordable to implement than biometric systems but are more secure than passwords. Today, many organizations with low to medium security requirements are looking to smartcard technology as a means to tighten up authentication security.

Encryption

Encryption is the process of encoding data so that, without the appropriate unlocking code, the encrypted data can't be read. Encryption is used as a means of protecting data from being viewed by unauthorized users. If you have ever used a secure website, you have used encryption.

On private networks, encryption is generally not a big issue. Modern network operating systems often implement encryption so that passwords are not transmitted openly throughout the network. On the other hand, normal network transmissions are not usually encrypted, although they can be if the need arises. A far more common use for encryption is for data that is sent across a public network such as the Internet, or across wireless networks where outside users may be able to gain access to the data. In both of these cases, there is plenty of opportunity for someone to take the data from the network and then read the contents of the packets. This process is often referred to as *packet sniffing*.

NOTE

Encryption for Encryption's Sake   With so many server and client operating systems now supporting encryption mechanisms, there is often a temptation to implement encryption even on networks that have very little to gain from it. This perspective comes from the idea that the encryption functionality is free, or at least has already been paid for. The reality is that on most wired networks, there is little to gain from implementing encryption in terms of increased security. Instead, there are the hidden costs of configuring, troubleshooting, and supporting the operating systems and other devices that are used with encrypted communications. As with any other network feature or function, the pros of increased security from encryption must be weighed with the cons of the additional administrative overhead.

By sniffing packets from the network and reading their contents, unauthorized users can gain access to private information. They can also alter the information in the packet. But packet sniffing is not possible, or at least made extremely difficult, with encrypted data. Without the necessary code to decrypt the data, the sniffer can see only jumbled code. There is a chance that the sniffer might be capable of working out what the code is, but the stronger the form of encryption used, the more difficult it is for the sniffer to work out the code. Therefore, the stronger the encryption method used, the better protected the data is.

A number of encryption methods are commonly used, including

▶ IP Security (IPSec)

▶ Secure Sockets Layer (SSL)

▶ Triple Data Encryption Standard (3DES)

▶ Pretty Good Privacy (PGP)

For more information on the characteristics of these encryption protocols, see Chapter 8, "Remote Access and Security Protocols."

Implementing Encryption

Regardless of which encryption method or protocol is used, network administrators must be aware that providing encryption for network traffic is not without its considerations. These include the following:

▶ **Network traffic overhead**—Encrypting data on a network increases the volume of traffic. Even if, as it is with some encryption methods, the size of the data packets that traverse the network do not increase in size, there is often traffic associated with the setup and breakdown of encrypted communication sessions. When deciding to implement encryption, consider this increase in network traffic. You may also need to consider whether networking equipment such as routers can support the chosen encryption method in their current configuration.

▶ **Processor overhead**—Although modern encryption protocols are designed to be as lightweight as possible, there is still always an overhead associated with encrypting or decrypting data. In a small environment with just a few computers, this overhead may be negligible, and server or workstation performance may not be affected. In larger environments, however, or with servers that handle large amounts of network traffic, the overhead associated with encryption must be considered more carefully. For example, a server that was coping, but near acceptable performance thresholds, without encryption, may be pushed into the realms of unacceptable performance with the implementation of a technology such as IPSec. Admittedly, environments where such a calculation may come into play might be able to easily justify an investment in more powerful hardware, but it is the responsibility of the network administrator to make management aware of these types of considerations when a new technology is being contemplated.

▶ **Supported operating systems**—Not all operating systems support all encryption mechanisms. For example, Microsoft Windows Server 2003 relies on IPSec as the primary means of encryption, and Windows XP Professional Edition also supports IPSec, as does Windows 2000 Professional. Earlier versions of Windows, such as Windows 98 and Windows Me, however, do not support IPSec without additional client software. For this reason, you need to be aware of what encryption mechanisms your client systems support before performing an implementation.

Another key consideration when using encryption, particularly from a connectivity perspective, is that some operating systems can be configured to deny requests from clients not using encryption. Windows Server 2003, for example, supports a policy that blocks any connection requests made without IPSec. This kind of policy should be implemented only after all the client systems have been configured to use IPSec encryption. Otherwise, they will not be able to connect to the server.

> **NOTE**
>
> **Public Key Infrastructure (PKI)**   No discussion of encryption would be complete without the inclusion of Public Key Infrastructure (PKI). However, the role of PKI in encryption is often misunderstood. The main misconception about PKI is that it provides encryption services, which it does not. Instead, PKI provides a mutually accessible certification authority from which encryption protocols such as IPSec and SSL can obtain, exchange, and transmit keys, in the form of certificates. These certificates then provide a common mechanism by which data can be encrypted and decrypted.

Intranets and Extranets

Objective:
3.9 Identify the main characteristics and purpose of extranets and intranets.

Over recent years, the terms *intranet* and *extranet* have established themselves firmly in the IT vocabulary. Even so, many people are still unsure about what exactly defines, or is defined by, either an intranet or an extranet.

Intranets

The term *intranet* is commonly used to describe a web-based application that provides tools for groups of people to work together collaboratively. These tools might include group-based scheduling systems, message boards, task lists, chat rooms, and file sharing systems. The key element of an intranet is that only people within an organization can access it. Intranets are typically hosted, maintained, and operated completely independently from an organization's external web presence, even though some of the information provided through both mechanisms might be the same. Intranets are typically not high security solutions because access is already limited to users within the corporate network infrastructure. As with all things technology related, however, there are always exceptions.

> ### TIP
>
> **Intranet Protocols** Because they are typically accessed using web browsers and hosted by web server applications, intranets rely on protocols such as the Hypertext Transfer Protocol (HTTP) and File Transfer Protocol (FTP).

The popularity of intranets has grown dramatically over recent years, due in part to the increasing simplicity of web server software, but mostly because of the availability of easily customizable intranet applications. In addition, a number of companies now produce intranet "appliances" that provide all the typical intranet tools and features in a dedicated hardware device. These devices can further simplify the deployment and management of an intranet. Figure 11.9 shows an example of an intranet.

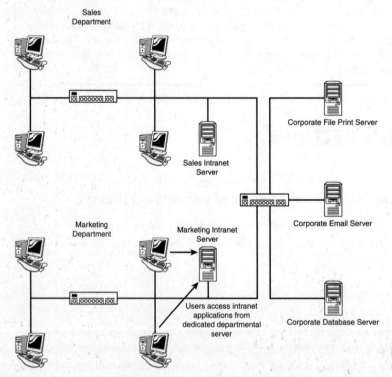

FIGURE 11.9 An example of an intranet.

Intranets are commonly identified by the following characteristics:

▶ **Limited access**—Access to an intranet is normally limited to users, or a subgroup of users, within the organization.

▶ **Browser based**—Most intranets operate as web server based applications, and so are accessed through a web browser.

▶ **Types of application**—Although no specific rules define what applications an intranet can host, the most common are collaborative, "groupware" applications like those described earlier.

> **NOTE**
>
> **Intranet**   Technically, any privately operated network to which external access is restricted could be considered an intranet. In common terms, though, the description provided in this section is the most common interpretation of the term *intranet*.

Almost every business environment can benefit from the deployment of intranet-type applications, and chances are that most mid- to large-sized organizations already have an intranet in place.

Extranets

Any network that operates outside the physical and logical boundaries of an organization can be called an extranet. That means that any network on which remote access services are provided could, technically, be considered an extranet. Commonly, though, the term *extranet* describes a system or application, hosted within an organization, that is securely made available to selected people outside an organization.

> **NOTE**
>
> **Portals**   The word *portal* is sometimes used to describe both intranets and extranets. The word is appropriate because portal is often used to describe a gateway or access point into another place. In the case of intranets and extranets, that "place" would be the applications available after accessing the intranet or extranet.

As an example, consider a manufacturing company that provides a system via which clients can check on the status of orders, query the company's inventory, or examine sales information such as catalogs and brochures. Because the clients are outside the organization, this would be considered an extranet. The key consideration to this model is that the company providing the system controls access to the extranet. In other words, only selected clients and associates are provided with access, and they may even be required to access the extranet over secure virtual private networking (VPN) links. Contrast this with the model used by, for example, online bookstores, where anyone can access the site, even though a username and password are subsequently required to place or track orders. Although the bookstore could decide to prevent a certain user from accessing the site, it is unlikely to do so. Figure 11.10 shows an example of an extranet.

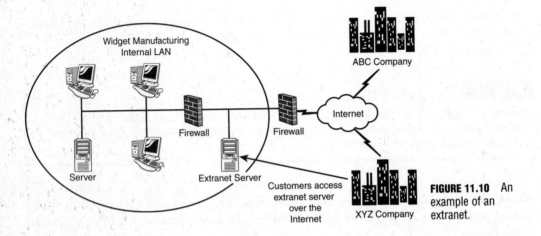

FIGURE 11.10 An example of an extranet.

Extranets are commonly identified by the following characteristics:

▶ **Users are outside the hosting organization**—Access to the extranet system is made available to individuals and organizations not directly affiliated with the host organization.

▶ **Only the owner of the system grants access**—Access to the extranet is normally granted and controlled by the operating organization.

▶ **Secure**—Extranets are typically secure, and connection to the extranet may require the use of secure communication channels such as a VPN.

Typically, though not exclusively, extranet applications, like intranet applications, are hosted on a web server and accessed through a web browser. This has an additional advantage in an extranet; it alleviates any requirements for extranet clients to have special software or applications installed to access the extranet.

Whether your organization operates an extranet depends on the need to grant access to outside users. If you do not want to grant users outside your organization access to applications within it, you will not need to concern yourself with an extranet.

Chapter Summary

Network security is a complex subject, and it should be a primary focus for any network administrator.

Being able to effectively secure a network involves understanding the risks that can be a threat to the network as well as what the result of a breach in security might entail.

There is a distinction between physical security and logical security. Physical security involves physically protecting equipment and data by controlling access to the systems that hold that data. Logical security involves protecting the data on a network from being accessed by unauthorized personnel.

Network operating systems include features that allow you to protect the data on a network by providing authentication capabilities, logon restrictions, file system rights, and in some cases, auditing. Depending on the environment, you might not use all these features, but you are sure to use some of them.

Two important elements of a network security implementation are the use of proxy servers and firewall systems. A firewall system provides protection to the network by controlling the traffic that passes between internal and external networks. Proxy servers allow you to centralize access to the Internet and therefore provide a way to control and monitor network access.

Understanding how implementing security features such as port blocking and encryption affect the network and the users on it is another important aspect of network security.

As well as implementing measures that serve to protect the network, you must also be able to detect intrusions to the network and provide procedures that define what steps should be taken when a breach does occur. All these elements must be combined to have an effective network security policy.

Many organizations now use intranets and extranets to provide additional functionality to the network. These web server–based systems are accessed through web browsers, providing an easy method of access without the need for additional software.

Key Terms

- application gateway firewall
- authentication
- caching proxy server
- circuit-level firewall
- DMZ
- encryption
- extranet
- file system security
- firewalls
- inheritance

- ▶ intranet
- ▶ logical security
- ▶ MAC address
- ▶ NAT
- ▶ packet filtering

- ▶ password policy
- ▶ personal firewalls
- ▶ physical security
- ▶ port number
- ▶ proxy server

Apply Your knowledge

Exercises

11.1 Activating Logon Auditing on a Windows 2000 Server

Many different elements go into developing an effective security strategy. Two of these elements are configuring and setting up a password policy and configuring system auditing. In this exercise, you learn the procedures involved in activating the auditing feature on a Windows 2000 Server system. (Remember that to enable auditing, you need to have administrative privileges.)

Estimated time: 15 minutes

1. Select Start, Programs, Administrative Tools, and then select Local Security Policy. The Local Security Settings dialog box, shown in Figure 11.11, appears.

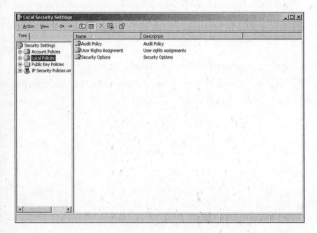

FIGURE 11.11   The Local Security Settings dialog box in Windows 2000 Server.

2. On the left side of the dialog box, click on the Local Policies folder, and then double-click the Audit Policy file folder on the right side of the dialog box. The auditable policies are displayed. Figure 11.12 shows the auditable policies.

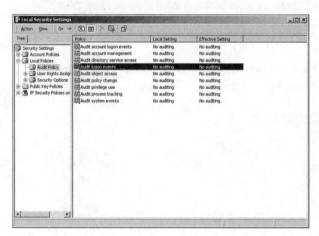

FIGURE 11.12 The auditable policies on a Windows 2000 Server system.

3. Double-click the Audit Logon Events icon. This opens the Local Security Policy Setting dialog box, which is shown in Figure 11.13.

FIGURE 11.13 The Local Security Policy Setting dialog box in Windows 2000 Server.

4. Select the Success and Failure check boxes to audit both successful and failed logon attempts, and then click OK.

5. View the Local and Effective Setting columns to view the new auditing configuration. (Note that if the domain-level security policy is defined for these values, they will override the local security policy settings.)

11.2 Setting Password Policies

As a network administrator, you might be required to establish a password policy for the organization. In this exercise, you identify where password policies are set in Windows 2000 and how to set them. Specifically, you set a specific maximum password age.

Estimated time: 10 minutes

1. Select Start, Programs, Administrative Tools, and then select Domain Security Policy from the menu. The Domain Security Policy dialog box, shown in Figure 11.14, appears.

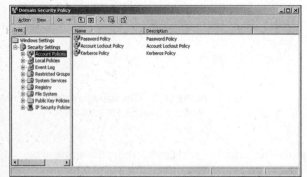

FIGURE 11.14   The Domain Security Policy dialog box in Windows 2000.

2. On the left side of the dialog box, click the Account Policies icon, and then double-click the Password Policy option on the right side of the dialog box. The password policy options are displayed.

3. Double-click the Maximum Password Age option. The Security Policy Setting dialog box, which is shown in Figure 11.15, appears.

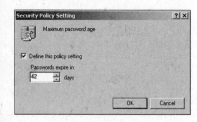

FIGURE 11.15   The Security Policy Setting dialog box in Windows 2000.

4. In the Passwords Expire In field, enter the number of days before the password expires. Click OK. The new password policy is now active for the system.

11.3 Testing Password Strength

Network administrators are required to set strong passwords and ensure that users also set strong passwords. In this exercise, you test password strength.

Estimated time: 10 minutes

1. Log on to the Internet, and go to http://www.securitystats.com/tools/password.php. You arrive at the Secure Stats website.

2. In the Enter a Password field, enter a sample password, and click Submit.

3. The password strength is displayed in a bar graph, ranging from Weak Passwords to Strong Passwords. After getting the results on the password strength, try to increase the password's strength by using the advice offered under the To Increase the Strength of Your Password, Consider One or More of the Following area of the screen. Write down on a piece of paper what passwords you try, so that you can see the progression from a weak to a strong password.

4. Continue experimenting until you get the message "Congratulations! You've supplied a sample password that is difficult to guess and hard to crack. It is recommended that you use passwords of this type."

Exam Questions

1. Which of the following are benefits of using a proxy server? (Choose the three best answers.)

   ○ **a.** It allows costs associated with Internet access to be reduced.

   ○ **b.** It provides a central point of Internet access.

   ○ **c.** It allows Internet access to be controlled.

   ○ **d.** It allows hostnames to be resolved to IP addresses.

2. On a packet-filtering firewall, which of the following is not used as a criterion for making forwarding decisions?

   ○ **a.** IP address

   ○ **b.** MAC address

   ○ **c.** TCP/IP port

   ○ **d.** NetBIOS service name

3. What is the basic reason for implementing a firewall?

   ○ **a.** It reduces the costs associated with Internet access.

   ○ **b.** It provides NAT functionality.

   ○ **c.** It provides a mechanism to protect one network from another.

   ○ **d.** It allows Internet access to be centralized.

4. Which of the following is the strongest password?

   ○ **a.** *password*

   ○ **b.** *WE300GO*

   ○ **c.** *l00Ka1ivE*

   ○ **d.** *lovethemusic*

5. Which of the following statements would you associate with an extranet? (Choose the two best answers.)

   ○ **a.** It is typically hosted by a web server application and accessed through a web browser.

   ○ **b.** It is available only to users within an organization.

   ○ **c.** It is used to provide application access to users outside an organization.

   ○ **d.** Security is generally not a priority.

6. When defining a password policy for an organization, which of the following would you consider setting? (Choose the three best answers.)

   ○ **a.** Minimum password length

   ○ **b.** Password expiration period

   ○ **c.** Prevention of password reuse

   ○ **d.** Maximum password length

7. What is the name for an area that is connected to a firewall but is neither in the private network area nor the public network area?

   ○ **a.** Area of no return

   ○ **b.** Demilitarized zone

   ○ **c.** No man's land

   ○ **d.** Forbidden zone

8. At which two layers of the OSI model does a packet-filtering firewall operate? (Choose the two best answers.)

   ○ **a.** Network

   ○ **b.** Data-link

   ○ **c.** Transport

   ○ **d.** Application

9. You have installed a proxy server on a network and configured it to allow all the hosts on the internal network to access the Internet through it. None of the users on the internal network are able to access the Internet, although they could before you implemented the proxy server. What is the most likely cause of the problem?

   ○ **a.** The proxy server is not configured correctly.

   ○ **b.** The Internet connection is not working.

   ○ **c.** The web browser on the client system needs to be reconfigured to use a proxy server.

   ○ **d.** The HTTP proxy service is not enabled on the system.

10. What is the purpose of auditing?

   ○ **a.** It allows you to be notified when a security breach is detected.

   ○ **b.** It allows you to determine whether there has been a security breach.

   ○ **c.** It allows you to prevent security breaches.

   ○ **d.** It allows you to control Internet access from a single point.

11. After noticing that there have been several attempts to access your network from the Internet, you decide to block port 53. Which of the following services is associated with port 53?

   ○ **a.** NTP

   ○ **b.** DNS

   ○ **c.** SMTP

   ○ **d.** POP3

12. At which level of the OSI model does a circuit-level firewall operate?

   ○ **a.** Transport

   ○ **b.** Data-link

   ○ **c.** Network

   ○ **d.** Physical

13. Which of the following is not a valid file permission on a Unix/Linux system?

    ○ a. Read

    ○ b. Write

    ○ c. Execute

    ○ d. Erase

14. You suspect that an employee in the company has been logging on to the system from a remote connection and attempting to look through files that he should not have access to. Which mechanism could you use to discover the identity of the person trying to dial in?

    ○ a. Auditing

    ○ b. File permissions

    ○ c. Password policy

    ○ d. Intruder detection

15. Which of the following network operating system platforms uses inheritance filters to prevent file permissions from flowing through the directory structure?

    ○ a. NetWare

    ○ b. Linux

    ○ c. Windows 2000

    ○ d. Windows 98

16. Which of the following is not a valid file permission on a NetWare server?

    ○ a. Read

    ○ b. Write

    ○ c. Full Control

    ○ d. Modify

17. Your company is moving from a client-based email system to a web-based solution. After all the users have been successfully moved to the new system, what are you likely to do on the corporate firewall? (Choose the two best answers.)

    ○ a. Block port 53

    ○ b. Block port 110

    ○ c. Block port 80

    ○ d. Block port 25

18. Which of the following is considered a physical security measure?

    ○ **a.** Password policy

    ○ **b.** Locks on equipment cabinets

    ○ **c.** Auditing policy

    ○ **d.** Firewall

19. Which of the following is not a valid file permission on a Windows 2000 NTFS partition?

    ○ **a.** Full Control

    ○ **b.** Read

    ○ **c.** Modify

    ○ **d.** Change

20. You are a network administrator for a small company in Alaska that makes knitted hats. It is expected that your company will experience huge growth, and a competitive company is seeking the design for your company's latest toque, which is code-named "Frost Killer." Your manager is concerned that a rogue employee might be preparing to sell the design to the competition, so you have been given the task of securing the company's data on your Windows 2000 server. Which of the following would you do?

    ○ **a.** Block ports.

    ○ **b.** Use a proxy server.

    ○ **c.** Implement file system security.

    ○ **d.** Install a firewall.

Answers to Exam Questions

1. **a, b, c.** A proxy server allows the costs associated with Internet access to be reduced, provides a central point of Internet access, and allows Internet access to be controlled. Answer d describes the function of a DNS server. For more information, see the section "Proxy Servers," in this chapter.

2. **d.** Firewalls do not make forwarding decisions based on the NetBIOS service name, which is fictitious. All the other answers are valid means by which a firewall can make filtering decisions. For more information, see the section "Firewalls," in this chapter.

3. **c.** Implementing a firewall allows you to have protection between networks, typically from the Internet to a private network. All the other answers describe functions offered by a proxy server. Note that some firewall systems do offer NAT functionality, but NAT is not a firewall feature; it is an added benefit of these systems. For more information, see the section "Firewalls," in this chapter.

4. **c.** Strong passwords include a combination of letters and numbers and upper- and lowercase letters. In this question Answer c is by far the strongest password. Answer a is not a strong password because it is a standard word, contains no numbers, and is all in lowercase. Answer b mixes letters and numbers, and it is not a recognized word, so it is a strong password, although it is not as strong as Answer c. Answer d is too easy to guess and contains no numbers. For more information, see the section "Physical and Logical Security," in this chapter.

5. **a, c.** Extranets are typically web server[en]based applications accessed through a web browser. Applications on an extranet are made available to users outside the organization. Because they are accessed by outside users, security is a major concern. For more information, see the section "Intranets and Extranets," in this chapter.

6. **a, b, c.** When creating a password policy, you should set a minimum password length, parameters limiting reusing the old password, and a password expiration period. You may even want to set a maximum password length, though most operating systems have a built in maximum. For more information, see the section "Physical and Logical Security," in this chapter.

7. **b.** A DMZ is an area of a network where you would place systems that must be accessed by users outside the network. All the other answers are invalid. For more information, see the section "Firewalls," in this chapter.

8. **a, b.** Packet-filtering firewalls work at the data-link and network layers of the OSI model. They do not operate at the Application or Transport layers of the OSI model. For more information, see the section "Firewalls," in this chapter.

9. **c.** For web browsers to access the Internet through a proxy server, they must be correctly configured. Given the scenario, Answer c is the most likely answer, even though all the other answers could be possible explanations for the problem described. For more information, see the section "Proxy Servers," in this chapter.

10. **b.** Auditing is a process of reviewing security logs so that breaches can be detected. Answer a describes the function of alerting. The other answers are not valid. For more information, see the section "Understanding How Security Affects a Network," in this chapter.

11. **b.** DNS uses port 53. NTP uses TCP/IP port 123, SMTP uses port 25, and POP3 uses port 110. For more information, see the section "Understanding How Security Affects a Network," in this chapter.

12. **a.** A circuit-level firewall works at the transport layer of the OSI model. None of the other answers are valid. For more information, see the section "Firewalls," in this chapter.

13. **d.** Erase is not a valid file permission on Linux or Unix systems. Read, Write, and Execute are all valid Linux file permissions. For more information, see the section "Physical and Logical Security," in this chapter.

14. **a.** To determine the user ID of a person trying to log on, you would implement auditing. File permissions, password policies, and intruder detection would not help you to do this. For more information, see the section "Understanding How Security Affects a Network," in this chapter.

15. **a.** Novell NetWare uses filters to prevent file permissions from flowing through the directory tree. None of the other network operating systems use inheritance filters as part of their file system security structure. For more information, see the section "Physical and Logical Security," in this chapter.

16. c. The Full Control permission is associated with NTFS file system on Windows servers. The equivalent permission on NetWare is Supervisor. All the other answers are valid NetWare file permissions. For more information, see the section "Physical and Logical Security," in this chapter.

17. b, d. Because users will access their email via a web browser, the firewall will not need to accommodate POP3 (port 110) and SMTP (port 25). Blocking port 53 would disable DNS lookups, and blocking port 80 would disable web browsing (HTTP). For more information, see the section "Understanding How Security Affects a Network," in this chapter.

18. b. Locks on a cabinet would be considered a physical security measure. All the other answers are considered logical security measures. For more information, see the section "Physical and Logical Security," in this chapter.

19. d. Change is not a valid NTFS file permission. All the other permissions are valid on an NTFS partition. For more information, see the section "Physical and Logical Security," in this chapter.

20. c. Implementing file system permissions can help secure data on the internal network. Blocking ports would prevent external users but would likely have no effect on internal users. The same is true of implementing a proxy server. Answer d is not a valid option. For more information, see the section "Physical and Logical Security," in this chapter.

Suggested Readings and Resources

1. Habraken, Joe. *Absolute Beginner's Guide to Networking*, fourth edition. Que Publishing, 2003.

2. Eric Maiwald. *Network Security: A Beginner's Guide, Second Edition*. McGraw-Hill Osborne Media, 2003.

3. Northcutt, Steven, David McLachlan, Judy Novak. *Network Intrusion Detection*, third edition. Sams Publishing, 2002.

4. Zwicky, Elizabeth D., Simon Cooper, Brent Chapman, Deborah Russell. *Building Internet Firewalls*, second edition. O'Reilly & Associates, 2000.

5. William R. Cheswick, Steven M. Bellovin, Aviel D. Rubin. *Firewalls and Internet Security: Repelling the Wily Hacker, Second Edition*. Addison-Wesley Professional, 2003.

6. Linux security information, www.linuxsecurity.com.

7. Windows security information, http://www.windowsecurity.com/.

8. Apple/Mac OS security information, http://www.securemac.com.

9. Computer Security Institute, www.gocsi.com.

10. Computer networking tutorials and advice, compnetworking.about.com.

11. "TechEncyclopedia," www.techencyclopedia.com.

12

VLANs, Antivirus, Fault Tolerance, and Disaster Recovery

Objectives

This chapter covers the following CompTIA-specified objectives for the "Network Implementation" section of the Network+ exam:

3.8 Identify the main characteristics of VLANs (virtual local area networks).

▶ VLANs are used in modern networks to create divisions within the networks. Although they are not as widely implemented as some other network technologies, VLANs are deployed in many organizations.

3.10 Identify the purpose, benefits, and characteristics of using antivirus software.

▶ Viruses and malicious software are serious threats to today's networks. Antivirus software is a integral part of a proactive antivirus strategy.

3.11 Identify the purpose and characteristics of fault tolerance:

▶ **Power**   ▶ **Storage**

▶ **Link redundancy**   ▶ **Services**

▶ For a network to be effective as a business tool, it must be available. In the quest for network availability, many technologies are employed so that failure of a specific piece of equipment does not necessarily mean that the network becomes unavailable.

3.12 Identify the purpose and characteristics of disaster recovery:

▶ **Backup/restore**   ▶ **Hot and cold spares**

▶ **Offsite storage**   ▶ **Hot, warm, and cold sites**

▶ The old saying goes "when things go wrong, as they usually will." The need for businesses to ensure the availability of the network and the data on it, no matter what the circumstance, is a key consideration in network planning. A network administrator plays a key role in this strategy.

Outline

Study Strategies

▶ Review and identify the function of a VLAN.

▶ Identify the ways in which a VLAN can be implemented.

▶ Understand the signs and symptoms of viruses.

▶ Review and compare the common types of malicious software.

▶ Identify and compare the characteristics of the various RAID levels.

▶ Understand the strategies used to create a fault tolerant solution.

▶ Review the types of backup options and environments for which they are suited.

▶ Review the Notes, Tips, and Exam Alerts in this chapter. Make sure that you understand the information in the Exam Alerts. If you don't understand the topic referenced in an Exam Alert, refer to the information in the chapter text and then read the Exam Alert again.

Introduction

When you come right down to it, the most important responsibility of network administrators is to ensure data availability. When users, customers, or clients need access to network data, it should be ready to go. Many organizations depend on data availability; without it, they could not function.

Two key strategies help ensure data availability: fault tolerance and disaster recovery. To fulfill the role of network administrator, it is essential that you have a clear understanding of how to use these strategies.

In addition to fault tolerance and disaster recovery, two additional objectives covered in this chapter have to do with managing malicious software and segmenting the LAN. Software designed to help manage the threat of malicious software such as viruses is an important part of a secure network design. Such software is now mandatory for systems connected to a network and strongly recommended for systems not even connected to a network.

This chapter begins by examining virtual LANs (VLANs), revealing how this technology can be used to help secure a network by segmentation.

VLANs

Objective:

3.8 Identify the main characteristics of VLANs.

The word *virtual* is used a lot in the computing world—perhaps too often. In the case of VLANs, the word *virtual* does little to help explain the technology. Perhaps a more descriptive name for the VLAN concept might have been *segmented LAN*.

> **TIP**
>
> **802.1q**   802.1q is the Institute of Electrical and Electronics Engineers (IEEE) specification developed to ensure interoperability of VLAN technologies from the various vendors.

VLANs are used for network segmentation, a strategy that significantly increases the performance capability of the network, removes potential performance bottlenecks, and can even increase network security. A VLAN is a group of computers connected together that act as if they are on their own network segments, even though they might not be. For instance, suppose that you work in a three-story building in which the advertising employees are spread over all three floors. A VLAN can let all the advertising personnel be combined and access network resources as if they were connected on the same segment. This virtual segment can be isolated from other network segments. In effect, it would appear to the advertising group that they were on a network by themselves.

VLANs offer some clear advantages. Being able to create logical segmentation of a network gives administrators flexibility beyond the restrictions of the physical network design and cable infrastructure. VLANs allow for easier administration because the network can be divided into well-organized sections. Further, you can increase security by isolating certain network segments from others. For example, you can segment the marketing personnel from finance or the administrators from the students. VLANs can ease the burden on overworked routers and reduce broadcast storms. Table 12.1 summarizes the benefits of VLANs.

TABLE 12.1   Benefits of VLANs

Advantage	Description
Increased security	By creating logical (virtual) boundaries, network segments can be isolated.
Increased performance	By reducing broadcast traffic throughout the network, VLANs free up bandwidth.
Organization	Network users and resources that are linked and communicate frequently can be grouped together in a VLAN.
Simplified administration	With a VLAN the network administrator's job is easier when moving users between LAN segments, recabling, addressing new stations, and reconfiguring hubs and routers.

VLAN Membership

You can use several methods to determine VLAN membership or how devices are assigned to a specific VLAN. The following sections describe the common methods of determining how VLAN membership is assigned.

Protocol-Based VLANs

With protocol-based VLAN membership, computers are assigned to VLANs by using the protocol that is in use and the Layer 3 address. For example, this method allows an Internetwork Packet Exchange (IPX) network or a particular Internet Protocol (IP) subnet to have its own VLAN.

It is important to note that although VLAN membership may be based on Layer 3 information, this has nothing to do with routing or routing functions. The IP numbers are used only to determine the membership in a particular VLAN—not to determine routing.

Port-Based VLANs

Port-based VLANs require that specific ports on a network switch be assigned to a VLAN. For example, ports 1 through 8 may be assigned to marketing, ports 9 through 18 may be assigned to sales, and so on. Using this method, a switch determines VLAN membership by taking note of the port used by a particular packet. Figure 12.1 shows how the ports on a server could be used for port-based VLAN membership.

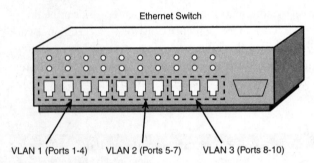

Ethernet Switch

VLAN 1 (Ports 1-4)   VLAN 2 (Ports 5-7)   VLAN 3 (Ports 8-10)

FIGURE 12.1   Port-based VLAN membership.

MAC Address–Based VLANs

As you may have guessed, the Media Access Control (MAC) address type of a VLAN assigns membership according to the MAC address of the workstation. To do this, the switch must keep track of the MAC addresses that belong to each VLAN. The advantage of this method is that a workstation computer can be moved anywhere in an office without needing to be reconfigured; because the MAC address does not change, the workstation remains a member of a particular VLAN. Table 12.2 provides an example of the membership of a MAC address–based VLAN.

TABLE 12.2   MAC Address–Based VLANs

MAC Address	VLAN	Description
44-45-53-54-00-00	1	Sales
44-45-53-54-13-12	2	Marketing
44-45-53-54-D3-01	3	Administration
44-45-53-54-F5-17	1	Sales

Although the acceptance and implementation of VLANs has been slow, the capability to logically segment a LAN provides a new level of administrative flexibility, organization, and security.

Viruses, Virus Solutions, and Malicious Software

Objective:

3.10 Identify the purpose, benefits, and characteristics of using antivirus software.

Viruses, spyware, worms, and other malicious code are an unfortunate part of modern computing. In today's world, an unprotected computer is at high risk of having some form of malicious software installed on the system. Even a protected system is still at risk; it's just that the risk is lower.

By definition, a virus is a self-replicating program that operates on a computer system without the user's knowledge. A viruses either attaches to or replaces system files, system executables, and data files. Once in, the virus can perform many different functions. For example, the virus may completely consume system resources making the system too slow to use, corrupt data, down a computer, or even compromise data integrity and availability.

To be considered a virus, the malicious program must meet two criteria: It must be self-replicating, and it must be able to execute itself. The following list examines the common types of viruses found today:

▶ **Boot sector virus**—Boot sector viruses target the boot record of a hard disk or floppy disk. To boot, floppy disks or hard drives contain an initial set of instructions that start the boot process. Boot sector viruses infect this program and activate when the system boots. This allows the virus to stay hidden in memory and operate in the background.

▶ **File Viruses**—These common viruses attack applications and program files. This type of virus often targets the .exe, .com, and .bat files either by destroying them, preventing applications from running, or by modifying them and using them to propagate the virus.

NOTE

Combining a Virus   Viruses are not necessarily either file viruses or a boot sector viruses; they can be both. One virus can be designed to both attack the boot sector and the applications.

▶ **Macro viruses**—The actual data, such as documents, spreadsheets, and so on, represents the most important and irreplaceable elements on a computer system. Macro viruses are designed to attack documents and files and therefore are particularly nasty.

Trojans, Worms, Spyware, and Hoaxes

There are other forms of malicious programs that by definition are not viruses but still threaten our computer systems.

A *Trojan horse* is a program that appears harmless or even helpful, but after being executed it performs an undesirable and malicious action. For example, a Trojan horse can be a program advertised to be a patch, a harmless application such as a calculator, or a product upgrade or enhancement. The Trojan horse is designed to fool the user to download and install the program. Once executed, the Trojan horse can perform the function it was actually designed to do. This may include crashing a system, data theft, and data corruption.

> **EXAM ALERT**
>
> **Trojan Horse** By strict definition, a Trojan horse is not a virus because it does not replicate and does not execute itself. This form of malicious code is installed by the user mistakenly and is often delivered through email or by downloading applications from the Internet.

Worms are similar to viruses in that they replicate, but they do not require a host file to spread from system to system. The difference between viruses and worms is that a worm does not attach itself to an executable program as do viruses. A worm is self-contained and does not need to be part of another program to propagate itself. This makes a worm capable of replicating at incredible speeds. This can cause significant network slow-downs as the worm spreads.

A worm can do any number of malicious actions including deleting files and sending documents via email without the user knowing. A worm may also carry another program designed to open a back door in the system used by spam senders to send junk mail and notices to a computer. When this back-door access is open to your system, it is vulnerable and susceptible to data theft, modification, or worse.

Spyware is a new threat that can be hidden and easy to get. Spyware is designed to monitor activity on a computer, such as a web surfing activity, and send that information out to a remote source. It is commonly installed along with a free program that may have been downloaded.

Spyware detection software is becoming increasingly popular and, given the information that can be stolen, should be considered an important part of a secure system.

One final consideration is that of virus hoaxes. The threat of virus activity is very real and as such we are alerted to it. Some take advantage of this to create elaborate virus hoaxes. Hoaxes often pop up on the computer screen or arrive in email warning of a virus or claiming that your system has contracted a virus. These are more annoying than dangerous but serve to confuse and complicate the virus issue.

> **NOTE**
>
> **Virus Types** Malicious code varies by the type of virus and also how the virus operates. For example, polymorphic viruses change themselves each time they infect a system. This makes them difficult to scan for because they are always changing their look. Stealth viruses become part of a program and make it appear like the program is operating normally when in fact a virus is at work. This too makes them difficult to scan for.

Protecting Computers from Viruses

The threat from malicious code is a very real concern. It is important to take the steps to protect our systems, and although it may not be possible to eliminate the threat, it is possible to significantly reduce that threat.

One of the primary tools used in the fight against malicious software is *antivirus software*. Antivirus software is available from a number of companies and each offers similar features and capabilities. The following is a list of the common features and characteristics of antivirus software:

▶ **Real-time protection**—An installed antivirus program should continuously monitor the system looking for viruses. If a program is downloaded, an application opened, or a suspicious email received, the real-time virus monitor detects and removes the threat. The virus application sits in the background largely unnoticed to the user.

▶ **Virus scanning**—An antivirus program must be capable of scanning selected drives and disks either locally or remotely. Scanning can either be run manually or be scheduled to run at a particular time.

▶ **Scheduling**—It is a best practice to schedule virus scanning to occur automatically at a predetermined time. In a network environment, this would typically occur off hours when the overhead of the scanning process won't impact users.

▶ **Live updates**—New viruses and malicious software are released with alarming frequency. It is recommended that the antivirus software be configured to receive virus updates regularly.

▶ **Email vetting**—Emails represent one of the primary sources for virus delivery. It is essential to use antivirus software that provides email scanning for both inbound and outbound email.

▶ **Centralized management**—If used in a network environment, it is a good idea to use software that supports managing the virus program from the server. Virus updates and configurations only need to be made on the server and not on each individual client station.

Managing the threat from viruses is considered a proactive measure with antivirus software being only part of the solution. A complete virus protection strategy requires many aspects to help limit the risk of viruses, including the following:

▶ **Develop in-house policies and rules**—In a corporate environment or even a small office it is important to establish what information can be placed onto a system. For example, should users be able to download programs from the Internet? Can users bring in their own floppy disks or other storage media?

▶ **Monitoring virus threats**—With new viruses coming out all the time, it is important to check whether new viruses have been released and what they are designed to do.

▶ **Educate users**—One of the keys to a complete antivirus solution is to train users in virus prevention and recognition techniques. If users know what they are looking for, it can prevent a virus from entering the system or the network. Back up copies of important documents. It should be mentioned that no solution is absolute and care should be taken to ensure the data is backed up. In the event of a malicious attack, redundant information is available in a secure location.

▶ **Automate virus scanning and updates**—Today's antivirus software can be configured to scan and update itself automatically. Because such tasks can be forgotten and overlooked, it is recommended to have these processes scheduled to run at predetermined times.

▶ **Email vetting**—Email is one of the commonly used virus delivery mechanisms. Antivirus software can be used to check inbound and outbound emails for virus activity.

Challenge

You are the administrator for a medium-sized network. Recently several viruses have come into the network and corrupted computers. The network consists of 100 desktop systems, 14 laptops that the sales team may take on the road, 21 remote users, and 3 servers.

Currently no virus solution strategy is in place. As such, you have been asked to design a virus strategy for the company that will secure the network from viruses including all computer and server systems. Furthermore, you need to create strict user policies for the prevention of future virus activity. The policy must include guidelines for email, unauthorized application installs, and file downloading.

For this exercise, determine the most cost-efficient and effective strategy for protecting the network. In addition, develop an organization virus policy that establishes a proactive virus prevention plan. Finally, the solution should include policies for new systems that may be added to the network.

Understanding Fault Tolerance

Objective:

3.11 Identify the purpose and characteristics of fault tolerance:

- ▶ Storage
- ▶ Link redundancy
- ▶ Power
- ▶ Services

In networking, *fault tolerance* refers to the capability for a device or system to continue operating in the event of a failure. Fault tolerance should not be confused with disaster recovery, which is the ability to respond to and recover from catastrophic events with no loss of data and no loss of data availability.

In practical terms, fault tolerance involves ensuring that when network hardware or software fails, users on the network can still access the data and continue working with little or no disruption of service. Developing a strong fault-tolerant system that ensures continual access to data is not easy, and it involves attention to many details. The following sections explore fault tolerance, establishing a fault-tolerant network design, and the impact failure can have on the network.

Today's business world relies heavily on networks and network servers. If these networks and servers were to fail, many businesses would be unable to function. Thus every minute a network is not available costs money. The exact amount of money depends on the size of the organization and can range from a mild economic inconvenience to a crippling financial blow. The potential impact of a network failure often dictates the fault tolerance measures an organization implements.

Unfortunately, no fault-tolerance measures can guarantee 100% availability to network data or services, and fault-tolerance solutions that strive to meet this goal can be expensive. But the costs associated with any fault-tolerance solution must be compared to the costs of losing access to network services and the reconstruction of network data.

Some hardware components are more likely than others to fail. Implementing a strong fault-tolerance strategy involves identifying the weakest links and employing strategies that can compensate when those weak links fail. Figure 12.2 provides a quick look at the failure rates of server hardware components.

As shown in Figure 12.2, 50% of all server failures can be attributed to hard disks. The hard disk is 50 times more likely to fail than the motherboard and 12 times more likely to fail than memory. It should come as no surprise that when configuring a fault-tolerant system, hard drives receive special attention; after all, they do hold all the data. (Of course, it would be unwise not to consider fault-tolerance measures for other hardware devices as well.) The following sections identify common fault tolerance measures, beginning with the best known: Redundant Array of Inexpensive Disks (RAID).

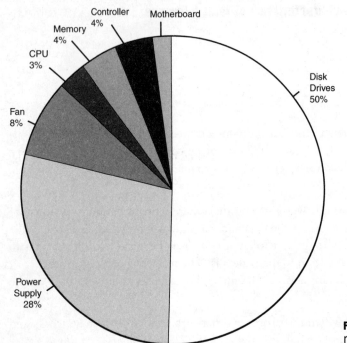

FIGURE 12.2 Server hardware failure rates.

RAID

RAID (Redundant Array of Inexpensive Disks)is a strategy for implementing fault-tolerance solutions that prevent data disruption due to hard disk failure. RAID combines multiple hard disks together in such a way that more than one disk is responsible for holding data. Instead of using a single large disk, information is written to several smaller disks.

Such a design offers two key advantages. First, the failure of one disk does not, in fault-tolerant RAID configurations, compromise the availability of data. Second, reading (and sometimes writing) to multiple smaller disks is often faster with multiple hard disks than when using one large disk, thus offering a performance boost.

The goals of a RAID solution are clear: Decrease the costs associated with downtime, secure network data, minimize network disruption, and (selfishly) reduce the stress on the network administrator(s). Because a well-designed RAID system can accomplish all these goals, RAID is widely implemented and found in organizations of all sizes.

Several RAID strategies are available, and each has advantages and disadvantages. It is important to know what you are protecting and why before you implement any RAID solution; the particular RAID strategy used depends on many factors, including associated costs, the server's role, and the level of fault tolerance required. The following sections discuss the characteristics of the various RAID strategies.

RAID 0

Although it is classified as a RAID level, RAID 0 is in fact not fault tolerant. As such, RAID 0 is not recommended for servers that maintain mission-critical data. RAID 0 works by writing to multiple hard drives simultaneously, allowing for faster data throughput. RAID 0 offers a significant performance increase over a single disk—but, as with a single disk, all data is lost if any disk in the RAID set fails. With RAID 0 you actually increase your chances of losing data compared to using a single disk because RAID 0 uses multiple hard disks, creating multiple failure points. Essentially, the more disks you use in the RAID 0 array, the more at risk the data is. A minimum of two disks is required to implement a RAID 0 solution.

RAID 0 writes data to the disks in the array by using a system called *striping*. Striping works by partitioning the hard disks into stripes and writing the data across the stripes, as shown in Figure 12.3. The striping strategy is also used by RAID 2, RAID 3, RAID 4, and RAID 5.

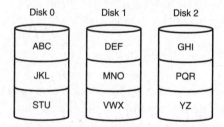

FIGURE 12.3 RAID 0 with disk striping.

Advantages of RAID 0

Despite the fact that it is not fault tolerant, RAID 0 is well suited for some environments. The following are some of the advantages of RAID 0:

- ▶ **Ease of implementation**—RAID 0 offers easy setup and configuration.

- ▶ **Good input/output (I/O) performance**—RAID 0 offers a significant increase in performance over a single disk and other RAID solutions by spreading data across multiple disks.

- ▶ **Minimal hardware requirements**—RAID 0 can be implemented with as few as two hard drives, making it a cost-effective solution for some network environments.

Disadvantages of RAID 0

You cannot have the good without the bad. For a number of reasons, a RAID 0 solution may not be appropriate:

▶ **No fault tolerance**—Employing a RAID solution that does not offer data protection is a major drawback. This factor alone limits a RAID 0 solution to only a few network environments.

▶ **Increased failure points**—A RAID 0 solution has as many failure points as there are hard drives. For instance, if your RAID 0 configuration has five disks and any one of those drives fails, the data on all drives will be lost.

▶ **Limited application**—Because of the lack of fault tolerance, a RAID 0 solution is practical for few applications. Quite simply, it's limited to environments where the performance of I/O outweighs the importance of data availability.

Despite its drawbacks, you might encounter RAID 0.

Recovering from a Failed RAID 0 Array

Anyone relying on a RAID 0 configuration to hold sensitive data is bold. The bottom line is, there is no way to recover from a failed RAID 0 array, short of restoring the data from backups. Both the server and the services it provides to the network are unavailable while you rebuild the drives and the data.

RAID 1

RAID 1 is a fault-tolerant configuration known as *disk mirroring*. A RAID 1 solution uses two physical disk drives. Whenever a file is saved to the hard disk, a copy of the file is automatically written to the second disk. The second disk is always an exact mirrored copy of the first one. Figure 12.4 illustrates a RAID 1 array.

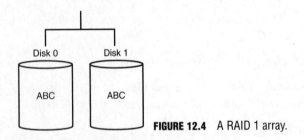

FIGURE 12.4 A RAID 1 array.

RAID 1 writes the same data to the hard drives simultaneously. The benefits of having a duplicate copy of all saved data are clear, and on the surface, RAID 1 may seem like a very fault-tolerant solution. However, it has a couple drawbacks. First, RAID 1 has high overhead because an entire disk must be used to provide the mirrored copy. Second, a RAID 1 solution is limited to two hard drives, which limits the available storage capacity.

Another RAID strategy that falls under the category of RAID 1 is disk duplexing. *Disk duplexing* is a mirrored solution that incorporates a second level of fault tolerance by using a separate hard disk controller for each hard drive. Putting the hard disks on separate controllers eliminates the controller as a single point of failure. The likelihood of a failed disk controller is not nearly as high as the likelihood of a failed hard disk, but the more failure points covered, the better. Figure 12.5 shows a disk duplexing configuration.

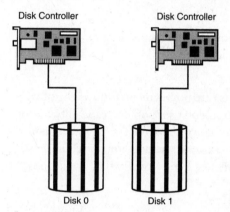

Disk Controller   Disk Controller

Disk 0   Disk 1   **FIGURE 12.5** A disk duplexing configuration.

> **NOTE**
>
> **Sizing the Mirror**   Because mirroring involves making a duplicate copy of the data, the volumes used on each disk are the same size. If you set up the mirrored environment with a 500MB volume and a 700MB volume, the result will be only a 500MB volume. The system uses the lowest common amount of free space to construct the mirrored volume.

Advantages of RAID 1

Although it is far from perfect, RAID 1 is widely implemented in many different network environments. The following are a few of the advantages of RAID 1:

- **Fault tolerance**—RAID 1 is a fault-tolerance solution that maintains a mirrored image of data on a second hard drive in case of failure. Disk duplexing adds extra fault tolerance by using dual hard drive controllers.

- **Reduced cost**—RAID 1 provides fault tolerance by using only two hard disks, thereby providing a cost-effective method of implementing a fault-tolerance solution.

- **Ease of implementation**—Implementing a RAID 1 solution is not difficult; it can be set up easily. The procedures and methods for implementing the hardware and software are well documented.

Disadvantages of RAID 1

Several factors exclude RAID 1 from being used in many network environments. The following are some of the disadvantages associated with RAID 1:

▸ **Limited disk capacity**—Because RAID 1 uses only two hard disks, limited disk space is available for use. Even if you purchased two 80GB drives, your network would have only 80GB of storage space. The applications and data storage needs of many of today's businesses would exceed this limitation quickly.

▸ **High disk space overhead**—RAID 1 has 50% overhead—that is, half the hard disk space needs to be used for RAID. So for every megabyte used for other purposes, another is needed for RAID.

▸ **Limited hot-swap support**—Because RAID 1 is often implemented through software rather than hardware, RAID 1 configurations often don't support the capability to hot swap drives, meaning that you might have to shut down the server to replace a damaged hard disk. In some environments, powering down a server is a major consideration that is avoided at all costs. In such environments, a software RAID 1 solution is not practical.

Although disk mirroring is a reliable fault-tolerance method, it provides for only a single disk failure.

Recovering from a Failed RAID 1 Array

RAID 1 can handle the failure of a single drive; if one fails, a complete copy of the data exists on an alternate hard drive. Recovering from a failed RAID 1 array typically involves breaking the mirror set, replacing the failed drive with a working one, and reestablishing the mirror. The data will be automatically rebuilt on the new drive.

The recovery process may cause network disruption while a new hard drive is installed. The server can continue to function with a single drive, but there is no fault tolerance until the RAID 1 array is rebuilt.

It is possible—however unlikely—for multiple drives to fail, and RAID 1 cannot handle such a situation.

RAID 2

A few RAID levels have fallen into obscurity, and it is unlikely that you will see them in modern network environments. RAID 2 falls into this category. RAID 2 is described here to provide a complete look at the RAID picture.

RAID 2 is a fault-tolerant RAID level that writes error-correction data across several disks and uses this code to re-create data in case of failure. RAID 2 offers an error-detection method that uses *hamming code*. Hamming code was designed to be used with drives with no built-in error detection. SCSI hard disks today all have built-in error-detection, making this feature useless. RAID 2 no longer has any real-world practical applications.

RAID 3

RAID 3 is another obsolete RAID level. RAID 3 stripes data across several hard disks, like RAID 0 does, but it also uses an additional disk for parity information. If a hard drive fails, the separate parity disk can be used to re-create the missing data, and business can continue without disruption to network service. Using a dedicated disk as a parity disk puts undue stress on a single disk because the parity information is constantly being written to the disk. The increased workload placed on a single disk can slow performance and cause the disk to fail more quickly than the other disks in the array.

RAID 4

RAID 4, like RAID 3, stripes information across all hard drives and uses a single dedicated disk for parity information. The main difference between the two is that RAID 4 uses *block-level striping*. However, due to the use of a single parity disk, RAID 4 suffers from the same shortcomings as RAID 3, and you are unlikely to encounter it today.

> **NOTE**
>
> **Long Shots**   The chances of encountering RAID levels 2, 3, and 4 in a modern network environment are similar to the odds of being struck by lightning and winning the lottery on the same day.

RAID 5

RAID 5 is the preferred hard disk fault-tolerance strategy for most environments; it is trusted to protect the most sensitive data. RAID 5 stripes the data across all the hard drives in the array.

> **NOTE**
>
> **Drive Failures**   The key advantage of RAID 5 is that a single drive can fail, and the server can continue operation.

Instead of reserving a single disk for parity information as RAID 3 and 4 do, RAID 5 spreads parity information across all the disks in the array. Known as *distributed parity*, this approach allows the server to continue to function in the event of disk failure. The system can calculate the information missing from the failed drive by using the parity information on the disks. A minimum of three hard drives is required to implement RAID 5, but more drives are recommended, up to 32. When calculating how many drives you will be using in a RAID 5 array, remember that the parity distributed across the drives is equivalent to one disk. Thus if you have four 10GB hard disks, you will have 30GB of storage space.

You can expect to work with and maintain a RAID 5 array in your network travels. Figure 12.6 shows a RAID 5 array.

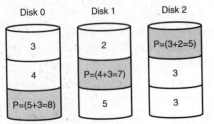

FIGURE 12.6   A RAID 5 array.

Advantages of RAID 5

RAID 5 has become a widely implemented fault-tolerance strategy for several reasons. The following are some of the key advantages of RAID 5:

- **Minimal network disruption**—When a hard disk crashes in a RAID 5 array, the rest of the drives continue to function with no disruption in data availability. Network users can keep working, and costs associated with network downtime are minimized. Although there is no disruption to data access, the performance of the system decreases until the drive has been replaced.

- **Performance**—Because RAID 5 can access several drives simultaneously, the read performance over that of a single disk is greatly improved. Increased performance is not necessarily a reason to use a fault-tolerant solution, but it is an added bonus.

- **Distributed parity**—By writing parity over several disks, RAID 5 avoids the bottleneck of writing parity to a single disk, which occurs with RAID 3 and 4.

Disadvantages of RAID 5

The disadvantages of RAID 5 are few, and the benefits certainly outweigh the costs. The following are the disadvantages of RAID 5:

- **Poor write performance**—Because parity is distributed across several disks, multiple writes must be performed for every write operation The severity of this performance lag depends on the application being used, but its impact is minimal enough to make it a factor in only a few environments.

- **Regeneration time**—When a hard disk is replaced in a RAID 5 array, the data must be regenerated on it. This process is typically performed automatically and demands extensive system resources. However, this factor is unlikely to become a concern.

- **Data limitations**—RAID 5 that is implemented using software may not be able to include the system or boot partitions in the stripe set, so you must use an alternative method to secure the system and boot partitions. For example, some organizations use

RAID 5 for data and a mirrored set to provide fault tolerance for the system and boot partitions. This limitation does not include hardware RAID 5 solutions, which can stripe the system and boot partitions.

Recovering from a RAID 5 Array Failure

RAID 5 ensures data availability even in the event of failed hard disks. A RAID 5 system can still service requests from clients in the event of a failure, by using the parity information from the other disks to identify the data that is now missing because it was on the failed drive.

At some point, you must replace the failed hard disks to rebuild the array. Some systems let you remove the failed hard drive (that is, they are hot swappable) and insert the new one without powering down the server. The new hard disk is configured automatically as part of the existing RAID 5 array, and the rebuilding of data on the new drive occurs automatically. Other systems may require you to power down the server to replace the drive. You must then manually perform the rebuild. Because RAID 5 continues to run after a disk failure, you can schedule a time to replace the damaged drive and minimize the impact on network users.

Hot Swap Versus Hot Spare

Two strategies are commonly associated with minimizing data disruption with RAID: *hot swappable drives* and *hot spare drives*. A hot spare drive sits unused in a RAID array, waiting to be called into action. For instance, if a hard disk fails in a RAID 5 array, the hot spare is already installed and ready to take over.

Hot swapping, on the other hand, refers to the ability to replace a device such as a hard disk without having to power down the system. Hot swapping is not reserved for hard disks; many other types of server and workstation hardware support hot swapping.

RAID 10

In some server environments, it makes sense to combine RAID levels. One such strategy is RAID 10, which combines RAID 1 and RAID 0. RAID 10 requires four hard disks—two for the data striping and two to provide a mirrored copy of the striped pair.

NOTE

Implementing RAID 10 There are various ways of implementing RAID 10, depending on how many drives you have available and what the system configuration is.

RAID 10 combines the performance benefits of RAID 0 with the fault-tolerant capability of RAID 1, without requiring the parity calculations. However, RAID 10 also combines the limitations of RAID 0 and RAID 1. Mirroring the drives somewhat reduces the performance capabilities of RAID 0, and the 50% overhead of a RAID 1 solution is still in effect. Even with these limitations, RAID 10 is well suited for many environments, and you might find yourself working with or implementing such a solution. Figure 12.7 shows a possible configuration for a RAID 10 solution.

> **NOTE**
>
> **What's in a Name?** RAID 10 has many names. It's sometimes referred to as RAID 1/0, RAID 0/1, or RAID 1+0.

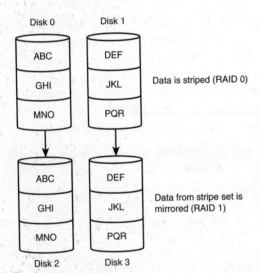

FIGURE 12.7 A RAID 10 solution.

Choosing a RAID Level

Deciding whether to use a fault-tolerant solution on a network is the first and most obvious step for you to take when you design a network. The next, less simple, decision is which RAID level to implement. Your first inclination might be to choose the best possible RAID solution, but your budget might dictate otherwise. Consider the following when choosing a specific RAID level:

▶ **Data protection and availability**—First and foremost, consider the effect of downtime on the organization. If minutes will cost the organization millions, you need a very strong fault-tolerant solution. On the other hand, if you can go offline for an hour or more and suffer nothing more than an inconvenience, a costly RAID solution might be overkill. Before choosing a RAID solution, be sure what impact data unavailability will have on you and your network.

▶ **Cost**—We would all like the best RAID solution, but high-end RAID solutions are out of the price range of many organizations. You are left to choose the best solution for the price.

▶ **Capacity**—Some organizations' data needs are measured in megabytes, and other organizations' needs are measured in gigabytes. Before choosing a RAID solution, you need to know the volume of data. RAID 1, for instance, provides far less space than RAID 5.

▶ **Performance**—Speed is an important consideration. With some RAID solutions the network suffers a performance hit, whereas with others performance can be increased over the performance using a single disk. Choosing the correct RAID solution might involve understanding the performance capabilities of each of the different RAID levels.

Table 12.3 summarizes the main characteristics of the various RAID levels.

REVIEW BREAK

TABLE 12.3   RAID Characteristics

RAID Level	Description	Key Features	Minimum Disks Required
RAID 0	Disk striping	No fault tolerance; improved I/O performance	2
RAID 1	Disk mirroring	Provides fault tolerance but at 50% disk overhead; can also be used with separate disk controllers, a strategy known as disk duplexing	2 (2 is also the maximum number of disks used for RAID 1.)
RAID 2	Disk striping with hamming code	Limited use	3
RAID 3	Disk striping with single-parity disk	Limited use	3
RAID 4	Disk striping with single-parity disk	Limited use	3
RAID 5	Disk striping with distributed parity	Widely used RAID solution; uses distributed parity	3
RAID 10	Striping with mirrored volumes	Increased performance with striping and offers mirrored fault tolerance	4

Hardware and Software RAID

After you've decided to implement a RAID solution, you must also decide whether to use a software or hardware RAID solution. The decision is not easy, and your budget might again be the deciding factor.

Software RAID is managed by the network operating system or third-party software and as such requires server resources to operate. As a result, the overhead associated with software RAID can affect the performance of the server by taking resource time away from other applications. Some variations of RAID require more from the server than others; for example, RAID 1 is commonly implemented using software RAID because it requires less overhead than RAID 5.

Software RAID has one definite advantage: It's inexpensive. For example, Linux, Windows 2000/2003/XP, and Mac OS X servers have RAID capability built in, allowing RAID to be implemented at no extra cost, apart from the costs associated with buying multiple disks. These operating systems typically offer support for RAID levels 0, 1, and 5.

Hardware RAID is the way to go if your budget allows. Hardware RAID uses its own specialized controller, which takes the RAID processing requirements away from the server. The server's resources can thus focus on other applications. Hardware RAID also provides the capability to use cache memory on the RAID controller, further adding to its performance capabilities over software RAID.

> **NOTE**
>
> **Arrays and Volumes**   When discussing RAID, you'll often encounter the terms *array* and *volume*. An *array* is a group of disks that are part of a single RAID configuration. For example, you would say, "There are two disks in a RAID 1 array." A *volume* is a logical disk space within an array. Typically, a volume only refers to data storage and capacity.

Other Fault-Tolerance Measures

Although hard drives represent the single largest failure point in a network, they are not the only failure points. Even the most costly RAID solution cannot save you from a faulty power supply or memory module. To fully address data availability, you must consider all hardware. This section provides a brief overview of some of the other common fault-tolerance measures you can take to further ensure data availability:

▶ Link redundancy

▶ Using uninterruptible power supplies (UPSs)

▶ Power supply fault tolerance

▶ Server and service fault tolerance

▶ Memory

▶ Managing processor failures

Link Redundancy

A faulty NIC can disable access to data quickly because a failed NIC effectively isolates a system. Several strategies are used to provide fault tolerance for NICs. Many systems employ a hot spare in the system that can be put to work as soon as the primary NIC fails.

Though a failed network card may not actually stop a system, it may as well. A network system that cannot access the network isn't much good. Though the chances of a failed network card are relatively low, our attempts to reduce the occurrence of downtime have led to the development of a strategy that provides fault tolerance for network connections.

Through a process called *adapter teaming*, groups of network cards are configured to act as a single unit. The teaming capability is achieved through software, either as a function of the network card driver or through specific application software. Adapter teaming is not widely implemented in smaller organizations however, the. benefits it offers makes it an important consideration. The result of adapter teaming is increased bandwidth, fault tolerance, and the ability to manage network traffic more effectively. These features are organized into three sections:

▶ **Adapter fault tolerance**—The basic configuration allows one network card to be configured as the primary device and others as secondary. If the primary adapter fails, one of the other cards can take its place without the need for intervention. When the original card is replaced, it resumes the role of primary controller.

▶ **Adapter load balancing**—Because software controls the network adapters, workloads can be distributed evenly among the cards so that each link is used to a similar degree. This distribution allows for a more responsive server because one card is not overworked while another is underworked.

▶ **Link aggregation**—This provides vastly improved performance by allowing more than one network card's bandwidth to be combined into a single connection. For example, through link aggregation, four 100MBps network cards can provide a total of 400MBps bandwidth. Link aggregation requires that both the network adapters and the switch being used support it. In 1999, the IEEE ratified the 802.3ad standard for link aggregation, allowing compatible products to be produced.

NOTE

Warm Swaps Some systems support *warm swaps*. Warm swapping involves powering down an individual bus slot to change a NIC. Doing so prevents you from having to power down the entire system to replace a NIC.

Using Uninterruptible Power Supplies

No discussion of fault tolerance can be complete without a look at power-related issues and the mechanisms used to combat them. When you're designing a fault-tolerant system, your planning should definitely include UPSs. A UPS serves many different functions and is a major part of server consideration and implementation.

On a basic level, a UPS is a box that holds a battery and a built-in charging circuit. During times of good power, the battery is recharged; when the UPS is needed, it's ready to provide power to the server. Most often, the UPS is required to provide enough power to give the administrator time to shut down the server in an orderly fashion, preventing any potential data loss from a dirty shutdown.

NOTE

Overloading UPSs   One mistake often made by administrators is the overloading of UPSs. UPSs are designed for server systems, and connecting monitors, printers, or other peripheral devices to them reduces their effectiveness.

Why Use a UPS?

Organizations of all shapes and sizes need UPSs as part of their fault-tolerance strategies. A UPS is as important as any other fault-tolerance measure. Three key reasons make a UPS necessary:

▶ **Data availability**—The goal of any fault-tolerance measure is data availability. A UPS ensures access to the server in the event of a power failure—or at least as long as it takes to save your file.

▶ **Data loss**—Fluctuations in power or a sudden power down can damage the data on the server system. In addition, many servers take full advantage of caching, and a sudden loss of power could cause the loss of all information held in cache.

▶ **Hardware damage**—Constant power fluctuations or sudden power downs can damage hardware components within a computer. Damaged hardware can lead to reduced data availability while the hardware is being repaired.

Power Threats

In addition to keeping a server functioning long enough to safely shut it down, a UPS also safeguards a server from inconsistent power. This inconsistent power can take many forms. A UPS protects a system from the following power-related threats:

▶ **Blackout**—A total failure of the power supplied to the server.

▶ **Spike**—A spike is a short (usually less than a second) but intense increase in voltage. Spikes can do irreparable damage to any kind of equipment, especially computers.

▶ **Surge**—Compared to a spike, a surge is a considerably longer (sometimes many seconds) but usually less intense increase in power. Surges can also damage your computer equipment.

▶ **Sag**—A sag is a short-term voltage drop (the opposite of a spike). This type of voltage drop can cause a server to reboot.

▶ **Brownout**—A brownout is a drop in voltage supply that usually lasts more than a few minutes.

Many of these power-related threats can occur without your knowledge; if you don't have a UPS, you cannot prepare for them. Forthe investment, it is worth buying a UPS, if for no other reason than to sleep better at night.

Power Supplies

If you work with servers or workstations, you know that from time to time a power supply will fail. When it fails in a workstation, you simply power down the system and replace the power supply. On a server, where downtime is often measured in dollars and cents, powering down to replace a faulty power supply can be a major issue.

You can prepare for a faulty power supply by using redundant, hot-swappable power supplies. As you might expect, such a strategy has associated costs that must be weighed against the importance of continual access to data.

Server and Services Fault Tolerance

In addition to providing fault tolerance for individual hardware components, some organizations go the extra mile to include entire servers in the fault-tolerant design. Such a design keeps servers and the services they provide up and running.

When it comes to server fault tolerance, two key strategies are used: *standby servers* and *server clustering*.

Using Standby Servers

In addition to instituting fault-tolerance measures for individual components, many larger organizations use server fault-tolerance measures. In this scenario, if one server fails, a second is fully configured and waiting to take over. Using this configuration, if a server fails, the network services it provided to the network will become available in a short amount of time using the redundant server. The second server is sometimes located in a separate building, in case of fire or flood damage to the location where the first server is kept.

Another strategy used for complete server and network service fault tolerance is *server failover*. A server failover configuration has two servers wired together, with one acting as the primary server and the other acting as the secondary server. The systems synchronize data between them, ensuring that they are always current with each other. If the secondary server detects that the primary is offline, it switches to failover mode and becomes the primary server for the network. It then is responsible for providing any missing network services. The whole procedure is transparent to the network user, and very little downtime, if any, is experienced.

As you might imagine, the costs associated with having a redundant server are very high. For this reason, few organizations use the failover and hot-spare server measures.

Server Clustering

Continuing our journey into incredibly expensive fault-tolerance strategies, we come to server clustering. For companies that cannot afford even a second of downtime, the costs of server clustering are easily justified.

Server clustering involves grouping several computers into one logical unit. This strategy can, depending on the configuration, provide fault tolerance as well as increased performance and load balancing. Because the servers within the cluster are in constant contact with each other, they are able to detect and compensate for a failing server system. A well-configured server cluster provides failover without any disruption to network users.

The advantages of clustering are obvious. Clustering affords the highest possible availability of data and network services. Clusters are the foundational configuration for the "five nines" level of service—that's 99.999% uptime, which translates to less than 10 minutes of downtime in a year.

The fundamental downside to server clustering is its cost. Clustering requires a separate network to be constructed between the servers, installation and configuration of additional software, additional hardware, and additional administrative support.

Memory Failures

After memory is installed and confirmed to be working, it generally works error free. Sometimes, however, memory is at the root of system problems. Unfortunately, fault-tolerance strategies for memory are limited. Memory doesn't support hot swapping, so you have to power down the server during memory replacement. The best you can do is minimize the impact of the failure.

Some environments have spare memory available at all times in case of failure. When memory does fail, a spare is ready to go. Such planning requires considerable forethought, but when you need such a solution, the preparation pays off.

Managing Processor Failures

Processors are hardy, and processor failure is extremely uncommon. In fact, processor failure is so unusual that few organizations include processors in their fault-tolerance designs. Environments that consider processors may have a spare or, more likely, a standby server (discussed previously in this chapter).

Some multiprocessor machines have a built-in safeguard against a single processor failure. In such a machine, the working processor maintains the server while a replacement for the nonfunctioning processor is found.

Disaster Recovery

Objective:

3.12 Identify the purpose and characteristics of disaster recovery:

▶ Backup/restore

▶ Offsite storage

▶ Hot and cold spares

▶ Hot, warm, and cold sites

Besides implementing fault-tolerance measures in a network you need to consider disaster recovery—the things to do when your carefully implemented fault-tolerance measures fail. Disaster recovery and fault tolerance are two separate entities, and both are equally important. *Disaster recovery* is defined as measures that allow a network to return to a working state.

Backups and backup strategies are key components of disaster recovery. The following sections identify the various backup strategies commonly used and why these strategies are such an important part of a network administrator's role.

Backup Methods

You can choose from several backup methods. Don't select one at random; choose carefully, to match the needs of your organization.

> **EXAM ALERT**
>
> **Tape Cleaning Tips**   When backing up to tape, you must periodically clean the tape drive with a cleaning cartridge. If your system is unable to access a tape, you should first try another tape. If that doesn't work, use a cleaning tape. Remember these tips for the exam!

The backup method you choose will most likely be affected by the amount of time you have available. Many organizations have a time window in which backup procedures must be conducted. Outside that window, the backup procedure can impede the functioning of the network by slowing down the server and the network. Organizations with large amounts of data require more time for a backup than those with small amounts of data. Although both small and large organizations require full backups, the strategy each uses will be different. With that in mind, let's look at the various backup methods, which include full backups, incremental backups, and differential backups.

Full Backups

If you have time, a full backup is usually the best type of backup. A *full backup*, also referred to as a normal backup, copies all the files on the hard disk. In case of disaster, the files from a single backup set can be used to restore the entire system.

Despite the advantages of full backups, they are not always a practical solution. Depending on the amount of data that needs to be backed up, the procedure can take a long time. Many administrators try to run full backups in the off hours, to reduce the impact on the network. Today, many networks do not have off hours, making it difficult to find time to squeeze in full backups.

Full backups are often used as the sole backup method in smaller organizations that have only a few gigabytes of data. Larger organizations that utilize hundreds of gigabytes of data storage are unlikely to rely on full backups as their sole backup strategy.

Backups and Security

Having your entire hard drive stored on a single tape has obvious advantages but also some not-so-obvious disadvantages, including security concerns. A tape holding all your sensitive data can be restored by you or by anyone who has access to the tape. There are well-documented cases of stolen tapes and the resulting stolen data. When you make any backups, you're responsible for storing the tapes in a secure location.

Incremental Backups

An *incremental backup* is much faster than a full backup because only the files that have changed since the last full or incremental backup are included in it. For example, if you do a full backup on Tuesday and an incremental on Thursday, only the files that have changed since Tuesday will be backed up. Because an incremental backup copies less data than a full backup, backup times are significantly reduced.

On the other hand, incremental backups take longer to restore than full backups. When you are restoring from an incremental backup, you need the last full backup tape and each incremental tape done since the last full backup. In addition, these tapes must be restored in order. Suppose that you do a full backup on Friday and incremental backups on Monday, Tuesday, and Wednesday. If the server fails on Thursday, you will need four tapes: Friday's full backup and the three incremental backups.

Differential Backups

Many people confuse differential backups and incremental backups, but they are very different from one another. Whereas an incremental backup backs up everything from the last full or incremental backup, a *differential backup* backs up only the files that have been created or changed since the last full backup.

When restoring from a differential backup, you need only two tapes: the latest full backup and the latest differential. Depending on how dynamic the data is, the differential backup could still take some time. Essentially, differential backups provide the middle ground between incremental and full backups.

EXAM ALERT

What to Use in a Backup Cycle   In a backup cycle, incremental backups and a differential backup must be combined with a full backup to get a complete copy of the data on a drive.

EXAM ALERT

Understand the Backup Types   For the Network+ exam, make sure that you understand what is involved in backing up and restoring data for all the backup types (for example, how many tapes are used and in what order they must be restored).

REVIEW BREAK

A Comparison of Backup Methods

The backup software determines what data has changed since the last full backup, by checking a setting known as the *archive bit*. When a file is created, moved, or changed, the archive bit is set to indicate that the changed file must be backed up.

Full backups do not concern themselves with the archive bit because all data is backed up. However, a full backup resets the archive bit after the files have been copied to the tape. Differential backups use the archive bit but do not clear it because the information is needed for the next differential backup. Incremental backups clear the archive bit so that unnecessary files aren't backed up. Table 12.4 summarizes the characteristics of the different backup methods.

TABLE 12.4   Comparison of Backup Methods

Method	What Is Backed Up	Restore Procedure	Archive Bit
Full	All data	All data is restored from a single tape.	Does not use the archive bit but clears it after files have been copied to tape
Incremental	All data changed since the last full or incremental backup	The restore procedure requires several tapes: the latest full backup and all incremental tapes since the last full backup.	Uses the archive bit and clears it after a file is saved to disk
Differential	All data changed since the last full backup	The restore procedure requires the latest full backup tape and the latest differential backup tape.	Uses the archive bit but does not clear it

EXAM ALERT

Clearing the Archive Bit   On the Network+ exam it is likely that you will be asked to identify what backup methods clear the archive bit from a changed or created file.

Backup Rotation Schedules

You can use a backup rotation schedule in conjunction with a backup method. Organizations use many different rotations, but most are variations on a single popular rotation strategy: the *Grandfather-Father-Son (GFS)* rotation.

GFS is the most widely used rotation method. It uses separate tapes for monthly, weekly, and daily backups. A common GFS strategy requires 12 tapes. Four tapes are used for daily backups, Monday through Thursday; these are the son tapes. Five tapes are used for weekly backups, perhaps each Friday; these are the father tapes. Finally, three tapes are used for a monthly rotation; these are the grandfather tapes.

Using the GFS rotation, you can retrieve lost information from the previous day, previous week, and several previous months. Adding tapes to the monthly rotation lets you go back even further to retrieve data. Of course, the further back you go, the less current (and perhaps less usable) the information is. More tapes also make the rotation more complex.

Many organizations don't follow the GFS strategy by the book; instead, they create their own backup regimes. Regardless of the backup strategy used, a well-designed backup rotation is an integral part of system administration and should follow guidelines that allow for several retrieval points.

Backup Best Practices

When you're designing a backup strategy, consider some general best practices. These best practices ensure that when you need it, the backup you are depending on will be available:

- ▶ **Test your backups**—After a backup is completed, you have no idea whether the backup was successful and whether you will be able to retrieve needed data from it. Learning this information after your system has crashed is too late. To make sure that the backups work, it is important to periodically restore them.

- ▶ **Confirm the backup logs**—Most backup software generates log files after a backup procedure. After a backup is completed, read the backup logs to look for any documented errors that may have occurred during the backup procedure. Keep in mind that reading the backup-generated logs is no substitute for occasionally testing a restore. A completely unsuccessful backup might generate no documented errors.

- ▶ **Label the backup cartridges**—When you use many tapes in a rotation, label the cartridges to prevent reusing a tape and recording over something you need. The label should include the date of the backup and whether it was a full, incremental, or differential backup.

- ▶ **Rotate backups offsite**—Keeping all the tape backups in the server room or elsewhere in the same location as the server can be a problem. If the server location is damaged (by fire or flood, for example), you could lose all the data on the server as well as all your backups. Use an offsite tape rotation scheme to store current copies of backups in a secure offsite location.

- ▶ **Use new tapes**—Over time, tape cartridges can wear out and become unreliable. To combat this problem, periodically introduce new tapes into the tape rotation and destroy the old tapes.

- ▶ **Password-protect the backups**—As an added measure of security, it is a good idea to password-protect your backups. That way, if they fall into the wrong hands, they are protected by a password.

TIP

Write Protection   Tape cartridges often use a write protection tab similar to the ones found on 3.5-inch floppy disks. It is a good idea to write-protect a tape cartridge after a backup so that it will not be overwritten accidentally.

Designing an effective backup strategy is one of the most important considerations for a network administrator, and therefore, it is an important topic area for the Network+ exam. Remember that the preservation of data is a foremost consideration when approaching network management.

Offsite Storage

The type of backup to use and the frequency of these backups are critical considerations for any organization. Another backup decision that must be made is how and where backups are to be stored. It is easy to perform a backup and store the tapes onsite, perhaps in a locked room, but backup tapes rotation schedules should include a consideration for offsite backup.

Offsite data storage is an important element because it allows backups to be accessed should the original location be unavailable. Even though the key feature of backups is its role in guaranteeing the availability of data, it is not without its risks.

For many organizations, backups are often the weak link in the security chain because the item of most value to an organization, and to a criminal, is normally the data. Many security measures can be used to protect data while it is inside a controlled environment. But what happens when it is taken outside that environment?

When a data backup leaves your server environment, the degree of control over that tape and the data on it is diminished. An organization can spend millions of dollars building a state-of-the-art server environment, but if the security of data backups is not fully considered, it really is a false sense of security. Here are some precautions that you can take to protect your valuable data when it leaves the server environment:

▶ **Password protection**—Tape backup software commonly has a password feature that allows each tape to be password-protected. The password must be entered before the tape is restored or viewed.

▶ **Physical locks**—Use physically lockable tape cases for transporting the tapes. As well as providing protection against data theft, tape cases also provide a degree of protection against accidental damage.

▶ **Registered couriers**—When transferring tapes between sites, use a trusted company employee or a registered secure courier service.

▶ **Secure storage**—Ensure that the location at which the tapes are stored is sufficiently secure. Having an employee take tapes home may provide a cheap offsite storage system, but it provides a low level of security for your valuable data.

▶ **Verification of data integrity**—If possible, when backup tapes reach their destination, they should be checked to ensure that they are the correct tapes and that they contain the correct data.

▶ **Encryption**—If facilities exist and the data is deemed sufficiently vital, the use of a data encryption system should be considered.

▶ **Knowledge restriction**—Confine knowledge of the backup and storage procedures to only those individuals who need the information.

The safety of backed-up data should be given at least the same considerations as the safety of data held inside your environment. When data leaves your site, it is exposed to a wide range of threats. Securing data when it leaves the site is a major security task for any organization.

Hot and Cold Spares

The impact that a failed component has on a system or network depends largely on predisaster preparation and on the recovery strategies used. Hot and cold spares represent a strategy for recovering from failed components.

Hot Spare and Hot Swapping

Hot spares give system administrators the ability to quickly recover from component failure. A hot spare, for example, is widely used by the RAID system to automatically failover to a spare hard drive should one of the other drives in the RAID array fail. A hot spare does not require any manual intervention, rather a redundant drive resides in the system at all times, just waiting to take over if another drive fails. With the RAID array continuing to function, the failed drive can be removed at a later time. Even though hot-spare technology adds an extra level of protection to your system, after a drive has failed and the hot spare has been used, the situation should be remedied as soon as possible.

Hot swapping is the ability to replace a failed component while the system is running. Perhaps the most commonly identified hot-swap component is the hard drive. In certain RAID configurations, when a hard drive crashes, hot swapping allows you simply to take the failed drive out of the server and install a new one.

The benefits of hot swapping are clear in that it allows a failed component to be recognized and replaced without compromising system availability. Depending on the system's configuration, the new hardware will normally be recognized automatically by both the current hardware and the operating system. Today, most internal and external RAID subsystems support the hot swapping feature. Some other hot swappable components include power supplies and hard disks.

Cold Spare and Cold Swapping

The term *cold spare* refers to a component such as a hard disk that resides within a computer system but requires manual intervention in case of component failure. A hot spare engages automatically, but a cold spare may require configurations settings or some other action to engage it. A cold spare configuration typically requires a reboot of the system.

The term *cold spare* has also been used to refer to a redundant component stored outside the actual system but kept in case of component failure. To replace the failed component with a cold spare, the system would need to be powered down.

Cold swapping refers to replacing components only after the system is completely powered off. This strategy is by far the least attractive for servers because the services provided by the server will be unavailable for the duration of the cold swap procedure. Modern systems have come a long way to ensure that cold swapping is a rare occurrence. For some situations and for some components, however, cold swapping is the only method to replace a failed component.

> **NOTE**
>
> **Warm Swapping**   The term *warm swap* is sometimes applied to a device that can be replaced while the system is still running but that requires some kind of manual intervention to disable the device before it can be removed. Using a PCI hot plug is technically a warm swap strategy because it requires that the individual PCI slot be powered down before the PCI card is replaced. Of course, a warm swap is not as efficient as a hot swap, but it is far and away better than a cold swap.

Hot, Warm, and Cold Sites

A disaster recovery plan may include the provision for a recovery site that can be brought quickly into play. These sites fall into three categories: hot, warm, and cold. The need for each of these types of site depends largely on the business you are in and the funds available. Disaster recovery sites represent the ultimate in precautions for organizations that really need it. As a result, they aren't cheap.

The basic concept of a disaster recovery site is that it can provide a base from which the company can be operated during a disaster. The disaster recovery site is not normally intended to provide a desk for every employee but is intended more as a means to allow key personnel to continue the core business function.

In general, a *cold recovery site* is a site that can be up and operational in a relatively short time span, such as a day or two. Provision of services, such as telephone lines and power, is taken care of, and the basic office furniture may be in place, but there is unlikely to be any computer equipment, even though the building may well have a network infrastructure and a room ready to act as a server room. In most cases cold sites provide the physical location and basic services.

Cold sites are useful if there is some forewarning of a potential problem. Generally, cold sites are used by organizations that can weather the storm for a day or two before they get back up and running. If you are the regional office of a major company, it might be possible to have one of the other divisions take care of business until you are ready to go, but if you are the one and only office in the company, you might need something a little hotter.

For organizations with the dollars and the desire, *hot recovery sites* represent the ultimate in fault-tolerance strategies. Like cold recovery sites, hot sites are designed to provide only enough facilities to continue the core business function, but hot recovery sites are set up to be ready to go at a moment's notice.

A hot recovery site includes phone systems with the phone lines already connected. Data networks are also be in place, with any necessary routers and switches plugged in and ready to go. Hot sites may have desktop PCs installed and waiting, and server areas replete with the necessary hardware to support business-critical functions. In other words, within moments, the hot site can become a fully functioning element of an organization. Key to this is having network data available and current.

The issue that confronts potential hot recovery site users is simply that of cost. Office space is expensive at the best of times, but having space sitting idle 99.9 percent of the time can seem like a tremendously poor use of money. A popular strategy to get around this problem is to use space provided in a disaster recovery facility, which is basically a building, maintained by a third-party company, in which various businesses rent space. Space is apportioned, usually, on how much each company pays.

Sitting in between the hot and cold recovery sites is the *warm site*. A warm site typically has computers but not configured ready to go. This means that data may need to be upgraded or other manual interventions performed before the network is again operational. The time it takes to get a warm site operational lands right in the middle of the other two options as does the cost.

EXAM ALERT

Hot, Warm, and Cold A hot site mirrors the organization's production network and will be able to assume network operations at a moment's notice. Warm sites have the equipment needed to bring the network to an operational state but require configuration and potential database updates. Warm sites have network data but may not be completely up-to-date. A cold site has the space available with basic service but typically requires equipment and maybe data delivery.

Chapter Summary

In some networks, VLANs are used to segment a LAN into logical segments. This segmentation allows for increased organization and security for the logical LANs. Once a LAN is divided, broadcasts are isolated to the segmented LAN segment.

Antivirus software has become an important part of today's network environment. Such software is designed to detect and remove many different types of malicious software including viruses, worms, spyware, and Trojan horses.

This chapter also explored two important networking concepts: fault tolerance and disaster recovery. Although many people think fault tolerance and disaster recovery are one and the same, they are in fact different, but equally important, concepts.

Fault tolerance usually refers to the measures network administrators use to ensure that data and network services are always available to network users. A strong fault-tolerance strategy does not happen by accident; rather, you must consider many factors when choosing the best fault-tolerance strategies for a specific organization.

Because availability is such a huge issue and server downtime is so costly, most hardware components within a server need to be considered part of a fault-tolerance solution. Hard drives typically receive the most attention because they're 50% more likely to fail than any other component. The mechanism used to protect against such failures is RAID.

Several RAID levels are available today. The most common are RAID levels 0, 1, and 5. Although RAID 0 is a RAID level, it does not offer any fault tolerance, but it does offer performance improvements over using a single disk. RAID 1 uses disk mirroring to establish fault tolerance but suffers from 50% overhead and limited storage capacity. The RAID level of choice for organizations that can afford it is RAID 5. RAID 5 stripes data and parity information over several disks. The parity information can be used to re-create data in the event that a hard drive in the array fails.

Other fault-tolerance measures include using UPSs, redundant components, and sometimes redundant servers.

Disaster recovery involves having in place measures that can be used when the system goes down. To protect data from disaster, you need backups. Three key types of backups are available: full, incremental, and differential. A full backup makes a copy of all data, an incremental backup makes a copy of the data that has changed since the last full backup or the latest incremental backup, and a differential backup saves everything that has changed since the last full backup.

In addition to backup methods, a backup rotation strategy ensures that data is sufficiently recoverable. The most common backup rotation strategy is the GFS rotation. This type of rotation requires numerous tapes for daily, weekly, and monthly backups.

Key Terms

- archive bit
- backup rotation
- blackout
- brownout
- differential backup
- disaster recovery
- disk mirroring
- disk striping with parity
- fault tolerance
- full backup
- GFS
- incremental backup
- MAC address–based VLAN
- memory
- NIC

- port-based VLAN
- power supply
- processor
- protocol-based VLAN
- RAID
- RAID 0
- RAID 10
- sag
- server clustering
- spike
- standby server
- surge
- UPS
- VLAN

Apply Your Knowledge

Exercise

10.1   Performing a Full Backup

You have recently been employed as the network administrator for a large pharmaceutical company. On your first day of work, you notice that no backup has been performed for more than six months. You immediately decide to perform a full backup and schedule backups to occur at regular intervals.

You use Windows 2000 Server's Backup Wizard utility to back up a few data files and automate the process to recur automatically based on a schedule you construct.

Estimated time: 20 minutes

1. Select Start, Programs, Accessories, System Tools, Backup. The Backup [Untitled] screen appears.

2. Select the Schedule Jobs tab and click the Add Job button. The Backup Wizard screen appears.

3. Click Next on the Backup Wizard screen.

4. Choose Back Up Selected Files, Drives, or Network Data and click Next.

5. Select the data you want to back up. The window contains a directory of files similar to Windows Explorer, with one added twist: A check box appears next to each directory item. Click the box to select an item to be backed up. Note that if you click on a folder, you will back up everything from that point in the directory down.

6. Choose one or two folders that contain a few files. Click Next.

7. Choose the media type to which you want to save your data. In this project, you'll save your back-up to disk, so choose the File in the Backup Media Type drop-down box.

8. If the directory you want to use doesn't exist, you can create it by clicking the Browse button and navigating to where you want to put the backup file you are about to create. (Click the New Folder icon in the browse window.)

9. Specify the type of backup you want to perform. Choose Normal and click Next.

10. Select Verify Data After Backup if you want the operating system to check to make sure that the backup has been made. Click Next.

NOTE

Test Recoveries   Continue to perform test recoveries to be sure that you can restore your data.

---

11. Choose whether you want to add this backup to the end of any previous backups or whether you want to replace an old backup with this new one. For this project, choose Replace the Data on the Media with This Backup. Click Next.

12. The next window lets you assign Backup Label and Media Label names. Leave the defaults in place and click Next. A Set Account Information dialog box might appear. Windows 2000 allows you to run the job under another account name/password if you want. If you get this choice, enter your administrator account username and password. (The password will be whatever you estab-lished when you installed Windows 2000 Server or whatever you changed it to.)

13. The When to Backup screen appears. Give the backup job you are creating the name BackupTest and click Set Schedule.

14. The Schedule Job screen appears, and you can schedule when you want the backup job to occur. Set whatever schedule you want and click OK. You return to the When to Backup Screen; click Next.

15. On the Completing the Backup Wizard screen, click Finish to create the job. The backup utility cre-ates the job, and the folders/files you selected will be backed up according to the schedule you selected.

16. You can view the status of the backup job or make changes to it by using the Task Scheduler. To use the Task Scheduler, choose Start, Settings, Control Panel. When the Control Panel opens, double-click the Scheduled Tasks icon. You should see the backup job you just created. You can double-click it to edit the job.

Exam Questions

1. What is the minimum number of disks required for a RAID 5 array?

   ○   **a.** 2

   ○   **b.** 5

   ○   **c.** 1 physical and 1 logical

   ○   **d.** 3

2. What RAID level uses disk mirroring to provide fault tolerance?

   ○   **a.** RAID 1

   ○   **b.** RAID 0

   ○   **c.** RAID 5

   ○   **d.** RAID 2

3. Which of the following backup methods require the archive bit to be cleared? (Choose the two best answers.)

   ○   **a.** Full

   ○   **b.** Incremental

   ○   **c.** Differential

   ○   **d.** Mirror image

4. As network administrator, you have been asked to implement a backup and restore method that requires only a total of two tape sets. Which of the following backup pairs would you use?

   ○   **a.** Full, incremental, and differential

   ○   **b.** Differential, incremental

   ○   **c.** Full, differential

   ○   **d.** This cannot be done.

5. Which of the following are valid ways to assign computers to a VLAN? (Choose the three best answers.)

   ○ a. Protocol assignment

   ○ b. Port-based assignment

   ○ c. NetBIOS computer name

   ○ d. MAC address

6. How many hard disks are required to establish a RAID 1 solution?

   ○ a. 8

   ○ b. 4

   ○ c. 6

   ○ d. 2

7. You are the network administrator for a company that operates from 7 a.m. to 9 p.m. Monday through Friday. Your boss requires that a backup be performed nightly but does not want the back-up to interfere with network operations. Full backups have been started at 9:30 p.m. and have taken until 8 a.m. to complete. What strategy would you suggest to correct the backup issue?

   ○ a. Weekly full backups, incremental backups on Mondays, and differential backups every other weekday

   ○ b. Full backup performed on the weekend and incremental backups performed on weekdays

   ○ c. Differential backups performed on weekends and a full backup every other weekday evening

   ○ d. Weekly full backups combined with weekend differential backups

8. Which of the following power-related problems is associated with a short-term voltage drop?

   ○ a. Surge

   ○ b. Brownout

   ○ c. Sag

   ○ d. Spike

9. Which of the following fault-tolerant RAID levels offers the best read and write performance?

   ○ a. RAID 0

   ○ b. RAID 1

   ○ c. RAID 5

   ○ d. RAID 10

10. Which of the following are fault-tolerance measures associated with network adapters? (Choose the two best answers.)

    ○ **a.** Warm swapping

    ○ **b.** Adapter teaming

    ○ **c.** Packet fragment recovery

    ○ **d.** Secondary I/O recovery

11. Which of the following devices cannot be implemented in a fault-tolerant configuration?

    ○ **a.** Power supply

    ○ **b.** Processor

    ○ **c.** NIC

    ○ **d.** Memory

12. What is the storage capacity of a RAID 1 array that uses two 40GB hard disks?

    ○ **a.** 80GB

    ○ **b.** 40GB minus the parity calculation

    ○ **c.** 40GB

    ○ **d.** 80GB minus the parity calculation

13. Which of the following are valid reasons to use a UPS? (Choose the three best answers.)

    ○ **a.** Data availability

    ○ **b.** To prevent damage to hardware

    ○ **c.** Increased network speeds

    ○ **d.** To prevent damage to data

14. How many tapes are typically used in a GFS tape rotation?

    ○ **a.** 14

    ○ **b.** 13

    ○ **c.** 12

    ○ **d.** 11

15. As a network administrator, you have been asked to implement a RAID solution that offers high performance. Fault tolerance is not a concern. Which RAID level are you likely to use?

    ○ a. RAID 0

    ○ b. RAID 1

    ○ c. RAID 2

    ○ d. RAID 5

    ○ e. RAID 10

16. What is the best way to verify that your backup procedures are working?

    ○ a. Check the system logs.

    ○ b. Perform periodic test restores.

    ○ c. Introduce new cartridges into the tape rotation.

    ○ d. Use the Verify option when backing up data.

17. Which of the following recovery sites requires the delivery of computer equipment and an update of all network data?

    ○ a. Cold site

    ○ b. Warm site

    ○ c. Hot site

    ○ d. None of the above

18. Which of the following uses redundant hard disk controllers?

    ○ a. Disk duplexing

    ○ b. RAID 0

    ○ c. Disk duplication

    ○ d. RAID 5

19. You have installed five 15GB hard disks for your server in a RAID 5 array. How much storage space will be available for data?

    ○ a. 75GB

    ○ b. 60GB

    ○ c. 30GB

    ○ d. 45GB

20. While digging through an old storage closet, you find two 10GB hard disks. What RAID levels could you implement with them? (Choose the two best answers.)

    ○ **a.** RAID 5

    ○ **b.** RAID 0

    ○ **c.** RAID 10

    ○ **d.** RAID 1

Answers to Exam Questions

1. **d.** At least three hard disks are required in a RAID 5 array. None of the other answers are valid. For more information, see the section "Understanding Fault Tolerance" in this chapter.

2. **a.** Disk mirroring is defined by RAID 1. Raid 0 is disk striping, which offers no fault tolerance. RAID 5 is disk striping with parity. RAID 2 is not a commonly implemented RAID level. For more information, see the section "Understanding Fault Tolerance" in this chapter.

3. **a, b.** The archive bit is reset in both a full backup and an incremental backup. Differential backups do not change the status of the archive bit. Mirror image is not an accepted backup type. For more information, see the section "Disaster Recovery" in this chapter.

4. **c.** A full backup combined with a differential backup requires only two tapes to do a complete restore, assuming that each backup set fits on a single tape. Full and incremental backups might need more than two tapes. Differential and incremental backups must be combined with a full backup to be effective. Answer d is not valid. For more information, see the section "Disaster Recovery" in this chapter.

5. **a, b, d.** VLANs can be created by using protocol assignments, by defining the ports on a device as belonging to a VLAN, or by using MAC addresses. VLANs cannot be created by using the NetBIOS computer name. For more information, see the section "VLANs" in this chapter.

6. **d.** Two disks are required to create a RAID 1 array. All the other answers are invalid. For more information, see the section "Understanding Fault Toleranc," in this chapter.

7. **b.** By making a full backup on the weekend and incremental backups during the week, you should be able to complete the backups without interfering with the normal working hours of the company. All the other answers are invalid. For more information, see the section "Disaster Recovery" in this chapter.

8. **c.** A sag is a short-term voltage drop. A brownout is also a voltage drop, but it lasts longer than a sag. A surge is an increase in power that lasts a few seconds. A spike is a power increase that lasts a few milliseconds. For more information, see the section "Understanding Fault Tolerance" in this chapter.

9. **d.** RAID 10 offers the performance advantages of RAID 0 and the fault-tolerance capabilities of RAID 1. RAID 0 is not a fault-tolerant solution. RAID 1 and RAID 5 offer fault tolerance but do not increase performance. For more information, see the section "Understanding Fault Tolerance" in this chapter.

10. **a, b.** In server systems, warm swapping allows network adapters to be swapped out without the server being powered off. Adapter teaming allows multiple NICs to be logically grouped together. If one of the NICs fails, the other NICs in the group can continue to provide network connectivity. Adapters in a team can also be grouped together to increase the available bandwidth. Answers c and d are not valid answers. For more information, see the section "Understanding Fault Tolerance" in this chapter.

11. **d.** There is no accepted fault-tolerance strategy for coping with a failed memory module. All the other hardware components listed can be implemented in a fault-tolerant configuration. For more information, see the section "Understanding Fault Tolerance" in this chapter.

12. **c.** A RAID 1 array requires an amount of disk space equivalent to that of the mirrored drive. Therefore, in a RAID 1 array of 80GB, only 40GB will be available for data storage. None of the other answers are valid. For more information, see the section "Understanding Fault Tolerance" in this chapter.

13. **a, b, d.** UPSs can prevent damage to hardware and damage to data caused by fluctuations in the power supply. They can also promote the availability of data by keeping a server running in the event of a power outage. A UPS does not increase the speed of the network. For more information, see the section "Understanding Fault Tolerance" in this chapter.

14. **c.** The standard GFS rotation uses 12 tapes. None of the other answers are valid. For more information, see the section "Disaster Recovery" in this chapter.

15. **a.** RAID 0 offers the highest level of performance but does not offer any fault tolerance. If the performance of RAID 0 is required along with fault tolerance, RAID 10 is a better choice. RAID 1 offers fault tolerance but no increase in performance. For more information, see the section "Understanding Fault Tolerance" in this chapter.

16. **b.** Performing periodic test restores is the only way to be absolutely sure that your backup and restore procedures and systems are working correctly. All the other options are best practices, but doing a test restore is the only way to be sure that the backups are working. For more information, see the section "Disaster Recovery" in this chapter.

17. **a.** A cold site provides an alternate location but typically not much more. A cold site often requires the delivery of computer equipment and other services. For more information, see the section "Hot, Warm, and Cold Sites" in this chapter.

18. **a.** Disk duplexing is an implementation of RAID 1 (disk mirroring) that places each of the drives on a separate controller. None of the other answers are valid. For more information, see the section "Understanding Fault Tolerance" in this chapter.

19. **b.** In a RAID 5 configuration, a space equivalent to one whole drive is used for the storage of parity information. In this question, this requirement equates to 15GB. Therefore, in a 75GB RAID 5 array, 60GB is available for data storage. None of the other answers are valid. For more information, see the section "Understanding Fault Tolerance" in this chapter.

20. **b, d.** Both RAID 0 and RAID 1 use two disks. The difference between the two implementations is that RAID 1 offers fault tolerance through disk mirroring, whereas RAID 0 stripes the data across the drives but does not offer any fault tolerance. RAID 5 requires at least three disks, and RAID 10 requires at least four disks if the entire hard disk is to be used. For more information, see the section "Understanding Fault Tolerance" in this chapter.

Suggested Readings and Resources

1. Olexa, Ron. *Implementing 802.11, 802.16, and 802.20 Wireless Networks: Planning, Troubleshooting, and Operations* (Communications Engineering). Newnes Publishing, 2004.

2. "Wikipedia," www.wikipedia.org.

3. Computer networking device information, www.3com.com.

4. "Computer Networking Tutorials and Advice," compnetworking.about.com.

5. "TechEncyclopedia," www.techencyclopedia.com.

6. "Networking Technology Information from Cisco," www.cisco.com/public/products_tech.shtml.

CHAPTER 13

Troubleshooting Tools and Utilities

Objectives

This chapter covers the following CompTIA-specified objectives for the "Network Support" section of the Network+ exam.

4.1 Given a troubleshooting scenario, select the appropriate network utility from the following:

- ▶ **Tracert/traceroute**

- ▶ **ping**

- ▶ **arp**

- ▶ **netstat**

- ▶ **nbtstat**

- ▶ **ipconfig/ifconfig**

- ▶ **winipcfg**

- ▶ **nslookup/dig**

- ▶ Many TCP/IP troubleshooting utilities are available. Knowing which one to use in a given scenario is an essential skill for the real world and the Network+ exam.

4.2 Given output from a network diagnostic utility (for example, those utilities listed in objective 4.1), identify the utility and interpret the output.

- ▶ With the wide range of troubleshooting tools available to you, tracking down a network problem is easier than ever. But to put the information provided by the tools to good use, you must effectively interpret the tool's output.

Outline

Study Strategies

▶ Read the information presented in the chapter, paying special attention to tables, Notes, and Exam Alerts.

▶ This chapter discusses specific utilities that are used in troubleshooting scenarios. Try to experiment with each of the utilities discussed to familiarize yourself with their usage, and the output that they generate.

▶ Most of the utilities discussed have a built-in help feature that discusses the options available for each command in more detail. Use this to learn more about the options available for the command.

▶ Complete the Challenge Exercises, and the Exercises at the end of the chapter. These exercises are designed to give you practical experience of using the utilities discussed.

▶ Complete the Exam Questions at the end of the chapter. They are designed to simulate the type of questions you will be asked in the Network+ exam.

Introduction

There are two certainties in the networking world. The first is that you will be working on networks that use Transmission Control Protocol/Internet Protocol (TCP/IP). The second is that at some point, you will be troubleshooting those networks. This chapter focuses on identifying the TCP/IP utilities commonly used when working with TCP/IP networks and explains how to use those utilities in the troubleshooting process.

> **EXAM ALERT**
>
> **Windows Versus Unix and Linux** Previous versions of the Network+ exam have focused very strongly on Windows operating system utilities at the expense of other platforms such as Unix and Linux. Although there is still a bias toward Windows in the newest version of the Network+ exam, Unix and Linux are now better represented. This is reflected in the objectives for the Network+ exam, and as a result, in the coverage in this book.

Troubleshooting Tools

Objective:

4.1 Given a troubleshooting scenario, select the appropriate network utility from the following:

▶ Tracert/traceroute

▶ ping

▶ arp

▶ netstat

▶ nbtstat

▶ ipconfig/ifconfig

▶ winipcfg

▶ nslookup/dig

The best way to work through this chapter is to try each of the utilities as they are discussed. This will give you a better idea of how the tools are used and what they are designed to do. These tools are the core utilities used in the troubleshooting of TCP/IP networks and are used extensively in real-world environments. The following sections describe these utilities:

▶ ping

▶ Tracert/traceroute

▶ arp

- ► netstat

- ► nbtstat

- ► ipconfig/ifconfig

- ► winipcfg

- ► nslookup/dig

- ► route

Note that not all the tools discussed here are available on every operating system. However, the discussion begins by looking at one that is not only available on all platforms but also is arguably the most used—and most useful—of all troubleshooting utilities: ping.

> **NOTE**
>
> Many of the utilities discussed in this chapter have a help facility that can be accessed by typing the command followed by a "/?" or a "-?". On a Windows system, for example, you can get help on the netstat utility by typing the command netstat /? Sometimes, using a utility with an invalid switch will also bring up the help screen.

The ping Utility

ping is a command-line utility designed to test connectivity between systems on a TCP/IP-based network. Its basic function is to answer one simple question: "Can I connect to another host?" ping can be a network administrator's right hand; most TCP/IP troubleshooting procedures begin with the ping utility and, if necessary, work from there. We say "if necessary" because the information provided by the ping command can often isolate the cause of a problem so well that further action is not needed.

> **EXAM ALERT**
>
> **Command Output** For each of the commands discussed in this chapter, make sure that you are able to identify the output. On the Network+ exam, you will likely be asked to identify the output from these commands. This aspect of each tool's use is covered in more detail later in this chapter.

ping works by using Internet Control Message Protocol (ICMP) packets to ascertain whether another system is connected to the network and can respond. A successful ping request requires that a packet, called an *ICMP echo request*, be sent to a remote host. If the remote host receives the packet, it sends an *ICMP echo reply* in return, and the ping is a success. Figure 13.1 shows the output from a successful ping request on a Windows Server 2003 system.

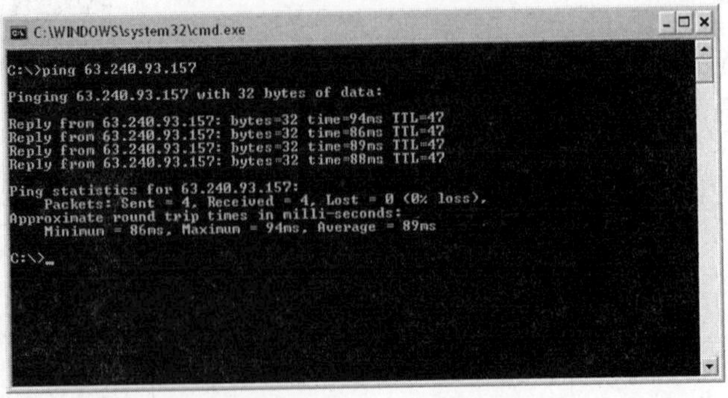

FIGURE 13.1 A successful ping request.

Notice in Figure 13.1 that four packets are sent to the remote host. These packets are 32 bytes in size and took 94ms, 86ms, 89ms, and 88ms to reach their destination. The time= section of the ping command output is often important because a high number could indicate congestion on the network or a routing problem. The version of the ping utility shown in Figure 13.1 is from a Windows Server 2003 system. Other versions might send more packets or larger packets.

Sometimes ping requests fail. When a ping fails, you know that you are unable to connect to a remote host. Figure 13.2 shows the output from a failed ping command.

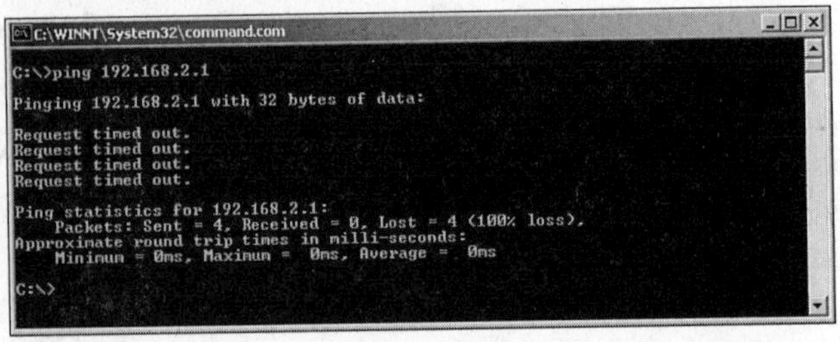

FIGURE 13.2 A failed ping request.

Troubleshooting with ping

Although ping does not completely isolate problems, you can use it to help identify where a problem lies. When troubleshooting with ping, you take the following steps:

1. ping the IP address of your local loopback, using the command ping 127.0.0.1. If this command is successful, you know that the TCP/IP protocol suite is installed correctly on your system and functioning. If you are unable to ping the local loopback, TCP/IP might need to be reloaded or reconfigured on the machine you are using.

2. ping the IP address assigned to your local network interface card (NIC). If the ping is successful, you know that your interface is functioning on the network and has TCP/IP correctly installed. If you are unable to ping the local interface, TCP/IP might not be bound correctly to the card, or the network card drivers might be improperly installed.

NOTE

The Loopback Adapter The *loopback* is a special function within the TCP/IP protocol stack that is provided for troubleshooting purposes. The Class A IP address 127.X.X.X is reserved for the loopback; although convention dictates that you use 127.0.0.1, you can use any address in the 127.X.X.X range, except for the network number itself (127.0.0.0) and the broadcast address (127.255.255.255). You can also `ping` by using the default hostname for the local system, which is called `localhost` (for example, `ping localhost`).

3. `ping` the IP address of another knowing working node on your local network. By doing so you can determine whether the computer you are using can see other computers on the network. If you can `ping` other devices on your local network, you have network connectivity.

   If you cannot `ping` other devices on your local network and you were able to `ping` your local network card, you might not be connected to the network correctly, or there might be a cable problem on the computer.

4. After you've confirmed that you have network connectivity for the local network, you can verify connectivity to a remote network by sending a `ping` to the IP address of the default gateway.

5. If you are able to `ping` the default gateway, you can verify remote connectivity by sending a `ping` the IP address of a system on a remote network.

EXAM ALERT

Connectivity Problems On the Network+ exam, you might be asked to relate the correct procedure for using `ping` for a connectivity problem.

TIP

Testing TCP/IP Installations To test a system to see whether TCP/IP is installed, working, and configured correctly, you can `ping` the loopback address and then `ping` the IP address of the local system (`localhost`).

By using just the `ping` command in the manner described, you can confirm network connectivity to not only the local network but also to a remote network. The whole process requires as much time as it takes to type in the command—and you can do it all from a single location.

If you are an optimistic person, you can perform step 5 first. If that works, all the other steps will also work, saving you the need to test them. If your step 5 trial fails, you can go back to step 1 and start the troubleshooting process from the beginning.

> **TIP**
>
> **ping Using DNS**   The ping examples used in this section show the ping command using the IP address of the remote host. It is also possible to ping the Domain Name Service (DNS) name of the remote host (for example, ping www.comptia.org, ping server1); this, of course, can be done only if your network uses a DNS server. On a Windows-based network, you can also ping by using the Network Basic Input/Output System (NetBIOS) computer name.

Switches for ping

If you've spent any time working with command-line utilities, you no doubt already know that every command is accompanied by a number of *switches*, or options. The switches let you customize the behavior of the command. Although some switches (we'll call them that from now on) are rarely used, others come in handy under a number of circumstances.

> **EXAM ALERT**
>
> **Switches**   Even the most obscure switches for the commands discussed in this chapter might appear on the Network+ exam.

The ping command offers several switches, the most widely used, -t, sends continuous packets rather than just a few. This switch sets the ping command to continue to ping the remote host until it is stopped by keyboard input. This switch is particularly helpful when you're troubleshooting connectivity issues such as a suspect cable. Table 13.1 shows the some of the more useful switches available for the ping command on a Windows 2000 or Windows Server 2003 system.

> **EXAM ALERT**
>
> **More Options**   Newer versions of Windows such as Windows XP and Windows Server 2003 have more switches for the ping command. These extra switches are not included on the Network+ exam.

TABLE 13.1   ping Switches on a Windows 2000 System

Switch	Description
-t	pings a device on the network until stopped. To stop it, press Ctrl+C.
-a	Tells the ping utility to resolve the IP address to a hostname as well as perform the ping.
-n count	Specifies the number of ping requests to send to the remote host. Example: ping -n 15 <IP address>.
-l size	Specifies the size of the ping request to send.

TABLE 13.1 *Continued*

Switch	Description
-f	Specifies that the "Don't Fragment" flag is set in the packet.
-i TTL	Specifies the time to live for the packet.
-v TOS	Specifies the type of service for the packet to be sent.
-r count	Records the route hops that the packet takes on its journey.
-w timeout	Specifies the timeout, in milliseconds, during which the ping utility should wait for each reply.

EXAM ALERT

More Switches Of the switches listed in Table 13.1, the ones most likely to appear on the Network+ exam are the -t, -a, and -n switches.

NOTE

ping Example Scenario Suppose that you have been asked to troubleshoot a computer system that is unable to print to a network printer. You have verified that the computer is logged on to the network with the correct username and password and that the printer is online and functioning. However, you still cannot print.

ping Example Solution In this scenario, it would be a good idea to use the ping command to determine whether the computer can see the printer. To do this, you can ping the IP address of the printer. If you successfully ping the printer, you know that the printer is working, as least as far as network connectivity is concerned. If you are unable to ping the network printer, there is a network problem. Try to ping a different device on the network; if you're successful, the network problem is likely with the printer.

The Trace Route Utility (Tracert/traceroute)

As great as ping is, sometimes it just isn't enough. In such cases, you need to reach for something a little stronger. Trace route is a TCP/IP utility used to track the path a packet takes to reach a remote host. Each of the network operating systems covered by Network+ provides a trace route utility, but the name of the command and the output vary slightly in each. Table 13.2 shows the trace route command syntax used in various operating systems.

NOTE

Order of commands Even though CompTIA lists Tracert and traceroute before the ping utility in the Network+ objectives, we decided to discuss ping first because it naturally leads into a discussion of the trace route utility.

TABLE 13.2   Trace Route Utility Commands

Operating System	Trace Route Command Syntax
Windows 2000/NT	`tracert <IP address>`
Novell NetWare	`iptrace`
Linux/Unix	`traceroute <IP address>`
Macintosh	`traceroute <IP address>`

What exactly does the trace route command trace? The simple answer, of course, is routes. Local area networks (LANs) and wide area networks (WANs) can have several routes that packets can follow to reach their destinations. These routes are kept in routing tables. Systems use the information from these routing tables to tell the packets how they will travel through the network. The trace route utility lets you track the path a packet takes through the network. Figure 13.3 shows the results of a successful trace route command in Windows Server 2000.

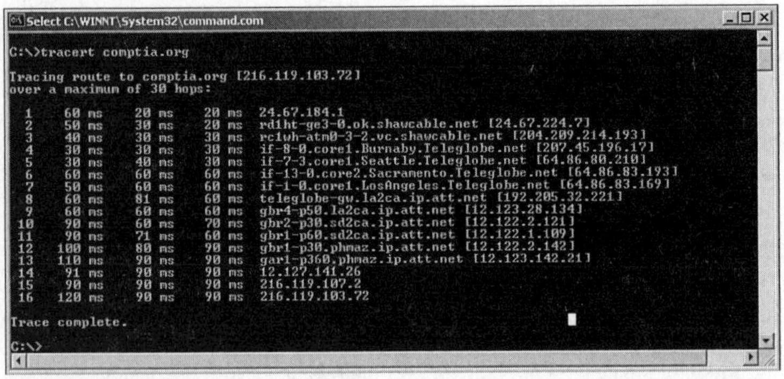

FIGURE 13.3   A successful trace route command in Windows 2000.

Not all trace route commands are as successful as the one in Figure 13.3. A trace route command that has an asterisk (*) in the entries shows that the particular hop was timed out. Several consecutive asterisks indicate a problem with the routing information or congestion on the network. Figure 13.4 shows an example of a failed trace route command.

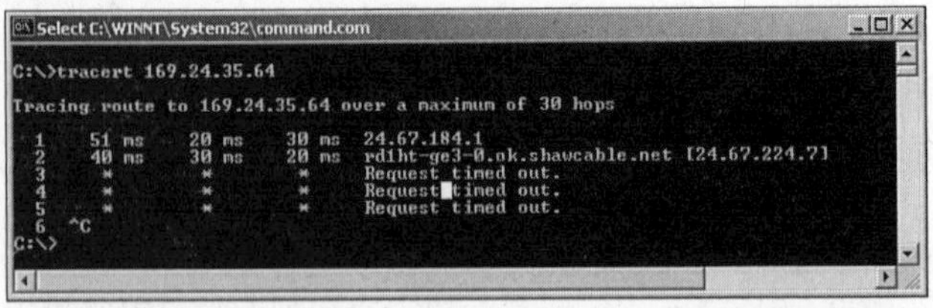

FIGURE 13.4   A failed trace route command from a Windows 2000 system.

EXAM ALERT

Isolating Bottlenecks   Because trace route reports the amount of time it takes to reach each host in the path, it is a useful tool for isolating bottlenecks in a network. You need to know this for the exam.

In the example shown in Figure 13.4, the route is traced over a number of hops before it times out on the next hop of the route. In this example, pressing Ctrl+C terminates the trace; but if the trace route command were left to its own devices, it would run to 30 steps, like the successful trace.

In a network troubleshooting situation, trace route is often used in concert with `ping`. First, you use trace route to determine where on a route the connectivity problem lies. Then, from the point of the problem, you can determine the possible cause of the problem by using `ping`.

NOTE

Trace Route Example Scenario   Suppose that a user on your network complains that she is unable to access files located in an offsite location. However, she can access all files within the local network.

Trace Route Example Solution   In this case, you could use the trace route command to determine how far the packet travels before it fails. You would probably perform the trace route command with the IP address of the computer holding the files in the offsite location. The results from the command would determine how far the packet reaches before it's dropped.

The `arp` Utility

As discussed in Chapter 6, "Working with TCP/IP," Address Resolution Protocol (ARP) is the part of the TCP/IP suite that resolves IP addresses to Media Access Control (MAC) addresses. Such a translation is necessary because even though systems use IP addresses to find each other, the low-level communication between devices occurs using the MAC address.

When two systems on an IP network want to communicate, they first establish each other's location by using the IP address. Then, ARP requests are sent to ascertain the MAC address of the devices so that they can communicate with each other. In a sense, the IP address can be thought of as the name by which a system can be found in a phone book. The MAC address is the actual phone number used to establish communication.

The ARP Cache

ARP translations are typically stored locally on systems in the ARP cache. But how does the MAC address from another computer system end up in your system's ARP cache? Each time you access another host, your system broadcasts to the ARP component of every host on the network. Because the IP address is embedded in the request, all systems other than the chosen one ignore the request, but the target system receives the request and replies accordingly. At this point both hosts record each other's MAC address in their local ARP cache, and these entries remain in the cache until they are timed out, which depends on how often they are accessed. If the ARP entry is reused, the time period is extended further.

The ARP table can hold two different types of entries: static and dynamic. Static entries do not expire and can be added to the ARP cache manually via the `-s` switch. Dynamic entries are added as the system accesses other hosts on the network.

> **TIP**
>
> **ARP and OSI**   ARP operates at the network layer of the Open Systems Interconnect (OSI) model.

To view the ARP cache on a Windows 2000 computer, you use the arp -a command. Figure 13.5 shows an example of an ARP cache, the result of using arp -a.

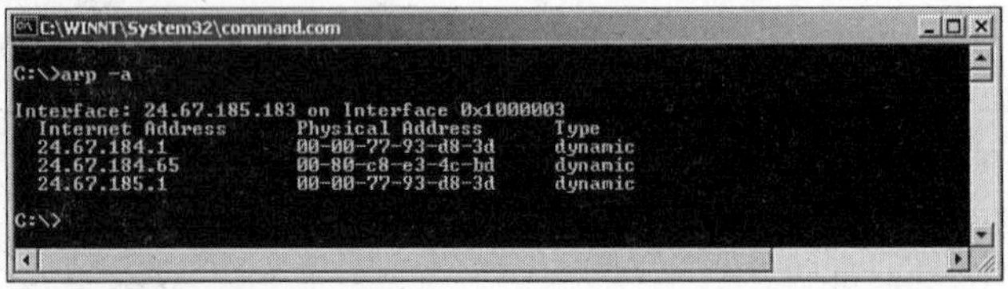

```
C:\WINNT\System32\command.com                                    _|□|x|

C:\>arp -a

Interface: 24.67.185.183 on Interface 0x1000003
  Internet Address      Physical Address      Type
  24.67.184.1           00-00-77-93-d8-3d     dynamic
  24.67.184.65          00-00-c8-e3-4c-bd     dynamic
  24.67.185.1           00-00-77-93-d8-3d     dynamic

C:\>
```

FIGURE 13.5   An ARP cache.

Switches for arp

As with the other command-line utilities discussed in this chapter, arp has a few associated switches. Table 13.3 lists some of the switches commonly used with the arp command.

TABLE 13.3   Commonly Used arp Command Switches

Switch	Description
-a	Displays the current ARP entries. If there is more than one interface, ARP resolution for each interface is displayed.
inet_addr	Resolves the MAC address of a remote system identified in the inet_addr field.
-N if_addr	Displays the ARP entries for a specific network interface.
-d inet_addr	Deletes the entry for the specified host.
-s inet_addr eth_addr	Allows you to add a static entry to the ARP cache. Must be used with both the IP address (inet_addr) and the MAC address (eth_addr).

> **NOTE**
>
> arp **Example Scenario**   Suppose that you receive a message on a client machine, stating that a duplicate IP address is being used on the network. What do you do?
>
> arp **Example Solution**   The arp command is well suited for troubleshooting duplicate IP addresses on a network. The ARP cache holds information, which includes the MAC address and its associated IP address. From this information, it is possible to determine where the IP conflict lies.

The netstat Utility

The netstat utility displays packet statistics such as how many packets have been sent and received from and to the system, as well as other related protocol information. It is also used to view both inbound and outbound TCP/IP network connections. This utility is popular with seasoned network administrators whose information needs go far beyond what utilities such as ping can provide.

On a Windows system, there are essentially four columns to view when using the netstat command without switches. The first is Proto, which identifies the protocol being used. The second is the Local Address column, which specifies the local address and the local port being used. Next is the Foreign Address column, which identifies the destination address and port used. Finally, the State column lists whether the connection has been established; this column is used to determine the current status of your TCP connections.

As with the other command-line utilities, you can use a number of available switches with the netstat command. Without using any of these switches, the output from a netstat command would resemble the output shown in Figure 13.6. Note that in its default usage, the netstat command shows outbound connections that have been established by TCP.

FIGURE 13.6   Output from a netstat command in Windows 2000.

Switches for netstat

A handful of switches are used with the netstat command. Table 13.4 shows the various switches on a Windows system.

TABLE 13.4   netstat Switches on Windows

Switch	Description
-a	Displays a list of the current connections and listening ports on the system.
-e	Displays statistical information for the network interfaces.

(continues)

TABLE 13.4 *Continued*

Switch	Description
-n	Specifies IP addresses and port numbers in numeric form rather than as hostnames if resolution is available and has been performed.
-p proto	Shows a list of the connections, on a per-protocol basis, where proto is the protocol.
-r	Displays the routing table for the system.
-s	Displays a complete list of protocol statistics, on a protocol-by-protocol basis, including TCP, UDP, and IP.
interval	Redisplays selected statistics, pausing the number of seconds specified by the interval second between each display. You can stop the updates by pressing Ctrl+C. If the interval switch is omitted, netstat prints the current configuration information once.

Of these switches, you're likely to use one far more than any other: -r. The netstat -r command provides an easy way to see the routes configured on the system.

In time, you will be able to read a routing table and determine whether there is a routing problem on the network. Figure 13.7 shows the output from the netstat -r command.

TIP

Viewing Routing Information   The route print command can be used to view the routing information.

EXAM ALERT

netstat -r **Command**   The netstat -r command is commonly used to view routing information. You are likely to be asked about it on the Network+ exam.

NOTE

netstat **Example Scenario**   Suppose that you are unable to access a system on a remote network, but you know that the system is up and running. What should you try?

netstat **Example Solution**   It might be necessary to view the current routing table by using the netstat -r command to determine whether the route to the remote host is correct.

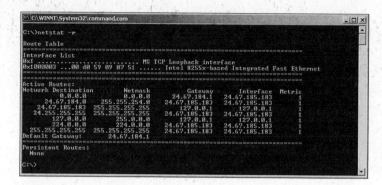

FIGURE 13.7 Output from the
`netstat -r` command.

The `nbtstat` Utility

The NetBIOS statistic utility, `nbtstat`, can be used to display protocol and statistical information for NetBIOS over TCP/IP (sometimes called NetBT) connections. Among other things, the `nbtstat` utility displays the NetBIOS names of systems that have been resolved.

Because `nbtstat` is used for the resolution of NetBIOS names, it's available only on Windows systems. Neither NetWare nor Linux supports NetBIOS, or subsequently nbstat.

Table 13.5 shows some of the most frequently used switches for `nbtstat`.

TABLE 13.5 `nbtstat` Switches

Switch	Description
-a	(Adapter status) Lists the NetBIOS resolution table of a remote system identified by its hostname.
-A	(Adapter status) Lists the NetBIOS resolution table for a remote system identified by its IP address.
-c	(Cache) Lists the NetBIOS name cache along with the IP address of each name in the cache.
-n	(Names) Displays the NetBIOS local name table.
-r	(Resolved) Provides statistical information about resolutions.
-R	(Reload) Reloads the NetBIOS names from the LMHOSTS file.
-S	(Sessions) Shows the NetBIOS sessions table, with the state of connection on a hostname basis.

When you look at the output from certain `nbtstat` commands, you may see reference to a scope ID. Do not confuse this with Dynamic Host Configuration Protocol (DHCP) scopes. In NetBIOS, you can create scopes to logically group systems together. It is this grouping that the scope ID information refers to.

Figure 13.8 shows the output from using `nbtstat -r` in Windows 2000.

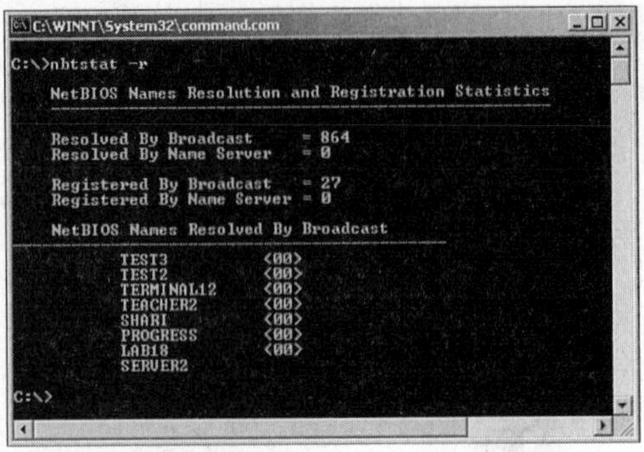

FIGURE 13.8 The output from the `nbtstat -r` command.

NOTE

nbstat Example Scenario Suppose that a Windows system is having problems communicating with another system on the network. You can connect to the system by using an IP address but not by using the NetBIOS name. What should you do?

nbstat Example Solution To solve the problem, check to see whether NetBIOS name resolution is operating correctly by looking at the list of resolved names in the NetBIOS name cache. You get to the NetBIOS name cache by using the `nbtstat` command.

The `ipconfig` and `ifconfig` Utilities

When it comes to troubleshooting connectivity on a network, you won't get too far without first determining the current TCP/IP configuration of the systems in question. Two utilities, `ipconfig` and `ifconfig`, can provide much of the information you will require. The `ipconfig` utility shows the TCP/IP configuration of Windows systems, whereas `ifconfig` is used on Linux, Unix, and Macintosh systems. In both cases, the same utility that you can use to obtain configuration information can also be used to perform certain configuration tasks. We'll look at the two utilities separately, beginning with `ipconfig`.

The `ipconfig` Utility

The `ipconfig` utility shows the TCP/IP configuration information for all network cards installed in a Windows system. Information provided includes the IP address, the subnet mask, and the current default gateway. To find additional information, the `ipconfig` command is often used with the `/all` switch, which then yields additional information on Windows Internet Name Service (WINS) servers, DNS configuration, the MAC address of the interface, and whether DHCP is enabled. If DHCP is enabled, information about the DHCP address lease is provided, including how much time is left on the lease.

Because it provides such a wealth of information, `ipconfig` is the utility of choice for network administrators looking for configuration information; therefore, you can expect it to be on the Network+ exam. Figure 13.9 shows the output from the `ipconfig /all` command.

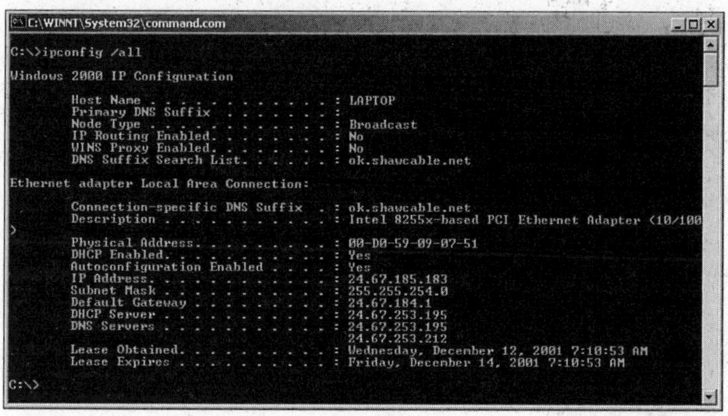

```
C:\C:\WINNT\System32\command.com                                    _ □ x

C:\>ipconfig /all

Windows 2000 IP Configuration

        Host Name . . . . . . . . . . . . : LAPTOP
        Primary DNS Suffix  . . . . . . . :
        Node Type . . . . . . . . . . . . : Broadcast
        IP Routing Enabled. . . . . . . . : No
        WINS Proxy Enabled. . . . . . . . : No
        DNS Suffix Search List. . . . . . : ok.shawcable.net

Ethernet adapter Local Area Connection:

        Connection-specific DNS Suffix  . : ok.shawcable.net
        Description . . . . . . . . . . . : Intel 8255x-based PCI Ethernet Adapter (10/100
>
        Physical Address. . . . . . . . . : 00-D0-59-09-07-51
        DHCP Enabled. . . . . . . . . . . : Yes
        Autoconfiguration Enabled . . . . : Yes
        IP Address. . . . . . . . . . . . : 24.67.185.183
        Subnet Mask . . . . . . . . . . . : 255.255.254.0
        Default Gateway . . . . . . . . . : 24.67.184.1
        DHCP Server . . . . . . . . . . . : 24.67.253.195
        DNS Servers . . . . . . . . . . . : 24.67.253.195
                                            24.67.253.212
        Lease Obtained. . . . . . . . . . : Wednesday, December 12, 2001 7:10:53 AM
        Lease Expires . . . . . . . . . . : Friday, December 14, 2001 7:10:53 AM

C:\>
```

FIGURE 13.9   Output from the ipconfig /all command.

Only a limited number of switches are available for the ipconfig command, but they are important. Table 13.6 lists some of the commonly used switches and what they do.

TABLE 13.6   Commonly Used ipconfig Switches

Switch	Description
/?	Provides a list of the switches available for the ipconfig command. Exact switches vary between Windows platforms.
/all	Displays all TCP/IP configuration information.
/renew	Releases all TCP/IP information and then queries a DHCP server for new information. After the command is issued, you can use ipconfig /all to confirm that the ipconfig /renew command was successful.
/release	Releases the DHCP lease. The result is that the system will not have any IP configuration information.
/registerdns	Re-registers the system's name with DNS servers and also refreshes the DHCP lease. This command is particularly useful in environments such as Windows 2000 and Windows Server 2003 that use Dynamic DNS (DDNS).

TIP

Multiple NICs   Using the ipconfig command with the flags listed in Table 13.6 will affect all the interfaces on the system. This is fine if you have only one network interface, but on systems with more than one network interface it's possible to specify which interface rather than have the command applied to all interfaces.

The ifconfig Utility

As mentioned previously, ipconfig is a Windows-based utility. The equivalent on a Linux, Unix, or Macintosh system is ifconfig. Because Linux relies more heavily on command-line utilities than Windows, the Linux and Unix version of `ifconfig` provides much more functionality than `ipconfig`. On a Linux or Unix system you can get information about the usage of the `ifconfig` command by using `ifconfig --help`. Figure 13.10 shows the output from the basic `ifconfig` command run on a Linux system.

FIGURE 13.10   Output from an `ifconfig` command on a Linux system.

The `winipcfg` Utility

`winipcfg` is the Windows 95, Windows 98, and Windows Me equivalent of the `ipconfig` command. Although it provides similar information to `ipconfig`, it is a graphical utility rather than a command-line utility. The `winipcfg` dialog box, shown in Figure 13.11, has two parts. The top part of the dialog box displays information such as the hostname and the address of the DNS server; the bottom part of the dialog box displays the local IP configuration information. The information shown includes the MAC address, IP address, subnet mask, gateway, and DHCP address and lease information.

TIP

The `ipconfig` Command Line   You can use `ipconfig` from the command line on Windows 95, Windows 98, and Windows Me systems.

TIP

Running the `winipcfg` Utility   You can run the `winipcfg` utility from within Windows clients by selecting Start, Run, and then typing `winipcfg` in the dialog box.

NOTE

`winipcfg` Example Scenario   Suppose that you are working from home and although you are able to use your system normally, you are unable to log on to the Internet. What should you do?

`winipcfg` Example Solution   You can use the `winipcfg` utility on your computer to determine whether you are getting a valid IP address from the Internet service provider's (ISP's) DHCP server. If an IP address is listed, it might not be valid. Use the Renew All button to refresh and reload the TCP/IP configuration.

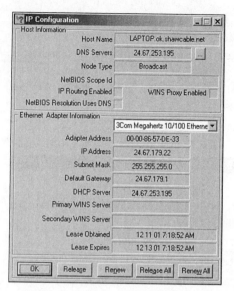

FIGURE 13.11   The winipcfg utility dialog box on a Windows Me system.

DNS Diagnostic Tools (nslookup/dig)

The nslookup and dig utilities are TCP/IP diagnostic tools that can be used to troubleshoot DNS problems. They let you interact with a DNS server and locate records by performing manual DNS lookups. nslookup is used on Windows systems, whereas Linux, Unix, and Macintosh systems support both dig and nslookup.

The basic syntax of both commands is that you add the IP address of the DNS server after the command. Figure 13.12 shows an example of nslookup usage and its output.

```
C:\WINNT\System32\command.com

C:\>nslookup 24.67.253.212
Server:  ns1ht.ok.shawcable.net
Address:  24.67.253.195

Name:    ns2ht.ok.shawcable.net
Address:  24.67.253.212

C:\>
```

FIGURE 13.12   nslookup output.

nslookup

Using nslookup, you can run manual name resolution queries against DNS servers, get information about the DNS configuration of your system or specify what kind of DNS record should be resolved.

If you provide a server name with nslookup, the command performs a DNS lookup and returns the IP address for the server name you entered. If you provide an IP address with nslookup, the command performs a reverse DNS lookup and provides you with the server name.

Entering nslookup by itself at the command prompt and pressing Enter starts the nslookup utility in interactive mode. Instead of being returned to the command prompt, you stay in the utility and receive a > prompt. At the > prompt, you can issue more commands or switches. A list of some of the nslookup switches for the interactive mode on a Windows 2000 or Windows Server 2003 system is provided in Table 13.7. You can get a full list of the switches by typing ? at the > command prompt.

TABLE 13.7 nslookup Switches in Interactive Mode

Switch	Description
option	Sets a switch
all	Displays a list of the currently set switches, including the current server and domain
[no]debug	Turns display of debug information print on/off
[no]d2	Turns display of exhaustive debugging information on/off
[no]defname	Causes the domain specified in defname to be appended to each query
[no]recurse	Specifies that the query should be recursive
[no]search	Specifies that nslookup should use the domain search list
[no]vc	Specifies that nslookup should use a virtual circuit
domain=NAME	Sets the default domain name to the name specified in NAME
srchlist=N1[/N2/.../N6]	Sets the domain to N1 and the search order to the values specified inside [ ]
root=NAME	Sets the root server to the root server specified in NAME
retry=X	Specifies the number of retries, where X is the number
timeout=X	Sets the initial timeout value, in seconds, to the value specified in X
type=X	Specifies the type of query that nslookup should perform, such as A, ANY, CNAME, MX, NS, PTR, SOA, or SRV
querytype=X	The same switches as for type
class=X	Specifies the query class
[no]msxfr	Tells nslookup to use the Microsoft fast zone transfer system
server NAME	Sets the default server to the value specified in NAME
exit	Exits the nslookup program and returns you to the command prompt

NOTE

nslookup Example Scenario   Suppose that you are experiencing problems using the Internet, but you have verified that the IP configuration of your workstation is valid, and you are able to `ping` a remote server by using its IP address. What should you do?

nslookup Example Solution   To solve your problem, use `nslookup` to validate the configuration and function of your DNS servers.

dig

As mentioned, on a Linux, Unix, or Macintosh system you can also use the `dig` command to perform manual DNS lookups. `dig` performs the same basic task as `nslookup` but with one major distinction; the `dig` command does not have an interactive mode and instead uses only command-line switches to customize results. Figure 13.13 shows an example of the output from a manual name resolution request with the `dig` command.

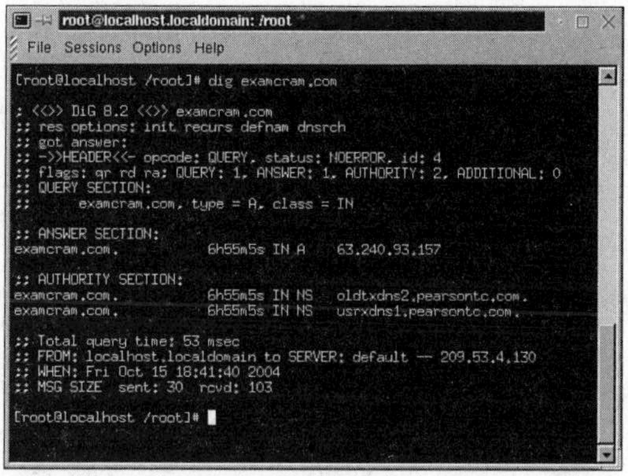

FIGURE 13.13   Output from `dig` command on a Linux system.

The route Utility

A rather odd omission from the CompTIA Network+ objectives is the `route` command. We're not sure why they elected not to include it; but because it is an often-used and very handy tool, we cover it here. Based on the fact that `route` is not included in the objectives, we can say with some confidence that you will not be asked about it on the exam as it pertains to this objective. However, you never know when CompTIA might decide that it fits into another objective.

NOTE

Linux and the route Command   The discussion here focuses on the Windows `route` command, but other operating systems have equivalent commands. On a Linux system, for example, the command is also `route`, but the usage and switches are different.

The `route` command lets you display and modify the routing table on your Windows and Linux systems. Figure 13.14 shows the output from a `route print` command on a Windows 2000 system.

FIGURE 13.14   The output from a `route print` command on a Windows 2000 system.

As well as displaying the routing table, the Windows version of the `route` command has a number of other switches, detailed in Table 13.8. For complete information about all the switches available with the `route` command in Windows 2000 or Windows Server 2003, use the command `route` at the command line. To see a list of the `route` command switches on a Linux system, use the command `route --help`.

TABLE 13.8   Switches for the `route` Command, in Windows 2000

Switch	Description
add	Allows you to add a route to the routing table.
delete	Allows you to remove a route from the routing table.
change	Allows you to modify an existing route.
-p	When used with the `add` command, makes the route permanent. If the `-p` switch is not used when a route is added, the route is lost upon reboot.
print	Allows you to view the routing table of the system.
-f	Removes all gateway entries from the routing table.

Challenge

As a network administrator, you need to be familiar with what diagnostic tools are available, what purpose they are used for, and what operating system platforms they are supported by.

To reinforce this knowledge, complete the following table by providing the missing information. The completed table should match the information presented in the solution table on Page 577. The first line of the table has been completed as an example.

(continues)

(continued)

Question Table:

Utility	Platforms Supported	Description
Nslookup	Windows, Unix, Linux, Mac	Command line utility used to view and troubleshoot DNS configurations.
Winipcfg	Windows	Graphical utility used to view TCP/IP configurations and renew dynamically assigned IP address information.
Dig	Unix, Linux, Mac	Command line utility used to view and troubleshoot configuration.
Ifconfig	Unix, Linux, Mac	Command line utility used to view TCP/IP configuration information.
Tracert		Command line utility used to track the path a packet takes as it traverses the network.
Nbtstat	Windows	Command line utility used to display protocol and statistical information for NetBIOS over TCP/IP connections.
Ping	Windows, Unix, Linux, Mac	Command line utility used to verify connectivity between two devices on a network.

Solution Table:

Utility	Platforms Supported	Description
Nslookup	Windows, Unix, Linux, Mac	Command line utility used to view and troubleshoot DNS configurations.
Winipcfg	Windows	Graphical utility used to view TCP/IP configurations and renew dynamically assigned IP address information.
Dig	Unix, Linux, Mac	Command line utility used to view and troubleshoot DNS configuration.
Ifconfig	Unix, Linux, Mac	Command line utility used to view TCP/IP configuration information.
Tracert	Windows	Command line utility used to track the path a packet takes as it traverses the network.
Nbtstat	Windows	Command line utility used to display protocol and statistical information for NetBIOS over TCP/IP connections.
Ping	Windows, Unix, Linux, Mac	Command line utility used to verify connectivity between two devices on a network.

Using Diagnostic Utilities

Objective:

Given output from a network diagnostic utility (for example: those utilities listed in objective 4.1), identify the utility and interpret the output.

The utilities described in the previous section provide you with a comprehensive toolkit for troubleshooting problems on a TCP/IP-based network. So far we have discussed the tools and looked at when and why you might use them. In this section, we'll look more closely at what you can learn from the information these tools provide. This information is what you will use to locate and fix problems on the network.

> **EXAM ALERT**
>
> **Know the Command Output**   On the Network+ exam, you will be asked to identify the output from a given command. It is also highly likely that you will be asked to interpret the information provided by a command.

ping

As was discussed earlier, `ping` is perhaps the most widely used of all network tools; it is primarily used to verify connectivity between two network devices. On a good day, the results from the `ping` command will be successful, and the sending device will receive a reply from the remote device. Not all `ping` results are that successful, however, and to be able to effectively use `ping`, you must be able to interpret the results of a failed `ping` command.

When you're troubleshooting with the `ping` command, four key error messages can be returned: two of the error messages are common, and two are a little less common. The following sections describe these results of a `ping` command.

The Destination Host Unreachable Message

The Destination Host Unreachable error message means that a route to the destination computer system cannot be found. To remedy this problem, you might need to examine the TCP/IP configuration or routing information on the local host to confirm that the configuration is correct or, if static routes are being used, verify that the local routing table is configured correctly. Listing 13.1 shows an example of a `ping` failure that gives the Destination Host Unreachable message.

LISTING 13.1   A `ping` Failure with the Destination Host Unreachable
```
Pinging 24.67.54.233 with 32 bytes of data:
Destination host unreachable.
Destination host unreachable.
```

LISTING 13.1 *continued*

```
Destination host unreachable.
Destination host unreachable.
Ping statistics for 24.67.54.233:
    Packets: Sent = 4, Received = 0, Lost = 4 (100% loss),
    Minimum = 0ms, Maximum =  0ms, Average =  0ms
```

The Request Timed Out Message

The Request Timed Out error message is common when you use the ping command. Essentially, this error message indicates that your host did not receive the ping message back from the other host within the designated time period. This is typically an indicator that the destination device is not connected to the network, is powered off, or is not configured correctly; however it could also mean that some intermediate device is not operating correctly. In some rare cases, it can also indicate that there is so much congestion on the network that timely delivery of the ping message could not be completed. It might also mean that the ping is being sent to an invalid IP address or that the system is not on the same network as the remote host, and an intermediary device is not configured correctly. In any of these cases, the failed ping should initiate a troubleshooting process that may involve other tools, manual inspection, and possibly reconfiguration. Listing 13.2 shows the output from a ping to an invalid IP address.

LISTING 13.2   Output for a ping to an Invalid IP Address

```
C:\>ping 169.76.54.3
Pinging 169.76.54.3 with 32 bytes of data:
Request timed out.
Request timed out.
Request timed out.
Request timed out.
Ping statistics for 169.76.54.3:
    Packets: Sent = 4, Received = 0, Lost = 4 (100%
Approximate round trip times in milliseconds:
    Minimum = 0ms, Maximum =  0ms, Average =  0ms
```

Refer to section "Troubleshooting with ping" earlier in this chapter for information on what troubleshooting procedures you can use with ping.

When running ping, you might receive some successful replies from the remote host intermixed with Request Timed Out errors. This is often a result of a congested network. An example follows; notice that the example in Listing 13.3, which was run on a Windows Server 2003 system, uses the -t switch to generate continuous pings.

LISTING 13.3   The -t Switch Generating Continuous pings

```
C:\>ping -t 24.67.184.65
Pinging 24.67.184.65 with 32 bytes of data:
```

(continues)

LISTING 13.3   *continued*

```
Reply from 24.67.184.65: bytes=32 time=55ms TTL=127
Reply from 24.67.184.65: bytes=32 time=54ms TTL=127
Reply from 24.67.184.65: bytes=32 time=27ms TTL=127
Request timed out.
Request timed out.
Request timed out.
Reply from 24.67.184.65: bytes=32 time=69ms TTL=127
Reply from 24.67.184.65: bytes=32 time=28ms TTL=127
Reply from 24.67.184.65: bytes=32 time=28ms TTL=127
Reply from 24.67.184.65: bytes=32 time=68ms TTL=127
Reply from 24.67.184.65: bytes=32 time=41ms TTL=127
Ping statistics for 24.67.184.65:
    Packets: Sent = 11, Received = 8, Lost = 3 (27% loss),
Approximate round trip times in milliseconds:
    Minimum = 27ms, Maximum =  69ms, Average =  33ms
```

In this example, three packets were lost. If you experienced this type of error frequently, you would need to determine what was causing packets to be dropped from the network.

The Unknown Host Message

The Unknown Host error message is generated when the hostname of the destination computer cannot be resolved. This error usually occurs when you `ping` an incorrect hostname, as shown in the following example, or when trying to use `ping` with a hostname when hostname resolution (via DNS or a HOSTS text file) is not configured:

```
C:\>ping www.comptia.ca
Unknown host www.comptia.ca
```

If the `ping` fails, you need to verify that the `ping` is being sent to the correct remote host. If it is, and if name resolution is configured, you have to dig (excuse the pun) a little more to find the problem. This error might indicate a problem with the name resolution process, and you might need to verify that the DNS or WINS server is available. Other commands, such as `nslookup`, can help in this process.

> **NOTE**
>
> **Security Settings and Connection Errors**   A remote host connection error can sometimes be caused by your server's security settings. For example, the IPSec policies might restrict access to certain hosts. You might need to disable security measures temporarily when you're troubleshooting errors.

The Expired TTL Message

The Time to Live (TTL) is an important consideration in understanding the `ping` command. The function of the TTL is to prevent circular routing, which occurs when a `ping` request keeps looping through a series of hosts. The TTL counts each hop along the way toward its destination device. Each time it counts one hop, the hop is subtracted from the TTL. If the TTL reaches 0, the TTL has expired, and you get a message like the following:

```
Reply from 24.67.180.1: TTL expired in transit
```

If the TTL is exceeded with ping, you might have a routing problem on the network. You can modify the TTL for ping on a Windows system by using the ping -i command.

> **NOTE**
>
> **More on ping**   As you can see from each of the ping examples, a common set of information is provided each time you run ping. This summary can be useful for getting an overall picture of the ping information.

The tracert Command

The tracert command, which is short for *trace route*, does exactly what its name implies—it traces the route between two hosts by using Internet Control Message Protocol (ICMP) echo packets to report back at every step in the journey. The tracert command provides a lot of useful information, including the IP address of every router connection it passes through, and in many cases the name of the router (although this depends on the router's configuration). tracert also reports the length, in milliseconds, of the round-trip the packet made from the source location to the router and back. This information can tell you a lot about where network bottlenecks or breakdowns may be. Listing 13.4 shows an example of a successful tracert command on a Windows Server 2003 system.

LISTING 13.4   A tracert Command
```
C:\>tracert 24.7.70.37
Tracing route to c1-p4.sttlwa1.home.net [24.7.70.37]
over a maximum of 30 hops:
  1    30 ms    20 ms    20 ms  24.67.184.1
  2    20 ms    20 ms    30 ms  rd1ht-ge3-0.ok.shawcable.net
  [24.67.224.7]
  3    50 ms    30 ms    30 ms  rc1wh-atm0-2-1.vc.shawcable.net
  [204.209.214.193]
  4    50 ms    30 ms    30 ms  rc2wh-pos15-0.vc.shawcable.net
 [204.209.214.90]
  5    30 ms    40 ms    30 ms  rc2wt-pos2-0.wa.shawcable.net
  [66.163.76.37]
  6    30 ms    40 ms    30 ms  c1-pos6-3.sttlwa1.home.net [24.7.70.37]
Trace complete.
```

The tracert display on a Windows-based system includes several columns of information. The first column represents the hop number. The next three columns indicate the round-trip time, in milliseconds, that a packet takes in its attempts to reach the destination. The last column is the hostname and the IP address of the responding device.

Of course, not all tracert commands are successful. Listing 13.5 shows the output from a tracert command that doesn't manage to get to the remote host.

LISTING 13.5   A tracert Command That Doesn't Get to the Remote Host

```
C:\>tracert comptia.org
Tracing route to comptia.org [216.119.103.72]
over a maximum of 30 hops:
  1     27 ms     28 ms     14 ms   24.67.179.1
  2     55 ms     13 ms     14 ms   rd1ht-ge3-0.ok.shawcable.net
     [24.67.224.7]
  3     27 ms     27 ms     28 ms   rc1wh-atm0-2-1.shawcable.net
     [204.209.214.19]
  4     28 ms     41 ms     27 ms   rc1wt-pos2-0.wa.shawcable.net
     [66.163.76.65]
  5     28 ms     41 ms     27 ms   rc2wt-pos1-0.wa.shawcable.net
     [66.163.68.2]
  6     41 ms     55 ms     41 ms   c1-pos6-3.sttlwa1.home.net
     [24.7.70.37]
  7     54 ms     42 ms     27 ms   home-gw.st6wa.ip.att.net
     [192.205.32.249]
  8      *         *         *       Request timed out.
  9      *         *         *       Request timed out.
 10      *         *         *       Request timed out.
 11      *         *         *       Request timed out.
 12      *         *         *       Request timed out.
 13      *         *         *       Request timed out.
 14      *         *         *       Request timed out.
 15      *         *         *       Request timed out.
```

In this example, the tracert only gets to the seventh hop, at which point it fails; this failure indicates that the problem lies on the far side of the device in step 7 or on the near side of the device in step 8. In other words, the device at step 7 is functioning but might not be able to make the next hop. The cause of the problem could be a range of things, such as an error in the routing table or a faulty connection. Alternatively, the seventh device might be operating 100%, but Device 8 might not be functioning at all. In any case, you can isolate the problem to just one or two devices.

The tracert command can also help you isolate a heavily congested network. In the following example, the trace route packets fail in the midst of the tracert but subsequently are able to continue. This behavior can be an indicator of network congestion, as shown in Listing 13.6.

LISTING 13.6   A Trace Route Packet Failure During the tracert

```
C:\>tracert comptia.org

Tracing route to comptia.org [216.119.103.72]over a maximum of 30 hops:
  1     96 ms      96 ms      55 ms   24.67.179.1
  2     14 ms      13 ms      28 ms   rd1ht-ge3-0.ok.shawcable.net [24.67.224.7]
  3     28 ms      27 ms      41 ms   rc1wh-atm0-2-1.shawcable.net [204.209.214.19]
  4     28 ms      41 ms      27 ms   rc1wt-pos2-0.wa.shawcable.net
➡ [66.163.76.65]
  5     41 ms      27 ms      27 ms   rc2wt-pos1-0.wa.shawcable.net
➡ [66.163.68.2]
  6     55 ms      41 ms      27 ms   c1-pos6-3.sttlwa1.home.net [24.7.70.37]
  7     54 ms      42 ms      27 ms   home-gw.st6wa.ip.att.net [192.205.32.249]
  8     55 ms      41 ms      28 ms   gbr3-p40.st6wa.ip.att.net [12.123.44.130]
  9      *          *          *      Request timed out.
 10      *          *          *      Request timed out.
 11      *          *          *      Request timed out.
 12      *          *          *      Request timed out.
 13     69 ms      68 ms      69 ms   gbr2-p20.sd2ca.ip.att.net [12.122.11.254]
 14     55 ms      68 ms      69 ms   gbr1-p60.sd2ca.ip.att.net [12.122.1.109]
 15     82 ms      69 ms      82 ms   gbr1-p30.phmaz.ip.att.net [12.122.2.142]
 16     68 ms      69 ms      82 ms   gar2-p360.phmaz.ip.att.net [12.123.142.45]
 17    110 ms      96 ms      96 ms   12.125.99.70
 18    124 ms      96 ms      96 ms   light.crystaltech.com [216.119.107.1]
 19     82 ms      96 ms      96 ms   216.119.103.72
Trace complete.
```

> **NOTE**
>
> **route Interpretation**   This section explores the results from the Windows `tracert` command, but the information provided is equally relevant to interpreting `traceroute` command results from Unix, Linux, or Macintosh systems.

Generally, `tracert` allows you to identify the location of a problem in the connectivity between two devices. After you have determined this location, you might need to use a utility such as `ping` to continue troubleshooting. In many cases, as in the examples provided in this chapter, the routers might be on a network such as the Internet and so not be within your control. In that case, there is little you can do except inform your ISP of the problem.

The traceroute Command

As discussed, the `traceroute` command performs the same function as `tracert`, but can be used on Unix, Linux, and Macintosh systems. Output from the `traceroute` command is almost identical to that produced by `tracert` on a Windows system, but for the purpose of comparison you can see an example of the output from a `traceroute` command run on a Linux system in Listing 13.7.

LISTING 13.7 Output from a traceroute Command on a Linux System

```
[root@localhost /root]#traceroute 22tecmet44.com
1  d207-81-224-254.bchsia.telus.net (207.81.224.254)   10.304 ms
➡  10.224 ms  10.565 ms
2  208.181.240.22 (208.181.240.22)  9.764 ms  9.784 ms  9.427 ms
3  vancbc01br01.bb.telus.com (154.11.10.58)  16.771 ms  17.664 ms
➡  17.456 ms
4  nwmrbc01gr01.bb.telus.com (154.11.10.54)  15.407 ms  14.622 ms
➡  14.249 ms
5  if-6-0.core1.VBY-Burnaby.Teleglobe.net (207.45.196.17)  14.966 ms
➡  13.942ms  14.992 ms
6  ix-4-0.core1.VBY-Burnaby.Teleglobe.net (207.45.196.14) 17.653 ms
➡  17.666 ms  18.356 ms
7  GE3-0.WANA-PACNW.IP.GROUPTELECOM.NET (66.59.190.5)   18.426 ms
➡ 17.626 ms 18.395 ms
8  216.18.31.161 (216.18.31.161)  18.454 ms  17.610 ms  17.467 ms
9  h209-139-197-237.gtst.groulecom.net (209.139.197.237)  19.412 ms
➡  19.326ms  18.434 ms
10  host-65-61-192-186.inptnet.com (65.61.192.186)  74.120 ms 20.041 ms
➡  21.091 ms
11  dhweb11.d66534host.com (65.61.222.201)  19.188 ms 20.083 ms
➡  19.658 ms
```

As mentioned earlier, from a troubleshooting perspective, the information provided by `traceroute` can be interpreted in almost the same exact way as with `tracert`.

The arp Command

As discussed earlier in this chapter, the `arp` command displays a listing of the IP address to MAC address resolutions that have been performed by the system. The `arp` command can be used on all commonly used operating systems, and in each case it presents essentially the same information.

In practical terms, the information provided by the `arp` utility is of little use beyond the aforementioned role of identifying the origin of a duplicate IP address. Even so, you still need to be able to identify and interpret the output from an `arp` command for both the Network+ exam and the real world. With that in mind, Listing 13.8 shows the output from the `arp -a` command.

LISTING 13.8 Output from an arp -a Command on a Windows XP Professional System

```
C:\>arp -a
Interface: 192.168.1.100 --- 0x2
  Internet Address      Physical Address       Type
```

LISTING 13.8 *continued*

```
192.168.1.1        00-0c-41-a8-5a-ee    dynamic
192.168.1.101      00-60-08-17-63-a0    dynamic
209.22.34.63       00-fd-43-23-f4-e4    static
```

As you can see, there are three entries in the arp table of this system. For each entry, the IP address and the resolved hardware (MAC) address that corresponds to that address is shown. Two of the entries are dynamic, whereas the other is static. Generally, dynamic entries will give you few problems because the automatic resolution process is almost always successful. Static entries, in other words those that have been entered manually, are another matter. If for some reason you decide to add static entries to the arp table, and you then subsequently have problems accessing that host, check the information for the arp entry to ensure that it is correct. Although the arp command will not allow you to add a static entry to the arp table that does not conform to the syntax for either the IP address or the MAC address, it doesn't stop from you entering the *wrong* information for either of these fields.

The `netstat` Command

As discussed earlier in this chapter, the netstat command displays the protocol statistics and current TCP/IP connections. Used without any switches, the netstat command shows the active connections for all outbound TCP/IP connections. In addition, several switches are available that change the type of information displayed by netstat.

The following sections show the output from several netstat switches and identify and interpret the output from each command.

`netstat -e`

The netstat -e command shows the activity for the NIC and displays the number of packets that have been both sent and received. Listing 13.9 shows an example of the netstat -e command.

LISTING 13.9 **Example of the `netstat  -e` Command**

```
C:\WINDOWS\Desktop>netstat -e
Interface Statistics

                      Received          Sent

Bytes                 17412385          40237510
Unicast packets          79129             85055
Non-unicast packets        693               254
Discards                     0                 0
Errors                       0                 0
Unknown protocols          306
```

As you can see, the `netstat` `-e` command shows more than just the packets that have been sent and received. The following list briefly explains the information provided in the `netstat` `-e` command:

▶ **Bytes**—The number of bytes that have been sent or received by the NIC since the computer was turned on.

▶ **Unicast packets**—Packets sent and received directly to this interface.

▶ **Non-unicast packets**—Broadcast or multicast packets picked up by the NIC.

▶ **Discards**—The number of packets rejected by the NIC, perhaps because they were damaged.

▶ **Errors**—The errors that occurred during either the sending or receiving process. As you would expect, this column should be a low number. If it is not, it could indicate a problem with the NIC.

▶ **Unknown protocols**—The number of packets that were not recognizable by the system.

netstat -a

The `netstat` `-a` command displays statistics for both the TCP and User Datagram Protocol (UDP). Listing 13.10 shows an example of the `netstat` `-a` command.

LISTING 13.10 Example of the `netstat` `-a` Command

```
C:\WINDOWS\Desktop>netstat -a

Active Connections

  Proto  Local Address          Foreign Address         State
  TCP    laptop:1027            LAPTOP:0                LISTENING
  TCP    laptop:1030            LAPTOP:0                LISTENING
  TCP    laptop:1035            LAPTOP:0                LISTENING
  TCP    laptop:50000           LAPTOP:0                LISTENING
  TCP    laptop:5000            LAPTOP:0                LISTENING
  TCP    laptop:1035            msgr-ns41.msgr.hotmail.com:1863
➡ ESTABLISHED
  TCP    laptop:nbsession       LAPTOP:0                LISTENING
  TCP    laptop:1027            localhost:50000         ESTABLISHED
  TCP    laptop:50000           localhost:1027          ESTABLISHED
  UDP    laptop:1900            *:*
  UDP    laptop:nbname          *:*
  UDP    laptop:nbdatagram      *:*
  UDP    laptop:1547            *:*
  UDP    laptop:1038            *:*
  UDP    laptop:1828            *:*
  UDP    laptop:3366            *:*
```

As you can see, the output includes four columns, which show the protocol, local address, foreign address, and state of the port. The TCP connections show the local and foreign destination address and the current state of the connection. UDP, however, is a little different; it does not list a state status because, as mentioned throughout this book, UDP is a connectionless protocol and does not establish connections. The following list briefly explains the information provided by the `netstat -a` command:

▶ **Proto**—The protocol used by the connection.

▶ **Local Address**—The IP address of the local computer system and the port number it is using. If the entry in the local address field is an asterisk (*), it indicates that the port has not yet been established.

▶ **Foreign Address**—The IP address of a remote computer system and the associated port. When a port has not been established, as with the UDP connections, *:* appears in the column.

▶ **State**—The current state of the TCP connection. Possible states include established, listening, closed, and waiting.

netstat -r

The `netstat -r` command is often used to view the routing table for a system. A system uses a routing table to determine routing information for TCP/IP traffic. Listing 13.11 shows an example of the `netstat -r` command from a Windows Me system.

> **NOTE**
>
> **Getting Routing Information** The routing information provided by the `netstat -r` command on a Windows system is the same as that produced by the `route print` command.

LISTING 13.11 Example of the `netstat -r` Command

```
C:\WINDOWS\Desktop>netstat -r
Route table


===========================================================================
===========================================================================
Active Routes:
Network Destination        Netmask          Gateway    Interface  Metric
          0.0.0.0          0.0.0.0      24.67.179.1  24.67.179.22       1
       24.67.179.0    255.255.255.0     24.67.179.22  24.67.179.22       1
      24.67.179.22  255.255.255.255       127.0.0.1     127.0.0.1       1
   24.255.255.255  255.255.255.255     24.67.179.22  24.67.179.22       1
         127.0.0.0        255.0.0.0        127.0.0.1     127.0.0.1       1
```

(continues)

LISTING 13.11 *continued*

```
        224.0.0.0       224.0.0.0     24.67.179.22   24.67.179.22      1
  255.255.255.255  255.255.255.255   24.67.179.22                 2    1
Default Gateway:        24.67.179.1
============================================================================
Persistent Routes:
  None
```

NOTE

TCP Information in Windows   In some versions of Windows, the TCP connection information section at the bottom of the screen is not shown.

---

netstat -s

The netstat -s command displays a number of different statistics related to the TCP/IP protocol suite. Understanding the purpose of every field in the output is beyond the scope of the Network+ exam, but for your reference, Listing 13.12 shows sample output from the netstat -s command.

LISTING 13.12   Example of the netstat -s Command

```
C:\>netstat -s

IP Statistics

      Packets Received                    = 389938
      Received Header Errors              = 0
      Received Address Errors             = 1876
      Datagrams Forwarded                 = 498
      Unknown Protocols Received          = 0
      Received Packets Discarded          = 0
      Received Packets Delivered          = 387566
      Output Requests                     = 397334
      Routing Discards                    = 0
      Discarded Output Packets            = 0
      Output Packet No Route              = 916
      Reassembly Required                 = 0
      Reassembly Successful               = 0
      Reassembly Failures                 = 0
      Datagrams Successfully Fragmented   = 0
      Datagrams Failing Fragmentation     = 0
      Fragments Created                   = 0


ICMP Statistics

                            Received      Sent
      Messages              40641         41111
```

LISTING 13.12 *continued*

```
Errors                        0          0
Destination Unreachable     223        680
Time Exceeded                24          0
Parameter Problems            0          0
Source Quenches               0          0
Redirects                     0         38
Echos                     20245      20148
Echo Replies              20149      20245
Timestamps                    0          0
Timestamp Replies             0          0
Address Masks                 0          0
Address Mask Replies          0          0

TCP Statistics

Active Opens                    = 13538
Passive Opens                   = 23132
Failed Connection Attempts      = 9259
Reset Connections               = 254
Current Connections             = 15
Segments Received               = 330242
Segments Sent                   = 326935
Segments Retransmitted          = 18851

UDP Statistics

Datagrams Received      = 20402
No Ports                = 20594
Receive Errors          = 0
Datagrams Sent          = 10217
```

The `nbtstat` Command

As discussed earlier, the `nbtstat` command is used on Windows platforms to show protocol and statistic information for NetBIOS over TCP/IP (NetBT) traffic. Because Microsoft now prefers the Domain Name Service (DNS) over the Windows Internet Name Service (WINS) for name resolutions, the need to use `nbtstat` in troubleshooting scenarios is somewhat reduced. However, you should still be aware of the information that `nbtstat` provides. Listing 13.13 shows the result of one of the most common uses for `nbtstat`—`nbtstat -r`.

LISTING 13.13   Output from the `nbtstat -r` Command

```
C:\>Netstat -r
    NetBIOS Names Resolution and Registration Statistics
    ----------------------------------------------------
    Resolved By Broadcast      = 722
```

(continues)

LISTING 13.13 *continued*

```
    Resolved By Name Server   = 29

    Registered By Broadcast   = 7
    Registered By Name Server = 0

    NetBIOS Names Resolved By Broadcast
    -------------------------------------------------------
          SALES             <00>
          ADMIN             <00>
          ROUTER1           <00>
          FWALL-1           <00>
          MAILSERV          <00>
          WORKSTATION2      <00>
          WORKSTATION3      <00>
```

EXAM ALERT

Don't Confuse Your Rs Don't get confused between `nbtstat -r` and `netstat -r`. `nbtstat -r` shows a list of the NetBIOS names that have been resolved via broadcasts or by some other name resolution method such as a WINS server. `netstat -r` displays the routing table for the system.

As you can see, the information provided by the `nbtstat -r` command is straightforward. The first part of the listing defines the number of resolutions that have been achieved via broadcast or through a name server. It also shows the number of times that this system has been registered via a broadcast or by a name server. Below that are listed the NetBIOS names of other computers that have been resolved by this system.

The `ipconfig` Command

The `ipconfig` command is a technician's best friend when it comes to viewing the TCP/IP configuration of a Windows system—at least most Windows-based systems. The `ipconfig` command cannot be used on Windows 95 and Windows 98 systems. Used on its own, the `ipconfig` command shows basic information such as the name of the network interface, the IP address, the subnet mask, and the default gateway. Combined with the `/all` switch, it shows a detailed set of information, as you can see in Listing 13.14.

LISTING 13.14 Example of the `ipconfig /all` Command

```
C:\>ipconfig /all
Windows 2000 IP Configuration
    Host Name . . . . . . . . . . . . : server
    Primary DNS Suffix  . . . . . . . : write
    Node Type . . . . . . . . . . . . : Broadcast
```

LISTING 13.14 *continued*

```
    IP Routing Enabled. . . . . . . . : Yes
    WINS Proxy Enabled. . . . . . . . : No
    DNS Suffix Search List. . . . . . : write
                                        ok.anyotherhost.net
Ethernet adapter Local Area Connection:

    Connection-specific DNS Suffix  . : ok.anyotherhost.net
    Description . . . . . . . . . . . : D-Link DFE-530TX PCI Fast Ethernet
    Physical Address. . . . . . . . . : 00-80-C8-E3-4C-BD
    DHCP Enabled. . . . . . . . . . . : Yes
    Autoconfiguration Enabled . . . . : Yes
    IP Address. . . . . . . . . . . . : 24.67.184.65
    Subnet Mask . . . . . . . . . . . : 255.255.254.0
    Default Gateway . . . . . . . . . : 24.67.184.1
    DHCP Server . . . . . . . . . . . : 24.67.253.195
    DNS Servers . . . . . . . . . . . : 24.67.253.195
                                        24.67.253.212
    Lease Obtained.. . . . . : Thursday, February 07, 2002 3:42:00 AM
    Lease Expires .. . . . . : Saturday, February 09, 2002 3:42:00 AM
```

As you can imagine, you can use the output from an `ipconfig /all` command in a massive range of troubleshooting scenarios. Table 13.9 lists some of the most common troubleshooting symptoms, along with where to look for clues about solving them in the `ipconfig /all` output.

EXAM ALERT

Check the `ipconfig` Information   When looking at `ipconfig` information, make sure that all information is present and correct. For example, a missing or incorrect default gateway parameter would limit communication to the local segment. Be sure to know this for the exam.

TABLE 13.9   Common Troubleshooting Symptoms That `ipconfig` Can Help Solve

Symptom	Field to Check in `ipconfig` Output
User is unable to connect to any other system.	Make sure the TCP/IP address and subnet mask are correct. If the network uses DHCP, make sure DHCP is enabled.
User is able to connect to another system on the same subnet but is not able to connect to a remote system.	Make sure the default gateway is correctly configured.
User is unable to browse the Internet.	Make sure the DNS server parameters are configured correctly.
User is unable to browse more remote subnets	Make sure the WINS server or DNS server parameters are configured correctly, if applicable.

EXAM ALERT

Identify the `ipconfig` Output Be prepared to identify the output from an `ipconfig` command in relationship to a troubleshooting scenario for the Network+ exam.

The `ifconfig` Command

Like `ipconfig`, `ifconfig` is often the starting point of any connectivity troubleshooting procedure. The difference, as has already been discussed, is that whereas `ipconfig` is used on Windows systems, `ifconfig` is used on Unix, Linux, and Macintosh systems.

As you saw earlier, the basic information provided by `ifconfig` includes the hardware (MAC) address of the installed network adapters, as well as the IP address, subnet mask, and default gateway parameters. It also provides information on the number of packets sent and received by the interface. A high number in any of the error categories might indicate a problem with the network adapter. A high number of collisions may indicate a problem with the network itself. Listing 13.15 shows sample output from the `ifconfig` command.

LISTING 13.15 Example Output from an `ifconfig` Command

```
eth0      Link encap:Ethernet   HWaddr 00:60:08:17:63:A0
          inet addr:192.168.1.101  Bcast:192.168.1.255  Mask:255.255.255.0
          UP BROADCAST RUNNING  MTU:1500  Metric:1
          RX packets:911 errors:0 dropped:0 overruns:0 frame:0
          TX packets:804 errors:0 dropped:0 overruns:0 carrier:0
          collisions:0 txqueuelen:100
          Interrupt:5 Base address:0xe400

lo        Link encap:Local Loopback
          inet addr:127.0.0.1  Mask:255.0.0.0
          UP LOOPBACK RUNNING  MTU:3924  Metric:1
          RX packets:18 errors:0 dropped:0 overruns:0 frame:0
          TX packets:18 errors:0 dropped:0 overruns:0 carrier:0
          collisions:0 txqueuelen:0
```

Although the `ifconfig` command displays the IP address, subnet mask, and default gateway information for both the installed network adapter and the local loopback adapter, it does not report DCHP lease information. Instead, you can use the `pump  -s` command to view detailed information on the DHCP lease including the assigned IP address, the address of the DHCP server, and the time remaining on the lease. The `pump` command can also be used to release and renew IP addresses assigned via DHCP and to view DNS server information.

The issues and suggested solutions described in Table 13.9 for using `ipconfig` on Windows systems are equally applicable to basic troubleshooting with `ifconfig` on a Linux, Unix, or Macintosh system. The only thing to remember is that you might need to run both `ifconfig` and push `-s` to gain all the information required. Also, you may find that the additional statistical information provided by the `ifconfig` command points toward other sources of a problem, such as a faulty network adapter, or a high level of traffic on the network.

The `winipcfg` Command

On a Windows 98 Second Edition or Windows Me system, the `winipcfg` command is used instead of the `ipconfig` command. The difference between the two utilities is that `winipcfg` is a graphical utility. Figure 13.15 shows the `winipcfg` graphical screen.

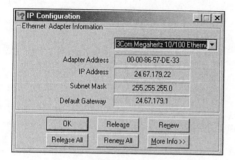

FIGURE 13.15 The basic `winipcfg` screen.

As you can see, in basic mode, `winipcfg` shows information including the Media Access Control (MAC) address and IP address of the interface, the subnet mask, and the default gateway. For detailed information, similar to that produced with `ipconfig /all`, a More Info button allows you to switch into a much more detailed screen (see Figure 13.16).

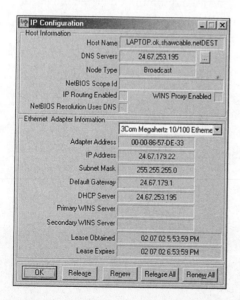

FIGURE 13.16 A detailed `winipcfg` screen.

The same troubleshooting scenarios, with the same solutions, apply to `winipcfg` as to `ipconfig`. Refer to Table 13.9 to see some explanations of common problems and solutions.

The `Nslookup/dig` Commands

The final commands we will interpret the output for in this chapter are the `Nslookup` and `dig` commands. As discussed earlier in this chapter, the `Nslookup` and `dig` commands are used most often when troubleshooting name resolution issues. `Nslookup` is used for Windows systems, whereas `dig` is used on Unix, Linux, and Macintosh systems. We'll look at the output created by each of these commands separately.

Nslookup

The most common use of `Nslookup` is to perform a simple manual name resolution request against a DNS server. Listing 13.16 shows the output from this process on a Windows XP Professional system.

LISTING 13.16   Output from a Manual Name Resolution Using `Nslookup`

```
C:/>Nslookup examcram.com
Server:   nen.bx.ttfc.net
Address:  209.55.4.155

Name:     examcram.com
Address:  63.240.93.157
```

There are two sections to the information provided by `Nslookup`. The first part provides the hostname and IP address of the DNS server that performed the resolution. The second part is the domain name that was resolved along with its corresponding IP address. From a troubleshooting perspective, you can use this information if you suspect that a record held on a DNS server is incorrect.

You can also verify that the DNS server is operating correctly by specifying the DNS server against which the resolution should be performed. For example, consider Listing 13.17, which shows a failed resolution run against a specified DNS server.

LISTING 13.17   Example Output from an `Nslookup` Command

```
C:/>Nslookup examcram.com 209.56.43.130
Server:   heittm.bx.ttc.net
Address:  209.56.43.130

DNS request timed out.
    timeout was 2 seconds.
```

By adding the IP address of the DNS server to the Nslookup command syntax, the resolution request is directed at that server. As you can see, the request timed out, which most often indicates that the DNS server is down or inaccessible.

Challenge

In this Challenge Exercise, you will use Nslookup in interactive mode to perform some basic tasks like viewing help information, and performing manual DNS lookups. This exercise assumes that you are using a Windows XP system, and that you have a DNS server configured.

1. Click Start, Run. In the Open field, type **CMD** and then click OK. A command prompt dialog will open.

2. At the command prompt, type **Nslookup** and press Enter. You should receive output showing the hostname of your default DNS server, and its IP address. You will also be presented with a > prompt.

3. At the > prompt, type a question mark (?) and press Enter. A list of the available options in interactive mode will be displayed. Use the scrollbar at the right side of the command dialog box if information at the top of the listing has been pushed off the screen.

4. At the > prompt, type **SET ALL**. A list of the current configured options will be displayed, along with other information, such as the domain in which your system is configured.

5. To perform a manual name resolution, at the > prompt, type a domain name such as comptia.org, or examcram.com. View the results.

6. Perform a manual name resolution to a domain that does not exist, such as notrealdomain.com or baddomain.com. View the results.

7. Type **Exit** at the > prompt to close the interactive mode. Close the command prompt.

dig

dig is generally considered a more powerful tool than Nslookup, but in the course of a typical network administrator's day, the minor limitations of Nslookup are unlikely to be too much of a factor. Instead, dig is often simply the tool of choice for DNS information and troubleshooting on Unix, Linux, or Macintosh systems. Like Nslookup, dig can be used to perform simple name resolution requests. Listing 13.18 shows the output from this process.

LISTING 13.18 Output from a Name Resolution Request on the Domain examcram.com Performed with dig

```
; <<>> DiG 8.2 <<>> examcram.com
;; res options: init recurs defnam dnsrch
;; got answer:
;; ->>HEADER<<- opcode: QUERY, status: NOERROR, id: 4
;; flags: qr rd ra; QUERY: 1, ANSWER: 1, AUTHORITY: 2, ADDITIONAL: 0
;; QUERY SECTION:
```

(continues)

LISTING 13.18 *continued*

```
;;     examcram.com, type = A, class = IN

;; ANSWER SECTION:
examcram.com.          7h33m IN A     63.240.93.157

;; AUTHORITY SECTION:
examcram.com.          7h33m IN NS    usrxdns1.pearsontc.com.
examcram.com.          7h33m IN NS    oldtxdns2.pearsontc.com.

;; Total query time: 78 msec
;; FROM: localhost.localdomain to SERVER: default -- 209.53.4.130
;; WHEN: Sat Oct 16 20:21:24 2004
;; MSG SIZE  sent: 30  rcvd: 103
```

As you can see, dig provides a number of pieces of information in the basic output, more so than nslookup. Administrators can gain information from three key areas of the output: the Answer Section, the Authority Section, and the last four lines of the output.

The Answer Section of the output provides the name of the domain or host being resolved, along with its IP address. The "A" in the results line indicates the record type being resolved. In this case it is an Alias record, the standard type of DNS record used to define IP address to hostname resolutions.

The Authority Section provides information on the authoritative DNS servers for the domain against which the resolution request was performed. This information can be useful in determining whether the correct DNS servers are considered authoritative for a domain.

The last four lines of the output, which don't have a section name, show how long the name resolution request took to process, in this case 78 milliseconds, and the IP address of the DNS server that performed the resolution. It also shows the date and time of the request, and the size of the packets sent and received.

Chapter Summary

Knowing how to troubleshoot network connectivity is an important part of a network administrator's role. Fortunately, many utilities are designed to make the process of determining and correcting connectivity issues easier. The most common utilities for this type of troubleshooting include `ping`, `ipconfig`, `ifconfig`, `tracert`, `traceroute`, `nbstat`, and `netstat`.

In addition to knowing what utility to use and where, you need to be able to interpret the output from those commands. This ability allows you to identify configuration problems with a system, the network to which it is attached, and even remote hosts on other networks.

The tools discussed in this chapter represent an important part of any network administrator's toolbox. You will find that your knowledge of these utilities will prove to be useful for much more than just passing the CompTIA Network+ exam.

Key Terms

- `arp`
- ARP cache
- `dig`
- ICMP
- `ifconfig`
- `ipconfig`
- localhost
- `nbtstat`

- `netstat`
- `nslookup`
- `ping`
- pump
- `route`
- trace route
- `winipcfg`

Apply Your Knowledge

Exercises

13.1 Using the `ipconfig` Command

By using the troubleshooting commands, you can reinforce the knowledge you need for the Network+ exam. In this exercise you use a Windows Server 2003 system to view the information provided by the `ipconfig` command. The exercise also works on other versions of Windows, including Windows 2000 and Windows XP.

Estimated time: 10 minutes

1. Open a command prompt by selecting Start, Run and then typing **cmd** in the Run dialog box. Click OK, and a command prompt dialog box opens.

2. At the command prompt, type **ipconfig**. Note what information is displayed.

3. At the command prompt, type **ipconfig /all**. Note what additional information is displayed.

4. Determine whether you are using DHCP by looking for the entry for the DHCP server. If you are using DHCP, when was your address assigned? How much time is left on the lease?

5. If you are using DHCP, attempt to renew the address lease by using the command ipconfig /renew. Note whether you are able to renew the lease.

6. To see the updated lease information, type **ipconfig /all**. The date and time for the DHCP lease information should now be updated. Leave the command prompt dialog open. You can use it in the next exercise.

13.2 Using the ping Utility

In this exercise, you follow the ping troubleshooting sequence. How far you go depends on your network connectivity. If you are able to connect to the Internet, you should be able to complete all the steps in this exercise.

Estimated time: 10 minutes

1. In the command prompt dialog, ping the local loopback of your system by using the command ping 127.0.0.1.

2. Determine your IP address by using the ipconfig command.

3. ping the IP address of your system by using the ping *<IP ADDRESS>* command.

4. Use the ipconfig command to determine the address of your default gateway and then ping it.

5. ping a remote host. If you are able to determine (from the address) that your DNS server is on a remote network, ping that. Otherwise, you can try ping 63.240.93.157.

6. If you have DNS capability (which is likely, if you are connected to the Internet), you can also try to ping a remote host by its hostname (for example, ping examcram.com). Leave the command prompt dialog open. You can use it in the next exercise.

13.3 Using the arp Command

In this exercise, you use the arp command to look at the local ARP cache and observe the process of the ARP cache being updated. As in the previous exercise, being connected to a network makes a big difference in the amount and variety of information displayed in this exercise.

Estimated time: 10 minutes

1. In the command prompt dialog, view the ARP cache on your local system by using the `arp -a` command. Note how many devices are listed in the ARP cache.

2. Determine the IP address of your default gateway by using the `ipconfig` command. `ping` the IP address of your default gateway system. Does the first `ping` take longer than the subsequent pings? If so, why do you think it does? Immediately run the `ping` utility again. Is the first `ping` quicker than the first `ping` of the first attempt?

3. Using the `arp -a` command again, view the ARP cache. Note whether any entries have been added. Write down the IP address and MAC address of the default gateway; you'll use them later in the exercise.

4. By using the `ipconfig` command, determine the IP address of your default gateway and then `ping` the address.

5. Immediately view the ARP cache again. Note whether any new entries have been added.

6. Wait about three minutes and then view the ARP cache again. Is the entry for the default gateway still there?

7. Using the information you wrote down in step 3, add a static entry for your default gateway by using the following command:

   ```
   arp -s <IP ADDRESS OF DEFAULT GATEWAY>
      <MAC ADDRESS OF DEFAULT GATEWAY>
   ```

   For help with the syntax, type **arp** at the command line to display the help screen.

8. After you have successfully added the new entry, view the ARP cache. The static entry should now be listed.

9. Delete the static entry you just created by using the following command:

   ```
   arp -d <IP ADDRESS OF DEFAULT GATEWAY>
   ```

10. View the ARP cache one last time, to ensure that the static entry has been removed. Leave the command prompt dialog open. You can use it in the next exercise.

13.4 Using the Trace Route Utility

In this exercise, you use the `tracert` command to look at how a trace route works.

Estimated time: 10 minutes

1. In the command prompt dialog, ascertain the IP address of your DNS server by using the `ipconfig /all` command.

2. Trace the route to your DNS server by using the command `tracert <ADDRESS OF DNS SERVER>`. Note how many hops you are from your DNS server and how long the round-trip took.

3. Trace the route to the CompTIA web server by using the command `tracert www.comptia.org`. Note how many hops you are away from the web server and how long the round-trip took.

4. Use the same command as in step 3, but add the -d switch to the command line, as follows: `tracert www.comptia.org.com -d`. Note what changes in the output from the command.

Exam Questions

1. Which of the following TCP/IP utilities can be used to view routing tables on a Windows 2000 system? (Choose the two best answers.)

   - ○ a. `netstat`
   - ○ b. `nbtstat`
   - ○ c. `route`
   - ○ d. `ping`
   - ○ e. `tracert`

2. Which of the following commands can be used to purge and reload the remote cache name table?

   - ○ a. `nbtstat -R`
   - ○ b. `nbtstat -n`
   - ○ c. `nbtstat -r`
   - ○ d. `nbtstat -S`

3. You are trying to use the `tracert` command to determine the route a packet takes. You receive five successful hops, followed by several asterisks (*). What is the likely cause of the problem?

   - ○ a. The destination host is not online.
   - ○ b. The router at step 4 or 5 has a problem.
   - ○ c. The router at step 5 or 6 has a problem.
   - ○ d. The router at step 5 is not powered on.

4. Which of the following commands can be used to display the protocol statistics on a per-protocol basis?

   - ○ a. `netstat -S`
   - ○ b. `netstat -r`
   - ○ c. `netstat -R`
   - ○ d. `netstat -s`
   - ○ e. `netstat -a`

5. The following is output from which of the following commands?

```
Active Connections
Proto Local Address Foreign Address State
TCP    laptop:1026    127.0.0.1:50000 ESTABLISHED
TCP    laptop:50000   127.0.0.1:1026  ESTABLISHED
```

    ○ **a.** nbtstat

    ○ **b.** netstat

    ○ **c.** arp

    ○ **d.** ipconfig

6. You are trying to ping a remote host with the command ping desertforme.co.uk. The ping returns an Unknown Host error message. What is the cause of the problem?

    ○ **a.** The remote host is not responding.

    ○ **b.** The name of the destination computer cannot be resolved.

    ○ **c.** The route to the destination computer is incorrect.

    ○ **d.** WINS is not configured.

7. From your Linux system, you try unsuccessfully to ping a remote host on another network. What utility might you use to determine where the packet was dropped?

    ○ **a.** arp

    ○ **b.** tracert

    ○ **c.** traceroute

    ○ **d.** nbtstat

8. You are troubleshooting a client connectivity problem in which a system is unable to log on to the network. The client system uses the Linux operating system. Which of the following commands would you use to view the current TCP/IP configuration?

    ○ **a.** ipconfig

    ○ **b.** ipconfig /all

    ○ **c.** ifconfig

    ○ **d.** config

9. Which of the following switches is used on a Windows Server 2003 system to perform a continuous ping?

   ○ **a.** -c

   ○ **b.** -d

   ○ **c.** -t

   ○ **d.** -ct

10. You are attempting to troubleshoot an IP configuration problem on a Windows 98 system. Which of the following commands could you use to view the TCP/IP configuration information? (Choose the two best answers.)

    ○ **a.** winipcfg

    ○ **b.** ifconfig

    ○ **c.** config

    ○ **d.** ipconfig

11. You are troubleshooting a connectivity problem in which the user is unable to connect to any systems on remote networks. Connectivity to systems on the local network appears to work correctly. Based on the following output from an `ipconfig /all` command, what is the most likely cause of the problem?

```
C:\>ipconfig /all
Windows 2000 IP Configuration
      Host Name . . . . . . . . . . . . . : server
      Primary DNS Suffix  . . . . . . . : write
      Node Type . . . . . . . . . . . . : Broadcast
      IP Routing Enabled. . . . . . . . : Yes
      WINS Proxy Enabled. . . . . . . . : No
      DNS Suffix Search List. . . . . . : write
                                          ok.anyotherhost.net
Ethernet adapter Local Area Connection:

Connection-specific DNS Suffix  . : ok.anyotherhost.net
Description . . . . . . . . . . . : D-Link DFE-530TX PCI Fast Ethernet
Physical Address. . . . . . . . . : 00-80-C8-E3-4C-BD
DHCP Enabled. . . . . . . . . . . : Yes
Autoconfiguration Enabled . . . . : Yes
IP Address. . . . . . . . . . . . : 24.67.184.65
Subnet Mask . . . . . . . . . . . : 255.255.254.0
Default Gateway . . . . . . . . . :
DHCP Server . . . . . . . . . . . : 24.67.253.195
DNS Servers . . . . . . . . . . . : 24.67.253.195
                                    24.67.253.212
      Lease Obtained.. . . . . : Thursday, February 07, 2002 3:42:00 AM
      Lease Expires .. . . . . : Saturday, February 09, 2002 3:42:00 AM
```

    ○ **a.** The DNS server information is missing.

    ○ **b.** The node type is set to broadcast.

    ○ **c.** The default gateway parameter is missing.

    ○ **d.** DHCP is enabled.

12. Which utility is used to view NetBIOS over TCP/IP statistics?

    ○ **a.** `ping -t`

    ○ **b.** `netstat`

    ○ **c.** `nbtstat`

    ○ **d.** `arp`

    ○ **e.** `tracert`

13. Consider the following output from the `netstat -e` command. What might you determine from this information?

```
                        Received              Sent

Bytes                   17412385              40237510
Unicast packets         79129                 85055
Non-unicast packets     693                   254
Discards                0                     0
Errors                  2233654               0
Unknown protocols       306
```

    ○ **a.** The NIC in this system is faulty.

    ○ **b.** This is normal.

    ○ **c.** Errors are being generated on the network, but not by this system.

    ○ **d.** This system is generating errors.

14. Which utility would produce the following output?

```
6  55 ms  27 ms  42 ms  so-1-0-0.XL1.VAN1.NET [152.63.137.130]
7  55 ms  41 ms  28 ms  0.so-7-0-0.TL1.VAN1.NET [152.63.138.74]
8  55 ms  55 ms  55 ms  0.so-2-0-0.TL1.SAC1.NET [152.63.8.1]
9  83 ms  55 ms  55 ms  0.so-7-0-0.XL1.SAC1.NET [152.63.53.249]
10 82 ms  41 ms  55 ms  POS6-0.BR5.SAC1.NET [152.63.52.225]
11 55 ms  68 ms  55 ms  uu-gw.ip.att.net [192.205.32.125]
12 55 ms  68 ms  69 ms  tbr2-p013802.ip.att.net [12.122.11.229]
13 96 ms  69 ms  82 ms  tbr1-p012801.ip.att.net [12.122.11.225]
14 82 ms  82 ms  69 ms  tbr2-p012402.ip.att.net [12.122.11.221]
15 82 ms  83 ms  68 ms  gbr2-p20.ip.att.net [12.122.11.254]
```

```
16  55 ms   69 ms   69 ms  gbr1-p60.ip.att.net [12.122.1.109]
17  123 ms  96 ms   96 ms  gbr1-p30.ip.att.net [12.122.2.142]
18  83 ms   96 ms   97 ms  gar1-p360.ip.att.net [12.123.142.21]
19  96 ms   82 ms   96 ms  12.127.141.26
20  124 ms  96 ms   96 ms  216.119.107.2
21  124 ms  82 ms   110 ms  216.119.103.72
```

○ **a.** nbtstat -R

○ **b.** netstat -R

○ **c.** arp -s

○ **d.** tracert

15. Examine the following output from the `tracert` command. What, if anything, is wrong with this trace route?

```
C:\>tracert 24.7.70.37
Tracing route to c1-pos6-3.sttlwa1.home.net [24.7.70.37] over a maximum of 30
hops:
  1    30 ms   20 ms   20 ms  24.67.184.1
  2    20 ms   20 ms   30 ms  rd1ht-ge3-0.ok.shawcable.net [24.67.224.7]
  3    50 ms   30 ms   30 ms  rc1wh-atm0-2-1.vc.shawcable.net [204.209.214.193]
  4    50 ms   30 ms   30 ms  rc2wh-pos15-0.vc.shawcable.net [204.209.214.90]
  5    30 ms   40 ms   30 ms  rc2wt-pos2-0.wa.shawcable.net [66.163.76.37]
  6    30 ms   40 ms   30 ms  c1-pos6-3.sttlwa1.home.net [24.7.70.37]
Trace complete.
```

○ **a.** The IP address is invalid.

○ **b.** There is nothing wrong with this output.

○ **c.** The trace was not completed.

○ **d.** The maximum hop count has restricted the number of hops reported.

16. Examine the following output from the `ping` command. Based on this information, what are you likely to check first in your troubleshooting process? (Choose the two best answers.)

```
Pinging 24.67.54.233 with 32 bytes of data:
Destination host unreachable.
Destination host unreachable.
Destination host unreachable.
Destination host unreachable.
Ping statistics for 24.67.54.233:
    Packets: Sent = 4, Received = 0, Lost = 4 (100% loss),
Approximate round trip times in milliseconds:
    Minimum = 0ms, Maximum =  0ms, Average =  0ms
```

○ **a.** That the remote host is online

○ **b.** The default gateway setting of the system

○ **c.** The routing table on the system

○ **d.** The patch cable for the system

17. Which of the following tools can you use to perform manual DNS lookups on a Linux system? (Choose two.)

○ **a.** dig

○ **b.** nslookup

○ **c.** tracert

○ **d.** Dnslookup

18. Which of the following commands would generate a Request Timed Out error message?

○ **a.** ping

○ **b.** netstat

○ **c.** ipconfig

○ **d.** nbtstat

19. Which of the following commands would you use to add a static entry to the ARP table of a Windows 2000 system?

○ **a.** arp -a <IP ADDRESS> <MAC ADDRESS>

○ **b.** arp -s <MAC ADDRESS> <IP ADDRESS>

○ **c.** arp -s <IP ADDRESS> <MAC ADDRESS>

○ **d.** arp -i <IP ADDRESS> <MAC ADDRESS>

20. Which command created the output shown here?

```
Server:   nen.bx.ttfc.net
Address:  209.55.4.155

Name:     examcram.com
Address:  63.240.93.157
```

○ **a.** nbtstat

○ **b.** ipconfig

○ **c.** tracert

○ **d.** NSLOOKUP

Answers to Exam Questions

1. **a, c.** Both `route` and `netstat` can be used to view the routing table on a Windows 2000 system. `nbtstat` is used to view NetBIOS over TCP/IP statistics, and `ping` is used to test connectivity between two devices. `tracert` is used to trace the route between two devices on a network. For more information, see the section "Troubleshooting Tools," in this chapter.

2. **a.** The `nbtstat -R` command purges and reloads the remote cache name table. The `-n` switch displays the local name table, `-r` provides resolution information, and `-S` shows the NetBIOS session table. For more information, see the section "Troubleshooting Tools," in this chapter.

3. **c.** The router at step 5 or 6 is the likely source of the problem. Because all steps up to and including step 5 have been successful, the problem lies either on the far side of Router 5 or the near side of the router in step 6. Answer a is incorrect because if the destination host were not online, you would receive no successful replies. Answer b is incorrect because if the router at step 4 were having a problem, you would receive only four successful replies and not five. Answer d is incorrect because if the router were powered off, you would receive no successful replies. For more information, see the section "Using Diagnostic Utilities," in this chapter.

4. **d.** The `netstat -s` command displays statistics on a per-protocol basis. The `-S` and `-R` switches are not valid with `netstat`. Answer b (`-r`) causes `netstat` to display the routing table, and Answer e (`-a`) checks connections. For more information, see the section "Troubleshooting Tools," in this chapter.

5. **b.** The output is from a `netstat` command. All the other utilities listed provide different output. For more information, see the section "Troubleshooting Tools" in this chapter.

6. **b.** In this case, the problem is caused because the hostname of the destination computer cannot be resolved. In Answer a, the hostname would have to first be resolved before you could draw this conclusion. Answer c is incorrect; if the route to the destination could not be determined, you would receive a Destination Unreachable message. Answer d is incorrect because WINS is not used for name resolution on the Internet. For more information, see the section "Using Diagnostic Utilities," in this chapter.

7. **c.** On a Linux system, the `traceroute` command can be used to track the path a packet takes between hosts on the network. Of the commands listed, only `traceroute` can perform this function on a Linux system. `Tracert` is the equivalent of the `traceroute` command on Windows systems. The `arp` utility is used to view IP address to MAC address resolutions that have been performed by the system. The `nbtstat` utility is used to view NetBIOS over TCP/IP statistics. For more information, see the section "Troubleshooting Tools," in this chapter.

8. **c.** The `ifconfig` command displays the configuration of the network interfaces on a Linux system. Answers a and b are Windows-based utilities, and Answer d is a NetWare command. For more information, see the section "Troubleshooting Tools," in this chapter.

9. **c.** The `ping -t` command issues a continuous stream of `ping` requests until it is interrupted. None of the other answers are valid switches for the `ping` command. For more information, see the section "Troubleshooting Tools," in this chapter.

10. **a, d.** The `winipcfg` and `ipconfig` commands can be used to verify IP information on a Windows 98 client system. The `ipconfig` command is run from the Windows command prompt, while `winipcfg` is a graphical utility. The `ifconfig` utility is used on Linux and OS/2 systems to view and set interface configurations. The `config` utility is used on NetWare to view configuration information. For more information, see the section "Using Diagnostic Utilities," in this chapter.

11. **c.** The default gateway parameter is missing from the TCP/IP configuration. For more information, see the section "Using Diagnostic Utilities," in this chapter.

12. **c.** The `nbtstat` command can be used to view NetBIOS over TCP/IP statistics. The `ping` command is used to test connectivity between devices, `netstat` is used to view TCP/IP protocol statistics, the `arp` command is used to view a list of IP address to MAC address resolutions, and `tracert` is used to track the path between two devices on the network. For more information, see the section "Troubleshooting Tools," in this chapter.

13. **c.** A high number of errors in the Received column in the `netstat -e` output indicates that errors are being generated on the network. However, the 0 value in the Sent column suggests that this system is not generating the errors. The other answers for this question are not valid. For more information, see the section "Using Diagnostic Utilities," in this chapter.

14. **d.** The output is from the Windows `tracert` command. All the other utilities listed provide different output. For more information, see the section "Troubleshooting Tools," in this chapter.

15. **b.** This is normal output from a `tracert` command. For more information, see the section "Using Diagnostic Utilities," in this chapter.

16. **b, c.** A Destination Host Unreachable message in response to a `ping` suggests either a problem with the default gateway or an error in the routing table. Answer a is incorrect; if the remote host were online, the `ping` should be successful. Answer d would result in a series of Request Timed Out errors. For more information, see the section "Using Diagnostic Utilities," in this chapter.

17. **a, b.** Both the `dig` and `nslookup` commands can be used to perform manual DNS lookups on a Linux system. You cannot perform a manual lookup with the `tracert` command. There is no such command as `dnslookup`. For more information, see the section "Troubleshooting Tools," in this chapter.

18. **a.** The `ping` command generates a Request Timed Out error when it is unable to receive a reply from the destination system. None of the other commands produce this output. For more information, see the section "Using Diagnostic Utilities," in this chapter.

19. **c.** This command would correctly add a static entry to the ARP table. None of the other answers are valid ARP switches. For more information, see the section "Troubleshooting Tools," in this chapter.

20. **d.** The output shown was produced by the `nslookup` command. The other commands listed produce different output. For more information, see the section "Using Diagnostic Utilities," in this chapter.

Suggested Readings and Resources

1. Sloan, Joseph D. *Network Troubleshooting Tools* (O'Reilly System Administration). O'Reilly & Associates, 2001.

2. Habraken, Joe. *Absolute Beginner's Guide to Networking*, fourth edition. Que Publishing, 2003.

3. Sugano, Alan. *The Real-world Network Troubleshooting Manual: Tools, Techniques, and Scenarios* (Administrator's Advantage Series). Charles River Media, 2004.

4. Hunt, Craig. *TCP/IP Network Administration*, third edition. O'Reilly & Associates, 2002.

5. Searchable database of Linux command manual pages, http://man.linuxquestions.org/.

6. Computer networking tutorials and advice, compnetworking.about.com.

7. "TechEncyclopedia," www.techencyclopedia.com.

CHAPTER 14

Troubleshooting Network Connectivity

Objectives

This chapter covers the following CompTIA-specified objectives for the "Network Support" section of the Network+ exam:

4.3 Given a network scenario, interpret visual indicators (for example, link LEDs [Light Emitting Diode] and collision LEDs [Light Emitting Diode]) to determine the nature of a stated problem.

▶ Sometimes finding the source of a problem is as simple as looking at indicator lights. Many network devices have visual indicators that help you troubleshoot.

4.4 Given a troubleshooting scenario involving a client accessing remote network services, identify the cause of the problem (for example, file services, print services, authentication failure, protocol configuration, physical connectivity, and SOHO [Small Office/Home Office] router).

▶ Remote connectivity is now common. Although many LAN troubleshooting procedures apply equally to remote connectivity, you need to be aware of some additional considerations.

4.5 Given a troubleshooting scenario between a client and the following server environments, identify the cause of a stated problem:

▶ **Unix/Linux/Mac OS X Server**   ▶ **Windows**

▶ **NetWare**   ▶ **Appleshare IP (Internet Protocol)**

▶ Client connectivity errors are an inevitable part of a network administrator's day-to-day activity. Most problems can be fixed easily and quickly; however, you need to know what you are looking for to get users back online in the shortest time possible.

4.6 Given a scenario, determine the impact of modifying, adding, or removing network services (for example: DHCP [Dynamic Host Configuration Protocol], DNS [Domain Name Service], and WINS [Windows Internet Name Server]) for network resources and users.

▶ As a network administrator, you need to be aware of the impact that adding or removing services to and from the network will have on network availability.

Outline

Study Strategies

▶ Read through the information presented in this chapter, paying special attention to Exam Alerts, Notes, and Tips.

▶ After reading the section "Interpreting Visual Indicators," familiarize yourself with the LEDs on network equipment to which you have access.

▶ Review the troubleshooting scenarios and solutions presented throughout the chapter. They provide practical examples of situations where you might apply the information presented in this chapter.

▶ Review the "Troubleshooting Checklists" section, which provides guidance on possible causes and potential solutions to common networking issues.

▶ Complete the Challenge Exercises and end of chapter exercise.

▶ Complete the "Exam Questions" at the end of the chapter.

Introduction

As a network administrator, you will be called on to fix all manner of client and remote connectivity issues, from the simple and straightforward to the complex and bizarre.

Although troubleshooting is a skill best gained through experience, many basic procedures, processes, and tools can help you track down and fix problems as they occur. Often, some of the most simple fixes, such as checking that cables are plugged in, are all that is needed to get a user back on to the network. In other cases, though, you'll need to delve deeper into your technical know-how and use your intuition to crack a problem.

In the following sections, we'll discuss some of the tools and procedures that will become the mainstays of your connectivity troubleshooting practices. Combined with real-world experience, these will help you to identify and fix problems more quickly and more effectively. We'll begin our discussion with one of a network administrator's best friends—the LED.

Interpreting Visual Indicators

Objective:

4.3 Given a network scenario, interpret visual indicators (for example, link LEDs [Light Emitting Diode] and collision LEDs [Light Emitting Diode]) to determine the nature of a stated problem.

One of the easiest ways to spot signs of trouble on a network or with a network component is to look at the LEDs that appear on most network components. Many devices used in modern networks—such as hubs, routers, switches, and even NICs—have LEDs that let you know what, if anything, is going wrong. The following sections examine some of the common networking devices and what you can learn from their LEDs.

LEDs on Networking Devices

If you have seen a hub or a switch, you have no doubt noticed the LEDs on the front of the device. Each individual RJ-45 socket has one or two dedicated LEDs. These LEDs are designed to provide the network administrator with a quick idea of the status of a connection or to a potential problem. Table 14.1 provides some examples of link-light indicators functioning on a typical hub.

Note that the LEDs' sequencing and meanings vary among the different hub manufacturers and therefore may be different from those listed in Table 14.1. Check the manual for the networking equipment you are working with to effectively interpret the visual indicators.

TABLE 14.1   Example Link-Light Indicator LED States for a Network Hub or Switch

LED State	Meaning
Solid green	A device is connected to the port, but there is no activity on the device.
Blinking green	There is activity on the port. The connected system is sending or receiving data.
No LED lit	There is no detectable link. Either there's a problem with the connection between the device and the hub (such as an unplugged cable) or the remote system is powered down.
Fast continuous blinking for extended periods	This often indicates a fault with the connection, which can commonly be attributed to a faulty network card or a bad RJ-45 connector.
Blinking amber	There are collisions on the network. A few orange LEDs flashing intermittently are okay, but continuously blinking amber LEDs indicate a problem.

In addition to link-light indicators, some hubs and switches have port-speed LEDs that, when lit, indicate the speed at which the connected device is functioning. Some also have LEDs that indicate whether the link is operating in full-duplex mode. These LEDs are often labeled FDX, FX, FD, or Full. Figure 14.1 shows an example of LEDs on an Ethernet switch.

> **EXAM ALERT**
>
> **Do You Have a Faulty Patch Cable?**   If a connection LED on a hub is not lit, all the physical connections appear complete, and the connected system is powered on, you might have a faulty patch cable. You should know this for the exam.

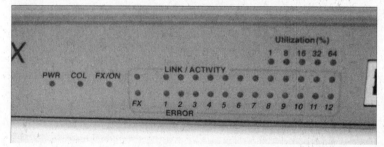

FIGURE 14.1   LEDs on an Ethernet switch.

By understanding the function of the lights on networking devices, you can tell at a glance the status of a device and the systems connected to it. Take the time to familiarize yourself with the specific indicator lights on the network devices you work with and their various states.

LEDs on NICs and Other Devices

In addition to hubs and switches, most other networking devices have LEDs that provide a variety of information. Most NICs have at least one LED that indicates whether there is a link between the system and the network into which it is plugged. The link light operates at a physical level; in other words, it should be lit when the PC is on, regardless of whether the networking software is loaded, the network configuration is correct, or the user is logged on to the network. In addition to the link LED, many NICs have additional lights to indicate the speed at which the network connection is established and/or when there is network activity on the link. Figure 14.2 shows a NIC that has a link light (right), an activity LED (middle), and an LED that indicates whether the link is at 100Mbps (left).

FIGURE 14.2   A NIC with indicator LEDs.

LEDs are also included on cable modems and DSL modems, which are commonly used in small or home office networks for Internet connectivity

As already explained, the number of LEDs on a device and their functionality depends on the device. For example, the cable modem we use has four LEDs: one that indicates that the modem is online, a Send indicator, a Receive indicator, and one labeled Message. On another Internet connection, this time with a DSL modem, we have six LEDs. One shows that the device is powered, and one flashes to indicate that the device is operating normally. Then there is a link light for both the local network and the ADSL connection, and both the local network and ADSL connections have a separate LED that flashes to indicate activity on the links.

NOTE

Reading the Lights   The trick to using indicator lights on networking equipment is knowing how they function in normal operation. Then, when a deviation occurs, you can recognize that something is wrong.

Using LEDs in Troubleshooting

The usefulness of LEDs in troubleshooting scenarios cannot be overstated. LEDs provide an instant, visual indicator about the state of a network link. In some cases, as with collision lights, they can even alert you to problems on the network. Understanding how to interpret information provided by LEDs is important for the real world and for the Network+ exam.

To demonstrate how LEDs can be used for troubleshooting, consider the sample network layout in Figure 14.3.

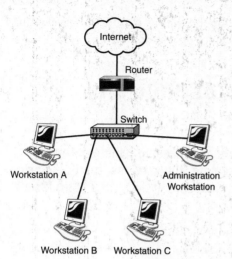

FIGURE 14.3 A sample network.

Imagine a scenario in which a user who is working at Workstation A calls and tells you she is unable to access the Internet. The Internet connection could be down, but by connecting to the Internet yourself, you determine that it is working correctly; therefore, it is safe to assume that the problem is on the user's end rather than with the Internet connectivity. You also check with the users on Workstations B and C, both of whom report that everything is working normally as far as they are concerned. Next, you decide to visit Workstation A to see whether you can ping the Internet router. Before you begin the ping test, you look at the back of the system and see that the link LED on the NIC is not lit. You can be fairly sure at this point that the ping test will not work because without the link light, there is no connectivity between the NIC and the switch.

Now you have narrowed the problem to one of a few things. Either the NIC in Workstation A or the cable between the workstation and the switch is faulty. Less likely, though still possible, is that the port on the switch to which the user is connected is faulty.

The easiest way to test whether the cable is the problem is to unplug the known working cable from Workstation B or C and plug it in to Workstation A. When you try this, if the link light on the NIC does not come on, you can deduce that the NIC is most likely the cause of the fault. If the light does come on, you can deduce that either the port on the switch or the original cable between Workstation A and the switch is faulty. The next step is to swap the cable out or try the original cable in another port switch.

EXAM ALERT

Identify the Link Lights Expect to be asked to identify the purposes of link lights on the Network+ exam. You might be presented with diagrams and asked how you would use LEDs in the troubleshooting process.

Whatever the actual problem, link lights play an important role in the troubleshooting process. They give you an easy method of seeing what steps do and don't work.

Troubleshooting Remote Connectivity

Objective:

4.4 Given a troubleshooting scenario involving a client accessing remote network services, identify the cause of the problem (for example, file services, print services, authentication failure, protocol configuration, physical connectivity, and SOHO [Small Office/Home Office] router).

As networks have moved away from single locations, and working from home, or *telecommuting*, has increased in popularity, a new world of troubleshooting has opened up: that of remote connectivity errors. Remote connectivity errors are bugs that prevent you from connecting to the office network, from remotely dialing in to your home computer, or from logging on to your ISP and subsequently the Internet. People have come to rely on this ability to remotely access the office, and the Internet has become so closely integrated with modern business that many organizations come to a standstill without it.

> **NOTE**
>
> **Troubleshooting Print Services and File Services**   The wording for the CompTIA objective covered by this section includes *file services* and *print services*. Because the troubleshooting steps for these specific points are the same in a remote connectivity scenario as in a local connectivity scenario, we have chosen to cover this material only once under the section "Troubleshooting Client Connectivity Errors" later in this chapter.

Although many means and methods are available for establishing remote connectivity, network administrators can focus their attention on some common hotspots when troubleshooting errors, including authentication failure, protocol configuration problems, and physical connectivity. You also need to consider, though to a lesser extent, problems with file and print services that may look like a remote connectivity problem when they are not.

We'll start our discussion at remote connectivity troubleshooting by looking at some of the steps involved in troubleshooting the physical connection.

Troubleshooting Physical Connectivity

When you're troubleshooting remote connectivity errors, it is often easy to forget the most basic troubleshooting practices. By this we mean ensuring that all the physical connections are in place. When you suspect a physical connectivity problem, here are a few key places to look:

▶ **Faulty cable**—Either through accident or by wear and tear, sometimes cables break. If you suspect a faulty cable as the cause of a connectivity error, replace the cable with one that is known to be working to confirm your suspicion.

▶ **Improperly connected cable**—Troubleshooting a connectivity issue might be as simple as plugging in a cable. Make sure that all cables are securely attached to the correct ports.

▶ **Incorrect cable**—If you are troubleshooting a new connection, make sure that the correct cable is being used.

▶ **Faulty interface**—A faulty network card can stop data flow in a hurry.

▶ **Faulty networking devices**—Hubs, switches, and routers may be the sources of your problem; just because the lights are on, don't assume that a device is working correctly. If possible, substitute the device for one that is known to be working so that you can eliminate it from your inquiries.

Also try these troubleshooting measures:

▶ **Use observation techniques and connectivity tools**—Approach physical connectivity problems methodically and use tools such as ping and tracert (Windows) or traceroute (Unix, Linux, Mac) to locate problems. Most networking devices have indicator LEDs that you can use to determine the status of the device.

▶ **Be aware of EMI and crosstalk**—As discussed in Chapter 2, you must be aware of the effects of electromagnetic interference (EMI) and crosstalk on network media. If you have an intermittent or hard-to-trace problem, you should certainly consider this factor.

NOTE

Physical Connectivity Example Scenario   One of your company's remote users calls you and is angry that he is unable to dial in and access the local network from his remote location. He insists he is using the correct username and password.

Physical Connectivity Example Solution   When you receive calls for remote connectivity errors, try to think of problems associated with physical connectivity. If the user is accessing a remote location using a modem, confirm that the modem is correctly cabled both in the computer and into the phone jack. If the user requires a network card to access remote services, make sure that the network cable is installed correctly. You can also try a different jack and phone cable.

Now that we have looked at some of the more general considerations of remote connectivity troubleshooting from a physical perspective, we'll focus specifically on some of the commonly used remote access technologies.

Many methods are used to establish remote connections. Some, such as POTS, involve dialing in directly to the corporate network across the public telephone network. Others, such as cable and DSL, use the Internet as a mechanism to establish Virtual Private Networks (VPNs). Because broadband connectivity, such as DSL and cable, is now increasingly common, we'll start our discussion there.

DSL Troubleshooting Procedures

Troubleshooting DSL is similar to troubleshooting any other Internet connection. The following are a few things to check when users are experiencing problems with a DSL connection:

▶ **Physical connections**—The first place to look when troubleshooting a DSL problem is the network cable connections. From time to time, these cables can come loose or inadvertently be detached, and they are often overlooked as the cause of a problem. DSL modems typically have a minimum of three connections: one for the DSL line, one for the local network, and one for the power. Make sure that they are all plugged in appropriately.

▶ **The NIC**—While you're checking the cable at the back of the system, take a quick look to see whether the network card LED is lit. If it is not, something could be wrong with the card. It might be necessary to swap out the network card and replace it with one that is known to be working.

▶ **Drivers**—Confirm that the network card is installed and has the correct drivers. Many times, simply using the most up-to-date driver can resolve connectivity issues.

▶ **Protocol configuration**—The device you are troubleshooting might not have a valid IP address. Confirm the IP address by using the appropriate tool for the operating system being used—for example, `winipcfg`, `ipconfig`, or `ifconfig`. If the system requires the automatic assignment of an IP address, confirm that the system is set to obtain an IP address automatically. It might be necessary to use the `ipconfig /release` and `ipconfig /renew` commands to get a new IP address.

▶ **DSL LEDs**—Each DSL box has an LED on it. The light sequences are often used to identify connectivity problems or problems with the box itself. Refer to the manufacturer's website for specific information about error codes and LEDs, but remember the basics—a link light should be on to indicate that the physical connection is complete, and a flashing LED indicates that there is activity on the connection.

> **EXAM ALERT**
>
> **Remember the Visual Indicators** When troubleshooting remote connectivity on a cable or DSL modem, use the LEDs that are always present on these devices to aid in your troubleshooting process.

Ultimately, if none of these steps cure or indicate the cause of the problem, you might have to call the DSL provider for assistance. You can find more information about using technical support services later in this chapter, in the section "Calling Technical Support."

NOTE

DSL Example Scenario   You are unable to get onto the Internet using a DSL connection. You look at the indicator lights on the DSL modem and notice that the Ethernet link light is lit, but that the ADSL link light is not. What should you do?

DSL Example Solution   Verify that the phone cable between the modem and the wall jack are connected correctly. If the connection appears complete, consider trying another cable between the DSL modem and the wall jack. If that fails, or you do not have another cable available, contact the DSL service provider's technical support line.

Cable Troubleshooting Procedures

In general, cable Internet access is a low-maintenance system with few problems. When problems do occur, you can try various troubleshooting measures:

▶ **Check the user's end**—Before looking at the cable modem, make sure that the system is configured correctly and that all cables are plugged in. If a hub or switch is used to share the cable Internet access among a group of computers, make sure that the hub or switch is on and functioning correctly.

▶ **Check the physical connections**—Like DSL modems, cable modems have three connections: one for the cable signal, one for the local network, and one for the power. Make sure that they are all plugged in appropriately.

▶ **Ensure that the protocol configuration on the system is valid**—If an IP address is assigned via DHCP, the absence of an address is a sure indicator that connectivity is at fault. Try obtaining a new IP address by using the appropriate command for the operating system platform you are using. If the IP addresses are statically configured, make sure that they are set correctly. Trying to use any address other than that specified by the ISP might prevent a user from connecting to the network.

▶ **Check the indicator lights on the modem**—Most cable modems have indicator lights that show the status of the modem. Under normal conditions, a single light labeled Ready or Online should be lit. Most cable providers provide a manual with the modem that details the functions of the lights and what they indicate in certain states. Generally, any red light is bad. Flashing LEDs normally indicate traffic on the connection.

▶ **Cycle the power on the modem**—Cycling the power on the modem is a sure-fire way of resetting it.

▶ **Call the technical support line**—If you are sure that the connectors are all in place and the configuration of the system is correct, the next step is to call the technical support line of the cable provider. If the provider is experiencing problems that affect many users, you might get a message while you're on hold, informing you of the fact. If not, you will eventually get to speak to someone who can help you troubleshoot the problem. One of the good things about cable access is that the cable company can remotely monitor and reset the modem. It should be able to tell you whether the modem is functioning correctly.

Unless the modem is faulty, which is not that common, by this point the user should be back on the Internet or at least you should fully understand why the user cannot connect. If the problem is with the cable provider's networking equipment, you and the user simply have to wait for the system to come back on.

> **NOTE**
>
> **Cable Example Scenario**   Suppose that you are troubleshooting a user's cable Internet connection and are unable to get an IP address. What should you do?
>
> **Cable Example Solution**   Verify that the protocol configuration is correct and that all cables are connected correctly. During your investigation, you notice that the Online light of the cable modem is red. After you cycle the power to the modem, the light remains red; you are still unable to obtain a valid IP address. The next step is to contact the cable service provider's technical support line.

Home Satellite Troubleshooting Procedures

Your ability to troubleshoot satellite Internet connections might be limited. Home satellite Internet is a line-of-sight wireless technology, and the installation configuration must be very precise. Because of this requirement, many satellite companies insist that the satellite be set up and configured by trained staff members. In fact, if you install a satellite system in a way that does not accord with the manufacturer's recommendations, you might void any warranties.

Given this limitation, troubleshooting satellite connections often requires you to concentrate less on connectivity issues and more on physical troubleshooting techniques. Perhaps more than for any other Internet technology, calls to technical support occur very early in the troubleshooting process.

Wireless Troubleshooting Procedures

Wireless Internet access requires a wireless network adapter and a wireless access service from a Wireless Internet Service Provider (WISP). Troubleshooting wireless access is normally confined to ensuring that the adapter is functioning correctly and configured properly.

The main factors that can affect wireless access are environmental conditions and outside interference. Many people who live in areas that often have fog or other damp conditions experience poor performance (or none at all) from wireless Internet service. In other areas, the conditions are perfect for wireless communication. Electrical interference can also be a factor.

Here are some specific things you should check when troubleshooting a wireless connection:

- **Check the configuration of the wireless interface**—This step includes checking to make sure that the system is recognizing the device, that the drivers are enabled and configured, and that all protocols and bindings are correct.

- **Move the computer around to find out whether it's in a dead spot**—Some construction materials or electrical equipment can block or weaken the signal. Moving around will help you discover this kind of problem.

- **Check with other people**—If possible, and if you know other people who have the same Internet access method, check to see whether they are also experiencing problems. It might be that there is a problem with the service rather than just the user's system.

If you are sure that everything is configured correctly, you might have to contact the wireless provider to see whether anything is amiss.

Given the availability, speed, and relatively low cost of other Internet access methods, wireless Internet access seems like it might take some time to get a foothold in the Internet access market. But for people who simply have to have 100% mobility, or those in areas that do not have access to other broadband Internet access methods such as DSL or cable, it's the way to go.

POTS Troubleshooting Procedures

Troubleshooting a dial-up connection problem can be tricky and time-consuming because you must consider many variables. In fact, of the remote connectivity mechanisms discussed in this chapter, you are far more likely to have problems with a POTS connection than any of the others. The following are some places to start your troubleshooting under various conditions.

> **NOTE**
>
> **Technical Support**   In some cases, users may not use an ISP at all and instead dial another system on the corporate network directly. In that case, all the troubleshooting steps in this section apply, except that you have to rely on the technical support capabilities of the person responsible for the remote system rather than the ISP if you have a problem.

If the user is unable to dial out, try the following:

- **Check physical connections**—The most common problem with modem connections is that something has become unplugged; modems rarely fail after they initially work. For an external modem, you also need to verify that the modem has power.

▶ **Check that there is a dial tone on the line**—You can do this by plugging a normal phone into the socket and seeing whether you can dial out. Also, a modem generally has a speaker, and you can set up the modem to use the speaker so that you can hear what is going on.

If the user can dial out but cannot connect to the network, try the following:

▶ **Make sure that the user is dialing the correct number**—This suggestion sounds obvious, but sometimes numbers change or are entered incorrectly.

▶ **Call the ISP**—You can call the ISP to determine whether it is having problems.

▶ **Check the modem speaker**—Find out whether you are getting busy signals from the ISP by turning on the modem speaker.

If the user can dial out and can get a connection but is then disconnected, try the following:

▶ **Make sure that the modem connection is configured correctly**—The most common modem configuration is 8 data bits, 1 stop bit, and no parity (commonly referred to as *eight-one-none*).

▶ **Check the username and password**—Make sure that the correct username and password combination is configured for the dial-up connection.

▶ **Verify that the connection settings are correct**—Pay particular attention to things such as the IP address. Nearly all ISPs assign IP addresses through DHCP, and trying to connect with a statically configured IP address is not permitted.

▶ **Make sure that the user has not exceeded a preset connection time limit**—Some ISPs restrict the number of monthly access hours. If the user has such a plan, check to make sure that some time credit is left.

▶ **Try specifying a lower speed for the connection**—Modems are designed to negotiate a connection speed with which both devices are comfortable. Sometimes, during the negotiation process, the line can be dropped. Initially setting a lower speed might get a connection. You can then increase the modem speed to accommodate a better connection.

Call Waiting

If you are troubleshooting a dial-up connection that randomly slows down or disconnects completely, check to see whether the line has a call-waiting function on it. As you probably know, when call waiting is used, a tone informs you during the call that someone is trying to get through. This tone interferes with the modem connection and can cause it to either slow down for a period of time or drop the connection altogether.

(continues)

(continued)

Call-waiting problems are difficult to troubleshoot because they occur only when a call is coming in and when you are on that line. Moving the system to another line might make the connection work properly and leave all concerned scratching their heads. The good news is that the solution to the call-waiting problem is simple. The telephone company can give you a code to add to the beginning of the modem dial string to temporarily disable call waiting for the duration of the call. In most cases, the telephone company or ISP can help you configure the disabling of call waiting if you need such help.

Troubleshooting Poor Connection Speeds

Even if you are not having a problem connecting, you might find that the speed of modem connections is problematic. Such problems are not uncommon. The modem might say it can handle a certain speed, and the ISP might advertise the same, but often you simply cannot get the maximum supported speed on a dial-up connection. There are many possible reasons; some of them you can do something about, and some of them you can't. Here are some of the reasons speeds might not be as fast as expected:

▶ **Poor line quality**—In some areas, the quality of the telephone lines and exchange equipment can reduce the maximum possible connection speed.

▶ **Incorrectly configured modem**—The modem configuration is important in ensuring the highest possible connection speed. In particular, for external modems, the configuration of the serial port the modem is connected to should be checked. Defaults sometimes restrict the speed of the port. Generally, though, an incorrectly configured modem or serial port will prevent the modem from making a connection at all, not just impact the speed.

▶ **Poor-quality modems**—Perhaps less of an issue now than in the past, poor-quality modems can contribute to poor connection speeds and connectivity problems. Paying the extra money for a good-quality modem is worth the savings in frustration alone.

After saying all this, it is worth mentioning that after you establish a connection, whatever the speed, you are still at the mercy of the ISP. Even a 56Kbps link might be too slow if the ISP's networking equipment or Internet connection can't keep up with demand. Unfortunately, there is no way to know whether the bottleneck is with the ISP or the modem.

Modem-Specific Troubleshooting

Typically, modems are reliable devices. They have no moving parts, and chances are that after you have installed, configured, and tested a modem, you won't have to play around with it again. However, there can be exceptions, and you should be aware of the following modem-specific troubleshooting measures:

▶ **Make sure that you have the latest drivers**—For any type of modem, make sure that the latest drivers are installed. The drivers supplied with modems typically are not up-to-date, and a visit to the modem manufacturer's website (from another computer) might yield more up-to-date drivers. Try to avoid using generic drivers or those provided with operating systems where possible. Even if they work, which they often don't, they probably won't offer all the features of the proper drivers.

▶ **Check for resource conflicts**—On older PCs, make sure that there are no conflicts between internal modems and other system resources. For external devices, make sure that serial ports are enabled and configured correctly.

▶ **Check for firmware updates**—Both internal and external modems have updatable firmware chips. Check the modem manufacturer's website to ensure that you have the latest version of the firmware. (Note that firmware updates should be completed only if they fix a specific problem you are having.)

If you are confident that a modem is installed and configured correctly, but it's still not working properly, you can test and configure it by using special commands called the *AT command set*. These commands are mentioned briefly in Chapter 3, "Networking Components and Devices," but they are worthy of a more detailed discussion here; they are often useful for troubleshooting modems and related connectivity problems.

You can use AT commands through a communications application to talk directly to the modem. On Windows platforms, you can use the HyperTerminal utility. On most common Linux distributions, you can use the `minicom` utility. After you have established a session with the modem, you can issue AT commands directly to the modem, which will respond different ways, depending on the command. Table 14.2 lists some of the most commonly used AT commands.

TABLE 14.2 Commonly Used AT Commands

AT Command	Result
ATA	Sets the modem to auto-answer.
ATH	Hangs up an active connection.
ATD	Dials a number.
ATZ	Resets the modem.
ATI3	Displays the name and model of the modem.

In general, getting the modem to respond to an ATZ command is a good enough indicator that the modem is functioning.

NOTE

POTS Example Scenario A customer calls and complains that she is often disconnected during a dial-up session. Other times, the connection is fine. What should you do?

POTS Example Solution You check all the modem configurations, and they appear to be correct. Find out whether call waiting is enabled on the line; if it is, modify the modem dial string to disable call waiting before dialing an Internet connection.

Calling Technical Support

When troubleshooting any kind of Internet access, there is a chance that your efforts will not be successful and that you will need to call technical support. If you find yourself in such a situation, you can take the following steps to ensure that you get the answers you need:

- ▶ **Be prepared**—Have on hand all the information you might be asked for. This includes account numbers, user IDs for the connection, and other information. Do not give technical support representatives the administrator or equivalent account information for your system.

- ▶ **Be prepared to wait**—Many service providers seem to think that a 20-minute (or more) wait is a reasonable level of customer service. Even if you don't agree, there is little you can do about it, so call from a hands-free phone or headset if possible so that you can do other things while you wait.

- ▶ **Try fixes during the call**—If possible, avoid ending a technical support call to try things and then calling back if they don't work. Make the call while you're in front of the system with the problem. You are far more likely to get a speedy resolution if you can try fixes with the tech support representative on the phone.

With the help of a technical support staff person, you should be able to correct the problem. But what if you are on the other end of the phone? What if you are the one trying to solve remote connectivity problems for a customer? The next section offers some guidance.

Troubleshooting Authentication Failure

Authentication problems are typically the first place to look when a user is experiencing remote connectivity errors. All forms of remote connectivity should require some form of authentication to confirm that those trying to access the remote resources have permission to do so. Most of us are aware of authentication in the form of usernames and passwords.

As a network administrator, you can expect to become familiar with authentication troubleshooting. Often, authentication errors result from users incorrectly entering usernames and/or passwords. As you might expect and hope, when this happens, users cannot access the network. Many systems use case-sensitive passwords; when you are troubleshooting authentication failure, be sure that you know whether case-sensitive passwords are required.

TIP

Caps Lock   If you're troubleshooting authentication failure, make sure that Caps Lock is turned off on the keyboard.

Authentication issues can also arise as a result of permissions changes in users' accounts. In all kinds of networks, network administrators need to sometimes make changes to accounts. Whether due to security reasons, network maintenance, or an accident, at some point accounts change. When incorrect changes to accounts are made, it is the responsibility of the network administrator to correct them before the user tries to log on, or at least to notify the user of a potential problem. If you're troubleshooting remote connectivity and you have confirmed that the correct username and password are used, confirm that everything is as it should be with the user's account.

Another and perhaps least likely cause for authentication failure is a downed authentication server. If the server providing the authentication for the remote access goes down, then no one who is authenticated through that server will be able to log on. In such a circumstance, you are likely to receive numerous calls regarding authentication difficulty—not just one or two.

NOTE

Authentication Example Scenario   Suppose that you are employed to provide telephone support for a large ISP. A customer calls, complaining that she is unable to dial in to your ISP service and access the Internet.

Authentication Example Solution   When isolating remote connectivity errors, first determine whether customers are using the correct authentication information. In this case, it would be necessary to confirm that the correct username and password are being used. If you are using an authentication system that is case sensitive, make sure that the correct case is being used.

Troubleshooting Protocol Configuration Problems

Many, but not all, of the problems you encounter with remote connectivity can be addressed with the measures listed previously. Even so, you might encounter a time when you have confirmed that the network user is using the correct username and password combination, that no changes have been made to the user's account information, that all physical connections are in place, and that the user still cannot establish a remote connection.

The next most likely client connectivity problem is protocol configuration. Protocol configuration issues are usually on the client side of the network. Each client computer must have a unique address to participate on the network. Failure to obtain addressing information could indicate a problem with a DHCP server. Check the DHCP server to make sure that it is functioning and that addresses are available for assignment.

One of the most frustrating troubles to deal with as an administrator is duplicate IP addresses. This problem usually is the result of manually assigning IP addresses or improperly configuring subnet assignments on multiple DHCP servers. However, such occurrences are rare.

> **NOTE**
>
> **Unauthorized Configurations**   Some operating systems are better at protecting against unauthorized configuration changes than others. Windows 2000, Windows Server 2003, and Linux, for example, require special rights to change network configurations. Windows 95 and Windows 98, on the other hand, do not. If you are working on an operating system that does not control reconfigurations, be sure to check carefully for changes.

Administrators should also be aware of whether the client operating system will automatically assign private IP addresses when the DHCP server cannot be located. On a Windows 2000, Windows Server 2003 or Windows XP client, if the client runs `ipconfig` and reports an IP address beginning with 169, you know that the client has been provided with an address via APIPA, and that the DHCP server is either down, unreachable, or has run out of available IP addresses for assignment.

Beyond basic protocol issues such as addressing, remote connectivity troubleshooting also brings with it the additional considerations of authentication protocols. Although there are nuances to troubleshooting specific protocols that are beyond the scope of this book and the Network+ exam, one rule applies to all. If a client in a remote connectivity solution is configured to use one type of authentication protocol, and the server to which they are connecting does not support that protocol, the connection will be refused. Even though this statement might seem obvious, you would be surprised at just how often authentication protocol mismatch is identified as the cause of a problem.

> **EXAM ALERT**
>
> **Check the Authentication Protocol**   If a client is attempting to connect to a remote system using one authentication protocol, and the remote access server does not support that protocol, the connection will be refused.

Troubleshooting a Small Office/Home Office Router

In the Network+ objectives, CompTIA specifically cites a Small Office/Home Office (SOHO) router as a component of remote connectivity troubleshooting, and with good reason. As more people choose to use broadband Internet connectivity methods such as cable and DSL, the use of compact hub/router and switch/router combinations has become common. Although these devices provide a range of features that allow an Internet connection to be managed, used, and shared more effectively, they also introduce another, sometimes complex element into to remote connectivity troubleshooting process. Figure 14.4 shows an example of an SOHO router.

FIGURE 14.4 A typical SOHO router.

Most SOHO routers are, in fact, more than routers. Most are also Ethernet hubs or switches, making it possible to share an Internet connection with other systems on the network. They also typically provide basic firewall capabilities and in most cases DHCP server functionality. Further, some SOHO routers also provide 802.11x wireless capabilities, turning your home office or small office into a wireless hotspot.

With so many features, you would think that these devices would be expensive, but in reality they are not. A device that offers all the features described costs less than $100. That's a lot of bang for your buck, which is just one more reason why these little boxes of tricks have become so popular.

Configuration

The most common configuration method for SOHO routers is through a browser interface, though some models also use a custom application for this purpose. Configuration is generally straightforward because SOHO routers are designed to be home user friendly. Some allow you to switch between a basic and advanced user interface, "hiding" the more complex configuration tasks from people who do not need to see them. Some of these more complex tasks might include the configuration of port forwarding, which is a process associated with NAT, and MAC address spoofing, which is sometimes required by ISPs. Whatever the requirements, you need to become familiar with the configuration processes for your specific SOHO router if you are to configure it properly.

Troubleshooting

Because a SOHO router is a network device, the rules and procedures applied to other troubleshooting scenarios are valid. If you are experiencing Internet connectivity issues on a network with a SOHO router, the first step is to ensure that the SOHO router is powered on, and that all the network connections are complete and secure. As mentioned earlier, many networking devices use LEDs to indicate the status of connections. SOHO routers are no exception. Familiarize yourself with the diagnostic LEDs on your SOHO router so that you can interpret the information they provide accordingly.

Outside of physical connections, you are most likely to troubleshoot problems with the firmware on the router. *Firmware* refers to the configuration application discussed earlier. Router manufacturers update these applications from time to time to fix issues or add features. Check the website of your router manufacturer periodically to see whether there are any updates that you need to install. Typically, updating firmware is a straightforward process that involves downloading and installing an application, much like you would an application for a PC.

If you suspect that a configuration problem exists, consider whether the router has ever functioned correctly. If you are experiencing problems with the initial setup, you may need to delve into the inner workings of the router firmware, though most often the default configurations of a router work well, albeit without all the additional configuration and security measures. If the device has already been in use for some time and has simply developed a problem, you may find that a simple power-down, power-up procedure can fix a problem. If that fails, you may have to contend with a faulty device. However, the absence of fans or other moving parts makes such instances rare. Once SOHO routers are in and working, they tend to stay that way.

Of course, it may be that you simply need to exclude the router from your "inquiries." One of the easiest ways to test whether the SOHO router is the cause of a problem is to remove it from the communications chain and plug a PC directly into the broadband interface (be that cable or DSL). If the PC is configured to obtain an IP address automatically, it should be able to get an IP address from the ISP just as easily as it would from the SOHO router. If the system subsequently works fine and can access the Internet, you know that the problem lies with the SOHO router and not the system configuration. Obviously, the reverse applies as well: If the PC doesn't work, the problem is likely with the PC and not the SOHO router. Although it has happened, it is unlikely that both would be faulty at the same time.

> **NOTE**
>
> **Hard Reset** In addition to being able to reset the router through a web browser interface, some SOHO routers also have a physical button in an inconspicuous place that will allow you to reset the device to its factory default settings. This can be particularly useful if you want to start from a clean, known configuration, or if you cannot find the administrative password. In the same way, though, an inadvertent pressing of this button can erase previous configurations or settings, which might lead to the report of a problem in the first place.

However, you need to be aware that unless the PC itself is running a firewall in this configuration, it is exposed to Internet-borne threats. Even connecting a system without a firewall to the Internet for a very short time will likely result in your system being hacked. By a short time, we are talking in the region of 15 minutes, but if you get unlucky it could be immediate. For that reason, you should either install a software firewall on the system before you connect directly to the Internet, or if you choose to forgo this cautionary step, make sure that you are only connected for the shortest amount of time possible.

The bottom line with troubleshooting SOHO routers is to treat them just like you would any other networking device. Apart from the basics such as checking connectivity (both physically and logically) and ensuring that the device is powered on, there is little you can do without developing an understanding of the administration tools associated with the device. For that reason, it is worth gaining a basic understanding of these tools before a problem develops instead of having to troubleshoot and learn how to use the tools at the same time.

Troubleshooting Client Connectivity Errors

Objective:

4.5 Given a troubleshooting scenario between a client and the following server environments, identify the cause of a stated problem:

▶ Unix/Linux/Mac OS X Server

▶ NetWare

▶ Windows

▶ Appleshare IP (Internet Protocol)

Any network administrator is likely to tell you that client connectivity errors are one of the most common sources of network-related problems. Client connectivity errors range from plain old user error to more complex protocol and cabling issues. Sometimes, even administrators make mistakes that can impact users!

With so many possibilities, it is no wonder that client connectivity persists as one of the biggest network troubleshooting hotspots. The following sections explore the common sources of client connectivity problems and provide scenarios that network administrators might encounter.

> **NOTE**
>
> **Just the Basics** CompTIA chooses to identify specific operating systems under this objective. However, to pass the Network+ exam, you are not expected to have a detailed understanding of each of these operating systems. Instead, you should focus on the general troubleshooting steps and procedures involved in client connectivity issues.

Protocol Errors

The client system has to have a protocol assigned or bound to its NIC to access resources. You can use specialized tools to verify that a protocol is being used by the system; for example, on Windows 2000/XP/2003 systems you use the `ipconfig` command, on older Windows client systems you use the `winipcfg` command, and on Linux and Macintosh systems you can use the `ifconfig` command.

Protocol-Specific Issues

You need to consider a number of factors related to network protocols when you troubleshoot client connectivity. The following list describes some of the protocol-specific issues you should consider in such a situation:

▶ **Transmission Control Protocol/Internet Protocol (TCP/IP)**—For a system to operate on a TCP/IP-based network, it must have at the least a unique IP address, the correct subnet mask for the network to which it is connected, and (for cross-network connectivity) a default gateway entry. In addition, a Domain Name Service (DNS) server address is also very likely to be required.

▶ **Internetwork Packet Exchange/Sequenced Packet Exchange (IPX/SPX)**—Each system on an IPX/SPX network must have a unique address, although the addresses are generated and assigned automatically.

▶ **Network BIOS Extended User Interface (NetBEUI)**—Each system on a network that uses NetBEUI must have a unique name to identify the computer on the network. For name resolution between network segments, a network needs either a Windows Internet Naming System (WINS) server or manual name resolution through an `LMHOSTS` file.

▶ **AppleTalk**—Each system on an AppleTalk network must have a unique address. If AppleTalk over TCP/IP is being used, make sure that the system is configured with a valid IP address, subnet mask, and (if needed) a default gateway.

On networks that use TCP/IP, DHCP is often used to automatically assign protocol information to clients. When DHCP is not used, protocol information has to be entered manually, and many errors can arise—most commonly duplicate IP addresses.

EXAM ALERT

APIPA Addresses Remember that Windows systems use APIPA. If they are configured to use DHCP but cannot obtain an address from a server, they will self-assign an IP address from the 169.254.x.x range. Non-APIPA systems that cannot obtain an IP address from a DHCP server will typically self-assign an IP address of 0.0.0.0.

When protocol settings are correctly configured, protocol problems are infrequent. Unless settings are manually changed, little can go wrong.

Authentication

Before users can log on to any system, their identities must be verified. By far the most common type of authentication used is the standard username and password combination. When a user account is created, it is good practice for the administrator to set a password. The user should change that password immediately so that the administrator no longer knows it.

Users should be forced to change their logon passwords periodically, although that often creates the problem of users forgetting their passwords. Mechanisms should therefore be in place that allow users to get new passwords quickly.

Most user password problems can be traced to users entering an incorrect password or entering the correct password incorrectly. All common operating systems offer the capability for the administrator to change a user's password, but none offer the capability to determine the user's existing password. Therefore, if a user does forget his or her password, a new one has to be created and issued.

Little can be done about users incorrectly typing passwords, except that you can encourage them to be careful. Note that all commonly used network operating systems, with the exception of Novell NetWare, use case-sensitive passwords. Therefore, if a user is having trouble logging on, she should make sure that the Caps Lock key is on or off as appropriate.

Permissions Errors

Access to applications and data across the network is controlled by permissions. Permissions are responsible for protecting the data on the network and ensuring that only those who should have access to it do.

The first rule of permissions troubleshooting is to remember that permissions do not change themselves. If a user cannot access a file, the first question to the user should always be, "Could you ever access the file?" If the user says "Yes, but now I can't access the file," you should check server change logs or documentation to see whether any changes have been made in the permissions structure.

If no changes have been made, verify that the user is in fact allowed access to that file or directory. In large environments, trying to keep track of who should have access to what can be a tricky business—one that is best left to defined policies and documentation.

The following are some other items you should consider when troubleshooting permissions problems:

▶ On some operating systems, rights and permissions can be inherited from parent directories or other directories that are higher in the directory structure. A change in the permissions assignments at one level may have an effect on a lower level in the directory tree.

▶ File permissions can be gained from objects other than the user's account. Depending on the operating system being used, rights can also be gained from group membership, other network objects, or security equivalence. When you are troubleshooting a permissions problem, be sure that you understand where rights are supposed to originate.

▶ File attributes can override file permissions, and they can prevent actions from being performed on certain files. To the uninitiated, this might seem like a file permissions problem, but in fact it is correct operation. For example, on a NetWare file system, the Rename Inhibit permission prevents changes to the name of a file, even if the user has the Supervisor file system permission.

▶ Determine that there is actually a problem. Users sometimes decide to clean up by deleting files they think are no longer used. Permissions may have been set that prevent users from doing this, and rightly so, but the user might identify this as a permissions problem and report it as such. To a lesser extent, the same situation can occur if a user tries to manipulate a file while it is in use by another application or user.

Application Problems and File Permissions

A malfunctioning application can sometimes be traced back to a file permissions problem. Many types of applications write temporary files, which they then need to delete when a certain operation is completed or the application is closed. File permissions and attributes can prevent this process, and in some cases, the result is that the application misbehaves or stops working completely. If you have an application problem you can't nail down, make sure that it is not related to file permissions or attribute problems.

Troubleshooting permissions problems can be both challenging and enjoyable. As with many other IT troubleshooting scenarios, you can solve most permissions problems effectively if you fully understand what you are troubleshooting and the factors that affect the situation. Also in common with other troubleshooting scenarios, you need to approach the problem methodically.

Physical Connectivity Errors

Although many of the problems associated with client connectivity can be traced to software-based problems such as configuration, authentication, and permissions issues, physical connectivity is often the root of the problem. As we have already discussed, when you are troubleshooting physical connectivity errors, the first place to look is at the network cables. Physical connectivity errors can also involve the devices used to establish the physical client/server connectivity.

> **NOTE**
>
> **Cooling Fans**   Most networking devices have only one moving part: the cooling fan. Do not underestimate the importance of the fan, and always make sure that hubs, switches, and routers have adequate cooling and that the fan is working.

Troubleshooting physical connectivity errors often requires some trial and error. For example, you might switch a cable to a different port in a hub to test whether the port is at fault or replace a cable or NIC with one that is known to be working to see whether it fixes the problem. If you are fortunate enough to have them, you can use instruments and devices aimed at reducing the hit-or-miss approach to the troubleshooting process, but they are costly devices and actually often come in a distant second to the trial-and-error method.

Now that you have had a quick overview of the common client connectivity issues, it is time to test your knowledge with some scenarios.

> **NOTE**
>
> **Troubleshooting Scenario**   A user calls and says that he is unable to log on to the network. After checking that he is using the correct username and password combination, you decide that there may be a connectivity issue, so you visit the user at his desk.
>
> **Troubleshooting Solution**   Upon reaching the user's desk, you determine that the cable is indeed plugged in to the NIC, but you also notice that the link light on the NIC is not on. As a precaution, you attempt to log on anyway, but you are unsuccessful. You receive a message saying that no logon server could be found. Noting the connection number for the wall socket to which the problem system is connected, you proceed to the server room to check the switch to which the system is connected. You check the physical connection into the switch, and everything appears to be in order. You grab a spare network cable and head back to the user's desk. You swap out the existing cable with the new one, and the link light comes on. The user attempts to log on again and is successful.

> **NOTE**
>
> **Troubleshooting Scenario**   You receive several calls from users on the second floor, reporting that they have become disconnected from the network. You know that on the second floor there is a printer with a network connection, so you attempt to `ping` the IP address of the printer but are unsuccessful. What could be the problem?
>
> **Troubleshooting Solution**   Because numerous people are reporting problems, you can be sure that the problem is not with a specific workstation or network connection. The problem is more likely with one of the switches used for second-floor connections. On reaching the server room, you notice that one of the switches in the rack is powered off and that none of the LEDs on it are lit. All the other switches in the rack are on and operating correctly. After checking that the power cord is firmly inserted, you attempt to cycle the power on the failed switch; nothing happens. You deduce that the switch must have failed and proceed to replace with a spare hub as a temporary measure.

Challenge—Part 1

In this Challenge exercise, you walk through a basic troubleshooting process—the type of scenario you will find yourself in frequently as a network administrator. The Challenge exercise is divided into three parts. Part 1 describes the problem and provides some options for a first step in the troubleshooting process. Part 2 identifies the best course of action from Part 1 and continues the troubleshooting process with more information and more options. Finally, Part 3 describes the last part of the scenario and provides another set of options along with a solution.

Remember, this exercise is based on how you might best handle the situation in the real world. There may be more than one right answer for each step of the exercise. Your task is to choose the *best* approach.

Scenario: You are the senior network administrator for a large insurance company. The network is a 100BaseT infrastructure, with 6 fileservers and 260 Windows XP Professional workstations. You work in a 15-story office tower in downtown Chicago.

At 7:20 one morning, a user calls to report a problem accessing the network from her PC on the third floor. No other users have reported any problems yet, but it is likely that no other employees have arrived for work yet. Workers in the department on the third floor typically do not start before 9:00 a.m.

Which of the following troubleshooting steps are you most likely to perform first?

1. Leave your desk on the tenth floor and go to visit the user at her desk.

2. Visit the equipment room on the eighth floor to determine whether the port link light on the switch to which the user is connected is lit.

3. Ascertain the IP address of the user's workstation and try to `ping` it.

4. `ping` one of the servers on the network.

5. Ask the user for her username and password so that you can attempt to log on with her account.

Select your answer and write the number here: _____

See Part 2 of this Challenge exercise for explanations.

Troubleshooting Checklists

In a real-world networking environment, you will be expected to be able to troubleshoot many different areas. You can expect to be tested on them on the CompTIA exam. The following sections provide some troubleshooting checklists that can help you review some of the various troubleshooting areas.

Troubleshooting Cable Problems

Cable accounts for a great many of the problems on a network. There are many places to look when you suspect a cable-related problem. If you suspect that cable is at the bottom of your network troubles, consider the following areas:

▶ **Loose connections**—Verify that cables are securely attached and that they are attached to the correct ports.

▶ **Poorly crimped or bent cable**—Sometimes a chair running over a cable or a cable that has a poor crimp can cause problems.

▶ **Incorrect cable length**—Recall from Chapter 2, "Cabling Standards, Media, and Connectors," that cables cannot exceed a specified maximum length.

▶ **Cable placement**—Care must be taken when cables are run too closely to strong electrical devices. If cables are run too closely to electrical devices, you need to make sure that they are designed for the task.

▶ **Termination**—If you are using a bus topology, make sure that the correct termination is being used.

Troubleshooting Network Connectivity

As a network administrator, you can expect to troubleshoot a number of connectivity issues. These might come in the form of local connectivity errors or remote connectivity errors. Either way, most of the troubleshooting techniques are the same. If you are struggling with connectivity issues, confirm the following:

▶ **Username/password**—Your first consideration when determining connectivity issues is to confirm that the correct username and password configuration is used. Often, this is as far as your troubleshooting needs to go.

▶ **Configuration**—It might be necessary to confirm that the network settings on the client computer have not changed.

▶ **Account Status**—Verify that the user has an active account on the network and that it has the correct permissions set. It is often a good idea to try to log on with a known working account from the client's system, which will allow you to isolate the problem to the computer or the user account.

▶ **Physical connections**—Check to see whether a cable has come unplugged. As we have already discussed, correcting connectivity issues may be as simple as reconnecting a cable.

▶ **NIC**—From time to time, NICs fail. To confirm that a card is working, you might need to swap out the card with one that is known to be working.

Troubleshooting Network Printing

The time between a failed print job and a call to the network administrator is measured in milliseconds. Printing is one of the services that network users expect to be working, and it is the administrator's job to make sure that it is available. When you find yourself on the hot seat, trying to get a printer back up and running, confirm the following:

▶ **Printer online status**—Confirm that the printer is online and ready to go. If there is a problem with the printer itself, the printer might display error messages on an LCD panel or use LEDs to indicate a problem.

▶ **Printer functioning**—Nearly all printers have a test print feature. You can use it to make sure that the printer itself is functioning correctly.

▶ **Printer connectivity**—Verify that the printer is visible to the network. If the printer is connected directly to the network using TCP/IP, for example, you can ping the printer to test for connectivity.

▶ **Client configuration**—Make sure that the computers that are trying to access the printer are configured correctly to use that printer. Often, several printers are used in networks, and it might be necessary to confirm that the client is configured to send a print job to a particular printer.

▶ **Permissions**—On many operating systems, it is possible to set permissions to allow or deny users access to a printer. Verify that the correct permissions have been set.

▶ **Check logs**—Network operating systems log printer activity. Monitoring printer logs can often provide clues as to the source of a problem.

▶ **Driver software**—Today's modern operating systems have a number of mechanisms to ensure that the correct print driver is used when connecting to a network printer. However, there are still occasions when the wrong driver gets installed, or the installed driver becomes corrupt. If you are having problems isolating a printing issue, consider reinstalling or replacing the printer driver.

Troubleshooting Data Access

The inability to access data is not always a result of connectivity errors. Improperly set data security can prevent a user's access. If a user is unable to access data, there are a few key areas to verify:

▶ **Proper network login**—Sometimes people use a shortcut or try to access data without being properly logged on to the network. Verify that users are correctly logged on to the network and that any necessary network drives are connected.

▶ **Permissions**—Access to data through the network is controlled by access permissions. When you are troubleshooting data access, make sure that the permissions are set correctly.

▶ **Connectivity**—Verify that the system that maintains the data is available. Many organizations use multiple servers to hold data. Confirm that the server is available. What can seem like a problem accessing a file can mask a potentially larger problem such as a disk or server failure.

▶ **Data integrity**—Sometimes data itself can be corrupt. This is the worst-case scenario, and the robust nature of today's file systems ensures that it occurs rarely. This is when you need backups.

▶ **Viruses**—In some cases, viruses may be your problem. You can use a virus-checking program to determine whether indeed this is the problem.

Troubleshooting NICs

When NICs are configured correctly and verified to be working, very little goes wrong with them. Despite their dependability, NICs can give you a little grief. When you are troubleshooting a NIC, consider the following:

▶ **Resource settings**—NICs require specific computer resources to operate. After you install a card or add new devices, check for device conflicts.

▶ **Speed settings**—If you are not getting the expected speed from the NIC, confirm the speed settings and, if applicable, the duplex settings.

▶ **Protocols**—For the NIC to work on the network, it must have a valid protocol assigned to it. Often, protocol information is provided via DHCP on TCP/IP networks. A protocol issue is usually not a problem with the card itself, although a problem with the NIC can disguise itself as a protocol problem on occasion. If you are using multiple NICs in a system, each card needs at least one protocol assigned to it.

▶ **Faulty card**—Some NICs are faulty when they ship from the manufacturer, and some are damaged through poor handling. Whatever the case, the NIC you are troubleshooting might actually be faulty. To test for this, you can swap the card with one that is known to be working.

Challenge—Part 2

Explanation: In this case, you are most likely to choose option 3 (ascertain the IP address of the user's workstation and try to `ping` it). A successful `ping` confirms that network connectivity exists. A failed `ping` confirms that network connectivity is the cause of the problem.

You are less likely to choose option 1 (Leave your desk on the tenth floor and go to visit the user at her desk) because this will take more time, and chances are that the first thing you will do when you arrive at the user's desk is use `ping` to verify connectivity.

Option 2 (visit the equipment room on the eighth floor to determine whether the port link light on the switch to which the user is connected is lit) may let you determine whether physical connectivity exists between the workstation and the network switch, but it will not confirm protocol configurations, whereas using `ping` will.

Option 4 (`ping` one of the servers on the network) would achieve little apart from confirming that you have network connectivity.

Option 5 (ask the user for her username and password so that you can attempt to log on with her account) is not a valid troubleshooting step at this stage. You would ask a user for her username and password only if you suspected an authentication issue.

Scenario (continued): You attempt to `ping` the user's workstation, and all the `ping`s are returned successfully. In this one step, you have confirmed that the physical connectivity between your workstation and the user's is complete, and that the configuration of protocols on the user's workstation (and your own) is correct. Which of the following steps are you most likely to perform next?

1. Give the user your username and password to see whether she can log on with your credentials.

2. Ask the user for her username and password.

3. Have the user restart her system to get another IP address from the DHCP server.

4. Reboot the server on the third floor, working on the assumption that there are no other users at work yet so no one else will be affected.

5. Check the account details for the user to make sure that there are no restrictions preventing her from logging on to the network.

Select your answer and write the number here: _____

See Part 3 of this Challenge exercise for explanations.

Adding, Modifying, or Removing Network Services

Objective:

4.6 Given a scenario, determine the impact of modifying, adding, or removing network services (for example, DHCP [Dynamic Host Configuration Protocol], DNS [Domain Name Service], and WINS [Windows Internet Name Service]) for network resources and users.

All network services require a certain amount of network resources to function. The amount of resources required depends on the exact service being used. Before implementing or removing any service on a network, it is important to understand the impact that these services can have on the entire network. To provide some idea of the demands various services place on the network, this section outlines some of the most common network services and the impact their addition, modification, or removal might have on the network and clients.

Adding, Modifying, or Removing DHCP

As discussed back in Chapter 6, "Working with TCP/IP," DHCP automatically assigns TCP/IP addressing to computers when they join the network and automatically renews the addresses before they expire. The advantage of using DHCP is the reduced number of addressing errors, which makes network maintenance much easier. Remember from earlier in this chapter that each computer on a TCP/IP network requires a unique IP address.

One of the biggest benefits of using DHCP is that the reconfiguration of IP addressing can be performed from a central location, with little or no effect on the clients. In fact, you can reconfigure an entire IP addressing system without the user even noticing. There is, as always, a cost associated with everything good, and with DHCP, the cost is increased network traffic.

DHCP Traffic

You know what the function of DHCP is and the service it provides to the network, but what impact does the DHCP service have on the network itself? Some network services can consume huge amounts of network bandwidth, but DHCP is not one of them. The traffic generated between the DHCP server and the DHCP client is minimal during normal usage periods.

EXAM ALERT

DHCP and Broadcast Traffic The majority of DHCP traffic is broadcast based. Therefore, one of the effects of implementing DHCP is an increase in broadcast-related traffic. However, such an increase has little impact on the overall amount of network traffic.

The bulk of the network traffic generated by DHCP occurs during two phases of the DHCP communication process: when the lease of the IP address is initially granted to the client system and when that lease is renewed. The entire DHCP communication process takes less than a second, but if there are many client systems, the communication process can slow down the network.

For most network environments, the traffic generated by the DHCP service is negligible. For environments where DHCP traffic is a concern, you can reduce this traffic by increasing the lease duration for the client systems, thereby reducing communication between the DHCP client and the server.

DHCP Leases

Some network administrators choose to allow infinite DHCP leases, but this strategy is not always practical. In any network, there can be changes; for example, computers can be added or taken away, remote laptops can be used to connect to the main LAN, and NICs might need to be replaced. In addition, on a wireless network users frequently may move between parts of the network. If a system is removed from a network that uses infinite DHCP leases, the IP address used by the removed system will be unavailable for reuse. A better option is to choose long duration periods ranging from one to two weeks. This ensures that the IP address will be able to be reused in the future.

If DHCP functionality is removed from the network (which is unusual), each system needs to be manually configured with IP addressing information.

DHCP is covered in greater detail in Chapter 6.

Adding, Modifying, or Removing DNS

As previously mentioned, the function of DNS is to resolve hostnames to IP addresses. Without such a service, network users would have to identify a remote system by its IP address rather than by its easy-to-remember hostname. Alternatively, name resolutions can be accomplished statically, using the HOSTS file on the client system. If you are using a DNS server, the IP address of the DNS server is required. DNS server addresses can be entered manually, or they can be supplied through a DHCP server.

Like DHCP, the amount of traffic generated by DNS is relatively low, and given that the majority of network activities now involve or require a hostname resolution at some point, this minimal overhead is easily justified. As for the impact of removing DNS, well, quite simply it would make many aspects of network use, such as web browsing, difficult. A more detailed discussion of DNS is presented in Chapter 6.

Adding, Modifying, or Removing WINS

WINS is used on Microsoft networks to facilitate communications between computers by resolving NetBIOS names to IP addresses. Each time a computer starts up, it registers itself with a WINS server by contacting that server over the network. If the system then needs to contact another system, it can contact the WINS server to get the NetBIOS name resolved to an IP address. If you are thinking about not using WINS, you should know that the alternative is for computers to identify themselves and resolve NetBIOS names to IP addresses via broadcasts. Broadcasts are inefficient because all data is transmitted to every device on the network segment. Broadcasts can be a significant problem for large network segments. Also, if a network has more than one segment, you will be unable to browse to remote segments because broadcasts are not typically forwarded by routers, which should eliminate this method of resolution.

Because WINS actually removes the broadcast communications generated on a network, it has a positive impact on network resources and bandwidth usage. This does not mean that WINS does not generate any network traffic—just that the traffic is more organized and efficient. The amount of network traffic generated by WINS clients to the WINS server is minimal and should not have a negative impact in most network environments.

> **NOTE**
>
> **WINS Traffic** When you are estimating the amount of traffic WINS will generate, it is important to consider the network topology and the design or configuration of the routers in the network.

WINS server information can be entered manually into the TCP/IP configuration on a system, or it can be supplied via DHCP. If the WINS server addresses change and the client configuration is being performed manually, each system needs to be reconfigured with the new WINS server addresses. If you are using DHCP, you need to update only the DHCP scope with the new information.

Removing WINS from a network increases the amount of broadcast traffic and can potentially limit browsing to a single segment.

> ## Challenge—Part 3
>
> Explanation: The best course of action from those described is option 5 (check the account details for the user to make sure that there are no restrictions preventing her from logging on to the network).
>
> You would not choose option 1 (give the user your username and password to see whether she can log on with your credentials). This represents a great security risk, not to mention that such an action would almost certainly be in violation of the corporate computer usage policy (assuming one exists).

(continues)

(continued)

You would not choose option 2 (ask the user for her username and password) yet. You may get to a point where you ask for a username and password to attempt a logon, but there are many other things to check first. If you did get the username and password from the user, you must ensure that the user changes her password immediately following to ensure password confidentiality.

As you have ascertained that the protocol configuration is working correctly via `ping`, there is little value in having the user release and renew her IP address (option 3).

You would not choose option 4 (reboot the server on the third floor, working on the assumption that there are no other users at work yet so noone else will be affected). Rebooting a server is generally a pre-meditated decision, and even though no other users would be affected, the server may be hosting services or applications that need to be running at all times. Additionally, rebooting the server is unlikely to fix the issue anyway. All signs point to a problem with the users logon.

Scenario (continued): While checking the user's account details, you notice a time restriction that prevents the user from logging on to the network before 8:00 a.m. The time now is 7:27 a.m. Which of the following steps are you most likely to take?

1. Change the user's account details so that she can log on to the network immediately.

2. Give the user a username and password from another account that does not have time restrictions applied to it.

3. Inform the user that she will need to wait until 8:00 a.m. before she can log on to the network.

4. Tell the user that you are working on the problem; then go and get yourself some coffee. Call the user back at 8:05 a.m. and tell her that it was hard going, but you fixed the problem.

Select your answer and write the number here: _____

Explanation: The best choice from those listed is option 3. The best course of action is to politely inform the user of the cause of the problem and tell her that if she attempts a logon after 8:00 a.m. there should not be any problems. It should be noted that in a real-world scenario, the user likely would have received an information message related to the logon time restrictions, but sometimes users will close warning or information dialogs without reading them.

You are unlikely to choose option 1 (change the user's account details so that she can log on to the network immediately). Restrictions on logon times are made for specific reasons, and as network administrator you are unlikely to change them just because a user is unable to log on.

You would not choose option 2 (give the user a username and password from another account that does not have time restrictions applied to it). There may be a good reason why the user should not be able to log on to the system. You would never give the user another user account so that she could gain access.

You would not choose option 4 (tell the user that you are working on the problem, go and get some coffee, and then call the user back at 8:05 a.m. and tell her that it was hard going, but you fixed the problem). We hope that we don't need to explain why!

Chapter Summary

This chapter focuses on the processes and procedures involved with troubleshooting remote client connectivity.

Many network devices, such as switches and hubs, have indicator lights that provide information about the status of the device and systems connected to it. Indicator lights provide an easy way to determine whether devices are functioning properly.

Today, small offices and home networks alike rely on Internet access for remote access to either the Internet, or directly to the corporate network to facilitate telecommuting or home working. There are many different ways to get Internet access, including using DSL, cable, home satellite, wireless, and POTS.

How you troubleshoot each type of Internet connectivity depends on the exact type being used. General troubleshooting guidelines include using observation techniques, confirming physical connectivity, and verifying the protocol configuration.

As an administrator in today's networks, you will probably find yourself troubleshooting client connectivity errors. Three common troubleshooting areas for remote access include authentication failure, protocol configuration problems, and physical connectivity problems. Before calling for technical support, network administrators should verify functionality in each of these areas.

Networks today run a variety of services that provide functionality to client systems. Adding, removing, or modifying the configuration of these services can have a direct impact on the functionality of the network. As a network administrator, be aware of and anticipate this impact before it affects the ways in which clients interact with the network.

Key Terms

- cable Internet
- cabling
- client configuration
- collision lights
- configuration
- DHCP
- DNS
- DSL
- LEDs
- link lights
- permissions
- physical connections
- POTS
- protocols
- satellite Internet
- SOHO router
- troubleshooting
- WINS
- wireless Internet

Apply Your Knowledge

Exercises

14.1 Examining the Output from a Successful `ping`

When you're troubleshooting and managing networks, using and interpreting the results from diagnostic utilities is an important skill to learn. In this exercise, you take a look at the output for a successful `ping`.

This exercise assumes that you are using Windows XP.

Estimated time: 10 minutes

1. Open a command prompt on your system by selecting Start, Run. In the Open field of the Run dialog box, type cmd and click OK.

2. At the command prompt, type the command ping examcram.com. You should receive four Reply From messages indicating a successful `ping`.

3. Determine the minimum, maximum, and average times taken to complete the round-trip.

14.2 Simulating a Bad Connection or a Communication Problem

This exercise shows you how to simulate a bad connection or communication problem by disconnecting the network cable during a continuous `ping` of a remote host.

This exercise assumes that you are using Windows 2000 and have an Internet connection.

Estimated time: 10 minutes

1. At the command prompt, type the command ping -t examcram.com.

2. After the pinging process has started, unplug the cable from the NIC in your system. Look at the screen. What message do you receive?

3. Plug the cable back in to the NIC. The output from the command should return to the normal Reply From messages.

4. Press Ctrl+C to stop the `ping` process. Leave the command screen open, but minimize it.

14.3 Simulating What Happens When the Default Gateway Parameter on a System Is Missing or Incorrectly Configured

This exercise shows how to simulate a missing or incorrectly configured default gateway parameter. This exercise assumes that you are using Windows XP.

Estimated time: 5 minutes

1. From the Start menu, locate the shortcut for My Network Places. Then right-click the shortcut and select Properties. The Network and Dial-up Connections dialog box appears.

2. Right-click the Local Area Connection icon (or whatever your network connection is called) and select Properties from the menu. The Local Area Connection Properties dialog box appears.

3. Select Internet Protocol (TCP/IP) from the This Connection Uses the Following Items area of the screen and then click the Properties button. The Internet Protocol (TCP/IP) Properties dialog box appears.

CAUTION

Record Your Settings   Before you complete step 4, make a note of all the current settings for your TCP/IP configuration. If you are using DHCP, this might be as simple as noting that addresses will be assigned via DHCP. If you are using static addresses, double-check the information you have noted before proceeding to step 4.

---

4. Select the Use the Following IP Address radio button. Enter the private address **192.168.2.1** and the subnet mask **255.255.255.0**. Leave the Default Gateway field blank. The screen should look like the dialog box shown in Figure 14.5.

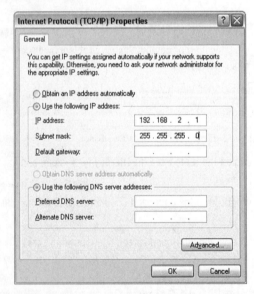

FIGURE 14.5   The Internet Protocol (TCP/IP) Properties dialog box.

5. Click OK to return to the Local Area Connection Properties dialog box. Click OK, and the system initializes the new TCP/IP settings.

6. Restore the command prompt that was minimized in step 4 of Exercise 14.2.

7. Type the command ping 63.240.93.157. What is the result?

8. Repeat steps 1 through 3 and use the information you originally collected before step 4 to restore your original configuration.

Exam Questions

1. You have been contracted to isolate the cause of a client connectivity error on a network. Which of the following areas is likely to be your starting point in the troubleshooting process?

   - ○ **a.** Confirm that the cable distance does not exceed the specified maximum length to the client system.

   - ○ **b.** Replace the NIC in the client computer.

   - ○ **c.** Verify the authentication information.

   - ○ **d.** Verify the protocol configuration.

2. You are installing a NIC into a an older computer system. After it is installed, the system does not recognize it. Which of the following should be confirmed? (Choose the two best answers.)

   - ○ **a.** Verify that the card has a unique IP address.

   - ○ **b.** Verify that the NIC has a unique IRQ.

   - ○ **c.** Verify that the NIC is Ethernet compatible.

   - ○ **d.** Verify that there are no I/O conflicts.

3. During a visual inspection, you notice that one of the indicator lights on your hub is continuously and rapidly flashing, even though you know that no one is using the PC connected to that port. How might you interpret the LED?

   - ○ **a.** The system connected to the port is not powered on.

   - ○ **b.** You are using a crossover cable.

   - ○ **c.** This is normal activity.

   - ○ **d.** You might have a faulty NIC.

4. Marvin, a network user, calls you and is upset because he is unable to log on to the network. Which of the following are valid troubleshooting steps that would help isolate the problem? (Choose the three best answers.)

   - ○ **a.** Try logging on with a different username and password combination.

   - ○ **b.** Verify Marvin's logon information.

   - ○ **c.** `ping` the server.

   - ○ **d.** Run `ifconfig` on the server to verify that the IP address is correct.

5. Joan, a worker in the payroll group, calls you and states that she is unable to print to a network printer. You confirm that other members of the payroll group can print and that Joan's account has permissions to the printer. Which of the following is a likely cause of her inability to print?

   ○ a. The printer is in a different domain.

   ○ b. The printer is offline.

   ○ c. Joan is not correctly logged on to the network.

   ○ d. There is a paper jam in the printer.

6. You are working with a network switch. Each port on the switch has a single LED to indicate link and activity. You notice a solid green light on several of the hub ports. What does this most likely indicate?

   ○ a. Collisions on the port

   ○ b. A connected device with no activity on the device

   ○ c. A connected device sending information to the network

   ○ d. A crossover cable connecting the device to the hub

7. A user calls you to say that he is unable to access a certain file on the server. You establish that the user has accessed the file before and that the user has the appropriate permissions, even though he is assigned permissions at the directory level rather than to the file itself. Which of the following are possible causes of the problem? (Choose the three best answers.)

   ○ a. The user has become disconnected from the server.

   ○ b. The file has been moved or deleted.

   ○ c. The file has become infected with a virus.

   ○ d. The file system on the server has become corrupted.

8. Which of the following need to be verified when you are troubleshooting client connectivity errors? (Choose the three best answers.)

   ○ a. Protocol configurations

   ○ b. Authentication

   ○ c. Logon permissions

   ○ d. File permissions

9. You are troubleshooting a network printer in a busy accounting office. When you try to ping the printer, some of the ping requests are returned, but others are not. What is the most likely explanation of this problem?

   ○ **a.** The printer keeps going online and offline.

   ○ **b.** The network is congested or the NIC in the printer is unable to keep up with the printing demands.

   ○ **c.** The network cable connecting the printer is faulty.

   ○ **d.** The NIC in the printer is faulty.

10. A user calls you to report that he is experiencing problems accessing a file on the server. On quizzing the user, you determine that he has not accessed the file before. Which of the following should be your next troubleshooting step?

   ○ **a.** Set the file permission so that the user can access the file.

   ○ **b.** Reset the user's password.

   ○ **c.** Reboot the server to reinitialize the permissions set.

   ○ **d.** Determine whether the user should have access to the file.

11. While troubleshooting your Windows 2000 server, you disable WINS. What effect is this most likely to have on network users?

   ○ **a.** Users cannot be assigned IP addresses dynamically.

   ○ **b.** Users cannot resolve hostnames to IP addresses.

   ○ **c.** Users cannot browse across subnets.

   ○ **d.** Authentication for new users fails.

12. Which of the following commands would you use to check whether a modem is working through a communications program?

   ○ **a.** ARP

   ○ **b.** ATZ

   ○ **c.** ATG

   ○ **d.** AMP

13. Which of the following is *most* likely to be the cause of slow connections over a dial-up link?

   ○ **a.** No dial tone

   ○ **b.** Incorrect modem configuration

   ○ **c.** Poor line quality

   ○ **d.** Incorrect serial port configuration

14. When using cable Internet access, which of the following is not a valid troubleshooting step?

    ○ **a.** Plugging the cable connection into a TV

    ○ **b.** Ensuring that all physical connections are in place

    ○ **c.** Calling the support line of the cable service provider

    ○ **d.** Checking to make sure that you have a valid IP address

15. While troubleshooting a Linux server, you disable the DNS service. What effect will this most likely have on the network?

    ○ **a.** Users will not be able to receive IP addresses dynamically.

    ○ **b.** Users will not be able to connect to servers using hostnames.

    ○ **c.** DNS broadcast traffic will increase.

    ○ **d.** Systems cannot use VPNs.

16. As the network administrator for a very large network, you have been asked to reduce the traffic generated by the DHCP service. Which of the following would be the best course of action?

    ○ **a.** Reinstall DHCP.

    ○ **b.** Increase the DHCP lease time.

    ○ **c.** Decrease the DHCP lease time.

    ○ **d.** Manually assign DHCP addresses.

17. When contacting technical support personnel, which of the following information should you be prepared to give? (Choose the three best answers.)

    ○ **a.** Administrator passwords for your server systems

    ○ **b.** Account information for the dial-up account

    ○ **c.** Details of what fixes you have already tried

    ○ **d.** A detailed description of the problem

18. A user calls to report a problem with his workstation when trying to connect to the server. You are able to connect to the server without a problem. When you visit the user's desk, you notice that the link light on the network card is not lit. Which of the following is not a possible cause of the problem?

    ○ **a.** The NIC in the workstation

    ○ **b.** The NIC in the server

    ○ **c.** The patch cable between the user's system and the switch

    ○ **d.** The network switch port to which the user is connected

19. A user calls to tell you that after a lunch break he cannot log on to the network. The user's workstation is a Windows XP system with a 10BaseT network connection connected to a network with one Windows 2000 Server on it. The user was able to log on before lunch, and then he logged off before he left. What should you ask the user to check first?

   - ○ **a.** Is the network cable securely plugged in to the back of the workstation?

   - ○ **b.** Are you using the right password?

   - ○ **c.** Is the Caps Lock key off?

   - ○ **d.** Are you using the right username?

20. Which of the following is not a valid troubleshooting step when you are having connectivity problems with a cable modem?

   - ○ **a.** Use the AT command set to initialize the modem.

   - ○ **b.** Cycle the power on the modem.

   - ○ **c.** Check all the physical connections to the modem and the network.

   - ○ **d.** Verify the network settings.

Answers to Exam Questions

1. **c.** Checking to make sure that the authentication information is correct is the simplest of the steps listed and is also the most likely source of the problem. All the other options are valid troubleshooting steps, but you should check the authentication information first. For more information, see the section "Troubleshooting Client Connectivity Errors" in this chapter.

2. **b, d.** When installing a any new device into a system, you must ensure that there are no resource conflicts. On older systems, this includes verifying that there are no IRQ or I/O address conflicts. Answer a is not correct because a valid IP address would not affect whether the system is able to recognize the card. Answer c is not valid. For more information, see the section "Troubleshooting Checklists" in this chapter.

3. **d.** When an LED is continually and rapidly flashing, but you know that there are no users or applications using network resources, you might have a faulty NIC in the system. None of the other answers are valid explanations for this scenario. For more information, see the section "Interpreting Visual Indicators" in this chapter.

4. **a, b, c.** Verifying that the user is using the correct logon information is the first troubleshooting step. Next, you should attempt to log on using another user account, which helps you verify that the workstation connectivity is correct. You can also `ping` the logon server, which enables you to ensure that it is up and running. Answer d is not a valid troubleshooting step because it is a Linux utility. For more information, see the section "Troubleshooting Client Connectivity Errors" in this chapter.

5. **c.** Of the answers provided, the most likely is that the user is not logged on to the network. Because you have confirmed that the other members of the payroll group are able to print, the problem lies with the user and not with some other aspect of the network or the printer. For more information, see the section "Troubleshooting Client Connectivity Errors" in this chapter."

6. **b.** A solid green indicator light normally indicates that the device is connected but not sending any data. Collisions are normally indicated by a rapidly flashing LED, and a device sending data normally causes the LED to flash sporadically. The use of a crossover cable to connect the device to the hub causes a connectivity failure, and in that case the LED would most likely not be lit at all. For more information, see the section "Interpreting Visual Indicators" in this chapter.

7. **a, b, c.** It could be that the user has been disconnected from the server or that the file has been moved or deleted. Less likely is that the file was infected by a virus, rendering it unusable. Answer d is not correct because if you have been able to certify the user's file permissions, there is not an apparent problem with the file system on the server. For more information, see the section "Troubleshooting Client Connectivity Errors" in this chapter.

8. **a, b, c.** Client connectivity problems are normally due to authentication problems, but they can also be attributed to the protocol configuration on the workstation and logon permissions. File permissions do not represent a valid troubleshooting step when you're verifying client connectivity. For more information, see the section "Troubleshooting Client Connectivity Errors" in this chapter.

9. **b.** If you're trying to `ping` a remote system and you receive intermittent Request Timed Out errors, these errors might indicate a congested network or trouble with the NIC in the remote system. All the other answers are valid, although they are much less likely than Answer b. For more information, see the section "Troubleshooting Client Connectivity Errors" in this chapter.

10. **d.** Before you assign permissions in a case like this, it is important to verify that the user is supposed to have access to the file in the first place. Answer a is not valid because you must verify that the user should have access to the file before granting permissions. Because the user is able to log on to the server, resetting the password is not a valid troubleshooting step. Restarting the server is also not a valid troubleshooting step. For more information, see the section "Troubleshooting Client Connectivity Errors" in this chapter.

11. **c.** If you disable WINS, users may be unable to browse across subnets. Of the choices given, this is the most likely. Answer a describes what would happen if you disabled DHCP, and Answer b describes what would happen if you disabled DNS. Answer d is invalid. For more information, see the section "Adding, Modifying, or Removing Network Services" in this chapter.

12. **b.** The ATZ command resets the modem. If the command can be executed successfully, the modem is working correctly. None of the other commands are valid AT command set commands. For more information, see the section "Troubleshooting Remote Connectivity" in this chapter.

13. **c.** Poor line quality is often the cause of performance issues with dial-up links. Answer a is incorrect. The lack of a dial tone would mean that no link could be established—not even a slow one. Answers b and d are incorrect. Incorrect modem or serial port configuration can result in poor performance, but they would more likely result in the modem failing to establish a link. For more information, see the section "Troubleshooting Remote Connectivity" in this chapter.

14. **a.** Although the physical connections for cable TV and a cable modem are the same, the data signal on a coaxial cable would be ignored by a TV, making this an invalid troubleshooting step. All the other steps are valid troubleshooting steps. For more information, see the section "Troubleshooting Remote Connectivity" in this chapter.

15. **b.** If you disable the DNS service, users will not be able to contact servers on the network by using the hostnames and will instead have to use IP addresses. Answer a describes the DHCP service, so disabling DNS will not affect IP address assignment. DNS resolutions cannot be achieved via broadcasts, so these will not increase as a result. Answer d is not valid. For more information, see the section "Adding, Modifying, or Removing Network Services" in this chapter.

16. **b.** If you increase the DHCP lease duration, there will be fewer lease renewal requests on the system. However, this brings with it many other considerations that might make it impractical. None of the other strategies would reduce DHCP-related traffic. For more information, see the section "Adding, Modifying, or Removing Network Services" in this chapter.

17. **b, c, d.** When contacting technical support, be prepared to give the username and password for the account, information about what fixes you have attempted, and a detailed description of the problem. Do not, however, give a technical support person passwords for the user accounts—especially the Administrator account—on the internal network. For more information, see the section "Troubleshooting Remote Connectivity" in this chapter.

18. **b.** The NIC in the server would not cause the problem in this scenario because you are still able to access the server. All the other answers could be the potential cause of the problem. For more information, see the section "Interpreting Visual Indicators" in this chapter.

19. **c.** Windows XP systems use case-sensitive passwords. When a user enters a password, if the Caps Lock key is on and the user doesn't realize it, the password will be entered in the wrong case. All the other troubleshooting steps are valid, but you would perform Answer a first. For more information, see the section "Troubleshooting Client Connectivity Errors" in this chapter.

20. **a.** The AT command set is for use with conventional modems, not with cable or DSL modems. All the other steps are valid for troubleshooting cable modems. For more information, see the section "Troubleshooting Remote Connectivity" in this chapter.

Suggested Readings and Resources

1. Ogletree, Terry William. *Upgrading and Repairing Networks, Fourth Edition.* Que Publishing, 2003.

2. Habraken, Joe. *Absolute Beginner's Guide to Networking*, fourth edition. Que Publishing, 2003.

3. Sugano, Alan. *The Real-world Network Troubleshooting Manual: Tools, Techniques, and Scenarios (Administrator's Advantage Series).* Charles River Media, 2004.

4. Hunt, Craig. *TCP/IP Network Administration*, third edition. O'Reilly & Associates, 2002.

5. "Computer Networking Tutorials and Advice," compnetworking.about.com.

6. "TechEncyclopedia," www.techencyclopedia.com.

7. Network+ network protocol tutorial, www.learnthat.com/courses/computer/networkplus/network11.shtml.

Troubleshooting Procedures and Best Practices

Objectives

This chapter covers the following CompTIA-specified objectives for the "Network Support" section of the Network+ exam:

4.7 Given a troubleshooting scenario involving a network with a particular physical topology (for example: bus, star, mesh, or ring) and including a network diagram, identify the network area affected and the cause of the stated failure.

▶ Physical topology problems are infrequent, but they do occur. You will need to be able to identify the symptoms of a topology error and the steps necessary to correct them.

4.8 Given a network troubleshooting scenario involving an infrastructure (for example, wired or wireless) problem, identify the cause of a stated problem (for example, bad media, interference, network hardware or environment).

▶ Although wiring is resilient to failure, it can and does become faulty. It can also be affected by outside sources, which can create some challenges for troubleshooters. In addition, the devices used to create networks can fail, which often renders entire sections of a network, or the whole network, unusable.

4.9 Given a network problem scenario, select an appropriate course of action based on a logical troubleshooting strategy. This strategy can include the following steps:

▶ **Identify the symptoms and potential causes.**

▶ **Identify the affected area.**

▶ **Establish what has changed.**

▶ **Select the most probable cause.**

▶ **Implement an action plan and solution including potential effects.**

▶ **Test the result.**

▶ **Identify the results and effects of the solution.**

▶ **Document the solution and process.**

▶ For troubleshooting to be successful, it must be approached in a structured manner. These steps describe a troubleshooting methodology that has been proven in the field.

Outline

Study Strategies

▶ Review and identify the order of the troubleshooting steps as identified by the Comptia objectives.

▶ Pay close attention to the "Troubleshooting Scenario and Solution" sidebars. They focus on specific areas of knowledge for the Network+ exam.

▶ Identify the various topology errors paying close attention to the types of errors associated with a particular topology.

▶ Review the components in a network infrastructure that may require troubleshooting (media and hardware).

▶ Review the wireless standards presented in Table 15.2 and specific wireless troubleshooting considerations.

▶ Review the Notes, Tips, and Exam Tips in this chapter. Make sure you understand the information in the Exam Tips. If you don't understand the topic referenced in an Exam Tip, refer to the information in the chapter text and then read the exam tip again.

Introduction

Even the most well-designed and maintained networks will fail at some point. Such a failure might be as dramatic as a failed server taking down the entire network or as routine as a single computer system being unable to print. Regardless of the problem you face, as a network administrator, you will spend a sizable portion of your time troubleshooting problems with the network, the devices connected to it, and the people who use it. In each case, the approach to the problem is as important as the troubleshooting process itself. Although some steps are common to the troubleshooting process, few problems you face will be alike because so many variables are involved.

As you will see in this chapter, troubleshooting is about more than just fixing a problem: It includes isolating the problem and taking the appropriate actions to prevent it from happening again. The ability to effectively troubleshoot network-related problems goes beyond technical knowledge and includes the ability to think creatively to get to the root of a problem. In addition, strong communication skills can turn a difficult and seemingly impossible troubleshooting task into an easy one. Although the role of the network administrator can be a cellular one, you will be surprised at just how much interaction there is with users and at how important this element of your role will be.

This chapter provides a comprehensive look into the many facets that make up an effective troubleshooting strategy. In addition, it examines specific skills and techniques you can use to quickly isolate a network-related problem. It also examines scenarios in which these troubleshooting skills come into play.

> **NOTE**
>
> **Who Says?**   Ask 10 network administrators about troubleshooting best practices, and you will no doubt get 15 different answers. There really is no universally accepted definition or procedural acceptance of troubleshooting best practices. With this in mind, the information provided in this chapter specifies troubleshooting best practices identified by CompTIA. Whether these are the best practices in real-world application is a matter of debate. However, there is no debate that these are the best practices that will be on the exam.

Troubleshooting Basics

There is really no magic or innate ability that makes a good network troubleshooter. You will hear tales of people who have a gift for troubleshooting, but there is nothing necessarily gifted about those who can troubleshoot well. Instead, good troubleshooters have a special combination of skills. The ability to competently and confidently troubleshoot networks comes from experience, a defined methodology, and sometimes just plain luck.

One of the factors that make troubleshooting such a difficult task is the large number of variables that can come into play. Although it is difficult to preemptively list all the factors you have to consider while troubleshooting networks, this chapter lists a few to make you start thinking in the right direction. When you are troubleshooting, thinking in the right direction is half the battle. Considering that most network administrators spend the majority of their troubleshooting time working on the devices connected to the network rather than on the network infrastructure itself, it is worth looking at some of the factors that can affect troubleshooting of devices connected to the network. First, let's look at the difference between troubleshooting a server and troubleshooting a workstation system.

Troubleshooting Servers and Workstations

One often overlooked but important distinction in troubleshooting networks is the difference between troubleshooting a server computer and troubleshooting a workstation system. Although the fundamental troubleshooting principles of isolation and problem determination are often the same in different networks, the steps taken for problem resolution are often different from one network to another. Make no mistake: When you find yourself troubleshooting a server system, the stakes are much higher than with workstation troubleshooting, and therefore it's considerably more stressful. Let's take a look at a few of the most important distinctions between workstation and server troubleshooting:

▶ **Pressure**—It is difficult to capture in words the pressure you feel when troubleshooting a downed server. Troubleshooting a single workstation with one anxious user is stressful enough, and when tens, hundreds, or even thousands of users are waiting for you to solve the problem, the pressure can be enough to unhinge even the most seasoned administrator.

▶ **Planning**—Troubleshooting a single workstation often requires very little planning. If work needs to be done on a workstation, it can often be done during a lunch break, after work, or even during the day. If work needs to be done on a server, particularly one that is heavily accessed, you might need to wait days, weeks, or even months before you have a good time to take down the server so that you can work on it and fix the problem.

▶ **Time**—For many organizations, every minute a server is unavailable is measured as much in dollars as it is in time. Servers are often relied on to provide 24-hour network service—and anything less is often considered unacceptable. Although it might be necessary to take a server down at some point for troubleshooting, you will be expected to account for every minute that it is down.

▶ **Problem determination**—Many people who have had to troubleshoot workstation systems know that often finding the problem involves a little trial and error. (Swap out the RAM; if that doesn't work, replace the power supply, and so on.) Effective server troubleshooting involves very little trial and error—if any at all. Before the server is powered down, the administrator is expected to have a good idea of the problem.

▶ **Expertise**—Today, many people feel comfortable taking the case off their personal computers to add memory, replace a fan, or just have a quick peek. Although it is based on the same technologies as PC hardware, server hardware is often more complex, and those who manage and maintain servers are expected to have an advanced level of hardware and software knowledge, often reinforced by training and certifications.

These are just a few of the differences in the troubleshooting practices and considerations between servers and workstations. As this chapter discusses troubleshooting, attention is focused mainly on the server side of troubleshooting. This helps explain why some of the troubleshooting procedures might seem rigid and unnecessary on a workstation level.

General Troubleshooting Considerations

Knowing the differences between procedures and approaches for troubleshooting servers and for troubleshooting workstations is valuable, but there are a seemingly endless number of other considerations. Each of these other factors can significantly affect the way you approach a problem on the network. The following list contains some of the obvious and perhaps not so obvious factors that come into play when troubleshooting a network:

▶ **Time**—The time of day can play a huge role in the troubleshooting process. For instance, you are likely to respond differently to a network problem at 10 a.m., during high network use, than at 8 p.m., when the network is not being utilized as much. The response to network troubleshooting during high-use periods is often geared toward a Band-Aid solution, just getting things up and running as soon as possible. Finding the exact cause of the problem and developing a permanent fix generally occurs when there is more time.

▶ **Network size**—The strategies and processes used to troubleshoot small networks of 10 to 100 computer systems can be different from those used to troubleshoot networks consisting of thousands of computers.

▶ **Support**—Some network administrators find themselves working alone, as a single IT professional working for a company. In such cases, the only available sources might include telephone, Internet, or manufacturer support. Other network administrators are part of a large IT department. In that type of environment, the troubleshooting process generally includes a hierarchical consultation process.

▶ **Knowledge of the network**—It would be advantageous if there was uniformity in the installation of all networks, but there isn't. You could be working on a network with ring, bus, or star topology. Before you start troubleshooting a network, you need to familiarize yourself with its layout and design. The troubleshooting strategies you employ will be affected by your knowledge of the network.

▶ **Technologies used**—Imagine being called in to troubleshoot a wide area network (WAN) that includes multiple Linux servers, a handful of NetWare servers, an old Windows NT 3.51 server, and multiple Macintosh workstations. Your knowledge of these technologies will dictate how, if at all, you are going to troubleshoot the network. There is no shame in walking away from a problem you are unfamiliar with. Good network administrators always recognize their knowledge boundaries.

These are just a few of the factors that will affect your ability to troubleshoot a network. There are countless others—far too many to list.

> **EXAM ALERT**
>
> **Workstations and Servers**   The Network+ exam does not require you to identify any specific differences between workstation and server troubleshooting but does require background knowledge of general troubleshooting procedures and the factors that influence how a network problem is approached.

The Art of Troubleshooting

Objective:

4.9 Given a network problem scenario, select an appropriate course of action based on a logical troubleshooting strategy. This strategy can include the following steps:

▶ Identify the symptoms and potential causes.

▶ Identify the affected area.

▶ Establish what has changed.

▶ Select the most probable cause.

▶ Implement an action plan and solution, including potential effects.

▶ Test the result.

▶ Identify the results and effects of the solution.

▶ Document the solution and process.

There is little question that at some point in your networking career, you will be called on to troubleshoot network-related problems. Correctly and swiftly identifying these problems is not done by accident; rather, effective troubleshooting requires attention to some specific steps and procedures. Although some organizations have documented troubleshooting procedures for their IT staff members, many do not. Whether you find yourself using these exact steps in your job is debatable, but the general principles remain the same. The CompTIA objectives list the troubleshooting steps as follows:

1. Identify the symptoms and potential causes.

2. Identify the affected area.

3. Establish what has changed.

4. Select the most probable cause.

5. Implement an action plan and solution, including potential effects.

6. Test the result.

7. Identify the results and effects of the solution.

8. Document the solution and process.

The following sections examine each area of the troubleshooting process.

Identify the Symptoms and Potential Causes

Troubleshooting a network can be difficult at the best of times, but trying to do it with limited information makes it that much harder. Trying to troubleshoot a network without all the information can, and often will, cause you to troubleshoot the wrong problem. Without the correct information, you could literally find yourself replacing a toner cartridge when someone actually just used the wrong password.

With this in mind, the first step in the troubleshooting process is to establish exactly what the symptoms of the problem are. This stage of the troubleshooting process is all about information gathering. To get this information, you need knowledge of the operating system used, good communication skills, and a little patience. It is important to get as much information as possible about the problem before you charge out the door with that toner cartridge under your arm. You can glean information from three key sources: the computer (in the form of logs and error messages), the computer user experiencing the problem, and your own observation. These sources are examined in the following sections.

Information from the Computer

If you know where to look and what to look for, a computer can help reveal where a problem lies. Many operating systems provide error messages when a problem is encountered. A Linux system, for example, might present a Segmentation Fault error message, which often indicates a memory-related error. Windows, on the other hand, might display an Illegal Operation error message to indicate a possible memory or application failure. Both of these system error messages can be cross-referenced with the operating system's website information to identify the root of the problem. The information provided in these error messages can at times be cryptic, so finding the solution might be tricky.

In addition to the system-generated error messages, network operating systems can be configured to generate log files after a hardware or software failure. An administrator can then view these log files to see when the failure occurred and what was being done when the crash occurred. Windows 2000/2003/XP displays error messages in the Event Viewer, Linux stores many of its system log files in the /var/log directory, and NetWare creates a file called abend.log, which contains detailed information about the state of the system at the time of the crash. When you start the troubleshooting process, make sure that you are familiar enough with the operating system being used to be able to determine whether it is trying to give you a message.

> **EXAM ALERT**
>
> **Error Message Storage**   For the Network+ exam, you do not need to know where error messages are stored on the respective operating systems; you only need to know that the troubleshooting process requires you to read system-generated log errors.

Information from the User

Getting accurate information from a computer user or anyone with limited technical knowledge can be difficult. Having a limited understanding of computers and technical terminology can make it difficult for a nontechnical person to relay the true symptoms of a problem. However, users can convey what they are trying to do and what is not working. When you interview an end user, you will likely want the following information:

▶ **Error frequency**—If it is a repeating problem, ask for the frequency of the problem. Does the problem occur at regular intervals or sporadically? Does it happen daily, weekly, or monthly?

▶ **Applications in use**—You will definitely want to know what applications were in use at the time of the failure. Only the end user will know this information.

▶ **Past problems**—Ask whether this error has been a problem in the past. If it has and it was addressed, you might already have your fix.

▶ **User modifications**—A new screensaver, a game, or other such programs have ways of ending up on users' systems. Although many of these applications can be installed successfully, sometimes they create problems. When you are trying to isolate the problem, ask the user whether any new software additions have been made to the system.

▶ **Error messages**—Network administrators cannot be at all the computers on a network all the time. Therefore, they are likely to miss an error message when it is displayed onscreen. The end user might be able to tell you what error message appeared.

> **NOTE**
>
> **Installation Policies**   Many organizations have strict policies about what can and cannot be installed on computer systems. These policies are not in place to exercise the administrator's control but rather to prevent as many crashes and failures as possible. Today many harmless-looking freeware and trial programs have Trojan viruses or spyware attached. When executed they can cause considerable problems on a system.

NOTE

Gathering Information   Your communication skills will be most needed when you are gathering information from end users.

Observation Techniques

Finding a problem often involves nothing more than using your eyes, ears, and nose to locate the problem. For instance, if you are troubleshooting a workstation system and you see a smoke cloud wafting from the back of the system, looking for error messages might not be necessary. If you walk into a server room and hear the CPU fan grinding, you are unlikely to need to review the server logs to find the problem.

Observation techniques often come into play when you're troubleshooting connectivity errors. For instance, looking for an unplugged cable and confirming that the light-emitting diode (LED) on the network interface card (NIC) is lit requires observation on your part. Keeping an eye as well as a nose out for potential problems is part of the network administrator's role and can help in identifying a situation before it becomes a problem.

EXAM ALERT

Observation Techniques   For the Network+ exam, remember that observation techniques play a large role in the preemptive troubleshooting process, which can result in finding a small problem before it becomes a large one.

Challenge

A user calls you to complain that she is unable to logon to the network. You confirm that she is using the correct username and password and that the account is active. She was able to access the network the previous day and no software changes have been made to the server or workstation and no other users have reported a similar problem. Given the information provided, what can likely be excluded as the cause of the logon problem and identify a potential cause.

Effective Questioning Techniques

Regardless of the method you are using to gather information about a problem, there are some important questions you will need to have answered. When approaching a problem, consider the following questions:

▶ Is only one computer affected, or has the entire network gone down?

▶ Is the problem happening all the time, or is it intermittent?

▶ Does the problem happen during specific times, or does it happen all the time?

▶ Has this problem occurred in the past?

▶ Has any network equipment been moved recently?

▶ Have any new applications been installed on the network?

▶ Has anyone else tried to correct the problem; if so, what has that person tried?

▶ Is there any documentation that relates to the problem or to the applications or devices associated with the problem?

By answering these questions, as well as others, you will gain a better idea of exactly what the problem is.

Identifying the Affected Area

Some computer problems are isolated to a single user in a single location; others affect several thousand users spanning multiple locations. Establishing the affected area is an important part of the troubleshooting process, and it often dictates the strategies you use in resolving the problem.

> **EXAM ALERT**
>
> **Be Thorough** On the Network+ exam, you might be provided with either a description of a scenario or a description augmented by a network diagram. In either case, you should read the description of the problem carefully, step by step. In most cases, the correct answer is fairly logical, and the wrong answers can be identified easily.

Problems that affect many users are often connectivity issues that disable access for many users. Such problems can often be isolated to wiring closets, network devices, and server rooms. The troubleshooting process for problems isolated to a single user often begins and ends at that user's workstation. The trail might indeed lead you to the wiring closet or server, but that is not likely where the troubleshooting process would begin. Understanding who is affected by a problem can provide you the first clues about where the problem exists.

As a practical example, assume that you are troubleshooting a client connectivity problem whereby a Windows client is unable to access the network. You can try and ping the server from that system, and, if it fails, ping the same server from one or two more client systems. If only the one ping to the server fails, just the single system likely is the problem. If all tested client systems are unable to ping the server, the troubleshooting procedure will not focus on the clients but more toward something common to all three, such as the DHCP server or network hub.

NOTE

Troubleshooting Scenario   You are a network administrator managing a network that has four separate network segments: sales, administration, payroll, and advertising. Late on Tuesday evening, you get a call from several members of the sales staff, complaining that they are unable to access a network printer.

Troubleshooting Solution   Because the reported problem has a common thread, the sales department, it is likely that there is a connectivity issue with the network segment the sales group is on. The problem could be a downed router, switch hub, or authentication server. Whatever the cause, you can more easily isolate the problem if you know the location. Consider how this troubleshooting scenario would be handled differently if the error reports came simultaneously from the sales, payroll, and advertising groups.

Establishing What Has Changed

Whether there is a problem with a workstation's access to a database or an entire network, keep in mind that they were working at some point. Although many claim that the "computer just stopped working," it is unlikely. Far more likely is that there have been changes to the system or the network that caused the problem. As much as users try to convince you that computers do otherwise, computer systems do not reconfigure themselves. Therefore, establishing what was done to a system will lead you in the right direction to isolate and troubleshoot a problem.

Changes can occur on the network, server, or workstation. Each of these is discussed in the following sections.

EXAM ALERT

The Obvious Solutions   In the Network+ exam, avoid discounting a possible answer because it seems too easy. Many of the troubleshooting questions are based on possible real-world scenarios, many of which do have easy or obvious solutions.

Changes to the Network

Most of today's networks are dynamic and continually growing to accommodate new users and new applications. Unfortunately, these network changes, although intended to increase network functionality, may inadvertently cause additional problems. For instance, a new computer system added to a network might be installed with a duplicate computer name or IP address, which would prevent another computer that has the same name or address from accessing the network. Other changes that can create problems on the network include adding or removing a hub or switch, changing the network's routing information, or adding or removing a server. In fact, almost every change that the network administrator makes to the network can potentially have an undesirable impact elsewhere on the network. For this reason, all changes made to the network should be fully documented and fully thought out.

> **NOTE**
>
> **Faulty Hardware** Although recent changes to systems or networks account for many network problems, some problems do happen out of the blue. Faulty hardware is a good example.

Changes to the Server

Part of a network administrator's job involves some tinkering with the server. Although this might be unavoidable, it can sometimes lead to several unintentional problems. Even the most mundane of all server tasks can have a negative impact on the network. The following are some common server-related tasks that can cause problems:

▶ **Changes to user accounts**—For the most part, changes to accounts do not cause any problems, but sometimes they do. If after making changes to user accounts a user or several users are unable to log on to the network or access a database, the problem is likely related to the changes made to the accounts.

▶ **Changes to permissions**—Data is protected by permissions that dictate who can and cannot access the data on the drives. Permissions are an important part of system security, but changes to permissions can inadvertently prevent users from being able to access specific files.

▶ **Patches and updates**—Part of the work involved in administering networks is to monitor new patches and updates for the network operating system and install them as needed. It is not uncommon for an upgrade or a fix to an operating system to cause problems on the network.

▶ **New applications**—From time to time, new applications and programs—such as productivity software, firewall software, or even virus software—have to be installed on the server. When any kind of new software is added to the server, it might cause problems on the network. Knowing what has recently been installed can help you isolate a problem.

▶ **Hardware changes**—Either because of failure or expansion, hardware on the server might have to be changed. Changes to the hardware configuration on the server can cause connectivity problems.

Changes to the Workstation

The changes made to the systems on the network are not always under the control of the network administrator. Often, the end user performs configuration changes and some software installations. Such changes can be particularly frustrating to troubleshoot, and many users are unaware that the changes they make can cause problems. When looking for changes to a workstation system, consider the following:

▶ **Network settings**—One of the configuration hotspots for workstation computer systems is the network settings. If a workstation is unable to access the network, it is a good idea to confirm that the network settings have not been changed.

▶ **Printer settings**—Many printing problems can be isolated to changes in the printer configuration. Some client systems, such as Linux, are more adept at controlling administrative configuration screens than others; for example, Windows leaves such screens open to anyone who wants to change the configuration. When printing problems are isolated to a single system, changes in the configuration could be the cause.

▶ **New software**—Many users love to download and install nifty screensavers or perhaps the latest 3D adventure games on their work computers. The addition of extra software can cause the system to fail. Confirm with the end user that new software has not been added to the system recently.

> **NOTE**
>
> **Troubleshooting Scenario**   A system that could previously log on to the network now receives an error message, saying that it cannot log on due to a duplicate IP address.
>
> **Troubleshooting Solution**   A duplicate IP address means that two systems on the network are attempting to connect to the network using the same IP address. As you know, there can be only one. This often happens when a new system has been added to a network where Dynamic Host Configuration Protocol (DHCP) is not being used.

Selecting the Most Probable Cause of the Problem

There can be many different causes for a single problem on a network, but with appropriate information gathering, it is possible to eliminate many of them. When looking for a probable cause, it is often best to look at the easiest solution first and then work from there. Even in the most complex of network designs, the easiest solution is often the right one. For example, if a single user cannot log on to a network, it is best to confirm network settings before replacing the NIC. Remember, though, that at this point you are only trying to determine the most probable cause, and your first guess might in fact be incorrect. It might take a few tries to determine the correct cause of the problem.

> **NOTE**
>
> **Troubleshooting Scenario**   A user calls you to inform you that she is unable to access email. After asking a few questions, you determine that the user has only recently started with the company and has been unable to get email since her start date.
>
> **Troubleshooting Solution**   In this scenario, there can be several causes of the problem: perhaps network connectivity, perhaps a bad NIC, or perhaps (most likely) email has never been configured on her workstation. Check to see whether email has been configured. If it has not, configure it. If it has been configured and it is working correctly, consider the next most likely cause of the problem.

> **NOTE**
>
> **Escalation Procedures**   One important but often neglected parts of the planning process is the development of escalation procedures. Although many technicians have difficulty admitting that they might need help with a problem, sometimes they need to do it. Unless formal escalation procedures are defined by an organization, the rule of thumb is simply to determine the closest available suitable source of help and start from there.

Implement an Action Plan and Solution, Including Potential Effects

After identifying a cause, but before implementing a solution, develop a plan for the solution. This is particularly a concern for server systems in which taking the server offline is a difficult and undesirable prospect. After identifying the cause of a problem on the server, it is absolutely necessary to plan for the solution. The plan must include details around when the server or network should be taken offline and for how long, what support services are in place, and who will be involved in correcting the problem.

Planning is an important part of the whole troubleshooting process and may involve formal or informal written procedures. Those who do not have experience troubleshooting servers may be wondering about all the formality, but this attention to detail ensures the least amount of network or server downtime and the maximum data availability.

As far as workstation troubleshooting is concerned, rarely is a formal planning procedure required, and this makes the process easier. Planning for workstation troubleshooting typically involves arranging a convenient time with end users to implement a solution.

With the plan in place, you should be ready to implement a solution—that is, apply the patch, replace the hardware, plug in a cable, or implement some other solution. Ideally, your first solution would fix the problem, although unfortunately this is not always the case. If your first solution does not fix the problem, you will need to retrace your steps and start again.

It is important that you attempt only one solution at a time. Trying several solutions at once can make it unclear which one actually corrected the problem.

> **TIP**
>
> **Rollback Plans**   A common and mandatory step that you must take when working on servers and some mission-critical workstations is to develop a rollback plan. The purpose of a rollback plan is to provide a method to get back to where you were before attempting the fix. Troubleshooting should not make the problem worse. Have an escape plan!

Testing the Results

After the corrective change has been made to the server, network, or workstation, it is necessary to test the results—never assume. This is where you find out whether you were right and the remedy you applied actually worked. Don't forget that first impressions can be deceiving, and a fix that *seems* to work on first inspection may not actually have corrected the problem.

The testing process is not always as easy as it sounds. If you are testing a connectivity problem, it is not difficult to ascertain whether your solution was successful. However, changes made to an application or to databases are typically much more difficult to test. It might be necessary to have people who are familiar with the database or application run the tests with you in attendance. For example, suppose that you are troubleshooting an accounting program installed in a client/server configuration. Network clients access the accounting program and the associated data from the server. Recently, all network accountants only receive outdated data when using the application. You, being a network administrator and not an accountant, may have never used the program and therefore cannot determine the outdated data from current data. Perhaps you don't even know how to load the data in the application. How can you possibly determine whether you have corrected the problem?

Even from this simple example, we can see that the process of testing results may require the involvement of others including end users, managers, other members of the IT team, support professionals associated with third-party applications, and so on.

> **NOTE**
>
> **Avoiding False Starts**   When you have completed a fix, test it as thoroughly as you can before informing users of the fix. Users would generally rather wait for a real fix than have two or three false starts.

In an ideal world, you want to be able to fully test a solution to see whether it indeed corrects the problem. However, you might not know whether you were successful until all users have logged back on, the application has been used, or the database has been queried. As a network administrator, you will be expected to take the testing process as far as you realistically can, even though you might not be able to simulate certain system conditions or loads. The true test will be in a real-world application.

> **NOTE**
>
> **Virus Activity**   Keep in mind when troubleshooting a network or systems on a network that the problem might be virus related. Viruses can cause a variety of problems that can often disguise themselves as other problems. Part of your troubleshooting toolkit should include a bootable virus disk with the latest virus definitions. Indicators that you might have a virus include increased error messages and missing and corrupt files.

Identify the Results and Effects of the Solution

Sometimes, you will apply a fix that corrects one problem but creates another problem. Many such circumstances are difficult to predict—but not always. For example, you might add a new network application, but the application requires more bandwidth than your current network infrastructure can support. The result would be that overall network performance would be compromised.

Everything done to a network can have a ripple effect and negatively affect another area of the network. Actions such as adding clients, replacing hubs, and adding applications can all have unforeseen results. It is difficult to always know how the changes you make to a network are going to affect the network's functioning. The safest thing to do is assume that the changes you make are going to affect the network in some way and realize that you just have to figure out how. This is where you might need to think outside the box and try to predict possible outcomes.

Understanding Potential Impacts of Solutions You Choose

It is important to remember that the effects of a potential solution may be far-reaching. As a real example, a few years ago, a mid-sized network hired an IT consultant to address a problem of lost data stored on local client hard disks. His solution was to install a new client/server application that would store data and graphics on a centralized file server. With all data stored centrally, data, including backups, could be easily managed and controlled. The solution was implemented and tested on some client systems, and the application worked.

At first only a few users used the application, but within months most users were transferring large files back and forth from the file server. Network monitoring tools revealed that the network could not handle the load of the new application, and network performance was far below an acceptable level, leaving network users frustrated with wait times.

It turned out that the IT consultant failed to identify an infrastructure problem. Although the network used switches and 10/100 Mbps NICs, Cat3 cable was used throughout most of the network. Cat3 UTP cable provides 10Mbps network speeds, not enough bandwidth for the number of users accessing the application.

This situation provides an example of how the troubleshooting process can easily go wrong. The first problem may have been addressed—decentralized storage on client systems—but the effects of that solution created a much bigger problem. Using CompTIA's troubleshooting process, how could this situation have been avoided?

Documenting the Solution

Although it is often neglected in the troubleshooting process, documentation is as important as any of the other troubleshooting procedures. Documenting a solution involves keeping a record of all the steps taken during the fix—not necessarily just the solution.

For the documentation to be of use to other network administrators in the future, it must include several key pieces of information. When documenting a procedure, include the following information:

▶ **Date**—When was the solution implemented? It is important to know the date because if problems occur after your changes, knowing the date of your fix makes it easier to determine whether your changes caused the problems.

▶ **Why**—Although it is obvious when a problem is being fixed why it is being done, a few weeks later, it might become less clear why that solution was needed. Documenting why the fix was made is important because if the same problem appears on another system, you can use this information to reduce time finding the solution.

▶ **What**—The successful fix should be detailed, along with information about any changes to the configuration of the system or network that were made to achieve the fix. Additional information should include version numbers for software patches or firmware, as appropriate.

▶ **Results**—Many administrators choose to include information on both successes and failures. The documentation of failures may prevent you from going down the same road twice, and the documentation of successful solutions can reduce the time it takes to get a system or network up and running.

▶ **Who**—It might be that information is left out of the documentation, or someone simply wants to ask a few questions about a solution. In both cases, if the name of the person who made a fix is in the documentation, she can easily be tracked down. Of course, this is more of a concern in environments where there are a number of IT staff, or if system repairs are performed by contractors instead of actual company employees.

TIP

Log Books   Many organizations require that a log book be kept in the server room. This log book should maintain a record of everything that has been done on the network. In addition, many organizations require that administrators keep a log book of all repairs and upgrades made to networks and workstations.

NOTE

Troubleshooting Scenario   You have been away on a sunny vacation for three weeks, and when you return, there are several error messages on your company's server.

Troubleshooting Solution   Part of the role of a network administrator is to review the network documentation. To troubleshoot this scenario, look for any documented changes made to the system in your absence. Specifically, look for network configuration changes and added software applications or operating system patches. It is likely that one of these modifications will be at the root of the problem.

Troubleshooting Topology Errors

Objective:

4.7 Given a troubleshooting scenario involving a network with a particular physical topology (for example: bus, star, mesh, or ring) and including a network diagram, identify the network area affected and the cause of the stated failure.

As discussed in Chapter 1, "Introduction to Networking," several different topologies are used for networks. Each of these different types of network designs has failure points specific to the topology being used. To get a better idea of what is involved in troubleshooting these topology errors, the following sections provide specific troubleshooting scenarios and identify the potential causes of the problems.

Bus Network Errors

Recall from Chapter 1 that a bus topology connects all computer stations in a linear fashion. In the early days of Ethernet, the bus topology was the most widely used topology, and network administrators during that time were experienced with the techniques involved in troubleshooting a bus network.

Before looking at specific bus troubleshooting scenarios, let's review the following characteristics of the bus topology:

▶ The cable used on a bus network has two distinct physical endpoints. Each of these cable ends requires a terminator. Terminators are used to absorb electronic signals so that they are not reflected back on the media, compromising data integrity. A failed or missing terminator renders the entire network segment unusable.

▶ The addition, removal, or failure of a device on the network might prevent the entire network from functioning. Also, the coaxial cable used in a bus network can be damaged easily. Moving cables to add or remove devices can cause cable problems.

▶ A bus topology must be continuous. A break in the cable at any point renders the entire segment unusable. If the location of the break in the cable is not apparent, you can check each length of cable systematically from one end to the other to identify the location of the break, or you can use a tool such as a time domain reflectometer.

▶ One end of the bus network should be grounded. Intermittent problems or a high occurrence of errors may indicate poor or insufficient grounding.

Now that we have looked at some of the considerations for bus topologies, we examine some possible troubleshooting scenarios and solutions.

> **NOTE**
>
> **Troubleshooting Scenario**   You have been called in to troubleshoot a network. The network has six computers and one printer connected in a bus topology. You question the network users and discover that although all devices on the network can access each other's system, data failures are occurring intermittently, and some print jobs are failing.
>
> **Troubleshooting Solution**   Intermittent data failures on a bus network can be the result of improper termination or grounding. Improper termination can also prevent the network from functioning altogether. A bus network requires a 50-ohm terminator on each of the physical ends of the bus. One of the ends of the bus also needs to be grounded.

> **NOTE**
>
> **Troubleshooting Scenario**   You have been asked to come in on the weekend and install two new computer systems for the new employees who are starting Monday. On Monday morning, all employees are able to use their local computer resources but are unable to print or access the Internet through the proxy server. What is the likely cause of the problem?
>
> **Troubleshooting Solution**   Network failure after the installation of new systems on a bus topology can often be traced to improper cabling during the installation. If devices are unable to access network resources, you should ensure that the network is properly cabled, with all the network devices connected to each other.

> **NOTE**
>
> **Troubleshooting Scenario**   You are called to troubleshoot a bus topology. When you arrive, you find that none of the devices on the network can communicate with each other. Using the information provided in Figure 15.1, identify the cause of the problem.
>
> **Troubleshooting Solution**   The cable in a bus network segment must be a contiguous length. In Figure 15.1, you can see a break in the cable that would stop Workstations A, B, and C from accessing Workstations D, E, and F. However, because the terminators are at each end of the broken segment, neither part of the network sections would be able to function.

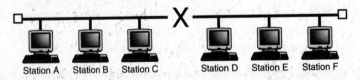

Station A   Station B   Station C   Station D   Station E   Station F   **FIGURE 15.1**   A bus network failure.

Star Network Errors

A star network is the most commonly used network topology today. With a star topology, each computer connects to a centralized device, and each system requires its own cable.

Troubleshooting a star network has different considerations from troubleshooting a bus topology. As a network administrator today, you can expect to troubleshoot star networks.

The following list contains a few of the main characteristics of the star topology and some pointers to potential steps you can take when troubleshooting a star network:

▶ Each device on the network requires its own cable, which is connected to a centralized device such as a hub. A cable failure should affect only the device connected to that cable length.

▶ Devices can be added or removed from a star network without affecting the existing users on the network. If other stations are affected by the addition or removal of devices, there might be a problem with a hub or switch.

▶ A centralized device provides a single point of failure in a star network. If a hub were to fail, for instance, all devices connected to it would be unable to access the network. When you know this and the fact that a cable problem should affect only a single system, you can significantly reduce the amount of time needed to isolate a problem in a star network.

▶ Hubs and switches have indicator lights, or LEDs, that show the states of connected devices as well as representations of network utilization and collision statistics. You can use the lights as a resource when troubleshooting a problem. No lights means no power. Most modern hubs and switches cannot operate without power.

▶ Hubs and switches can be connected to each other to provide more capacity on the network. If all the devices connected to one hub can see each other but not the rest of the network, you should suspect a problem with the hub-to-hub or switch-to-switch connection.

Challenge

After an unhealthy lunch, you receive several calls from network users, complaining that they are unable to access the network. Upon further investigation, you confirm that all the users are members of the sales department. Using Figure 15.2 as a reference, what is the likely cause of the problem?

NOTE

Troubleshooting Scenario A single user calls you, complaining that he is unable to access the star network. Upon investigation, you discover that neither the NIC LED nor the LED associated with that user's computer on the hub is lit. What steps can you take to identify the problem?

Troubleshooting Solution In this scenario, you can take troubleshooting steps from both the workstation and the wiring closet. The first step is to check the physical connections between the two devices. If they are okay, consider trying another network cable or another port on the hub or switch. If it is convenient, you could try the network cable in an alternative system to see whether the problem lies with the workstation's NIC.

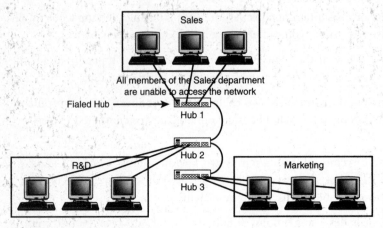

FIGURE 15.2 A star topology failure.

Ring Network Errors

A ring topology is not commonly used in today's network environments, but just in case you are working with a ring network, it is worthwhile knowing what to look for when troubleshooting one. The following is a review of the characteristics of a ring topology:

▶ A break anywhere in the ring prevents all clients from accessing the network. When new systems are added to a ring network, the ring is broken, and the network will be unavailable.

▶ Only one computer can send data onto the network at a time, and the sending computer must have access to the *token* to send the data.

▶ Ring topologies are seen in Token Ring and Fiber Distributed Data Interface (FDDI) networks. Each of these systems uses fault-tolerant strategies.

▶ Physical ring topologies use an actual cable in a ring formation; logical ring topologies use a MAU/MSAU, a device similar to a hub, to perform the ring function internally. The physical layout of the logical ring topology resembles that of a star network.

> **EXAM ALERT**
>
> **Ring Failures** For the exam, remember that a physical ring topology will fail if there is a break anywhere in the media. A logical ring network has a single point of failure, the MSAU. If the MSAU fails, all clients connected to the device will not be able to access the network.

Mesh Network Errors

A mesh topology offers high redundancy by providing several paths for data to reach its destination. In a true mesh network, each device on the network is connected to every other device, and if one cable fails, there is another to provide an alternative data path. Given the number of cables involved, a mesh network can be somewhat tricky to troubleshoot.

> **NOTE**
>
> **Troubleshooting Scenario**   All users of a ring network are unable to log on to the network. After checking the connectivity between the workstation and the multistation access unit (MSAU), you are satisfied that all the workstation connections are secure and correct. What is the problem?
>
> **Troubleshooting Solution**   Ensure that the ring is complete. On an MSAU, the ring completion is achieved by connecting the first MSAU in the ring to the last one. If the ring connection is not complete, devices on the network will not be able to communicate with each other.

Let's review the characteristics of a mesh topology and look at some of the factors that can affect troubleshooting in mesh systems:

▶ A mesh topology interconnects all devices on the network, offering the highest level of redundancy of all the topologies. In a pure mesh environment, all devices are directly connected to all other devices. In a hybrid mesh environment, some devices are connected only to certain others in the topology.

▶ Although a mesh topology can accommodate failed links, mechanisms should still be in place so that failed links are detected and reported.

▶ Design and implementation of a true mesh network can be complex and often requires specialized hardware devices.

Wired mesh networks are so rare that it's unlikely that you will be faced with troubleshooting one, but there will likely be questions on the Network+ exam that focus on mesh networks.

> **NOTE**
>
> **Troubleshooting Scenario**   After numerous problems with connectivity between remote sites, your manager asks to you to design and specify a new topology that has the maximum amount of fault tolerance.
>
> **Troubleshooting Solution**   You can implement a mesh topology between all your WAN devices and configure the topology to accommodate a network link failure.

Troubleshooting Wired and Wireless Infrastructure-Related Problems

Objective:

4.8 Given a network troubleshooting scenario involving an infrastructure (for example, wired or wireless) problem, identify the cause of a stated problem (for example, bad media, interference, network hardware or environment).

You will no doubt find yourself troubleshooting wiring and infrastructure problems much less frequently than you'll troubleshoot client connectivity problems—and thankfully so. Wiring- and infrastructure-related problems can be difficult to trace, and sometimes a costly solution is needed to remedy the situation. When troubleshooting these problems, a methodical approach is likely to pay off.

Wiring problems are related to the actual cable used in a network. For the purposes of the Network+ exam, infrastructure problems are classified as those related to network devices such as hubs, switches, and routers.

Troubleshooting Wiring

Troubleshooting wiring involves knowing what wiring your network uses and where it is being used.

Determining Your Wiring

As mentioned in Chapter 2, "Cabling Standards, Media, and Connectors," the cable used has certain limitations, in terms of both speed and distance. It might be that the network problems are the result of trying to use a cable in an environment or a way for which it was not designed. For example, you might find that a network is connecting two workstations that are 130 meters apart with Category 5 UTP cabling. Category 5 UTP is specified for distances up to 100 meters, so exceeding the maximum cable length could be a potential cause of the problem.

> **NOTE**
>
> **Cable Distances**   Look at cable distances carefully. When you are running cables along walls, across ceilings, and along baseboards, the distances can add up quickly. For this reason, carefully consider the placement of the wiring closet and ensure that you are able to reach all extents of your network while staying within the specified maximum cable distances.

Determining the type of cable used by a network is often as easy as reading the cable. The cable should be stamped with its type—whether it is, for example, UTP Category 5, RG-58, or something else. As you work with the various cable types used to create networks, you'll get to the point where you can easily identify them. However, be careful when identifying cable types because some cable types are almost indistinguishable. After you have determined the cable being used, you can compare the characteristics and limitations of that cable against how it is being used on the network.

> **TIP**
>
> **Cable Types**   The type of cable used in a network is an important fact and one that should be included in the network documentation.

Where the Cable Is Used

Imagine that you have been called in to track down a problem with a network. After some time, you discover that clients are connected to the network via standard UTP cable run down an elevator shaft. Recall from Chapter 2 that UTP has poor resistance to electromagnetic interference (EMI), and therefore UTP and the electrical equipment associated with elevators react to each other like oil and water. The same can be said of cables that are run close to fluorescent light fittings. Such problems might seem farfetched, but you would be surprised at just how many environments you will work in that have random or erratic problems that users have lived with for a long time and not done anything about.

NOTE

Risers   In many buildings, risers are used for running cables between floors. A *riser* is a column that runs from the bottom of the building to the top. Risers are used for running all kinds of cables, including electrical and network cables.

Part of troubleshooting wiring problems is to identify where the cable is run to isolate whether the problem is a result of crosstalk or EMI. Be aware of problems associated with interference and the distance limitations of the cable being used.

NOTE

Test Cable   Never assume that the cable you are using is good until you test it and confirm that it is good. Sometimes cables break, and bad media can cause network problems.

If you find a problem with a network's cable, you can do various things to correct the problem. For cables that exceed the maximum distance, you can use a repeater to regenerate the signal, try to reroute the cable over a more economical route, or even replace the type of cable with one that has greater resistance to attenuation. The method you choose often depends on the network's design and your budget.

For cable affected by EMI or other interference, consider replacing the cable with one that is more resistant to such interference or rerouting the cable away from the source of the interference. If you do reroute cable, pay attention to the maximum distance, and make sure that as you're curing one problem you don't create another.

Troubleshooting Infrastructure Hardware

If you are looking for a challenge, troubleshooting hardware infrastructure problems is for you. It is often not an easy task and usually involves many processes, including baselining and performance monitoring. One of the keys to identifying the failure of a hardware network device is to know what devices are used on a particular network and what each device is designed to do. Some of the common hardware components used in a network infrastructure are shown in Table 15.1.

TABLE 15.1 Common Network Hardware Components, Their Function and Troubleshooting Strategies

Networking Device	Function	Troubleshooting and Failure Signs
Hubs	Hubs are used with a star network topology and UTP cable to connect multiple systems to a centralized physical device.	Because hubs connect multiple network devices, if many devices are unable to access network, the hub may have failed. When a hub fails, all devices connected to it will be unavailable to access the network. Additionally, hubs use broadcasts and forward data to all the connected ports increasing network traffic. When network traffic is high and the network operating slowly, it may be necessary to replace slow hubs.
Switches	Like hubs, switches are uses with a star topology to create a connectivity device.	The inability of several network devices to access the network may indicate a failed switch. If the switch fails, all devices connected to the switch will be unable to access the network. Switches forward data only to the intended recipient allowing them to better manage data that hubs.
Routers	Routers are used to separate broadcast domains and to connect different networks.	If a router fails, network clients will be unable to access remote networks connected by the router. For example, if clients access a remote office through a network router and the router fails, the remote office would be unavailable. Testing router connectivity can be done using utilities such as `ping` and `tracert`.
Bridges	Bridges are commonly used to connect network segments within the same network. Bridges manage the flow of traffic between these network segments.	A failed bridge would prevent the flow of traffic between network segments. If communication between network segments has failed, it may be due to a failed bridge.
Wireless Access Points	Wireless access points provide the bridge between the wired and wireless network.	If wireless clients are unable to access the wired network, the WAP may have failed. However, there are many configuration settings to verify first.

For more information on network hardware devices and their function, refer to Chapter 3 "Networking Components and Devices."

Baselines and Performance Monitoring

Often, the only way to know whether the network is suffering from poor performance is to compare its current performance to its past performance, to see whether it has changed. Such a comparison is done by using *baselines*. Baselines measure network performance and provide a means of comparison when troubleshooting network performance.

Performing baselines on the network is not a one-time task. For baselines to be useful, they must be performed periodically. As a network expands, introducing new users and new applications, baselines can let you know whether the network infrastructure can carry the load. As a rough estimate, consider the following guidelines in determining the frequency of network baselines:

▶ **Changes to network applications**—Some applications are more bandwidth-hungry than others. Installing the latest and greatest application might be too much for the existing network infrastructure to handle. To determine whether this is the case, perform baselines before and after installing a new application.

▶ **Addition of users**—Network performance can slow down if too many users are on the system, using the same resources. If several new users are to be added to a network, a preemptive troubleshooting step would be to obtain baseline performance before and after the new clients are added.

▶ **Changes to the network hardware**—Changes such as installing a new NIC in the server or adding an additional hub can have an impact on the network's overall performance.

▶ **Software upgrade**—If you have to upgrade your network operating system, you should obtain a baseline. A network designed for and working with Linux might struggle if, for example, it were switched to Windows 2003.

TIP

Baseline Strategy   To get an accurate and comparable measurement, perform baselines during both peak and nonpeak times.

NOTE

Troubleshooting Scenario   Users on your network have been complaining that network performance has been slow, and many of their everyday tasks are taking longer than they used to. What should you do?

Troubleshooting Solution   Take a baseline and compare it with information from your baseline history. Interpret the information to see whether there is actually a problem or whether users are just perceiving a problem that does not actually exist. If you determine that there is a problem, you need to find out whether there have been any changes to the network that might account for the slow network performance, such as changes to the hardware or software configurations.

Troubleshooting Wireless Connections

Wireless networks do not require physical cable to connect computers; rather, they use a wireless media such as radio frequency. The benefits of such a configuration are clear—users have access to files and resources without the need for physical connections. Wireless networking eliminates cable faults and cable breaks. It does, however, introduce its own considerations such as signal interference and security.

The following list summarizes the characteristics of a wireless network:

▶ A wireless network allows for a remote connection without requiring cumbersome cabling.

▶ Users can be added to an existing network without disruption to current users.

▶ Common media types for wireless networks include infrared, radio waves, and satellite communication. The most common method used for wireless local area network (WLAN) implementations is radio waves.

▶ It is possible to eavesdrop on wireless signals. Therefore, security must be carefully considered.

▶ Wireless communication has limited speed compared to cabled Ethernet networks.

▶ Some types of wireless communications require a point-to-point direct line-of-sight connection.

When it comes to troubleshooting wireless connections, there are many potential causes including: poor and low-grade signals, channel/SSID conflict, and loss of contact with the wireless access point and more.

Wireless Signal Quality

Because wireless signals travel through the atmosphere, they are subjected to all sorts of environmental and external factors. This includes storms and the number of walls, ceilings, and so on, that the signal must pass through. Just how weakened the signal becomes depends on the building material used and the level of RF interference. All these elements serve to decrease the power of the wireless signal.

> **NOTE**
>
> **Signal Strength** — Wireless signals degrade depending on the construction material used. Signals passing through concrete and steel are particularly weakened.

If you are troubleshooting a wireless connection that has a particularly weak signal, you can do a few things to help increase the power of that signal:

▶ **Antenna**—Perhaps the first and most obvious thing to do is to make sure that the antenna on the AP is positioned for best reception; this often takes a little trial and error to get the placement right. Today's wireless access cards commonly ship with diagnostic software that displays signal strength and make it easy to find the correct position.

▶ **Device placement**—One factor that can degrade wireless signals is RF interference. Because of this, it is important to try and keep wireless devices away from appliances that output RF noise. This includes microwaves, certain cordless devices using the same frequency such as phones, and electrical devices.

▶ **Network location**—Although there may be limited choice, as much as possible it is important to try to reduce the number of obstructions that the signal must pass through. Every obstacle strips a little more power from the signal. The type of material a signal must pass through also can have a significant impact on the signal integrity.

▶ **Boost signal**—If all else fails, it is possible to purchase devices, such as wireless repeaters, that can amplify the wireless signal. The device takes the signal and amplifies it so that it has greater strength. This also increases the distance that the client system can be placed from the WAP.

To successfully manage the wireless signals you need to know the wireless standard that you are using. The standards used today specify range distances, RF ranges, and speeds. It may be that the wireless standard is not capable of doing what you need. Table 15.2 highlights the characteristics of common wireless standards.

TABLE 15.2   Comparing Wireless Standards

Standard	Speed	Range	Frequency	Concerns
802.11a	Up to 54Mbps	25–75 feet	5GHz	Not compatible with 802.11g or 802.11b.
802.11b	Up to 11Mbps	Up to 150 feet	2.4GHz	May conflict with other devices using the 2.4GHz range.
802.11g	Up to 54Mbps	Up to 150 feet	2.4GHz	May conflict with other devices using the 2.4GHz range.
Bluetooth	720Kbps	33 feet	2.4GHz	May conflict with other devices using the 2.4GHz range.

As you can see in Table 15.2, the speeds are listed with the "up to" disclaimer. This is because each standard will decrease the data rate if there is interference. 802.11b wireless link offers speeds up to 11Mbps, but it will automatically back down from 11Mbps to 5.5, 2, and 1Mbps when the radio signal is weak or when interference is detected. 802.11g auto rate sensing rates are 1, 2, 5.5, 6, 9, 12, 18, 24, 36, 48, and 54Mbps. Finally, 802.11a provides rates up to 54Mbps, but will automatically back down to rates 48, 36, 24, 18, 12, 9, and 6Mbps.

EXAM ALERT

Wireless Standards Be prepared to answer questions on the specific characteristics of wireless standards on the Network+ exam.

NOTE

Troubleshooting Scenario Users connecting to a wireless access point are experiencing random problems such as lost connections, poor speed, and network errors.

Troubleshooting Solution Check to see whether the wireless devices are operating within the accepted range of the wireless access point. Also find out whether any environmental considerations have not been fully taken into account, such as construction materials and heavy machinery that can interfere with the quality of the signal.

Wireless Channels

RF channels are important parts of wireless communications. A *channel* is the band of frequency used for the wireless communication. Each standard specifies the channels that can be used. The 802.11a standard specifies radio frequency ranges between 5.15 and 5.875GHz. In contrast, 802.11b and 802.11g standards operate between the 2.4 to 2.497GHz range. As far as channels are concerned, 802.11a has a wider frequency band, allowing more channels and therefore more data throughput. As a result of the wider band, 802.11a supports up to eight nonoverlapping channels. 802.11b/g standards use the smaller band and support only up to three nonoverlapping channels.

It is recommended that the nonoverlapping channels be used for communication. In the U.S., 802.11b/g use 11 channels for data communication as mentioned; three of these—channels 1, 6, and 11—are nonoverlapping channels. Most manufacturers set their default channel to one of the nonoverlapping channels to avoid transmission conflicts. With wireless devices you have the option of selecting which channel your WLAN operates on to avoid interference from other wireless devices that operate in the 2.4GHz frequency range.

When troubleshooting a wireless network, be aware that overlapping channels can disrupt the wireless communications. For example, in many environments, WAPs are inadvertently placed close together—perhaps two access points in separate offices located next door to each other or between floors. Signal disruption will result if there is channel overlap between the access points. The solution here is to try and move the access point to avoid the problem with the overlap, or change channels to one of the other nonoverlapping channels. For example, switch from channel 6 to channel 11.

As far as troubleshooting is concerned, you would typically change the channel of a wireless device only if there is a channel overlap with another device. If a channel must be changed, it must be changed to another nonoverlapping channel.

> **NOTE**
>
> **Troubleshooting Utilities**—When troubleshooting a wireless problem in Windows, the `ipconfig` command can be used to see the status of IP configuration. Similarly, the `ifconfig` command can be used in Linux. In addition, Linux users can use the `iwconfig` command to view the state of your wireless network. Using `iwconfig`, you can view such important information as the link quality, WAP MAC address, data rate, and encryption keys, which can be helpful in ensuring that the parameters within the network are consistent.

SSIDs

The Service Set Identifier (SSID) is a configurable client identification that allows clients to communicate to a particular base station. In application, only clients configured with the same SSID can communicate with base stations having the same SSID. SSID provide a simple password arrangement between base stations and clients.

As far as troubleshooting is concerned, if a client is not able to access a base station, make sure that they are both using the same SSID. Incompatible SSIDs are sometimes found when clients move computers, such as laptops, between different wireless networks. They obtain an SSID from one network, and, if the system is not rebooted, the old SSID won't allow communication to a different base station.

WEP Settings

The Wired Equivalent Privacy (WEP) is a security protocol for wireless networks that encrypts transmitted data. WEP is easy to configure with only three possible security options: Off (no security), 64-bit (basic security), and 128-bit (stronger security). WEP is not difficult to crack, and using it reduces performance slightly.

If your network operates with WEP turned off, your system is open for someone to access your data. Depending on the sensitivity of your data you can choose between the 64-bit or 128-bit encryption. Although the 128-bit WEP encryption provides greater security, it does so at a performance cost; 64-bit offers less impact on system performance and less security.

As far as troubleshooting is concerned, for wireless communication to take place, wireless devices must all use the same WEP setting. Most devices are set to Off by default; if changed, all clients must use the same settings.

WAP Coverage

Like any other network media, WAPs have a limited transmission distance. This limitation is an important consideration when deciding where a WAP should be placed on the network. When troubleshooting a wireless network, pay close attention to the distance client systems are away from the WAP.

When faced with a problem where client systems cannot consistently access the WAP, you could try moving the access point to better cover the area, but then you may disrupt access for users in other areas. So what can be done to troubleshoot WAP coverage?

Depending on the network environment, the quick solution may be to throw money at the problem and purchase another access point, cabling, and other hardware to expand the transmission area. However, there are a few things to try before installing another wireless access point. The following list starts with the least expensive solution and progresses to the most expensive:

▸ **Increase transmission power**—Some access points have a setting to adjust the transmission power output. By default, most of these settings will be set to the maximum output; however, it is worth verifying just in case. As a side note, the transmission power can be decreased if trying to reduce the dispersion of radio waves beyond the immediate network. Increasing the power provides clients stronger data signals and greater transmission distances.

▸ **Relocate the WAP**—When wireless client systems suffer from connectivity problems, the solution may be as simple as relocating the WAP to another location. It may be that it is relocated across the room, a few feet away, or across the hall. Finding the right location will likely take a little trial and error.

▸ **Adjust or replace antennas**—If the access point distance is not sufficient for some network clients, it may be necessary to replace the default antenna used with both the WAP and the client with higher end antennas. Upgrading an antenna can make a big difference in terms of transmission range. Unfortunately, not all WAPs have replaceable antennas.

▸ **Signal amplification**—RF amplifiers add significant distance to wireless signals. An RF amplifier increases the strength and readability of the data transmission. The amplifier provides improvement of both the received and transmitted signals, resulting in an in increase wireless network performance.

▸ **Use a repeater**—Before installing a new WAP, you may first want to think about a wireless repeater. When set to the same channel as the WAP, the repeater takes the transmission and repeats it. So, the WAP transmission gets to the repeater and then the repeater duplicates the signal and passes it forward. It is an effective strategy to increase wireless transmission distances.

Wireless Troubleshooting Checklist

Poor communication between wireless devices has many different potential causes. The following is a review checklist of wireless troubleshooting presented in this chapter:

▶ **Auto transfer rate**—By default, wireless devices are configured to use the strongest, fastest signal. If experiencing connectivity problems between wireless devices, try using the lower transfer rate in a fixed mode to achieve a more stable connection. For example, you can manually choose the wireless transfer rate and instead of using 11Mbps, the highest rate for 802.11b, try 5.5Mbps, 2Mbps, or 1 Mbps. The higher the transfer rate is, the shorter the connection distance is.

▶ **Router placement**—If signal strength is low, try moving the access point to a new location. Moving it just a few feet can make the difference.

▶ **Antenna**—The default antenna shipped with wireless devices may not be powerful enough for a particular client system. Better quality antennas can be purchased for some WAPs, which will boost the distance the signal can go.

▶ **Building obstructions**—Wireless RF communications are weakened if they have to travel through obstructions such as metal and concrete.

▶ **Conflicting devices**—Any device that uses the same frequency range as the wireless device can cause interference. For example, 2.4GHz phones can cause interference with devices using the 802.11g standard.

▶ **Wireless channels**—If connections are inconsistent, try changing the channel to another nonoverlapping channel.

▶ **Protocol issues**—If an IP address is not assigned to the wireless client, an incorrect SSID or incorrect WEP settings can prevent a system from obtaining IP information.

▶ **SSID**—The SSID number used on the client system must match the one used on the WAP. Typically, the default SSID assigned is sufficient but may need to be changed if switching a laptop between different WLANs.

▶ **WEP**—If WEP is enabled, the encryption type must match what is set up in the WAP.

Reviewing Wireless Settings

Now that we have reviewed key wireless settings, let's take a look at an actual wireless connection configuration. Figure 15.3 shows the connection status of a wireless device.

As you can see from the diagram, this wireless connection uses an SSID password of Blitzz, an infrastructure wireless network design, and an 11Mbps transfer rate. However, there are two potential concerns with this connection. First, the connection is using an overlapping channel—1, 6, and 11 are the nonoverlapping channels for this standard. If a channel conflict arises, this may need to be switched. Also, the default security setting has WEP turned off. For better security, both the WAP and the card should be configured with better security. Figure 15.4 shows the Settings dialog box for this connection.

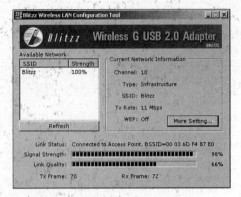

FIGURE 15.3 Wireless configuration information.

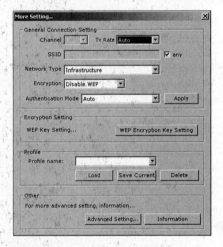

FIGURE 15.4 Modifying wireless settings.

As shown in Figure 15.4, you can adjust many settings for troubleshooting or security reasons. These settings include the following:

▶ **Channel**—If needed, the channel can be changed using the drop-down menu.

▶ **TX Rate**—The transfer rate is typically set to Auto by default. This allows the maximum connection speed. However, it is possible to drop the speed down to increase the distance that the signal travels and boost signal strength due to poor environmental conditions.

▶ **SSID**—This setting allows you to change the SSID to match that used by the WAP to which you are trying to connect.

▶ **Network Type**—This is where the network can be set to use the ad-hoc or infrastructure network design.

▶ **Encryption**—It is advised that this not be set with no security. The default setting leaves the system open to attack. The security setting must match that of the WAP.

▶ **Authentication Mode**—This setting is typically set to Auto but dictates how communication between the two devices will be authenticated. Forcing an authentication mode increases system security.

▶ **WEP Encryption Key**—This setting identifies the level of encryption required. High encryption may have an impact on overall network performance. Figure 15.5 shows the options for this system.

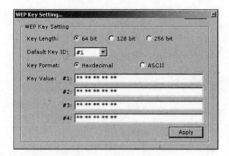

FIGURE 15.5   Encryption settings.

Chapter Summary

Troubleshooting networks is an activity with which network administrators become very familiar. Successful troubleshooting does not happen by accident; rather, the troubleshooting process follows some defined procedures. These procedures include the following:

1. Identify the symptoms and potential causes.

2. Identify the affected area.

3. Establish what has changed.

4. Select the most probable cause.

5. Implement an action plan and solution, including potential effects.

6. Test the result.

7. Identify the results and effects of the solution.

8. Document the solution and process.

You can use several strategies when troubleshooting different topologies, and each topology has unique troubleshooting considerations. When you are troubleshooting a network, it is necessary to identify the topology being used and think about the troubleshooting strategies associated with that particular topology.

At times, you might find yourself troubleshooting wiring and infrastructure problems. Although they are less common than other troubleshooting areas, wiring and network devices should be considered possible causes of a problem. Tracking down infrastructure problems often requires using documentation and network maps or taking baselines to compare network performance.

There are several areas to consider when troubleshooting a wireless network. Many problems are related to poor signal strength, low transmission rates, and limited distances.

Key Terms

- 802.11a
- 802.11b
- 802.11g
- antenna
- attenuation
- baseline
- Bluetooth
- bus
- EMI
- frequency
- hub
- ifconfig

▶ interference

▶ ipconfig

▶ log file

▶ media

▶ mesh

▶ MSAU

▶ NIC

▶ protocol

▶ ring

▶ SSID

▶ star

▶ switch

▶ termination

▶ topology

▶ WEP

▶ wireless

▶ wireless access point (WAP)

▶ wireless channel

Apply Your Knowledge

Exercises

15.1   Using the Internet to Interpret Error Log Messages and Propose Possible Solutions

As a network administrator, you have been given the task of installing and configuring a new printer on a Windows 2000 computer system. However, each time you stop and restart the Windows 2000 system you receive the following error message:

```
STOP: 0x0000009F (0x00000100, 0x8a8a0030, 0x8a8a0030, 0x8a8c2d90)
DRIVER_POWER_STATE_FAILURE
```

To fix the Windows 2000 system, you need to find the solution to the problem.

Estimated time: 10 minutes

1. Go to www.microsoft.com.

2. From the Support links select bar, choose the Support link and then select the Knowledge Base option from the drop-down menu.

3. In the Search drop-down box on the left side of the screen, click the down arrow and then select Windows 2000.

4. In the Search dialog box, type the problem. In this case, you are looking for the cause of the reboot error and the STOP: 0x0000009F message. Type STOP: 0x0000009F in the Search box and then click the Search Now button to begin the search. You might have to scroll down the page to see the results.

5. The solutions search should produce numerous articles pertaining to your search. Find the article titled "You receive a 'STOP: 0x0000009F' error when you shut down or restart a Windows 2000-based computer."

6. Select the article to find a possible solution to the preceding error message.

Exam Questions

1. Which of the following wireless protocols operates at 2.4GHz? (Select two.)

   ○ a. 802.11a

   ○ b. 802.11b

   ○ c. 802.11g

   ○ d. 802.11t

2. Under which of the following circumstances would you change the default channel on an access point?

   ○ a. When there is a channel overlap between access points

   ○ b. To release and renew the SSID

   ○ c. To increase the WEP security settings

   ○ d. To decrease WEP security settings

3. A client on your network has had no problem accessing the wireless network, but recently the client moved to a new office. Since the move she has been unable to access the network. Which of the following is most likely the cause of the problem?

   ○ a. The SSID on the client and the WAP are different.

   ○ b. The SSID has been erased.

   ○ c. The client has incorrect WEP settings.

   ○ d. The client system has moved too far away from the access point.

4. You have just configured a wireless connection using the Bluetooth standard. At what speed does Bluetooth operate?

   ○ a. 350Mbps

   ○ b. 720Kbps

   ○ c. 200Kbps

   ○ d. 11Mbps

5. You have just purchased a new wireless access point that uses no WEP security by default. You change the security settings to use 128-bit encryption. How must the client systems be configured?

    ◯ **a.** All client systems must be set to 128-bit encryption.

    ◯ **b.** The client system will inherit security settings from the WAP.

    ◯ **c.** WEP does not support 128-bit encryption.

    ◯ **d.** The client WEP settings have to be set to auto detect.

6. Which of the following should you consider when troubleshooting wiring problems? (Choose the three best answers.)

    ◯ **a.** The distance between devices

    ◯ **b.** Interference

    ◯ **c.** Atmospheric conditions

    ◯ **d.** Connectors

7. You get numerous calls from users who are unable to access an application. Upon investigation, you find that the application has crashed. You restart the application, and it appears to run okay. What is the next step in the troubleshooting process?

    ◯ **a.** Email the users and let them know that they can use the application again.

    ◯ **b.** Test the application to ensure that it is operating correctly.

    ◯ **c.** Document the problem and the solution.

    ◯ **d.** Reload the application executables from the CD and restart it.

8. A user calls to inform you that she is having a problem accessing her email. What is the next step in the troubleshooting process?

    ◯ **a.** Document the problem.

    ◯ **b.** Make sure that the user's email address is valid.

    ◯ **c.** Discuss the problem with the user.

    ◯ **d.** Visit the user's desk to reload the email client software.

9. You have successfully fixed a problem with a server and have tested the application and let the users back on the system. What is the next step in the troubleshooting process?

    ◯ **a.** Document the problem.

    ◯ **b.** Restart the server.

    ◯ **c.** Document the problem and the solution.

    ◯ **d.** Clear the error logs of any reference to the problem.

10. You are called in to troubleshoot a problem with the NIC on a server that has been running well for some time. The server reports a resource conflict. What would be the next step in the troubleshooting process?

    ○ a. Change the NIC.

    ○ b. Consult the documentation to determine whether there have been any changes to the server configuration.

    ○ c. Download and install the latest drivers for the NIC.

    ○ d. Reload the protocol drivers for the NIC and set them to use a different set of resources.

11. You are troubleshooting a network problem on a network that has a star topology. Four segments are on the network: sales, marketing, admin, and research. Three users from the admin department call you, reporting problems accessing the server. Where are you most likely to look for the source of the problem?

    ○ a. The users' workstations

    ○ b. The server

    ○ c. The switch that services the admin segment

    ○ d. The switch that services the sales segment

12. You are troubleshooting an infrastructure problem and suspect the problem may be the network media. Which of the following must be considered when troubleshooting network media? (Choose two)

    ○ a. Where the media is used

    ○ b. Media frequency output/input ratio

    ○ c. Media type

    ○ d. Media Voltage

13. When you are troubleshooting connectivity on a wireless portion of a LAN, which of the following would you verify? (Choose the two best answers.)

    ○ a. That there is a line of sight between the workstation and the wireless access point

    ○ b. The distance between the workstations and the wireless access point

    ○ c. Hardware resource conflicts on the workstation with the wireless NIC

    ○ d. Cable termination

14. You are adding a new system to a network that uses a physical ring topology. Which of the following statements is true?

    ○ **a.** All network users will not be affected by the addition of the new system.

    ○ **b.** The network will be unavailable while the new system is added.

    ○ **c.** As long as a port is available in the MSAU, network users will not be disrupted.

    ○ **d.** The MSAU will need to be powered down during the installation, affecting only the users connected to that particular MSAU.

15. A user calls to inform you that she is unable to print. Upon questioning her, you determine that the user has just been moved from the second floor to the third floor. The user connects to the printer via a wireless router on the first floor. You need to allow the user to print but do not want to purchase another WAP or disrupt other wireless users. Which of the following might you do?

    ○ **a.** Move the WAP to allow the client system to access the network and therefore the printer.

    ○ **b.** Search for RF interference on the 2.4GHz range.

    ○ **c.** Change the channel.

    ○ **d.** Configure an RF repeater to forward the wireless communications.

16. You are troubleshooting a problem with a bus topology network. Users are reporting that they are sometimes unable to access the network, but it is fine at other times. Which of the following might you consider? (Choose the two best answers.)

    ○ **a.** Faulty hubs or switch

    ○ **b.** Improper or faulty termination

    ○ **c.** Improper grounding

    ○ **d.** Cable lengths in excess of 100 meters

17. You have been called in to troubleshoot a problem with a specific application on a server system. The client is unable to provide any information about the problem except that the application is not accessible. Which of the following troubleshooting steps should you perform first?

    ○ **a.** Consult the documentation for the server.

    ○ **b.** Consult the application error log on the server.

    ○ **c.** Reboot the server.

    ○ **d.** Reload the application from the original CD.

18. Users are occasionally experiencing problems accessing network resources. You suspect that the NIC on the server might not be able to keep up with the demands placed on it. Which of the following troubleshooting steps would you perform first?

   ○ **a.** Replace the NIC with one that offers better levels of performance.

   ○ **b.** Check to see whether updated drivers are available for the card.

   ○ **c.** Perform a baseline to determine whether the card is having a problem coping.

   ○ **d.** Swap the card with one that is known to be working, to see whether there is a problem with the card.

19. Which of the following wireless standards specifies an RF of 5GHz?

   ○ **a.** 802.11a

   ○ **b.** 802.11b

   ○ **c.** 802.11g

   ○ **d.** 802.11g

20. A user is having problems logging on to the server. Each time she tries, she receives a "server not found" message. After asking a few questions, you deduce that the problem is isolated to this single system. Which of the following are possible explanations to the problem? (Choose the two best answers.)

   ○ **a.** The protocol configuration on the workstation is incorrect.

   ○ **b.** A hub may have failed.

   ○ **c.** The cable has become disconnected from the user's workstation.

   ○ **d.** The server is down.

Answers to Exam Questions

1. **b and c.** Wireless standards specify an RF range on which communications are sent. The 802.11b and 802.11g standards use the 2.4GHz range. 802.11a is incorrect as it uses the 5GHz range and 802.11t is not avalid standard.For more information, see the section "Troubleshooting Wireless Connections," in this chapter.

2. **a.** Ordinarily the default channel used with a wireless device is adequate; however, it may be necessary to change the channel if there is overlap with another nearby access point. The channel should be changed to another nonoverlapping channel. Changing the channel would not impact the WEP security settings. For more information, see the section "Troubleshooting Wireless Connections," in this chapter.

3. **d.** A WAP has a limited distance that it can send data transmissions. When a client system moves out of range, it won't be able to access the WAP. Many strategies exist to increase transmission

distances, including RF repeaters, amplifiers, and buying more powerful antennas.The problem is not likely related to the SSID or WEP settings as the client had access to the network before and no settings were changed. For more information, see the section "Troubleshooting Wireless Connections," in this chapter.

4. **b.** Bluetooth is a wireless standard commonly used to interconnect peripheral devices to the computer system. Bluetooth operates at 720Kbps. For more information, see the section "Troubleshooting Wireless Connections," in this chapter.

5. **a**. On a wireless connection between an access point and the client, each system must be configured to use the same WEP security settings. In this case, they must both be configured to use 128-bit encryption.For more information, see the section "Troubleshooting Wireless Connections," in this chapter.

6. **a, b, d.** When you're troubleshooting a wiring problem, consider the distance between devices, interference such as crosstalk and EMI, and the connection points. Answer c is not correct because bound media (that is, cables) are not affected by atmospheric conditions. For more information, see the section "Troubleshooting Wiring," in this chapter.

7. **b.** After you have fixed a problem, you should test it fully to ensure that the network is operating correctly before allowing users to log back on. The steps described in Answers a and c are valid, but only after the application has been tested. Answer d is not correct; you would reload the executable only as part of a systematic troubleshooting process, and because the application loads, it is unlikely that the executable has become corrupt. For more information, see the section "The Art of Troubleshooting," in this chapter.

8. **c.** Not enough information is provided to make any real decision about what the problem might be. In this case, the next troubleshooting step would be to talk to the user and gather more information about exactly what the problem might be. All the other answers are valid troubleshooting steps, but only after the information gathering has been completed. For more information, see the section "The Art of Troubleshooting," in this chapter.

9. **c.** After you have fixed a problem, tested the fix, and let users back on to the system, you should create detailed documentation that describes the problem and the solution. Answer a is incorrect because you must document both the problem and the solution. It is not necessary to restart the server, so Answer b is incorrect, and Answer d would be performed only after the documentation for the system has been created. For more information, see the section "The Art of Troubleshooting," in this chapter.

10. **b.** In a server that has been operating correctly, a resource conflict could indicate that a device has failed and is causing the conflict. More likely, a change has been made to the server, and that change has created a conflict. Although all the other answers represent valid troubleshooting steps, it is most likely that there has been a change to the configuration. For more information, see the section "The Art of Troubleshooting," in this chapter.

11. **c.** In this scenario, the common denominator is that all the users reporting a problem are connected to the same network switch. Therefore, this would be the first place to look for a problem. Because more than one user has a problem, looking at the users' workstations is not the best troubleshooting step. Because you have not received any other calls from other departments, it is

unlikely that there is a problem with the server. Because no users from the sales department have reported problems, there is unlikely to be a problem with the sales section of the network. For more information, see the section "Troubleshooitng Topology Errors," in this chapter.

12. **a, c.** When troubleshooting media, you will need to know the type of media being used. This will allow you to know the characteristics of the media and if it is being used correctly on the network. You will also want to know where the media is being used. If it is being used in an area that causes interference, then another media type or another location may be required. see the section "Troubleshooting Wiring," in this chapter.

13. **b, c.** Wireless devices can operate only within a certain distance from the access point. Operating outside this distance can cause problems with the signal. Also, just as with wired NICs, you must take into account resources when you install wireless NICs in devices. Answer a is not correct because wireless devices do not need a line of sight between sending and receiving devices. Cable termination is not an issue for wireless devices, and so Answer d is not a valid answer. For more information, see the section "Troubleshooting Wireless Connections," in this chapter.

14. **b.** A physical ring topology uses a length of cable to form the ring function. A single break in this cable will take the entire network offline. To add a new system to a physical ring network, the ring must be broken. Therefore, the addition of the new client system will affect all network users.

15. **d.** By the description it sounds like the client has moved beyond the reach of the WAP. To try to accommodate the client, an RF repeater could be used to duplicate and forward the wireless signal. It would not be wise to move the wireless access point because the move might put it out of reach for other network users.Changung the wireless channel would not help but would prevent the user from accessing the WAP altogether.

16. **b, c.** A bus network must have a terminator at each physical end of the bus. It must also be grounded at one end. Improper grounding or faulty termination can lead to random network problems such as those described. Answer a is not correct because 10Base2 networks do not use hubs or switches. 10Base2 has a maximum cable length of 185 meters; therefore, Answer d is not valid either. For more information, see the section "Troubleshooting Topology Errors," in this chapter.

17. **a.** When you are working on an unfamiliar system, the first step should be to consult the documentation to gain as much information as you can about the server and the applications that run on it. All the other troubleshooting steps are valid, but they would be performed only after the information gathering process is complete. For more information, see the section "The Art of Troubleshooting," in this chapter.

18. **c.** By performing a baseline, it is possible to determine whether there is actually a problem with the NIC or whether the problem lies with another part of the server or network. All the answers are valid, but they would be performed only after the actual problem had been determined. For more information, see the section "Troubleshooting the Infrastructure," in this chapter.

19. **a.** The 802.11a wireless standard uses the 5GHz frequency range. 802.11b/g use the 2.4GHz range.'For more information, see the section "Troubleshooting Wireless Connections," in this chapter.

20. **a, c.** The information provided indicates that this user is the only one experiencing a problem. After determining the scope of the problem, we can assume that the issue must lie with something directly connected with that system. In this case, it is likely that the configuration of the workstation or the physical connectivity is to blame. ""For more information, see the section "The Art of Troubleshooting," in this chapter.

Suggested Readings and Resources

1. Habraken, Joe. *Absolute Beginner's Guide to Networking*, fourth edition. Que Publishing, 2003.

2. Ogletree, Terry William. *Upgrading and Repairing Networks, Fourth Edition*. Que Publishing, 2003.

3. Groth, David, Jim McBee. *Cabling: The Complete Guide to Network Wiring*. Sybex, 2001.

4. Network cabling information, www.techfest.com/networking/cabling.htm.

5. "TechEncyclopedia," www.techencyclopedia.com.

6. Network cabling help, www.datacottage.com.

PART II

Final Review

Fast Facts

Practice Exam

Fast Facts

Network+

The fast facts listed in this chapter are designed as a refresher for some of the key knowledge areas required to pass the Network+ certification exam. If you can spend an hour prior to your exam reading through this information, you will have a solid understanding of the key information required to succeed in each major area of the exam. You should be able to review the information presented here in less than an hour.

This summary cannot serve as a substitute for all the material supplied in this book. However, its key points should refresh your memory on critical topics. In addition to the information in this chapter, remember to review the glossary terms because they are intentionally not covered here.

CompTIA uses the following job domains, which are discussed in this book, to arrange the objectives for the Network+ exam:

- ► 1.0—Media and Topologies
- ► 2.0—Protocols and Standards
- ► 3.0—Network Implementation
- ► 4.0—Network Support

1.0—Media and Topologies

Understanding media and topologies is important when designing and troubleshooting networks. Therefore, CompTIA includes many questions on the exam related to commonly used network media. In addition, the exam includes questions that test your knowledge of the various network topologies.

Network Types and Physical and Logical Topologies

The following are some of the important aspects of network types:

- There are two types of computer networks:

  - **Peer-to-peer networks**—Peer-to-peer networks are useful for only relatively small networks. They are often used in small offices or home environments.

  - **Client/server networks**—Client/server networks, also called *server-centric networks*, have clients and servers. Servers provide centralized administration, data storage, and security. The client system requests data from the server and displays the data to the end user.

The following are some of the important aspects of network topologies:

- Network topologies can be defined on a physical level or on a logical level.

- The bus network topology is also known as a *linear bus* because the computers in such a network are linked together using a single cable called a *trunk*, or *backbone*. The following are important features of the bus topology:

  - The computers can be connected to the backbone by a cable, known as a *drop cable*, or, more commonly, directly to the backbone, via T connectors.

  - At each end of the cable, terminators prevent the signal from bouncing back down the cable.

  - If a terminator is loose, data communications may be disrupted. Any other break in the cable will cause the entire network to fail.

  Table 1 shows the advantages and disadvantages of the bus topology.

TABLE 1 Bus Topology: Features, Advantages, and Disadvantages

Features	Advantages	Disadvantages
It uses a single length of cable.	It is inexpensive and easy to implement.	It does not scale well that is, it cannot be expanded easily.
Devices connect directly to the cable.	It doesn't require special equipment.	A break in the cable renders the entire segment unusable.
The cable must be terminated at both ends.	It requires less cable than other topologies.	It is difficult to troubleshoot.

- In a star topology, each device on the network connects to a centralized device via a single cable. The following are important features of the star topology:

▶ Computers in a star network can be connected and disconnected from the network without affecting any other systems.

▶ In a star configuration all devices on the network connect to a central device, and this central device creates a single point of failure on the network.

▶ The most common implementation of the physical star topology is the Ethernet 10BaseT standard.

Table 2 lists the features, advantages, and disadvantages of the star topology.

TABLE 2   Star Topology: Features, Advantages, and Disadvantages

Features	Advantages	Disadvantages
Devices connect to a central point.	It can be easily expanded without disruption to existing systems.	It requires additional networking equipment to create the network layout.
Each system uses an individual cable to attach.	A cable failure affects only a single system.	It requires considerably more cable than other topologies, such as the linear bus.
Multiple stars can be combined to create a hierarchical star.	It is easy to troubleshoot.	Centralized devices create a single point of failure.

▶ In the ring topology, the network layout forms a complete ring. Computers connect to the network cable directly or, far more commonly, through a specialized network device. Breaking the loop of a ring network disrupts the entire network. Even if network devices are used to create the ring, the ring must still be broken if a fault occurs or the network needs to be expanded. Table 3 lists the features, advantages, and disadvantages of the ring topology.

TABLE 3   Ring Topology: Features, Advantages, and Disadvantages

Features	Advantages	Disadvantages
Devices are connected in a closed loop or ring.	It is easy to troubleshoot.	A cable break can disrupt the entire network.
Dual-ring configuration can be used for fault tolerance.	Can be implemented in a fault tolerant configuration.	Network expansion creates network disruption.

▶ The mesh topology requires each computer on the network to be individually connected to each other device. This configuration provides maximum reliability and redundancy for the network. Table 4 lists the features, advantages, and disadvantages of the mesh topology.

TABLE 4   Mesh Topology: Features, Advantages, and Disadvantages

Features	Advantages	Disadvantages
A true mesh uses point-to-point connectivity between all devices.	Multiple links provide fault tolerance and redundancy.	It is difficult to implement.
A hybrid mesh uses point-to-point connectivity between certain devices, but not all of them.	The network can be expanded with minimal or no disruption.	It can be expensive because it requires specialized hardware and cable.

▶ Wireless networks operating in the infrastructure mode use a centralized device known as a *wireless access point* (WAP) that transmits signals to devices with wireless network interface cards (NICs) installed in them.

▶ The ad-hoc wireless topology does not use an AP, but rather all devices connect together in a peer-to-peer configuration.

Standards and Access Methods

The following are descriptions of the Institute of Electrical and Electronics Engineers (IEEE) 802 standards:

▶ **802.1, internetworking**—Defines internetwork communications standards between devices and includes specifications for routing and bridging.

▶ **802.2, the LLC sublayer**—Defines specifications for the Logical Link Control (LLC) sublayer in the 802 standard series.

▶ **802.3, CSMA/CD**—Defines the carrier-sense multiple-access with collision detection (CSMA/CD) media access method used in Ethernet networks. This is the most popular networking standard used today.

▶ **802.4, a token passing bus (rarely used)**—Defines the use of a token-passing system on a linear bus topology.

▶ **802.5, Token Ring networks**—Defines Token Ring networking.

▶ **802.6, metropolitan area network (MAN)**—Defines a data transmission method called distributed queue dual bus (DQDB), which is designed to carry voice and data on a single link.

▶ **802.7, Broadband Technical Advisory Group**—Defines the standards and specifications of broadband communications methods.

▶ **802.8, Fiber-Optic Technical Advisory Group**—Provides assistance to other IEEE 802 committees on subjects related to the use of fiber-optics.

▶ **802.9, Integrated Voice and Data Networks Group**—Works on the advancement of integrated voice and data networks.

▶ **802.10, network security**—Defines security standards that make it possible to safely and securely transmit and exchange data.

▶ **802.11, wireless networks**—Defines standards for wireless LAN communication.

▶ **802.12, 100BaseVG-AnyLAN**—Defines a standard for high-speed LAN technologies.

The Network+ exam focuses on the LAN standards 802.2, 802.3, 802.5, and 802.11.

Access methods govern the way in which systems access the network media and send data. Following are the key aspects of the CSMA/CD access method:

▶ CSMA/CD, which is defined in the IEEE 802.3 standard, is the most popular media access method because it is associated with Ethernet networking, which is by far the most popular networking system.

▶ CSMA/CD is known as a *contention media access method* because systems contend for access to the media.

▶ Closely connected to the CSMA/CD access method is CSMA/CA. Instead of collision detection (CD), collision avoidance (CA) is used. Wireless 802.11 standards use the CSMA/CA access method.

Table 5 shows the advantages and disadvantages of CSMA/CD.

TABLE 5 Advantages and Disadvantages of CSMA/CD

Advantages	Disadvantages
It has low overhead.	Collisions degrade network performance.
It is able to utilize all available bandwidth when possible.	Priorities cannot be assigned to certain nodes.
	Performance degrades exponentially as devices are added.

Token passing is an access method specified in IEEE 802.5. Following are the important facts about token-passing networks:

▶ On a token-passing network, a packet called a *token* is passed among the systems on the network. The network has only one token, and a system can send data only when it has possession of the token.

▶ All cards in a token-passing network must operate at the same speed.

▶ Because a system can transmit only when it has the token, there is no contention, as with CSMA/CD.

▶ Ring networks are most commonly wired in a star configuration. In a Token Ring network, a multistation access unit (MSAU) is equivalent to a hub or switch on an Ethernet network.

▶ To connect MSAUs, the ring in (RI) and ring out (RO) configuration must be properly set.

Table 6 shows the advantages and disadvantages of token-passing networks.

TABLE 6   Advantages and Disadvantages of Token-Passing Networks

Advantages	Disadvantages
No collisions mean more consistent performance in high-load configurations.	The generation of a token creates network overhead.
Performance is consistently predictable, making token passing suitable for time-sensitive applications.	Network hardware is more complex and expensive than that used with other access methods.
	The maximum speed is limited due to the overhead of token passing and regeneration.

Media Considerations and Limitations

As a data signal travels through a specific media, it may be subjected to a type of interference known as *electromagnetic interference* (EMI). Following are important EMI facts:

▶ Many different factors cause EMI; common sources include computer monitors and fluorescent lighting fixtures.

▶ Copper-based media are prone to EMI, whereas fiber-optic cable is completely resistant to it.

Data signals may also be subjected to something commonly referred to as *crosstalk*, which occurs when signals from two cables in close proximity to one another interfere with each other.

Media has maximum lengths because a signal weakens as it travels farther from its point of origin. The weakening of data signals as they traverse the media is referred to as *attenuation*.

Two types of signaling methods are used to transmit information over network media:

▶ **Baseband**—Baseband transmissions typically use digital signaling over a single channel or frequency; the transmissions themselves take the form of either electrical pulses or light. Ethernet networks use baseband transmissions.

Using baseband transmissions, it is possible to transmit multiple signals on a single cable by using a process known as *multiplexing*.

▶ **Broadband**—Broadband signaling uses analog signals in the form of optical or electromagnetic waves over multiple transmission frequencies.

Dialog Modes

There are three main dialog modes:

▶ **Simplex**—The simplex mode allows only one-way communication through the media. A good example of simplex is a radio or television signal: There is only one transmitting device, and all other devices are receiving devices.

▶ **Half-duplex**—Half-duplex allows each device to both transmit and receive, but only one of these processes can occur at a time.

▶ **Full-duplex**—Full-duplex allows devices to receive and transmit simultaneously. A 100Mbps network card in full-duplex mode can operate at 200Mbps.

Wireless

▶ 802.11 represents the IEEE designation for wireless networking. There are four primary wireless networking specifications under the 802.11 banner: 802.11, 802.11a, 802.11b, and 802.11g. All four use the Ethernet protocol and the CSMA/CA access method. Table 7 reviews 802.11 wireless standards.

TABLE 7   802.11 Wireless Standards
Summary of Wireless Standards

IEEE Standard	Frequency/ Media	Speed	Topology	Transmission Range	Access Method
802.11	2.4GHz RF	1 to 2 Mbps	Ad-hoc/ infrastructure	25 to 75 feet indoors; range can be affected by building materials.	CSMA/CA

(continues)

TABLE 7 *continued*
Summary of Wireless Standards

IEEE Standard	Frequency/ Media	Speed	Topology	Transmission Range	Access Method
802.11	2.4GHz RF	1 to 2 Mbps	Ad-hoc/ infrastructure	25 to 75 feet indoors; range can be affected by building materials.	CSMA/CA
802.11a	5GHz	Up to 54 Mbps	Ad-hoc/ infrastructure	25 to 75 feet indoors; range can be affected by building materials.	CSMA/CA
802.11b	2.4GHz	Up to 11Mbps	Ad-hoc/ infrastructure	Up to 150 feet indoors; range can be affected by building materials.	CSMA/CA
802.11g	2.4GHz	Up to 54Mbps	Ad-hoc/ infrastructure	Up to 150 feet indoors; range can be affected by building materials.	CSMA/CA

▶ Bluetooth is a wireless standard used for many purposes, including connecting peripheral devices to a system. Bluetooth uses a low-cost, short-range radio link to create a link to replace many of the cords that used to connect devices. Table 8 shows the characteristics of Bluetooth.

▶ Infrared wireless networking uses infrared beams to send data transmissions between devices. Infrared wireless networking offers higher transmission rates reaching 10Mbps to 16Mbps.

TABLE 8   Summary of Bluetooth

Specification	Bluetooth
Topology	Ad hoc
Spread spectrum	FHSS
Media	2.4GHz RF
Speed	720Kbps
Range	10 meters in optimal conditions

Wireless interference:

▶ **Radio frequency interference**—Wireless technologies such as 802.11b/g use RF range of 2.4GHz and so do many other devices such as cordless phones, microwaves, and so on. Devices that share the channel can cause noise and weaken the signals.

▶ **Electrical interference**—Electrical interference comes from devices such as computers, fridges, fans, lighting fixtures, or any other motorized devices. The impact electrical interference has on the signal is depends on the proximity of the electric device to the wireless access point. Advances in wireless technologies and in electrical devices, have reduced the impact these types of devices have on wireless transmissions.

▶ **Environmental factors**—Weather conditions can have a huge impact on wireless signal integrity. Lighting for instance can cause electrical interference, and fog can weaken signals as they pass through.

Network Media

There are two distinct types of twisted-pair cable: unshielded twisted pair (UTP) and shielded twisted pair (STP). STP has extra shielding within the casing, so it copes with interference and attenuation better than regular UTP. UTP is much more common in modern network implementations.

The Electronic Industries Association/Telecommunications Industry Association (EIA/TIA) has specified seven categories of twisted-pair cable:

▶ **Category 1**—Voice-grade UTP telephone cable. Due to its susceptibility to interference and attenuation and its low bandwidth capability, Category 1 UTP is not practical for network applications.

▶ **Category 2**—Data-grade cable capable of transmitting data up to 4Mbps. Category 2 cable is, of course, too slow for networks. It is unlikely that you will encounter Category 2 used on any network today.

▶ **Category 3**—Data-grade cable capable of transmitting data up to 10Mbps. A few years ago, Category 3 was the cable of choice for twisted-pair networks. As network speeds pushed the 100Mbps speed limit, Category 3 became ineffective. Category 3 cabling can be used up to 100 meters.

▶ **Category 4**—Data-grade cable that has potential bandwidth of 16Mbps. Category 4 cable was often implemented in the IBM Token Ring networks.

▶ **Category 5**—Data-grade cable capable of transmitting data at 100Mbps. Category 5 is the cable of choice on twisted-pair networks and is commonly associated with Fast Ethernet technologies.

▸ **Category 5e**—Data-grade cable used on networks that run at up to 1000Mbps. Category 5e cabling can be used up to 350 meters, depending on the implementation.

▸ **Category 6**—High-performance UTP cable capable of transmitting data at over 1000Mbps. Category 6 cabling is rated up to 550 meters depending on the implementation.

The networking standard used defines what speed the network will operate at, not the network cabling. Cables do not operate at a certain speed. All the network cabling needs to do is support that speed as a minimum.

Fiber-optic cables are not susceptible to EMI or crosstalk, giving fiber-optic cable an obvious advantage over copper-based media. The loss of signal strength on fiber-optic cable is referred to as *chromatic dispersion*.

Two types of optical fiber are available: single-mode and multimode.

SC, ST, LC, and MT-RJ connectors are associated with fiber cabling. ST connectors offer a twist-type attachment, and SC and LC are push-on connectors. MT-RJ is somewhat similar in appearance to an RJ-45 connector but is longer. MT-RJ connectors have a flange, like an RJ-45 connector, to secure the cable in place.

RJ-45 connectors are used with the 8-wire UTP cable used in network implementations. RJ-11 connectors are used with the 4-wire UTP cable associated with telephone systems.

F-Type connectors are used with coaxial cable. In network implementations, they are most commonly associated with connecting cable modems to incoming cable connections.

IEEE 1394 (FireWire) can use either a 4-pin or a 6-pin connector.

Table 9 summarizes the characteristics of the types of network cable.

TABLE 9   Summary of Cable Characteristics

Media	Resistance to Attenuation	Resistance to EMI/ Crosstalk	Cost of Implementation	Difficulty of Implementation
Thin coax	Moderate	Moderate	Low	Low
UTP	Low	Low	Low	Low
STP	Moderate	Moderate	Moderate	Low
Fiber-optic	Very high	Very high	Very high	Moderate

IEEE Ethernet Networking Standards

The following tables (Table 10 through Table 15) provide a summary of the IEEE Ethernet networking standards covered in the Network+ exam objectives.

TABLE 10   Summary of 10BaseT Characteristics

Characteristic	Description
Transmission method	Baseband
Speed	10Mbps
Total distance/segment	100 meters
Cable type	Category 3, 4, or 5 UTP or STP
Connector	RJ-45

TABLE 11   Summary of 10BaseFL Characteristics

Characteristic	Description
Transmission method	Baseband
Speed	10Mbps
Total distance/segment	2000 meters
Cable type	Single mode/Multimode fiber
Connector	Fiber connectors

TABLE 12   Summary of 100BaseX Standards

Characteristic	100BaseTX	100BaseT4	100BaseFX
Transmission method	Baseband	Baseband	Baseband
Speed	100Mbps	100Mbps	100Mbps
Distance	100 meters	100 meters	412 meters (multimode, half-duplex)
			10,000 meters (single-mode, full-duplex)
Cable type	Category 5 UTP, STP	Category 3, 4, 5	Fiber-optic
Connector type	RJ-45	RJ-45	SC, ST, MIC

TABLE 13 Summary of 1000BaseT

Characteristic	Description
Transmission method	Baseband
Speed	1000Mbps
Total distance/segment	100 meters
Cable type	Category 5 or better
Connector type	RJ-45

TABLE 14 Summary of Fiber-Optic Based 1000BaseX (gigabit Ethernet) Standards

Characteristic	1000BaseSX	1000BaseLX	1000BaseCX
Transmission method	Baseband	Baseband	Baseband
Speed	1000Mbps	1000Mbps	1000Mbps
Distance	Half-duplex 275 (62.5 micron multimode fiber); half-duplex 316 (50 micron multimode fiber); full-duplex 275 (62.5 micron multimode fiber); full-duplex 550 (50 micron multimode fiber)	Half-duplex 316 (multimode and single-mode fiber); full-duplex 550 (multimode fiber); full-duplex 5000 (single-mode fiber)	25 meters for both full-duplex and half-duplex operations
Cable type	62.5/125 and 50/125 multimode fiber	62.5/125 and 50/125 multi-mode fiber; two 10-micron single-mode optical fibers	Shielded copper cable
Connector type	SC connector	SC connector	9-pin shielded connector, 8-pin Fibre Channel type 2 connector

TABLE 15 Summary of IEEE 802.3ae 10 Gigabit Ethernet Characteristics

	10GbaseSR	10GbaseLR	10GbaseER
Transmission method	Baseband	Baseband	Baseband
Speed	10000Mbps	10000Mbps	10000Mbps
Distance	33m/300m	10,000m	40,000m

TABLE 15   *continued*

	10GbaseSR	10GbaseLR	10GbaseER
Cable type	62.5 micron Multimode Fibre/50 Micron Multimode fiber	Single mode Fiber	Single mode Fiber
Connector type	Fiber	Fiber	Fiber

Network Devices

Both hubs and switches are used in Ethernet networks. The following facts are relevant to hubs:

▶ Token Ring networks, which are few and far between, use special devices called multi-station access units (MSAUs) to create the network.

▶ The function of a hub is to take data from one of the connected devices and forward it to all the other ports on the hub.

▶ Most hubs are referred to as *active* because they regenerate a signal before forwarding it to all the ports on the device. To do this, the hub needs a power supply.

▶ Passive hubs do not need power because they don't regenerate signals.

The following facts are relevant to switches:

▶ Rather than forward data to all the connected ports, a switch forwards data only to the port on which the destination system is connected.

▶ A switch makes forwarding decisions based on the Media Access Control (MAC) addresses of the devices connected to it to determine the correct port.

▶ In cut-through switching, the switch begins to forward the packet as soon as it is received.

▶ In store-and-forward switching, the switch waits to receive the entire packet before beginning to forward it.

▶ In fragment-free switching, the switch reads only the part of the packet that enables it to identify fragments of a transmission.

▶ Switches reduce collisions by a process called *microsegmentation*. Each port on a switch is a dedicated link between the switch and the connected computer.

The following facts are relevant to both hubs and switches:

▶ Hubs and switches have two types of ports: medium-dependent interface (MDI) and medium-dependent interface crossed (MDI-X).

▶ A straight-through cable is used to connect systems to the switch or hub using the MDI-X ports.

▶ In a crossover cable, Wires 1 and 3 and Wires 2 and 6 are crossed.

▶ Both hubs and switches use light-emitting diodes (LEDs) to indicate certain connection conditions. At the very least, a link light on the hub indicates the existence of a live connection.

▶ Both hubs and switches are available in managed and unmanaged versions. A managed device has an interface through which it can be configured to perform certain special functions.

Bridges are used to divide up networks and thus reduce the amount of traffic on each network.

A bridge functions by blocking or forwarding data, based on the destination MAC address written into each frame of data.

Unlike bridges and switches, which use the hardware-configured MAC address to determine the destination of the data, routers use software-configured network addresses to make decisions.

With distance-vector routing protocols, each router communicates all the routes it knows about to all other routers to which it is directly attached.

Routing Information Protocol (RIP) is a distance-vector routing protocol for both Transmission Control Protocol (TCP) and Internetwork Packet Exchange (IPX).

Modems translate digital signals from a computer into analog signals that can travel across conventional phone lines.

Modems are controlled through a series of commands known as the Hayes AT command set:

Command	Result
ATA	Answers an incoming call
ATH	Hangs up the current connection
ATZ	Resets the modem
ATI3	Displays modem identification information

Following is a summary of UART chip speeds:

UART Chip	Speed (bps)
8250	9,600
16450	115,200
16550	115,200
16650	430,800
16750	921,600
16950	921,600

Table 16 summarizes the various devices used in networks.

TABLE 16   Networking Devices Summary

Device	Function/Purpose	Key Points
Hub	Connects devices on a twisted-pair network.	A hub does not perform any tasks besides signal regeneration.
Switch	Connects devices on a twisted-pair network.	A switch forwards data to its destination by using the MAC address embedded in each packet.
Bridge	Divides networks to reduce overall network traffic.	A bridge allows or prevents data from passing through it by reading the MAC address.
Router	Connects networks together.	A router uses the software-configured network address to make forwarding decisions.
Gateway	Translates from one data format to another.	Gateways can be hardware- or software-based. Any device that translates data formats is called a gateway.
CSU/DSU	Translates digital signals used on a LAN to those used on a WAN.	CSU/DSU functionality is sometimes incorporated into other devices, such as a router with a WAN connection.
Network card	Enables systems to connect to the network.	Network interfaces can be add-in expansion cards, PCMCIA cards, or built-in interfaces.
ISDN terminal adapter	Connects devices to ISDN lines.	ISDN is a digital WAN technology often used in place of slower modem links. ISDN terminal adapters are required to reformat the data format for transmission on ISDN links.
Wireless AP	Provides network capabilities to wireless network devices.	An AP is often used to connect to a wired network, thereby acting as a link between wired and wireless portions of the network.
Modem	Provides serial communication capabilities across phone lines.	Modems modulate the digital signal into analog at the sending end and perform the reverse function at the receiving end.

2.0—Protocols and Standards

A MAC address is a 6-byte address that allows a NIC to be uniquely identified on the network. The first three bytes (00:D0:59) identify the manufacturer of the card; The last three bytes (09:07:51) are the Universal LAN MAC address, which makes the interface unique.

OSI Model

As data is passed up or down through the OSI model structure, headers are added (going down) or removed (going up) at each layer—a process called *encapsulation (added) or decapsulation (removed)*.

Table 17 provides a summary of the OSI model layers, and Table 18 shows how each device maps to the OSI model.

TABLE 17   Summary of the OSI Model

OSI Layer	Major Functions
Application	Provides access to the network for applications and certain end-user functions. Displays incoming information and prepares outgoing information for network access.
Presentation	Converts data from the application layer into a format that can be sent over the network. Converts data from the session layer into a format that can be understood by the application layer. Handles encryption and decryption of data. Provides compression and decompression functionality.
Session	Synchronizes the data exchange between applications on separate devices. Handles error detection and notification to the peer layer on the other device.
Transport	Establishes, maintains, and breaks connections between two devices. Determines the ordering and priorities of data. Performs error checking and verification and handles retransmissions, if necessary.
Network	Provides mechanisms for the routing of data between devices across single or multiple network segments. Handles the discovery of destination systems and addressing.
Data-link	Has two distinct sublayers: LLC and MAC. Performs error detection and handling for the transmitted signals. Defines the method by which the medium is accessed. Defines hardware addressing through the MAC sublayer.
Physical	Defines the physical structure of the network. Defines voltage/signal rates and the physical connection methods. Defines the physical topology.

When you take the Network+ exam, you may be asked to identify at what level of the OSI model common network devices operate. This information is provided in Table 18.

TABLE 18 Mapping Devices to the OSI Model

Device	OSI Layer at Which the Device Operates
Hub	Physical (Layer 1)
Switch	Data-link (Layer 2)
Bridge	Data-link (Layer 2)
Router	Network (Layer 3)
NIC	Data-link (Layer 2)
WAP	Data-link (Layer 2)

Application protocols map to the application, presentation, and session layers of the OSI model. Application protocols include AFP, FTP, TFTP, SFTP, SSH, Telnet, SCP, NNTP, NTP, NCP, and SNMP.

Transport protocols map to the transport layer of the OSI model and are responsible for the transporting of data across the network. Transport protocols include ATP, NetBEUI, SPX, TCP, and UDP.

The NetBEUI protocol uses names as addresses.

Network protocols are responsible for providing the addressing and routing information. Network protocols include IP, IPX, and DDP.

RIP is responsible for the routing of packets on an IPX/SPX network.

Table 19 provides information on each of the protocol suites included in the Network+ exam. Table 20 summarizes each of the commonly used protocols in the TCP/IP suite, Table 21 shows you the TCP/IP port assignments, and Table 22 describes the TCP/IP services covered on the Network+ exam.

TABLE 19 Protocol Summary

Protocol	Operating System Support	Routable?	Configuration	Primary Use
IPX/SPX	Used to be the default protocol for NetWare, but now TCP/IP is preferred; can also be used with Linux; Windows supports NWLink, a version of the IPX/SPX protocol suite created by Microsoft for cross-platform compatibility.	Yes	Very easy—most information is autoconfigured.	Primarily used on legacy Novell Networks.

TABLE 19 *Continued*

Protocol	Operating System Support	Routable?	Configuration	Primary Use
NetBEUI	Windows only	No	Easy network configuration, requiring only the computer's NetBIOS name.	Primarily used on smaller networks where routing is not required.
AppleTalk	Used by Macintosh; Yes with some support on other platforms.	Yes	Minimal configuration difficulty; requires a node address (automatically assigned when systems boot) and a network address.	Used on legacy Macintosh networks.
TCP/IP	Used by default with Unix, Linux, NetWare, and Windows systems; supported by Macintosh and just about every other computing platform available.	Yes	Comparatively difficult to configure; has a number of different configuration requirements.	Used on many networks of all shapes and sizes; is the protocol of the Internet.

TABLE 20 **Summary of Common TCP/IP Protocols**

Protocol	Full Name	Description
IP	Internet Protocol	Connectionless protocol used for moving data around a network.
TCP	Transmission Control Protocol	Connection-oriented protocol that offers flow control, sequencing, and retransmission of dropped packets.
UDP	User Datagram Protocol	Connectionless alternative to TCP used for applications that do not require the functions offered by TCP.
FTP	File Transfer Protocol	Protocol for uploading and downloading files to and from a remote host; also accommodates basic file management tasks.
SFTP	Secure File	Protocol for securely uploading and downloading files to and from a remote host. Based on SSH security.
TFTP	Trivial File Transfer Protocol	File transfer protocol that does not have the security or error checking of FTP. TFTP uses UDP as a transport protocol and is therefore connectionless. TFTP is often used to download operating system updates to network devices such as routers.
SMTP	Simple Mail Transfer Protocol	Mechanism for transporting email across networks.

TABLE 20 *Continued*

Protocol	Full Name	Description
HTTP	Hypertext Transfer Protocol	Protocol for retrieving files from a web server.
HTTPS	Hypertext Transfer Protocol Secure	Secure protocol for retrieving files from a web server.
POP3/IMAP4	Post Office Protocol version 3/Internet Message Access Protocol version 4	Used for retrieving email from a server on which the email is stored. Can only be used to retrieve mail. IMAP and POP cannot be used to send mail.
Telnet	Telnet	Allows sessions to be opened on a remote host.
SSH	Secure Shell	Allows secure sessions to be opened on a remote host.
ICMP	Internet Control Message Protocol	Used on IP-based networks for error reporting, flow control, and route testing.
ARP	Address Resolution Protocol	Resolves IP addresses to MAC addresses, to enable communication between devices.
RARP	Reverse Address Resolution Protocol	Resolves MAC addresses to IP addresses.
NTP	Network Time Protocol	Used to communicate time synchronization information between devices.
NNTP	Network News Transport Protocol	Facilitates the access and downloading of messages from newsgroup servers.
SCP	Secure Copy Protocol	Allows files to be copied securely between two systems. Uses Secure Shell (SSH) technology to provide encryption services.
LDAP	Lightweight Directory Access Protocol	Protocol used to access and query directory services systems such as Novell Directory Services and Microsoft Active Directory.
IGMP	Internet Group Management Protocol	Provides a mechanism for systems within the same multicast group to register and communicate with each other.
LPR	Line Printer Remote	Used to connect to and send print tasks to printers and print servers.

TABLE 21 **Summary of TCP/IP Port Assignments**

Protocol	Port Assignment
FTP	20
FTP	21
SSH	22

(continues)

TABLE 21 *Continued*

Protocol	Port Assignment
Telnet	23
SMTP	25
DNS	53
TFTP	69
HTTP	80
POP3	110
NNTP	119
NTP	123
IMAP4	143
SNMP	161
HTTPS	443

TABLE 22 Summary of TCP/IP Services

Service	Purpose/Function
DHCP/BOOTP	Automatically assigns IP addressing information. DHCP tracks what IP address is assigned to what system by way of the corresponding MAC address. DHCP is platform independent; for example, a Linux DHCP server could provide addresses for Windows or Macintosh systems. Likewise, a Windows DHCP server could provide addresses to Linux or Unix systems.
DNS	Resolves hostnames to IP addresses. Without DNS, name resolutions must be performed through a text file called HOSTS.
NAT	Translates private network addresses into public network addresses.
ICS	Allows a single Internet connection to be shared among multiple systems on the network.
WINS	Resolves NetBIOS names to IP addresses.
SNMP	Provides network management facilities on TCP/IP-based networks.
NFS	Service that provides file sharing between server and client. Typically associated with Unix and Linux operating systems, but versions are available for most commonly deployed operating systems.
Zero Configuration	Provides a system by which devices can communicate with no network configuration or setup.
SMB	Application and presentation layer protocol that provides access to file and print services on server platforms that provide SMB access.
AFP	Provides remote file system access on Apple networks.
LPD	Printing service that provides both server and client printing functions.

TCP/IP Addressing

In a network that does not use DHCP, you need to watch for duplicate IP addresses that prevent a user from logging on to the network.

Following is a description of the classes of IP addresses:

▶ A Class A address uses only the first octet to represent the network portion, a Class B address uses two octets, and a Class C address uses three octets.

▶ Class A addresses span from 1 to 126, with a default subnet mask of 255.0.0.0.

▶ Class B addresses span from 128 to 191, with a default subnet mask of 255.255.0.0.

▶ Class C addresses span from 192 to 223, with a default subnet mask of 255.255.255.0.

The 127 network ID is reserved for the local loopback.

An example of a valid IPv6 address is

```
42DE:7E55:63F2:21AA:CBD4:D773:CC21:554F
```

Subnetting is a process whereby parts of the node portion of the IP address are used to create more network IDs. This results in more network addresses but fewer node addresses per network. It also increases broadcast domains. New network IDs created through this process are called *subnet IDs*.

APIPA is a system used on Windows that allows a system to automatically assign itself an IP address in the absence of a DHCP server. APIPA uses IP addresses from the 169.254.x.x address range. APIPA does not assign a default gateway, so communication is limited to the local network, and only to other systems that also have APIPA assigned addresses.

Public Versus Private Networks

A public network is a network to which anyone can connect, such as the Internet. Internet Assigned Numbers Authority (IANA) is responsible for assigning IP addresses to public networks.

A private network is any network to which access is restricted. Reserved IP address ranges are 10.0.0.0, 172.16.0.0–172.31.0.0, and 192.168.0.0.

WAN Technologies

Table 23 summarizes the WAN technologies.

TABLE 23   WAN Technologies

WAN Technology	Speed	Supported Media	Switching Method Used	Key Characteristics
ISDN	BRI: 64Kbps to 128Kbps PRI: 1.5Mbps	Copper/fiber-optic	Can be used for circuit-switching or packet-switching	ISDN can be used to transmit all types of traffic, including voice, video, and data. BRI uses 2B+D channels, PRI uses 23B+D channels. B channels are ISDN uses the public network and requires dial-in access.
T-carrier (T1, T3)	T1: 1.544Mbps T3: 44.736Mbps	Copper/fiber-optic	Circuit switching	T-carrier is used to create point-to-point network connections for private networks.
FDDI	100Mbps	Fiber-optic	N/A	FDDI uses a dual-ring configuration for fault tolerance. FDDI uses a token-passing media-access method. FDDI uses beaconing for error detection.
X.25	56Kbps	Copper/fiber-optic	Packet switching	X.25 is limited to 56Kbps or 64Kbps. X.25 provides a packet-switching network over standard phone lines.
SONET	51.8Mbps to 2.4Gbps	Fiber-optic	N/A	SONET defines synchronous data transfer over optical cable. The European equivalent of SONET is SDH.

Remote Access and Security Protocols

When a connection is made to the RAS server, the client is authenticated, and the system that is dialing in becomes a part of the network.

RAS supports remote connectivity from all the major client operating systems.

Although the system is called RAS, the underlying technologies that enable the RAS process are dial-up protocols such as PPP and SLIP:

▶ SLIP also does not provide error checking or packet addressing, so it can be used only in serial communications.

▶ PPP provides a number of security enhancements compared to SLIP. The most important of these is the encryption of usernames and passwords during the authentication process.

Windows 2000 natively supports SLIP and PPP.

RDP protocol allows client systems to access and run applications on a server, using the resources of the server, with only the user interface, keystrokes, and mouse movement being transferred between the client and server computers.

IPSec is designed to encrypt data during communication between two computers. IPSec operates at the network layer of the OSI model and provides security for protocols that operate at higher layers of the OSI model.

L2TP is a combination of PPTP and Cisco's L2F technology and uses tunneling to deliver data. L2TP operates at the data-link layer, making it protocol independent.

SSL is a security protocol used on the Internet. Secure website URLs begin with https:// instead of http://. HTTPS connections require a browser to establish a secure connection. Secure SSL connections for web pages are made through port 443 by default.

Kerberos provides a method to verify the identity of a computer system over an insecure network connection.

The security tokens used in Kerberos are known as *tickets*.

3.0—Network Implementation

Fault tolerance involves ensuring that when network hardware or software fails, users on the network can still access the data and continue working with little or no disruption of service. One of the most common fault-tolerance solutions is RAID. Table 24 shows various RAID solutions.

TABLE 24   RAID Solutions

RAID Level	Description	Key Features	Minimum Disks Required
RAID 0	Disk striping	No fault tolerance; improved I/O performance	2
RAID 1	Disk mirroring	Provides fault tolerance but at 50% disk overhead; can also be used with separate disk controllers, a strategy known as *disk duplexing*	2 (2 is also the maximum number of disks used for RAID 1.)
RAID 2	Disk striping with hamming code	Limited use	3
RAID 3	Disk striping with single-parity disk	Limited use	3

(continues)

TABLE 24 *Continued*

RAID Level	Description	Key Features	Minimum Disks Required
RAID 4	Disk striping with single-parity disk	Limited use	3
RAID 5	Disk striping with distributed parity	Widely used RAID solution; uses distributed parity	3
RAID 10	Striping with mirrored volumes	Increased performance with striping and offers mirrored fault tolerance	4

Backups

Table 25 describes various backup strategies.

TABLE 25   Summary of Backup Strategies

Method	What Is Backed Up	Restore Procedure	Archive Bit
Full	All data	All data is restored from a single tape.	Does not use the archive bit but clears it after files have been copied to tape
Incremental	All data changed since the last full or incremental backup	The restore procedure requires several tapes: the latest full backup and all incremental tape since the last full backup.	Uses the archive bit and clears it after a file is saved to disk
Differential	All data changed since the last full backup	The restore procedure requires the latest full backup tape and the latest differential backup tape.	Uses the archive bit but does not clear it

Use an offsite tape rotation scheme to store current copies of backups in a secure offsite location.

Periodically introduce new tapes into the tape rotation and destroy the old tapes.

VLANs

VLANs are used to segment networks. This is often done for organizational or security purposes.

Client Connectivity

At the minimum, an IP address and a subnet mask are required to connect to a TCP/IP network. With just this minimum configuration, connectivity is limited to the local segment, and DNS and WINS resolution are not possible.

To connect to systems on other networks, a default gateway must be configured. This default gateway must be on the same network segment as the system in question.

The Client for Microsoft Networks is used on Windows client systems to facilitate connection to a Windows Server platform such as Windows 2000 Server or Windows Server 2003.

To log on to a NetWare server, you might need a username, password, tree name, and context. You also need either the Novell provided client software, or, on Windows platforms, the Client Services for NetWare (CSNW).

Security: Physical, Logical, Passwords, and Firewalls

Physical security refers to the issues related to the physical security of the equipment that composes or is connected to the network.

Logical security is concerned with security of data while it is on the systems connected to the network.

Common password policies typically specify a minimum length for passwords, password expiration, prevention of password reuse, and prevention of easy-to-guess passwords.

A password that uses eight case-sensitive characters, with letters, numbers, and special characters, often makes a strong password.

User-level security offers greater security than share-level security.

Table 26 shows file permissions for a Windows 2000 server/Windows Server 2003 system with the NTFS file system.

TABLE 26   File Permissions on a Windows 2000/2003 System

Right	Description
Full Control	Provides all rights
Modify	Allows files to be modified
Read & Execute	Allows files to be read and executed (that is, run)
List Folder Contents	Allows the files in a folder to be listed
Read	Allows a file to be read
Write	Allows a file to be written to

Valid file permissions on a Unix/Linux system include read, write, and execute.

NetWare has a complex file and folder permissions structure, which includes user rights, inheritance filters, and security equivalence.

When a user cannot access files that other users can access, verify that the correct permissions are set.

A *firewall* is a system or group of systems that controls the flow of traffic between two networks. A firewall often provides such services as NAT, proxy services, and packet filtering.

The TCP/IP protocol suite uses port numbers to identify what service a certain packet is destined for. By configuring the firewall to allow certain types of traffic, you can control the flow.

Proxy Servers

A proxy server acts as an intermediary between a user on the internal network and a service on the external network such as the Internet.

A proxy server enables a network to appear to external networks as a single IP address—the IP address of the external network interface of the proxy server.

A proxy server allows Internet access to be controlled. Having a centralized point of access allows for a great deal of control over the use of the Internet.

A proxy server can cache frequently accessed web pages, increasing the speed of delivery to clients, and reducing traffic in environments where many people access the same page.

Intranets and Extranets

An *intranet* is typically a web server-hosted application made available only to users within an organization.

An *extranet* is an application or system made available to users outside an organization. Access to the extranet is tightly controlled and secure.

Protocols associated with intranets and extranets include HTTP and FTP.

Port Blocking

Port blocking is one of the most widely used security methods on networks. Port blocking is associated with firewalls and proxy servers, although in fact it can be implemented on any system that provides a means to manage network data flow, according to data type. To implement port blocking effectively, you need to be aware of the TCP/IP port numbers associated with common protocols.

4.0—Network Support

Network support includes utilities for monitoring and troubleshooting the network.

TCP/IP Utilities

`ping` is a command-line utility designed to test connectivity between systems on a TCP/IP-based network. You can `ping` the IP address of the local loopback by using the command `ping 127.0.0.1`. If this command is successful, you know that the TCP/IP protocol suite is installed correctly on your system and functioning.

If you can `ping` a remote system by its IP address, but not by its hostname, there is a problem with name resolution.

If you cannot `ping` other devices on your local network and you were able to `ping` your local NIC, you might not be connected to the network correctly, or there might be a cable problem on the computer.

Trace route is a TCP/IP utility used to track the path a packet takes to reach a remote host and isolate where network problems might be.

Trace route reports the amount of time it takes to reach each host in the path. It is a useful tool for isolating bottlenecks in a network. Trace route is implemented through the `tracert` command on Windows systems and as the `traceroute` command on Unix, Linux, and Macintosh systems.

ARP resolves IP addresses to MAC addresses and as such operates at the network layer of the OSI model.

`netstat` is used to view both inbound and outbound TCP/IP network connections.

The `netstat -r` command can be used to display the routing table of the system.

`nbtstat` is used to display protocol and statistical information for NetBIOS over TCP/IP connections.

The `ipconfig` command shows the IP configuration information on a Windows system for all NICs installed.

The `ipconfig /all` command is used on a Windows system to display detailed TCP/IP configuration information.

The `ipconfig /renew` command is used on a Windows system to refresh the system's DHCP assigned IP address information.

When looking for client connectivity problems using `ipconfig`, you should ensure that the gateway is correctly set.

The `ifconfig` command is the Linux, Unix, and Macintosh equivalent of the `ipconfig` command.

`winipcfg` is the Windows 95, Windows 98, and Windows Me equivalent of the `ipconfig` command.

The `nslookup` command is a TCP/IP diagnostic tool used to troubleshoot DNS problems. `dig` can be used for the same purpose on Unix and Linux systems.

Media Tools and LEDs

Following is a list of media tools and LED guidelines:

- A wire crimper is a tool that you use to attach media connectors to the ends of cables.

- Media testers, also called cable testers, are used to test whether a cable is working properly.

- An optical cable tester performs the same basic function as a wire media tester, but on optical media.

- The hardware loopback tests the outgoing signals of a device such as a network card.

- If a connection LED on a hub is not lit when all the physical connections are correct and the connected system is powered on, you might have a faulty patch cable.

- If the LED on a network card is constantly lit, you might have a chattering network card.

- A sporadically flashing activity LED on a network device normally denotes activity on the connection and is completely normal.

Troubleshooting Steps

Given a network problem scenario, select an appropriate course of action based on a logical troubleshooting strategy. This strategy can include the following steps:

1. Identify the symptoms and potential causes.
2. Identify the affected area.
3. Establish what has changed.
4. Select the most probable cause.
5. Implement an action plan and solution, including potential effects.
6. Test the result.
7. Identify the results and effects of the solution.
8. Document the solution and process.

Practice Exam

This exam consists of 72 questions that reflect the material covered in this book. The questions are representative of the types of questions you should expect to see on the Network+ exam; however, they are not intended to match exactly what is on the exam.

Some of the questions require that you deduce the best possible answer. In other cases, you are asked to identify the best course of action to take in a given situation. You must read the questions carefully and thoroughly before you attempt to answer them. It is strongly recommended that you treat this exam as if it were the actual exam. When you take it, time yourself, read carefully, and answer all the questions to the best of your ability.

The answers to all the questions appear in the section following the exam. Check your letter answers against those in the answers section, and then read the explanations provided. You might also want to return to the chapters in the book to review the material associated with any incorrect answers.

1. Which layer of the OSI model is responsible for placing the signal on the network media?

   ○ a. Physical

   ○ b. Data-link

   ○ c. MAC

   ○ d. LLC

2. Which of the following 10GbE standards can be used over the greatest distance?

   ○ a. 10GbaseER

   ○ b. 10GbaseTX

   ○ c. 10GbaseSR

   ○ d. 10GbaseLR

3. You are a network administrator managing a midsize network that uses a NetWare print server, a Windows application server, and a Linux firewall server. One of your servers loses network connectivity; you type `ifconfig` at the command line to see whether the server has a valid IP address. Which server has lost connectivity?

   ○ a. The firewall server.

   ○ b. The print server.

   ○ c. The application server.

   ○ d. `ifconfig` is not a valid command on any of these platforms.

4. You are managing a network that uses both a Unix server and a Windows 2000 server. Which of the following protocols can you use to transfer files between the two servers?

   ○ a. Telnet

   ○ b. PPP

   ○ c. FTP

   ○ d. PPTP

5. You have been called by a user who complains that access to a web page is very slow. What utility can you use to find the bottleneck?

   ○ a. ping

   ○ b. Telnet

   ○ c. tracert

   ○ d. nbtstat

6. During a busy administrative week, you install a new virus suite in your network of 55 computers, a new RAID array in one of the servers, and a new office suite on 25 of the computer systems. After all the updates, you are experiencing system errors throughout the entire network. Which of the following would you do to help isolate the problem?

    ○ **a.** Disable the RAID array.

    ○ **b.** Uninstall the office suite.

    ○ **c.** Check the virus suite vendor's website for system patches or service packs.

    ○ **d.** Reinstall the virus software.

7. You are the administrator for a network with six Linux servers. You need to administer one of the servers from your Linux workstation at home. Specifically, you need to stop and start the Samba service on that server. Which of the following utilities are you most likely to use to do this?

    ○ **a.** Telnet

    ○ **b.** SSH

    ○ **c.** FTP

    ○ **d.** SFTP

8. When a system running TCP/IP receives a data packet, which of the following does it use to determine what service to forward the packet to?

    ○ **a.** Port number

    ○ **b.** Packet ID number

    ○ **c.** Data IP number

    ○ **d.** IP protocol service type

9. Which of the following backup methods clear the archive bit? (Choose the two best answers.)

    ○ **a.** Differential

    ○ **b.** Sequential

    ○ **c.** Full

    ○ **d.** Incremental

10. You are troubleshooting a server connectivity problem on your network—a Windows XP system is having trouble connecting to a Windows 2000 Server. Which of the following commands would you use to display per-protocol statistics on the workstation system?

   ○ **a.** `arp -a`

   ○ **b.** `arp -A`

   ○ **c.** `nbtstat -s`

   ○ **d.** `nbtstat -S`

   ○ **e.** `netstat -s`

11. You are working as a network administrator on a UNIX system. The system uses dynamic name resolution. What is used to dynamically resolve a hostname on a UNIX server?

   ○ **a.** IPX

   ○ **b.** ARP

   ○ **c.** DNS

   ○ **d.** LMHOSTS

12. During the night, one of your servers powers down. Upon reboot, print services do not load. Which of the following would be the first step in the troubleshooting process?

   ○ **a.** Examine the server log files.

   ○ **b.** Reboot the server.

   ○ **c.** Reinstall the printer.

   ○ **d.** Reinstall the printer software.

13. Which of the following technologies uses Category 5 cable?

   ○ **a.** 100BaseTX

   ○ **b.** Fiber-optic

   ○ **c.** 10Base5

   ○ **d.** 10Base2

14. Which of the following utilities can be used to view the current protocol connections on a system?

   ○ **a.** `ping`

   ○ **b.** `netstat`

   ○ **c.** Telnet

   ○ **d.** `tracert`

15. Which of the following protocols are part of the TCP/IP protocol suite? (Choose the three best answers.)

   ○   a. AFP

   ○   b. FTP

   ○   c. DHCP

   ○   d. HTTP

   ○   e. NCP

16. Which of the following are connectionless protocols? (Choose the two best answers.)

   ○   a. TCP

   ○   b. SPX

   ○   c. IPX

   ○   d. UDP

17. You have just configured a wireless AP for your network. You want to ensure that a minimal level of security is provided for the connection by encrypting the data as it travels between the wireless devices and the access point. Which of the following protocols are you most likely to use for this purpose? (Select two.)

   ○   a. WEP

   ○   b. SSL

   ○   c. WST

   ○   d. WPA

18. After several passwords have been compromised in your organization, you have been asked to implement a networkwide password policy. Which of the following represents the most practical and secure password policy?

   ○   a. Daily password changes

   ○   b. Weekly password changes

   ○   c. Monthly password changes

   ○   d. Password changes only after an account has been compromised

19. You are experiencing a problem with a workstation and want to `ping` the local host. Which of the following are valid ways to check your local TCP/IP connection? (Choose the two best answers.)

    ○ a. `ping host`

    ○ b. `ping localhost`

    ○ c. `ping 127.0.0.1`

    ○ d. `ping 127.0.0.0`

20. Which of the following network devices operates at the physical layer of the OSI model?

    ○ a. Router

    ○ b. Hub

    ○ c. Bridge

    ○ d. NIC

21. You have been asked to implement a RAID solution on one of your company's servers. You have two hard disks and two hard disk controllers. Which of the following RAID levels could you implement? (Choose the three best answers.)

    ○ a. RAID 0

    ○ b. RAID 1

    ○ c. Disk duplexing

    ○ d. RAID 10

    ○ e. RAID 5

22. Which of the following represents a Class B IP address?

    ○ a. 191.23.21.54

    ○ b. 125.123.123.2

    ○ c. 24.67.118.67

    ○ d. 255.255.255.0

23. What utility would produce the following output?

```
Proto  Local Address          Foreign Address              State
TCP    laptop:1028            LAPTOP:0                      LISTENING
TCP    laptop:1031            LAPTOP:0                      LISTENING
TCP    laptop:1093            LAPTOP:0                      LISTENING
TCP    laptop:50000           LAPTOP:0                      LISTENING
TCP    laptop:5000            LAPTOP:0                      LISTENING
TCP    laptop:1031            n218.audiogalaxy.com:ftp   ESTABLISHED
TCP    laptop:1319            h24-67-184-65.ok.shawcable.net:nbsess
```

○ **a.** netstat

○ **b.** nbtstat

○ **c.** ping

○ **d.** tracert -R

24. You have been called in to troubleshoot a problem with a newly installed email application. Internal users are able to communicate with each other via email, but neither incoming nor outgoing Internet email is working. You suspect a problem with the port-blocking configuration of the firewall system that protects the Internet connection. Which of the following ports would you allow, to cure the problems with the email? (Choose the two best answers.)

○ **a.** 20

○ **b.** 25

○ **c.** 80

○ **d.** 110

○ **e.** 443

25. What is the default subnet mask for a Class B network?

○ **a.** 255.255.255.224

○ **b.** 255.255.255.0

○ **c.** 127.0.0.1

○ **d.** 255.255.0.0

26. At which OSI layer does TCP operate?

○ **a.** Network

○ **b.** Transport

○ **c.** Session

○ **d.** Presentation

27. What is the basic purpose of a firewall system?

○ **a.** It provides a single point of access to the Internet.

○ **b.** It caches commonly used web pages, thereby reducing the bandwidth demands on an Internet connection.

○ **c.** It allows hostnames to be resolved to IP addresses.

○ **d.** It protects one network from another by acting as an intermediary system.

28. Email and FTP work at which layer of the OSI model?

   ○   **a.** Application

   ○   **b.** Session

   ○   **c.** Presentation

   ○   **d.** User

29. Your manager has become increasingly concerned about the safety of network transmissions. You are asked by your manager to recommend a security strategy that will protect both internal and external network transmissions. Which of the following might you suggest?

   ○   **a.** Kerberos v4 encryption

   ○   **b.** IPSec

   ○   **c.** NTFS v5

   ○   **d.** SSL

30. While reviewing the security logs for your server, you notice that a user on the Internet has attempted to access your internal mail server. Although it appears that the user's attempts were unsuccessful, you are concerned about the possibility that your systems may be compromised. Which of the following solutions are you most likely to implement?

   ○   **a.** A more secure password policy

   ○   **b.** A firewall system at the connection point to the Internet

   ○   **c.** File-level encryption

   ○   **d.** Kerberos authentication

31. Which of the following pieces of information is not likely to be supplied via DHCP?

   ○   **a.** IP address

   ○   **b.** NetBIOS computer name

   ○   **c.** Subnet mask

   ○   **d.** Default gateway

32. While troubleshooting a network connectivity problem, you notice that the network card in your system is operating at 10Mbps in half-duplex mode. At what speed is the network link operating?

   ○   **a.** 2.5Mbps

   ○   **b.** 5Mbps

   ○   **c.** 10Mbps

   ○   **d.** 11Mbps

33. Which of the following is a valid IPv6 address?

    ○ **a.** 42DE:7E55:63F2:21AA:CBD4:D773

    ○ **b.** 42CD:7E55:63F2:21GA:CBD4:D773:CC21:554F

    ○ **c.** 42DE:7E55:63F2:21AA

    ○ **d.** 42DE:7E55:63F2:21AA:CBD4:D773:CC21:554F

34. While troubleshooting a network connectivity problem on a Windows 2003 Server, you need to view a list of the IP addresses that have been resolved to MAC addresses. Which of the following commands would you use to do this?

    ○ **a.** `arp -a`

    ○ **b.** `nbtstat -a`

    ○ **c.** `arp -d`

    ○ **d.** `arp -s`

35. Which of the following statements best describes RAID 5?

    ○ **a.** A RAID 5 array consists of at least two drives. Parity information is written across both drives to provide fault tolerance.

    ○ **b.** A RAID 5 array consists of at least three drives and distributes parity information across all the drives in the array.

    ○ **c.** A RAID 5 array consists of at least three drives and stores the parity information on a single drive.

    ○ **d.** A RAID 5 array consists of at least four drives. The first and last drives in the array are used to store parity information.

36. Which of the following IEEE specifications does CSMA/CD relate to?

    ○ **a.** 802.1x

    ○ **b.** 802.2

    ○ **c.** 802.5

    ○ **d.** 802.3

37. While you are troubleshooting a sporadic network connectivity problem on a Windows 2003 system, a fellow technician suggests that you run the `ping -t` command. What is the purpose of this command?

    ○ **a.** It shows the route taken by a packet to reach the destination host.

    ○ **b.** It shows the time, in seconds, that the packet takes to reach the destination.

    ○ **c.** It allows the number of `ping` messages to be specific.

    ○ **d.** It `pings` the remote host continually until it is stopped.

38. Which of the following protocols supports multiple authentication methods such as smart cards and token cards?

    ○ **a.** PAP

    ○ **b.** CHAP

    ○ **c.** EAP

    ○ **d.** Multi-Chap v2

39. What type of physical topology is shown in the following diagram?

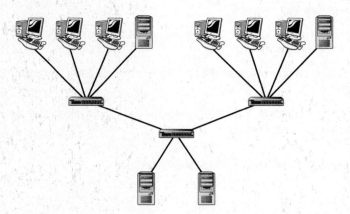

    ○ **a.** Star

    ○ **b.** Ring

    ○ **c.** Ad hoc

    ○ **d.** Mesh

40. A remote user calls you to report a problem she is having connecting to the corporate network over her DSL connection. The user is able to connect to the Internet and browse web pages, but she can't connect to the corporate remote access gateway. Which of the following troubleshooting steps would you perform first?

   ○ **a.** Check the corporate remote access gateway to see whether it is running and operating correctly.

   ○ **b.** Have the user reboot her system.

   ○ **c.** Have the user reconfigure the IP address on her system to one of the address ranges used on the internal corporate network, and then try again.

   ○ **d.** Have the user power cycle the DSL modem and try again.

41. You are implementing a security design for your wireless network. Which of the following security standards provides port-based network access control?

   ○ **a.** WEP

   ○ **b.** 802.1x

   ○ **c.** IPSec

   ○ **d.** Kerberos

42. What command would generate the following output?

```
7    60 ms    30 ms    40 ms   home-gw.st6wa.ip.att.net [192.205.32.249]
8    30 ms    40 ms    30 ms   gbr3-p40.st6wa.ip.att.net [12.123.44.130]
9    50 ms    50 ms    60 ms   gbr4-p10.sffca.ip.att.net [12.122.2.61]
10   60 ms    60 ms    60 ms   gbr3-p10.la2ca.ip.att.net [12.122.2.169]
11   90 ms    60 ms    70 ms   gbr6-p60.la2ca.ip.att.net [12.122.5.97]
```

   ○ **a.** `ipconfig`

   ○ **b.** `netstat`

   ○ **c.** `ping`

   ○ **d.** `tracert`

43. Your manager has asked you to implement security on your peer-to-peer network. Which of the following security models offers the highest level of security for this type of network?

   ○ **a.** Share level

   ○ **b.** User level

   ○ **c.** Password level

   ○ **d.** Layered

44. You are working on a Linux system and are having problems pinging a remote system by its hostname. DNS resolution is not configured for the system. What file might you look in to begin troubleshooting the resolution problem?

   ○ a. RESOLV

   ○ b. STATICDNS

   ○ c. PASSWD

   ○ d. HOSTS

45. You are tasked with specifying a way to connect two buildings across a parking lot. The distance between the two buildings is 78 meters. An underground wiring duct exists between the two buildings, although there are concerns about using it because it also houses high-voltage electrical cables. The budget for the project is tight, but your manager still wants you to specify the most suitable solution. Which of the following cable types would you recommend?

   ○ a. Fiber-optic

   ○ b. UTP

   ○ c. Thin coax

   ○ d. STP

46. You are attempting to configure a client's email program. The user can receive mail but is unable to send any. In the mail server configuration screen of the mail application, you notice that the Type of Outgoing Mail Server field is blank. This explains why the client is unable to send mail. Which of the following protocols are you most likely to enter as a value in the Type of Outgoing Mail Server field?

   ○ a. NMP

   ○ b. POP3

   ○ c. SMTP

   ○ d. IMAP

47. A user calls to inform you that she can't access the Internet from her system. When you visit the user, you run the `ipconfig /all` utility and see the following information. What is the most likely reason the user is having problems accessing the Internet?

```
C:\>ipconfig /all

Windows 2000 IP Configuration
         Host Name . . . . . . . . . . . . : LAPTOP
         Primary DNS Suffix  . . . . . . . :
         Node Type . . . . . . . . . . . . : Broadcast
         IP Routing Enabled. . . . . . . . : No
         WINS Proxy Enabled. . . . . . . . : No
```

```
Ethernet adapter Local Area Connection:
        Connection-specific DNS Suffix  . :
        Description . . . . . . . . . . . : Intel 8255x-based PCI
    Ethernet
        Physical Address. . . . . . . . . : 00-D0-59-09-07-51
        DHCP Enabled. . . . . . . . . . . : No
        IP Address. . . . . . . . . . . . : 192.168.2.1
        Subnet Mask . . . . . . . . . . . : 255.255.255.0
        Default Gateway . . . . . . . . . :
        DNS Servers . . . . . . . . . . . : 192.168.2.10
                                            192.168.2.20
```

    ○   **a.** The system is on a different subnet than the DNS servers.

    ○   **b.** DHCP is not enabled.

    ○   **c.** The subnet mask is incorrect.

    ○   **d.** The default gateway setting is not configured.

48. Your ISP account manager suggests that it might be appropriate for you to install a DNS server internally. Which of the following functions does the DNS server provide?

    ○   **a.** It performs network address translation services.

    ○   **b.** It streamlines the resolution of NetBIOS names to IP addresses.

    ○   **c.** It allows some hostname-to-IP address resolutions to occur internally.

    ○   **d.** It allows users to retrieve Internet web pages more quickly.

49. Which of the following is not one of the private address ranges?

    ○   **a.** 192.168.x.x

    ○   **b.** 10.x.x.x

    ○   **c.** 172.16.x.x

    ○   **d.** 224.181.x.x

50. Which of the following is a valid MAC address?

    ○   **a.** 00:D0:59:09:07:51

    ○   **b.** 00:D0:59

    ○   **c.** 192.168.2.1

    ○   **d.** 00FE:56FE:230F:CDA2:00EB:32EC

    ○   **e.** 00:DG:59:09:07:51

51. Which of the following protocols is *not* commonly associated with sharing and accessing files from a system?

    ○ a. NFS

    ○ b. SMB

    ○ c. RDP

    ○ d. AFP

52. Which of the following technologies can be implemented on a switch to create multiple separate networks?

    ○ a. Proxy

    ○ b. Subnet masking

    ○ c. NAS

    ○ d. VLAN

53. Which of the following protocols are responsible for network addressing? (Choose the two best answers.)

    ○ a. IP

    ○ b. SPX

    ○ c. IPX

    ○ d. TCP

54. Which of the following connectors are you most likely to associate with a connection to the PSTN?

    ○ a. RJ-PT

    ○ b. RJ-45

    ○ c. MTRJ

    ○ d. RJ-11

55. You are configuring dial-in remote access for several network users. Security is a primary concern. Which of the following protocols or services is used to authenticate remote access users?

    ○ a. RADIUS

    ○ b. IPSec

    ○ c. L2TP

    ○ d. PPTP

56. Which of the following connectors would you use when working with fiber-optic cable? (Choose the two best answers.)

○   **a.** RJ-11

○   **b.** SC

○   **c.** RJ-45

○   **d.** ST

○   **e.** BNC

○   **f.** Vampire tap

57. Which of the following is not a commonly implemented feature of a firewall system?

○   **a.** NAT

○   **b.** Packet filtering

○   **c.** Proxy

○   **d.** NAS

58. You are the network administrator for a Token Ring network. A NIC in a system fails, and you replace it with a new one. However, the system still cannot connect to the network. What is the most likely cause of the problem?

○   **a.** The NIC is set to the wrong ring speed.

○   **b.** The NIC is a 100Mbps card, and the ring is configured for only 10Mbps.

○   **c.** The NIC is set to full-duplex, and the ring is running at only half-duplex.

○   **d.** The NIC is faulty.

59. You have enabled HTTPS because of concerns about the security of your web server application, which runs on a web server system in the DMZ of your corporate network. However, remote users are now unable to connect to the application. Which of the following is the most likely reason for the problem?

○   **a.** Port 80 is being blocked on the corporate firewall.

○   **b.** Port 443 is being blocked on the corporate firewall.

○   **c.** Remote users need to enable HTTPS support in their web browsers.

○   **d.** Port 110 is being blocked on the corporate firewall.

60. Which of the following is a valid Class A IP address?

- ○ **a.** 124.254.254.254
- ○ **b.** 127.0.0.1
- ○ **c.** 128.16.200.12
- ○ **d.** 131.17.25.200

61. A user calls you from a hotel room. He has tried numerous times to dial in to the corporate RAS server, but the modem in his system is reporting a "no dial tone" error. When he plugs the hotel telephone back in to the phone socket, he gets a dial tone and can dial out successfully. What is the most likely cause of the problem?

- ○ **a.** The phone line in the room is analog.
- ○ **b.** The phone line in the room is faulty.
- ○ **c.** The modem is faulty.
- ○ **d.** The phone line in the room is digital.

62. Which of the following is not a valid file permission on a Windows 2000 system?

- ○ **a.** Read
- ○ **b.** Attribute
- ○ **c.** Execute
- ○ **d.** Write

63. What utility would you use to view the TCP connections that have been established between two systems?

- ○ **a.** netstat
- ○ **b.** nbtstat
- ○ **c.** tracert
- ○ **d.** ipconfig

64. Which of the following statements are true of a system that is using Zeroconf? (Choose three.)

    ⚬ **a.** The system must be able to assign itself an IP address without the need for a DHCP server.

    ⚬ **b.** The system must be able to resolve the hostname of another system to an IP address without the use of a DNS server.

    ⚬ **c.** The system must be able to locate or advertise services on the network without a directory services system.

    ⚬ **d.** The system must be able to assign itself a MAC address without contacting an address server.

65. On an AppleTalk network, what is the function of AARP?

    ⚬ **a.** It is a distance-vector routing protocol.

    ⚬ **b.** It allows the resolution of AppleTalk addresses to MAC addresses.

    ⚬ **c.** It allows the resolution of MAC addresses to AppleTalk addresses.

    ⚬ **d.** It is a link-state routing protocol.

66. What term is used to describe the process of using parts of the node address range of an IP address as network IDs?

    ⚬ **a.** Subnetting

    ⚬ **b.** Supernetting

    ⚬ **c.** Subnet masking

    ⚬ **d.** Super routing

67. Which of the following statements are true of subnetting? (Choose two.)

    ⚬ **a.** It results in more network addresses.

    ⚬ **b.** It results in more node addresses.

    ⚬ **c.** It results in fewer network addresses.

    ⚬ **d.** It results in fewer node addresses.

68. In a hardware loopback plug, which wire numbers are connected? (Choose the two best answers.)

- ○ **a.** 3 and 5
- ○ **b.** 1 and 3
- ○ **c.** 1 and 2
- ○ **d.** 3 and 4
- ○ **e.** 2 and 6

69. Which of the following network types is easiest to add new nodes to?

- ○ **a.** Bus
- ○ **b.** Ring
- ○ **c.** Star
- ○ **d.** Mesh

70. What kind of connector would you use to make a patch cable for a 10BaseT network?

- ○ **a.** RJ-45
- ○ **b.** RJ-11
- ○ **c.** RJ-13
- ○ **d.** BNC

71. Which TCP/IP port number is used by DNS?

- ○ **a.** 21
- ○ **b.** 25
- ○ **c.** 53
- ○ **d.** 110

72. What is the purpose of implementing fault tolerance?

- ○ **a.** It reduces the amount of time the administrator spends performing backups.
- ○ **b.** It promotes data availability by eliminating a single point of failure.
- ○ **c.** It allows systems to be brought back online more quickly.
- ○ **d.** It protects data from accidental deletion.

Answers to Exam Questions

1. **a.** The physical layer of the OSI seven-layer model is responsible for placing the signal on the network media. The data-link layer (Answer b) is responsible for physical addressing and media access. MAC and LLC (Answers c and d) are sublayers of the data-link layer. For more information, see Chapter 4, "The OSI Model."

2. **a.** 10GbaseER can be used over distances up to 40km. 10GbaseSR can be used over only relatively short distances—up to 300 meters. 10GbaseLR can be used over distances up to 10km. There is no 10 Gigabit Ethernet standard called 10GbaseTX. For more information, see Chapter 2, "Cabling Standards, Media, and Connectors."

3. **a.** The `ifconfig` command is used on a Linux system to determine the IP configuration of the system. With NetWare you use the `config` command to obtain information about network addresses. On a Windows 2000/2003 system, the `ipconfig` command is used to view the networking configuration, including the IP address. `ifconfig` can be used on Unix/Linux platforms to view the networking configuration. For more information, see Chapter 13, "Troubleshooting Tools and Utilities."

4. **c.** FTP can be used to transfer files between Windows and Unix systems. FTP is part of the TCP/IP protocol suite and is platform independent. The Telnet utility is used to open a virtual terminal session on a remote host (Answer a). PPP is used to establish communications over a serial link; thus, Answer b is incorrect. PPTP is used to establish a secure link over a public network such as the Internet (Answer d). For more information, see Chapter 6, "Working with TCP/IP."

5. **c.** `tracert` is a Windows command that can be used to display the full path between two systems, including the number of hops between the systems. The `ping` utility (Answer a) can be used to test connectivity between two devices, but it only reports the time taken for the round-trip; it does not give information about the time it takes to complete each hop in the route. The Telnet utility (Answer b) is used to open a virtual terminal session on a remote host. The `nbtstat` command (Answer d) is used to view statistical information about the NetBIOS status of a system. For more information, see Chapter 13.

6. **c.** Because the system errors are networkwide, it is likely that the cause of the problem in this scenario lies with the virus suite because it is installed on all computers. To troubleshoot such a problem, it would be a good idea to check for patches or updates on the vendor's website. A problem with a RAID array (Answer a) would affect only the server in which it is installed, not the entire network. Because the office suite (Answer b) was installed on only some of the systems, it can be eliminated as a problem because all the systems are affected. The virus software (Answer d) appears to be the cause of the problem, but reinstalling it is unlikely to help. For more information, see Chapter 15, "Troubleshooting Procedures and Best Practices."

7. **b.** Secure Shell (SSH) allows you to securely open a session on a remote Linux host and then administer that server. Telnet also provides remote administration capabilities, but it is not considered secure. Therefore, you are unlikely to use it as a means of remote administration across the Internet. The File Transfer Protocol (FTP) is a mechanism for transferring files to and from a remote server. It is not used for remote administration. The Secure File Transfer Protocol (SFTP) is a more secure version of FTP. For more information, see Chapter 6.

8. **a.** The service to which a data packet is destined is determined by the port number to which it is sent. Answers b, c, and d are not valid. For more information, see Chapter 6.

9. **c, d.** Both the full and incremental backup methods clear the archive bit, to indicate which data does and does not need to be backed up. In a differential backup (Answer a), the archive bit is not cleared. Sequential (Answer b) is not a type of backup. For more information, see Chapter 12, "VLANs, Antivirus, Fault Tolerance, and Disaster Recovery."

10. **e.** The `netstat -s` command can be used to display per-protocol statistics. The `arp` command (Answers a and b) is used to view a list of the IP address-to-MAC address resolutions performed by the system. The `nbtstat` utility (Answers c and d) is used to view protocol statistics for the NetBIOS protocol. For more information, see Chapter 13.

11. **c.** DNS is used on UNIX-based systems to resolve hostnames. IPX (Answer a) is a network layer connectionless protocol. ARP (Answer b) resolves IP addresses to MAC addresses. The LMHOSTS file (Answer d) is used on Windows systems to resolve NetBIOS names to IP addresses. For more information, see Chapter 6.

12. **a.** In this scenario your first step is to gather information by examining the server log files. When you have that information, you can proceed with the rest of the troubleshooting process. Rebooting the server (Answer b) is unlikely to cure the problem. Before you reinstall the printer (Answer c), you should examine the log files to see whether any problems are reported in the server log files. Before you reinstall the printer software (Answer d), examine the log files to see whether any problems are reported in the server log files. For more information, see Chapter 15.

13. **a.** 100BaseTX uses Category 5 cable. Fiber-optic (Answer b) is a type of cable. 10Base5 (Answer c) is an Ethernet networking standard that uses thick coaxial cable. 10Base2 (Answer d) is an Ethernet networking standard that uses thin coaxial cable. For more information, see Chapter 2.

14. **b.** The `netstat -a` command can be used to display the current connections and listening ports. The `ping` utility (Answer a) is used to test connectivity between two devices on a TCP/IP network. Telnet (Answer c) is an application-level protocol that allows a virtual terminal session on a remote host. The `tracert` utility (Answer d) allows a path to be traced between two hosts. For more information, see Chapter 13.

15. **b, c, d.** FTP, DHCP, and HTTP are all protocols in the TCP/IP protocol suite. AFP (Answer a) is part of the AppleTalk protocol suite. NCP (Answer e) is part of the IPX/SPX protocol suite. For more information, see Chapter 6.

16. **c, d.** UDP and IPX, are connectionless protocols. TCP (answer a) and SPX (Answer b) are connection-oriented protocol. For more information, see Chapter 5, "Overview of Network Protocols."

17. **a and d.** WEP and WPA are both security protocols associated with wireless networking. Both are designed to protect data as it is transmitted from one end point to another. However, it has been found that WEP is not as secure as once believed. WPA improves on WEP security by providing a stronger security design. For more information on wireless security, see Chapter 8, "Remote Access and Security Protocols."

18. **c.** Changing passwords too frequently is not practical, and changing them too infrequently represents a security risk. Monthly password changing is adequate for most environments. Changing passwords too frequently (Answers a and b) can cause problems because users might have problems remembering passwords and so use passwords that are too similar to one another. Although passwords should be changed if they are compromised, they should also be changed periodically, making Answer d incorrect. For more information, see Chapter 11, "Securing the Network."

19. **b, c.** To verify the IP configuration on a local computer system, you can either ping the localhost or the IP address 127.0.0.1. The default hostname for a system is localhost, not host, which means Answer a is incorrect. Answer d is not correct because this is the network address for the Class A loopback address, not a valid node loopback address. For more information, see Chapter 13.

20. **b.** A network hub operates at the physical layer of the OSI model. A router (Answer a) operates at the network layer of the OSI model. A bridge (Answer c) operates at the data-link layer of the OSI model. A NIC (Answer d) operates at the data-link layer of the OSI model. For more information, see Chapter 4.

21. **a, b, c.** With two hard disks and two controllers, you can implement RAID 0, RAID 1, and disk duplexing. RAID 5 (disk striping with parity; Answer e) requires a minimum of three disks to be implemented. RAID 10 (Answer d) is a combination of RAID 1 (disk mirroring) and RAID 0 (disk striping). RAID 10 requires a minimum of four disks. For more information, see Chapter 12.

22. **a.** The first octet of a Class B address must be in the range 128 to 191. Answers a and b represent Class A addresses. Class A addresses run from 1 to 126. Answer d is not a valid IP address. For more information, see Chapter 6.

23. **a.** The netstat utility can be used to display protocol statistics and TCP/IP network connections. The nbtstat utility (Answer b) shows statistical information about the NetBIOS over TCP/IP connections. The ping utility (Answer c) is used to test the connectivity between two devices on a TCP/IP network. The tracert utility (Answer d) traces the path between two hosts on a TCP/IP network. For more information, see Chapter 13.

24. **b, d.** TCP/IP port 25 is used by SMTP. TCP/IP port 110 is used by POP3. Because SMTP is used to send mail and POP3 is used to retrieve mail, port 25 and port 110 are the two ports that would need to be allowed for incoming and outgoing Internet email. TCP/IP port 21 (Answer a) is used by FTP. TCP/IP port 80 (Answer c) is used by HTTP. TCP/IP port 443 (Answer e) is used by HTTPS. For more information, see Chapter 6.

25. **d.** The default subnet mask for a Class B address is 255.255.0.0. Answer a is incorrect because it is not the default subnet mask for a Class B network. Answer b is the default subnet mask for a Class B network. Answer c is the local loopback address. For more information, see Chapter 6.

26. **b.** TCP operates at the transport layer of the OSI model. Answers a, c, and d are all incorrect. For more information, see Chapter 5.

27. **d.** The purpose of the firewall system is to protect one network from another. One of the most common places to use a firewall is to protect a private network from a public one such as the Internet. Answer a is incorrect because although a firewall can provide a single point of access, that is not its primary purpose. Answer b more accurately describes the function of a proxy server. Answer c describes the function of a DNS server. For more information, see Chapter 11.

28. **a.** Both email and FTP work at the application layer of the OSI model. Email and FTP are application layer protocols, not session layer protocols. User (Answer d) is not a layer of the OSI model. For more information, see Chapter 4.

29. **b.** IPSec is a security protocol that provides end-to-end security for network transmissions. This means that IPSec can be used to secure transmissions inside the network as well as those that travel beyond the LAN. IPSec can be used only on TCP/IP networks. If you are using another network protocol, you need to use a security protocol such as L2TP. Kerberos is an authentication system that provides a method to verify the identity of a computer system over an insecure network connection. NTFS is a file system with Windows 2000/XP/2003 that provides file level security using encryption. SSL is widely used to securely send credit card and other sensitive data to a vendor's website. For more information, see Chapter 8.

30. **b.** To prevent unauthorized access to a private network from the Internet, you can use a firewall server to restrict outside access. Implementing a more secure password policy (Answer a) is a good idea, but it is not the best choice of those available. Implementing a file-level encryption system (Answer c) is a good idea, but it is not the best choice of those available. Kerberos (Answer d) is an authentication system, not a method to prevent unauthorized access to the system. For more information, see Chapter 11.

31. **b.** A DHCP server does not supply NetBIOS computer names to client systems. The IP address (Answer a) is one of the pieces of information provided by DHCP. The subnet mask (Answer c) is one of the pieces of information provided by DHCP. The default gateway (Answer d) is one of the pieces of information supplied by DHCP. For more information, see Chapter 6.

32. **c.** Because the NIC is functioning at half-duplex 10Mbps, the transfer rate is 10Mbps. None of the other answers are correct. For more information, see Chapter 3, "Networking Components and Devices."

33. **d.** IPv6 uses a 128-bit address, which is expressed as eight octet pairs in hexadecimal format, separated by colons. Because it is hexadecimal, only numbers and the letters A through F can be used. An IPv6 address is composed of eight hexadecimal octets. Only numbers and the letters A through F can be used. For more information, see Chapter 6.

34. **a.** The arp -a command is used to display the IP addresses that have been resolved to MAC addresses. The nbtstat command (Answer b) is used to view protocol statistics for NetBIOS connections. arp -d (Answer c) is not a valid command. The arp -s command (Answer d) allows you to add static entries to the ARP cache. For more information, see Chapter 13.

35. **b.** A RAID 5 array consists of at least three hard disks and stripes parity information across all disks in the array. RAID 5 (disk striping with parity; Answer a) requires at least three drives. The parity information is stored in a stripe across all three drives in the array (Answer b). RAID 5 requires only three drives, which makes Answer d incorrect. For more information, see Chapter 12.

36. d. CSMA/CD relates to the IEEE specification 802.3. The 802.1x (Answer a) standard describes an authentication standard commonly used on wireless networks. The 802.2 (Answer b) standard defines the media access methods for various networking standards. The 802.5 (Answer c) standard defines Token Ring networking. For more information, see Chapter 1, "Introduction to Networking."

37. d. The `ping -t` command is used to send continuous `ping` requests to a remote system. The `ping` request will continue until it is manually stopped. The trace route utility (Answer a) performs this task. The `ping` command (Answer b) shows the amount of time a packet takes to complete the round-trip from the host to the destination. Answer c is incorrect because the `ping` command with the `-n` switch performs this task. For more information, see Chapter 13.

38. c. The Extensible Authentication Protocol (EAP) is an extension to PPP and supports multiple authentication methods, including token cards, Kerberos, one-time passwords, certificates, public key authentication, and smart cards. PAP is the least secure of the authentication methods because it uses unencrypted passwords. PAP is a basic encryption service that provides limited functionality and is not recommended for most environments. CHAP is a challenge/response authentication protocol not associated with smart cards or token cards. Multi-Chap v2 is not a valid option. For more information on authentication methods, refer to Chapter 8.

39. a. The diagram in the question shows a star topology. The star topology uses a centralized hub or switch to which all systems attach. Answers b, c, and d are all incorrect. The figure does not represent any of these network types. For more information, see Chapter 1 for information on network topologies.

40. a. In this scenario, you would first check the remote access gateway to see whether it is running and operating correctly. Because the user can browse web pages, this is not a connectivity problem. Answer b is incorrect because although rebooting the system might help, the system appears to be working correctly, and rebooting it is unlikely to cure the problem. The IP address configuration appears to be working because the user is able to access web pages and so Answer c is incorrect. The Internet connection appears to be working, so cycling the power on the DSL modem, as described in Answer d, is unlikely to help. For more information, see Chapter 15.

41. b. IEEE 802.1x defines a security standard for port-based, network access control. Originally designed for authentication on wired Ethernet networks, it has been adopted by 802.11 standards to provide authentication services for WLANs. WEP (Answer a) is a wireless security standard that offers encryption services but not port-based authentication. IPSec (Answer c) is a protocol designed to provide end-to-end security for network transmissions. Kerberos (Answer d) is an authentication system that provides a method to verify the identity of a computer system over an insecure network connection. For more information on security standards, see Chapter 8.

42. d. The output displayed in this question is from the Windows `tracert` utility. Answers a, b, and c are all incorrect. These utilities produce output that is different from the output shown. For more information, see Chapter 13.

43. b. User-level security is more secure than share-level security and requires a user to provide a login ID, usually a username and password combination to access network resources. Answer a is incorrect because share-level security is not as secure as user-level security. Answers c and d are not accepted terms for describing levels of security. For more information, see Chapter 11.

44. d. The HOSTS file is used to manually configure hostname resolution, and, if there is a problem with hostname resolution, entries in this file must be checked. Answers a and b are incorrect because files are not used on a Linux system. Answer c is incorrect because the PASSWD file is used to store user account information. For more information, see Chapter 6.

45. a. Fiber-optic cable provides the most resistance to EMI and therefore is often used in environ-ments where there is a risk of interference. Although it is inexpensive, UTP (Answer b) cable has very low resistance to EMI. Therefore, it should not be run near high-voltage electric cables. Thin coax (Answer c) has low resistance to EMI. Therefore, it should not be run near high-voltage elec-tric cables. STP (Answer d) has a good level of resistance to EMI, but it is still not as resistant as fiber optic. Not factoring in the cost, fiber optic is the most suitable solution. For more information, see Chapter 2.

46. c. SMTP is used for sending email. Answer a is not a valid answer. Answers b and d are incorrect because POP3 and IMAP are email retrieval protocols, not protocols for sending email. For more information, see Chapter 6.

47. d. The most likely cause of the problem is that the default gateway is not configured. Answer a is incorrect because from the output it appears that the DNS servers are on the same subnet as this system. Answer b does not apply because addressing is configured statically, so there is no DHCP service. This is not a problem, however. Answer c is incorrect because the subnet mask is the cor-rect default subnet mask for a Class C network. For more information, see Chapter 13.

48. c. DNS allows hostname resolutions to occur internally. In most cases companies use a DNS serv-er provided by the ISP. In some cases, however, it might be appropriate to have a DNS server on the internal network. Answer a is incorrect because NAT is normally a function of firewall or proxy servers. Answer b describes the purpose of a WINS server. Answer d describes the function of a proxy server. For more information, see Chapter 6.

49. d. Private address ranges are designed for use on private networks. The ranges are 192.168.X.X, 10.X.X.X, and 172.16.X.X–172.32.X.X. Answers a, b, and c are all valid private IP address ranges. For more information, see Chapter 6.

50. a. The MAC address is a 6-byte address expressed in six pairs of hexadecimal values. Because it is hexadecimal, only the letters A through F and numbers can be used. Answer b is incorrect because MAC addresses are expressed as six hexadecimal pairs. Answer c shows an example of an IPv4 address. Answer d shows an example of an IPv6 address. Answer e is incorrect because MAC addresses are expressed in hexadecimal; therefore, only the letters A through F and numbers can be used. For more information, see Chapter 3.

51. c. The Remote Desktop Protocol (RDP) is the protocol used in establishing and maintaining Microsoft Windows Terminal Services sessions. It is also used for applications that use Terminal Services technology, such as Remote Desktop. NFS (Answer a) is the default file access and shar-ing protocol used on Unix and Linux platforms. SMB (Answer b) is the default file access and sharing protocol used on Windows platforms. AFP (Answer d) is a file-sharing and access protocol associated with Apple Macintosh operating systems. For more information, see Chapter 6.

52. **d.** A VLAN is implemented on a switch to create multiple separate networks. A proxy server (Answer a) is used to control access to the Internet. Subnet masking (Answer b) is not a valid method of creating separate networks. NAS (Answer c) describes storage devices attached directly to the network media. For more information, see Chapter 12.

53. **a, c.** IP and IPX are responsible for network addressing. Answers b and d are incorrect because SPX and TCP are transport-layer protocols and so are not responsible for network addressing. For more information, see Chapter 5.

54. **d.** The RJ-11 connector is used for phone line connections, which is what you would be using to connect to the Public Switched Telephone Network (PSTN). There is no connector called RJ-PT (Answer a). RJ-45 (Answer b) connectors are used with UTP network cabling. MTRJ (Answer c) connectors are associated with fiber-optic cabling. For more information, see Chapter 2.

55. **a.** The RADIUS service provides authentication services for remote access users for a dial-up network. RADIUS uses a client-server model. IPSec (Answer b) is a protocol designed to encrypt local and remote network data communications. L2TP (Answer c) and PPTP (Answer d) are used to authenticate users over a VPN link. For more information, see Chapter 8.

56. **b, d.** Fiber-optic cable can use either SC or ST type connectors. RJ-11 connectors (Answer a) are associated with telephone cable, RJ-45 (Answer c) connectors are associated with UTP cable, and BNC connectors (Answer e) are associated with thin coaxial cable. For more information, see Chapter 2.

57. **d.** A firewall can provide several different services to the network, including NAT, proxy services, and packet filtering. NAS is not a function of a firewall server. Answers a, b, and c are all incorrect because NAT, packet filtering, and proxy functionality are all commonly implemented on firewall systems. For more information, see Chapter 11.

58. **a.** When a new NIC is installed on a Token Ring network, the speed of the card has to be set to match the speed used by the network. Answer b is incorrect because Token Ring networks operate at either 4Mbps or 16Mbps. Answer c is incorrect because full-duplex connections are not used on Token Ring networks. Answer d is incorrect because, although it is possible, a faulty card is not the most likely answer. For more information, see Chapter 1.

59. **b.** The most likely explanation is that port 443, the HTTPS default port, is being blocked by a corporate firewall. Port 80 (Answer a) is used by HTTP. All modern web browsers support HTTPS automatically; therefore, Answer c is incorrect. Port 110 (Answer d) is used by POP3. For more information, see Chapter 6.

60. **a.** Class A subnets use the range 1 to 126 for the value of the first octet. Answer b is the loopback address, which allows the IP stack functionality to be tested. Answers c and d are both addresses in the Class B range (128–191). Class A addresses run from 1 through 126. For more information, see Chapter 6.

61. **d.** Most modern phone systems are digital, and therefore, regular analog modems that require analog lines will not work. Answer a is incorrect because, if the phone line in the room were analog, the modem would probably work. Answer b is incorrect because, the phone line in the room is not faulty because the user is able to use it to call you and report the problem. Answer c is incorrect because if the modem can get as far as reporting a "no dial tone" error, it is most likely working correctly. For more information, see Chapter 8.

62. **b.** The attribute file permission is not a valid NTFS file permission. Answers a, c, and d are all incorrect because they are all valid file permissions on a Windows 2000/2003 system. For more information, see Chapter 11.

63. **a.** The netstat utility allows you to view the TCP/IP connections between two systems. The nbtstat utility (Answer b) is used to see the status of NetBIOS over TCP/IP connections. The tracert utility (Answer c) is used to track the path that a packet of data takes between two hosts. The ipconfig utility (Answer d) is used to view the IP addressing configuration information on a system. For more information, see Chapter 13.

64. **a, b, c.** For a system to be classed as a "zero configuration" system, it must be able to assign itself an IP address, resolve a hostname to an IP address without a DNS server, and locate system resources without a directory services system. Zero configuration does not require any kind of automatic MAC address assignment. MAC addresses, or hardware addresses, are configured directly on a network interface. For more information, see Chapter 6.

65. **b.** AARP is used to map the AppleTalk addresses to both Ethernet and Token Ring physical addresses. The distance-vector routing protocol used on AppleTalk networks is RMTP which makes Answer a incorrect. Answer c is incorrect because AARP resolves AppleTalk addresses to MAC addresses—not the other way around. AARP is not a link-state routing protocol. For more information, see Chapter 5.

66. **a.** The term *subnetting* is used to refer to the process of using parts of the node address range for network addressing purposes. *Supernetting* (Answer b) refers to the process of borrowing parts of the network address portion of an assigned address to be used for node addressing. *Subnet masking* (Answer c) is the term used to describe the process of applying a subnet mask to an address. Answer d is not a valid term. For more information, see Chapter 6.

67. **a, d.** The process of subnetting involves using parts of the node portion of the IP address to create more network addresses. The process of using parts of the network portion of the IP address to create more node addresses and fewer network addresses is called supernetting. For more information, see Chapter 6.

68. **b, e.** A hardware loopback plug connects the 2 and 6 wires and 1 and 3 wires to simulate a live network connection. Answers a, c, and d are all incorrect; these answers are not correct for the cable in a hardware loopback adapter. For more information, see Chapter 10.

69. **c.** Each node on a star network uses its own cable, which makes it easy to add users without disrupting current users. Adding a node to a bus network can sometimes involve breaking the segment, which makes it inaccessible to all other nodes on the network. This makes Answer a incorrect. Answer b is incorrect because a true ring network model would require that the ring be broken to add a new device. Answer d is incorrect because a mesh topology requires that every device be connected to every other device on the network. It is, therefore, difficult to expand a mesh network. For more information, see Chapter 1.

70. **a.** 10BaseT networks use twisted-pair cable and RJ-45 connectors. RJ-11 (Answer b) connectors are associated with telephone cable. RJ-T (Answer c) is not a valid type of connector. A BNC connector (Answer d) is associated with coaxial cable. The 10BaseT standard uses twisted-pair cable. For more information, see Chapter 2.

71. **c.** DNS uses TCP port 53. Port 21 (Answer a) is used by FTP. Port 25 (Answer b) is used by SMTP. Port 110 (Answer d) is used by POP3. For more information, see Chapter 6.

72. **b.** Fault tolerance promotes data availability by eliminating a single point of failure. Answer a is incorrect because, although fault tolerance may reduce the reliance on backups, they should still be performed. Answer c is incorrect because in the strict definition, being fault tolerant does not help a system get back online more quickly. Answer d is incorrect because being a fault tolerant system does not protect data from accidental deletion. For more information, see Chapter 12.

PART III

Appendixes

What's on the CD-ROM

The CD features an innovative practice test engine powered by MeasureUp, giving you yet another effective tool to assess your readiness for the exam.

Multiple Test Modes

MeasureUp practice tests are available in Study, Certification, Custom, Missed Question, and Non-Duplicate question modes.

Study Mode

Tests administered in Study Mode allow you to request the correct answer(s) and explanation to each question during the test. These tests are not timed. You can modify the testing environment *during* the test by selecting the Options button.

Certification Mode

Tests administered in Certification Mode closely simulate the actual testing environment you will encounter when taking a certification exam. These tests do not allow you to request the answer(s) and/or explanation to each question until after the exam.

Custom Mode

Custom Mode allows you to specify your preferred testing environment. Use this mode to specify the objectives you want to include in your test, the timer length, and other test properties. You can also modify the testing environment *during* the test by selecting the Options button.

Missed Question Mode

Missed Question Mode allows you to take a test containing only the questions you have missed previously.

Non-Duplicate Mode

Non-Duplicate Mode allows you to take a test containing only questions not displayed previously.

Random Questions and Order of Answers

This feature helps you learn the material without memorizing questions and answers. Each time you take a practice test, the questions and answers appear in a different randomized order.

Detailed Explanations of Correct and Incorrect Answers

You'll receive automatic feedback on all correct and incorrect answers. The detailed answer explanations are a superb learning tool in their own right.

Attention to Exam Objectives

MeasureUp practice tests are designed to appropriately balance the questions over each technical area covered by a specific exam.

Installing the CD

The minimum system requirements for the CD-ROM are

- ▶ Windows 95, 98, ME, NT4, 2000, or XP
- ▶ 7 MB disk space for testing engine
- ▶ An average of 1MB disk space for each test

To install the CD-ROM, follow these instructions:

NOTE

If you need technical support, contact MeasureUp at 678-356-5050 or email support@measureup.com. Additionally, you'll find Frequently Asked Questions (FAQs) at www.measureup.com.

---

1. Close all applications before beginning this installation.

2. Insert the CD into your CD-ROM drive. If the setup starts automatically, go to step 6. If the setup does not start automatically, continue with step 3.

3. From the Start menu, select Run.

4. Click Browse to locate the MeasureUp CD. In the Browse dialog box, from the Look In drop-down list, select the CD-ROM drive.

5. In the Browse dialog box, double-click on Setup.exe. In the Run dialog box, click OK to begin the installation.

6. On the Welcome screen, click MeasureUp Practice Questions to begin installation.

7. Follow the Certification Prep Wizard by clicking Next.

8. To agree to the Software License Agreement, click Yes.

9. On the Choose Destination Location screen, click Next to install the software to C:\Program Files\Certification Preparation.

NOTE

If you cannot locate MeasureUp Practice Tests through the Start menu, see the section later in this appendix entitled, "Creating a Shortcut to the MeasureUp Practice Tests."

---

10. On the Setup Type screen, select Typical Setup. Click Next to continue.

11. In the Select Program Folder screen, you can name the program folder your tests will be in. To select the default simply click Next, and the installation continues.

12. After the installation is complete, verify that Yes, I Want to Restart My Computer Now is selected. If you select No, I Will Restart My Computer Later, you will not be able to use the program until you restart your computer.

13. Click Finish.

14. After restarting your computer, choose Start, Programs, MeasureUp, MeasureUp Practice Tests.

15. On the MeasureUp Welcome screen, click Create User Profile.

16. In the User Profile dialog box, complete the mandatory fields and click Create Profile.

17. Select the practice test you want to access and click Start Test.

Creating a Shortcut to the MeasureUp Practice Tests

To create a shortcut to the MeasureUp Practice Tests, follow these steps:

1. Right-click on your desktop.

2. From the shortcut menu select New, Shortcut.

3. Browse to C:\Program Files\MeasureUp Practice Tests and select the MeasureUpCertification.exe or Localware.exe file.

4. Click OK.

5. Click Next.

6. Rename the shortcut MeasureUp.

7. Click Finish.

After you complete step 7, use the MeasureUp shortcut on your desktop to access the MeasureUp products you ordered.

Technical Support

If you encounter problems with the MeasureUp test engine on the CD-ROM, contact MeasureUp at 678-356-5050 or email support@measureup.com. Technical support hours are from 8:00 a.m. to 5:00 p.m. EST Monday through Friday. Additionally, you'll find Frequently Asked Questions (FAQs) at www.measureup.com.

If you want to purchase additional MeasureUp products, telephone 678-356-5050 or 800-649-1MUP (1687) or visit www.measureup.com.

Glossary

Numbers and Symbols

10Base2   An IEEE 802.3 specification for Ethernet at 10Mbps over thin coaxial cable. The maximum length of a 10Base2 segment is 185 meters (that is, 607 feet). 10Base2 operates at 10Mbps and uses a baseband transmission method.

10Base5   The IEEE 802.3 specification for 10Mbps Ethernet using thick coaxial cable. The maximum length of a 10Base5 segment is 500 meters (that is, 1,640 feet).

10BaseFL   The IEEE 802.3 specification for running Ethernet at 10Mbps over fiber-optic cable. The maximum length of a 10BaseFL segment is 2,000 meters.

10BaseT   The IEEE 802.3i specification for running Ethernet at 10Mbps over twisted-pair cabling. The maximum length of a 10BaseT segment is 100 meters (that is, 330 feet).

100BaseFX   The IEEE 802.3 specification for running Fast Ethernet at 100Mbps over fiber-optic cable. The maximum length of a 100BaseFX segment is 2,000 meters (6,561 feet), in full-duplex mode.

100BaseT   The IEEE 802.3 specification for running Ethernet at 100Mbps over twisted-pair cabling. The maximum length of a 100BaseT segment is 100 meters (that is, 330 feet).

100BaseT4   The IEEE specification that allows the use of Fast Ethernet (100Mbps) technology over existing Category 3 and Category 4 wiring, utilizing all four pairs of wires. The maximum length of a 100BaseT4 segment is 100 meters (that is, 330 feet).

100BaseTX   An IEEE 802.3u specification, also known as Fast Ethernet, for running Ethernet at 100Mbps over STP or UTP. The maximum length of a 100BaseTX segment is 100 meters (that is, 330 feet).

100BaseVG-AnyLAN   The IEEE 802.12 specification that allows data transmissions of 100Mbps over Category 3 cable, utilizing all sets of wires. *VG* in 100BaseVG-AnyLAN stands for *voice grade* because of its capability to be used over voice-grade cable. The maximum length of a 100BaseVG-AnyLAN segment is 100 meters (330 feet) on Category 3 cable, 150 meters (492 feet) on Category 5 cable, and 2,000 meters (6,561 feet) on fiber-optic cable.

1000BaseX   The IEEE 802.3z specification, also known as Gigabit Ethernet, that defines standards for data transmissions of 1000Mbps (1Gbps). 1000BaseX is most often associated with fiber or STP cable. 1000BaseX refers collectively to three distinct standards: 1000BaseLX, 1000BaseSX, and 1000BaseCX.

1000BaseT   IEEE 802.3ab standard that specifies Gigabit Ethernet over Category 5 UTP cable. The standard allows for full-duplex transmission using the four pairs of twisted cable.

1000BaseCX   IEEE 802.3z standard that uses a special shielded copper cable. 1000Base-CX can be used up to a maximum distance of 25 meters.

1000BaseLX   IEEE 802.3z standard that specifies Gigabit Ethernet over fiber-optic cable. 1000Base-LX can be used up to 5,000 meters.

1000BaseSX   IEEE 802.3z standard that specifies Gigabit Ethernet over fiber-optic cable.

10GbE   Term commonly used to refer to the 10Gbps Ethernet networking standards such as 10Gbase-ER, 10Gbase-LR, and 10Gbase-SR. 10 Gigabit Ethernet is defined in the IEEE 802.3ae standard.

10GbaseER   10Gbps Ethernet networking standard that can be used up to 40,000 meters.

10GbaseLR   10Gbps Ethernet networking standard that can be used up to 10,000 meters. 10Gbase-LR uses single mode fiber-optic cabling.

10GbaseSR   10Gbps Ethernet networking standard that can be used over relatively short distances, up to 300 meters.

A

access point   A transmitter and receiver (transceiver) device commonly used to facilitate communication between a wireless client and a wired network. Wireless APs are use with the wireless infrastructure network topology to provide a connection point between WLANs and a wired Ethernet LAN.

ACK   The acknowledgment message sent between two hosts during a TCP session.

ACL (access control list)   The list of trustees assigned to a file or directory. A trustee can be any object available to the security subsystem. The term ACL is also used with routers and firewall systems to refer to the list of permitted computers or users.

Active Directory   Active Directory is used in Windows network environments. It is a directory services system that allows network objects to be stored in a database. This database can then be divided up and distributed among different servers on the network.

active hub   A hub that has power supplied to it for the purposes of regenerating the signals that pass through it.

active termination   A termination system used on a SCSI bus. Unlike passive termination, which uses voltage resistors, active termination uses voltage regulators to create the termination voltage.

address   A set of numbers, used to identify and locate a resource or device on a network. An example is an IP address such as 192.168.2.1.

ad-hoc topology   Defines a wireless network layout whereby devices communicate directly between themselves without using an access point. Sometimes called an unmanaged or peer-to-peer wireless topology.

administrator   A person responsible for the control and security of the user accounts, resources, and data on a network.

Administrator account   On a Windows system, the default account that has rights to access everything and to assign rights to other users on the network. Unlike other user accounts, the Administrator account cannot be deleted.

ADSL (Asymmetric Digital Subscriber Line)   A service that transmits digital voice and data over existing (analog) phone lines.

AFP (Apple File Protocol)   File-sharing and access protocol implemented in Apple networks. AFP can be implemented over TCP/IP (AppleTalk over IP).

ANSI (American National Standards Institute)   An organization that publishes standards for communications, programming languages, and networking.

antivirus software   A software application that detects and removes virus programs.

APIPA (Automatic Private IP Addressing)   Technology implemented on certain Windows platforms through which a system assigns itself an IP address in the absence of a DHCP server. Addresses are assigned from the 169.254.x.x address range.

application layer   Layer 7 of the OSI model, which provides support for end users and for application programs using network resources.

application log   A log file on a Windows system that provides information on events that occur within an application.

archive bit   A flag that is set on a file after it has been created or altered. Some backup methods reset the flag to indicate that it has been backed up.

ARP (Address Resolution Protocol) A protocol in the TCP/IP protocol suite that is used to resolve IP addresses to MAC addresses. Specifically, the ARP command returns a layer 2 address for a layer 3 address.

ARP table A table of entries used by ARP to store resolved ARP requests. Entries can also be stored manually.

array A group of devices arranged in a fault-tolerant configuration. *See also* RAID.

attenuation The loss of signal that is experienced as data is transmitted over distance and across the network media.

authentication The process by which a user's identity is validated on a network. The most common authentication method is a username and password combination.

B

B (bearer) channel In ISDN, a 64Kbps channel that carries data. *See also* D channel.

backbone A network segment that acts as a trunk between other network segments. Backbones are typically high-bandwidth implementations such as fiber-optic cable.

backup schedule A document or plan that defines what type of backups are made, when, and what data is backed up.

bandwidth The width of the range of electrical frequencies, or amount of channels that the media can support. Bandwidth correlates to the amount of data that can traverse the media at one time, but other factors determine what the maximum speed supported by a cable will be.

baseband A term applied to any media capable of carrying only a single data signal at a time. *Compare with* broadband.

baseline A measurement of performance of a device or system for the purposes of future comparison. Baselining is a common server administration task.

baud rate The speed or rate of signal transfer. Baud rate bandwidth is measured in cycles per second, or Hertz (Hz). The word *baud* is derived from the name of French telegraphy expert J. M. Baudot.

binary A base 2 numbering system used in digital signaling. It uses only the numbers 1 and 0.

Bindery The name of the user account information database on NetWare servers up to and including NetWare 3.x.

binding The process of associating a protocol with a NIC.

biometrics The science and technology of measuring and analyzing biological data. Biometrics is used for security purposes, to analyze and compare characteristics such as voice patterns, retina patterns, and hand measurements.

BIOS (Basic Input/Output System) A basic set of instructions that a device needs to operate.

bit An electronic digit used in the binary numbering system. Bit is a contraction of the terms *binary* and *digit*.

blackout A total loss of electrical power.

Blue Screen of Death The term for the blue-screen STOP errors that occur and halt the system on Windows server based systems.

Bluetooth   A low-cost, short-range RF technology designed to replace many of the cords that used to connect devices. Bluetooth uses 2.4Ghz RF and provides transmission speeds up to 16Mbps.

BNC (Bayonet Neill Concelman)   A family of connectors typically associated with thin coaxial cabling and 10Base2 networks. BNC connectors use a twist and lock mechanism to connect devices to the network.

bound media   A term used to describe any media that have physical constraints, such as coaxial, fiber-optic, and twisted pair. *Compare with* unbound media.

boundless media   *See* unbound media.

BRI (Basic Rate Interface)   An ISDN digital communications line that consists of three independent channels: two B channels, each at 64Kbps, and one D channel, at 16Kbps. ISDN BRI is often referred to as 2B+D. *See also* ISDN, PRI.

bridge   A device that connects and passes packets between two network segments that use the same communications protocol. Bridges operate at the data-link layer of the OSI model. A bridge filters, forwards, or floods an incoming frame based on the MAC address of that packet.

bridging address table   A list of MAC addresses that a bridge keeps and uses when it receives packets. The bridge uses the bridging address table to determine which segment the destination address is on before it sends the packet to the next interface or drops the packet (if it is on the same segment as the sending node).

broadband   A communications strategy that uses analog or digital signaling over multiple communications channels.

broadcast   A packet delivery system in which a copy of a packet is given to all hosts attached to the network.

broadcast storm   An undesirable condition in which broadcasts become so numerous as to bog down the flow of data across the network.

brouter   A device that can be used to combine the benefits of both routers and bridges. Its common usage is to route routable protocols at the network layer of the OSI model and to bridge nonroutable protocols at the data-link layer.

brownout   A short-term decrease in the voltage level, usually caused by the startup demands of other electrical devices.

buffer   An area of memory in a device used to store data before it is forwarded to another device or location.

bus topology   A linear LAN architecture in which all devices are connected to a common cable, referred to as a bus or backbone.

byte   A set of bits (usually 8 bits) that operate as a unit to signify a character.

C

cable modem   A device that provides Internet access over cable television lines.

cable tester   A device used to check for electrical continuity along a length of cable. *Cable tester* is a generic term that can be applied to devices such as volt/ohm meters and TDRs.

caching-only server   A type of DNS server that operates the same way as secondary servers except that a zone transfer does not take place when the caching-only server is started.

carrier   A signal that carries data. The carrier signal is modulated to create peaks and troughs, which represent binary bits.

CDDI (Copper Distributed Data Interface)   An implementation of the FDDI standard that uses copper cable rather than optical cable.

Centronics connector   A connector that uses clips that snap into place to secure the connector. Used with external SCSI devices and some printer connections.

change control   A process in which a detailed record of every change made to the network is documented.

channel   A communications path used for data transmission.

checksum   A basic method of error checking that involves calculating the sum of bytes in a section of data and then embedding the result in the packet. When the packet reaches the destination, the calculation is performed again, to make sure that the value is still the same.

CIDR (classless interdomain routing)   An IP addressing scheme that allows a single IP address to designate many unique IP addresses. CIDR addressing uses an IP address followed by a "/" and the IP network prefix. An example CIDR address would be 192.168.100.0/16. CIDR is sometimes referred to as *supernetting*.

circuit switching   A method of sending data between two parties, in which a dedicated circuit is created at the beginning of the conversation and broken at the end. All data transported during the session travels over the same path, or circuit.

Class A network   A TCP/IP network that uses addresses from 1 to 126 and supports up to 126 subnets with 16,777,214 unique hosts each.

Class B network   A TCP/IP network that uses addresses from 128 to 191 and supports up to 16,384 subnets with 65,534 unique hosts each.

Class C network   A TCP/IP network that uses addresses from 192 to 223 and supports up to 2,097,152 subnets with 254 unique hosts each.

client   A node that uses the services from another node on a network.

client/server networking   A networking architecture in which front-end, or client, nodes request and process data stored by the back-end, or server, node.

clustering   A technology that allows two or more computers to act as a single system to provide improved fault tolerance, load balancing, and failover capability.

coaxial cable   A data cable, commonly referred to as *coax*, that is made of a solid copper core insulated and surrounded by braided metal and covered with a thick plastic or rubber covering. Coax is the standard cable used in cable television and in older bus topology networks.

config   A command used on a NetWare server to see basic information such as the server name, NDS information, and the details of network interface configurations.

collision   The result of two frames transmitting simultaneously on an Ethernet network and colliding, thereby destroying both frames.

collision domain   A segment of an Ethernet network that is between managing nodes, where only one packet can be transmitted at any given time. Switches, bridges, and routers can be used to segment a network into separate collision domains.

collision light   An LED on networking equipment that flashes to indicate a collision on the network. A collision light can be used to determine whether the network is experiencing many collisions.

COM port (communication port)   A connection through which serial devices and a computer's motherboard can communicate. A COM port requires standard configuration information, such as an IRQ, an I/O address, and a COM port number.

communication   The transfer of information between nodes on a network.

concentrator   A device that combines several communications channels into one. It is often used to tie multiple terminals together into one line.

connectionless communication   Packet transfer in which delivery is not guaranteed.

connection-oriented communication   Packet transfer in which delivery is guaranteed.

connectivity   The linking of nodes on a network for communication to take place.

copy backup   Normally, a backup of the entire hard drive. A copy backup is similar to a full backup, except that the copy backup does not alter the state of the archive bits on files.

cost   A value used to encourage or discourage the use of a certain route through a network. Routes that are to be discouraged are assigned a higher cost, and those that are to be encouraged are assigned a lower cost. *See also* metric.

cracker   A person who attempts to break software code or gain access to a system to which he or she is not authorized. *See also* hacker.

cracking   The process of attempting to break software code, normally to defeat copyright protection or alter the software's functioning. Also the process of attempting to gain unauthorized access to a computer system. *See also* hacking.

CRC (cyclical redundancy check)   A method used to check for errors in packets that have been transferred across a network. A computation bit is added to the packet and recalculated at the destination to determine whether the entire content of the packet has been transferred correctly.

crimper   A tool used to join connectors to the ends of network cables.

crossover cable A UTP cable in which the 1 and 3 wires and the 2 and 6 wires are crossed for the purposes of placing the transmit line of one device on the receive line of the other. Crossover cables can be used to directly connect two devices—for example, two computer systems—or as a means to expand networks that use devices such as hubs or switches.

crosstalk Electronic interference caused when two wires are too close to each other, and interference is caused by the adjacent cable.

CSMA/CA (carrier-sense multiple-access with collision avoidance) A contention media access method that uses collision-avoidance techniques.

CSMA/CD (carrier-sense multiple-access with collision detection) A contention media access method that uses collision-detection and retransmission techniques.

cut-through packet switching A switching method that does not copy the entire packet into the switch buffers. Instead, the destination address is captured into the switch, the route to the destination node is determined, and the packet is quickly sent out the corresponding port. Cut-through packet switching maintains a low latency.

D

D (delta) channel The channel used on ISDN to communicate signaling and other related information. Use of the D channel leaves the B channels free for data communication. *See also* B channel.

D-shell connector A connector shaped like the letter D and uses pins and sockets to establish connections between peripheral devices, using serial or parallel ports. The number that follows *DB* in the name of a D connector is the number of pins used for connectivity; for example, a DB-9 connector has 9 pins, and a DB-25 connector has 25 pins.

daemon A service or process that runs on a Unix or Linux server.

DAS (dual attached station) A device on an FDDI network that is connected to both rings. *Compare with* SAS.

DAT (digital audio tape) A tape recording technology that uses the helical scan recording method. This technology has been used in videotape recorders and VCRs since the 1950s.

Data field In a frame, the field or section that contains the data.

datagram An information grouping transmitted as a unit at the network layer. *See also* packet.

data-link layer Layer 2 of the OSI model, which is above the physical layer. Data comes off the cable, goes through the physical layer, and goes into the data-link layer. The data-link layer has two distinct sublayers: MAC and LLC.

DB-9 A 9-pin connector used for serial port or parallel port connection between PCs and peripheral devices.

DB-25 A 25-pin connector used for serial port or parallel port connection between PCs and peripheral devices.

DDNS (dynamic DNS)   A form of DNS that allows systems to be registered and deregistered with the DNS system dynamically. DDNS is facilitated by DHCP, which passes IP address assignments to the DNS server for entry into the DNS server records. This is in contrast with the conventional DNS system, in which entries must be made manually.

DDS (digital data storage)   A format for storing computer data on a DAT. DDS-formatted tapes can be read by either a DDS or DAT drive. The original DDS standard specified a 4mm tape cartridge with a capacity of 1.3GB. Subsequent implementations of DDS have taken the capacity to 40GB with compression.

dedicated line   A dedicated circuit used in WANs to provide a constant connection between two points.

default gateway   Normally a router or a multihomed computer to which packets are sent when they are destined for a host on a different network.

Delete or Erase   A right given to users that allows them to delete a file or files in a directory or to delete a directory.

demarcation point   The point at which communication lines enter a customer's premises. Sometimes shortened to simply "demarc."

destination address   The network address to which data is being sent.

DHCP (Dynamic Host Configuration Protocol)   A protocol that provides dynamic IP addressing to workstations on the network.

dial-up networking   Refers to the connection of a remote node to a network using POTS.

differential backup   A backup of only the data that has been created or changed since the previous full backup. In a differential backup, the state of the archive bits is not altered.

directory services   A system that allows network resources to be viewed as objects stored in a database. This database can then be divided up and distributed among different servers on the network. Examples of directory services systems include Novell Directory Services and Microsoft Active Directory.

disaster recovery plan   A plan for implementing duplicate computer services in the event of a natural disaster, a human-made disaster, or another catastrophe. A disaster recovery plan includes offsite backups and procedures to activate information systems in alternative locations.

disk duplexing   A fault-tolerant standard based on RAID 1 that uses disk mirroring with dual disk controllers.

disk mirroring   A fault-tolerant standard that is defined as RAID 1 and mirrors data between two disks to create an exact copy.

disk striping   An implementation of RAID in which data is distributed across multiple disks in a stripe. Some striping implementations provide performance improvements (RAID 0), whereas others provide fault tolerance (RAID 5).

distance-vector routing A type of routing in which a router uses broadcasts to inform neighboring routers on the network of the routes it knows about. *Compare with* link-state routing.

DLT (digital linear tape) A high-performance and high-capacity tape backup system that offers capacities up to 220GB with compression.

DMA (direct memory access) The process of transferring data directly into memory at high speeds, bypassing the CPU and incurring no processor overhead.

DNS (Domain Name Service) A system used to translate domain names, such as www.quepublishing.com, into IP addresses, such as 165.193.123.44. DNS uses a hierarchical namespace that allows the database of hostname-to-IP address mappings to be distributed across multiple servers.

domain A logical boundary of an Active Directory Structure on Windows Servers. Also, a section of the DNS namespace.

domain name server A server that runs application software that allows the server to perform a role associated with the DNS service.

DoS (Denial of Service) attack A type of hacking attack in which the target system is overwhelmed with requests for service, resulting in it not being able to service any requests—legitimate or otherwise.

downtime A period of time during which a computer system or network is unavailable. This may be due to scheduled maintenance or to hardware or software failure.

drive mapping A process through which an alias makes a network path appear as if it were a local drive.

DSL (Digital Subscriber Line) A public network technology that delivers high bandwidth over conventional copper wiring over limited distances.

DSU (data service unit) A network communications device that formats and controls data for transmission over digital lines. A DSU is used in conjunction with a CSU.

DTE (data terminal equipment) A device used at the user end of a user network interface that serves as a data source, a destination, or both. DTE devices include computers, protocol translators, and multiplexers.

dumb terminal A keyboard/monitor combination that allows access to a multiuser system but provides no processing or storage at the local level.

duplexing In RAID, a RAID 1 mirror set in which each drive is connected to a separate controller to eliminate the single point of failure that the controller created.

dynamic routing A routing system that allows routing information to be communicated between devices automatically and can recognize changes in the network topology and update routing tables accordingly. *Compare with* static routing.

dynamic window A flow control mechanism that prevents the sender of data from overwhelming the receiver. The amount of data that can be buffered in a dynamic window varies in size, hence its name.

E

(EAP) Extensible Authentication Protocol An extension of the PPP protocol that supports authentication methods more secure than a standard username and password combination. EAP is commonly used as an authentication protocol for token cards, smart cards, and digital certificates.

EMI (electromagnetic interference) External interference of electromagnetic signals that causes a reduction of data integrity and increased error rates in a transmission medium.

encapsulation A technique used by protocols in which header and/or trailer information is added to the protocol data unit as it is passed down through the protocol stack on a sending system. The reverse process, called *decapsulation*, is performed at the receiving system as the packet travels up through the protocol suite.

encryption The modification of data for security purposes prior to transmission so that it is not comprehendible without the decoding method.

ESD (electrostatic discharge) A condition created when two objects of dissimilar electrical charge come into contact with each other. The result is that a charge from the object with the higher electrical charge discharges itself into the object with the lower-level charge. This discharge can be harmful to computer components and circuit boards.

Ethernet The most common LAN technology. Ethernet can be implemented using coaxial, twisted-pair, or fiber-optic cable. Ethernet typically uses the CSMA/CD media access method and has various implementation standards.

Event Viewer A utility available on Windows server systems commonly used for gathering systems information and used in the troubleshooting process.

EXT2 The default file system used in Linux systems.

F

F-Type Screw type connector used with coaxial cable. In computing environments, most commonly used to connect cable modems to ISP equipment or incoming cable feeds.

failover The automatic switching from one device or system to another. Servers can be configured in a failover configuration so that if the primary server fails, the secondary server takes over automatically.

Fast Ethernet The IEEE 802.3u specification for data transfers of up to 100Mbps over twisted-pair cable. *See also* 100BaseFX, 100BaseTX, 100BaseT, and 100BaseT4.

fault tolerance The capability of a component, system, or network to endure a failure.

FDDI (Fiber Distributed Data Interface) A high-speed data transfer technology designed to extend the capabilities of existing LANs by using a dual-ring topology and a token-passing access method.

FDM (Frequency-Division Multiplexing) A technology that divides the output channel into multiple smaller-bandwidth channels, each of which uses a different frequency range.

fiber-optic cable   Also known as fiber optics or optical fiber, a physical medium capable of conducting modulated light transmissions. Compared with other transmission media, fiber-optic cable is more expensive, but it is not susceptible to EMI or crosstalk, and it is capable of very high data rates and increased distances.

fibre channel   A technology that defines full gigabit-per-second data transfer over fiber-optic cable. Commonly used with storage area network (SAN) implementations.

firewall   A program, system, device, or group of devices that acts as a barrier between one network and another. Firewalls are configured to allow certain types of traffic to pass while blocking others.

FireWire   A high-speed serial bus technology that allows up to 63 devices to be connected to a system. FireWire provides sufficient bandwidth for multimedia operations and supports hot swapping and multiple speeds on the same bus.

fixed wireless   A technology that provides data communication capabilities between two fixed locations. Fixed wireless can be used as a private networking method but is also becoming increasingly common as an Internet access method.

flow control   A method of controlling the amount of data transmitted within a given period of time. There are different types of flow control. *See also* dynamic window, static window.

FQDN (fully qualified domain name)   The entire domain name that specifies the name of the computer as well as the domain in which it resides and the top-level DNS domain (for example, www.marketing.quepublishing.com).

fragment-free switching   A switching method that uses the first 64 bytes of a frame to determine whether the frame is corrupted. If this first part is intact, the frame is forwarded.

frame   A grouping of information transmitted as a unit across the network at the data-link layer of the OSI model.

Frame Length field   In a data frame, the field that specifies the length of a frame.

Frame Type field   In a data frame, the field that names the protocol being sent in the frame.

frequency   The number of cycles of an alternating current signal over a unit of time. Frequency is expressed in Hertz.

FTP (File Transfer Protocol)   A protocol that provides for the transfer of files between two systems. FTP is part of the TCP/IP protocol suite and operates at layer 7 of the OSI model.

full backup   A backup in which files, regardless of whether they have been changed, are copied to the backup media. In a full backup, the archive bits of the files are reset.

full-duplex   A system in which data is transmitted in two directions simultaneously. *Compare with* half-duplex.

G

gateway   A hardware or software solution that enables communications between two dissimilar networking systems or protocols. A gateway can operate at any layer of the OSI model but is commonly associated with the Application layer.

Gb (gigabit)   1 billion bits or 1,000Mb.

Gbps (gigabits per second)   The throughput of a given network medium in terms of 1 billion bps.

GFS (Grandfather-Father-Son)   A backup strategy of maintaining backups on a daily, weekly, and monthly schedule. Backups are made on a five-day or seven-day schedule. A full backup is performed at least once a week. On all other days full, incremental, or differential backups (or no backups at all) are performed. The daily incremental, or differential, backups are known as the *son*. The *father* is the last full backup in the week (the weekly backup). The *grandfather* is the last full backup of the month (the monthly backup).

Gigabit Ethernet   An IEEE 802.3 specification that defines standards for data transmissions of 1Gbps. *See also* 1000BaseX.

guaranteed flow control   A method of flow control in which the sending and receiving hosts agree on a rate of data transmission. After the rate is determined, the communication takes place at the guaranteed rate until the sender is finished. No buffering takes place at the receiver.

H

hacker   A person who carries out hacking on a computer software program. *See also* cracker.

half-duplex   A connection in which data is transmitted in both directions but not simultaneously. *Compare with* full-duplex.

handshake   The initial communication between two data communication devices, during which they agree on protocol and transfer rules for the session.

hardware address   The hardware-encoded MAC address burned into every NIC.

hardware loopback   A device that is plugged into an interface for the purposes of simulating a network connection and thus enabling the interface to be tested as if it is operating while connected.

High-Speed Token Ring   A version of Token Ring that has a maximum speed of 100Mbps. This is in contrast with other Token Ring standards, which have maximum speeds of 4Mbps or 16Mbps.

hop   The means by which routing protocols determine the shortest way to reach a given destination. Each router constitutes one hop; so if a router is four hops away from another router, there are three routers, or hops, between itself and the destination. In some cases, the final step is also counted as a hop.

host   Typically refers to any device on the network that has been assigned an IP address.

host ID An identifier used to uniquely identify a client or resource on a network.

hostname A name assigned to a system for the purposes of identifying it on the network in a more user-friendly manner than by the network address.

HOSTS file A text file that contains host-name-to-IP address mappings. All commonly used platforms accommodate static name resolution using the HOSTS file.

hot site A disaster recovery term used to describe an alternate network site that can be immediately functional in the event of a disaster at the primary site.

hot spare In a RAID configuration, a drive that sits idle until another drive in the RAID array fails, at which point the hot spare takes over the role of the failed drive.

hotspot An area in which an access point provides public wireless broadband network services to mobile visitors through a WLAN. Hotspots are often located in heavily populated places such as airports, hotels, and coffee shops.

hot swap The removal and replacement of a component in a system while the power is still on and the system is functioning.

HSSI (High Speed Serial Interface) The network standard for high-speed serial communications over WAN links, including various T-carrier technologies.

HTTP (Hypertext Transfer Protocol) A protocol used by web browsers to transfer pages, links, and graphics from the remote node to the user's computer.

HTTPS (Hypertext Transfer Protocol Secure) A protocol that performs the same function as HTTP but does so over an encrypted link, ensuring the confidentiality of any data that is uploaded or downloaded. Also referred to as S-HTTP.

hub A hardware device that acts as a connection point on a network that uses twisted-pair cable. Also known as a concentrator or a multiport repeater.

HyperTerminal A Windows-based communications program that allows users to establish host/shell access to a remote system.

I

IANA (Internet Assigned Numbers Authority) An organization responsible for IP addresses, domain names, and protocol parameters. Some functions of IANA, such as domain name assignment, have been devolved into other organizations.

ICMP (Internet Control Message Protocol) A network-layer Internet protocol documented in RFC 792 that reports errors and provides other information relevant to IP packet processing. Utilities such as ping and tracert use functionality provided by ICMP.

IDE (Integrated Drive Electronics) The most common type of disk drive used in PCs today. In these devices, the controller is integrated into the device.

IEEE (Institute of Electrical and Electronics Engineers) A professional organization that among other things, develops standards for networking and communications.

IEEE 1394 A standard that defines a system for connecting up to 63 devices on an external bus. IEEE 1394 is commonly used with consumer electronic devices such as video cameras and MP3 players. IEEE 1394 is based on a technology developed by Apple Computers called FireWire.

IEEE 802.1 A standard that defines the OSI model's physical and data-link layers. This standard allows two IEEE LAN stations to communicate over a LAN or WAN and is often referred to as the internetworking standard.

IEEE 802.1X An IEEE security standard designed for authenticating wireless devices. This standard uses the Extensible Authentication Protocol (EAP), to provide a central authentication server to authenticate each user on the network.

IEEE 802.2 A standard that defines the LLC sublayer of the data-link layer for the entire series of protocols covered by the 802.x standards. This standard specifies the adding of header fields, which tell the receiving host which upper layer sent the information.

IEEE 802.3 A standard that specifies physical-layer attributes, such as signaling types, data rates, and topologies, as well as the media access method used. It also defines specifications for the implementation of the physical layer and the MAC sublayer of the data-link layer, using CSMA/CD. This standard also includes the original specifications for Fast Ethernet.

IEEE 802.4 A standard that defines how production machines should communicate and establishes a common protocol for use in connecting these machines. It also defines specifications for the implementation of the physical layer and the MAC sublayer of the data-link layer, using Token Ring access over a bus topology.

IEEE 802.5 A standard used to define Token Ring. However, it does not specify a particular topology or transmission medium. It provides specifications for the implementation of the physical layer and the MAC sublayer of the data-link layer, using a token-passing media-access method on a ring topology.

IEEE 802.6 A standard that defines the distributed queue dual bus technology to transfer high-speed data between nodes. It provides specifications for the implementation of MANs.

IEEE 802.7 A standard that defines the design, installation, and testing of broadband-based communications and related physical media connectivity.

IEEE 802.8 A standard that defines a group, called the Fiber Optic Technical Advisory Group, that advises the other 802 standard committees on various fiber-optic technologies and standards.

IEEE 802.9 A standard that defines the integration of voice and data transmissions using isochronous Ethernet.

IEEE 802.10 A standard that focuses on security issues by defining a standard method for protocols and services to exchange data securely by using encryption mechanisms.

IEEE 802.11   The original IEEE wireless standard defining standards for wireless LAN communication.

IEEE 802.11a   A wireless networking standard operating in the 5GHz band. 802.11a supports a maximum theoretical data rate of 54 Mbps. Depending on interference, 802.11a could have a range of 150 feet at the lowest speed setting. Higher speed transmissions would see a lower range. 802.11a uses the CSMA/CA media access method and is not compatible with 802.11b and 802.11g.

IEEE 802.11b   A commonly deployed IEEE wireless standard that uses the 2.4GHz RF range and offers speeds up to 11Mbps. Under ideal conditions, the transmission range can be as far as 75 meters.

IEEE 802.11g   An IEEE wireless standard that is backward compatible with 802.11b. 802.11g offers a data rate of 54Mbps. Like 802.11b, 802.11g uses the 2.4GHz RF range.

IEEE 802.12   A standard that defines 100BaseVG-AnyLAN, which uses a 1Gbps signaling rate and a special media access method that allows 100Mbps data traffic over voice-grade cable.

IETF (Internet Engineering Task Force)   A group of research volunteers responsible for specifying the protocols used on the Internet and for specifying the architecture of the Internet.

ifconfig   A command used on Linux, Unix, and OS/2 systems to obtain configuration for and configure network interfaces.

IGMP (Internet Group Management Protocol)   Protocol used for communication between devices within the same multicast group. IGMP provides a mechanism for systems to detect and make themselves aware of other systems in the same group.

IMAP (Internet Message Access Protocol)   A protocol that allows email to be retrieved from a remote server. It is part of the TCP/IP protocol suite, and it is similar in operation to POP but offers more functionality.

incremental backup   A backup of only files that have been created or changed since the last backup. In an incremental backup, the archive bit is cleared to indicate that a file has been backed up.

infrared   A wireless data communication method that uses light pulses in the infrared range as a carrier signal.

infrastructure topology   Wireless topology that defines a wireless network comprised of an access point connected to a wired LAN. Wireless devices communicate with the wired LAN through the access point (AP).

inherited rights   The file system or directory access rights valid at a given point as a result of those rights being assigned at a higher level in the directory structure.

intelligent hub/switch   A hub or switch that contains some management or monitoring capability.

intelligent UPS   A UPS that has associated software for monitoring and managing the power provided to the system. For information to be passed between the UPS and the system, the UPS and system must be connected, which is normally achieved through a serial or USB connection.

interface   A device, such as a card or a plug, that connects pieces of hardware with a computer so that information can be moved from place to place (for example, between computers and printers, hard disks, and other devices, or between two or more nodes on a network). Also, the part of an application or operating system that the user sees.

interference   Anything that can compromise the quality of a signal. On bound media, crosstalk and EMI are examples of interference. In wireless environments, atmospheric conditions that degrade the quality of a signal would be considered interference.

internal IPX address   A unique eight-digit hexadecimal number used to identify a server running IPX/SPX. It is usually generated at random when the server is installed.

internal loopback address   Functionality built into the TCP/IP protocol stack that allows one to verify the correct functioning of the stack by pinging any address in the 127.x.x.x range, except the network address (127.0.0.0) or the broadcast address (127.255.255.255). The address 127.0.0.1 is most commonly used.

Internet domain name   The name of an area of the DNS namespace. The Internet domain name is normally expressed along with the top-level domain to which it belongs (for example, comptia.org).

Internet layer   In the TCP/IP architectural model, the layer responsible for addressing, packaging, and routing functions. Protocols that operate at this layer are responsible for encapsulating packets into Internet datagrams. All necessary routing algorithms are run here.

internetwork   A group of networks connected by routers or other connectivity devices so that the networks function as one network.

intrusion detection   The process or procedures that provide a warning of successful or failed unauthorized access to a system.

I/O (input/output)   An operation in which data is either entered into a computer or taken out of a computer.

IP (Internet Protocol)   A network-layer protocol, documented in RFC 791, that offers a connectionless internetwork service. IP provides features for addressing, packet fragmentation and reassembly, type-of-service specification, and security.

IP address   The unique address used to identify the network number and node address of a device connected to a TCP/IP network. IP addresses are typically expressed in dotted decimal format, for example, 192.168.1.1

ipconfig   A Windows NT/2000 command that provides information about the configuration of the TCP/IP parameters, including the IP address.

IPSec (IP Security)   A protocol used to provide strong security standards for encryption and authentication on VPNs.

IPv6 (Internet Protocol version 6)   The new version of IP, which has a larger range of usable addresses than the current version of IP, IPv4, and enhanced security.

IPX (Internetwork Packet Exchange)   A network-layer protocol usually used by Novell's NetWare. IPX provides connectionless communication, supporting packet sizes up to 64KB.

IPX/SPX (Internetwork Packet Exchange/Sequenced Packet Exchange) The default protocol used in NetWare networks. It is a combination of IPX, to provide addressing, and SPX, to provide guaranteed delivery for IPX. IPX/SPX is similar in nature to its counterpart, TCP/IP.

IPX address The unique address used to identify a node in a network.

IRQ (interrupt request) A number assigned to a device in a computer that determines the priority and path in communications between a device and the CPU.

IrDA Wireless networking technology that uses infrared beams to send data transmissions between devices.

IRTF (Internet Research Task Force) The research arm of the Internet Architecture Board that performs research in the areas of Internet protocols, applications, architecture, and technology.

ISA (Industry Standard Architecture) The standard of the older, more common, 8-bit and 16-bit bus and card architectures.

ISDN (Integrated Services Digital Network) An internationally adopted standard for providing end-to-end digital communications between two points. ISDN is a dial-up technology allowing data, voice, and other source traffic to be transmitted over a dedicated link.

ISDN terminal adapter A device that enables communication over an ISDN link.

ISO (International Organization for Standardization) A voluntary organization founded in 1946 that is responsible for creating international standards in many areas, including communications and computers. This also includes the development of the OSI model.

ISP (Internet service provider) A company or an organization that provides facilities for clients to access the Internet.

J

jumpered (or jumpering) Refers to the physical placement of shorting connectors on a board or card.

jumperless A term used to describe devices configured via a software utility rather than by physical jumpers on the circuit board.

K

Kb (kilobit) 1,000 bits.

KB (kilobyte) 1,000 bytes.

Kerberos Network authentication protocol designed to ensure that the data sent across networks is encrypted and safe from attack. Its primary purpose is to provide authentication for client/server applications.

kernel The core of an operating system. The kernel provides basic functions and services for all other parts of the operating system, including the interface with which the user interacts.

L

L2TP (Layer 2 Tunneling Protocol)   A dial-up VPN protocol that defines its own tunneling protocol and works with the advanced security methods of IPSec. L2TP allows PPP sessions to be tunneled across an arbitrary medium to a home gateway at an ISP or a corporation.

LAN (local area network)   A group of connected computers located in a single geographic area—usually a building or office that share data and services.

laser printer   A type of printer that uses electrophotography as the means of printing images on paper.

latency   The delay induced by a piece of equipment or device used to transfer data.

LC   Media connector used with fiber-optic cabling.

LDAP   Protocol used to access and query compliant directory services systems such as Microsoft Active Directory or Novell Directory services.

learning bridge   A bridge that builds its own bridging address table instead of requiring someone to enter information manually. Most modern bridges are learning bridges. Also called a smart bridge.

legacy   An older computer system or technology.

line conditioner   A device used to stabilize the flow of power to the connected component. Also known as a power conditioner or voltage regulator.

link light   An LED on a networking device such as a hub, switch, or NIC. The illumination of the link light indicates that, at a hardware level, the connection is complete and functioning.

link-state routing   A dynamic routing method in which routers tell neighboring routers of their existence through packets called link-state advertisements (LSAs). By interpreting the information in these packets, routers can create maps of the entire network. *Compare with* distance-vector routing.

Linux   A Unix-like operating system kernel created by Linus Torvalds. Linux is distributed under an open-source license agreement, as are many of the applications and services that run on it.

LLC (logical link control) layer   A sublayer of the data-link layer of the OSI model. The LLC layer provides an interface for network-layer protocols and the MAC sublayer.

LMHOSTS file   A text file used in a Windows network environment that contains a list of NetBIOS hostname-to-IP address mappings used in TCP/IP name resolution.

logical addressing scheme   The addressing method used in providing manually assigned node addressing.

logical topology   The appearance of the network to the devices that use it, even if in physical terms the layout of the network is different. *See also* physical topology.

loop   A continuous circle that a packet takes through a series of nodes in a network until it eventually times out.

loopback plug   A device used for loopback testing.

loopback testing   A troubleshooting method in which the output and input wires are crossed or shorted in a manner that allows all outgoing data to be routed back into the card.

LPD (Line Printer Daemon)   Service on a system (normally Unix or Linux) that acts as a print server. Print jobs are submitted to the LPD application using a protocol such as LPR.

LPR (Line Printer Remote)   Network service that allows printing jobs to be sent to a remote print service such as LPD.

LTO (Linear Tape Open)   An open standard that allows both high storage capacity and fast data access in tape backup systems.

M

MAC (Media Access Control) address   A six-octet number, described in hexadecimal, that uniquely identifies a host on a network. It is a unique number that is burned into the network interface.

Mac OS X   Version 10 of an operating system designed for Macintosh computer systems. Mac OS X represents a complete shift in Apple operating systems because it is based on Unix code and as such can be managed using Unix utilities and procedures.

MAC layer   In the OSI model, the lower of the two sublayers of the data-link layer. It is defined by the IEEE as being responsible for interaction with the physical layer.

MAN (metropolitan area network)   A network that spans a defined geographical location such as a city or suburb.

master name server   The supplying name server that has authority in a DNS zone.

MAU (media access unit)   A transceiver specified in IEEE 802.3. Not to be confused with a Token Ring multistation access unit, which is abbreviated MSAU.

Mb (megabit)   1 million bits. Used to rate transmission transfer speeds.

MB (megabyte)   1 million bytes. Usually refers to file size.

Mbps (megabits per second)   The number of millions of bits that can travel across a given medium in a second.

MDI (medium-dependent interface)   A type of port found on Ethernet networking devices such as hubs and switches in which the wiring is straight through. MDI ports are sometimes referred to as uplink ports and are intended for use as connectivity points to other hubs and switches.

MDI-X (medium-dependent interface crossed)   A type of port found on Ethernet networking devices in which the wiring is crossed so that the transmit line of one device becomes the receive line of the other. MDI-X is used to connect hubs and switches to client computers.

memory address   The label assigned to define the location in memory where information is stored.

metric   A value that can be assigned to a route to encourage or discourage the use of the route. *See also* cost.

MIB (Management Information Base) A data set that defines the criteria that can be retrieved and set on a device, using SNMP.

microsegmentation The process of using switches to divide a network into smaller segments.

microwaves A wireless technology sometimes used to transmit data between buildings and across vast distances.

mirroring A fault-tolerant technique in which an exact duplicate of data on one volume is created on another. Mirroring is defined as RAID 1. *See* RAID.

modem (modulator-demodulator) A device used to modulate and demodulate the signals that pass through it. It converts the direct current pulses of the serial digital code from the controller into the analog signals that are compatible with the telephone network.

MSAU (multistation access unit) A device used in an IBM Token Ring network. It organizes the connected nodes into an internal ring and uses the RI and RO connectors to expand to other MSAUs on the network. Sometimes referred to as MAU.

MTBF (mean time between failure) The amount of time, normally expressed in hours, that represents the average amount of time a component will function before it fails.

MTRJ Media connector used with fiber-optic cabling.

MTTF (mean time to fix) The amount of time it normally takes to fix a problem or swap out a component.

multicast A single-packet transmission from one sender to a specific group of destination nodes.

multihomed A term used to refer to a device that has more than one network interface.

multiplatform A term used to refer to a programming language, technology, or protocol that runs on different types of CPUs or operating systems.

multiplexing Multiplexing is a technique of combining multiple channels over a transmission path and then recovering or demultiplexing the separate channels at the receiving end. Examples include FDM, TDM, CDM, and WDM.

multiprocessor A term that refers to the use of multiple processors in a single system.

multitasking The running of several programs simultaneously. In actuality, during multitasking the processor is sharing its time between the programs, and it only appears as if they are running concurrently.

N

name server A server that contains a databases of name resolution information used to resolve network names to network addresses.

NAT (Network Address Translation) A standard that enables the translation of IP addresses used on one network to a different IP address that is acceptable for use on another network. This translation allows multiple systems to access an external network, such as the Internet, through a single IP address.

NBNS (NetBIOS name server)   A central server that provides name resolution for NetBIOS names to IP addresses. Commonly referred to as a WINS server.

nbtstat   A Windows operating system command-line utility that displays protocol statistics and current TCP/IP connections using NetBIOS over TCP/IP (NBT).

NCP (NetWare Core Protocol)   A protocol that provides a method for hosts to make calls to a NetWare server for services and network resources. NCP is part of the IPX/SPX protocol suite.

NDS (Novell Directory Services)   A standards-compliant directory services system implemented by Novell in NetWare 4.x. Subsequently renamed eDirectory.

NetBEUI (NetBIOS Extended User Interface)   A nonroutable, Microsoft-proprietary networking protocol designed for use in small networks.

NetBIOS (Network Basic Input/Output System)   A software application that allows different applications to communicate between computers on a LAN.

netstat   A Windows operating system command-line utility that displays protocol statistics and current TCP/IP network connections.

NLM (NetWare loadable module)   A service or process that runs on a NetWare server.

NLSP (NetWare Link Services Protocol)   A link-state routing protocol used on networks that use Novell's IPX/SPX protocol suite.

network card   *See* NIC.

network ID   The part of a TCP/IP address that specifies the network portion of the IP address. The network ID is determined by the class of the address, which in turn is determined by the subnet mask used.

network interface layer   The bottom layer of the TCP/IP architectural model, which is responsible for sending and receiving frames.

network layer   Layer 3 of the OSI model, which is where routing based on node addresses (that is, IP or IPX addresses) occurs.

network operating system   An operating system that runs on the servers on a network. Network operating systems include NetWare, Unix, Windows NT Server, and Windows 2000/2003 Server.

newsgroup   A discussion group that focuses on a specific topic and is made up of a collection of messages posted to an Internet site. Newsgroups are useful resources for support personnel.

NFS (Network File System)   File sharing and access protocol most commonly associated with Unix and Linux systems.

NIC (network interface card)   A hardware component that serves as the interface, or connecting component, between a network and the node. It has a transceiver, a MAC address, and a physical connector for the network cable. Also known as a network adapter or a network card.

NIS (Network Information Services)   The user, group, and security information database utilized in a Unix internetwork.

NMS (Network Management System) An application that acts as a central management point for network management. Most NMS systems use SNMP to communicate with network devices.

NNTP (Network News Transfer Protocol) An Internet protocol that controls how news articles are to be queried, distributed, and posted. NNTP uses port 119.

noise Another name for EMI. *See* EMI.

NTP (Network Time Protocol) A protocol used to communicate time synchronization information between devices on the network. NTP is part of the TCP/IP protocol suite. NTP uses port 123.

O

operating system The main computer program that manages and integrates all the applications running on a computer. The OSs handles all disk interactions with the processor.

OSI (Open Systems Interconnect) reference model A seven-layer model created by the ISO to standardize and explain the interactions of networking protocols.

OSPF (Open Shortest Path First) A link-state routing protocol used on TCP/IP networks. *Compare with* distance-vector routing.

P

packet filtering A firewall method in which each packet that attempts to pass through the firewall is examined to determine its contents. The packet is then allowed to pass, or it is blocked, as appropriate.

packet sniffer A device or an application that allows data to be copied from the network and analyzed. In legitimate applications, it is a useful network troubleshooting tool.

PAN (personal area network) A network layout whereby devices work together in close proximity to share information and services, commonly using technologies such as Bluetooth or infrared.

passive hub A hub that has no power and therefore does not regenerate the signals it receives. *Compare with* active hub.

passive termination A SCSI bus terminator that uses a terminating resistor pack placed at the end of the bus. This resistor relies on the interface card to provide it with a consistent level of power.

password A set of characters used with a username to authenticate a user on a network and to provide the user with rights and permissions to files and resources.

patch A fix for a bug in a software application. Patches can be downloaded from the Internet to correct errors or security problems in software applications.

patch cable A cable, normally twisted-pair, used to connect two devices together. Strictly speaking, a patch cable is the cable that connects a port on a hub or switch to the patch panel, but today people commonly use the term to refer to any cable connection.

patch panel A device in which the cables used in coaxial or twisted-pair networks converge and are connected. The patch panel is usually in a central location.

PCAnywhere   A software program that allows users to gain control of a computer remotely.

PCI (Peripheral Component Interconnect)   A relatively new high-speed bus designed for Pentium systems.

PCMCIA (Personal Computer Memory Card International Association)   An industry group organized in 1989 to promote standards for credit card–sized devices such as memory cards, modems, and network cards. Almost all laptop computers today have multiple PCMCIA slots. PCMCIA cards are now generally referred to simply as PC cards.

peer-to-peer networking   A network environment that does not have dedicated servers, where communication occurs between similarly capable network nodes that act as both clients and servers.

permissions   Authorization provided to users that allows them to access objects on a network. The network administrators generally assign permissions. *Permissions* is slightly different from but often used with *rights*.

physical address   The MAC address on every NIC. The physical address is applied to a NIC by the manufacturer and, except for rare occurrences, are never changed.

physical layer   Layer 1 of the OSI model, where all physical connectivity is defined.

physical topology   The actual physical layout of the network. Common physical topologies include star, bus, and ring. *Compare with* logical topology.

ping   A TCP/IP protocol stack utility that works with ICMP and uses echo requests and replies to test connectivity to other systems.

plenum   The space between the structural ceiling and a drop-down ceiling that is commonly used for heating, ventilation, and air-conditioning systems as well as for running network cables.

plug and play   An architecture designed to allow hardware devices to be detected by the operating system and for the driver to be automatically loaded.

polling   The media-access method for transmitting data in which a controlling device is used to contact each node to determine whether it has data to send.

PoP (point-of-presence)   The physical location where a long-distance carrier or a cellular provider interfaces with the network of the local exchange carrier or local telephone company.

POP (Post Office Protocol)   A protocol that is part of the TCP/IP protocol suite and is used for retrieving mail stored on a remote server. The most commonly used version of POP is POP3. POP is an Application layer protocol.

port   In physical networking terms, a pathway on a networking device that allows other devices to be connected. In software terms, a port is the entry point into an application, system, or protocol stack.

port mirroring   A process by which two ports on a device, such as a switch, are configured to receive the same information. Port mirroring is useful in troubleshooting scenarios.

POTS (plain old telephone system) The current analog public telephone system. *See also* PSTN.

PPP (Point-to-Point Protocol) A common dial-up networking protocol that includes provisions for security and protocol negotiation and provides host-to-network and switch-to-switch connections for one or more user sessions.

PPPoE (Point-to-Point Protocol over Ethernet) Internet connection authentication protocol that uses two separate technologies, Ethernet and the point-to-point protocol (PPP), to provide a method for multiple users to share a common Digital Subscriber Line (DSL), cable modem, or wireless connection to the Internet.

PPTP (Point-to-Point Tunneling Protocol) A protocol that encapsulates private network data in IP packets. These packets are transmitted over synchronous and asynchronous circuits to hide the underlying routing and switching infrastructure of the Internet from both senders and receivers.

presentation layer Layer 6 of the OSI model, which prepares information to be used by the application layer.

PRI (Primary Rate Interface) A high-level network interface standard for use with ISDN. PRI is defined as having a rate of 1.544Mbps, and it consists of a single 64Kbps D channel plus 23 T1 B channels for voice or data. *See also* BRI, ISDN.

primary name server The DNS server that offers zone data from files stored locally on the machine.

private network A network to which access is limited, restricted, or controlled. Most corporate networks are private networks. *Compare with* public network.

proprietary A standard or specification created by a single manufacturer, vendor, or other private enterprise.

protocol A set of rules or standards that control data transmission and other interactions between networks, computers, peripheral devices, and operating systems.

proxy A device, an application, or a service that acts as an intermediary between two hosts on a network, eliminating the capability for direct communication.

proxy server A server that acts as a go-between for a workstation and the Internet. A proxy server typically provides an increased level of security, caching, NAT, and administrative control.

PSTN (public switched telephone network) A term that refers to all the telephone networks and services in the world. The same as POTS, PSTN refers to the world's collection of interconnected public telephone networks that are both commercial and government owned. All of the PSTN is digital, except the connection between local exchanges and customers (which is called the local loop or last mile), which remains analog.

public network A network, such as the Internet, to which anyone can connect with the most minimal of restrictions. *Compare with* private network.

punchdown block   A device used to connect network cables from equipment closets or rooms to other parts of a building. Connections to networking equipment such as hubs or switches are established from the punchdown block. Also used in telecommunications wiring for distributing phone cables to their respective locations throughout the building.

punchdown tool   A hand tool that enables the connection of twisted-pair wires to wiring equipment such as a patch panel.

R

RADIUS (Remote Authentication Dial-in User Service)   A security standard that employs a client-server model to authenticate remote network users. Remote users are authenticated using a challenge and response mechanism between the remote access server and the RADIUS server.

RAID (Redundant Array of Inexpensive Disks) A method of storing data on multiple hard drives, allowing the overlapping of I/O operations. Depending on the level of RAID, there are either fault-tolerant or performance advantages.

RAID 0   A RAID configuration that employs data striping but lacks redundancy because no parity information is recorded (*see* RAID 5). As a result, RAID 0 offers no fault tolerance, but it does offer increased performance. Requires a minimum of two disks.

RAID 1   A fault-tolerant method that uses disk mirroring to duplicate the information stored on a disk. Also referred to as disk duplexing when the two drives in a RAID 1 array are connected to separate disk controllers.

RAID 2   A fault-tolerant method that uses disk striping with error correction.

RAID 3   A fault-tolerant method that uses disk striping with a single disk for parity.

RAID 4   A fault-tolerant method that uses disk striping with a single disk for parity. Striping is done across the disks in blocks.

RAID 5   A fault-tolerant method that uses disk striping with distributed parity. Striping is done across the disks in blocks.

RAID 10   Also referred to as RAID 1/0, a RAID configuration in which stripe sets (RAID 0) are mirrored (RAID 1). This combination provides the fault-tolerant aspects of RAID 1 and the performance advantages of RAID 0.

RARP (Reverse Address Resolution Protocol) A protocol, part of the TCP/IP protocol suite, that resolves MAC addresses to IP addresses. Its relative ARP resolves IP addresses to MAC addresses. RARP resides on the network layer of the OSI model.

RAS (Remote Access Service)   A Windows NT/2000 service that allows access to the network through remote connections.

RDP (Remote Desktop Protocol) Presentation layer protocol that supports traffic between a Windows terminal client and Windows Terminal Server. RDP is also used for the Remote Desktop feature of Windows XP and Windows Server 2003.

read-only An assigned right that allows the user to open a file and look at the contents or to execute the file if it is an application. The user cannot change the file or delete it.

read-write An assigned right that allows the user to open a file, change a file, or execute a file. The user cannot delete a read-write file in some network operating systems but can in others. The user can create new files in the directory if she is granted read-write permissions to a directory.

remote control In networking, having physical control of a remote computer through software such as PCAnywhere or Microsoft Systems Management Server.

remote node A node or a computer connected to a network through a remote connection. Dialing in to the Internet from home is an example of the remote node concept.

repeater A device that regenerates and retransmits signals on a network. Repeaters are usually used to strengthen signals going long distances.

resolver A system that is requesting the resolution of a name to an IP address. This term can be applied to both DNS and WINS clients.

resource conflict A problem that occurs when multiple devices are using the same IRQ or I/O address at the same time, usually causing the devices to fail and the program to halt.

restore To transfer data from backup media to a server. The opposite of back up.

RFC (Request for Comments) The process by which standards relating to the Internet, the TCP/IP protocol suite, and associated technologies are created, commented on, and approved.

RG-58 A designation for the coaxial cable used in thin coaxial networks that operate on the Ethernet standard.

RI (ring in) A connector used in an IBM Token Ring network on an MSAU to expand to other MSAUs on the network. The counterpart to the RO, the RI on the MSAU connects to the media to accept the token from the ring.

rights An authorization provided to users that allows them to perform certain tasks. The network administrator generally assigns rights. Slightly different from but often used with the term *permissions*.

RIP (Routing Information Protocol) A protocol that uses hop count as a routing metric to control the direction and flow of packets between routers on an internetwork. There are versions of RIP for use on both TCP/IP- and IPX/SPX-based networks.

RJ-11 connector A connector that is used with telephone systems and can have up to six conductors.

RJ-45 connector An connector that is used with twisted-pair cable and can support eight conductors for four pairs of wires.

RO (ring out) A connector used in an IBM Token Ring network on an MSAU to expand to other MSAUs on the network. The counterpart to the RI, the RO on the MSAU connects to the medium to send the token out to the ring.

root   The top level of a file system or a directory services structure. Also, the name of the default administrative account on Unix and Linux systems. Also, the term used to describe the top level of the Domain Name Service namespace.

route   The entire path between two nodes on a network.

router   A device that works at the network layer of the OSI model to control the flow of data between two or more network segments.

RS-232   A communications standard that defines the flow of serial communications and the particular functions assigned to the wires in a serial cable.

S

sag   A momentary drop in the voltage provided by a power source.

Samba   Service that runs on a Unix or Linux system that provides file and print services available to Windows clients without the need for additional client software. Samba is a variation of the Server Message Block (SMB) protocol.

SAP (Service Advertising Protocol)   A NetWare protocol used on an IPX network. SAP maintains server information tables, listing each service that has been advertised to it, and provides this information to any nodes that attempt to locate a service.

SAP (Service Advertising Protocol) agent   A router or another node on an IPX network that maintains a server information table. This table lists each service that has been advertised to it and provides this information to any nodes that attempt to locate a service.

SAS (Single Attached Station)   In an FDDI system, a device that is attached to only one of the two rings. *Compare with* DAS.

SCP (Secure Copy Protocol)   Basic file copying protocol that uses Secure Shell (SSH) technology to provide security to the transfer.

SCSI (Small Computer System Interface)   A technology defined by a set of standards originally published by ANSI for use with devices on a bus known as a SCSI bus. SCSI is commonly implemented to support high-speed storage systems.

SCSI bus   The high-speed channel between the SCSI devices on a chain. The SCSI bus architecture contains a multithreaded I/O interface that can process multiple I/O requests at the same time.

SCSI bus termination   The use of a set of electrical resistors called terminators at the extreme ends of the SCSI bus to reflect the electrical impulses being transmitted across the bus.

SCSI ID   A number assigned to a SCSI device to identify the device and its priority when two or more devices are competing for the right to send data on the bus.

secondary name server   A type of DNS server that gets its zone data from another DNS name server that has authority in that zone.

Security log A log located in the Windows Event Viewer that provides information on audit events that the administrator has determined to be security related. These events include logons, attempts to log on, attempts to access areas that are denied, and attempts to log on outside normal hours.

security policy In general terms, a written policy that defines the rules and regulations pertaining to the security of company data and the use of computer systems. More specifically, the policy configuration on a server system or a firewall that defines the security parameters for a system.

segment A physical section of a network.

server A network node that fulfills service requests for clients. Usually referred to by the type of service it performs, such as file server, communications server, or print server.

server-based application An application run from a network share rather than from a copy installed on a local computer.

server-based networking A network operating system dedicated to providing services to workstations, or clients. *See also* client/server networking.

service pack A software update that fixes multiple known problems and in some cases provides additional functionality to an application or operating system.

session A dialog between two computers.

session layer Layer 5 of the OSI model, which establishes, manages, and terminates sessions between applications on different nodes.

SFTP (Secure File Transfer Protocol) A implementation of the File Transfer Protocol (FTP) that uses Secure Shell (SSH) technology to provide additional authentication and encryption services for file transfers.

shared system The infrastructure component routed directly into the backbone of an internetwork for optimal systems access. It provides connectivity to servers and other shared systems.

shell An interface, graphical or otherwise, that enables a user to access the functionality of an operating system.

SLIP (Serial Line Internet Protocol) A protocol that uses encapsulation to allow TCP/IP to be transmitted over asynchronous lines, such as standard telephone lines. Previously used for most Internet access, SLIP has been largely replaced by PPP because of SLIP's lack of error-checking capabilities.

SMDS (Switched Multimegabit Data Service) A data transmission system that uses public lines at speeds between 1.544Mbps (T1) and 44.736Mbps, using cell relay and fixed-length cells. Defined in IEEE 802.6.

SMB (Server Message Block) Native file sharing and access protocol used on Windows platforms.

SMP (symmetric multiprocessing) The utilization of multiple processors on a single system.

SMTP (Simple Mail Transfer Protocol) An Internet protocol used for the transfer of e-mail messages and attachments.

SNAP (SubNetwork Access Protocol)   An Internet protocol that specifies a standard method of encapsulating IP datagrams and ARP messages on a network.

SNMP (Simple Network Management Protocol)   A protocol that provides network devices with a method to monitor and control network devices; manage configurations, statistics collection, performance, and security; and report network management information to a management console. SNMP is part of the TCP/IP protocol suite.

SNMP agent   A software component that allows a device to communicate with, and be contacted by, an SNMP management system.

SNMP trap   An SNMP utility that sends an alarm to notify the administrator that something within the network activity differs from the established threshold, as defined by the administrator.

socket   A logical interprocess communications mechanism through which a program communicates with another program or with a network.

socket identifier   An 8-bit number that is used to identify the socket and is used by IPX when it needs to address a packet to a particular process running on a server. The developers and designers of services and protocols usually assign socket identifiers. A socket identifier is also known as a socket number.

SONET (Synchronous Optical NETwork)   A U.S. standard for data transmission that operates at speeds up to 2.4Gbps over optical networks referred to as OC-*x*, where *x* is the level. The international equivalent of SONET is Synchronous Digital Hierarchy (SDH).

source address   The address of the host that sent the frame. The source address is contained in the frame so that the destination node knows who sent the data.

source-route bridge   A bridge used in source-route bridging to send a packet to the destination node through the route specified by the sending node.

spike   An instantaneous, dramatic increase in the voltage input to a device. Spikes are responsible for much of the damage done to network hardware components.

SPX (Sequenced Packet Exchange)   A protocol used in conjunction with IPX when guaranteed delivery is required. SPX is used mainly in NetWare network environments. SPX operates at the Transport layer of the OSI model.

SSH (Secure Shell)   An application, like Telnet, that allows a session to be opened on a remote host. SSH differs from Telnet in that it provides additional authentication methods and encryption for data as it traverses the network. SSH uses TCP/IP port 22.

SSID (Service Set Identifier)   A unique client identifier sent over the WLAN that acts as a simple password used for authentication between a wireless client and an access point. The SSID is used to differentiate between networks, and, therefore, the client system and the AP must use the same SSID.

SSL (Secure Sockets Layer)   A method of securely transmitting information to and receiving information from a remote website. SSL is implemented through the HTTPS. SSL operates a the Presentation layer of the OSI model and uses TCP/IP port 443.

STA (Spanning Tree Algorithm) A standard defined by IEEE 802.1 as part of STP to eliminate loops in an internetwork with multiple paths.

static IP address An IP address that is assigned to a network device manually, as opposed to dynamically via DHCP.

static routing A routing method in which all routes must be entered into a device manually and in which no route information is exchanged between routing devices on the network. *Compare with* dynamic routing.

static window A mechanism used in flow control that prevents the sender of data from overwhelming the receiver. The amount of data that can be buffered in a static window is configured dynamically by the protocol.

station IPX address A 12-digit number used to uniquely identify each device on an IPX network. The station IPX address is derived directly from the MAC address of the network interface.

Storage Area Network (SAN) A subnetwork of storage devices, usually found on high-speed networks and shared by all servers on a network.

store-and-forward A fast-packet-switching method that produces a higher latency than other switching methods because the entire contents of the packet are copied into the onboard buffers of the switch. CRC calculations are performed before the packet can be passed on to the destination address.

STP (shielded twisted pair) Twisted-pair network cable that has shielding to insulate the cable from EMI.

STP (Spanning Tree Protocol) A protocol developed to eliminate the loops caused by the multiple paths in an internetwork. STP is defined in IEEE 802.1.

subdomain A privately controlled segment of the DNS namespace that exists under other segments of the namespace as a division of the main domain. Sometimes also called a child domain.

subnet A logical division of a network, based on the address to which all the devices on the network are assigned.

subnet mask A 32-bit address used to mask, or screen, a portion of an IP address to differentiate the part of the address that designates the network and the part that designates the host from one another.

subnetting The process of using parts of the node portion of an assigned IP address to create more network IDs. Although subnetting increases the number of network IDs, it decreases the number of node addresses available for each network ID.

supernetting The process of aggregating IP network addresses and using them as a single network address range.

Supervisor account In a NetWare network, a default account that has rights to access everything and to assign rights to other users on the network.

surge A voltage increase that is less dramatic than that of a spike but can last a lot longer. Sometimes referred to as a swell. The opposite of brownout.

surge protector An inexpensive and simple device that is placed between a power outlet and a network component to protect the component from spikes and surges. Also known as a surge suppressor.

SVC (switched virtual circuit) A virtual circuit that is established dynamically on demand to form a dedicated link and is then broken when transmission is complete.

switch A Layer 2 networking device that forwards frames based on destination addresses.

SYN A message sent to initiate a TCP session between two devices. The proper term is *synchronization packet*.

synchronous transmission A digital signal transmission method that uses a precise clocking method and a predefined number of bits sent at a constant rate.

System log A log, accessed through Event Viewer on Windows Server platforms, that provides information and warnings on events logged by operating system components and hardware devices. These events include driver failures, device conflicts, read/write errors, timeouts, and bad block errors.

T

T-line A digital communication line used in WANs. Commonly used T designations are T1 (Trunk Level 1) and T3 (Trunk Level 3). It is also possible to use only part of a T1 line, which then becomes known as *fractional T1*. T1 lines support a data transmission rate of up to 1.544 Mbps.

TCP (Transmission Control Protocol) A connection-oriented, reliable data transmission communication service that operates at the transport layer of the OSI model. TCP is part of the TCP/IP protocol suite.

TCP/IP (Transmission Control Protocol/Internet Protocol) A suite of protocols that includes TCP and IP. TCP/IP was originally designed for use on large internetworks but has now become the de facto protocol for networks of all sizes.

TCP/IP socket A socket, or connection to an endpoint, that is used in TCP/IP communication transmissions.

TDI (Transport Driver Interface) A kernel-mode network interface that is exposed at the upper edge of all Windows NT transport protocol stacks. The highest-level protocol driver in every such stack supports the TDI interface for still higher-level kernel-mode network clients.

TDR (time-domain reflectometer) A device used to test copper cables to determine whether and where a break is on the cable. For optical cables, an optical TDR is used.

Telnet A standard terminal emulation protocol in the TCP/IP protocol stack. Telnet is used to perform terminal emulation over TCP/IP via remote terminal connections, enabling users to log in to remote systems and use resources as if they were connected to a local system.

Terminal Services A service on Windows server platforms that allows clients to connect to the server as if it were a multiuser operating system. All the processing for the client session is performed on the server, with only screen updates and user input being transmitted across the network connection.

TFTP (Trivial File Transfer Protocol) A simplified version of FTP that allows file transfers but does not offer any security or file management capabilities. TFTP uses TCP/IP port 69.

thick coaxial The thick cable most commonly used as the backbone of a coaxial network. It is approximately .375 inches in diameter.

Thick Ethernet The IEEE 802.3 standard 10Base5, which describes Ethernet networking using thick coaxial cabling. Also called ThickNet.

thin client An application run from a back-end server system such as Microsoft Terminal Services. The processing tasks are all performed at the terminal server rather than on the client. In basic usage, only screen updates are sent from the terminal server, and only keyboard and mouse data is sent to the terminal server.

Thin Ethernet The 802.3a standard 10Base2, which describes Ethernet networking using thin coaxial cabling. Also referred to as ThinNet.

thin coaxial Cable that is thinner than thick coaxial cable but still about .25 inches in diameter. It is commonly used in older bus topologies.

TIA (Telecommunications Industry Association) An organization that, along with EIA, develops standards for telecommunications technologies.

token A frame that provides controlling information. In a Token Ring network, the node that possesses the token is the one that is allowed to transmit next.

Token Ring An IBM-proprietary token-passing LAN topology defined by IEEE standard 802.5. It operates at either 4Mbps or 16Mbps, in a star topology.

Token Ring adapter Traditionally an ISA or a Microchannel device with 4Mbps or 16Mbps transfer capability that is used to connect nodes to a Token Ring network.

tone generator A device used with a tone locator to locate and diagnose problems with twisted-pair cabling. Commonly referred to as a fox and hound.

topology The shape or layout of a physical network and the flow of data through the network. *See also* logical topology, physical topology.

trace route A function of the TCP/IP protocol suite, implemented in utilities such as `traceroute` and `tracert`, that allows the entire path of a packet to be tracked between source and destination hosts. It is used as a troubleshooting tool.

transmit To send data using light, electronic, or electric signals. In networking, this is usually done in the form of digital signals composed of bits.

transparent bridging A situation in which the bridges on a network tell each other which ports on the bridge should be opened and closed, which ports should be forwarding packets, and which ports should be blocking packets—all without the assistance of any other device.

transport layer Layer 4 of the OSI model. Protocols at this layer perform functions such as segmenting data so that it can be sent over the network and then reassembling the segmented data on the receiving end. The transport layer also deals with some of the errors that can occur in a stream of data, such as dropped and duplicated packets.

TTL (Time To Live) A value assigned to a packet of data to prevent it from moving around the network indefinitely. The TTL value is decremented each time the packet crosses a router, until it reaches 0, at which point it is removed from the network.

twisted-pair A type of cable that uses multiple twisted pairs of copper wire.

U

UART (Universal Asynchronous Receiver/Transmitter) A chip that is responsible for communications carried over a serial port; it converts between data bits and serial bits.

UDP (User Datagram Protocol) A communications protocol that provides connectionless, unreliable communications services and operates at the transport layer of the OSI model. It requires a network-layer protocol such as IP to guide it to the destination host.

unbound media (or boundless media) A term used to describe any media that do not have physical constraints. Examples of unbound media include infrared, wireless, and microwave. *Compare with* bound media.

UNC (Universal Naming Convention) An industry naming standard for computers and resources that provides a common syntax that should work in most systems, including Windows, Unix, and NetWare. An example of a UNC name is *servername**sharename*.

unicast Communication that takes place over a network between a single sender and a single receiver.

UPS (uninterruptible power supply) A system that provides protection against power surges and power outages. During blackouts, a UPS gives you time to shut down systems or devices on the network before the temporary power interruption becomes permanent. A UPS is also referred to as battery backup.

uptime The amount of time that a device has been on and operating.

URL (uniform resource locator) A name used to identify a site and subsequently a page on the Internet. An example of a URL is www.quepublishing.com/products.

USB (universal serial bus) A type of interface between a computer system and peripheral devices. The USB interface allows you to add or remove devices without shutting down the computer. USB supports up to 127 devices. USB supports auto detection and plug and play.

user account An account that an end user uses when logging in to a network. It contains the rights and permissions assigned to the user.

UTP (unshielded twisted pair) A type of cable that uses multiple twisted pairs of copper wire in a casing that does not provide much protection from EMI. The most common network cable in Ethernet networks, UTP is rated in categories including Category 1 through Category 5, as well as Category 5e and Category 6.

V

virtual memory A process for paging or swapping data from memory to disk in order to increase the amount of RAM available to a system.

virus A software program designed specifically to affect a system or network adversely. A virus is usually designed to be passed on to other systems with which it comes in contact.

VLAN (virtual LAN) A group of devices located on one or more different LAN segments, whose configuration is based on logical instead of physical connections. This allows the devices to operate as if they were connected to the same physical switch, regardless of whether they are connected to the same switch.

volume set Multiple disks or partitions of disks that have been configured to read as one drive.

VPN (virtual private network) A network that uses a public network such as the Internet as a backbone to connect two or more private networks. A VPN provides users with the equivalent of a private network in terms of security. VPNs can also be used as a means of establishing secure remote connectivity between a remote system and another network.

W

WAN (wide area network) A data communications network that serves users across a broad geographical area. WANs often use transmission devices such as modems or CSUs/DSUs to carry signals over leased lines or over common carrier lines.

WAP (wireless access point) A network device that offers connectivity between wireless clients and (usually) a wired portion of the network.

web server A server that runs an application and makes the contents of certain directories on that server, or other servers, available to clients for download, via a protocol such as HTTP.

WEP (Wired Equivalent Privacy) Data encryption method used to protect the transmission between 802.11 wireless clients and access points. WEP security has come under scrutiny because it uses an insufficient key length and provides no automated method for distributing the keys.

WiFi A voluntary standard that manufacturers can adhere to, which aims to create compatibility between wireless devices. WiFi is an abbreviation of the phrase WIreless FIdelity

window flow control A flow control method in which the receiving host buffers the data it receives and holds it in the buffer until it can be processed. After the data is processed, an acknowledgment is sent to the sender. *See also* dynamic window, static window.

WINS (Windows Internet Name Service) A NetBIOS name-to-IP address resolution service that runs on Windows server platforms.

WINS database   A dynamically built database of NetBIOS names and IP addresses used by WINS.

wireless channel   Term used to refer to the band of frequency used for wireless communications. Each IEEE wireless standard specifies the channels that can be used.

wire crimper   A tool used to create networking cables. The type of wire crimping tool used depends on the cable being made.

wireless networking   Networking that uses any unbound media, such as infrared, microwave, or radio waves.

WISP (Wireless Internet Service Provider)   A service provider that specializes in offering users wireless access to the Internet, often including hotspot access.

WLAN (Wireless LAN)   A local area network created using wireless transmission methods such as radio or infrared rather than traditional wired solutions.

workstation   A client computer on a network that does not offer any services of its own but uses the services of the servers on the network.

WPA (Wi-Fi Protected Access)   Data encryption method used on 802.11 wireless LANs. WPA is an industry-supported standard designed to address security shortcomings of WEP.

Z

zone   A logical grouping of network devices in an AppleTalk network. Also, an area of the DNS namespace.

zone transfer   The passing of DNS information from one name server to a secondary name server.

Index

How can we make this index more useful? Email us at indexes@quepublishing.com

I

How can we make this index more useful? Email us at indexes@quepublishing.com

J - K

L

link-state, 138-139

TCP/IP, 216

RTMP (Routing Table Maintenance Protocol), 210

SAP (Service Advertising Protocol), 204

SCP (Secure Copy Protocol), 259

security, 346-355, 724-725

IPSec, 347-348

Kerberos, 354-355

L2TP, 348-349

SSL, 349-350

SFTP (Secure File Transfer Protocol), 253

SLIP (Serial Line Internet Protocol), 342, 448

SMB (Server Message Block), 278

SMTP (Simple Mail Transfer Protocol), 201, 254

SNMP (Simple Network Management Protocol), 201

agents, 274

communities, 276-277

components, 273

identifiers, 276

management systems, 274

MIBs, 275-276

versions, 275

SPX, 178, 201, 204

SSL (Secure Sockets Layer), 349-350

STP (Spanning Tree Protocol), 132

summary of, 719-720

TCP (Transmission Control Protocol), 178, 201, 250, 716

TCP/IP. *See* TCP/IP

Telnet, 256

TFTP (Trivial File Transfer Protocol), 253-254

transport (OSI model), 178-179, 199-202, 719

UDP (User Datagram Protocol), 178, 202, 251, 254

VPN (virtual private networks), 298, 345

Zeroconf, 277

ZIP (Zone Information Protocol), 210

proxy servers, 270, 485-488, 728

PSTN (public switched telephone network), 447

public networks, 241-243, 723

address ranges, 243

WANs, 297-299

public switched telephone network. *See* **PSTN**

punchdown tools, 442-443

put command, 253

PVCs (permanent virtual circuits), 315

Q - R

querytype=X switch, 574

-r count switch, 563

-r switch, 568

-R switch, 569

rack mounts, 129

radio frequency interference, 711

RADIUS (Remote Authentication Dial-In User Service), 354

RADSL (ISDN DSL), 318

RAID (Redundant Array of Inexpensive Disks), 520-521

choosing levels, 528-529

hardware, 529-530

RAID 0, 521-522

RAID 1, 522-5234

RAID 10, 527-528

RAID 2, 524

RAID 3, 525

RAID 4, 525

RAID 5, 525-527

software, 529-530

solutions, 725-726

RAS (remote access service), 339-340, 450, 724

RDP (Remote Desktop Protocol), 346, 725

receiving devices, 200

Recovery console (Windows 2000), 408

Redundant Array of Inexpensive Disks. *See* **RAID**

X - Y - Z